CoreMicroeconomics

CoreMicroeconomics
Third Edition

Eric P. Chiang
Florida Atlantic University
Gerald W. Stone
Metropolitan State University of Denver

Worth Publishers
A Macmillan Higher Education Company

Senior Vice President, Editorial and Production: Catherine Woods
Publisher: Charles Linsmeier
Marketing Manager: Tom Digiano
Marketing Assistant: Tess Sanders
Senior Development Editor: Bruce Kaplan
Associate Development Editor: Mary Walsh
Editorial Consultant: Paul Shensa
Associate Media Editor: Lindsay Neff
Director of Market Research and Development: Steven Rigolosi
Director of Print and Digital Development: Tracey Kuehn
Associate Managing Editor: Lisa Kinne
Senior Project Editor: Georgia Lee Hadler
Copy Editor: Martha Solonche
Art Director: Babs Reingold
Senior Designer: Kevin Kall
Interior Designer: Amanda Kavanagh
Cover Designers: Amanda Kavanagh/Kevin Kall
Photo Editor: Christine Buese
Photo Researcher: Julie Tesser
Production Manager: Barbara Anne Seixas
Supplements Production Manager: Stacey Alexander
Supplements Project Editor: Edgar Bonilla
Layout Designer and Illustrations: TSI Graphics
Composition: TSI Graphics
Manufactured in China by RR Donnelley
Cover Photo: Tatiana Nikolaevna Kalashinikova/Getty Images

Credits for chapter opening photographs can be found on page CR-1, which is an extension of this copyright page.

ISBN-13: 978-1-4292-7847-8
ISBN-10: 1-4292-7847-1

Library of Congress Control Number: 2013951032

Manufactured in China by RR Donnelley

Fifth printing

Worth Publishers
41 Madison Avenue
New York, NY 10010
www.worthpublishers.com

To John and Tina Chiang, my parents,
who instilled in me a work ethic
that allowed me to pursue endless
opportunities

About the Author

Eric P. Chiang received his bachelor's degree in economics from the University of Nevada Las Vegas, and his master's and doctorate in economics from the University of Florida. His first academic position was at New Mexico State University. Currently, Eric is an associate professor and graduate director of the Department of Economics at Florida Atlantic University. Eric also serves as the director of instructional technology for the College of Business.

In 2009, Eric was recipient of Florida Atlantic University's highest teaching award, the Distinguished Teacher of the Year. He also received the Stewart Distinguished Professorship awarded by the College of Business among numerous other teaching awards. He has published twenty-five articles in peer-reviewed journals on a range of subjects including technology spillovers, intellectual property rights, telecommunications, and health care. His research has appeared in leading journals, including the *Review of Economics and Statistics*, the *Journal of Technology Transfer*, and the *Southern Economic Journal*. He has presented papers at all major economics conferences and at universities across the country and around the world.

As an instructor who teaches both face-to-face and online courses, Eric uses a variety of technological tools including clickers, text-response systems, and homework management systems to complement his active learning style lectures. As an administrator in the College of Business, Eric's role as director of instructional technology involves assisting instructors with effectively implementing classroom technologies. In this position, Eric also ensures that the quality of online courses meets accreditation standards including those set by AACSB.

In addition to his dedication to teaching economic principles and his administrative duties, Eric devotes time to new research in economic education. His current research agenda focuses on the effects of online versus face-to-face courses and the power of visual learning. The third edition of *CoreMicroeconomics* embodies Eric's devotion to economic education and the benefits of adapting to the new, often creative ways in which students learn and instructors teach.

In his spare time, Eric enjoys studying cultures and languages, and travels frequently. He has visited all fifty U.S. states, many of them to run half-marathons, and over seventy countries, and enjoys long jogs and walks when he travels in order to experience local life to the fullest.

Memorial to Jerry Stone

Worth Publishers regrets to inform you that Jerry Stone passed away after a difficult battle with cancer at the end of August 2010. Jerry Stone had a remarkable career as a longtime teacher at Metropolitan State University of Denver and as an author of two successful principles of economics textbooks. Those who knew Jerry miss his steadfast commitment to the teaching of economics, a legacy that lives on in each new edition of *CoreMicroeconomics.* Jerry Stone long-believed that the best principles of economics textbooks are authored by people invested in their students' classroom experience. The decisions made in the shaping of the second edition were educated by Jerry's thirty-plus years in the classroom and by the team of instructors that contributed to every aspect of the media and supplements package. The second edition was Jerry's accomplishment: a book envisioned, designed, and executed to be the principles of economics book that teaches better than any other textbook on the market.

Brief Contents

Preface xxvii

CHAPTER 1 Exploring Economics 1

CHAPTER 2 Production, Economic Growth, and Trade 27

CHAPTER 3 Supply and Demand 51

CHAPTER 4 Markets and Government 79

CHAPTER 5 Elasticity 101

CHAPTER 6 Consumer Choice and Demand 131

CHAPTER 7 Production and Costs 163

CHAPTER 8 Perfect Competition 189

CHAPTER 9 Monopoly 215

CHAPTER 10 Monopolistic Competition, Oligopoly, and Game Theory 245

CHAPTER 11 The Labor Market 275

CHAPTER 12 Land, Capital Markets, and Innovation 309

CHAPTER 13 Externalities and Public Goods 335

CHAPTER 14 Network Goods 365

CHAPTER 15 Poverty and Income Distribution 387

CHAPTER 16 International Trade 413

Sources for By the Numbers S-1
Glossary G-1
Credits for Chapter Opening Photographs CR-1
Index I-1

Contents

Preface **xxvii**

1 Exploring Economics

BY THE NUMBERS: Economic Issues Are All Around Us 3

What Is Economics About? 2

Why Should One Study Economics? 4
Microeconomics Versus Macroeconomics 4
Economic Theories and Reality 5
Model Building 5
Ceteris Paribus: All Else Held Constant 6
Efficiency Versus Equity 6
Positive Versus Normative Questions 7
Issue: Have Smartphones and Social Media Made Life Easier? 6

Key Principles of Economics 8

Principle 1: Economics Is Concerned with Making Choices with Limited Resources 8
Principle 2: When Making Decisions, One Must Take into Account Tradeoffs and Opportunity Costs 8
Principle 3: Specialization Leads to Gains for All Involved 9
Principle 4: People Respond to Incentives, Both Good and Bad 9
Principle 5: Rational Behavior Requires Thinking on the Margin 10
Principle 6: Markets Are Generally Efficient; When They Aren't, Government Can Sometimes Correct the Failure 10
Principle 7: Institutions and Human Creativity Help Explain the Wealth of Nations 11
Summing It All Up: Economics Is All Around Us 12
Issue: Do Economists Ever Agree on Anything? 13

ADAM SMITH (1723–1790) 12

Chapter Summary 14 ■ Key Concepts 16
Questions and Problems 16 ■ Answers to Questions in Checkpoints 17

Appendix: Working with Graphs and Formulas 18
Graphs and Data 18
Time Series 18
Scatter Plots 18
Pie Charts 19
Bar Charts 20
Simple Graphs Can Pack In a Lot of Information 20
A Few Simple Rules for Reading Graphs 21
Graphs and Models 21
Linear Relationships 22
Computing the Slope of a Linear Line 22
Nonlinear Relationships 23
Computing the Slope of a Nonlinear Curve 23
Ceteris Paribus, Simple Equations, and Shifting Curves 24
Ceteris Paribus: All Else Equal 24
Simple Linear Equations 24
Shifting Curves 25
Correlation Is Not Causation 26

2 Production, Economic Growth, and Trade

BY THE NUMBERS: Growth, Productivity, and Trade Are Key to Our Prosperity 29

Basic Economic Questions and Production 28
Basic Economic Questions 28
Economic Systems 30
Resources and Production 30
Land 30
Labor 30
Capital 31
Entrepreneurial Ability 31
Production and Efficiency 31

Production Possibilities and Economic Growth 32
Production Possibilities 32
Opportunity Cost 34
Increasing Opportunity Costs 34
Economic Growth 35
Expanding Resources 36
Technological Change 37

Summarizing the Sources of Economic Growth 38

Issue: Will Renewable Energy Be the Next Innovative Breakthrough? 39

Specialization, Comparative Advantage, and Trade 40

Absolute and Comparative Advantage 40

The Gains from Trade 42

Practical Constraints on Trade 45

Issue: Do We Really Specialize in That? Comparative Advantage in the United States and China 43

DAVID RICARDO (1772–1823) 40

Chapter Summary 46 ■ Key Concepts 48

Questions and Problems 48 ■ Answers to Questions in Checkpoints 50

3 Supply and Demand

BY THE NUMBERS: The World of Markets 53

Markets 52

The Price System 54

Issue: Do Markets Exist for Everyone, Including Dogs and Cats? 54

Demand 55

Willingness-to-Pay: The Building Block of Market Demand 55

The Law of Demand: The Relationship Between Quantity Demanded and Price 56

The Demand Curve 57

Determinants of Demand 58

- Tastes and Preferences 58
- Income 58
- Prices of Related Goods 59
- The Number of Buyers 59
- Expectations About Future Prices, Incomes, and Product Availability 59

Changes in Demand Versus Changes in Quantity Demanded 60

Supply 61

The Relationship Between Quantity Supplied and Price 61

The Law of Supply 62

The Supply Curve 62

Market Supply Curves 62

Determinants of Supply 62
Production Technology 63
Costs of Resources 63
Prices of Other Commodities 63
Expectations 64
Number of Sellers 64
Taxes and Subsidies 64
Changes in Supply Versus Changes in Quantity Supplied 64

Market Equilibrium 66

Moving to a New Equilibrium: Changes in Supply and Demand 68
Predicting the New Equilibrium When One Curve Shifts 68
Predicting the New Equilibrium When Both Curves Shift 70

Issue: Two-Buck Chuck: Will People Drink $2-a-Bottle Wine? 70

ALFRED MARSHALL (1842–1924) 68

Chapter Summary 72 ■ Key Concepts 74
Questions and Problems 74 ■ Answers to Questions in Checkpoints 78

4 Markets and Government

BY THE NUMBERS: Price Controls and Supports in the Economy Today 81

Consumer and Producer Surplus: A Tool for Measuring Economic Efficiency 82

Using Consumer and Producer Surplus: The Gains from Trade 85

The Consequences of Deviating from Market Equilibrium 85
When Prices Exceed Equilibrium 85
When Prices Fall Below Equilibrium 86
Market Failure 87
Lack of Competition 87
Information Is Not Shared by All Parties 87
The Existence of External Benefits or Costs 87
The Existence of Public Goods 88
Market Efficiency Versus Equity 88

Issue: Can Markets Accurately Predict the Future? 88

Price Ceilings and Price Floors 89

Price Ceilings 89
Price Floors 91

Issue: Are Price Gouging Laws Good for Consumers? 92

NOBEL PRIZE: PAUL A. SAMUELSON (1915–2009) 87

Chapter Summary 94 ■ Key Concepts 96
Questions and Problems 96 ■ Answers to Questions in Checkpoints 99

5 Elasticity

BY THE NUMBERS: Elasticity: How Markets React to Price Changes 103

Elasticity of Demand 104

Price Elasticity of Demand as an Absolute Value 104
Measuring Elasticity with Percentages 105
Elastic and Inelastic Demand 105
  Elastic 105
  Inelastic 105
  Unitary Elasticity 106
Determinants of Elasticity 107
  Substitutability 107
  Proportion of Income Spent on a Product 107
  Luxuries Versus Necessities 107
  Time Period 107
Computing Price Elasticities 108
  Using Midpoints to Compute Elasticity 108

Total Revenue and Other Measures of Elasticity 109

Elasticity and Total Revenue 110
  Inelastic Demand 110
  Elastic Demand 111
  Unitary Elasticity 111
  Elasticity and Total Revenue Along a Straight-Line (Linear) Demand Curve 111
Other Elasticities of Demand 112
  Cross Elasticity of Demand 112
  Income Elasticity of Demand 113

Issue: Using Loss Leaders to Generate Higher Total Revenue 114

Elasticity of Supply 115

Time and Price Elasticity of Supply 116
  The Market Period 116
  The Short Run 116
  The Long Run 116

Taxes and Elasticity 118

Taxes on Income Sources and Their Economic Burden 118
Taxes on Spending and the Incidence of Taxation 119
Elasticity of Demand and Tax Burdens 119
Elasticity of Supply and Tax Burdens 121

Issue: Are Sales Taxes Fair to Low-Income Households? 122

Chapter Summary 124 ▪ Key Concepts 126
Questions and Problems 126 ▪ Answers to Questions in Checkpoints 129

6 Consumer Choice and Demand

BY THE NUMBERS: How Do We Decide What to Buy? 133

The Budget Line and Choices 134

The Budget Line 134
Changes to the Budget Line 135
Changes to the Price of a Good 135
Changes to Income 135

Issue: Smaller Cars and Larger Homes: A Permanent Trend? 136

Marginal Utility Analysis 137

Preferences and Utility 137
Total and Marginal Utility 138
The Law of Diminishing Marginal Utility 139
Maximizing Utility 139
Deriving Demand Curves 142
Limitations of Marginal Utility Analysis 143

Behavioral Economics 144

Sunk Cost Fallacy 145
Framing Bias 145
Overconfidence 146
Overvaluing the Present Relative to the Future 146
Altruism 147

Issue: Tipping and Consumer Behavior 147

JEREMY BENTHAM (1748–1832) 138

Chapter Summary 149 ▪ Key Concepts 151
Questions and Problems 151 ▪ Answers to Questions in Checkpoints 153

Appendix: Indifference Curve Analysis 155

Indifference Curves and Consumer Preferences 155
Properties of Indifference Curves 156
Indifference (or Preference) Maps 156
Optimal Consumer Choice 157
Using Indifference Curves 157
Deriving Demand Curves 158
Income and Substitution Effects 159

Appendix Key Concepts 161 ■ Appendix Questions and Problems 161
Answers to Appendix Checkpoint Question 162

7 Production and Costs

BY THE NUMBERS: Innovation, Productivity, and Costs Rule Business 165

Firms, Profits, and Economic Costs 164

Firms 164
Entrepreneurs 166
Sole Proprietors 166
Partnerships 166
Corporations 166
Profits 168
Economic Costs 168
Sunk Costs 168
Economic and Normal Profits 169
Short Run Versus Long Run 170

Issue: The Vast World of Corporate Offshoring and Profits 167

Production in the Short Run 171

Total Product 171
Marginal and Average Product 172
Increasing and Diminishing Returns 173

Costs of Production 174

Short-Run Costs 174
Fixed and Variable Costs 174
Marginal Cost 175
Average Costs 176
Short-Run Cost Curves for Profit-Maximizing Decisions 177
Average Variable Cost (AVC) 177
Average Total Cost (ATC) 178
Marginal Cost (MC) 178

Long-Run Costs 178
Long-Run Average Total Cost 179
Economies and Diseconomies of Scale 179
Economies of Scope 180
Role of Technology 181
Issue: How Large Are Fixed Costs? A Look at the Pharmaceutical and Software Industries 181

Chapter Summary 183 ■ Key Concepts 185
Questions and Problems 185 ■ Answers to Questions in Checkpoints 187

8 Perfect Competition

BY THE NUMBERS: Perfect Competition and Efficiency 191

Market Structure Analysis 192

Primary Market Structures 192
Perfect Competition 192
Monopolistic Competition 192
Oligopoly 193
Monopoly 193
Defining Perfectly Competitive Markets 193
The Short Run and the Long Run (A Reminder) 194

Perfect Competition: Short-Run Decisions 195

Marginal Revenue 195
Profit-Maximizing Output 195
Economic Profits 196
Five Steps to Maximizing Profit 196
Normal Profits 198
Loss Minimization and Plant Shutdown 198
The Short-Run Supply Curve 200

Perfect Competition: Long-Run Adjustments 201

Adjusting to Profits and Losses in the Short Run 202
Competition and the Public Interest 204
Long-Run Industry Supply 205
Summing Up 207
Issue: Can Businesses Survive in an Open-Source World? 204
Issue: Globalization and "The Box" 206

NOBEL PRIZE: HERBERT SIMON (1916–2001) 200

Chapter Summary 209 ■ Key Concepts 211
Questions and Problems 211 ■ Answers to Questions in Checkpoints 213

9 Monopoly

BY THE NUMBERS: Monopoly and Market Power 217

Monopoly Markets 218

Sources of Market Power 218
  Control Over a Significant Factor of Production 218
  Economies of Scale 218
  Government Franchises, Patents, and Copyrights 219
Monopoly Pricing and Output Decisions 219
  MR < P for Monopoly 220
  Equilibrium Price and Output 221
  Using the Five Steps to Maximizing Profit 221
  Monopoly Does Not Guarantee Economic Profits 222

Issue: "But Wait . . . There's More!" The Success and Failure of Infomercials 223

Comparing Monopoly and Competition 224

Higher Prices and Lower Output from Monopoly 224
Rent Seeking and X-Inefficiency 225
Monopolies and Innovation 226
Benefits Versus Costs of Monopolies 226

Price Discrimination 227

Perfect (First-Degree) Price Discrimination 227
Second-Degree Price Discrimination 228
Third-Degree Price Discrimination 229

Issue: Is Flexible Ticket Pricing the New Form of Price Discrimination? 230

Regulation and Antitrust 231

Regulating the Natural Monopolist 231
  Marginal Cost Pricing Rule 232
  Average Cost Pricing Rule 232
  Regulation in Practice 232
Antitrust Policy 233
The Major Antitrust Laws 234
Defining the Relevant Market and Market Power 234
  Concentration Ratios 235
  Herfindahl-Hirschman Index 235
  Applying the HHI 236

Contestable Markets 236
The Future of Antitrust Policy 236

NOBEL PRIZE: GEORGE STIGLER (1911–1991) 233

Chapter Summary 238 ■ Key Concepts 240
Questions and Problems 240 ■ Answers to Questions in Checkpoints 242

10 Monopolistic Competition, Oligopoly, and Game Theory

BY THE NUMBERS: Product Differentiation and Market Share 247

Monopolistic Competition 248

Product Differentiation and the Firm's Demand Curve 248
The Role of Advertising 249
Price and Output Under Monopolistic Competition 250
Comparing Monopolistic Competition to Perfect Competition 252
Issue: Do Brands Really Represent Pricing Power? 250

Oligopoly 253

Defining Oligopoly 253
Cartels: Joint Profit Maximization and the Instability of Oligopolies 253
The Kinked Demand Curve Model and the Stability of Oligopolies 255

Game Theory 256

Basic Game Setup and Assumptions 258
Simultaneous Versus Sequential-Move Games 258
Simultaneous-Move Games 258
Nash Equilibrium 260
Nash Equilibrium: A Personal Example 260
Issue: Mission ~~Im~~possible: The Power of Focal Points in a Simulated Mission 261

Applications of Game Theory 262

The Prisoner's Dilemma 262
The Classic Prisoner's Dilemma 263
Other Examples of Prisoner's Dilemma Outcomes 264
Resolving the Prisoner's Dilemma 264
Repeated Games 265
Grim Trigger 265
Trembling Hand Trigger 265
Tit-for-Tat 265
Using Sequential-Move Analysis to Model Repeated Games 266

Leadership Games 266
Chicken Games 267
Summary of Market Structures 268

NOBEL PRIZE: JOHN NASH 257

Chapter Summary 270 ■ Key Concepts 272
Questions and Problems 272 ■ Answers to Questions in Checkpoints 274

11 The Labor Market

BY THE NUMBERS: Your Wages and Your Job After College 277

Competitive Labor Supply 278

Individual Labor Supply 278
  Substitution Effect 278
  Income Effect 279
Market Labor Supply Curves 279
Factors That Change Labor Supply 280
  Demographic Changes 280
  Nonmoney Aspects of Jobs 280
  Wages in Alternative Jobs 280
  Nonwage Income 281

Competitive Labor Demand 281

Marginal Revenue Product 281
Factors That Change Labor Demand 283
  Changes in Product Demand 283
  Changes in Productivity 284
  Changes in the Prices of Other Inputs 284
Elasticity of Demand for Labor 284
Factors That Affect the Elasticity of Demand for Labor 284
  Elasticity of Demand for the Product 284
  Ease of Input Substitutability 284
  Labor's Share of Total Production Costs 285
Competitive Labor Market Equilibrium 285

Issue: Reality TV and the Labor Market for Entertainers 286

Economic Discrimination 287

Becker's Theory of Economic Discrimination 287
Segmented Labor Markets 288
Public Policy to Combat Discrimination 290
  The Equal Pay Act of 1963 290
  Civil Rights Act of 1964 291
  Executive Order 11246—Affirmative Action 291
  Age, Disabilities, and Sexual Orientation 291

Labor Unions and Collective Bargaining 292

Types of Unions 292
Benefits and Costs of Union Membership 292
Brief History of American Unionism 293
Union Versus Nonunion Wage Differentials 295

Issue: Will Public Unions Become an Endangered Species? 296

The Changing World of Work 297

Jobs of the Past Versus the Present 297
Future Jobs in the U.S. Economy 297

NOBEL PRIZE: GARY BECKER 288

Chapter Summary 298 ■ Key Concepts 300
Questions and Problems 300 ■ Answers to Questions in Checkpoints 301

Appendix: Imperfect Labor Markets 303

Monopoly Power in Product Markets 303
Monopsony 304

KARL MARX (1818–1883) 306

Appendix Key Concepts 307 ■ Appendix Summary 307
Appendix Questions and Problems 307 ■ Answers to Appendix Checkpoint Question 308

12 Land, Capital Markets, and Innovation

BY THE NUMBERS: Innovation Is the Cornerstone of Growth 311

Land and Physical Capital 312

Land 312
Physical Capital 313
Present Value Approach 315
Rate of Return Approach 316

Financial Capital 317

Banks and Borrowing 317
Bonds (Debt Capital) 318
Stocks (Equity Capital) 319
Venture Capital and Private Equity 320

Issue: Venture Capital: A Few Success Stories and One Big Missed Opportunity 321

Investment in Human Capital 322

Education and Earnings 322
Education as Investment 322
Equilibrium Levels of Human Capital 324
Implications of Human Capital Theory 325
Human Capital as Screening or Signaling 325
On-the-Job Training 325

Issue: The Role of Educational Systems in Human Capital Accumulation 326

Entrepreneurship and Innovation 327

Entrepreneurship 327
Innovation and the Global Economy 328

Chapter Summary 329 ■ Key Concepts 331
Questions and Problems 331 ■ Answers to Questions in Checkpoints 332

13 Externalities and Public Goods

BY THE NUMBERS: The Environment and Sustainability 337

Externalities 338

Negative Externalities 338
The Coase Theorem 340
Positive Externalities 341
Limitations 342

Public Goods 343

What Are Public Goods? 343
The Demand for Public Goods 344
Optimal Provision of Public Goods 345
Common Property Resources 345

Issue: Tragedy of the Commons: The Perfect Fish 346

Environmental Policy 347

Government Failure 348
Intergenerational Questions 348
Socially Efficient Levels of Pollution 349
Overview of Environmental Policies 350
Command and Control Policies 350
Market-Based Policies 351
  Emissions Taxes 351
  Marketable or Tradable Permits 351
  Other Market-Based Policies 352

Issue: Cap-and-Trade: The Day Liberal Environmentalists and Free-Market Conservatives Agreed 353

Putting It All Together: An Analysis of Climate Change 354

Understanding Climate Change 355
Unique Timing Aspects 356
Public Good Aspects 356
Equity Aspects 356
Finding a Solution 357

NOBEL PRIZE: RONALD COASE (1910–2013) 341
NOBEL PRIZE: ELINOR OSTROM (1933–2012) 357

Chapter Summary 359 ■ Key Concepts 361
Questions and Problems 361 ■ Answers to Questions in Checkpoints 363

14 Network Goods

BY THE NUMBERS: How We Are Connected Today 367

What Is a Network Good? 368

Types of Network Goods 368
Network Effects 368

Demand Curve for a Network Good 370

Demand for a Fixed Capacity Network Good 370
Deriving the Full Network Demand Curve 371
Examples of Network Demand Curve Pricing in Our Daily Lives 372

Market Equilibrium for a Network Good 372

Economies of Scale and Marginal Cost 373
Finding an Equilibrium in the Market for Network Goods 373
Network Goods Can Face a Virtuous Cycle or a Vicious Cycle Very Quickly 374

Issue: The Broadband Effect: Virtuous and Vicious Cycles in Network Goods 375

Competition and Market Structure for Network Goods 376

Competition and Pricing Strategies 376
Capturing New Customers Using Teaser Strategies 376
Retaining Existing Customers Using Lock-In Strategies 377
Using Market Segmentation to Maximize Profits 377

Issue: Do Exclusive Marketing Deals Lock In Customers? 377

Should Network Goods Be Regulated? 379

Promoting Network Competition with Interconnection 380
Industry Standards and Network Compatibility 380
Does Interconnection Improve Efficiency in Network Industries? 381
Can Poor Regulation Be Worse Than No Regulation? 381

Chapter Summary 382 ■ Key Concepts 384
Questions and Problems 384 ■ Answers to Questions in Checkpoints 386

15 Poverty and Income Distribution

BY THE NUMBERS: Poverty and the Economy 389

The Distribution of Income and Wealth 390

Life Cycle Effects 390
The Distribution of Income 390
Personal or Family Distribution of Income 391
Lorenz Curves 392
Gini Coefficient 393
The Impact of Redistribution 394
Causes of Income Inequality 396
Human Capital 396
Other Factors 397

Poverty 398

Measuring Poverty 399
The Incidence of Poverty 400
Depth of Poverty 401
Alternative Measures of Poverty 402

Issue: Why Do We Use an Outdated Measure of Poverty? 403

Causes of Poverty 403
Eliminating Poverty 403

Issue: What Is Considered "Poor" Around the World? 404

Reducing Income Inequality 404
Increasing Economic Growth 405
Rawls and Nozick 405
Mobility: Are Poor Families Poor Forever? 406

Chapter Summary 408 ■ Key Concepts 410
Questions and Problems 410 ■ Answers to Questions in Checkpoints 412

16 International Trade

BY THE NUMBERS: International Trade 415

The Gains from Trade 416

Absolute and Comparative Advantage 416
Gains from Trade 418
Practical Constraints on Trade 419
Issue: The Challenge of Measuring Imports and Exports in a Global Economy 419

The Terms of Trade 420

Determining the Terms of Trade 421
The Impact of Trade 422
How Trade Is Restricted 422
Effects of Tariffs and Quotas 424
Issue: Do Foreign Trade Zones Help or Hurt American Consumers and Workers? 426

Arguments Against Free Trade 427

Traditional Economic Arguments 427
Infant Industry Argument 427
Antidumping 428
Low Foreign Wages 428
National Defense Argument 428
Recent Globalization Concerns 429
Trade and Domestic Employment 429
Trade and the Environment 429
Trade and Its Effect on Working Conditions in Developing Nations 430

Chapter Summary 432 ■ Key Concepts 434
Questions and Problems 434 ■ Answers to Questions in Checkpoints 437

Sources for By the Numbers S-1
Glossary G-1
Credits for Chapter Opening Photographs CR-1
Index I-1

Preface

Every instructor faces the same problem, every day, with every class: How many students can we reach today? Can we reach each one?

Every time I teach principles of microeconomics, I keep in mind that many of my students are learning about economics for the first time, and how they perceive *my* course may influence their perceptions of economics for a long time. I take this challenge seriously each time I enter a classroom.

I have taught over 10,000 students since 2001—in small classrooms, large auditoriums, online classes, day classes, and evening classes. The diversity of my students has provided abundant examples of learning by experience. Each setting provides a laboratory for using innovative teaching techniques to motivate students to appreciate the endless possibilities that thinking like an economist can provide.

The challenge, of course, is reaching each and every student. This challenge has been compounded by the increasing number of ways in which students learn.

A critical component of a positive first experience in microeconomics is a good textbook. The best textbooks fascinate students by conveying interesting and intuitive examples while providing a guide to understanding difficult and often frustrating concepts in a principles of microeconomics course. Therefore, in my search for a textbook, I desired a book that was written by an author who shared a similar teaching philosophy, one who loves teaching and has spent her or his career in the classroom. I believe that the best principles of microeconomics textbooks are authored by people invested in their students' classroom experience.

I found that author in Gerald Stone, a lifelong teacher, and his text *CoreMicroeconomics*. The concept was novel: Based on a comprehensive survey of what instructors actually had time to cover in their classes, the text covered the core chapters that all instructors taught. Additional material was kept to a minimum. This had several benefits. First, no longer would students be overwhelmed by a huge tome that gave the impression that microeconomics was all about topic after topic—after topic after topic. Second, because *CoreMicroeconomics* was shorter than the standard text, it offered a corresponding price break. My students were grateful that they paid only for chapters taught in the course. Third, once relieved of the pressure to cover most of a text, I could devote more time to enriching the learning experience of my students. Since I began using *CoreMicroeconomics*, I have been afforded the time to discuss more current events, to engage my students with more applications of key concepts, and to devote classroom time to active learning exercises.

The Story of *CoreMicroeconomics* Transformed

Intrigued by the promise of *CoreMicroeconomics,* I became involved in the development of the text as an accuracy checker for the first edition, then on the technology side with the development of *EconPortal,* an online homework and course management system that became a standard offering with the second edition. Hired as a faculty editor in 2009, I saw firsthand how the many parts of the textbook were all linked, from the author-written *CourseTutor,* Test Bank, and PowerPoint slides, to the multimedia and graphing tools created for *EconPortal.*

In early 2010, Gerald Stone was diagnosed with cancer, and could not continue authorship of *CoreMicroeconomics.* In May 2010, he invited me to Littleton, Colorado, where we shared a long discussion about our teaching experiences. Like a teacher bestowing wisdom to a pupil but with the relaxed nature of lifelong friends, he shared words of advice and encouragement. I was pleased to discover that Jerry looked beyond the textbook to the entire learning experience of students and to the teaching experience of fellow instructors, as demonstrated by his close involvement with the supplements. After all, Jerry was one of the creators of the first computerized test bank. His holistic approach to learning and teaching, which I will explain in more detail later in this preface, mirrored my own. As a result of this meeting and further discussions, he asked me to take over the authorship of *CoreMicroeconomics* with the third edition, with the expectation that I would carry *CoreMicroeconomics* forward to a new generation of students and instructors with new needs. Sadly, Jerry passed away a few months after our meeting in Littleton.

My expectations were rather modest at that time. I had inherited a fantastic legacy. I knew that I could bring some innovations to the textbook on the pedagogical side based on what I had discovered teaching large numbers of students every semester. I assumed that my contributions on the content side of the textbook would be greater than the often cursory revisions of other texts that I examined (revisions often limited to changing some boxes and updating data), but I thought that my additions would be minimal. As for the broader learning experience, I assumed that I would continue enhancing the content in *EconPortal* (now renamed *LaunchPad*) as the importance of technology resources increase in higher education. Was I surprised!

Looking back at that time and evaluating what I have done, I am astounded at the amount of effort I chose to devote to the third edition to reach this generation of students and to assist this generation of teachers. The textbook and its learning and teaching package have been more than just revised. It is more appropriate to think of this as a transformation, from a high-quality textbook by a great educator to a textbook and its related course materials that engage and accommodate the changing nature of the classroom for today's instructors and students alike. Here's why this new edition is a transformation.

The Textbook: Innovations in Pedagogy

I knew I could use my classroom experience to bring pedagogical innovations to the text to reach students better. I developed three key pedagogical innovations.

Visual Chapter Summaries

Chapter summaries in nearly all principles of microeconomics textbooks are text-based. Some use bullet points to highlight key points, while others summarize each section of the chapter into a paragraph or two. Surveys of students have found that many students tend to skip the chapter summaries, or at best skim through them. Although chapter summaries contain the main points from each chapter, they often do little to help students *retain and understand* information other than iterating the content in an abridged manner.

I took a different approach in creating each chapter summary. People are naturally visual learners. Numerous studies have shown that adding a picture to a concept's description significantly improves the retention of that concept. Therefore, the chapter summaries contain multiple visual elements, such as pictures, graphs, and other contextually rich features to help aid in the review and retention of chapter content. The chapter summaries also are inspired by the use of concept maps common in textbooks in other disciplines, such as psychology, in which concepts are linked to one another in a logical manner. In this book, each chapter summary appears as a colorful two-page spread, with concepts and features flowing naturally from one section to another.

Each visual chapter summary complements the traditional text-based section reviews called Checkpoints, which appear at the end of each major section of a chapter. Each Checkpoint contains bullet points of the main concepts discussed within each section followed by a critical thinking question. In sum, the combination of text- and visual-based summaries provides students with more than one approach to reviewing and retaining concepts from each chapter.

A Greater Visual Dimension

As with the chapter summaries, so with the chapter text preceding it. I brought in more photos, again to help students retain key concepts. I tried to make these photos directly recognizable to students and their way of life. Other texts have photos: I would like to think that the ones used here are more interesting and better utilized to portray concepts.

The Data Dimension

Students today are bombarded with data and data graphs in the popular press and online. Students need to become good consumers of data to make sound decisions. Students who are equipped with skills to analyze the abundance of data that accompany their lives tend to make better decisions when it comes to seeking a career, deciding where to live, or even whom to marry. The presence of data has become a common component of the choices we make, and this textbook reinforces this skill with the By the Numbers feature.

The previous edition introduced the By the Numbers feature in a limited number of chapters. By the Numbers aims to provide students with a practical connection between economic concepts and empirical data. Now, By the Numbers appears in every chapter, always on the third page, presenting data, data graphs, and pictures focused around a theme based on the content contained in the chapter. Students are not expected to have read the chapter prior to examining the feature, although doing so may provide a deeper understanding of what the data convey.

Our goal is for students to become more comfortable examining and evaluating data. Viewing data in By the Numbers is not effective if comprehension is not achieved. To assess a student's understanding of the data, each chapter now contains two Using the Numbers questions based on data appearing in By the Numbers. Each question requires students to read data from various data graphs, compare trends, and to make conclusions about what the data convey. The questions can be assigned, used for in-class discussion, or used as a starting point for students to explore a topic in further depth. The data sources have been gathered at the back of the book in Sources for By the Numbers. This way they can be used if desired without getting in the way.

All of these pedagogical innovations should help students understand and retain information, whether they are comfortable with old text-heavy ways or the more visual and data-driven ways we see more frequently today.

The Textbook: Innovations in Content

In taking over the authorship of *CoreMicroeconomics,* I had assumed I would improve the text but thought this would be a straightforward task. I was surprised by the extent of the content changes I made to transform this text into something compelling to my students. These changes came about mainly due to three factors: changes in approach and emphasis in economic theory because of the need to explain pressing problems, the natural progression of economics research, and changes in the student body.

It may be useful to present key changes in microeconomics in three ways.

1. *Chapters that provided a strong foundation.* I found that there was a group of chapters that provided a very strong foundation for learning topics. For example, Chapter 4, Markets and Government, presents expanded coverage of consumer surplus and producer surplus at the beginning of the chapter to emphasize the importance of these welfare measures in economic analysis. Chapter 6, Consumer

Choice and Demand, begins with an analysis of budget lines and consumer choice, leading to a section on marginal utility analysis. These chapters underwent greater changes than other chapters, such as Chapter 8, Perfect Competition, which in the second edition presented the perfect competition model so clearly and revealed its use as a benchmark so concisely that I did not want to tamper with it too much. I added "Five Steps to Profit Maximization," a pedagogical device for understanding market structure figures in Chapters 8–10.

2. *Chapters that changed because of the progression of economic research.* I discovered that while all of microeconomics has been affected by the rapid pace of economic research, three chapters were changed significantly.
   a. *Behavioral Economics.* Chapter 6, Consumer Choice and Demand, now contains a new section on behavioral economics. My students are fascinated by such topics as framing and the perils of overconfidence. This section follows the material on budget lines, consumer choice, and marginal analysis giving students a fuller understanding of decision-making theory.
   b. *Game Theory.* The previous edition contained a section on game theory in Chapter 10, Monopolistic Competition, Oligopoly, and Game Theory. Now, game theory is presented in two sections: The first focuses on strategic thinking and Nash equilibrium, and the second focuses on applications of game theory, including the analysis of games that fall under the categories of Prisoner's Dilemma, repeated games, leadership, and chicken games. This has the benefit of adding new applications for instructors who want to enhance their coverage of game theory, while letting other instructors concentrate on the rudiments of game theory in the first section.
   c. *New Chapter: Network Goods.* Research on networks and network goods has exploded in recent years as networks such as Facebook have become crucial in the lives of many people. My students appreciate studying them. I thought it best to include a brand new chapter (Chapter 14, Network Goods) to give these goods the analysis they deserve, rather than trying to shoehorn them into another chapter.
3. *Chapters that changed because of changes in the student body.* I realized that some material in the second edition was just too tough for my students, as currently presented. I reworked Chapter 4, now entitled Markets and Government. My students need to know early in the course that market failure exists, but an in-depth treatment needs to wait until they have a more solid grounding in standard micro building blocks such as costs, profit maximization, and market power. Trimming back the early market failure material substantially let me add some material on using consumer and producer surplus. I moved the analysis of price ceilings and price floors from Chapter 3 to Chapter 4 to incorporate the effects of welfare measures on consumer and producer welfare.

This is just a brief summary of the key changes in the textbook. Every chapter was changed to some degree, some to a great extent, others to a lesser extent. See the chapter-by-chapter explanations later in this preface to see the wide range of changes to the content of the text.

The Text: Vivid Examples for Students

Another way I have transformed this textbook has been to replace just about all of the Issues. Each chapter now has two Issues that appeal to the diverse body of students studying microeconomics. Here are some of my favorites:

Chapter 1: Have Smartphones and Social Media Made Life Easier?
Chapter 2: Will Renewable Energy Be the Next Innovative Breakthrough?
Chapter 4: Are Price-Gouging Laws Good for Consumers?
Chapter 5: Are Sales Taxes Fair to Low-Income Households?

Chapter 7: How Large Are Fixed Costs? A Look at the Pharmaceutical and Software Industries
Chapter 9: Is Flexible Ticket Pricing the New Form of Price Discrimination?
Chapter 11: Reality TV and the Labor Market for Entertainers
Chapter 12: The Role of Educational Systems in Human Capital Accumulation

A Holistic Approach to Learning and Teaching

Earlier I mentioned that Jerry Stone and I shared a holistic approach to teaching principles of microeconomics. By holistic, I refer to how all elements of a course, including lectures, discussions, online assignments and resources, and assessment tools, are connected to one another in a logical and cohesive manner that facilitates both the learning process by students and the teaching process by instructors. Unlike other books on the market, I did not want to create a bunch of supplements merely to accompany the text. Instead, the resources produced for this third edition of *CoreMicroeconomics* were created to complement a suite of learning and teaching approaches used in higher education today, including the increased presence of online, hybrid, and active learning classrooms in addition to the traditional lecture- and discussion-based classes.

A Suite of Learning and Teaching Approaches

I was pleased to discover that transforming the text with my current students in mind actually freed up time to consider active learning methodologies for them. Instructors often encourage or even require students to read their textbook prior to the related lecture. When students do, class time can be used more effectively to refine the knowledge learned through independent study and to engage in activities that apply that knowledge. In order to facilitate the active learning approach to the classroom, a textbook must be approachable to a student seeing a concept for the first time.

This edition was written with this active learning objective in mind. Each chapter contains a wealth of vivid examples, intuitive explanations that build on one's natural instincts and innate knowledge. Further, the expanded use of photos and other visuals where appropriate helps to convey a concept or aid in the retention of an important lesson or key point.

Like a majority of instructors who utilize technological resources, I use a homework management system. I find that providing a seamless connection between technology resources and the textbook is a vital element for learning. Many publishers provide homework management systems that are generic in the sense that they are used in conjunction with *any* textbook. The disadvantage of this approach is that the content may not always reflect the style and content presented in the textbook. Therefore, it is important to me that I use a homework management system for which all content was created for *CoreMicroeconomics*; *LaunchPad* is the answer. Because *LaunchPad* corresponds directly with the textbook, I was able to contribute to its content and oversee all of the elements to ensure that the user experience of students and teachers is a positive one. Further, *LaunchPad* is compatible with most LMS systems (such as Blackboard) used by colleges and universities, allowing students to complete assignments and view grades without having to log into a separate system.

Outline of the Book and Changes in the Third Edition

Chapter 1: Exploring Economics

- Chapter opener changed from focus on growth to economics as a decision-making discipline.
- The ten Key Ideas of Section 2 have been trimmed to seven Key Principles. (Several of the more obscure ones have been dropped so that students will not have to struggle with things such as the money supply in the first chapter, something they will have little to no understanding of at the start of the course.)
- New Issue: Have Smartphones and Social Media Made Life Easier?
- New Issue: Do Economists Ever Agree on Anything?

A Unified Pedagogical Approach

Every chapter is structured around a common set of features including visual elements, applications, and end of chapter material unique to CoreMicroeconomics.

After studying this chapter you should be able to:

- Describe the nature and purposes of markets.
- Describe the nature of demand, demand curves, and the law of demand.
- Describe the determinants of demand and be able to forecast how a change in one or more of these determinants will change demand.
- Explain the difference between a change in demand and a change in quantity demanded.
- Determine market equilibrium price and output.
- Determine and predict how price and output will change given changes to supply and demand in the market.

LEARNING OBJECTIVES

Each chapter begins with a set of learning objectives which instructors can use for assessment and students can rely on to determine their depth of knowledge of economic concepts in the chapter.

What $60 billion global industry sells a product that many people typically can obtain easily from another source free of charge? The bottled water industry! This industry began its meteoric rise in the early 1990s, and today, the ubiquitous bottle of water has changed the way we live. It also has created new concerns regarding the environmental impact of the billions of plastic bottles used and discarded.

The bottled water industry took off as consumers changed their hydration habits, spurred by greater awareness of the health benefits of drinking water, including weight loss, illness prevention, and overall health maintenance. As water consumption increased, people started wanting something more than just ordinary water from the tap. They desired water that was purer, more consistent in taste, or infused with flavor or minerals. Plus, consumers wanted water that was easy to carry. Bottl
sumers wanted, and the market was willing to provide it.

Bottled water comes from many sources, both dome
of either spring water (from natural springs underneath
(ordinary tap water that undergoes a complex purificati
grew, new varieties of water were made available. Water t
springs, vitamin-infused water, flavored water, and carbo
choices consumers were given. The total amount of water
industry continued to increase as long as there were cust
the market.

In the late 2000s, falling incomes from a deteriorating gl
the harmful effects of discarded plastic bottles on the enviro
water purification devices, and even some laws against th
ally halted the market's growth. The economy has since im
industry responded to the environmental concerns by usi
plastic or by using new technologies to reduce the plastic
responding to the desires of consumers. As a result, sales in

Consumers have many choices of what water to buy an
bottled water market is one in which prices vary considera
of purchase. A single bottle of water of
$0.99 at a convenience store, $1.25 fro
and $3.00 or more at a theme park, sp
product be sold in different places at s

This chapter analyzes the various
different settings and circumstances.
tives into account in determining wha
what prices to charge. The interaction
determines the prices we pay.

In any given market, prices are d
factors determine what the market wil
the marketplace cause prices to chang
to supply and demand analysis. The b
chapter will let you determine why pr
in, and how many goods will be offer
ketplace. Later chapters use this same
wages are set and how personal incom

This chapter introduces some of t
understand how the forces of supply a
the law of demand, demand curves, th
curves, the determinants of supply, an

THE INTERACTION OF TEXT AND VISUALS THROUGHOUT

Research into how the mind processes information emphasizes the importance of pairing different mediums together to increase comprehension. Throughout the chapter, images and text are paired together: in the chapter opening story and chapter opening image; the By The Numbers visual display of data; the use of photographs and text to illustrate economic concepts; the pairing of figures and tables with relevant description; and the Visual Summaries that conclude each chapter.

Markets

markets Institutions that bring buyers and sellers together so they can interact and transact with each other.

A **market** is an institution that enables buyers and sellers to interact and transact with one another. A lemonade stand is a market because it allows people to exchange money for a product, in this case lemonade. Ticket scalping, which remains illegal or

BY THE NUMBERS

The outset of each chapter includes a By The Numbers—a visual display of data. By The Numbers emphasize the importance of data, helping students to become better consumers of data in their daily lives.

BY THE NUMBERS

The World of Markets

Markets form the foundation of all economic transactions. As various factors affect the supply and demand for goods and services, prices adjust upward or downward correspondingly to reach equilibrium.

The legalization of casinos in many states has resulted in dramatic growth in the industry. Top gaming revenues by state in 2011:

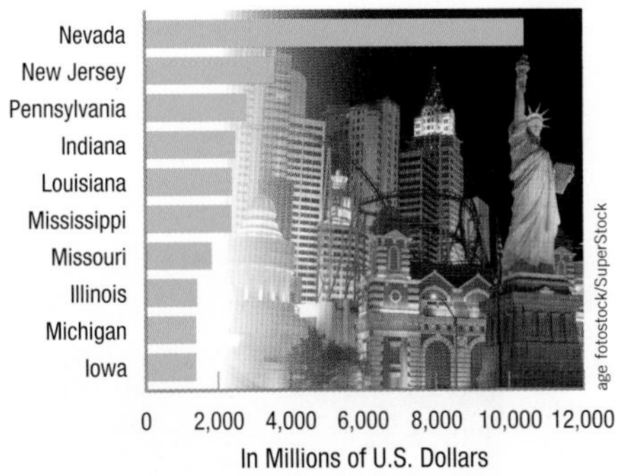

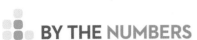

Prices for precious metals vary widely due to their relative demand and supply.

7,300,000,000
Total value (in U.S. dollars) of the worldwide virtual goods market associated with online gaming in 2012.

72,800,000,000
Total number of half-liter water bottles consumed in the United States in 2012 (over 220 bottles per person).

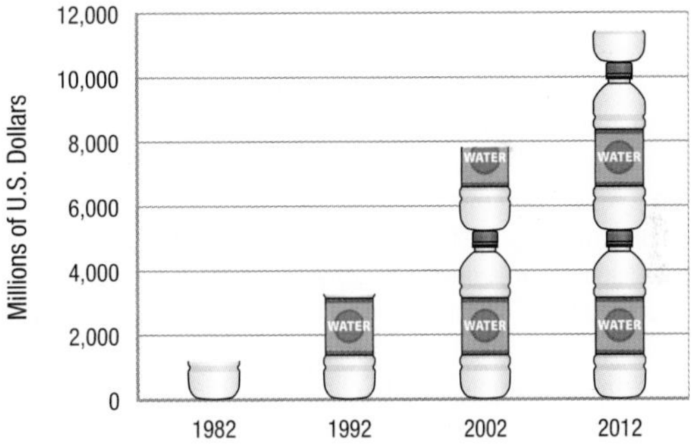

Total sales of bottled water in the United States took off in the 1990s and continued to grow steadily since.

University of Phoenix is the largest for-profit university with nearly 500,000 students.

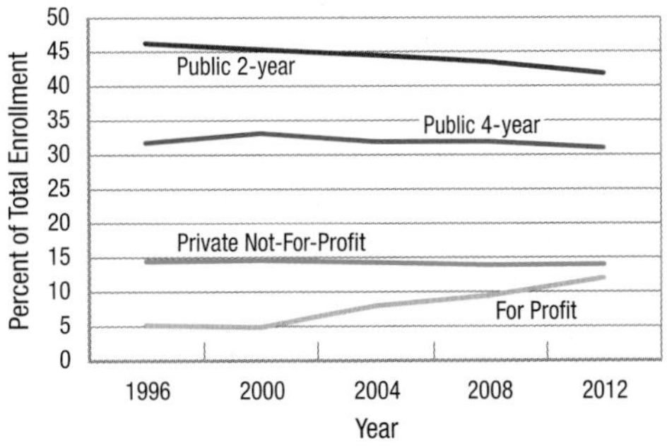

Enrollment at for-profit universities grew significantly over the past 16 years compared to not-for-profit institutions.

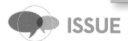

ISSUE

Features items from our economic world written for the third edition students in mind. Each Issue is kept to less than half a page to incentivize students to explore the world of economics around us.

ISSUE

Two-Buck Chuck: Will People Drink $2-a-Bottle Wine?

The great California wines of the 1990s put California vineyards on the map. Demand, prices, and exports grew rapidly. Overplanting of new grapevines was a result. When driving along Interstate 5 or Highway 101 north of Los Angeles, one can see vineyards extending for miles, and most were planted in the mid- to late 1990s. The 2001 recession reduced the demand for California wine, and a rising dollar made imported wine relatively cheaper. The result was a sharp drop in demand for California wine and a huge surplus of grapes.

Bronco Wine Company president Fred Franzia made an exclusive deal with Trader Joe's, an unusual supermarket that features exotic food and wine products. He bought the excess grapes at distressed prices, and in his company's modern plant produced inexpensive wines—chardonnay, merlot, cabernet sauvignon, shiraz, and sauvignon blanc—under the Charles Shaw label. Consumers flocked to Trader Joe's for wine costing $1.99 a bottle and literally hauled cases of wine out by the carload. In less than a decade, 400 million bottles of Two-Buck Chuck, as it is known, have been sold. This is not rotgut: The 2002 shiraz beat out 2,300 other wines to win a double gold medal at the 28th Annual International Eastern Wine Competition in 2004. Still, to many Napa Valley vintners it is known as Two-Buck Upchuck.

Two-Buck Chuck was such a hit that other supermarkets were forced to offer their own discount wines. This good, low-priced wine has had the effect of opening up markets. People who previously avoided wine because of the cost have begun drinking more. However, the influence of Two-Buck Chuck, which sold 60 million bottles in 2012, may be waning. In January 2013, Trader Joe's announced an increase in the price of the Two-Buck Chuck from $1.99 to $2.49 due to a poor grape harvest that raised the cost of producing the wine. Although the new price is still a bargain, the product that changed the wine industry may soon need another name.

joel zatz/Alamy

Predicting the New Equilibrium When Both Curves Shift When both supply and demand change, things get tricky. We can predict what will happen with price in some cases and output in other cases, but not what will happen with both.

Figure 12 portrays an increase in both demand and supply. Consider the market for corn. Suppose t … causes de… for corn

CHECKPOINT

MARKETS

- Markets are institutions that enable buyers and sellers to interact and transact business.
- Markets differ in geographical location, products offered, and size.
- Prices contain a wealth of information for both buyers and sellers.
- Through their purchases, consumers signal their willingness to exchange money for particular products at particular prices. These signals help businesses decide what to produce, and how much of it to produce.
- The market economy is also called the price system.

QUESTION: What are the important differences between the markets for financial securities such as the New York Stock Exchange and your local farmer's market?

...wers to the Checkpoint question can be found at the end of this chapter.

CHECKPOINT

Every section concludes with a set of review bullets that identify the key takeaways from that section of the chapter. Each CHECKPOINT also includes an open-ended critical thinking question. The answer can be found at the end of the chapter.

...emand

...ever you purchase a product, you are voting with your money. You are selecting one ...ct out of many and supporting one firm out of many, both of which signal to the ...ss community what sorts of products satisfy your wants as a consumer.

...onomists typically focus on wants rather than needs because it is so difficult to deter... what we truly need. Theoretically, you could survive on tofu and vitamin pills, living ... made of cardboar...

GRAPHS

Use Numbers not Symbols

Graphs use numbers on the horizontal and vertical axes whenever possible. This minimizes the level of abstraction that a student needs to understand economic models.

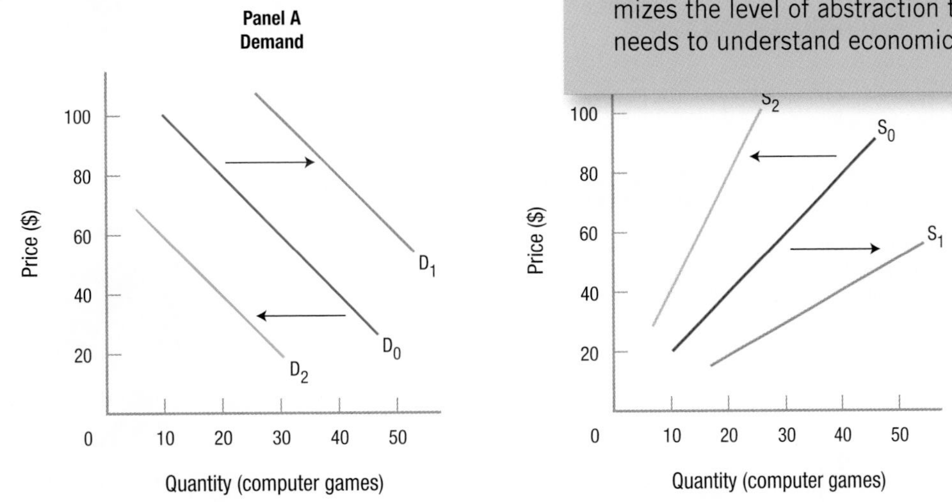

Determinants of Demand		Determinants of Supply	
Decrease in Demand	**Increase in Demand**	**Decrease in Supply**	**Increase in Supply**
Tastes and preferences fall	Tastes and preferences rise	Technology falls	Technology rises
Income falls (for normal goods)	Income rises (for normal goods)	Resource costs rise	Resource costs fall
Price of substitutes falls	Price of substitut...	...f product... ...sti...	Price of production substitute

VISUAL SUMMARY

Each chapter concludes with a two-page visual flow-chart of key concepts in the chapter. Instead of the traditional method of brief paragraphs of text (which are often read instead of the chapter text), the visual summaries pair images from the chapter with text to provide students with a deeper understanding of the relationship between terms and concepts in the chapter.

72

chapter summary

Section 1: **Markets**

A **market** is an institution that enables buyers and sellers to interact and transact with one another.

Corbis/SuperStock

Stars and Stripes/Alamy

Markets can be as simple as a lemonade stand, as large as an automobile lot, as valuable as the stock market, as virtual as an Internet shopping site, or as illegal as a ticket scalping operation.

Buyers and sellers communicate their desires in a market through the prices at which goods and services are bought and sold. Hence, a market economy is called a **price system.**

Robert Harding World Imagery/Corbis

Section 2: **Demand**

Demand refers to the goods and services people are willing and able to buy during a period of time. It is a horizontal summation of individual demand curves in a defined market.

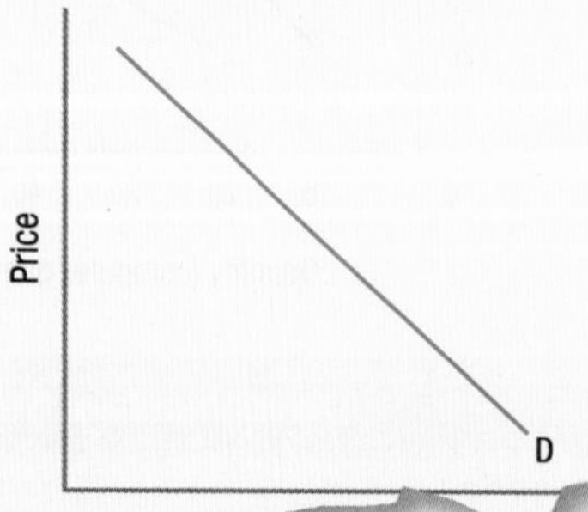

Alan Schein Photography/Corbis

Roller coasters are a lot of fun, but riding the same one over and over gives less satisfaction with each ride; therefore, willingness-to-pay falls with each ride.

Section 3: Supply

Supply analysis works the same way as demand, but looking at the market from the firm's point of view.

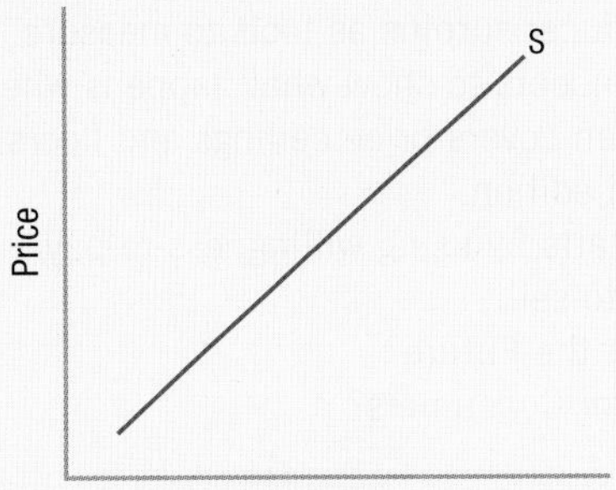

The **law of supply** states that as prices increase, firms want to supply more, and vice versa. It leads to an upward-sloping supply curve.

Philip Gostelow/Aurora Photos/Corbis

Determinants of Supply: How Supply Curves Shift

- ↑ Production technology: Supply shifts right.
- ↑ Cost of resources: Supply shifts left.
- ↑ Price of other commodities: Supply shifts left.
- ↑ Price expectations: Supply shifts left.
- ↑ Number of sellers: Supply shifts right.
- ↑ Taxes: Supply shifts left.
- ↑ Subsidies: Supply shifts right.

Section 4: Market Equilibrium

Market equilibrium occurs at the price at which the quantity supplied is equal to quantity demanded; in other words, where demand intersects supply.

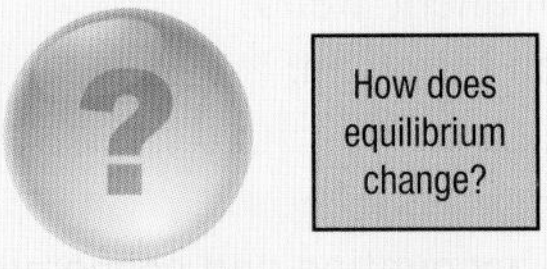

A shift in demand or supply will change equilibrium price and quantity.

Which curve slopes up and which slopes down? Two tricks to aid in memory:

- S"up"ply contains the word "up" for upward-sloping.
- Only the fingers on your right hand can make a "d" for demand. Hold that hand up in front of you!

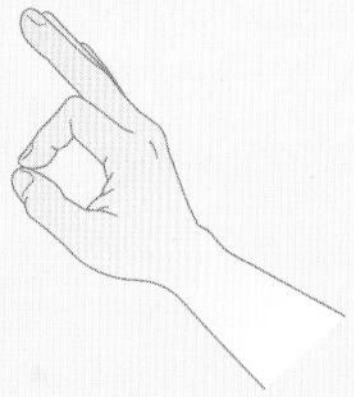

Chapter 2: Production, Economic Growth, and Trade

- New Figure 1: From Factors of Production to Output.
- New steps added on calculating opportunity costs in the comparative advantage section, with a new Table 1 summarizing the opportunity costs.
- New Issue: Will Renewable Energy Be the Next Innovative Breakthrough?
- New Issue: Do We Really Specialize in That? Comparative Advantage in the United States and China.

Chapter 3: Supply and Demand

- To explain where demand curves come from, a new section (and Figure 1) has been added on willingness-to-pay.
- The section on price ceilings and floors has been moved to Chapter 4.
- New Issue: Do Markets Exist for Everyone, Including Dogs and Cats?
- Figure 8, a summary figure, has been simplified.

Chapter 4: Markets and Government [title change]

- Second edition chapter had a long, tough section on market failure, and a history of the U.S. economy over the past 150 years. New third edition chapter prunes down the market failure material to approximately 1 page. The history section has been moved to the Web site.
- The chapter introduces consumer and producer surplus as tools to measure economic efficiency, then applies these concepts to show what happens when price is greater than or less than equilibrium, then covers price ceilings and floors. This is much more mainstream than the second edition.
- The consumer/producer surplus material starts by using willingness-to-pay (introduced in Chapter 3) and willingness-to-sell.
- New Issue: Can Markets Accurately Predict the Future?
- New Issue: Are Price-Gouging Laws Good for Consumers?

Chapter 5: Elasticity

- New separate section: Total Revenue and Other Measures of Elasticity.
- Cross elasticity is covered before income elasticity.
- New descriptive material (1½ pages) added to tax section.
- New Issue: Using Loss Leaders to Generate Higher Total Revenue.
- New Issue: Are Sales Taxes Fair to Low-Income Households?

Chapter 6: Consumer Choice and Demand

- New first section on budget lines and choices. Now covers how budget lines change based on prices or income.
- Second section on marginal utility analysis now combines parts of the first two sections in the second edition. The consumer surplus material has been removed because it is now discussed fully in Chapter 4.
- New third section on behavioral economics.
- New Issue: Smaller Cars and Larger Homes: A Permanent Trend?
- Appendix streamlined by dropping the long Issue on terrorism.

Chapter 7: Production and Cost

- Additional material makes the distinction between accounting and economic profits clearer, and emphasizes the fact that "zero economic profits" can still be a large accounting profit, depending on the opportunity costs of the firm.
- Focus on the AVC, ATC, and MC curves, with de-emphasis on the AFC curve.
- New Issue: The Vast World of Corporate Offshoring and Profits.
- New Issue: How Large Are Fixed Costs? A Look at the Pharmaceutical and Software Industries.

Chapter 8: Perfect Competition [title change]

- Chapter title changed to better capture what is covered in the chapter.
- New coverage of "Five Steps to Profit Maximization"—a method that will work for all market structures.
- Tables trimmed back.

Chapter 9: Monopoly

- Section 1 of the second edition divided into two sections: (1) Monopoly Markets, and (2) Comparing Monopoly and Competition.
- New coverage of "Five Steps to Profit Maximization."
- Section 2: New subsection on the benefits and costs of monopoly.
- New section combines regulation with antitrust, and trims some of the legal material in the antitrust coverage.
- Enhanced reliance on the concept of market power.
- New Issue: "But Wait . . . There's More!" The Success and Failure of Infomercials.
- New Issue: Is Flexible Ticket Pricing the New Form of Price Discrimination?

Chapter 10: Monopolistic Competition, Oligopoly, and Game Theory

- The major change is taking the section on game theory in the second edition and dividing it into two sections. Section 3, the first game theory section, now provides the introductory material, including the Nash equilibrium, and two examples. Section 4, the second game theory section, provides applications of game theory, with an emphasis on the Prisoner's Dilemma, repeated games, leadership, and chicken games.
- The first section on monopolistic competition now has more coverage of advertising.
- The section on oligopoly now has a fuller discussion of cartels and the incentive to cheat (with a new figure).
- New Issue: Mission ~~Im~~possible: The Power of Focal Points in a Simulated Mission.

Chapter 11: The Labor Market [new as a separate chapter]

- Major change: In the second edition, Chapter 11 included all of the factors including labor, and Chapter 12 included additional labor market issues. Thus, labor markets were divided over two chapters. In the third edition, all of labor is covered in Chapter 11, and the other factors are covered in Chapter 12.
- Labor market monopoly and monopsony are now covered in the chapter appendix, not the chapter body.
- New Issue: Reality TV and the Labor Market for Entertainers.
- New Issue: Will Public Unions Become an Endangered Species?

Chapter 12: Land, Capital Markets, and Innovation [new as a separate chapter]

- Land, capital, and innovation are now covered in a separate chapter, without labor.
- More coverage of land than in the previous edition.
- Financial capital section enhanced.
- New Issue: Venture Capital: A Few Success Stories and One Big Missed Opportunity.
- New Issue: The Role of Educational Systems on Human Capital Accumulation.

Chapter 13: Externalities and Public Goods

- Started the chapter with externalities rather than public goods because students typically find externalities easier to understand.

- Sections made more flexible so that instructors can cover externalities and public goods, and then skip environmental policy and climate change, if they wish.
- New Issue: Cap-and-Trade: The Day Liberal Environmentalists and Free-Market Conservatives Agreed.

Chapter 14: Network Goods [new chapter]

- Network goods are contemporary and of interest to students. Some network goods covered are software, wireless devices, and social networks such as Facebook.
- Network goods often have very large fixed costs but marginal costs close to zero.
- The demand curve for network goods is unlike the demand curves previously covered in the book because it slopes up initially and then slopes down.
- Full coverage of pricing strategies to attract and to lock in users.
- Issue: The Broadband Effect: Virtuous and Vicious Cycles in Network Goods.
- Issue: Do Exclusive Marketing Deals Lock In Customers?

Chapter 15: Poverty and Income Distribution

- New coverage of the 1% and the 99%.
- New subsection on the causes of poverty.
- Mobility of poor families moved from an Issue in the second edition into the chapter body. (The figure has been removed.)
- New Issue: What Is Considered "Poor" Around the World?

Chapter 16: International Trade

- Added discussion of three main reasons why nations trade: (1) Countries cannot produce everything they want (interindustry trade), (2) consumers desire variety (intraindustry trade), and (3) specialization increases total production and consumption (gains from trade).
- New Issue: The Challenge of Measuring Imports and Exports in a Global Economy.
- New Issue: Do Foreign Trade Zones Help or Hurt American Consumers and Workers?

CoreMedia Learning Suite: Transformed to Support Today's Students and Instructors

The CoreMedia Learning Suite establishes a new methodology behind creating great support materials for instructors and students. CoreMedia includes new and adapted resources engineered to match new approaches to classroom teaching and learning. Education research guides our decisions from the value of active learning classrooms to supporting hybrid and online education; each resource was crafted to support instructors and students understanding that no two classrooms are exactly the same. For more information on how each of the following resources supports different teaching and learning approaches, from traditional lectures to "flipped classrooms" or lecture capture to online or hybrid courses, please visit: www.coreecon.com.

For Instructors

Teaching Manual and Suggested Answers to Problems

Best Classroom Use: Traditional/Face-to-Face or Active-Learning/Face-to-Face

The Teaching Manual (TM) prepared by Mary H. Lesser (Lenoir-Rhyne University) is an ideal resource for many classroom teaching styles. The Teaching Manual focuses on expanding and enlivening classroom lectures by highlighting varied ways to bring real-world examples into the classroom. Portions of the Teaching Manual have been designed for use as student handouts. Every chapter of the Teaching Manual includes:

- *Chapter Overview*: A brief summary of the main topics in each chapter.

- *Ideas for Capturing Your Classroom Audience*: Written with experienced and novice instructors in mind, suggestions can be used for in-class demonstrations or enrichment assignments in on-site, hybrid, and online course formats.
- *Debate the Issues in the Chapter*: The TM reproduces the issues used in the chapter to spur student debate.
- *Examples Used in the End-of-Chapter Questions*: The TM provides the instructor with a succinct overview of those questions that refer to specific articles from major news sources that can be used to develop more in-depth analysis of current events.
- *For Further Analysis*: Each TM contains an additional extended example that can be used as a formatted, one-page handout, or posted online. It is designed for in-class group work or individual assignment. Learning objectives are specified and a one-page answer key is also available for reference or distribution.
- *Web-Based Exercises*: Each TM chapter includes a Web-based example that requires students to obtain information from a Web site and use it to answer a set of questions. As an in-class group exercise or an individual assignment, it can help students become better consumers of information and stronger evaluators of online data and research.
- *Tips from a Colleague*: Each chapter of the TM concludes with "tips," which share ideas about classroom presentation, use of other resources, and insights about topics that students typically find difficult to master.

Test Bank

Best Classroom Use: All Approaches

Coordinators: Jane Himarios (University of Texas at Arlington) and Eric Chiang (Florida Atlantic University)

Contributors and Accuracy Checkers: Dixie Button (Embry-Riddle Aeronautical University), Michael Fenick (Broward College), Scott Hegerty (Northeastern Illinois University), Fred May (Trident Technical College), Janet Wolcutt (Wichita State University), Sarah Jenyk (Youngstown State University), and Michael Dale (Trident Technical College).

The test bank contains nearly 4,000 carefully constructed, thoroughly edited and revised, and comprehensively accuracy checked questions. Each question was thoroughly reviewed by Jane Himarios and Eric Chiang; in fact, no component of the learning suite received as much scrutiny as the revision of the test bank.

- *New to this edition:* Each chapter features a set of *anchor questions* carefully selected by Eric Chiang as foundation questions around which a quiz, homework assignment, or test can be built.
- Each question has *skill descriptors* based on Bloom's Taxonomy and a *degree of difficulty* (easy, moderate, or difficult). *Easy* questions require students to recognize concepts and definitions; *moderate* questions require some analysis, including distinguishing between related concepts; and *difficult* questions usually require more detailed analysis.
- To further aid instructors in building tests, each question is referenced by the specific heading in the textbook. Questions are presented in the order in which concepts are presented in the book.
- The test bank includes questions with tables that students must analyze to solve for numerical answers. It contains questions based on graphs that appear in the book and require students to interpret information presented in the graph.

Computerized Test Bank

Wimba
people teach people

Best Classroom Use: Online and Hybrid Course Formats | Building Tests for Face-to-Face Instruction

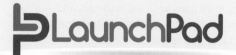

LaunchPad

Because technology should never get in the way

At Macmillan Higher Education, we are committed to providing online instructional materials that meet the needs of instructors and students in powerful, yet simple ways—powerful enough to dramatically enhance teaching and learning, yet simple enough to use right away.

We've taken what we've learned from thousands of instructors and the hundreds of thousands of students to create a new generation of Macmillan Higher Education technology—featuring **LaunchPad**. **LaunchPad** offers our acclaimed content curated and organized for easy assignability in a breakthrough user interface in which power and simplicity go hand in hand.

LaunchPad Units

Curated LaunchPad Units make class prep a whole lot easier. Combining a curated collection of video, simulations, animations, multimedia assignments, and e-book content, LaunchPad's interactive units give you a building block to use as-is, or as a starting point for your own learning units. An entire unit's worth of work can be assigned in seconds, drastically saving the amount of time it takes for you to have your course up and running.

- **Give students LearningCurve**—and get them more engaged with what they're learning. Powerful adaptive quizzing, a game-like format, direct links to the e-Book, instant feedback, and the promise of better grades make using LearningCurve a no-brainer. Customized quizzing tailored to each text adapts to student responses and provides material at different difficulty levels and topics based on student performance. Students love the simple yet powerful system and instructors can access class reports to help refine lecture content.

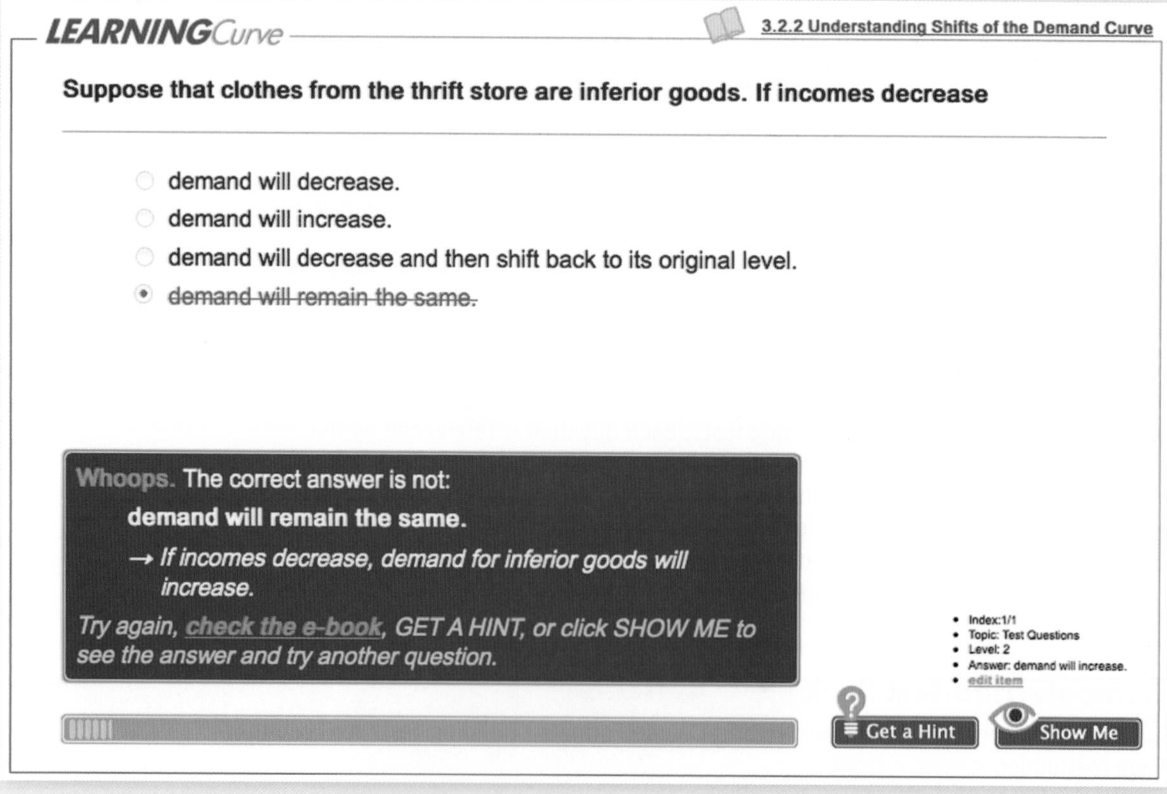

- **Everything is Assignable.** You can customize the LaunchPad Units by adding quizzes and other activities from our vast wealth of resources. You can also add a discussion board, a dropbox, and RSS feed, with a few clicks. LaunchPad allows you to customize your students' experience as much or as little as you'd like.
- **Useful Analytics.** The gradebook quickly and easily allows you to look up performance metrics for your whole class, for individual students and for individual assignments. Having ready access to this information can help in both lecture prep and in making office hours more productive and efficient.
- **An e-Book that delivers more than content.** Every LaunchPad e-Book comes with powerful study tools for students, video and multimedia content, and easy customization for instructors. Students can search, highlight, and bookmark, making it easier to study and access key content. And teachers can make sure their class gets just the book they want to deliver: customize and rearrange chapters, add and share notes and discussions, and link to quizzes, activities, and other resources.
- **Intuitive interface and design.** Students can be in only two places – either viewing the home page with their assigned content, or working to complete their assignments. Students' navigation options and expectations are clearly laid out in front of them at all times ensuring they can never get lost in the system.
- **Electronically graded graphing problems** replicate the paper and pencil experience better than any program on the market. Students are asked to draw their response and label each curve. The software automatically grades each response, providing feedback options at the instructor's discretion, including partial credit for incomplete, but not entirely incorrect, responses. Graphing questions are tagged to appropriate textbook sections and range in difficulty level and skill.

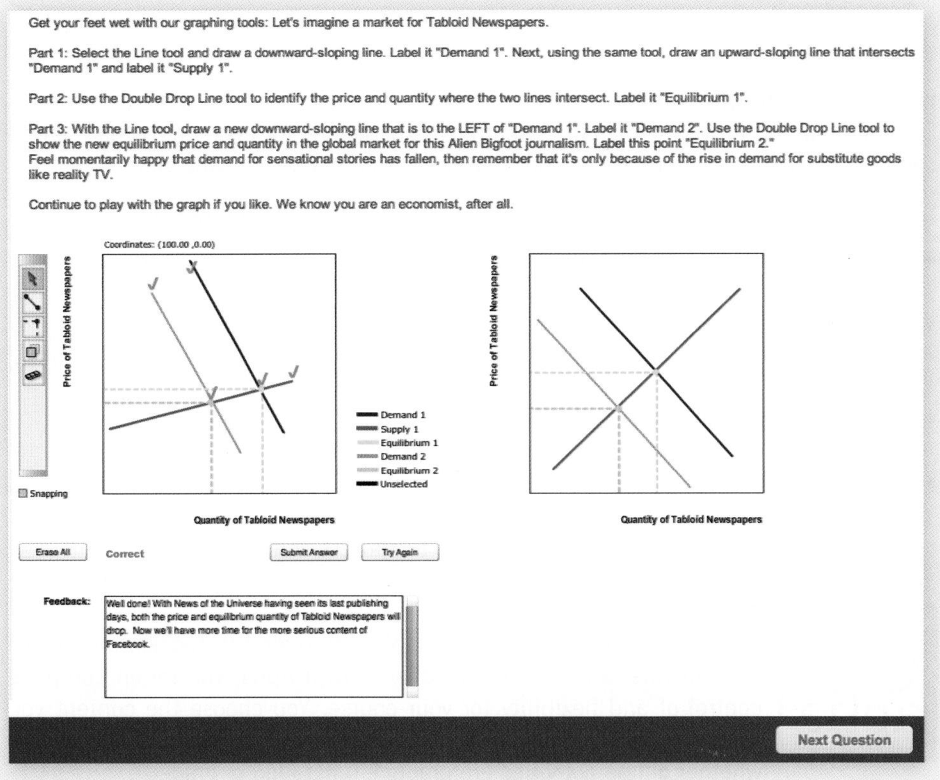

Diploma was the first software for PCs that integrated a test-generation program with grade-book software and online testing system. Diploma is now in its fifth generation. The Test Banks are available for both Windows and Macintosh users.

With Diploma, you can easily create and print test banks and write and edit questions. You can add an unlimited number of questions, scramble questions and distractors, and include figures. Tests can be printed in a wide range of formats. The software's unique synthesis of flexible word-processing and database features creates a program that is extremely intuitive and capable.

Two Sets of PowerPoint Slides

Best Classroom Use: Traditional/Face-to-Face or Active Learning/Face-to-Face

Dynamic PowerPoint Presentation by Eric Levy (Florida Atlantic University): PowerPoint slides designed with front-of-the-classroom presentation and visual learning in mind. This set of PowerPoint slides contains fully animated graphs, visual learning images, additional examples, links, and embedded questions. These slides may be customized by instructors and accessed via the catalog page at www.wortheconomics.com or within *LaunchPad* for *CoreMicroeconomics.*

Lecture PowerPoint Presentation consists of PowerPoint slides designed by Debbie Evercloud (University of Colorado, Denver) that provide graphs from the textbook, data, tables, and bulleted lists of key concepts suitable for lecture presentation. Key figures from the text are replicated and animated to demonstrate how they develop. These slides may be customized by instructors to suit individual needs. These files may be accessed on the catalog page at www.wortheconomics.com or within *LaunchPad* for *CoreMicroeconomics.*

Additional Online Offerings

sapling learning

www.saplinglearning.com

Sapling Learning provides interactive learning experiences for economics that significantly improve student comprehension, retention, and problem-solving skills.

Sapling Learning's system delivers unmatched benefits and capabilities including:

- **Proven Results**. Independent university studies have shown Sapling Learning improves student performance by 0.75 to a full letter grade.
- **Industry-Leading Support**. We match instructors with a Technology TA—PhD and master's-level subject experts—to provide software and course support throughout the semester.
- **Instant Student Feedback**. Our easy-to-use online homework assignments provide instant feedback and tutorials tailored to students' responses.
- **Performance Tracking**. Sapling Learning grades assignments, tracks student participation and progress, and compiles performance analytics—helping instructors save time and tailor assignments to address student needs.

aplia™

www.aplia.com/worth

Worth/Aplia courses are all available with digital textbooks, interactive assignments, and detailed feedback. With Aplia, you retain complete control of and flexibility for your course. You choose the content you want students to cover, and you decide how to organize it. You decide whether online activities are practice (ungraded or graded).

- **Extra problem sets** (derived from in-chapter questions in the book) suitable for homework and keyed to specific topics from each chapter
- **Regularly updated news analyses**

Interactive tutorials to assist with math and graphing
Instant online reports that allow instructors to target student trouble areas more efficiently

Further Resources Offered

CourseTutor

CourseTutor, revised by Albert J. Sumell (Youngstown State University) and Gregory Rose (Sacramento City College) is more than a traditional study guide. It originated as a study aid crafted by Gerald Stone to help students in his Saturday sections at Metropolitan State University of Denver.

Each chapter of the *CourseTutor* is divided into two basic sections: a six-step detailed walk-through of the material to help each student check his or her individual progress, followed by a section with standard study material such as fill-in, true/false, multiple-choice, and short essay questions. Both sections are designed for interactivity and many of these features can be found in a digital format within *LaunchPad* for *CoreMicroeconomics* including:

Solved Problems: developed by Irina Pritchett (North Carolina State University), the solved problems are designed for the online environment using a graphing and assessment engine. Students receive detailed feedback and guidance on where to go for further review.

Students learn by many different methods and *CourseTutor* provides a buffet of learning choices. Students select those methods that best help them learn. In this way, the *CourseTutor* was a precursor to the many adaptive methodologies at work in online learning software, including those found in *LaunchPad* for *CoreMicroeconomics.*

CourseSmart e-Books

www.coursesmart.com

CourseSmart e-Books offer the complete book in PDF format. Students can save money—up to 60% off the price of the printed textbook. In CourseSmart, students have the ability to take notes, highlight, print pages, and more. It is great alternative to renting a textbook and it is compatible with most mobile platforms.

i>clicker

Developed by a team of University of Illinois physicists, i>clicker is the most flexible and reliable classroom response system available. It is the only solution created *for educators, by educators*—with continuous product improvements made through direct classroom testing and faculty feedback. You'll love i>clicker, no matter your level of technical expertise, because the focus is on your teaching, not the technology. To learn more about packaging i>clicker with this textbook, please contact your local sales representative or visit www.iclicker.com.

LMS Integration

LaunchPad for *CoreMicroeconomics* can be fully integrated with any campus LMS including such features as single sign-on for students revisiting the site, gradebook integration for all activities completed in *LaunchPad,* as well as integration of assignments within the campus LMS for certain products. For more information on LMS integration, please contact your local publisher's representative.

Acknowledgments

No project of this scope is accomplished alone. *CoreMicroeconomics* and its suite of learning resources came together as a result of the dedication of many individuals who devoted incredible amounts of time to the project. These include reviewers of manuscript chapters, focus group participants, accuracy reviewers, supplements contributors, project specialists, and the production and editorial staff at Worth Publishers.

I want to thank those reviewers of the third edition who read through chapters in manuscript and offered many important suggestions that have been incorporated into this project. They include:

Bill Adamson, University of South Dakota
Stephen Bannister, University of Utah
Robert Burrus, University of North Carolina-Wilmington
Suparna Chakraborty, University of San Francisco
AnaMaria Conley, Regis University
Dale DeBoer, University of Colorado, Colorado Springs
Erwin Erhardt III, University of Cincinnati
Scott Gilbert, Southern Illinois University
Ross J. Hallren, University of Oklahoma
Moon Moon Haque, University of Memphis
Michael G. Heslop, Northern Virginia Community College
Ryan Herzog, Gonzaga University
Scott Hunt, Columbus State Community College
Sarah Jenyk, Youngstown State University
Janis Y. F. Kea, West Valley College
Barry Kotlove, Edmonds Community College
Larry Landrum, Virginia Western Community College
Jim Lee, Texas A&M University Corpus Christi
Sang H. Lee, Southeastern Louisiana University
Fred May, Trident Technical College
Robert McKizzie, Tarrant County College Southeast
Randy Methenitis, Richland College
Stan Mitchell, McLennan Community College
Douglas Orr, City College of San Francisco
Tomy Ovaska, Youngstown State University
Ravi Samitamana, Daytona State College
Albert J. Sumell, Youngstown State University
Deborah Thorsen, Palm Beach State College
Jane A. Treptow, Broward College
Christine Walthen, Middlesex County College
Wendy Wysocki, Monroe County Community College

I would like to thank those focus group participants who devoted a lot of time and effort to discussing the proposed revisions to the third edition and how this edition of *CoreMicroeconomics* can facilitate a broad range of learning and teaching approaches. Their suggestions (and criticisms) contributed immensely to the development of this project. They include:

Nelson Altamirano, National University
Dennis Avola, Framingham State University
Kristie Briggs, Creighton University
Bruce Brown, California Polytechnic University, Pomona
Parama Chaudhury, University College London
Salvador Contreras, University of Texas Pan American
Brent Evans, Mississippi State University
Virginia Fierro-Renoy, Keiser University
Melanie Fox, Austin College
Lisa Gloege, Grand Rapids Community College
Oskar Harmon, University of Connecticut
Ryan Herzog, Gonzaga University
Jennifer Imazeki, San Diego State University
Ahmed Kader, University of Nevada Las Vegas
Hossein Kazemi, Stonehill College
Steven Levkoff, University of California San Diego
Eric Levy, Florida Atlantic University
Rotua Lumbantobing, Westminster College
Shakun Mago, University of Richmond
Diego Mendez-Carbajo, Illinois Wesleyan University
Evelina Mengova, California State University Fullerton
Rebecca Moryl, Emmanuel College
James Murray, University of Wisconsin, La Crosse
Robert Pennington, University of Central Florida
Robert Rebelein, Vassar College
Matthew Rousu, Susquehanna University
Rochelle Ruffer, Nazareth College
Scott Simkins, North Carolina A&T University
Jim Wollscheid, University of Arkansas, Fort Smith
Madelyn Young, Converse College

I would like to thank my current and former student assistants who helped with data collection and shared ideas for examples that would click with college students today. These students include Alan Jagessar, Eileen Schneider, Phil Esterman, Enrique Valdes, Kevin Brady, Thomas Thornton, Brett Block, and Craig Haberstumpf. I also thank all of the students who have taken my principles courses. Their comments, body language, and facial expressions provided cues to whether my concept explanations and applications were clear and provided guidance on how to approach these topics in the book.

I would like to thank Jose Vazquez of the University of Illinois at Urbana-Champaign and Rochelle Ruffer of Nazareth College for their willingness to use the preliminary version of the third edition in their classes. The feedback I received from their experience as well as from their students allowed me to improve the textbook prior to its publication.

I am extremely grateful to Jane Himarios of the University of Texas at Arlington who not only oversaw the complete revision of the Test Bank but also took on the role of an expert accuracy checker. Further, Jane provided constant moral support throughout the project.

I want to thank James Watson for his tireless examination of the page proofs to ensure accuracy. Despite dozens of eyes that have read through manuscript and proofs, James still managed to catch errors that none of us want to see in the final product.

A huge debt of gratitude is owed to Lindsay Neff and the supplements authors. Lindsay did a remarkable job to get the best people to author the supplements. They include Jane Himarios of the University of Texas at Arlington who managed the revision of the Test Bank, Albert J. Sumell of Youngstown State University and Gregory Rose of Sacramento City College who revised the *CourseTutor,* Eric Levy of Florida Atlantic University who created the dynamic PowerPoint slides, and Solina Lindahl of California Polytechnic University–San Luis Obispo for coordinating the pedagogical resources available to instructors. I would also like to thank Ting Levy of Florida Atlantic University, Tamika Steward, James Watson and Brett Block for the development of materials for *LaunchPad* for *CoreMicroeconomics. CoreMicroeconomics* and the *CoreMedia* came together into a cohesive set of instructor and student resources because of their efforts.

I owe a significant debt to the team of technology specialists who created many fascinating digital resources for *CoreMicroeconomics.* I thank Tom Acox for his instrumental role in the development and management of the online resources, especially *LaunchPad.* There has been more than one occasion when a crisis situation with my class required immediate attention, and Tom was always available, day and night, to resolve the problem. He truly exemplifies his title as digital solutions manager.

I am truly indebted to Jeremy Brown, who over the years has taught me the tools and tricks of digital technology that have become indispensable in today's media-driven world. These tools include video editing, animation, and other visual effects, creating a professional Web site, and maximizing the effectiveness of social media. Whenever I have a technology-related question, I can count on Jeremy for an answer. His influence has given me the confidence to use cutting-edge technology to its maximum potential to the benefit of the *CoreMicroeconomics* suite of resources.

Several persons have provided inspiration for various teaching pedagogies as well as a willingness to lend an ear. These individuals include Gregory Rose of Sacramento City College, Djeto Assane of the University of Nevada Las Vegas, Yoram Bauman (Stand-up Economist), Janice Hauge of the University of North Texas, Marc Cannon, and William Bosshardt of Florida Atlantic University.

The production team at Worth is truly the best in the industry. My heartfelt thanks go to the entire team, including Kevin Kall, senior designer, for creating a fantastic set of interior and cover designs; Georgia Lee Hadler, senior project editor, for skillfully managing the copyediting and proofing of the book; Martha Solonche for her superb copyediting; Christine Buese and Julie Tesser for their immense efforts at finding and obtaining rights to the hundreds of photos used in the book; Mary Walsh for her meticulous work in preparing manuscripts for production; Tracey Kuehn, Barbara Seixas, and production specialists Susie Bothwell, Lisa Hankins, and Christina Welker. Each of these individuals made sure each part of the production process went smoothly. Thank you very much for a job well done.

I want to thank Charles Linsmeier, publisher of economics, for recruiting me for this project and making this collaboration with Jerry Stone a reality. Not only did Chuck sign me to Worth, he also has provided dedicated support throughout the entire process. I also thank Paul Shensa for this support from the beginning of the project to its completion. From his ideas on editorial changes to marketing, Paul is an indispensable resource for any author.

There is no one person I can thank more than Bruce Kaplan, senior development editor, who has guided me on the revision of *CoreMicroeconomics* from start to finish. Bruce had a long working relationship with Jerry Stone on his first two editions and was able to provide the continuity into the third edition without Jerry's presence. In fact, in my last conversation with Jerry Stone, he told me to "stick with Bruce; he's the best and will take you far." Jerry's words ring true each time I work with Bruce, who is the best editor and mentor an author can have.

You couldn't ask for a better marketing team than that at Worth. In the early stages of this edition, I had the pleasure of working with Scott Guile, whose enthusiasm is infectious and his efforts tireless. Scott's promotion left big shoes to fill, but the arrival of Tom Digiano as marketing manager provided a flawless transition. Tom's expertise in online homework systems and social media marketing is inspiring, and has encouraged me to push the boundaries to create wonderful marketing pieces that I am proud to put my name on. I thank Tom Kling for his role in motivating the sales reps to the benefits of this project, and for always making me feel at home during sales meetings. I thank the entire sales force, which devotes its time, effort, and passion to showcasing *CoreMicroeconomics* in a way that truly exemplifies its value to economics education.

I wish to thank Sarah Dorger, for without her efforts, my authoring role would not have happened. I thank Sharon Balbos, whose abundance of experience with textbook-related projects prior to *CoreMicroeconomics* helped me to develop a keen eye for detail that is vital to an author. I thank Craig Bleyer, who for many years encouraged me to become an author before I finally did. And I thank Catherine Woods and Elizabeth Widdicombe for supporting me as an author.

Finally, I thank Jerry Stone, a true friend and colleague who put his full trust in me when he offered me the opportunity to take over authorship of *CoreMicroeconomics* in 2010 and carry the book forward to a new generation of students and instructors with new needs. I wish Jerry were still here to collaborate on the textbook he created so successfully in the first two editions. I will never cease my efforts to make *CoreEconomics* a long-lasting legacy of Jerry's brilliance and dedication to students and instructors.

Eric P. Chiang

Eric P. Chiang

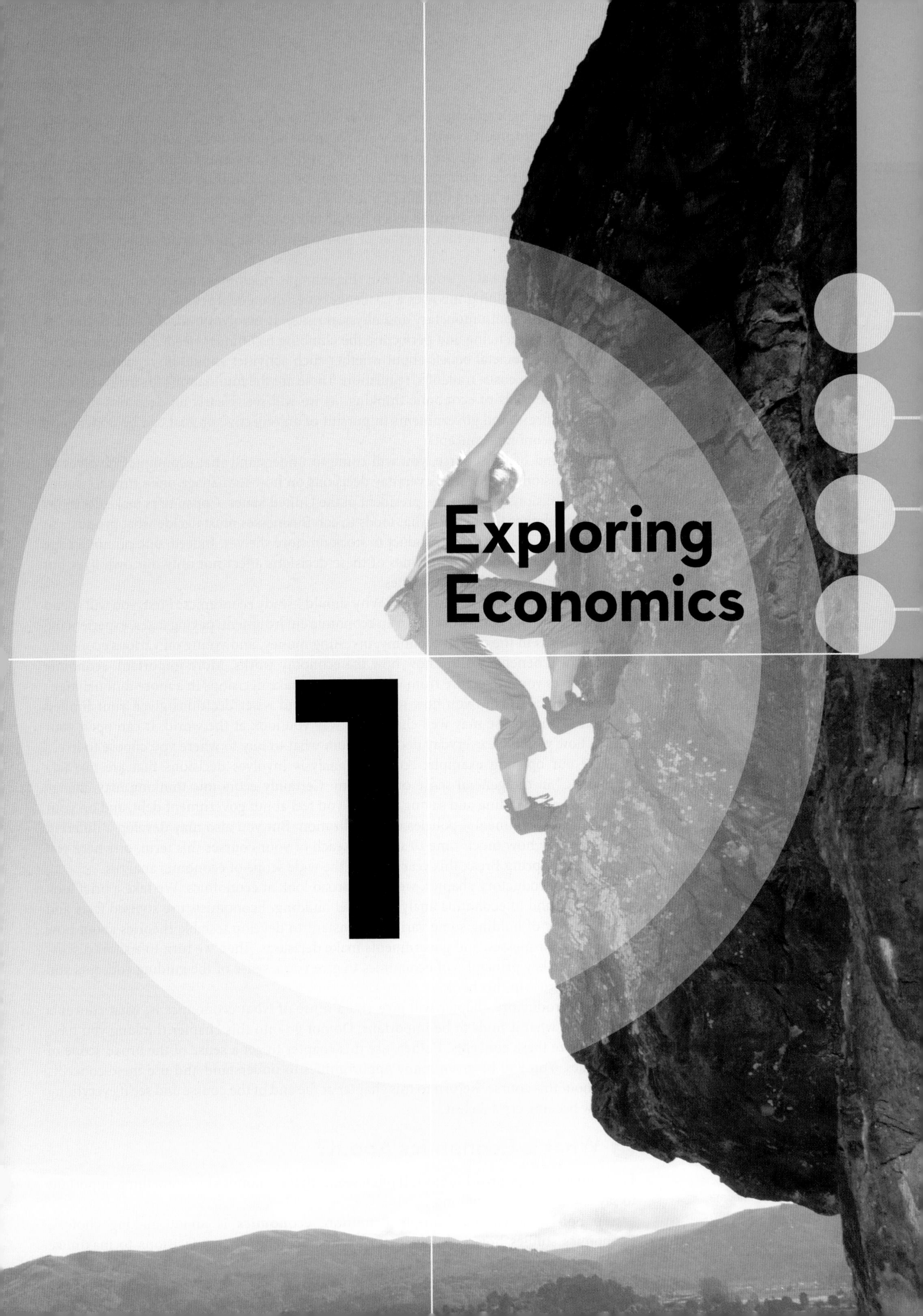

1 Exploring Economics

After studying this chapter you should be able to:

- Explain how economic analysis can be used in decision making.
- Differentiate between microeconomics and macroeconomics.
- Describe how economists use models.
- Describe the *ceteris paribus* assumption.
- Discuss the difference between efficiency and equity.
- Describe the key principles in economics.
- Apply the key principles to situations faced in your daily routine.

Perched high atop the 3,000-foot vertical monolith known as El Capitan, a climber gazes out upon a perfect view of Yosemite National Park. Holding onto the wall *with no rope,* one tiny slip of the foot will lead to certain death. Welcome to the sport of free soloing, an extreme form of rock climbing done *without* ropes or harnesses. Does this sound thrilling? Or perhaps crazy? Or even irrational? These are common thoughts that come to mind when people talk about the new wave of risky adventure sports. Would you think that whether or not to participate in such an activity is an economic question?

Most people probably wouldn't. But this example resembles an economic problem in many ways. Free soloing involves a challenge, one with a *benefit* (a sense of accomplishment) and a *cost* (both monetary and physical risks). It involves *tradeoffs*—the thousands of hours spent practicing and perfecting the climbing techniques needed to be successful. And it involves societal beliefs about whether such activities should be *regulated* or even banned. Benefits, costs, tradeoffs, regulation: These are the foundations for making a decision using the tools of economic thinking, as we will see. Nearly all decisions made by individuals, firms, and governments in pursuit of an objective or goal can be understood using these economic concepts.

By the end of this course, you will come to understand that economics involves all types of decisions, from small everyday decisions on how to manage one's time to world-changing decisions made by the president of the United States. Consumers make decisions about what clothes to buy and what foods to eat. Businesses must decide what products to make and how much of each product to stock on store shelves. Indeed, one cannot escape making decisions, and the outcomes of these decisions affect not only our own lives but those of entire societies and countries.

You still might be asking yourself: Why should I study economics? First, you will spend roughly the next 40 years working in an economic environment: paying taxes, experiencing ups and downs in the overall economy, investing money, and voting on various economic issues. It will benefit you to know how the economy works. More important, economic analysis gives you a structure from which you can make decisions in a more rational manner. Economics teaches you how to make better and wiser decisions given your limited resources. This course may well change the way you look at the world. It can open your eyes to how you make everyday decisions from what to buy to where you choose to live.

Like our opening example, economic analysis involves decisions that are not just "economic" in the general sense of the term. Certainly economic thinking may change your views on spending and saving, on how you feel about government debt, and on your opinion of environmental policies or globalization. But you also may develop a different perspective on how much time to study for each of your courses this term, or where you might go for Spring Break this year. Such is the wide scope of economic analysis.

In this introductory chapter, we take a broad look at economics. We take a brief look at a key method of economic analysis: model building. Economists use stylized facts and the technique of holding some variables constant to develop testable theories about how consumers, businesses, and governments make decisions. Then we turn to a short discussion of some key principles of economics to give you a sense of the guiding concepts you will come across in this book.

This introductory chapter will give you a sense of what economics is, what concepts it uses, and what it finds to be important. Do not go into this chapter thinking you have to memorize these concepts. Rather, use this chapter to get a sense of the broad scope of economics. You will be given many opportunities to understand and use these concepts throughout this course. Return to this chapter at the end of the course and see if everything has now become crystal clear.

What Is Economics About?

economics The study of how individuals, firms, and society make decisions to allocate limited resources to many competing wants.

Economics is a very broad subject. It often seems that economics has something important to say about almost everything.

To boil it down to a simple definition, **economics** is about making choices. Economics studies how individuals, firms, and societies make decisions to maximize

BY THE NUMBERS

Economic Issues Are All Around Us

Economics is one of the most popular college majors in the country. This is because so much of what we do, the decisions we face, and the issues we confront involve economics.

Each chapter in this book includes a By the Numbers box. It has two purposes. First, items in the feature preview some of the topics covered in the chapter. We hope these topics motivate you to read on. Second, the data explosion affecting our understanding of the world will only continue to accelerate. Numerical literacy will grow in importance. This By the Numbers box seeks to encourage a nonthreatening familiarity with data and numbers. At the end of each chapter, there are two Using the Numbers questions to test how well you understood the numbers.

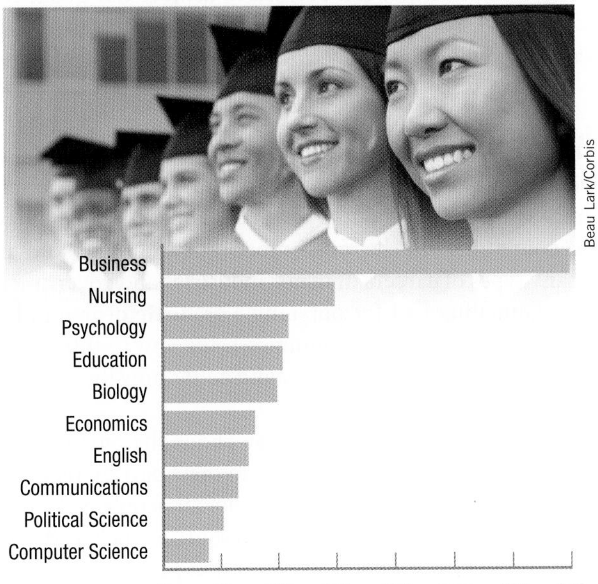

Total Number of Bachelor's Degrees (in thousands) Granted by Major in 2011

Business majors represented the largest number of college graduates in terms of the total number of bachelor's degrees granted in 2011. Economics majors represented the sixth most popular degree granted.

Technology Company CEO Majors:
1. Economics (22%)
2. Computer Science (20%)
3. Engineering (17%)

Fortune 100 Company CEO Majors:
1. Engineering (17%)
2. Economics (12%)
3. Business Administration (12%)

41%

Percent of Fortune 500 Companies (America's largest companies by revenue) founded by immigrants or their children.

$94,700

The median salary of workers with economics degrees after 15 years of work experience.

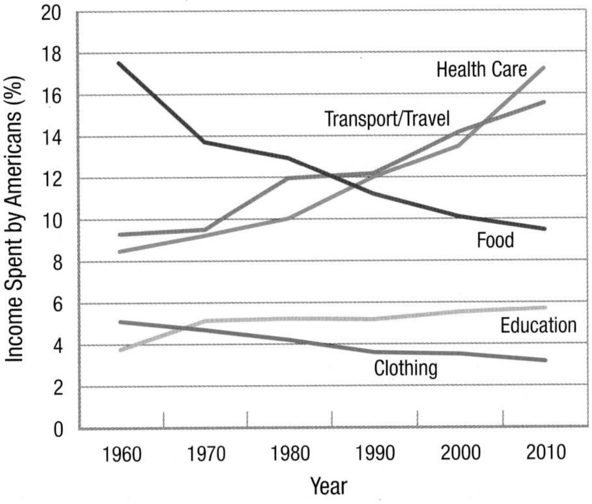

The average percentage of income Americans spent on food and clothing has fallen since 1960, but the percentage of income spent on travel, education, and health care has increased.

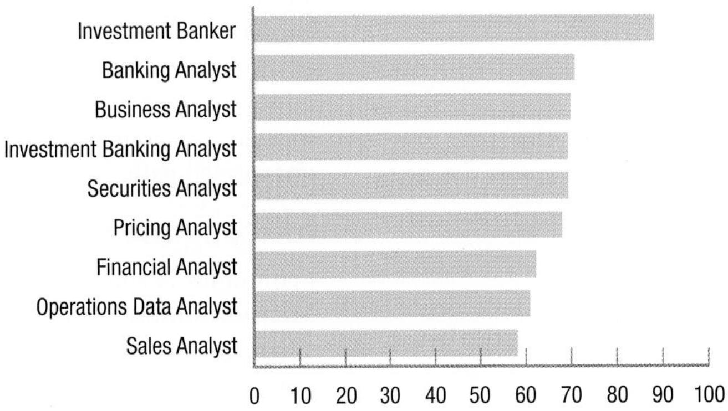

Median Salaries (in thousands)

What do economists do? Common jobs held by economists with bachelor's degrees and their median salaries.

their well-being given limitations. In other words, economics attempts to address the problem of having too many wants but too few resources to achieve them all, an important concept called **scarcity.** Note that scarcity is not the same thing as something being *scarce*. Although all resources are scarce, certain goods are less scarce than others. For example, cars are not very scarce—there are car dealerships around the country chock-full of cars ready to be sold, but that doesn't mean you can go out tonight and buy three. Scarcity refers to the fact that one must make choices given the resource limitations she or he faces.

scarcity Our unlimited wants clash with limited resources, leading to scarcity. Everyone (rich and poor) faces scarcity because, at a minimum, our time on earth is limited. Economics focuses on the allocation of scarce resources to satisfy unlimited wants.

What kind of limitations are we referring to here? It could be money, but money is not the only resource that allows us to achieve the life we want. It's also our time, our knowledge, our work ethic, and anything else that can be used to achieve our goals. It is this broad notion of economics being the study of how people make decisions to allocate scarce resources to competing wants that allows the subject to be applied to so many topics and applications.

Why Should One Study Economics?

The first answer that might come to mind as to why you are taking this course is "because you have to." Although economics is a required course for many college students, economics should be thought of as something much, much more. For example, studying economics can prepare you for many types of careers in major industries and government. Studying economics also is a great launching pad for pursuing a graduate degree in law, business, or other fields. More practically speaking, economics helps you to think more clearly about the decisions you make every day and to understand better how the economy functions and why certain things happen the way they do.

For example, economics has some important things to say about the environment. Most people care about the environment to some degree, and do their part by recycling, not littering, and turning off the lights when leaving a room. But not all people make decisions in the same way: Some might do much more to conserve resources, such as driving less or driving a more fuel efficient car, joining a local organization to plant trees, or even writing to policymakers to support sustainability legislation. The extent to which people participate in environmental activities depends on the benefit they perceive when pursuing such actions compared to the costs, which can include monetary costs, time and effort, and forgone opportunities such as driving a larger, more comfortable car. Economics looks at all of these factors to determine how people make decisions that affect the environment, which affects us all. Economics is a way of thinking about an issue, not just a discipline that has money as its chief focus.

Economists tend to have a rational take on nearly everything. Now all of this "analysis/speculation" may bring only limited insight in some cases, but it gives you some idea of how economists think. We look for rational responses to **incentives.** Incentives are the factors, both good and bad, that influence how people make decisions. For example, tough admissions requirements for graduate school provide an incentive for students to study harder in college, while lucrative commissions push car salespeople to sell even the ugliest or most unreliable car. Economics is all about how people respond to incentives. We begin most questions by considering how rational people would respond to the incentives that specific situations provide. Sometimes (maybe even often) this analysis leads us down an unexpected path.

incentives The factors that motivate individuals and firms to make decisions in their best interest.

Microeconomics Versus Macroeconomics

Economics is split into two broad categories: microeconomics and macroeconomics. **Microeconomics** deals with decision making by individuals, businesses, industries, and governments. It is concerned with issues such as which orange juice to buy, which job to take, and where to go on vacation, as well as which items a business should produce and what price it should charge, and whether a market should be left on its own or be regulated.

microeconomics The decision making by individuals, businesses, industries, and governments.

Microeconomics looks at how markets are structured. Some markets are very competitive, where many firms offer similar products; while other markets have only one or two large firms, offering little choice. What decisions do businesses make under different market structures? Microeconomics also extends to such topics as labor laws, environmental policy, and health care policy. How can we use the tools of microeconomics to analyze the costs and benefits of differing policies?

Macroeconomics, on the other hand, focuses on the broader issues we face as a nation. Most of us don't care whether an individual buys Nike or Merrell shoes. We *do* care whether prices of *all* goods and services rise. Inflation—a general increase in prices economy-wide—affects all of us. So does unemployment (virtually every person will at some point in their life be unemployed, even if it's just for a short time when switching from one job to another) and economic growth. What decisions do governments make to deal with macroeconomic problems such as inflation and recessions?

macroeconomics The broader issues in the economy such as inflation, unemployment, and national output of goods and services.

Macroeconomics uses microeconomic tools to answer some questions, but its main focus is on the broad aggregate variables of the economy. Macroeconomics has its own terms and topics, such as business cycles, recession, and unemployment. Macroeconomics looks at policies that increase economic growth, the impact of government spending and taxation, the effect of monetary policy on the economy, and inflation. It also looks closely at theories of international trade and international finance. All of these topics have broad impacts on our economy and our standard of living.

Still not clear? Here's an easy way to remember the difference between microeconomics and macroeconomics. Only one letter separates the two terms, so just remember that the "i" in microeconomics refers to "individual" entities (such as a person or a firm), while the "a" in macroeconomics refers to "aggregate" entities (such as cities or a nation as a whole).

Economics is a social science that uses many facts and figures to develop and express ideas. This inevitably involves numbers. For macroeconomics, this means getting used to talking and thinking in huge numbers: billions (nine zeros) and trillions (twelve zeros). Today we are talking about a federal government budget approaching $4 trillion. To wrap your mind around such a huge number, consider how long it would take to spend a trillion dollars if you spent a dollar every second, or $86,400 per day. To spend $1 trillion would require over 31,000 years. And the federal government now spends nearly 4 times this much in one year.

Although we break economics into microeconomics and macroeconomics, there is considerable overlap in the analysis. Both involve the analysis of how individuals, firms, and governments make decisions that affect the lives of people. We use simple supply and demand analysis to understand *both* individual markets and the general economy as a whole. You will find yourself using concepts from microeconomics to understand fluctuations in the macroeconomy.

Economic Theories and Reality

If you flip through any economics text, you'll likely see a multitude of graphs, charts, and equations. This book is no exception. The good news is that all of the graphs and charts become relatively easy to understand since they all basically read the same way. The few equations in this book stem from elementary algebra. Once you get through one equation, the rest are similar.

Graphs, charts, and equations are often the simplest and most efficient ways to express data and ideas. Equations are used to express relationships between two variables. Complex and wordy discussions can often be reduced to a simple graph or figure. These are efficient techniques for expressing economic ideas.

Model Building As you study economics this term, you will encounter stylized approaches to a number of issues. By *stylized,* we mean that economists boil down facts to their basic relevant elements and use assumptions to develop a stylized (simple) model to analyze the issue. There are always situations that lie outside these models, but they are the exception. Economists generalize about economic behavior and reach broadly applicable results.

We begin with relatively simple models, then gradually build to more difficult ones. For example, in the next chapter we introduce one of the simplest models in economics,

ceteris paribus Assumption used in economics (and other disciplines as well), where other relevant factors or variables are held constant.

efficiency How well resources are used and allocated. Do people get the goods and services they want at the lowest possible resource cost? This is the chief focus of efficiency.

equity The fairness of various issues and policies.

the production possibilities frontier that illustrates the limits of economic activity. This model has profound implications for the issue of economic growth. We can add in more dimensions and make the model more complex, but often this complexity does not provide any greater insight than the simple model.

Ceteris Paribus:* All Else Held Constant** To aid in our model building, economists use the ***ceteris paribus assumption: "Holding all other things equal." That means we will hold some important variables constant. For example, to determine how many songs you might be willing to download from iTunes in any given month, we would hold your monthly income constant. We then would change song prices to see the impact on the number purchased (again holding your monthly income constant).

Though model building can lead to surprising insights into how economic actors and economies behave, it is not the end of the story. Economic insights lead to economic theories, but these theories must then be tested. In some cases, such as the extent to which a housing bubble could lead to a financial crisis, economic predictions turned out to be false. Thus, model building is a *process*—models are created and then tested. If models fail to explain reality, new models are constructed.

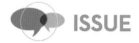

ISSUE

Have Smartphones and Social Media Made Life Easier?

Maxx-Studio/Shutterstock

Two decades ago, if your professor wanted to convey an important announcement about an upcoming class, she or he would have to wait until the next class period, or if more urgent, make a phone call to each student. Similarly, if you worked for a company, communications with your boss generally ended when you left the office for the day.

Today, we live in a society in which nearly everybody uses online technologies, whether it be for keeping up with friends on Facebook, writing a recommendation for a friend on LinkedIn, or completing homework using classroom management software. Further, we live in a world in which computers and phones are no longer fixed; instead, we carry miniature versions of them with us at all times. According to a Nielsen survey, over 55% of all American adults own a smartphone, and over 75% of those between the ages of 18 and 24 do. So how do these technologies affect our lives?

We can analyze this question using the standard economic benefit versus cost approach. On the benefit side, Internet and mobile technologies have clearly improved the speed and ease of communications, whether staying in touch with family and friends, or trying to locate a loved one at the mall (no more preplanned meeting locations required).

In addition to benefits, there are also costs. For example, greater ease of communications often comes with greater expectations. Several survey studies found that over 95% of Americans answer at least one work-related email or business phone call while on vacation. Students are expected to respond quickly to emails from professors. And even your friends might expect you to respond instantly to text messages and to "like" their latest posts on a social media site. Indeed, sometimes being too connected adds new pressures in life.

Each individual is unique and weighs the benefits and costs of technology differently. How you value these benefits and costs will ultimately determine how you choose to adapt to new and existing technologies. Economics involves all sorts of decisions, including how well connected we choose to be in life.

Efficiency Versus Equity

Efficiency deals with how well resources are used and allocated. No one likes waste. Much of economic analysis is directed toward ensuring that the most efficient outcomes result from public policy. *Production efficiency* occurs when goods are produced at the lowest possible cost, and *allocative efficiency* occurs when individuals who desire a product the most get those goods and services. As an example, it would not make sense for society to allocate to me a large amount of cranberry sauce—I would not eat it. Efficient policies are generally good policies.

The other side of the coin is **equity,** or fairness. Is it fair that the CEOs of large companies make hundreds of times more money than rank-and-file workers? Many think not. Is it fair that some have so much and others have so little? Again, many think not. There are many divergent views about fairness until we get to extreme cases. When just a few people earn nearly all of the income and control nearly all of a society's wealth, most people agree that this is unfair.

Throughout this course you will see instances where efficiency and equity collide. You may agree that a specific policy is efficient, but think it is unfair to some group of people. This will be especially evident when you consider tax policy and its impact on income distribution. Fairness, or equity, is a subjective concept, and each of us has different ideas about what is just and fair. When it comes to public policy issues, economics will help you see the tradeoffs between equity and efficiency, but you will ultimately have to make up your own mind about the wisdom of the policy given these tradeoffs.

Positive Versus Normative Questions

Returning to the example in the chapter opener, we ask ourselves many questions whenever a decision needs to be made or an issue is debated. Some questions involve the understanding of basic facts, such as how risky a particular sport is, or how much enjoyment one gets from participating in the sport. Economists call these types of questions **positive questions.** Positive questions (which need not be positive or upbeat in the literal sense) are questions that can be answered one way or another as long as the information is available. This does not mean that people will always agree on an answer, because facts and information can differ.

positive question A question that can be answered using available information or facts.

Another type of question that arises is how something ought to be, such as whether extreme sports should be banned or whether additional safety measures should be required. Economists call these types of questions **normative questions.** Normative questions involve societal beliefs on what should or should not be done; differing opinions on an issue can sometimes make normative questions difficult to resolve.

normative question A question that is based on societal beliefs on what should or should not take place.

Throughout this book, positive and normative questions will arise, which will play an important role in how individuals and firms make decisions, and how governments form policy proposals that may or may not become law. Indeed, economics encompasses many ideas and questions that affect everyone.

CHECKPOINT

WHAT IS ECONOMICS ABOUT?

- Economics is about making decisions under scarcity, in which wants are unlimited but resources are limited.
- Economics is separated into two broad categories: microeconomics and macroeconomics.
- *Microeconomics* deals with individuals, firms, and industries and how they make decisions.
- *Macroeconomics* focuses on broader economic issues such as inflation, employment and unemployment, and economic growth.
- Economics uses a stylized approach, creating simple models that hold all other relevant factors constant (*ceteris paribus*).
- Economists and policymakers often face a tradeoff between efficiency and equity.
- Positive questions can be answered with facts and information, while normative questions ask how something should or ought to be.

QUESTION: In each of the following situations, determine whether it is a microeconomic or macroeconomic issue.

1. Hewlett-Packard announces that it is lowering the price of its printers by 15%.
2. The president proposes a tax cut.
3. You decide to look for a new job.
4. The economy is in a recession, and the job market is bad.
5. The Federal Reserve announces that it is raising interest rates because it fears inflation.
6. You get a nice raise.
7. Average wages grew by 2% last year.

Answers to the Checkpoint questions can be found at the end of this chapter.

Key Principles of Economics

Economics has a set of key principles that show up continually in economic analysis. Some are more restricted to specific issues, but most apply universally. These principles should give you a sense of what you will learn in this course. In the following, we summarize seven key principles that will be applied throughout the entire book. By the end of this course, these principles should be crystal clear and you will likely find yourself using these principles throughout your life, even if you never take another economics course.

Principle 1: Economics Is Concerned with Making Choices with Limited Resources

Economics deals with nearly every type of decision we face every day. But when a typical person is asked what economics is about, the most common answer is "money." Why is economics commonly misconceived as dealing only with money? This may be due in part to how economics is portrayed in the news—dealing with financial issues, jobs and wages, and the cost of living, among other money matters. While money matters are indeed an important issue studied in economics, you now know that economics involves much, much more.

Economics is about making decisions on allocating limited resources to maximize an individual or society's well-being. Money is just one source of well-being, assuming that more money makes a person happier, all else equal. But other factors also improve a person's well-being, such as receiving a day off from work with pay. Even if one does not have a lot of money or free time, satisfaction can come from other activities or events, such as participating in a fun activity with friends or family, or watching one's favorite team win.

In sum, many aspects of life contribute to the well-being of individuals and of society. Unfortunately, often these are limited by various resource constraints. Therefore, one must think of economics in a broad sense of determining how best to manage all of society's resources (not just money) in order to maximize well-being. This involves tradeoffs and opportunity costs, which we consider next.

Tony Avelar/Bloomberg via Getty Images

Principle 2: When Making Decisions, One Must Take Into Account Tradeoffs and Opportunity Costs

Wouldn't it be great if we all had the resources of Mark Zuckerberg (the founder of Facebook) and could buy just about any material possession one could possibly want? Most likely we won't, so back to reality.

We all have limited resources. Some of us are more limited than others, but each of us, even Mark Zuckerberg, faces limitations (and not because Mark chooses to wear a $30 shirt instead of a $3,000 Brioni suit). For example, we all face time limitations: There are only 24 hours in a day, and some of that must be spent sleeping. The fact that we have many wants but limited resources (scarcity) means that we must make tradeoffs in nearly everything we do. In other words, we have to decide between alternatives, which always exist whenever we make a decision.

How is this accomplished? What factors determine whether you buy a nicer car or use the extra money to pay down debt? Or whether you should spend the weekend at a local music festival or use the time to study for an exam? Economists use an important term to help weigh the benefits and costs of every decision we make, and that term is **opportunity cost.** In fact, economics is often categorized as the discipline that always weighs benefits against costs.

opportunity cost The value of the next best alternative; what you give up to do something or purchase something.

At its very core, opportunity cost is determined by asking yourself, in any situation, "What could I be doing right now if I wasn't ______________ (fill in the activity)?" or "What could I have bought if I didn't buy this ______________ (fill in the last good or service you bought)?" In other words, opportunity cost measures the value of the next best alternative use of your time or money, or what you *give up* when you make an economic decision. And since there are always alternatives, one cannot avoid opportunity costs.

A common mistake that people make is that they sometimes do not fully take their opportunity costs into account. Have you ever camped out overnight in order to get tickets for a concert? Was it even worth going to the concert? Opportunity cost includes the value of everything you give up in order to attend the concert, including the cost of the tickets and transportation, and the time spent buying tickets, traveling to and from the venue, and of course attending the concert. The sum of all opportunity costs can sometimes outweigh the benefits.

Another example of miscalculating opportunity costs occurs when a student spends a copious amount of time to dispute a $15 parking ticket. Like the previous example, the opportunity cost (time and effort disputing the ticket which can be used for some other activity) may exceed the $15 savings if successful and certainly if the attempt to dispute the ticket fails.

In other cases, individuals do respond to opportunity costs. Why do many people choose a paper towel over a hand dryer in a public restroom when given the choice? It's because the opportunity cost of using the hand dryer is higher than using a paper towel.

Every activity involves opportunity costs. Sleeping, eating, studying, partying, running, hiking, and so on, all require that we spend resources that could be used on another activity. Opportunity cost varies from person to person. A company president rushing from meeting to meeting has a higher opportunity cost than a retired senior citizen, and therefore is more likely to choose the quickest option to accomplish day-to-day activities.

Opportunity costs apply to us as individuals and to societies as a whole. For example, if a country chooses to spend more on environmental conservation, it must use resources that could be used to promote other objectives, such as education and health care.

Principle 3: Specialization Leads to Gains for All Involved

Whenever we pursue an activity or a task, we use time that could be used for other activities or tasks. However, sometimes these other tasks are best left to others to perform. Life would be much more difficult if we all had to grow our own food. This highlights the idea that tradeoffs (especially with one's time) can lead to better outcomes if one is able to specialize in activities in which she or he is more proficient.

Suppose you and your roommate can each cook your own dinner and clean your own rooms. Alternatively, you might have your roommate clean both rooms (he's better at it than you) in exchange for you preparing dinner for two (you're a better cook). Using this arrangement, both tasks are completed in less time since each of you are specializing in the activity you're better at, plus both of you will benefit from a cleaner apartment and a tastier dinner.

Therefore, specialization in tasks in which one is more proficient can lead to gains for all parties as long as exchange is possible and those involved trade in a mutually beneficial manner. Each person is acting on the opportunity to improve his or her well-being, an example of how incentives affect people's lives.

Principle 4: People Respond to Incentives, Both Good and Bad

Each time an individual or a firm makes a decision, that person or firm is acting on an incentive that drives the individual or firm to choose an action. These incentives often occur naturally. For example, we choose to eat every day because we face an incentive to survive, and we study and work hard because we face an incentive to be successful in our careers. However, incentives also can be formed by policies set by government to encourage individuals and firms to act in certain ways, and by businesses to encourage consumers to change their consumption habits.

For example, tax policy rests on the idea that people follow their incentives. Do we want to encourage people to save for their retirement? Then let them deduct a certain amount that they can put into a tax-deferred retirement account. Do we want businesses to spend more to stimulate the economy? Then give them tax credits for new investment. Do we want people to go to college? Then give them tax advantages for setting up education savings accounts.

Tax policy is an obvious example in which people follow incentives. But this principle can be seen in action wherever you look. Want to encourage people to fly during the slow travel season? Offer price discounts or bonus frequent flyer miles for flying during that time. Want to spread out the dining time at restaurants? Give early-bird discounts to those willing to eat at 5:00 P.M. rather than at 7:30 P.M.

Note that in saying that people follow incentives, economists do not claim that everyone follows each incentive every time. Though you may not want to eat dinner at 5:00 P.M., there might be other people who are willing to eat earlier in return for a price discount.

If not properly constructed, incentives might lead to harmful outcomes. During the 2008 financial crisis, it became clear that the way incentives for traders and executives were set up by Wall Street investment banks was misguided. Traders and executives were paid bonuses based on short-term profits. This encouraged them to take extreme risks to generate quick profits and high bonuses with little regard for the long-term viability of the bank. The bank may be gone tomorrow, but these people still have those huge bonuses.

Eric Chiang

Would you pick it up? Who wouldn't?

Responding to badly designed incentives is often described as greed, but they are not always the same. If you found a $20 bill on the sidewalk, would you pick it up? Of course, but would that make you a greedy person? The stranger who accidentally dropped the bill an hour ago might think so, but you are just responding to an incentive to pick up the money before the next lucky person does. Could incentives ever be designed to prevent people from picking up money they find? It may surprise you that one industry has: In many casinos, it is prohibited to keep chips or money you find on the floor.

The natural tendency for society to respond to incentives leads individuals and firms to work hard and generate ideas that increase productivity, a measure of a society's capacity to produce that determines our standard of living. A worker who can do twice as much as another is likely to earn a higher salary, because productivity and pay tend to go together. The same is true for nations. Countries with the highest standards of living are also the most productive.

Principle 5: Rational Behavior Requires Thinking on the Margin

Have you ever noticed that when you eat at an all-you-can-eat buffet, you always go away fuller than when you order and eat at a non-buffet restaurant? Is this phenomenon unique to you, or is there something more fundamental? Remember, economists look at facts to find incentives to economic behavior.

In this case, people are just rationally responding to the price of *additional* food. They are thinking on the margin. In a non-buffet restaurant, dessert costs extra, and you make a decision as to whether the enjoyment you receive from the dessert (the marginal benefit) is worth the extra cost (the marginal cost). At the buffet, dessert is free, which means the marginal cost is zero. Even so, you still must ask yourself if dessert will give you satisfaction. If the dessert tastes terrible or adds unwanted calories to your diet, then you might pass on dessert even if it is free. But the fact that one is more likely to have dessert at a buffet than at a menu-based restaurant highlights the notion that people tend to think on the margin.

The idea of thinking on the margin applies to a society as well. Like asking ourselves whether we want another serving of dessert, a society must ask itself whether it wants a little bit more or a little bit less of something, and policymakers and/or citizens vote on such policy proposals. An example of society thinking on the margin is whether taxes should be raised a little to pay for other projects, or whether a country should send up another space exploration craft to study other planets.

Throughout this book, we will see examples of thinking on the margin. A business uses marginal analysis to determine how much of its products it is willing to supply to the market. Individuals use marginal analysis to determine how many hours to exercise or study. And governments use marginal analysis to determine how much pollution should be permitted.

Principle 6: Markets Are Generally Efficient; When They Aren't, Government Can Sometimes Correct the Failure

Individuals and firms make decisions that maximize their well-being, and markets bring buyers and sellers together. Private markets and the incentives they provide are the best mechanisms known today for providing products and services. There is no government food board that makes sure that bread, cereal, coffee, and all the other food products you demand are on your plate during the day. The vast majority of products we consume are privately provided.

Competition for the consumer dollar forces firms to provide products at the lowest possible price, or some other firm will undercut their high price. New products enter the market and old products die out. Such is the dynamic characteristic of markets.

What drives and disciplines markets? Prices and profits are the keys. Profits drive entrepreneurs to provide new products (think of Apple) or existing products at lower prices (think of Wal-Mart). When prices and profits get too high in any market, new firms jump in with lower prices to grab away customers. This competition, or sometimes even the threat of competition, keeps markets from exploiting consumers.

Individuals and firms respond to prices in markets by altering the choices and quantities of goods they purchase and sell, respectively. These actions highlight the ability of markets to provide an efficient outcome for all. Markets can achieve this efficiency without a central planner telling what people should buy or what firms should sell. This phenomenon that markets promote efficiency through the incentives faced by individuals and firms (as if they were guided by an omnipotent force) is referred to as the *invisible hand*, a term coined by Adam Smith, long considered the father of economics.

Oriental Touch/Robert Harding

Markets can be crowded and chaotic, but they generally promote an efficient outcome by bringing buyers and sellers together.

As efficient as markets usually are, society does not desire a market for everything. For example, markets for hard drugs or child pornography are largely deemed undesirable. In other cases, a market does not provide enough of a good or service, such as public parks or public education. For these products and services, markets can fail to provide an optimal outcome.

But when markets do fail, they tend to do so in predictable ways. Where consumers have no choice but to buy from one firm (such as a local water company), the market will fail to provide the best solution, and government regulation is often used to protect consumers. Another example is pollution: Left unregulated, companies often will pollute the air and water. Governments then intervene to deal with this market failure. Finally, people rely on information to make rational decisions. When information is not readily available or is known only to one side of the market, markets again can fail to produce the socially desirable outcome.

We also can extend the idea of market efficiency to the greater economy. The market forces of supply and demand generally keep the economy in equilibrium. But occasionally fluctuations in the macroeconomy will occur, and markets take time to readjust on their own. In some cases, the economy becomes stuck in a severe downturn. In these instances, government can smooth the fluctuations in the overall economy by using policies such as government spending or tax cuts. But remember, just because the government *can* successfully intervene does not mean it *always* successfully intervenes. The macroeconomy is not a simple machine. Successful policymaking is a tough task.

Principle 7: Institutions and Human Creativity Help Explain the Wealth of Nations

We have seen how individuals and firms make decisions to maximize their well-being, and how tradeoffs, specialization, incentives, and marginal analysis play an important role. We then saw how markets bring buyers and sellers together to promote better outcomes, and that governments sometimes step in when markets fail to produce the best outcome. But how does all of this affect the overall wealth of a nation? Two important factors influencing

ADAM SMITH (1723–1790)

When Adam Smith was four years old, he was kidnapped and held for ransom. Had his captors not taken fright and returned the boy unharmed, the history of economics might well have turned out differently.

Born in Kirkaldy, Scotland, in 1723, Smith graduated from the University of Glasgow at age 17 and was awarded a scholarship to Oxford. Smith considered his time at Oxford to be largely wasted. Returning to Scotland in 1751, Smith was named Professor of Moral Philosophy at the University of Glasgow.

After 12 years at Glasgow, Smith began tutoring the son of a wealthy Scottish nobleman. This job provided him with the opportunity to spend several years touring the European continent with his young charge. In Paris, Smith met some of the leading French economists of the day, which helped stoke his own interest in political economy. While there, he wrote a friend, "I have begun to write a book in order to pass the time."

Returning to Kirkaldy in 1766, Smith spent the next decade finishing *An Inquiry Into the Nature and Causes of the Wealth of Nations.* Before publication in 1776, he read sections of the text to Benjamin Franklin. Smith's genius was in taking the existing forms of economic analysis available at the time and putting them together in a systematic fashion to make sense of the national economy as a whole. Smith demonstrated how individuals left free to pursue their own economic interests end up acting in ways that enhance the welfare of all. This is Smith's famous "invisible hand." In Smith's words: "By directing that industry in such a manner as its produce may be of the greatest value, he intends only his own gain, and he is in this, as in many other cases, led by an invisible hand to promote an end which was no part of his intention."

How important was Adam Smith? He has been called the "father of political economy." Many of the foundations of economic analysis we use today are still based on Adam Smith's writings of several centuries ago.

Sources: Howard Marshall, *The Great Economists: A History of Economic Thought* (New York: Pitman Publishing, 1967; Paul Strathern, *A Brief History of Economic Genius* (New York: Texere), 2002; Ian Ross, *The Life of Adam Smith* (Oxford: Clarendon Press), 1995.

the wealth of nations are good institutions and human creativity.

Institutions include a legal system to enforce contracts and laws and to protect the rights of citizens and the ideas they create, a legislative process to develop laws and policies that provide incentives to individuals and firms to work hard, a government free of corruption, and a strong monetary system.

Equally as important as institutions is the ability of societies to create ideas. Ideas change civilizations. Ideas are the basis for creating new products and finding new ways to improve upon existing goods and services. Human creativity starts with a strong educational system, and builds with proper incentives that allow innovation and creativity to flourish into marketable outcomes to improve the lives of all.

Summing It All Up: Economics Is All Around Us

The examples presented in these key principles should have convinced you that economic decisions are a part of our everyday lives. Anytime we make a decision involving a purchase, or decide what we plan to eat, study, or do with our day, we are making economic decisions. Just keep in mind that economics is broader than an exclusive concern with money, despite the great emphasis placed on money in our everyday economic discussions.

Instead, economics is about making decisions when we can't have everything we want, and how we interact with others to maximize our well-being given limitations. The existence of well-functioning markets allows individuals and firms to come together to achieve good outcomes, and government institutions and policies provide incentives that can lead to a better standard of living for all residents.

The key principles discussed in this chapter will be repeated throughout this book, and you will learn more about these important principles as the term progresses. For now, realize that economics rests on the foundation of a limited number of important principles. Once you fully grasp these basic ideas, the study of economics will be both rewarding and exciting, because after this course you will discover and appreciate how much more you understand the world around you.

ISSUE

Do Economists Ever Agree on Anything?

> Give me a one-handed economist! All my economists say, "on one hand . . . on the other."
>
> Harry S Truman

President Truman once exclaimed that the country needed more *one-handed economists*. What did he mean by that? He was saying that anytime an economist talks about a solution to an economic problem, the economist will often follow that statement by saying "on the other hand . . .".

This story highlights the point that every issue can be viewed from different perspectives, so much so that economists seemingly disagree with one another on everything. Solutions often depend on how benefits and costs are measured. For example, suppose we debate whether gasoline taxes are too high. *On the one hand*, higher gasoline taxes will reduce oil consumption, reduce pollution, reduce traffic congestion, and generate money to promote public transportation such as buses, subways, and high-speed trains. *On the other hand*, higher gasoline taxes result in higher prices for most consumer goods due to higher transportation costs, and higher prices for gas and consumer goods affect lower-income households more since they spend a greater share of their money on such goods.

Different opinions about the relative weights of benefits and costs make economic policymaking challenging. Economic conditions are always changing. This is why economists rely so much on models and assumptions in order to prescribe a solution based on the conditions facing the economy.

But despite differences and frequent disagreements in economic policy, a recent survey of the IGM Economic Experts Panel, consisting of forty-one prominent economists from all different schools of thought, found that economists do agree on many things. First, most economists agree that specialization in activities leads to gains to all parties involved. Second, most economists agree that markets and competition promote efficiency. Third, most economists believe that stimulus programs and bailout packages do reduce unemployment (though not all believe such measures are worth their costs). Fourth, most economists believe flexible exchange rates are ideal. And finally, most economists believe that individuals and firms respond to incentives.

In sum, despite the constant bickering one often hears in economic policy debates, economists agree on a number of issues, and these are typically grounded in the key economic principles described in this chapter.

CHECKPOINT

KEY PRINCIPLES OF ECONOMICS

- Economics is concerned with making choices with limited resources.
- When making decisions, one must take into account tradeoffs and opportunity costs.
- Specialization leads to gains for all involved.
- People respond to incentives, both good and bad.
- Rational behavior requires thinking on the margin.
- Markets are generally efficient; when they aren't, government can sometimes correct the failure.
- Institutions and human creativity help explain the wealth of nations.

QUESTION: McDonald's introduced a premium blend of coffee that sells for more than its standard coffee. How does this represent thinking at the margin?

Answers to the Checkpoint question can be found at the end of this chapter.

chapter summary

Section 1: What Is Economics About?

Economics is the study of how individuals, firms, and societies make decisions to improve their well-being given limitations.

Scarcity is the idea that people have unlimited wants but limited resources. Resources can be money, time, ability, work ethic, or anything that can be used to generate productive outcomes.

Presselect/Alamy

Imageplus/Corbis

Scarce versus scarcity: Large uncut diamonds are scarce—only a few are found in the world each year—and are sold for millions of dollars each. A car, on the other hand, is less scarce, as car dealerships around the country have lots full of them. But both large diamonds and cars are subject to scarcity—many people want them, but can only buy what they can afford.

What Is the Difference Between Microeconomics and Macroeconomics?

- M"i"croeconomics deals with individual entities, such as individuals, firms, and industries (Remember "i" = "individual")
- M"a"croeconomics deals with aggregate entities, such as cities or the nation (Remember "a" = "aggregate" or "all")

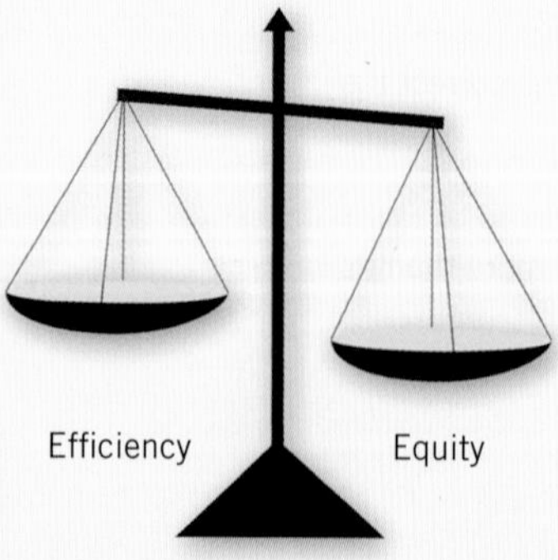

Fernando Jose Vascocelos Soares/Dreamstime.com

Economists and policymakers often confront the tradeoff between efficiency and equity. Efficiency reflects how well resources are used and allocated. Equity (or fairness) of an outcome is a subjective matter, where differences of opinion exist.

age fotostock/SuperStock

How governments deal with pollution is an important problem that can be addressed using economic analysis.

Economic analysis uses a stylized approach, where models boil issues and facts down to their basic relevant elements. To build models means that we make use of the *ceteris paribus* assumption and hold some important variables constant. This useful device often provides surprising insights about economic behavior.

Section 2: Key Principles of Economics

1. Economics Is Concerned with Making Choices with Limited Resources

Economics involves making decisions to maximize one's well-being, which can come from many sources, including money, time, happiness, or a fortuitous event.

Randy Faris/Corbis

"We should have done something different this weekend . . .".

2. When Making Decisions, One Must Take Into Account Tradeoffs and Opportunity Costs

Choice and scarcity force tradeoffs because we face unlimited wants but limited resources. We must make tradeoffs in nearly everything we do. Opportunity costs are resources (e.g., time and money) that could be used in another activity. Everything we do involves opportunity costs, the value of the next best alternative use of our resources.

3. Specialization Leads to Gains for All Involved

Specializing in tasks in which one is comparatively better at doing than another allows individuals to achieve productivity gains as long as the work is shared in a mutually beneficial manner.

4. People Respond to Incentives, Both Good and Bad

Incentives encourage people to work hard and be more productive.

Randy Faris/Corbis

Rewarding the top salesperson in the company creates a valuable incentive to work hard.

Julia Shin at Foodographer.net

Maximizing your food intake at a buffet is not thinking at the margin if you end up bloated from overeating.

5. Rational Behavior Requires Thinking on the Margin

When making a decision involving benefits and costs, one should continue to consume or produce as long as the marginal (additional) benefit exceeds the marginal (additional) cost.

6. Markets Are Generally Efficient; When They Aren't, Government Can Sometimes Correct the Failure

Markets bring buyers and sellers together. Competition forces firms to provide products at the lowest possible price. New products are introduced to the market and old products disappear. This dynamism makes markets efficient. In some instances though, markets might fail, such as in dealing with pollution, leading governments to intervene. During extended economic downturns, government can smooth fluctuations in the overall economy.

Henrik Jonsson/iStockphoto

Market equilibrium often is achieved by letting market participants make decisions freely.

7. Institutions and Human Creativity Help Explain the Wealth of Nations

Institutions include the legal system, laws and policies, a government free of corruption, and a strong monetary system. Ideas and innovation lead to new products and improve on existing ones, raising the standard of living of all residents.

KEY CONCEPTS

economics, p. 2
scarcity, p. 4
incentives, p. 4
microeconomics, p. 4
macroeconomics, p. 5
ceteris paribus, p. 6
efficiency, p. 6
equity, p. 6
positive question, p. 7
normative question, p. 7
opportunity costs, p. 8

QUESTIONS AND PROBLEMS

Check Your Understanding

1. What is wrong with the statement "Economics is everything to do with money"?
2. Does your going to college have anything to do with expanding choices or reducing scarcity? Explain.
3. What is the difference between a positive question and a normative question?
4. You normally stay at home on Wednesday nights and study. Next Wednesday night, your best friend is having his big 21st birthday party. What is the opportunity cost of going to the party?
5. What is the incentive to spend four years of one's life and tens of thousands of dollars to earn a college degree?
6. Why do markets typically lead to an efficient outcome for buyers and sellers?

Apply the Concepts

7. In contrasting equity and efficiency, why do high-tech firms seem to treat their employees better (better wages, benefits, working environments, vacations, etc.) compared to how landscaping or fast-food franchises treat their employees? Is this fair? Is it efficient?
8. Stores sometimes offer "mail-in rebates" to customers who purchase certain goods to get a portion of the purchase price refunded. Typically, a mail-in rebate requires proof of purchase (like a UPC from the actual product along with a store receipt) and a completed form to be mailed in for processing, with the rebate being mailed in the form of a check or a prepaid debit card six to eight weeks later. Why would some customers, but not all, take advantage of mail-in rebates?
9. The black rhinoceros is extremely endangered. Its horn is considered a powerful aphrodisiac in many Asian countries, and a single horn fetches many thousands of dollars on the black market, creating a great incentive for poachers. Unlike other stories of endangered species, this one might have a simple solution. Conservationists could simply capture as many rhinos as possible and remove their horns, reducing the incentive to poach. Do you think this will help reduce poaching? Why or why not?
10. Most amusement parks in the United States charge a fixed price for admission, which includes unlimited roller coaster rides for the day. Some people attempt to ride the roller coasters as often as possible in order to maximize the value of their admission. Why is riding a roller coaster at an amusement park over and over to "get your money's worth" not considered *thinking on the margin*?
11. With higher gasoline prices, the U.S. government wants people to buy more hybrid cars that use much less gasoline. Unfortunately, hybrids are approximately $4,000 to $5,000 more expensive to purchase than comparable cars. Because people follow incentives, what can the government do to encourage the purchase of hybrids?
12. Some colleges and universities charge tuition by the credit hour, while others charge tuition by the term, allowing students to take as many classes as they desire. How do these tuition structures affect the incentives students face when deciding how many

classes to take? Provide an example of a beneficial effect and an example of a potentially harmful effect resulting from the incentives created with each system. How does marginal analysis affect the incentives with each system?

In the News

13. *The New York Times* reported on January 18, 2012, in an article titled "What the Top 1% of Earners Majored In," that 8.2% of Americans who majored in economics for their undergraduate degree are in the top 1% of salary earners. Only those who majored in pre-med had a higher percentage in the top 1%. What might be some reasons why economics majors have done well in the job market?
14. Ticketmaster, the largest event ticket seller in the country, recently expanded its use of paperless tickets that requires buyers to pick up tickets on the day of the event and show identification (*Reuters,* "Paperless Tickets: Is Ticketmaster Hurting Consumers?," March 29, 2011) rather than mailing paper tickets weeks before the event. What are some reasons Ticketmaster is expanding this method of ticket delivery? How does this change the incentives in the secondary (resale) market?

Solving Problems

15. Suppose your favorite band is on tour and coming to your area. Tickets are $100, and you take a day off from work for which you could have earned $60. What is your opportunity cost of going to the concert?
16. Suppose you pay $10 to watch a movie at the local multiplex cinema, and then afterward sneak into the next theater to watch a second movie without paying. What would be your marginal cost of watching the second movie?

USING THE NUMBERS

17. According to By the Numbers, the average percentage of income spent on various items has changed since 1960.
    a. What percent of income did Food represent in 1960? In 2010? This represents a drop of approximately what percent? (Hint: it is *not* 8%.)
    b. What percent of income did Health Care represent in 1960? In 2010? This represents an increase of approximately what percent? (Hint: it is *not* 9%.)
18. According to By the Numbers, about how many economics degrees were awarded to college graduates in 2011? How does this number compare to the number of nursing degrees? Communications degrees?

ANSWERS TO QUESTIONS IN CHECKPOINTS

Checkpoint: What Is Economics About?

(1) microeconomics, (2) macroeconomics, (3) microeconomics, (4) macroeconomics, (5) macroeconomics, (6) microeconomics, (7) macroeconomics.

Checkpoint: Key Principles of Economics

McDonald's is adding one more product (premium coffee) to its line. Thinking at the margin entails thinking about how you can improve an operation (or increase profits) by adding to your existing product line or reducing costs.

Appendix
Working with Graphs and Formulas

After studying this appendix you should be able to:

- Describe the four simple forms of data graphs.
- Make use of a straightforward approach to reading graphs.
- Read linear and nonlinear graphs and know how to compute their slopes.
- Use simple linear equations to describe a line and a shift in the line.
- Explain why correlation is not the same as causation.

You can't watch the news on television or read a newspaper without seeing a graph of some sort. If you have flipped through this book, you have seen a large number of graphs, charts, and tables, and a few simple equations. This is the language of economics. Economists deal with data for all types of issues. Just looking at data in tables often doesn't help you discern the trends or relationships in the data.

Economists develop theories and models to explain economic behavior and levels of economic activity. These theories or models are simplified representations of real-world activity. Models are designed to distill the most important relationships between variables, and then these relationships are used to predict future behavior of individuals, firms, and industries, or to predict the future course of the overall economy.

In this short section, we will explore the different types of graphs you are likely to see in this course (and in the media) and then turn to an examination of how graphs are used to develop and illustrate models. This second topic leads us into a discussion of modeling relationships between data and how to represent these relationships with simple graphs and equations.

Graphs and Data

The main forms of graphs of data are time series, scatter plots, pie charts, and bar charts. Time series, as the name suggests, plots data over time. Most of the figures you will encounter in publications are time series graphs.

Time Series

Time series graphs involve plotting time (minutes, hours, days, months, quarters, or years) on the horizontal axis and the value of some variable on the vertical axis. Figure APX-1 illustrates a time series plot for civilian employment of those 16 years and older. Notice that since the early 1990s, employment has grown by almost 25 million for this group. The vertical strips in the figure designate the last three recessions. Notice that in cases when the recession hit, employment fell, then rebounded after the recession ended.

Scatter Plots

Scatter plots are graphs in which two variables (neither variable is time) are plotted against each other. Scatter plots often give us a hint if the two variables are related to each other in some consistent way. Figure APX-2 plots one variable, median household income, against another variable, percentage of Americans holding a college degree.

Two things can be seen in this figure. First, these two variables appear to be related to each other in a positive way. A rising percentage of college graduates leads to a higher median household income. It is not surprising that college degrees and earnings are related, because increased education leads to a more productive workforce, which translates into more income. Second, given that the years for the data are listed next to the dots, we can see that the percentage of the population with college degrees has risen significantly over the last half-century. From this simple scatter plot, we get a lot of information and ideas about how the two variables are related.

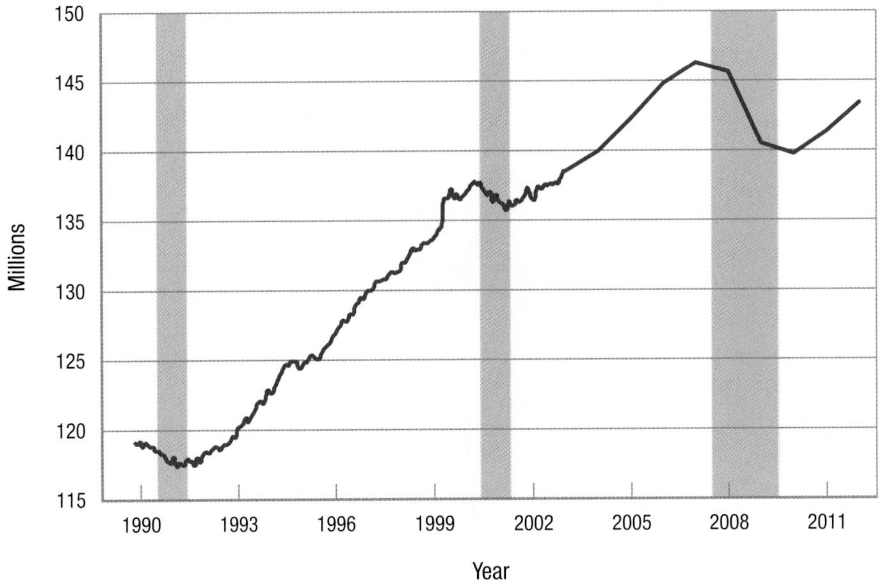

FIGURE APX-1

Civilian Employment, 16 Years and Older

This time series graph shows the number of civilians 16 years and older employed in the United States since 1990. Employment has grown steadily over this period, except in times of recession, indicated by the vertical strips. Note that employment fell during the recession, and then bounced back after each recession ended.

Pie Charts

Pie charts are simple graphs that show data that can be split into percentage parts that combined make up the whole. A simple pie chart for the relative importance of components in the consumer price index (CPI) is shown in Figure APX-3 on the next page. It reveals how the typical urban household budget is allocated. By looking at each slice of the pie, we get a picture of how typical families spend their income.

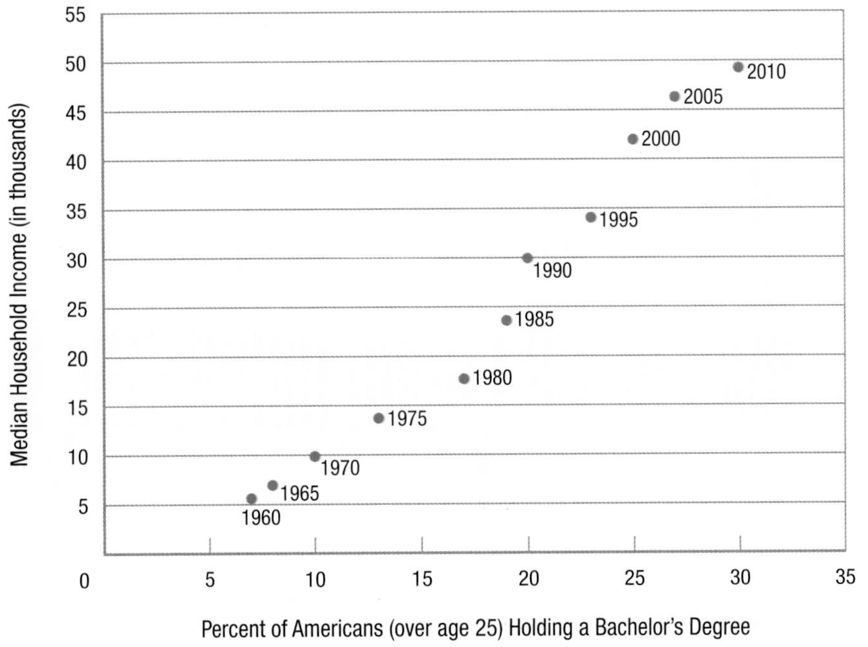

FIGURE APX-2

The Relationship Between the Median Household Income and the Percentage of Americans Holding a College Degree

This scatter diagram plots the relationship between median household income and the percentage of Americans holding a college degree. Median household income increased as a greater proportion of Americans earn college degrees. Note that the percentage of Americans earning college degrees has increased significantly in the last half-century.

FIGURE APX-3

Relative Importance of Consumer Price Index (CPI) Components (2011)

This pie chart shows the relative importance of the components of the consumer price index, showing how typical urban households spend their income.

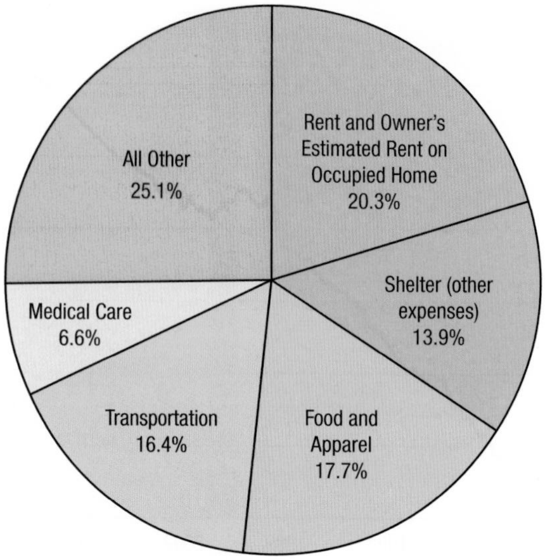

Bar Charts

Bar charts use bars to show the value of specific data points. Figure APX-4 is a bar chart showing the annual changes in real (adjusted for inflation) gross domestic product (GDP). Notice that over the last 50 years the United States has had only 7 years when GDP declined.

Simple Graphs Can Pack In a Lot of Information It is not unusual for graphs and figures to have several things going on at once. Look at Figure APX-5, illustrating the number of social media users as a percent of each age group. On the horizontal axis are the age groups in years. On the vertical axis is the percent of each age group that regularly used social media. Figure APX-5 shows the relationship between age and social media

FIGURE APX-4

Percent Change in Real (Inflation Adjusted) GDP

This bar chart shows the annual percent change in real (adjusted for inflation) gross domestic product (GDP) over the last 50 years. Over this period, GDP has declined only seven times.

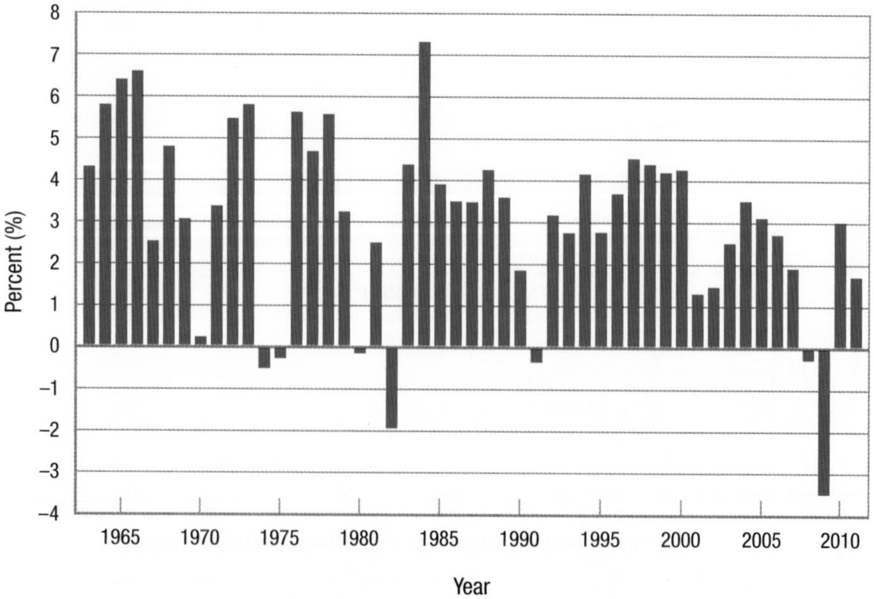

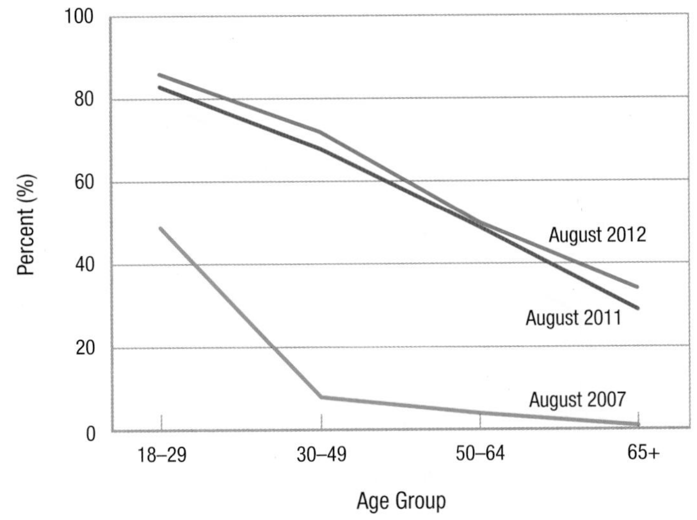

FIGURE APX-5

Social Media Usage Across Age Groups

These curves show the percentage of Americans using a social media site by age. The curves slope downward because older Americans are less likely to use social media than younger Americans. However, over time, more Americans in all age groups are using social media as evident by each point on the August 2011 curve being higher than the corresponding point on the August 2007 curve, and each point on the August 2012 curve being higher than the corresponding point on the August 2011 curve.

penetration for different periods. They include the most recent period shown (August 2012), a year previous (August 2011), and five years ago (August 2007).

You should notice two things in this figure. First, the relationship between the variables slopes downward. This means that older Americans are less likely to use social media than younger Americans. Second, use of social media has increased across all ages over the three periods studied (from August 2007 to August 2011 to August 2012) as shown by the position of the curves. Each point on the August 2007 curve is below the corresponding point on the August 2011 curve, which is subsequently below each point on the August 2012 curve.

A Few Simple Rules for Reading Graphs Looking at graphs of data is relatively easy if you follow a few simple rules. First, read the title of the figure to get a sense of what is being presented. Second, look at the label for the horizontal axis (x axis) to see how the data are being presented. Make sure you know how the data are being measured. Is it months or years, hours worked or hundreds of hours worked? Third, examine the label for the vertical axis (y axis). This is the value of the variable being plotted on that axis; make sure you know what it is. Fourth, look at the graph itself to see if it makes logical sense. Are the curves (bars, dots) going in the right direction?

Look the graph over and see if you notice something interesting going on. This is really the fun part of looking closely at figures both in this text and in other books, magazines, and newspapers. Often simple data graphs can reveal surprising relationships between variables. Keep this in mind as you examine graphs throughout this course.

One more thing. Graphs in this book are always accompanied by explanatory captions. Examine the graph first, making your preliminary assessment of what is going on. Then carefully read the caption, making sure it accurately reflects what is shown in the graph. If the caption refers to movement between points, follow this movement in the graph. If you think there is a discrepancy between the caption and the graph, reexamine the graph to make sure you have not missed anything.

Graphs and Models

Let's now take a brief look at how economists use graphs and models, also looking at how they are constructed. Economists use what are called *stylized graphs* to represent relationships between variables. These graphs are a form of modeling to help us simplify our analysis and focus on those relationships that matter. Figure APX-6 on the next page is one such model.

FIGURE APX-6

Studying and Your GPA

This figure shows a hypothetical linear relationship between average study hours and GPA. Without studying, a D average results, and with 10 hours of studying, a C average is obtained, and so on.

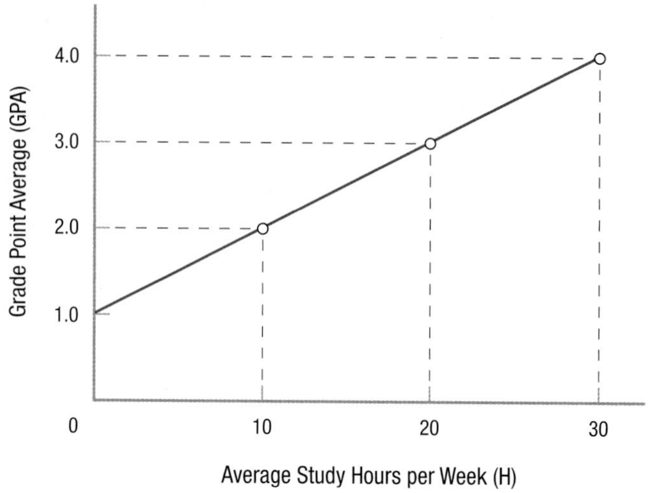

Linear Relationships

Figure APX-6 shows a linear relationship between average study hours and grade point average (GPA), indicating a higher GPA the more you study. By a linear relationship, we mean that the "curve" is a straight line. In this case, if you don't study at all, we assume you are capable of making Ds and your GPA will equal 1.0, not enough to keep you in school for long. If you hit the books for an average of 10 hours a week, your GPA rises to 2.0, a C average. Studying for additional hours raises your GPA up to its maximum of 4.0.

The important point here is that the curve is linear; any hour of studying yields the same increase in GPA. All hours of studying provide equal yields from beginning to end. This is what makes linear relationships unique.

Computing the Slope of a Linear Line

Looking at the line in Figure APX-6, we can see two things: The line is straight, so the slope is constant, and the slope is positive. As average hours of studying increase, GPA increases. Computing the slope of the line tells us how much GPA increases for every hour of additional studying. Computing the slope of a linear line is relatively easy and is shown in Figure APX-7.

FIGURE APX-7

Computing Slope for a Linear Line

Computing the slope is based on a simple rule: rise over run (rise divided by run). In the case of this straight line, the slope is equal to 0.1 because every 10 additional hours of studying yields a 1.0 increase in GPA.

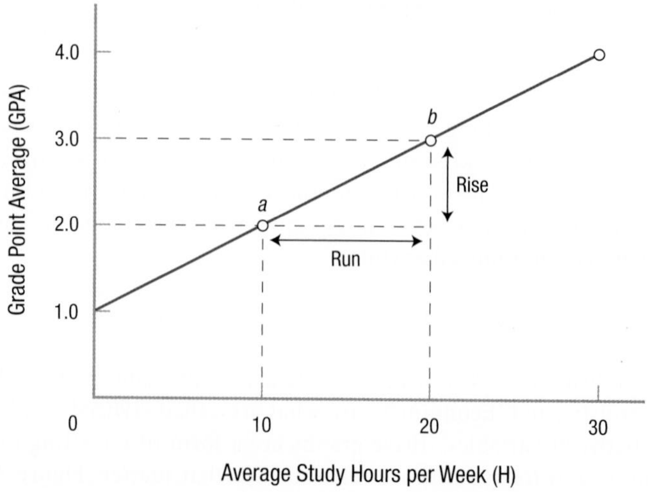

The simple rule for computing slope is: Slope is equal to rise over run (or rise ÷ run). Since the slope is constant along a linear line, we can select any two points and determine the slope for the entire curve. In Figure APX-7 we have selected points *a* and *b* where GPA moves from 2.0 to 3.0 when studying increases from 10 to 20 hours per week.

Your GPA increases by 1.0 for an additional 10 hours of study. This means that the slope is equal to 0.1 (1.0 ÷ 10 = 0.1). So for every additional hour of studying you add each week, your GPA will rise by 0.1. Thus, if you would like to improve your grade point average from 3.0 to 3.5, you would have to study five more hours per week.

Computing slope for negative relations that are linear is done exactly the same way, except that when computing the changes from one point to another, one of the values will be negative, making the relationship negative.

Nonlinear Relationships

It would be nice for model builders if all relationships were linear, but that is not the case. It is probably not really the case with the amount of studying and GPA either. Figure APX-8 depicts a more realistic nonlinear and positive relationship between studying and GPA. Again, we assume that one can get a D average (1.0) without studying and reach a maximum of straight As (4.0) with 30 hours per week.

Figure APX-8 suggests that the first few hours of study per week are more important to raising GPA than are the others. The first 10 hours of studying yields more than the last 10 hours: One goes from 1.0 to 3.3 (a gain of 2.3), as opposed to going only from 3.8 to 4.0 (a gain of only 0.2). This curve exhibits what economists call diminishing returns. Just as the first bite of pizza tastes better than the 100th, so the first 5 hours of studying brings a bigger jump in GPA than the 25th to 30th hours.

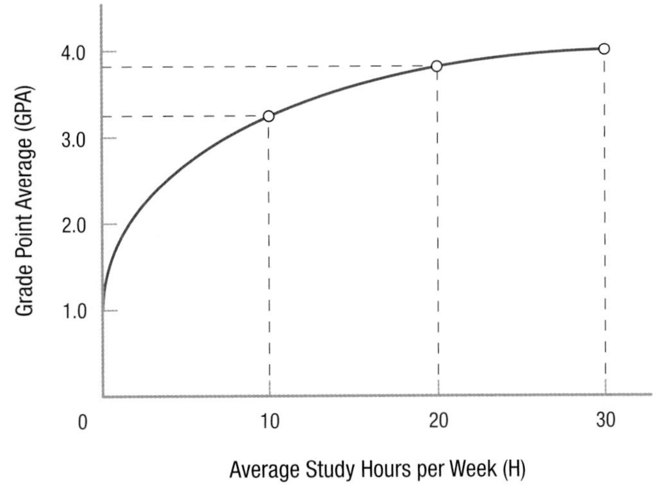

FIGURE APX-8

Studying and Your GPA (Nonlinear)

This nonlinear graph of study hours and GPA is probably more typical than the one shown in Figures APX-6 and APX-7. Like many other things, studying exhibits diminishing returns. The first hours of studying result in greater improvements to GPAs than further hours of studying.

Computing the Slope of a Nonlinear Curve

As you might suspect, computing the slope of a nonlinear curve is a little more complex than for a linear line. But it is not that much more difficult. In fact, we use essentially the same rise over run approach that is used for lines.

Looking at the curve in Figure APX-8, it should be clear that the slope varies for each point on the curve. It starts out very steep, then begins to level out above 20 hours of studying. Figure APX-9 on the next page shows how to compute the slope at any point on the curve.

Computing the slope at point *a* requires drawing a line tangent to that point, then computing the slope of that line. For point *a*, the slope of the line tangent to it is found by

FIGURE APX-9

Computing Slope for a Nonlinear Curve

Computing the slope of a nonlinear curve requires that you compute the slope of each point on the curve. This is done by computing the slope of a tangent to each point.

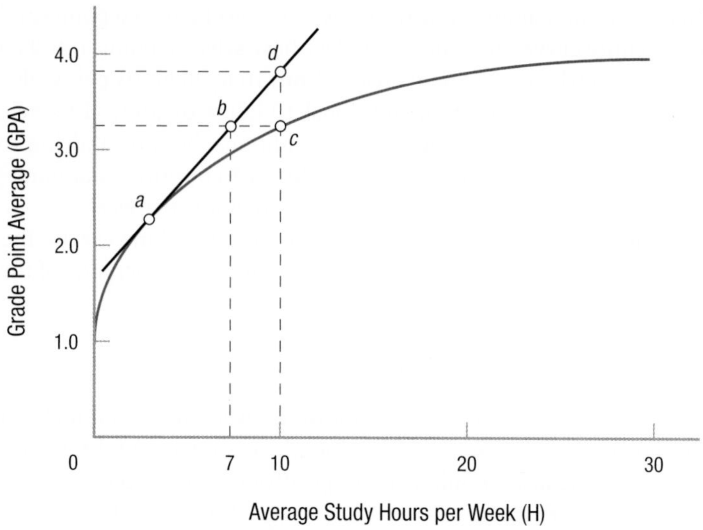

computing rise over run again. In this case, it is length $dc \div bc$ or $[(3.8 - 3.3) \div (10 - 7)] = 0.5 \div 3 = 0.167$. Notice that this slope is significantly larger than the original linear relationship of 0.1. If we were to compute the slope near 30 hours of studying, it would approach zero (the slope of a horizontal line is zero).

Ceteris Paribus, Simple Equations, and Shifting Curves

Hold on while we beat this GPA and studying example into the ground. Inevitably, when we simplify analysis to develop a graph or model, important factors or influences must be controlled. We do not ignore them, we hold them constant. These are known as *ceteris paribus* assumptions.

Ceteris Paribus: All Else Equal

By *ceteris paribus* we mean other things being equal or all other relevant factors, elements, or influences are held constant. When economists define your demand for a product, they want to know how much or how many units you will buy at different prices. For example, to determine how many DVDs you will buy at various prices (your demand for DVDs), we hold your income and the price of movie tickets and online movie downloads constant. If your income suddenly jumped, you would be willing to buy more DVDs at all prices, but this is a whole new demand curve. *Ceteris paribus* assumptions are a way to simplify analysis; then the analysis can be extended to include those factors held constant, as we will see next.

Simple Linear Equations

Simple linear equations can be expressed as: $Y = a + bX$. This is read as, Y equals a plus b times X, where Y is the variable plotted on the y axis and a is a constant (unchanging), and b is a different constant that is multiplied by X, the value on the x axis. The formula for our studying and GPA example introduced in Figure APX-6 is shown in Figure APX-10.

The constant a is known as the vertical intercept because it is the value of GPA when study hours (X) is zero, and therefore it cuts (intercepts) the vertical axis at the value of 1.0 (D average). Now each time you study another hour on average, your GPA rises by 0.1, so the constant b (the slope of the line) is equal to 0.1. Letting H represent hours of studying, the final equation is: GPA = $1.0 + 0.1H$. You start with a D average without

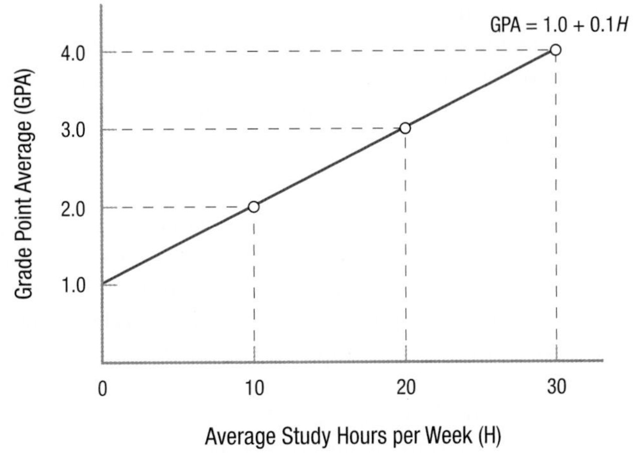

FIGURE APX-10

Studying and Your GPA: A Simple Equation

The formula for a linear relationship is $Y = a + bX$, where Y is the y axis variable, X is the x axis variable, and a and b are constants. For the original relationship between study hours and GPA, this equation is $Y = 1.0 + 0.1X$.

studying and as your hours of studying increase, your GPA goes up by 0.1 times the hours of studying. If we plug in 20 hours of studying into the equation, the answer is a GPA of 3.0 [$1.0 + (0.1 \times 20) = 1.0 + 2.0 = 3.0$].

Shifting Curves

Now let's introduce a couple of factors that we have been holding constant (the *ceteris paribus* assumption). These two elements are tutoring and partying. So, our new equation now becomes GPA $= 1.0 + 0.1H + Z$, where Z is our variable indicating whether you have a tutor or whether you are excessively partying. When you have a tutor, $Z = 1$, and when you party too much, $Z = -1$. Tutoring adds to the productivity of your studying (hence $Z = 1$), while excessive late-night partying reduces the effectiveness of studying because you are always tired (hence $Z = -1$). Figure APX-11 shows the impact of adding these factors to the original relationship.

With tutoring, your GPA-studying curve has moved upward and to the left. Now, because $Z = 1$, you begin with a C average (2.0), and with just 20 hours of studying (because of tutoring) you can reach a 4.0 GPA (point *a*). Alternatively, when you don't have tutoring and you party every night, your GPA–studying relationship has worsened (shifted downward and to the right). Now you must study 40 hours (point *c*) to accomplish a 4.0 GPA. Note that you begin with failing grades.

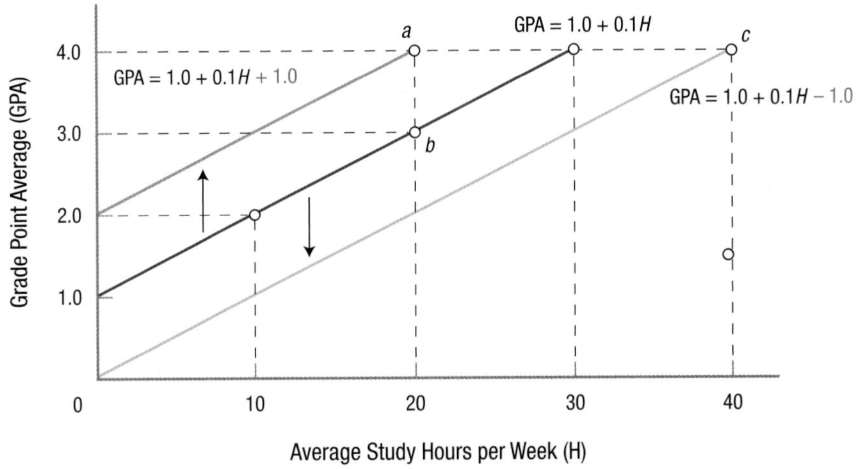

FIGURE APX-11

The Impact of Tutoring and Partying on Your GPA

The effect of tutoring and partying on our simple model of studying and GPA is shown. Partying harms your academic efforts and shifts the relationship to the right, making it harder to maintain your previous average (you now have to study more hours). Tutoring, on the other hand, improves the relationship (shifts the curve to the left).

The important point here is that we can simplify relationships between different variables and use a simple graph or equation to represent a model of behavior. In doing so, we often have to hold some things constant. When we allow those factors to change, the original relationship is now changed and often results in a shift in the curves. You will see this technique applied over and over as you study economics this term.

Correlation Is Not Causation

Just because two variables seem related or appear related on a scatter plot does not mean that one causes another. Economists 100 years ago correlated business cycles (the ups and downs of the entire economy) with sunspots. Because they appeared related, some suggested that sunspots caused business cycles. The only rational argument was that agriculture was the dominant industry and sunspots affected the weather; therefore, sunspots caused the economy to fluctuate.

Other examples of erroneously assuming that correlation implies causality abound, some of which can be preposterous or humorous. For example, did Facebook cause the Greek debt crisis? Both the number of Facebook users and the total Greek debt skyrocketed between the years of 2005 and 2011. Just because two variables appear to be related does not mean that one causes the other to change.

Understanding graphs and using simple equations is a key part of learning economics. Practice helps.

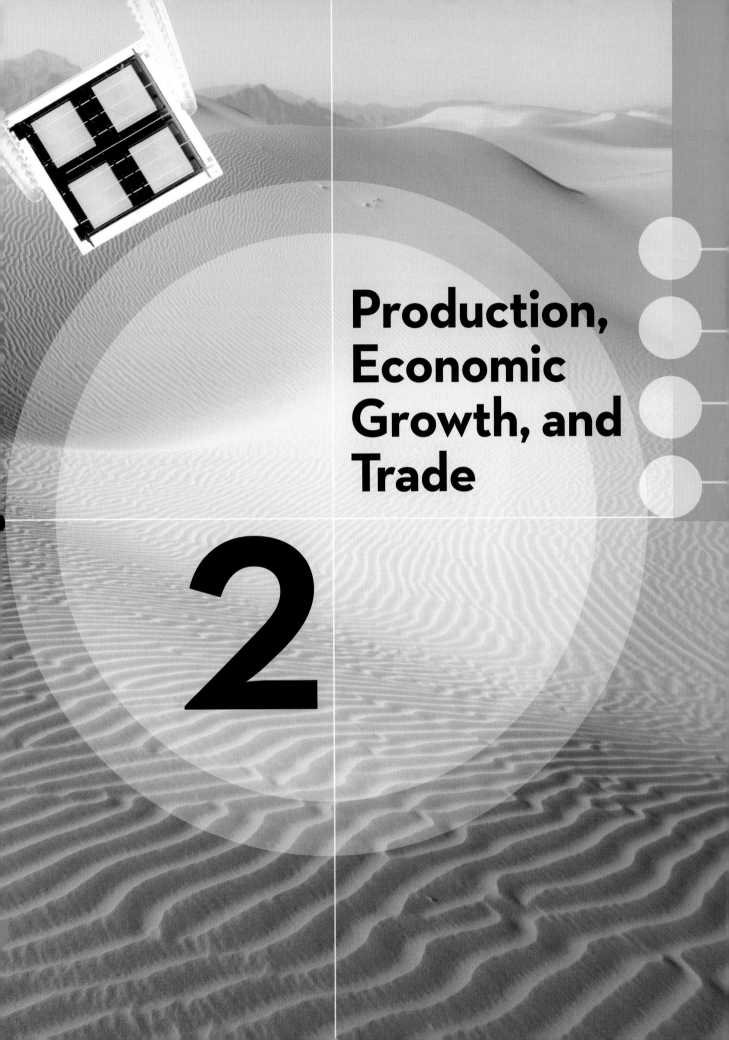

2

Production, Economic Growth, and Trade

After studying this chapter you should be able to:

- Describe the three basic questions that must be answered for any economy.
- Describe production and the factors that go into producing various goods and services.
- Describe the opportunity cost an economy incurs to increase the production of one product.
- Use a production possibilities frontier (PPF) to analyze the limits of production.
- Describe economic growth and how it is stimulated by education and training, capital accumulation, and technological improvements.
- Describe the concepts of absolute and comparative advantage and explain what they tell us about the gains from trade when countries specialize in certain products.
- Describe the practical constraints on free trade and how some industries might be affected.

Can a speck of sand be the most significant driver of economic growth of the last generation? Just about every piece of electronic and computing equipment contains a microchip, a tiny piece of circuitry that allows devices to function and to store immense amounts of data and multimedia. Most chips are made of silicon, which is nothing more than a basic element found in sand, and aside from oxygen is the most abundant element in the Earth's crust.

Extracting the silicon from the sand, melting it, and creating silicon wafers on which transistors are produced to create a functioning microchip is a complex process. More impressive is how efficient the process has become. A single chip smaller than the size of a dime can hold billions of transistors, enough to store and display all of the music, videos, and photos you could ever want on a single device.

Arguably no invention has transformed the economy more in the past 30 years than the development and advancement of the silicon chip. Technological change has made production methods more efficient, allowing countries to produce more goods and services using fewer physical and natural resources. And as we emphasized in the previous chapter on the importance of scarcity, determining how to achieve more using less—fewer resources—is one of the important goals of economics.

An industry that has experienced significant technological change is telecommunications. In 1950, long distance phone calls were placed with the assistance of live operators, every minute on the line costing the average consumer the equivalent of several hours pay. Today, with Internet communications technology allowing one to call virtually anyone in the world for pennies or less, the globe is shrinking as communications brings us closer together and contributes to greater productivity.

Another driver of economic growth is trade. Several centuries ago, individuals produced most of what they consumed. Today, most of us produce little of what we consume. Instead, we work at specialized jobs, then use our wages to purchase the goods we need.

Nearly every country engages in commercial trade with other countries to expand the opportunities for consumption and production by its people. As products are consumed, new products must be produced, allowing increased consumption in one country to spur economic growth in another. Given the ability of global trade to open economic doors and raise incomes, it is vital for economic growth in all nations.

This chapter gives you a framework for understanding economic growth. It provides a simple model for thinking about production, then applies this model to economies at large so you will know how to think about economic growth and its determinants. It then goes on to analyze international trade as a special case of economic growth. By the time you finish this chapter, you should understand the importance of economic growth and what drives it.

Basic Economic Questions and Production

Regardless of the country, its circumstances, or its precise economic structure, every economy must answer three basic questions.

Basic Economic Questions

The three basic economic questions that each society must answer are:

- What goods and services are to be produced?
- How are these goods and services to be produced?
- Who will receive these goods and services?

The response an economy makes to the first question—What goods and services should it produce?—depends on the goods and services a society wants. In a communist state, the government decides what a society wants, but in a capitalist economy, consumers signal what products they want by way of their demands for specific commodities. In the next chapter, we investigate how consumer demand for individual products is determined and how markets meet these demands. For now, we assume that consumers, individually and as a society, are able to decide on the mix of goods and services they most want, and that producers supply these items at acceptable prices.

BY THE NUMBERS

Growth, Productivity, and Trade Are Key to Our Prosperity

Over the last century, investment in education, infrastructure, and technology development, along with increased international trade, has resulted in increased productivity and growth, leading to higher incomes and standards of living around the world.

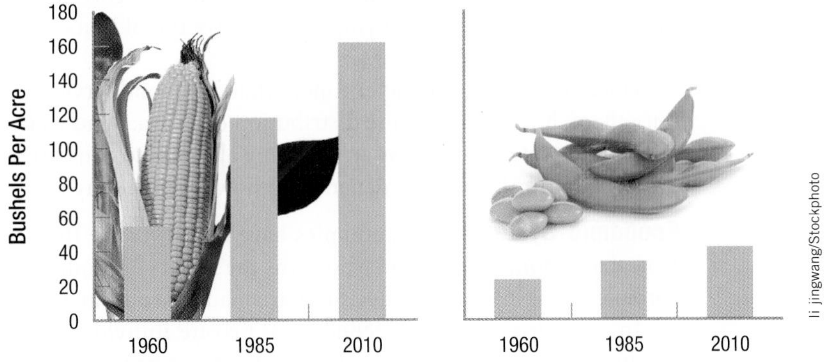

Farm productivity has dramatically increased since 1960 as a result of modern agricultural machinery and new seeds and fertilizers, resulting in higher yields per acre of crops such as corn and soybeans.

4–7%

Increase in a nation's economic output from increasing the average years of schooling by 1 year.

17

Number of countries in which the United States has a free trade agreement with as of 2012.

Firing workers can be costly in some countries. Firing a full-time worker with 20 years at the company costs roughly 70 weeks pay in Germany, but it is even more costly in China.

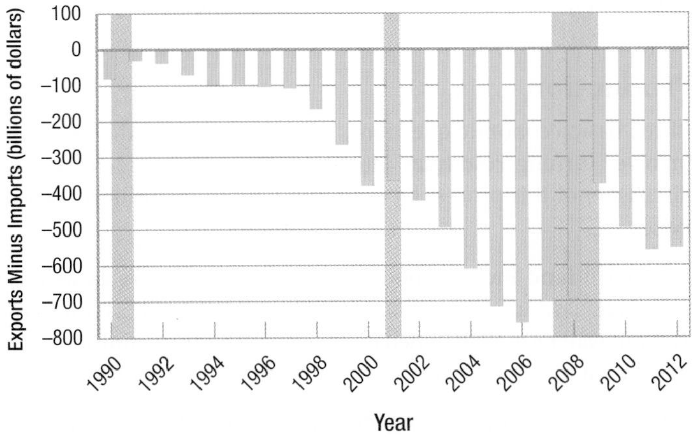

Our trade balance (exports minus imports) has grown steadily negative over the last two decades. During each of the last three recessions (shaded areas), our purchases of imports fell, improving our trade balance.

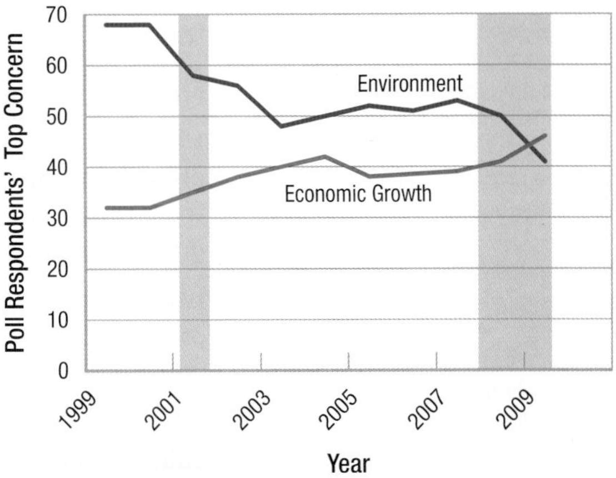

American attitudes about concerns for the environment or a preference for economic growth vary based on the state of the economy. As the economy enters a recession (shaded areas), the desire for economic growth increases while concern for the environment ebbs.

Once we know what goods a society wants, the next question its economic system must answer is, How are these goods and services to be produced? In the end, this problem comes down to the simple question of how land, labor, and capital should be combined to produce the desired products. If a society demands a huge amount of corn, for example, we can expect its use of land, labor, and capital will be different from a society that demands digital equipment. But even an economy devoted to corn production could be organized in different ways, perhaps relying on extensive use of human labor, or perhaps relying on automated capital equipment.

Once an economy has determined what goods and services to produce and how to produce them, it is faced with the distribution question: Who will get the resulting products? *Distribution* refers to the way an economy allocates to consumers the goods and services it produces. How this is done depends on how the economy is organized.

Economic Systems All economies have to answer the three basic economic questions. How that is done depends on who owns the factors of production (land, labor, capital, and entrepreneurship) and how decisions are made to coordinate production and distribution.

In *capitalist* or *market* economies, private individuals and firms own most of the resources. The what, how, and who decisions are determined by individual desires for products and profit-making decisions by firms. Product prices are the principal mechanism for communicating information in the system. Based on prices, consumers decide whether to buy or not, and firms decide how to employ their resources and what production technology to use. This competition between many buyers and sellers leads to highly efficient production of goods and services. Producers are free to survive or perish based on their efficiency and the quality of their products. The government's primary roles are protecting property rights, enforcing contracts between private parties, providing public goods such as national defense, and establishing and ensuring the appropriate operating environment for competitive markets. Today the U.S. economy is not a pure *laissez-faire* ("leave it alone," or minimal government role) market economy but more of a mixed economy with many regulations and an extended role for government.

In contrast, *planned* economies (socialist and communist) are systems in which most of the productive resources are owned by the state and most economic decisions are made by central governments. Big sweeping decisions for the economy, often called "five-year plans," are centrally made and focus productive resources on these priorities. Both the former Soviet Union and China (until quite recently) were highly centrally planned, and virtually all resources were government owned. Although Russia and China have moved toward market economies, a large portion of each country's resources is still owned by the state. Socialist countries (e.g., the Scandinavian nations of Europe) enjoy a high degree of freedom with a big role both for government services paid for by high taxes, and for highly regulated private businesses.

production The process of converting resources (factors of production)—land, labor, capital, and entrepreneurial ability—into goods and services.

resources Productive resources include land (land and natural resources), labor (mental and physical talents of people), capital (manufactured products used to produce other products), and entrepreneurial ability (the combining of the other factors to produce products and assume the risk of the business).

land Includes natural resources such as mineral deposits, oil, natural gas, water, and land in the usual sense of the word. The payment to land as a resource is called rent.

labor Includes the mental and physical talents of individuals who produce products and services. The payment to labor is called wages.

Resources and Production

Having examined the three basic economic questions, let's take a look at the production process. **Production** involves turning **resources** into products and services that people want. Let's begin our discussion of this process by examining the scarce resources used to produce goods and services.

Land For economists, the term **land** includes both land in the usual sense as well as all other natural resources that are used in production. Natural resources such as mineral deposits, oil and natural gas, and water are all included by economists in the definition of land. Economists refer to the payment to land as *rent.*

Labor **Labor** as a factor of production includes both the mental and physical talents of people. Few goods and services can be produced without labor resources. Improvement to labor capabilities from training, education, and apprenticeship programs—typically called human capital—all add to labor's productivity and ultimately to a higher standard of living. Labor is paid *wages.*

Capital **Capital** includes all manufactured products that are used to produce other goods and services. This includes equipment such as drill presses, blast furnaces for making steel, and other tools used in the production process. It also includes trucks and automobiles used by businesses, as well as office equipment such as copiers, computers, and telephones. Any manufactured product that is used to produce other products is included in the category of capital. Capital earns *interest*.

Note that the term *capital* as used by economists refers to real (or physical) capital—actual manufactured products used in the production process—not money or financial capital. Money and financial capital are important in that they are used to purchase the real capital that is used to produce products.

capital Includes manufactured products such as tractors, welding equipment, and computers that are used to produce other goods and services. The payment to capital is referred to as interest.

Entrepreneurial Ability **Entrepreneurs** *combine* land, labor, and capital to produce goods and services, and they assume the *risks* associated with running a business. Entrepreneurs combine and manage the inputs of production, and manage the day-to-day marketing, finance, and production decisions. Today, the risks of running a business are huge, as the many bankruptcies and failures testify. Globalization has opened many opportunities as well as risks. For undertaking these activities and assuming the risks associated with business, entrepreneurs earn *profits*.

entrepreneurs Entrepreneurs combine land, labor, and capital to produce goods and services. They absorb the risk of being in business, including the risk of bankruptcy and other liabilities associated with doing business. Entrepreneurs receive profits for this effort.

Production and Efficiency

Production turns *resources*—land, labor, capital, and entrepreneurial ability—into products and services. The necessary production factors vary for different products. To produce corn, for instance, one needs arable land, seed, fertilizer, water, farm equipment, and the workers to operate that equipment. Farmers looking to produce corn would need to devote hundreds of acres of open land to this crop, plow the land, plant and nurture the corn, and finally harvest the crop. Producing digital equipment, in contrast, requires less land but more capital and more highly skilled labor.

As we have seen, every country has to decide what to produce, how to produce it, and decide who receives the output. Countries desire to do the first two as efficiently as possible by choosing the production method that results in the greatest output using the least amount of resources. Figure 1 shows how factors of production enter into a production method to generate goods and services. Determining the production method is the role of a manager, who must decide how factors of production are best used. Economists refer to this actual choice as the production function, a concept that will be discussed in greater detail in a later chapter. For now, just understand that *how* resources are used is as important as the amount of resources available.

Productivity is a measure of efficiency determined by the amount of output produced given the amount of inputs used. But economists also use specific concepts to describe two different aspects of efficiency: production efficiency and allocative efficiency.

Production efficiency occurs when the mix of goods is produced at the lowest possible resource or opportunity cost. Alternatively, production efficiency occurs when as much output as possible is produced with a given amount of resources. Firms use the best technology available and combine the other resources to create products at the lowest cost to society.

production efficiency Goods and services are produced at their lowest resource (opportunity) cost.

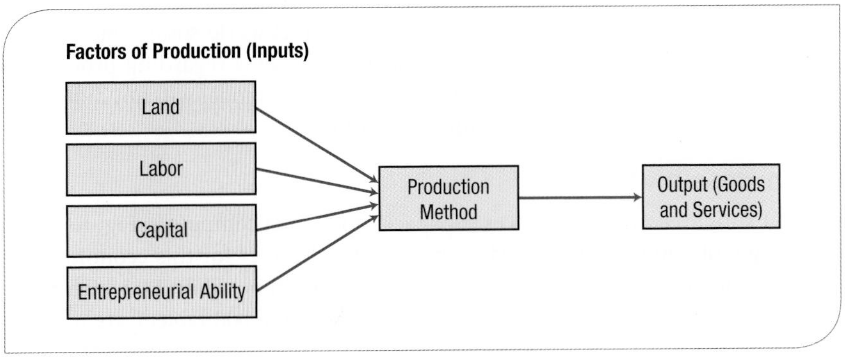

FIGURE 1

From Factors of Production to Output

Each of the four factors of production is employed in a production method in order to generate goods and services. The ability to use factors of production efficiently within a production method increases the amount of output given an amount of inputs used.

allocative efficiency The mix of goods and services produced is just what the society desires.

Allocative efficiency occurs when the mix of goods and services produced is the most desired by society. In capitalist countries, this is determined by consumers and businesses and their interaction through markets. The next chapter explores this interaction in some detail. Needless to say, it would be inefficient (a waste of resources) to be producing cassette tapes in the age of digital music players. Allocative efficiency requires that the right mix of goods be produced at the lowest cost.

Every economy faces constraints or limitations. Land, labor, capital, and entrepreneurship are all limited. No country has an infinite supply of available workers or the space and machinery that would be needed to put them all to work efficiently. No country can break free of these natural restraints. Such limits are known as production possibilities frontiers, and they are the focus of the next section.

CHECKPOINT

BASIC ECONOMIC QUESTIONS AND PRODUCTION

- Every economy must decide what to produce, how to produce it, and who will get what is produced.
- Production is the process of converting factors of production (resources)—land, labor, capital, and entrepreneurial ability—into goods and services.
- To the economist, land includes both land and natural resources. Labor includes the mental and physical resources of humans. Capital includes all manufactured products used to produce other goods and services. Entrepreneurs combine resources to manufacture products, and they assume the risk of doing business.
- Production efficiency requires that products be produced at the lowest cost. Allocative efficiency occurs when the mix of goods and services produced is just what society wants.

QUESTION: The one element that really seems to differentiate entrepreneurship from the other resources is the fact that entrepreneurs shoulder the *risk* of the failure of the enterprise. Is this important? Explain.

Answers to the Checkpoint question can be found at the end of this chapter.

Production Possibilities and Economic Growth

As we discovered in the previous section, all countries and all economies face constraints on their production capabilities. Production can be limited by the quantity of the various factors of production in the country and its current technology. Technology includes such considerations as the country's infrastructure, its transportation and education systems, and the economic freedom it allows. Although perhaps going beyond the everyday meaning of the word *technology,* for simplicity, we will assume that all of these factors help determine the state of a country's technology.

To further simplify matters, production possibilities analysis assumes that the quantity of resources available and the technology of the economy remain constant, and that the economy produces only two products. Although a two-product world sounds far-fetched, this simplification allows us to analyze many important concepts regarding production and tradeoffs. Further, the conclusions drawn from this simple model will not differ fundamentally from a more complex model of the real world.

Production Possibilities

Assume that our simple economy produces backpacks and tablet computers. Figure 2 with its accompanying table shows the production possibilities frontier for this economy. The table shows seven possible production levels (*a*–*g*). These seven possibilities, which range from 12,000 backpacks and zero tablets to zero backpacks and 6,000 tablets, are graphed in Figure 2.

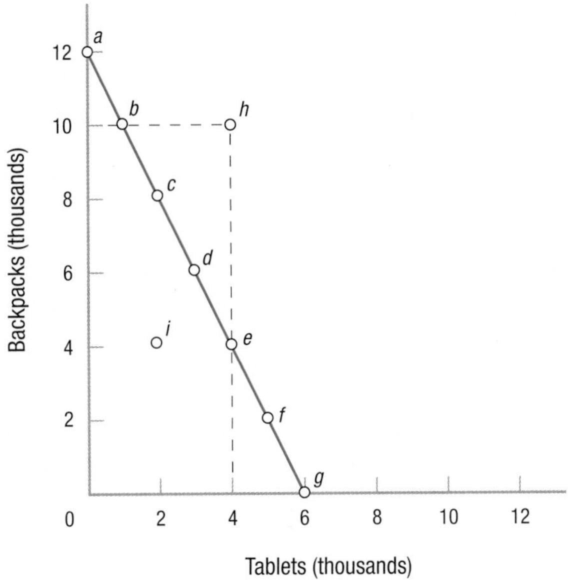

Possibility	Backpacks	Tablets
a	12,000	0
b	10,000	1,000
c	8,000	2,000
d	6,000	3,000
e	4,000	4,000
f	2,000	5,000
g	0	6,000

FIGURE 2

Production Possibilities Frontier

Using all of its resources, this stylized economy can produce many different mixes of backpacks and tablets. Production levels on, or to the left of, the resulting PPF are attainable for this economy. Production levels to the right of the PPF are unattainable.

When we connect the seven production possibilities, we delineate the **production possibilities frontier (PPF)** for this economy (some economists refer to this curve as the production possibilities curve). All points on the PPF are considered *attainable* by our economy. Everything to the left of the PPF is also attainable, but is an inefficient use of resources—the economy can always do better. Everything to the right of the curve is considered *unattainable.* Therefore, the PPF maps out the economy's limits; it is impossible for the economy to produce at levels beyond the PPF without an increase in resources or technology.

production possibilities frontier (PPF) Shows the combinations of two goods that are possible for a society to produce at full employment. Points on or inside the PPF are attainable, and those outside of the frontier are unattainable.

What the PPF in Figure 2 shows is that, given an efficient use of limited resources and taking technology into account, this economy can produce any of the seven combinations of tablets and backpacks listed, each of which represents a point of maximum output for the economy. If society wants to produce 1,000 tablets, it will only be able to produce 10,000 backpacks, as shown by point *b* on the PPF. Should the society decide that mobile Internet access is important, it might decide to produce 4,000 tablets, which would force it to cut backpack production down to 4,000, shown by point *e.* At each of these points, resources are fully employed in the economy, and therefore increasing production of one good requires giving up some production of the other. Also, the economy can produce any combination of the two products on or within the PPF, but not any combinations beyond it.

Contrast points *c* and *e* with production at point *i.* At point *i* the economy is only producing 2,000 tablets and 4,000 backpacks. Clearly, some resources are not being used. When fully employed, the economy's resources could produce more of both goods (point *d*).

Because the PPF represents a maximum output, the economy could not produce 4,000 tablets and still produce 10,000 backpacks. This situation, shown by point *h,* lies to the right of the PPF and hence outside the realm of possibility. Anything to the right of the PPF is impossible for our economy to attain.

opportunity cost The cost paid for one product in terms of the output (or consumption) of another product that must be forgone.

Opportunity Cost Whenever a country reallocates resources to change production patterns, it does so at a price. This price is called **opportunity cost.** Recall from Chapter 1 that opportunity cost is what you *give up* when making an economic decision. Here society is deciding how many backpacks and tablets to produce. If society decides to produce more tablets, it gives up the ability to produce more backpacks. Shown through the PPF, the opportunity cost of producing more of one good is determined by the amount of the other good that is given up. In moving from point *b* to point *e* in Figure 2, tablet production increases by 3,000 units, from 1,000 units to 4,000 units. In contrast, the country must forgo producing 6,000 backpacks because production falls from 10,000 backpacks to 4,000 backpacks. Giving up 6,000 backpacks for 3,000 more tablets represents an opportunity cost of 6,000 backpacks for these 3,000 tablets, or two backpacks for each tablet.

Opportunity cost thus represents the tradeoff required when an economy wants to increase its production of any single product. Governments must choose between guns and butter, or between military spending and social spending. Since there are limits to what taxpayers are willing to pay, spending choices are necessary. Think of opportunity costs as what you or the economy must give up to have more of a product or service.

Increasing Opportunity Costs In most cases, land, labor, and capital cannot easily be shifted from producing one good or service to another. You cannot take a semi-trailer and use it to plow a field, even though the semi and a top-of-the-line tractor cost about the same. The fact is that some resources are suited to specific sorts of production, just as some people seem to be better suited to performing one activity over another. Some people have a talent for music or art, and they would be miserable—and inefficient—working as accountants or computer programmers. Some people find they are more comfortable working outside, while others require the amenities of an environmentally controlled, ergonomically designed office.

© Lawrence Manning/Corbis

A magician might be perfect for a birthday party entertainer, but is probably less adept at baking the perfect birthday cake.

Thus, a more realistic production possibilities frontier is shown in Figure 3. This PPF is concave to (or bowed away from) the origin, because opportunity costs rise as more factors are used to produce increasing quantities of one product. Another way of saying this is that resources are subject to diminishing returns as more resources are devoted to the production of one product. Let's consider why this is so.

Let's begin at a point at which the economy's resources are strictly devoted to backpack production (point *a*). Now assume that society decides to produce 3,200 tablets. This will require a move from point *a* to point *b*. As we can see, 2,000 backpacks must be given up to get the added 3,200 tablets. This means the opportunity cost of 1 tablet is 0.625 backpacks ($2{,}000 \div 3{,}200 = 0.625$). This is a low opportunity cost, because those resources that are better suited to producing tablets will be the first ones shifted into this industry.

But what happens when this society decides to produce an additional 2,000 tablets, or moves from point *b* to point *c* on the graph? As Figure 3 illustrates, each additional tablet costs 2 backpacks because producing 2,000 more tablets requires the society to sacrifice 4,000 backpacks. Thus, the opportunity cost of tablets has more than tripled due to diminishing returns on the tablet side, which arise from the unsuitability of these new resources as more resources are shifted to tablets.

To describe what has happened in plain terms, when the economy was producing 12,000 backpacks, all its resources went into backpack production. Those members of the labor force who are engineers and electronic assemblers were probably not well suited to producing backpacks. As the economy reduces backpack production to start

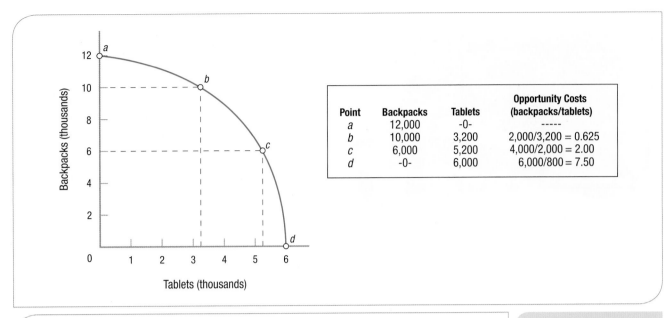

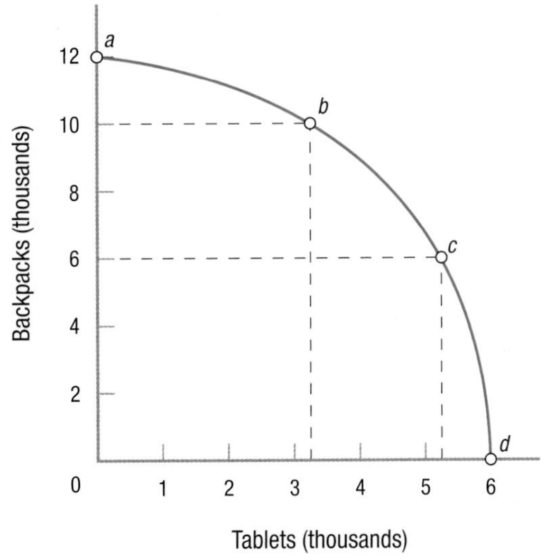

Point	Backpacks	Tablets	Opportunity Costs (backpacks/tablets)
a	12,000	-0-	-----
b	10,000	3,200	2,000/3,200 = 0.625
c	6,000	5,200	4,000/2,000 = 2.00
d	-0-	6,000	6,000/800 = 7.50

FIGURE 3

Production Possibilities Frontier (Increasing Opportunity Costs)

This figure shows a more realistic production possibilities frontier for an economy. This PPF is bowed out from the origin since opportunity costs rise as more factors are used to produce increasing quantities of one product or the other.

producing tablets, the opportunity cost of tablets was low, because the resources first shifted, including workers, were likely to be the ones most suited to tablet production and least suited to backpack manufacture. Eventually, however, as tablets became the dominant product, manufacturing more tablets required shifting workers skilled in backpack production to the tablet industry. Employing these less suitable resources drives up the opportunity costs of tablets.

You may be wondering which point along the PPF is the best for society. Economists have no grounds for stating unequivocally which mixture of goods and services would be ideal. The perfect mixture of goods depends on the tastes and preferences of the members of society. In a capitalist economy, resource allocation is determined largely by individual choices and the workings of private markets. We consider these markets and their operations in the next chapter.

Economic Growth

We have seen that PPFs map out the maximum that an economy can produce: Points to the right of the PPF are unattainable. But what if the PPF can be shifted to the right? This shift would give economies new maximum frontiers. In fact, we will see that economic growth can be viewed as a shift in the PPF outward. In this section, we use the production possibilities model to determine some of the major reasons for economic growth. Understanding these reasons for growth will enable us to suggest some broad economic policies that could lead to expanded growth.

The production possibilities model holds resources and technology constant to derive the PPF. These assumptions suggest that economic growth has two basic determinants: expanding resources and improving technologies. The expansion of resources allows producers to increase their production of all goods and services in an economy. Specific technological improvements, however, often affect only one industry directly. The development of a new color printing process, for instance, will directly affect only the printing industry.

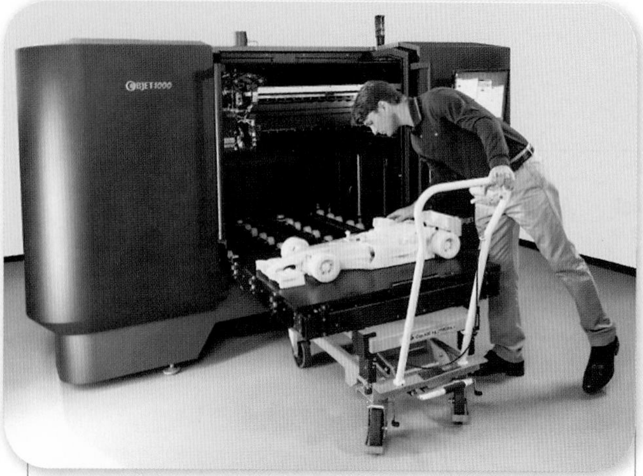

Courtesy of Stratasys Ltd.

"Beaming" objects might not be restricted to *Star Trek* fantasy with the development of 3D printers capable of reproducing objects. Could this be the next big technological advancement in printing?

Nevertheless, the ripples from technological improvements can spread out through an entire economy, just like ripples in a pond. Specifically, improvements in technology can lead to new products, improved goods and services, and increased productivity.

Sometimes technological improvements in one industry allow other industries to increase their production with existing resources. This means producers can increase output without using added labor or other resources. Alternatively, they can get the same production levels as before by using fewer resources than before. This frees up resources in the economy for use in other industries.

When the electric lightbulb was invented, it not only created a new industry (someone had to produce lightbulbs), but it also revolutionized other industries. Factories could stay open longer since they no longer had to rely on the sun for light. Workers could see better, thus improving the quality of their work. The result was that resources operated more efficiently throughout the entire economy.

The modern-day equivalent of the lightbulb might be the smartphone. Widespread use of these mobile devices enables people all across the world to produce goods and services more efficiently. Insurance agents can file claims instantly from disaster sites, deals can be closed while one is stuck in traffic, and communications have been revolutionized. Thus, this new technology has ultimately expanded time, the most finite of our resources. A similar argument could be made for the Internet. It has profoundly changed how many products are bought, sold, and delivered, and has expanded communications and the flow of information.

Expanding Resources The PPF represents the constraints on an economy at a specific time. But economies are constantly changing, and so are PPFs. Capital and labor are the principal resources that can be changed through government action. Land and entrepreneurial talent are important factors of production, but neither is easy to change by government policies. The government can make owning a business easier or more profitable by reducing regulations, or by offering low-interest loans or favorable tax treatment to small businesses. However, it is difficult to turn people into risk takers through government policy.

Increasing Labor and Human Capital A clear increase in population, the number of households, or the size of the labor force shifts the PPF outward, as shown in Figure 4. With added labor, the production possibilities available to the economy expand from PPF_0 to PPF_1. Such a labor increase can be caused by higher birthrates, increased immigration, or an increased willingness of people to enter the labor force. This last type of increase has occurred over the past several decades as more women have entered the labor force on a permanent basis. America's high level of immigration (both legal and illegal) fuels a strong rate of economic growth.

Rather than simply increasing the number of people working, however, the labor factor can also be increased by improving workers' skills. Economists refer to this as *investment in human capital.* Education, on-the-job training, and other professional training fit into this category. Improving human capital means people are more productive, resulting in higher wages, a higher standard of living, and an expanded PPF for society.

Capital Accumulation Increasing the capital used throughout the economy, usually brought about by investment, similarly shifts the PPF outward, as shown in Figure 4. Additional capital makes each unit of labor more productive and thus results in higher possible production throughout the economy. Adding robotics and computer-controlled machines to production lines, for example, means each unit of labor produces many more units of output.

The production possibilities model and the economic growth associated with capital accumulation suggest a tradeoff. Figure 5 illustrates the tradeoff all nations face between current consumption and capital accumulation.

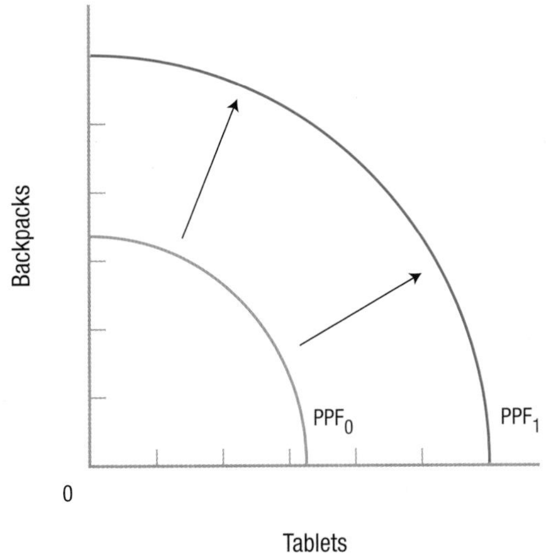

FIGURE 4

Economic Growth by Expanding Resources

A clear increase in population, the number of households, or the size of the labor force shifts the PPF outward. In this figure, a rising supply of labor expands the economy's production possibilities from PPF_0 to PPF_1.

Let's first assume that a nation selects a product mix in which the bulk of goods produced are consumption goods—that is, goods that are immediately consumable and have short life spans, such as food and entertainment. This product mix is represented by point *b* in Figure 5. Consuming most of what it produces, a decade later the economy is at PPF_b. Little growth has occurred, because the economy has done little to improve its productive capacity—the present generation has essentially decided to consume rather than to invest in the economy's future.

Contrast this decision with one in which the country at first decides to produce at point *a*. In this case, more capital goods such as machinery and tools are produced, while fewer consumption goods are used to satisfy current needs. Selecting this product mix results in the much larger PPF a decade later (PPF_a), because the economy steadily built up its productive capacity during those 10 years.

Technological Change Figure 6 on the next page illustrates what happens when an economy experiences a technological change in one of its industries, in this case the tablet industry. As the figure shows, the economy's potential output of tablets expands greatly, although its maximum production of backpacks remains unchanged. The area between the two curves

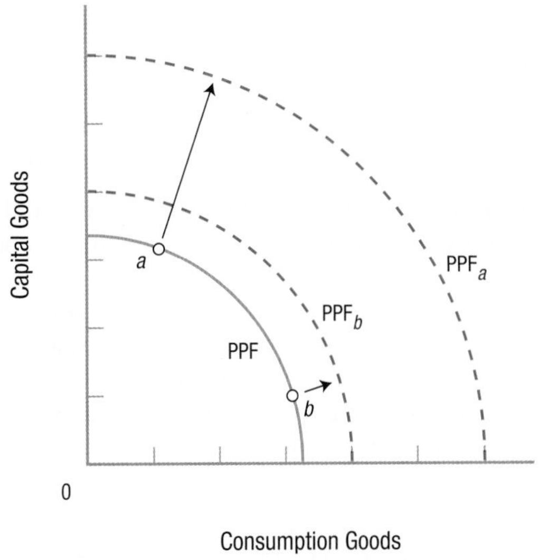

FIGURE 5

Consumption Goods and Capital Goods and the Expansion of the Production Possibilities Frontier

If a nation selects a product mix in which the bulk of goods produced are consumption goods, it will initially produce at point *b*. The small investment made in capital goods has the effect of expanding the nation's productive capacity only to PPF_b over the following decade. If the country decides to produce at point *a*, however, devoting more resources to producing capital goods, its productive capacity will expand much more rapidly, pushing the PPF out to PPF_a over the following decade.

FIGURE 6

Technological Change and Expansion of the Production Possibilities Frontier

In this figure, an economy's potential output of tablets has expanded greatly, while its maximum production of backpacks has remained unchanged. The area between the two curves represents an improvement in the society's standard of living, since more of both goods can be produced and consumed than before. Some of the resources once used for tablet production can be diverted to backpack production, even as the number of tablets produced increases.

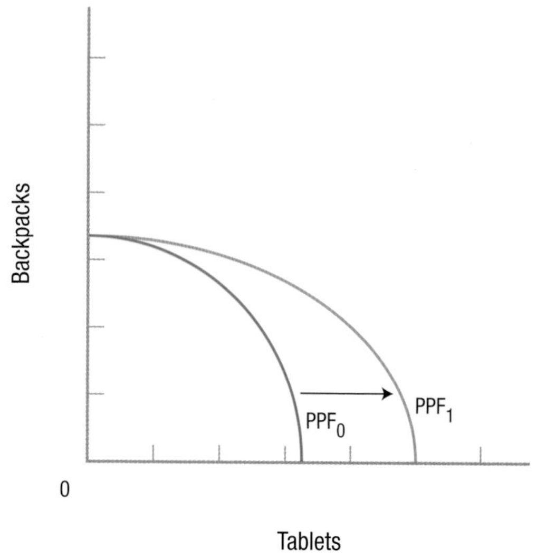

represents an improvement in the society's standard of living. People can produce and consume more of both goods than before: more tablets because of the technological advancement, and more backpacks because some of the resources once devoted to tablet production can be shifted to backpack production, even as the economy is turning out more tablets than before.

This example reflects the United States today, where the computer industry is exploding with new technologies. Companies such as Apple and Intel lead the way by relentlessly developing newer, faster, and more powerful products. Consequently, consumers have seen home computers go from clunky conversation pieces to powerful, fast, indispensable machines. Today's computers are more powerful than the mainframe supercomputers of just a few decades ago. And the latest developments in smartphones allow them to do what powerful computers did a decade ago.

Besides new products, technology has dramatically reduced the cost of producing tablets and other high-tech items, allowing countries to produce and consume more of other products, expanding the entire PPF outward. However, the effect of technology on an economy also depends on how well its important trade centers are linked together. If a country has mostly dirt paths rather than paved highways, you can imagine how this deficiency would affect its economy: Distribution will be slow, and industries will be slow to react to changes in demand. In such a case, improving the roads might be the best way to stimulate economic growth.

As you can see, there are many ways to stimulate economic growth. A society can expand its output by using more resources, perhaps by encouraging more people to enter the workforce or raising educational levels of workers. The government can encourage people to invest more, as opposed to devoting their earnings to immediate consumption. The public sector can spur technological advances by providing incentives to private firms to do research and development or underwrite research investments of its own.

Summarizing the Sources of Economic Growth Economic growth is driven by many factors, as we have seen. A study by the Organisation for Economic Co-operation and Development (OECD)[1] focused on what has been driving economic growth in twenty-one nations over the last several decades. The study first looked at contributions to economic growth from the macroeconomic perspective of added resources and technological improvements as we have been discussing in this chapter. It then looked at some benefits from good government policies that stimulate growth, and finally examined the industry and individual firm level for clues to the microeconomic sources of growth. The study showed

[1] *The Sources of Economic Growth in the OECD Countries* (Paris: Organisation for Economic Co-operation and Development), 2003.

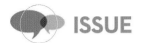

ISSUE

Will Renewable Energy Be the Next Innovative Breakthrough?

For much of modern history, economic growth has relied on the innovative abilities of humans to generate new ideas that translate into productive inputs and valued goods and services. The Industrial Revolution of the 19th century brought us innovations such as the telegraph, steel production, and railways. In the early 1900s, the automobile was invented, along with electricity and telecommunications. In the mid-1900s, commercial air travel and television were introduced. In the latter part of the 20th century, the invention of personal computing led to dramatic gains in productivity. And at the turn of the 21st century, the creation of the Internet once again changed the way we live.

These "waves of innovation," as described by economist William Baumol, contribute much of the economic growth we have seen over the past century. But to sustain such growth, innovation must not slow down. Instead, pressure to innovate has become more intense as the Earth's population grows and its resources diminish.

Hence, much attention has been placed on resource scarcity by focusing on expanding renewable resources, particularly energy sources such as those from the sun, wind, and water. Although the renewable energy industry is still developing, substantial strides have been made to increase investment in renewable energy.

The drawbacks of renewable energies are evident in the near term, as expensive solar panels, wind turbines, and hydroelectric dams cost much more to produce than traditional sources of energy such as coal mines and fossil fuels, let alone the often unsightly views such infrastructures create. But these obstacles are changing.

Today, countries around the world are finding innovative ways to incorporate renewable energy sources into their infrastructure, dramatically reducing the use of traditional energy. It may just be a matter of time before innovation finds ways to allow everybody to use the sun, wind, and rain to sustain our energy needs. Succeeding in this endeavor would be an innovative breakthrough that would add to the remarkable list of innovations in our history.

Orhan Çam/Dreamstime.com

The Bahrain World Trade Center incorporates wind turbines into the structure that provide much of the building's energy.

that some of the policies that have led to growth and subsequently higher standards of living in these countries include:

- Increasing business investment (physical capital).
- Increasing average education levels (human capital).
- Increasing research and development.
- Reducing both the level and variability of inflation.
- Reducing the tax burden.
- Increasing the level of international trade.

One important point to take away from this discussion is that our simple stylized model of the economy using only two goods gives a good first framework upon which to judge proposed policies for the economy. While not overly complex, this simple analysis is still quite powerful.

CHECKPOINT

PRODUCTION POSSIBILITIES AND ECONOMIC GROWTH

- A production possibilities frontier (PPF) depicts the different combinations of goods that a fully employed economy can produce, given its available resources and current technology (both assumed fixed in the short run).
- Production levels inside and on the frontier are possible, but production mixes outside the curve are unattainable.

- Because production on the frontier represents the maximum output attainable when all resources are fully employed, reallocating production from one product to another involves *opportunity costs*: The output of one product must be reduced to get the added output of the other. The more of one product that is desired, the higher its opportunity costs because of diminishing returns and the unsuitability of some resources for producing some products.
- The PPF model suggests that economic growth can arise from an expansion in resources or improvements in technology. Economic growth is an outward shift of the PPF.

QUESTION: Taiwan is a small mountainous island with 23 million inhabitants, little arable land, and few natural resources, while Nigeria is a much larger country with 7 times the population, 40 times more arable land, and tremendous deposits of oil. Given Nigeria's sizable resource advantage, why is Nigeria's total annual production only half the size of Taiwan's?

Answers to the Checkpoint question can be found at the end of this chapter.

Specialization, Comparative Advantage, and Trade

As we have seen, economics is all about voluntary production and exchange. People and nations do business with one another because all expect to gain from the transactions. Centuries ago, European merchants ventured to the Far East to ply the lucrative spice trade. These days, American consumers buy wines from Italy, cars from Japan, electronics from Korea, and millions of other products from countries around the world.

Many people assume that trade between nations is a zero-sum game—a game in which, for one party to gain, another party must lose. This is how poker works. If one player walks away from the table a winner, someone else must have lost. But this is not how voluntary trade works. Voluntary trade is a positive-sum game: Both parties to a transaction score positive gains. After all, who would voluntarily enter into an exchange if he or she did not believe there was some gain from it? To understand how all parties to an exchange (whether individuals or nations) can gain from it, we need to consider the concept of comparative advantage developed by David Ricardo roughly 200 years ago, and how this concept differs from the concept of absolute advantage.

DAVID RICARDO (1772–1823)

David Ricardo's rigorous, dispassionate evaluation of economic principles influenced generations of theorists, including such vastly different thinkers as John Stuart Mill and Karl Marx. Ricardo was born in London as the third of 17 children. At age 14 he joined his father's trading business on the London Stock Exchange. At 21, he started his own brokerage and within five years had amassed a small fortune.

While vacationing in Bath, England, he chanced upon a copy of Adam Smith's *The Wealth of Nations,* and decided to devote his energies to studying economics and writing. He once wrote to his lifelong friend Thomas Malthus (another prominent economist of the time) that he was "thankful for the miserable English climate because it kept him at his desk writing." Ricardo and Malthus corresponded on a regular basis, and their exchanges led to the development of many economic concepts still used today.

Later, as a member of the British Parliament, Ricardo was an outspoken critic of the 1815 Corn Laws, which placed high tariffs on imported grain to protect British landowners. Ricardo was a strong advocate of free trade, and his writings reflected this view. His theory of "comparative advantage" suggested that countries would mutually benefit from trade by specializing in export goods they could produce at a lower opportunity cost than another country. His classic example was trade in cloth and wine between Britain and Portugal.

Ricardo died in 1823 of an ear infection, leaving an enduring legacy of classical (pre-1930s) economic analysis.

Sources: E. Ray Canterbery, *A Brief History of Economics* (New Jersey: World Scientific), 2001; Howard Marshall, *The Great Economists: A History of Economic Thought* (New York: Pitman Publishing), 1967; Steven Pressman, *Fifty Major Economists, 2nd ed.,* (New York: Routledge), 2006.

Absolute and Comparative Advantage

Figure 7 shows hypothetical production possibilities curves for the United States and Mexico. To simplify the analysis, we assume that opportunity costs are constant (PPFs are straight lines); however, the same analysis applies to PPFs with increasing opportunity costs. Both countries are assumed to produce only crude oil and silicon chips. Given

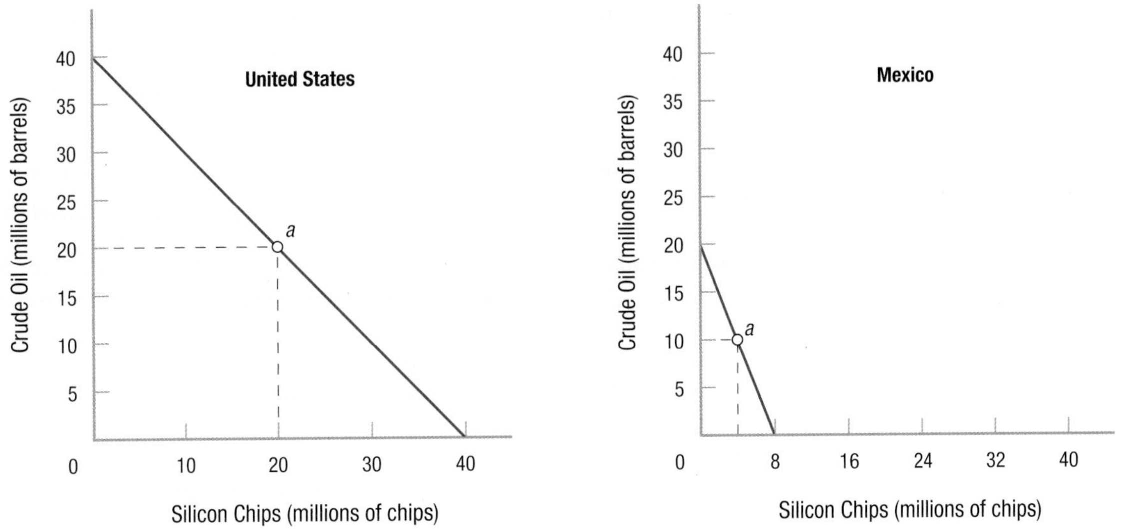

FIGURE 7

Production Possibilities for the United States and Mexico

One country has an absolute advantage if it can produce more of a good than another country. In this case, the United States has an absolute advantage over Mexico in producing both silicon chips and crude oil—it can produce more of both goods than Mexico can. Even so, Mexico has a comparative advantage over the United States in producing oil, since it can increase its output of oil at a lower opportunity cost than can the United States. This comparative advantage leads to gains for both countries from specialization and trade.

the PPFs in Figure 7, the United States has an **absolute advantage** over Mexico in producing both products. An absolute advantage exists when one country can produce more of a good than another country. In this instance, the United States can produce 2 times more oil (40 million versus 20 million barrels) and 5 times as many silicon chips (40 million versus 8 million chips) as Mexico.

absolute advantage One country can produce more of a good than another country.

At first glance you might wonder why the United States would even consider trading with Mexico. The United States has so much more production capacity than Mexico, so why wouldn't it just produce all of its own crude oil and silicon chips? The answer lies in comparative advantage.

One country has a **comparative advantage** in producing a good if its opportunity cost to produce that good is lower than the other country's. We can calculate each country's opportunity cost for each good using the production possibility frontiers in Figure 7.

comparative advantage One country has a lower opportunity cost of producing a good than another country.

If the United States uses all of its resources efficiently, it can produce a maximum of 40 million barrels of oil *or* 40 million silicon chips. It can also produce some of both goods, though clearly not 40 million of each, because in order to produce more of one good, it must reduce production of another (its opportunity cost). Because the PPF is linear, the tradeoff between oil and chips is constant. For the United States, it can substitute 1 million barrels of oil for 1 million silicon chips, which means it can produce 20 million barrels of oil and 20 million silicon chips. The opportunity cost for each good is summarized as follows:

- For every barrel of oil the United States produces, it must give up producing one silicon chip.
- For every silicon chip the United States produces, it must give up producing one barrel of oil.

Now let's look at Mexico. If it uses its resources efficiently, it can produce a maximum of 20 million barrels of oil *or* 8 million silicon chips. For Mexico, although the tradeoff between goods also is constant, the tradeoff is not one-for-one as in the United States. Because Mexico is better at producing oil than silicon chips, its opportunity cost for each good is as follows:

- For every barrel of oil Mexico produces, it must give up producing 0.4 silicon chips.
- For every silicon chip Mexico produces, it must give up producing 2.5 barrels of oil.

Note that the values of 0.4 and 2.5 are inverses of one another. In other words, 1/0.4 = 2.5, and 1/2.5 = 0.4. This relationship exists when calculating opportunity costs in a two-product economy.

Now that we have determined the opportunity cost of each good in both countries, we can conclude that Mexico has a comparative advantage over the United States in producing oil. This is because Mexico gives up only 0.4 chips for every barrel of oil it produces, while the United States must give up 1 chip. Thus, Mexico's opportunity cost of producing oil is less than that of the United States, giving Mexico a comparative advantage.

Conversely, the United States has a comparative advantage over Mexico in producing silicon chips: Producing a silicon chip in the United States costs one barrel of oil, whereas the same chip in Mexico costs two-and-a-half barrels of oil. Table 1 summarizes the opportunity costs of each good and which country has the comparative advantage.

TABLE 1 Comparing Opportunity Costs for Oil and Chip Production

	U.S. Opportunity Cost	Mexico Opportunity Cost	Comparative Advantage
Oil Production	1 chip	0.4 chips	Mexico
Chip Production	1 barrel of oil	2.5 barrels of oil	United States

Note that each country has a comparative advantage in one good, even though the United States has an absolute advantage in both goods. However, it is comparative advantage that generates gains from trade. These relative costs suggest that the United States should pour its resources into producing silicon chips, while Mexico specializes in crude oil. The two countries can then engage in trade to their mutual benefit. As long as relative production costs differ between countries, specialization and trade can be mutually beneficial, allowing all countries to consume more.

The same idea applies to individuals. Although we have focused on trade between countries, the concept of comparative advantage explains why individuals specialize in a few tasks and then trade with one another. For example, if you are relatively better at understanding economics than your roommate who is on the golf team, you might offer to tutor economics in exchange for golf lessons. Comparative advantage explains all trade: between individuals as well as between countries.

The Gains from Trade

To see how specialization and trade can benefit all trading partners, let's return to our example in which the United States has the ability to produce more of both goods than Mexico. Assume that each country is at first (before trade) operating at point *a*

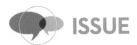

ISSUE

Do We Really Specialize in That? Comparative Advantage in the United States and China

What do tofu, edamame, ink, soy sauce, livestock feed, and soy milk have in common? They are all important products commonly made from soybeans. Although direct human consumption of soybeans in the United States is often confined to health food products and food in Asian restaurants, soybeans are much more important to the U.S. economy than most people think. The United States has a comparative advantage in soybean production. It produces and sells more soybeans than any other country, with much of it being sold to China.

How can a rich, technologically advanced country like the United States end up with a comparative advantage in an agricultural good like soybeans? Several factors play a role. First, the United States has an abundance of farmland ideal in climate and soil for soybean production. Second, modern fertilizers and seed technologies have made soybean production a much more innovative industry than in the past, allowing farms to increase soybean yields per acre of land. And third, a strong appetite for soy-based products, particularly in China, has made soybeans a very lucrative industry.

China is the second largest trading partner to the United States after Canada, trading $539 billion worth of goods between the countries in 2011. Yet, the top five U.S. export goods (items sold) and import goods (items bought) with China, listed below, may be surprising.

Top Five Exports to China (2011)

1. Machinery ($12.2 billion)
2. Soybeans ($10.7 billion)
3. Electrical goods ($10.1 billion)
4. Automobiles ($6.8 billion)
5. Aircraft ($6.4 billion)

Top Five Imports from China (2011)

1. Electrical goods ($98.7 billion)
2. Machinery ($94.9 billion)
3. Toys/sporting goods ($22.6 billion)
4. Furniture ($20.5 billion)
5. Footwear ($16.7 billion)

Although the United States sells a lot of machines and electrical goods to China (mostly specialized machinery and electronics used in factories and research labs), it buys significantly greater amounts of these products *from* China. In other words, the United States is a net buyer of machinery and electrical goods, industries that include many consumer technology goods we use, such as smartphones, computers, and digital equipment. Besides soybeans, paper pulp and copper are two other resource industries (not listed above) that constitute a large portion of U.S. sales *to* China.

In sum, specialization and trade are not as simple as they used to be. Products such as computers and electronics that once were the purview of "rich" countries such as the United States are now being manufactured in China and other countries, while improved technology in the agricultural and natural resource industries has given the United States a new form of specialization that would have been unheard of 50 years ago.

in Figure 7. At this point, both countries are producing and consuming only their own output; the United States produces and consumes 20 million barrels of oil and 20 million silicon chips; Mexico, 10 million barrels of oil and 4 million chips. Table 2 summarizes these initial conditions.

Initial Consumption-Production Pattern — **TABLE 2**

	United States	Mexico	Total
Oil	20	10	30
Chips	20	4	24

Now assume that Mexico focuses on oil, producing the maximum it can: 20 million barrels. We also assume both countries want to continue consuming 30 million barrels of oil between them. Therefore the United States only needs to produce 10 million barrels of oil because Mexico is now producing 20 million barrels. For the United States, this frees up some resources that can be diverted to producing silicon chips. Because each barrel of oil in the United States costs one chip, reducing oil output by 10 million barrels means that 10 million more chips can be produced.

TABLE 3 Production After Mexico Specializes in Producing Crude Oil

	United States	Mexico	Total
Oil	10	20	30
Chips	30	0	30

Table 3 shows each country's production after Mexico has begun specializing in oil production.

Notice that the combined production of crude oil has remained constant, but the total output of silicon chips has risen by 6 million chips. Assuming that the two countries agree to share the added 6 million chips between them equally, Mexico will now ship 10 million barrels of oil to the United States in exchange for 7 million chips. From the 10 million additional chips the United States produces, Mexico will receive 4 million (its original production) plus 3 million for a total of 7 million, leaving 3 million additional chips for U.S. consumption. The resulting mix of products consumed in each country is shown in Table 4. Clearly, both countries are better off, having engaged in specialized production and trade.

TABLE 4 Final Consumption Patterns after Trade

	United States	Mexico	Total
Oil	20	10	30
Chips	23	7	30

The important point to remember here is that even when one country has an absolute advantage over another, both countries still benefit from trading with one another. In our example, the gains were small, but such gains can grow. As two economies become more equal in size, the benefits of their comparative advantages grow.

Practical Constraints on Trade

Before leaving the subject of international trade and how it contributes to growth in both countries, we should take a moment to note some practical constraints on trade. First, every transaction involves costs, including transportation, communications, and the general costs of doing business. Even so, over the last several decades, transportation and communication costs have been declining all over the world, resulting in growing global trade.

Second, the production possibilities curves for nations are not linear, but rather governed by increasing costs and diminishing returns. Therefore, it is difficult for countries to specialize in producing one product. Complete specialization would be risky, moreover, because the market for a product can always decline, perhaps because the product becomes technologically obsolete. Alternatively, changing weather patterns can wreak havoc on specialized agricultural products, adding further instability to incomes and exports in developing countries.

Finally, although two countries may benefit from trading with one another, expanding this trade may well hurt some industries and individuals within each country. Notably, industries finding themselves at a comparative disadvantage may be forced to scale back production and lay off workers. In such instances, government may need to provide workers with retraining, relocation, and other help to ensure a smooth transition to the new production mix.

When the United States signed the North American Free Trade Agreement (NAFTA) with Canada and Mexico, many people experienced what we have just been discussing. Some U.S. jobs went south to Mexico because of low production costs. By opening up more markets for U.S. products, however, NAFTA did stimulate economic growth, such that retrained workers may end up with new and better jobs.

CHECKPOINT

SPECIALIZATION, COMPARATIVE ADVANTAGE, AND TRADE

- An absolute advantage exists when one country can produce more of some good than another.
- A comparative advantage exists if one country has lower opportunity costs of producing a good than another country. Both countries gain from trade if each focuses on producing those goods with which it has a comparative advantage.
- Voluntary trade is a positive-sum game, because both countries benefit from it.

QUESTION: Why do Hollywood stars (and many other rich individuals)—unlike most people—have full-time personal assistants who manage their personal affairs?

Answers to the Checkpoint question can be found at the end of this chapter.

chapter summary

Section 1: Basic Economic Questions and Production

Every economy must decide:

1. What to produce.
2. How to produce it.
3. Who will get the goods produced.

Rainer Plendl/Dreamstime. com

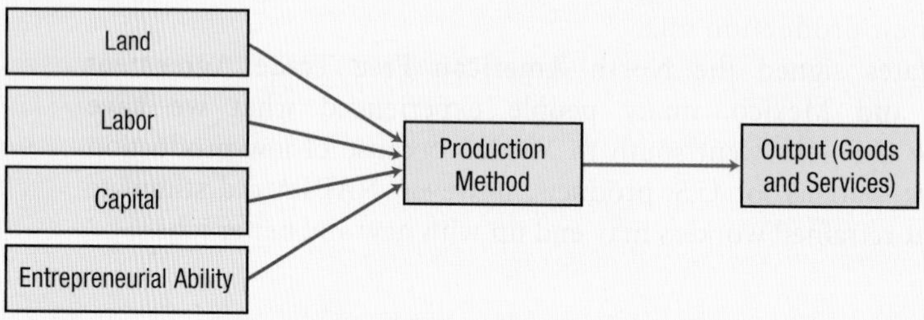

Using scarce resources productively leads to:

Production efficiency: Goods and services are produced at their lowest possible resource cost.

Allocative efficiency: Goods are produced according to what society desires.

Section 2: Production Possibilities and Economic Growth

The **production possibilities frontier (PPF)** shows the different combinations of goods that a fully employed economy can produce, given its available resources and current technology.

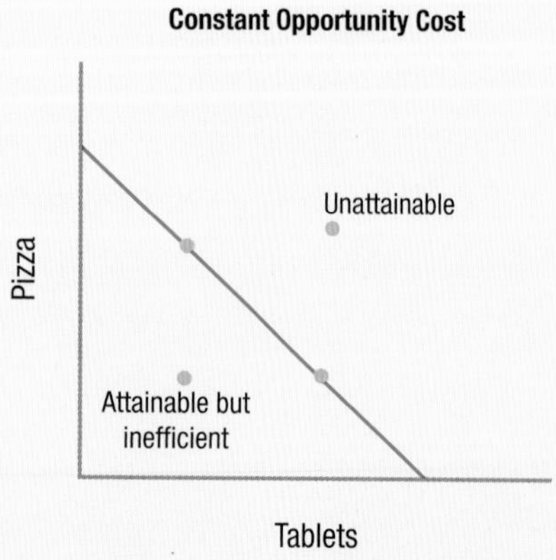

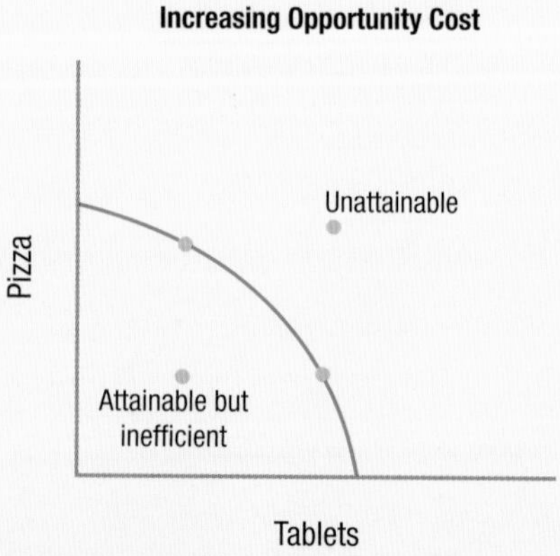

Production possibilities frontiers (PPFs) illustrate tradeoffs—if an economy operates at full employment (on the PPF), producing more of one good requires producing less of the other. A concave PPF shows how opportunity costs rise due to diminishing returns.

Some pizza makers were never meant to produce computers and some computer workers were never meant to produce pizza, increasing the opportunity cost of production as more of one good is produced.

The production possibilities model shows how economic growth can arise from an expansion in resources or from improvements in technology.

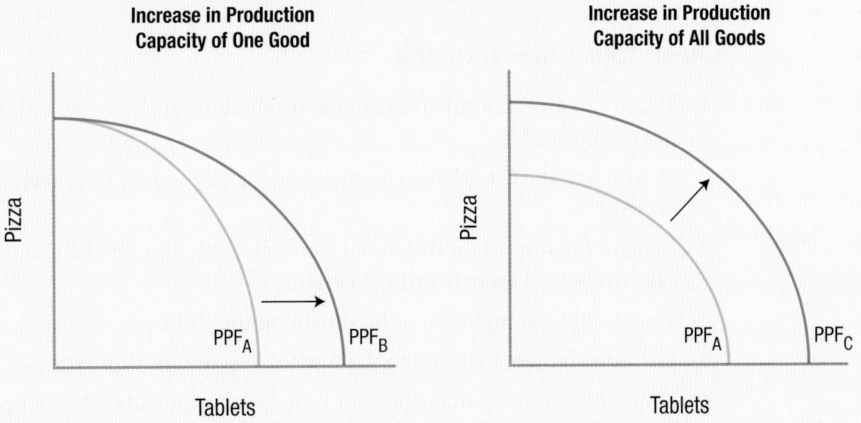

Changes in the PPF: From PPF_A to PPF_B: An increase in productivity in the production of one good (for example, an increase in the number of students studying computer engineering).

From PPF_A to PPF_C: An increase in productive capacity of both goods (for example, an increase in overall technology, or an increase in labor or capital resources).

Section 3: Specialization, Comparative Advantage, and Trade

An **absolute advantage** exists when one country can produce more of some good than another.

A **comparative advantage** exists when one country can produce a good at a lower opportunity cost than another.

Gains from trade result when a country specializes in the production of goods in which it has a comparative advantage, and trades these goods with another country. Trade is a positive-sum game. Both countries can benefit even if one country has an absolute advantage in both goods.

Calculating Opportunity Costs Using Production Numbers (units produced per day per worker)

	Australia	New Zealand
Boomerangs	20	8
Kiwi	12	16

- Opportunity cost of 1 boomerang in:
  Australia: 12 kiwi/20 boomerangs = 0.6 kiwi per boomerang
  New Zealand: 16 kiwi/8 boomerangs = 2 kiwi per boomerang
  Australia has a lower opportunity cost producing boomerangs
- Opportunity cost of 1 kiwi in:
  Australia: 20 boomerangs/12 kiwi = 1.7 boomerangs per kiwi
  New Zealand: 8 boomerangs/16 kiwi = 0.5 boomerangs per kiwi
  New Zealand has a lower opportunity cost producing kiwi

Countries export goods for which they have a comparative advantage, and import goods for which they do not, leading to gains from trade to both countries.

KEY CONCEPTS

production, p. 30
resources, p. 30
land, p. 30
labor, p. 30
capital, p. 31
entrepreneurs, p. 31
production efficiency, p. 31
allocative efficiency, p. 32
production possibilities frontier (PPF), p. 33
opportunity cost, p. 34
absolute advantage, p. 41
comparative advantage, p. 41

QUESTIONS AND PROBLEMS

Check Your Understanding

1. When can an economy increase the production of one good without reducing the output of another?
2. In which of the three basic questions facing any society does technology play the greatest role?
3. Explain the important difference between a straight line PPF and the PPF that is concave to (bowed away from) the origin.
4. How would unemployment be shown on the PPF?
5. List three factors that can contribute to an economy's growth.
6. How can a country that does not have an absolute advantage in producing goods still benefit from trade?

Apply the Concepts

7. China has experienced levels of economic growth in the last decade that have been about 5 times that of the United States (10% versus 2% per year in the United States). Has China's high growth rate eliminated scarcity in China?
8. Describe how a country producing more capital goods rather than consumption goods ends up in the future with a PPF that is larger than a country that produces more consumption goods and fewer capital goods.
9. The United States has an absolute advantage in making many goods, such as short-sleeved cotton golf shirts. Why do Indonesia and Bangladesh make these shirts and export them to the United States?
10. Why is it that America uses heavy street cleaning machines driven by one person to clean the streets, while China and India use many people with brooms to do the same job?
11. If specialization and trade as discussed in this chapter lead to a win-win situation in which both countries gain, why is there often opposition to trade agreements and globalization?
12. American attitudes about the tradeoff between the environment and economic growth shown in By the Numbers at the beginning of the chapter changed significantly when the economy entered a recession. However, during the recession in 2009, Americans were roughly equally split between their concerns for the environment and economic growth. What would you expect to find in a similar survey in a relatively poor developing nation?

In the News

13. According to a March 8, 2012, *New York Times* report, the 2011 earthquake in Japan that triggered a devastating tsunami led to a near complete shutdown of Japan's nuclear

energy industry, which generates one-third of the country's total electricity. The resulting energy crisis caused severe supply disruptions in nearly all industries. How do natural disasters such as the tsunami in Japan affect a country's ability to achieve economic growth? Illustrate your answer using a PPF.

14. The recession of 2007–2009 and the slow recovery led to severe budget cuts in state governments across the United States. Public colleges and universities, which are highly subsidized by state governments, saw dramatic cuts in their budgets, making it more difficult for students to attend school and/or complete their degrees. The *Chronicle of Higher Education* of January 17, 2012, argued that cuts to higher education will "imperil competitiveness" in America. How might the cost savings from reduced educational spending end up costing states even more in the future?

Solving Problems

15. Political commentators often make the argument that growth in another country (most notably China) is detrimental to the economic interests of the United States. Look back at Tables 2 to 4 in the Gains from Trade section of the chapter. Then, assume that Mexico doubles in size, and make those changes to Table 2. Reconstruct Tables 3 and 4 given Mexico's greater capacity. Has the United States benefited by Mexico being able to produce more?
16. The table below shows the potential output combinations of oranges and jars of prickly pear jelly (from the flower of the prickly pear cactus) for Florida and Arizona.
    a. Compute the opportunity cost for Florida of oranges in terms of jars of prickly pear jelly. Do the same for prickly pear jelly in terms of oranges.
    b. Compute the opportunity cost for Arizona of oranges in terms of jars of prickly pear jelly. Do the same for prickly pear jelly in terms of oranges.
    c. Would it make sense for Florida to specialize in producing oranges and for Arizona to specialize in producing prickly pear jelly and then trade? Why or why not?

Florida		Arizona	
Oranges	**Prickly Pear Jelly**	**Oranges**	**Prickly Pear Jelly**
0	10	0	500
50	8	20	400
100	6	40	300
150	4	60	200
200	2	80	100
250	0	100	0

USING THE NUMBERS

17. According to By the Numbers, in which period (1960 to 1985 or 1985 to 2010) did corn and soybean production increase faster in terms of yield per acre?
18. According to By the Numbers, in the period between 1990 and 2012, in how many years did the U.S. trade balance improve from the previous year and in how many years did the trade balance deteriorate (assume the trade balance deteriorated from 1989 [not shown in the figure] to 1990)?

ANSWERS TO QUESTIONS IN CHECKPOINTS

Checkpoint: Basic Economic Questions and Production

Typically, entrepreneurs put not only their time and effort into a business but also their money, often pledging private assets as collateral for loans. Should the business fail, they stand to lose more than their jobs, rent from the land, or interest on capital loaned to the firm. Workers can get other jobs, landowners can rent to others, and capital can be used in other enterprises. The entrepreneur must suffer the loss of personal assets and move on.

Checkpoint: Production Possibilities and Economic Growth

Although Nigeria has significantly more natural resources and labor (two important factors of production) than Taiwan, these resources alone do not guarantee a higher ability to produce goods and services. Factors of production also include physical capital (machinery), human capital (education), and technology (research and development), all of which Taiwan has in great abundance. Thus, despite the lack of land, labor, and natural resources, Taiwan is able to use its resources efficiently and expand its production possibilities well beyond that of Nigeria.

Checkpoint: Specialization, Comparative Advantage, and Trade

For Hollywood stars and other rich people, the opportunity cost of their time is high. As a result, they hire people at lower cost to do the mundane chores that each of us is accustomed to doing because our time is relatively less valuable.

3 Supply and Demand

After studying this chapter you should be able to:

- Describe the nature and purposes of markets.
- Describe the nature of demand, demand curves, and the law of demand.
- Describe the determinants of demand and be able to forecast how a change in one or more of these determinants will change demand.
- Explain the difference between a change in demand and a change in quantity demanded.
- Describe the nature of supply, supply curves, and the law of supply.
- Describe the determinants of supply and be able to forecast how a change in one or more of these determinants will change supply.
- Explain the difference between a change in supply and a change in quantity supplied.
- Determine market equilibrium price and output.
- Determine and predict how price and output will change given changes to supply and demand in the market.

What $60 billion global industry sells a product that many people typically can obtain easily from another source free of charge? The bottled water industry! This industry began its meteoric rise in the early 1990s, and today, the ubiquitous bottle of water has changed the way we live. It also has created new concerns regarding the environmental impact of the billions of plastic bottles used and discarded.

The bottled water industry took off as consumers changed their hydration habits, spurred by greater awareness of the health benefits of drinking water, including weight loss, illness prevention, and overall health maintenance. As water consumption increased, people started wanting something more than just ordinary water from the tap. They desired water that was purer, more consistent in taste, or infused with flavor or minerals. Plus, consumers wanted water that was easy to carry. Bottled water was the product consumers wanted, and the market was willing to provide it.

Bottled water comes from many sources, both domestic and foreign, and consists of either spring water (from natural springs underneath the earth) or purified water (ordinary tap water that undergoes a complex purification process). As the industry grew, new varieties of water were made available. Water that came from exotic faraway springs, vitamin-infused water, flavored water, and carbonated water were some of the choices consumers were given. The total amount of water produced for the bottled water industry continued to increase as long as there were customers willing to pay for it in the market.

In the late 2000s, falling incomes from a deteriorating global economy, concerns about the harmful effects of discarded plastic bottles on the environment, increased use of home water purification devices, and even some laws against the use of bottled water eventually halted the market's growth. The economy has since improved, and the bottled water industry responded to the environmental concerns by using bottles made from recycled plastic or by using new technologies to reduce the plastic content in water bottles, again responding to the desires of consumers. As a result, sales increased again in 2011.

Consumers have many choices of what water to buy and where to buy it. Even so, the bottled water market is one in which prices vary considerably depending on the location of purchase. A single bottle of water of the same brand might cost $0.69 at a grocery store, $0.99 at a convenience store, $1.25 from a vending machine, $1.49 at a local coffee shop, and $3.00 or more at a theme park, sports stadium, or movie theater. How can the same product be sold in different places at so many different prices?

This chapter analyzes the various factors influencing how consumers value goods in different settings and circumstances. We also study how producers take costs and incentives into account in determining what products to produce, how much to produce, and what prices to charge. The interaction between consumers and producers within a market determines the prices we pay.

In any given market, prices are determined by "what the market will bear." Which factors determine what the market will bear, and what happens when events that occur in the marketplace cause prices to change? For answers to these questions, economists turn to supply and demand analysis. The basic model of supply and demand presented in this chapter will let you determine why product sales rise and fall, what direction prices move in, and how many goods will be offered for sale when certain events happen in the marketplace. Later chapters use this same model to explain complex phenomena such as how wages are set and how personal income is distributed.

This chapter introduces some of the basic economic concepts you need to know to understand how the forces of supply and demand work. These concepts include markets, the law of demand, demand curves, the determinants of demand, the law of supply, supply curves, the determinants of supply, and market equilibrium.

Markets

markets Institutions that bring buyers and sellers together so they can interact and transact with each other.

A **market** is an institution that enables buyers and sellers to interact and transact with one another. A lemonade stand is a market because it allows people to exchange money for a product, in this case lemonade. Ticket scalping, which remains illegal or

BY THE NUMBERS

The World of Markets

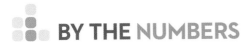

Markets form the foundation of all economic transactions. As various factors affect the supply and demand for goods and services, prices adjust upward or downward correspondingly to reach equilibrium.

The legalization of casinos in many states has resulted in dramatic growth in the industry. Top gaming revenues by state in 2011:

age fotostock/SuperStock

PjrStudio/Alamy

Prices for precious metals vary widely due to their relative demand and supply.

7,300,000,000

Total value (in U.S. dollars) of the worldwide virtual goods market associated with online gaming in 2012.

72,800,000,000

Total number of half-liter water bottles consumed in the United States in 2012 (over 220 bottles per person).

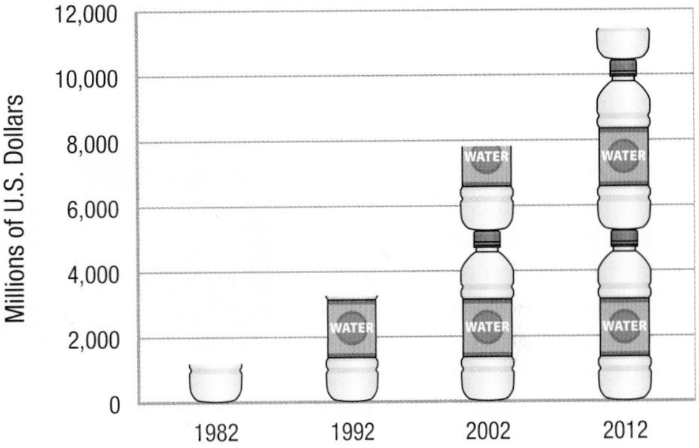

Total sales of bottled water in the United States took off in the 1990s and continued to grow steadily since.

ZUMA Wire Service /Alamy

University of Phoenix is the largest for-profit university with nearly 500,000 students.

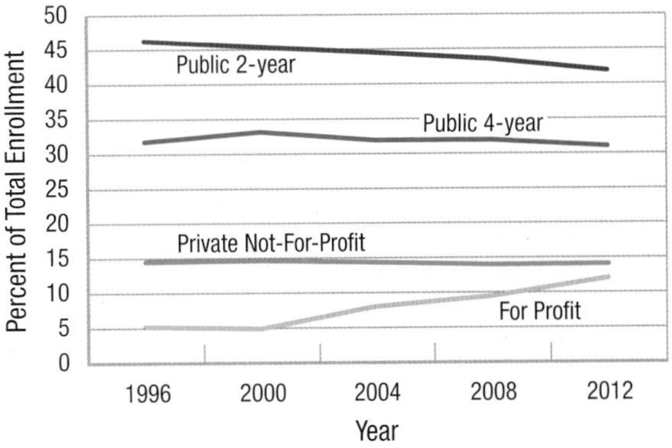

Enrollment at for-profit universities grew significantly over the past 16 years compared to not-for-profit institutions.

price system A name given to the market economy because prices provide considerable information to both buyers and sellers.

highly restricted in some states, similarly represents market activity since it leads to the exchange of money for tickets, whether it takes place in person outside the stadium or online.

The Internet, without a physical location, has dramatically expanded the notion of markets. Online market sites such as eBay permit firms and individuals to sell a large number of low-volume products, ranging from rare collectible items to an extra box of unused diapers, and still make money. This includes students who resell their textbooks on Amazon.com and Half.com. The Internet also has launched markets for virtual goods. For example, buying virtual tools, cash, and animals in online games has become an important part of social media sites.

Even though all markets have the same basic component—the transaction—they can differ in a number of ways. Some markets are quite limited because of their geographical location, or because they offer only a few different products for sale. The New York Stock Exchange serves as a market for just a single type of financial instrument, stocks, but it facilitates exchanges worth billions of dollars daily. Compare this to the neighborhood flea market, which is much smaller and may operate only on weekends, but offers everything from food and crafts to T-shirts and electronics. Cement manufacturers are typically restricted to local markets due to high transportation costs, whereas Internet firms can easily do business with customers around the world.

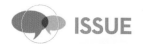

ISSUE

Do Markets Exist for Everyone, Including Dogs and Cats?

Over 78 million dogs and 86 million cats call the United States home, with many times more finding homes around the world. Over four in ten U.S. households include at least one pet, which is often treated as a beloved member of the family. The expenses associated with pet ownership often extend beyond the basic necessities of food and vet checkups.

Jefferson Graham

Total spending on pet-related products in the United States has increased every year since 2001, surpassing $50 billion in 2011. Even during the depths of the last economic downturn, spending on pets continued to increase. The seeming immunity of the pet goods market to economic hardships raises an interesting question of who the market is geared toward: the pets or their sometimes fanatical owners?

Pet goods manufacturers have increased the types of "consumer" goods and services for pets. These include a greater selection of pet foods and toys, but increasingly sellers are being more creative in their offerings. For example, the number of pet spas, pet hotels, and even pet airlines, allowing pets to bathe in luxury as they or their owners travel, has boomed over the past decade.

Pet consumerism has even gone high-tech. Since the introduction of tablets, programmers have introduced new tablet apps designed for cats, including games that are played feline versus human. Such apps highlight the ability of businesses to turn pets into consumers, whose desires (even if imagined by their owners) turn into actual purchases.

The power of consumer decisions extending beyond the wants of humans demonstrates the broad reach of markets. Because humans share a deep connection with their furry loved ones, they will often incorporate their pets' desires into real consumption choices. And based on the growth of this market, it's likely that dogs and cats will continue to be avid consumers in this market.

The Price System

When buyers and sellers exchange money for goods and services, accepting some offers and rejecting others, they are also doing something else: They are communicating their individual desires. Much of this communication is accomplished through the prices of items. If buyers value a particular item sufficiently, they will quickly pay its asking price. If they do not buy it, they are indicating they do not believe the item to be worth its asking price.

Prices also give buyers an easy means of comparing goods that can substitute for each other. If the price of margarine falls to half the price of butter, this will suggest to many consumers that margarine is a better deal. Similarly, sellers can determine what goods to sell by comparing their prices. When prices rise for tennis rackets, this tells sporting goods store operators that the public wants more tennis rackets, leading the store operators to order more. Prices, therefore, contain a huge amount of useful information for both consumers and sellers. For this reason, economists often call our market economy the **price system.**

CHECKPOINT

MARKETS

- Markets are institutions that enable buyers and sellers to interact and transact business.
- Markets differ in geographical location, products offered, and size.
- Prices contain a wealth of information for both buyers and sellers.
- Through their purchases, consumers signal their willingness to exchange money for particular products at particular prices. These signals help businesses decide what to produce, and how much of it to produce.
- The market economy is also called the price system.

QUESTION: What are the important differences between the markets for financial securities such as the New York Stock Exchange and your local farmer's market?

Answers to the Checkpoint question can be found at the end of this chapter.

Demand

Whenever you purchase a product, you are voting with your money. You are selecting one product out of many and supporting one firm out of many, both of which signal to the business community what sorts of products satisfy your wants as a consumer.

Economists typically focus on wants rather than needs because it is so difficult to determine what we truly need. Theoretically, you could survive on tofu and vitamin pills, living in a lean-to made of cardboard and buying all your clothes from thrift stores. Most people in our society, however, choose not to live in such austere fashion. Rather, they want something more, and in most cases they are willing and able to pay for more.

Willingness-to-Pay: The Building Block of Market Demand

Imagine sitting in your economics class around mealtime. In your rush to class, you did not have a chance to make a sandwich at home or to stop at the cafeteria on your way to class. You think about foods that sound appealing to you (just about anything at this point), and plan to go to the cafeteria immediately after class and buy a sandwich. Given your growling stomach, you think more about what you want on your sandwich and less about how much the sandwich will cost. In your mind, your **willingness-to-pay** for that sandwich can be quite high, say $10 or even more.

willingness-to-pay An individual's valuation of a good or service, equal to the most an individual is willing and able to pay.

Economists refer to willingness-to-pay as the maximum amount one would be willing to pay for a good or service, which represents the highest value that a consumer believes the good or service is worth. Of course, one always hopes that the actual price would be much lower. In your case, willingness-to-pay is the cutoff from buying a sandwich and not buying a sandwich.

Willingness-to-pay varies from person to person, from the circumstances each person is in to the number of sandwiches one chooses to buy. Suppose your classmate ate a full meal before she came to class. Her willingness-to-pay for a sandwich would be much lower than yours because she isn't hungry at that moment. Similarly, after you buy and consume your first sandwich, your willingness-to-pay for a second sandwich would decrease because you would be less hungry. The desires consumers have for goods and services that are expressed through their purchases are known as demands in the market.

Figure 1 on the next page illustrates how individuals' willingness-to-pay (WTP) is used to derive market demand curves. Suppose you are willing to pay up to $10 for the first sandwich and $4 for the second sandwich (shown in panel A), while Jane, your less-hungry classmate, would pay up to $6 for her first sandwich and only $2 for her second sandwich (shown in panel B). If we take the WTP for your two sandwiches and the WTP of Jane's two sandwiches and place all four values in order from highest to lowest, a two-person market for sandwiches is created as shown in panel C. Notice how the distance between steps becomes smaller in the two-person market. Now suppose we combine the WTPs for

FIGURE 1

From Individual Willingness-to-Pay to Market Demand

In panel A, you would be willing to pay up to $10 for your first sandwich and $4 for the second. Jane, however, is only willing to pay up to $6 for her first sandwich and $2 for a second (panel B). Placing the WTP for sandwiches by you and Jane in order from the highest to lowest value, we generate a market with two consumers shown in panel C. As more and more individuals are added to the market, the demand for sandwiches becomes a smooth downward-sloping line, shown in panel D.

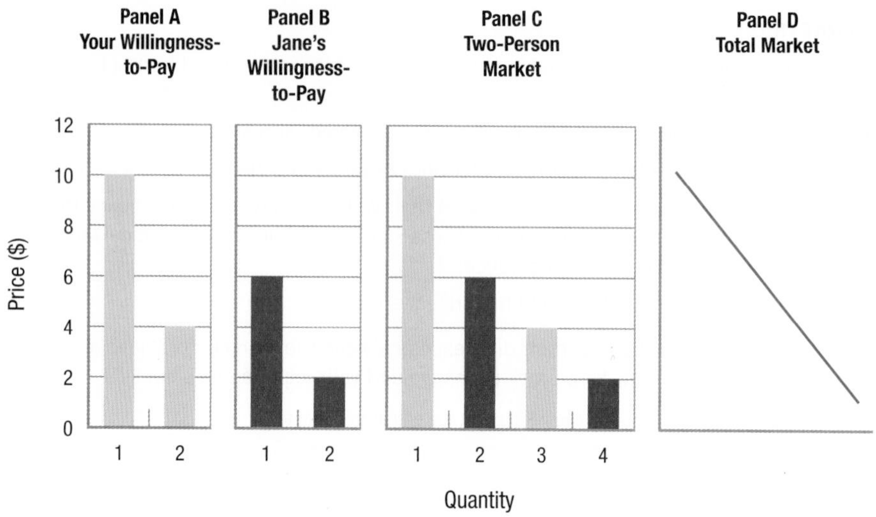

demand The maximum amount of a product that buyers are willing and able to purchase over some time period at various prices, holding all other relevant factors constant (the *ceteris paribus* condition).

law of demand Holding all other relevant factors constant, as price increases, quantity demanded falls, and as price decreases, quantity demanded rises.

everybody in the class (or for an entire city or country) into a single market. What would that diagram look like? In large markets, the difference in WTP between each unit of a good becomes so small that it becomes a straight line, as shown in panel D.

These illustrations show how ordinary demand curves, which we will discuss in detail in the remainder of this section, are developed from the perceptions of what individual consumers believe a good or service is worth to them (their willingness-to-pay). Let's now discuss an important characteristic of market demand.

The Law of Demand: The Relationship Between Quantity Demanded and Price

Demand refers to the goods and services people are willing and able to buy during a certain period of time at various prices, holding all other relevant factors constant (the *ceteris paribus* condition). Typically, when the price of a good or service increases (say your favorite café raises its prices), the quantity demanded will decrease because fewer and fewer people will be willing and able to spend their money on such things. However, when prices of goods or services decrease (think of sales offered the day after Thanksgiving), the quantity demanded increases.

In a market economy, there is a negative relationship between price and quantity demanded. This relationship, in its most basic form, states that as price increases, the quantity demanded falls, and conversely, as prices fall, the quantity demanded increases.

This principle, when all other factors are held constant, is known as the **law of demand.** The law of demand states that the lower a product's price, the more of that product consumers will purchase during a given time period. This straightforward, commonsense notion happens because, as a product's price drops, consumers will substitute the now cheaper product for other, more expensive products. Conversely, if the product's price rises, consumers will find other, less expensive products to substitute for it.

Peter Foley/Bloomberg via Getty Images

The day after Thanksgiving, dubbed "Black Friday," is when stores offer steep discounts to jumpstart the holiday shopping season. This leads to massive quantities of goods sold, in an example of the law of demand.

To illustrate, when videocassette recorders first came on the market 30 years ago, they cost $3,000, and few homes had one. As VCRs became less and less expensive, however, more people bought them, and others found more uses for them. Today, DVD players and digital video recorders (DVRs) are everywhere, and VCRs are essentially consigned to museums.

Digital music players have altered the structure of the music business, and digital cameras have essentially replaced cameras that use film.

Time is an important component in the demand for many products. Consuming many products—watching a movie, eating a pizza, playing tennis—takes some time. Thus, the price of these goods includes not only their monetary cost, but also the opportunity cost of the time needed to consume them. It follows that, all other things being equal, including the cost of a ticket, we would expect more consumers to attend a two-hour movie than a four-hour movie. The shorter movie simply requires less of a time investment.

The Demand Curve

The law of demand states that as price decreases, quantity demanded increases. When we translate demand information into a graph, we create a **demand curve.** This demand curve, which slopes down and to the right, graphically illustrates the law of demand. A demand curve shows both the willingness-to-pay for any given quantity and what the quantity demanded will be at any given price. In Figure 1, we saw how individual demands (measured by willingness-to-pay) can be combined to represent market demand, which can consist of many consumers. For simplicity, from this point we will assume that all demand curves, including those for individuals, are linear (straight lines).

demand curve A graphical illustration of the law of demand, which shows the relationship between the price of a good and the quantity demanded.

Suppose Abe and Betty are the only two consumers in the market for computer games. Figure 2 shows each of their annual demands using a demand schedule and a demand curve. A **demand schedule** is a table indicating the quantities consumers are willing to purchase at each price. Looking at the demand schedule, we can see that both Abe and Betty are willing to buy more computer games as the price decreases. When the price is $100, Abe is willing to buy 10 games while Betty buys none. When the price falls to $80, Abe is willing to buy 15 games and Betty would buy 5.

demand schedule A table that shows the quantity of a good a consumer purchases at each price.

We can take the values from the demand schedule in the table and graph them in a figure, with price shown on the vertical axis and computer games on the horizontal axis, following the convention in economics of always placing price on the vertical axis and quantity demanded on the horizontal axis. By doing so, we can create a demand curve for both Abe and Betty. Both the table and the graph convey the same information. They also both portray the law of demand. As the price decreases, Abe and Betty demand more computer games.

Although individual demand curves are interesting, market demand curves are far more important to economists, as they can be used to predict changes in product price

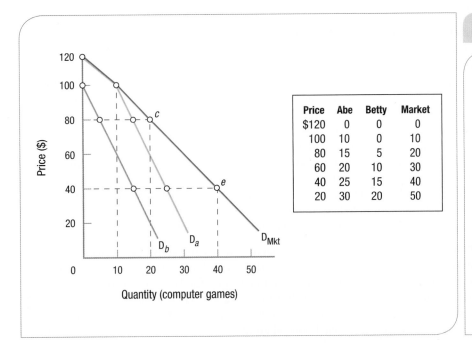

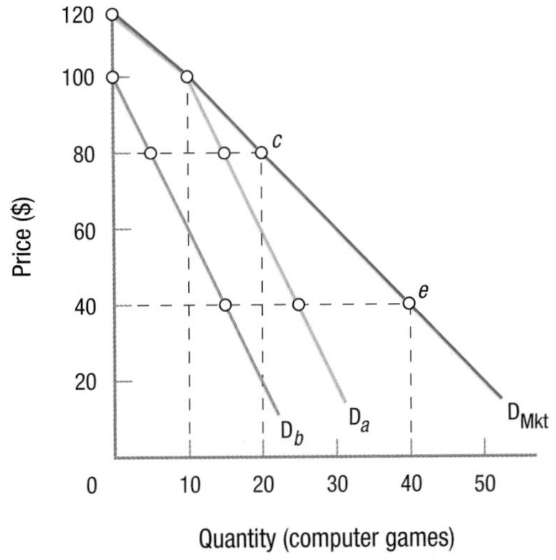

Price	Abe	Betty	Market
$120	0	0	0
100	10	0	10
80	15	5	20
60	20	10	30
40	25	15	40
20	30	20	50

FIGURE 2

Market Demand: Horizontal Summation of Individual Demand Curves

Abe and Betty's demand schedules (the table) and their individual demand curves (the graph) for computer games are shown. Abe will purchase 15 computer games when the price is $80, buy 25 games when the price falls to $40, and buy more as prices continue to fall. Betty will purchase 5 computer games when the price is $80 and buy 15 when the price falls to $40. The individual demand curves for Abe and Betty are shown as D_a and D_b, respectively, and are horizontally summed to get market demand, D_{Mkt}. Horizontal summation involves adding together the quantities demanded by each individual at each possible price.

and quantity. Further, one can observe what happens to a product's price and quantity and infer what changes have occurred in the market. Market demand is the sum of individual demands. To calculate market demand, economists simply add together how many units of a product all consumers will purchase at each price. This process is known as **horizontal summation.**

horizontal summation Market demand and supply curves are found by adding together how many units of the product will be purchased or supplied at each price.

Turning to the demand curves in Figure 2, two individual demand curves for Abe and Betty, D_a and D_b, are shown. For simplicity, let's assume they represent the entire market, but recognize that this process would work for any larger number of people. Note that at a price of $100 a game, Betty will not buy any, although Abe is willing to buy 10 games at $100 each. Above $100, therefore, the market demand is equal to Abe's demand. At $100 and below, however, we add both Abe's and Betty's demands at each price to obtain market demand. Thus, at $80, individual demand is 15 for Abe and 5 for Betty, therefore the market demand is equal to 20 (point *c*). When the price is $40 a game, Abe buys 25 and Betty buys 15, for a total of 40 games (point *e*). The heavier curve, labeled D_{Mkt}, represents this market demand; it is a horizontal summation of the two individual demand curves.

This all sounds simple in theory, but in the real world estimating market demand curves is a tricky business, given that many markets contain millions of consumers. Economic analysts and marketing professionals use sophisticated statistical techniques to estimate the market demand for particular goods and services in the industries they represent.

The market demand curve shows the maximum amount of a product consumers are willing and able to purchase during a given time period at various prices, all other relevant factors being held constant. Economists use the term determinants of demand to refer to these other, nonprice factors that are held constant. This is another example of the use of *ceteris paribus:* holding all other relevant factors constant.

Determinants of Demand

Up to this point, we have discussed only how price affects the quantity demanded. When prices fall, consumers purchase more of a product, thus quantity demanded rises. When prices rise, consumers purchase less of a product, thus quantity demanded falls. But several other factors besides price also affect demand, including what people like, what their income is, and how much related products cost. More specifically, there are five key **determinants of demand:** (1) tastes and preferences; (2) income; (3) prices of related goods; (4) the number of buyers; and (5) expectations regarding future prices, income, and product availability. When one of these determinants changes, the *entire* demand curve changes. Let's see why.

determinants of demand Nonprice factors that affect demand, including tastes and preferences, income, prices of related goods, number of buyers, and expectations.

Tastes and Preferences We all have preferences for certain products over others, easily perceiving subtle differences in styling and quality. Automobiles, fashions, phones, and music are just a few of the products that are subject to the whims of the consumer.

Remember Crocs, those brightly colored rubber sandals with the little air holes that moms, kids, waitresses, and many others favored recently? They were an instant hit. Initially, demand was D_0 in Figure 3. They then became such a fad that demand jumped to D_1 and for a short while Crocs were hard to find. Eventually Crocs were everywhere. Fads come and go, and now the demand for them settled back to something like D_2, less than the original level. Notice an important distinction here: More Crocs weren't sold because the *price* was lowered; the entire demand curve shifted rightward when they were hot and more Crocs could be sold at *all* prices. Now that the fad has subsided, fewer can be sold at all prices. It is important to keep in mind that when one of the determinants changes, such as tastes and preferences in this case, the *entire* demand curve shifts.

Income Income is another important factor influencing consumer demand. Generally speaking, as income rises, demand for most goods will likewise increase. Get a raise, and you are more likely to buy more clothes and acquire the latest technology gadgets. Your demand curve for these goods will shift to the right (such as from D_0 to D_1 in Figure 3). Products for which demand is positively linked to income—when income rises, demand for the product also rises—are called **normal goods.**

normal good A good for which an increase in income results in rising demand.

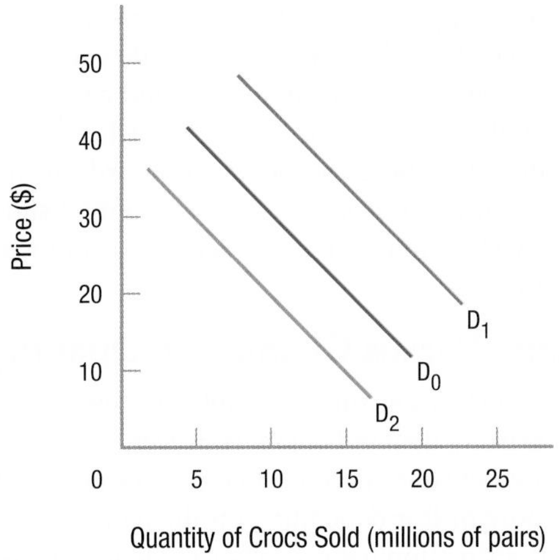

FIGURE 3

Shifts in the Demand Curve

The demand for Crocs originally was D_0. When they became a fad, demand shifted to D_1 as consumers were willing to purchase more at *all* prices. Once the fad cooled off, demand fell (shifted leftward) to D_2 as consumers wanted less at each price. When a determinant such as tastes and preferences changes, the *entire* demand curve shifts.

There are also some products for which demand declines as income rises, and the demand curve shifts to the left. Economists call these products **inferior goods.** As income grows, for instance, the consumption of discount clothing and cheap motel stays will likely fall as individuals upgrade their wardrobes and stay in more comfortable hotels when traveling. Similarly, when you graduate from college and your income rises, your consumption of ramen noodles will fall as you begin to cook tastier dinners and eat out more frequently.

inferior good A good for which an increase in income results in declining demand.

Prices of Related Goods The prices of related commodities also affect consumer decisions. You may be an avid concertgoer, but with concert ticket prices often topping $100, further rises in the price of concert tickets may entice you to see more movies and fewer concerts. Movies, concerts, plays, and sporting events are good examples of **substitute goods,** because consumers can substitute one for another depending on their respective prices. When the *price* of concerts rises, your *demand* for movies increases, and vice versa. These are substitute goods.

substitute goods Goods consumers will substitute for one another depending on their relative prices. When the *price* of one good rises and the *demand* for another good increases, they are substitute goods, and vice versa.

Movies and popcorn, on the other hand, are examples of **complementary goods.** These are goods that are generally consumed together, such that an increase or decrease in the consumption of one will similarly result in an increase or decrease in the consumption of the other—see fewer movies, and your consumption of popcorn will decline. Other complementary goods include cars and gasoline, hot dogs and hot dog buns, and ski lift tickets and ski rentals. Thus, when the *price* of lift tickets increases, the quantity of lift tickets demanded falls, which causes your *demand* for ski rentals to fall as well (shifts to the left), and vice versa.

complementary goods Goods that are typically consumed together. When the *price* of a complementary good rises, the *demand* for the other good declines, and vice versa.

The Number of Buyers Another factor influencing market demand for a product is the number of potential buyers in the market. Clearly, the more consumers there are who would be likely to buy a particular product, the higher its market demand will be (the demand curve will shift rightward). As our average life span steadily rises, the demands for medical services and retirement communities likewise increase. As more people than ever enter universities and graduate schools, demand for textbooks and backpacks increases.

Expectations About Future Prices, Incomes, and Product Availability The final factor influencing demand involves consumer expectations. If consumers expect shortages of certain products or increases in their prices in the near future, they tend to rush out and buy these products immediately, thereby increasing the present demand for the products. The demand curve shifts to the right. During the Florida hurricane season, when a large storm forms and begins moving toward the coast, the demand for plywood, nails, bottled water, and batteries quickly rises.

The expectation of a rise in income, meanwhile, can lead consumers to take advantage of credit in order to increase their present consumption. Department stores and furniture stores, for example, often run "no payments until next year" sales designed to attract consumers who want to "buy now, pay later." These consumers expect to have more money later, when they can pay, so they go ahead and buy what they want now, thereby increasing the present demand for the sale items. Again, the demand curve shifts to the right.

The key point to remember from this section is that when one of the determinants of demand changes, the *entire* demand curve shifts rightward (an increase in demand) or leftward (a decline in demand). A quick look back at Figure 3 shows that when demand increases, consumers are willing to buy more at all prices, and when demand decreases, they will buy less at all prices.

Changes in Demand Versus Changes in Quantity Demanded

When the price of a product rises, consumers simply buy fewer units of that product. This is a movement along an existing demand curve. However, when one or more of the determinants change, the entire demand curve is altered. Now at any given price, consumers are willing to purchase more or less depending on the nature of the change. This section focuses on this important distinction between *changes in demand* versus *changes in quantity demanded.*

change in demand Occurs when one or more of the determinants of demand changes, shown as a shift in the entire demand curve.

Changes in demand occur whenever one or more of the determinants of demand change and demand curves shift. When demand changes, the demand curve shifts either to the right or to the left. Let's look at each shift in turn.

Demand increases when the entire demand curve shifts to the right. At all prices, consumers are willing to purchase more of the product in question. Figure 4 shows an increase in demand for computer games; the demand curve shifts from D_0 to D_1. Notice that more computer games are purchased at all prices along D_1 as compared to D_0.

Now look at a decrease in demand, when the entire demand curve shifts to the left. At all prices, consumers are willing to purchase less of the product in question. A drop in consumer income is normally associated with a decrease in demand (the demand curve shifts to the left, as from D_0 to D_2 in Figure 4).

change in quantity demanded Occurs when the price of the product changes, shown as a movement along an existing demand curve.

Whereas a change in demand can be brought about by many different factors, a **change in quantity demanded** can be caused by only one thing: *a change in product price.* This is shown in Figure 4 as a reduction in price from \$80 to \$40, resulting in sales (quantity demanded) increasing from 20 (point *a*) to 40 (point *c*) games. This distinction between a change in demand and a change in quantity demanded is important. Reducing price to increase sales is different from spending a few million dollars on Super Bowl advertising to increase sales at all prices.

These concepts are so important that a quick summary is in order. As Figure 4 illustrates, given the initial demand D_0, increasing sales from 20 to 40 games can occur in

FIGURE 4

Changes in Demand Versus Changes in Quantity Demanded

A shift in the demand curve from D_0 to D_1 represents an *increase in demand,* and consumers will buy more of the product at each price. A shift from D_0 to D_2 reflects a *decrease in demand.* Movement along D_0 from point *a* to point *c* indicates an *increase in quantity demanded;* this type of movement can only be caused by a change in the price of the product.

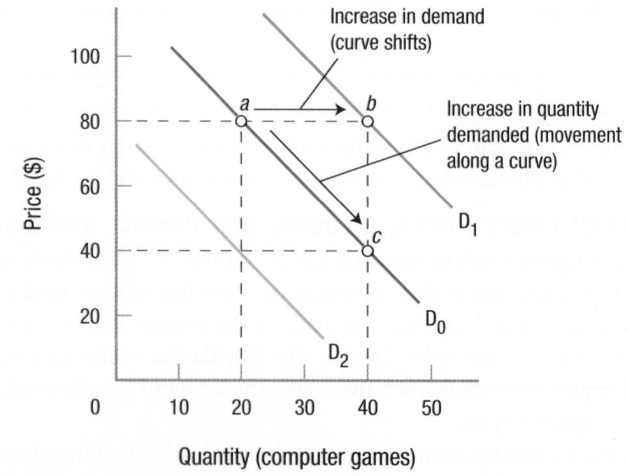

either of two ways. First, changing a determinant (say, increasing advertising) could shift the demand curve to D_1 so that 40 games would be sold at $80 (point *b*). Alternatively, 40 games could be sold by reducing the price to $40 (point *c*). Selling more by increasing advertising causes an increase in demand, or a shift in the entire demand curve. Simply reducing the price, on the other hand, causes an increase in quantity demanded, or a movement along the existing demand curve, D_0, from point *a* to point *c*.

CHECKPOINT

DEMAND

- A person's willingness-to-pay is the maximum amount she or he values a good to be worth at a particular moment in time and is the building block for demand.
- Demand refers to the quantity of products people are willing and able to purchase at various prices during some specific time period, all other relevant factors being held constant.
- The law of demand states that price and quantity demanded have an inverse (negative) relation: As price rises, consumers buy fewer units; as price falls, consumers buy more units. It is depicted as a downward-sloping demand curve.
- Demand curves shift when one or more of the determinants of demand change.
- The determinants of demand are consumer tastes and preferences, income, prices of substitutes and complements, the number of buyers in a market, and expectations about future prices, incomes, and product availability.
- A shift of a demand curve is a *change in demand*, and occurs when a determinant of demand changes.
- A *change in quantity demanded* occurs only when the price of a product changes, leading consumers to adjust their purchases along the existing demand curve.

QUESTIONS: Sales of electric plug-in hybrid cars are on the rise. The Chevrolet Volt is selling well, despite being priced almost double that of similar-sized gasoline-only cars in Chevrolet's line. Other manufacturers are adding plug-in hybrids to their lines at an astonishing pace. What has been the cause of the rising sales of plug-in hybrids? Is this an increase in demand or an increase in quantity demanded?

Answers to the Checkpoint questions can be found at the end of this chapter.

Supply

The analysis of a market economy rests on two foundations: supply and demand. So far, we've covered the demand side of the market. Let's focus now on the decisions businesses make regarding production numbers and sales. These decisions cause variations in product supply.

The Relationship Between Quantity Supplied and Price

Supply is the maximum amount of a product that producers are willing and able to offer for sale at various prices, all other relevant factors being held constant. The quantity supplied will vary according to the price of the product.

supply The maximum amount of a product that sellers are willing and able to provide for sale over some time period at various prices, holding all other relevant factors constant (the *ceteris paribus* condition).

What explains this relationship? As we saw in the previous chapter, businesses inevitably encounter rising opportunity costs as they attempt to produce more and more of a product. This is due in part to diminishing returns from available resources, and in part to the fact that when producers increase production, they must either have existing workers put in overtime (at a higher hourly pay rate) or hire additional workers away from other industries (again at premium pay).

Producing more units, therefore, makes it more expensive to produce each individual unit. These increasing costs give rise to the positive relationship between product price and quantity supplied to the market.

The Law of Supply

law of supply Holding all other relevant factors constant, as price increases, quantity supplied will rise, and as price declines, quantity supplied will fall.

Unfortunately for producers, they can rarely charge whatever they would like for their products; they must charge whatever the market will permit. But producers can decide how much of their product to produce and offer for sale. The **law of supply** states that higher prices will lead producers to offer more of their products for sale during a given period. Conversely, if prices fall, producers will offer fewer products to the market. The explanation is simple: The higher the price, the greater the potential for higher profits and thus the greater the incentive for businesses to produce and sell more products. Also, given the rising opportunity costs associated with increasing production, producers need to charge these higher prices to increase the quantity supplied profitably.

The Supply Curve

supply curve A graphical illustration of the law of supply, which shows the relationship between the price of a good and the quantity supplied.

Just as demand curves graphically display the law of demand, **supply curves** provide a graphical representation of the law of supply. The supply curve shows the maximum amounts of a product a producer will furnish at various prices during a given period of time. While the demand curve slopes *down* and to the right, the supply curve slopes *up* and to the right.[1] This illustrates the positive relationship between price and quantity supplied: the higher the price, the greater the quantity supplied.

Market Supply Curves

As with demand, economists are more interested in market supply than in the supplies offered by individual firms. To compute market supply, use the same method used to calculate market demand, horizontally summing the supplies of individual producers. A hypothetical market supply curve for computer games is depicted in Figure 5. The quantity of computer games that producers will offer for sale increases as the price of computer games rises. The opposite would happen if the price of computer games falls.

FIGURE 5

Supply of Computer Games

This supply curve graphs the supply schedule and shows the maximum quantity of computer games that producers will offer for sale over some defined period of time. The supply curve is positively sloped, reflecting the law of supply. In other words, as prices rise, quantity supplied increases; as prices fall, quantity supplied falls.

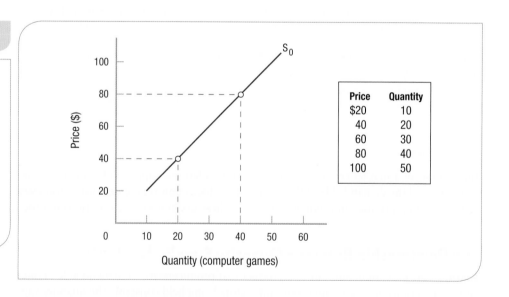

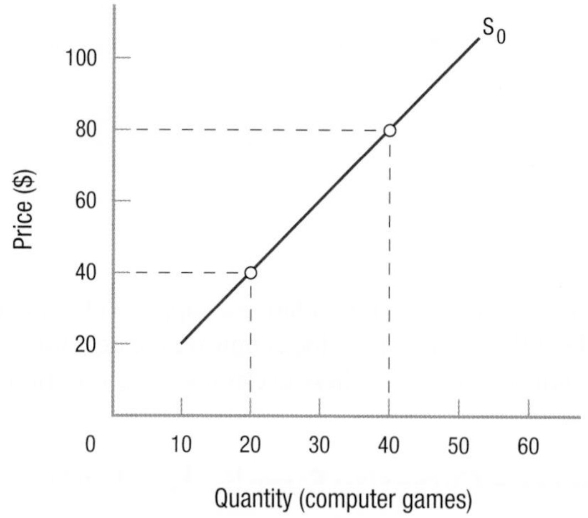

Price	Quantity
$20	10
40	20
60	30
80	40
100	50

Determinants of Supply

determinants of supply Nonprice factors that affect supply, including production technology, costs of resources, prices of other commodities, expectations, number of sellers, and taxes and subsidies.

Like demand, several nonprice factors help to determine the supply of a product. Specifically, there are six **determinants of supply:** (1) production technology, (2) costs of resources, (3) prices of other commodities, (4) expectations, (5) the number of sellers (producers) in the market, and (6) taxes and subsidies.

[1] There are some exceptions to positively sloping supply curves. But for our purposes, we will ignore them for now.

Production Technology Technology determines how much output can be produced from given quantities of resources. If a factory's equipment is old and can turn out only 50 units of output per hour, then no matter how many other resources are employed, those 50 units are the most the factory can produce in an hour. If the factory is outfitted with newer, more advanced equipment capable of turning out 100 units per hour, the firm can supply more of its product at the same price as before, or even at a lower price. In Figure 6, this would be represented by a shift in the supply curve from S_0 to S_1. At every single price, more would be supplied.

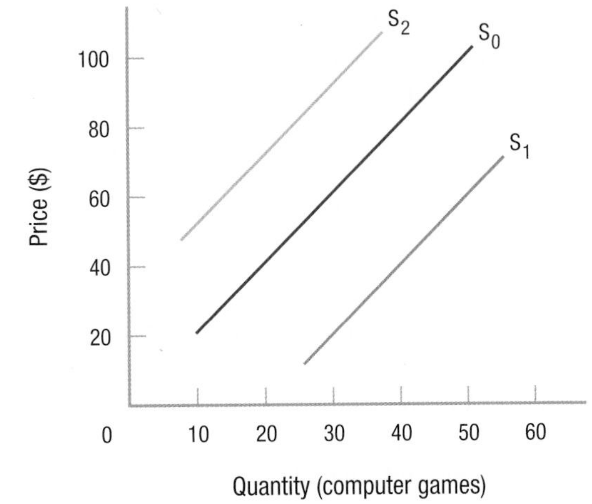

FIGURE 6

Shifts in the Supply Curve

The supply of computer games originally is S_0. If supply shifts to S_1, producers are willing to sell more at *all* prices. If supply falls, supply shifts leftward to S_2. Now firms are willing to sell less at each price. When a determinant of supply changes, the *entire* supply curve shifts.

Technology further determines the nature of products that can be supplied to the market. A hundred years ago, the supply of computers on the market was zero because computers did not yet exist. More recent advances in microprocessing and miniaturization brought a wide array of products to the market that were not available just a few years ago, including mini-tablets, auto engines that go 100,000 miles between tune-ups, and constant-monitoring insulin pumps that automatically keep a diabetic patient's glucose levels under control.

Costs of Resources Resource costs clearly affect production costs and supply. If resources such as raw materials or labor become more expensive, production costs will rise and supply will be reduced (the supply curve shifts to the left, from S_0 to S_2 in Figure 6). The reverse is true if resource costs drop (the supply curve shifts to the right, from S_0 to S_1). The growing power of microchips along with their falling cost has resulted in cheap and plentiful electronics and computers. Nanotechnology—manufacturing processes that fashion new products through the combination of individual atoms—may soon usher in a whole new generation of inexpensive products.

On the other hand, if the cost of petroleum goes up, the cost of products using petroleum in their manufacture will go up, leading to the supply being reduced (the supply curve shifts leftward). If labor costs rise because immigration is restricted, this drives up production costs of California vegetables (fewer farmworkers) and software in Silicon Valley (fewer software engineers from abroad) and leads to a shift in the supply curve to the left in Figure 6.

Prices of Other Commodities Most firms have some flexibility in the portfolio of goods they produce. A vegetable farmer, for example, might be able to grow celery or radishes, or some combination of the two. Given this flexibility, a change in the price of one item may influence the quantity of other items brought to market. If the price of celery should rise, for instance, most farmers will start growing more celery. And since they all have a limited amount of land on which to grow vegetables, this reduces the quantity of radishes they can produce. Hence, in this case, the rise in the price of celery may well cause a reduction in the supply of radishes (the supply curve for radishes shifts leftward).

Expectations The effects of future expectations on market supplies can be confusing, but it need not be. When sellers expect prices of a good to rise in the future, they are likely to restrict their supply in the current period in anticipation of receiving higher prices in some future period. Examples include homes and stocks—if you believe prices are going up, you'd be less likely to sell today, which decreases the supply of such goods (supply shifts to the left). Similarly, expectations of price reductions can increase supply as sellers try to sell off their inventories before prices drop (supply shifts to the right).

Eventually, if prices do rise in the next period, producers would increase the quantity supplied of the good; however, this would be due to the law of supply, not due to a shift of the supply curve. In other words, rising prices result in a movement along the supply curve. Only when producers anticipate a change in a future price, causing a reaction now, does supply shift.

Number of Sellers Everything else being held constant, if the number of sellers in a particular market increases, the market supply of their product increases. It is no great mystery why: Ten dim sum chefs can produce more dumplings in a given period than five dim sum chefs.

Taxes and Subsidies For businesses, taxes and subsidies affect costs. An increase in taxes (property, excise, or other fees) will shift supply to the left and reduce it. Subsidies are the opposite of taxes. If the government subsidizes the production of a product, supply will shift to the right and rise. A proposed new tax on expensive health care insurance plans may reduce supply (the tax is equivalent to an increase in production costs), while today's subsidies to ethanol producers expand ethanol production.

Changes in Supply Versus Changes in Quantity Supplied

change in supply Occurs when one or more of the determinants of supply change, shown as a shift in the entire supply curve.

change in quantity supplied Occurs when the price of the product changes, shown as a movement along an existing supply curve.

A **change in supply** results from a change in one or more of the determinants of supply; it causes the entire supply curve to shift. An increase in supply of a product, perhaps because advancing technology has made it cheaper to produce, means that more of the commodity will be offered for sale at every price. This causes the supply curve to shift to the right, as illustrated in Figure 7 by the shift from S_0 to S_1. A decrease in supply, conversely, shifts the supply curve to the left, since fewer units of the product are offered at every price. Such a decrease in supply is here represented by the shift from S_0 to S_2.

A change in supply involves a shift of the entire supply curve. In contrast, the supply curve does not move when there is a **change in quantity supplied.** Only a change in the price of a product can cause a change in the quantity supplied; hence, it involves a

FIGURE 7

Changes in Supply Versus Changes in Quantity Supplied

A shift in the supply curve from S_0 to S_1 represents an *increase in supply,* because businesses are willing to offer more of the product to consumers at *all* prices. A shift from S_0 to S_2 reflects a decrease in supply. A movement along S_0 from point *a* to point *c* represents an *increase in quantity supplied;* it results from an increase in the product's market price from $40 to $80.

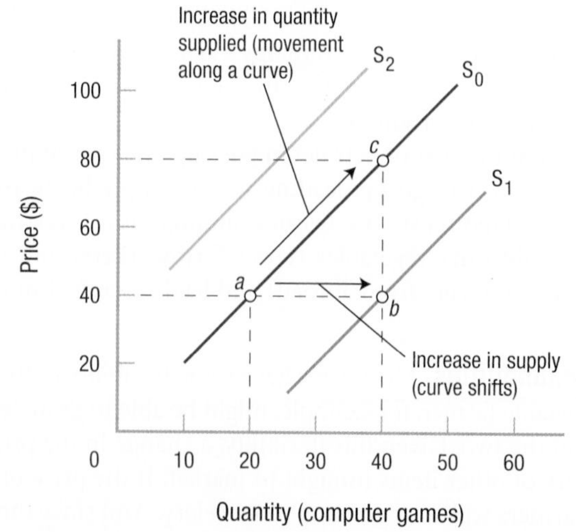

movement along an existing supply curve rather than a shift to an entirely different curve. In Figure 7, for example, an increase in price from \$40 to \$80 results in an increase in quantity supplied from 20 to 40 games, represented by the movement from point *a* to point *c* along S_0.

In summary, a change in supply is represented in Figure 7 by the shift from S_0 to S_1 or S_2, which involves a shift in the entire supply curve. For example, an increase in supply from S_0 to S_1 results in an increase in supply from 20 computer games (point *a*) to 40 (point *b*) provided at a price of \$40. More games are provided at the same price. In contrast, a change in quantity supplied is shown in Figure 7 as a movement along an existing supply curve, S_0, from point *a* to point *c* caused by an increase in the price of the product from \$40 to \$80.

As on the demand side, this distinction between changes in supply and changes in quantity supplied is crucial. It means that when a product's price changes, only quantity supplied changes—the supply curve does not move. A summary of the determinants for both supply and demand is shown in Figure 8.

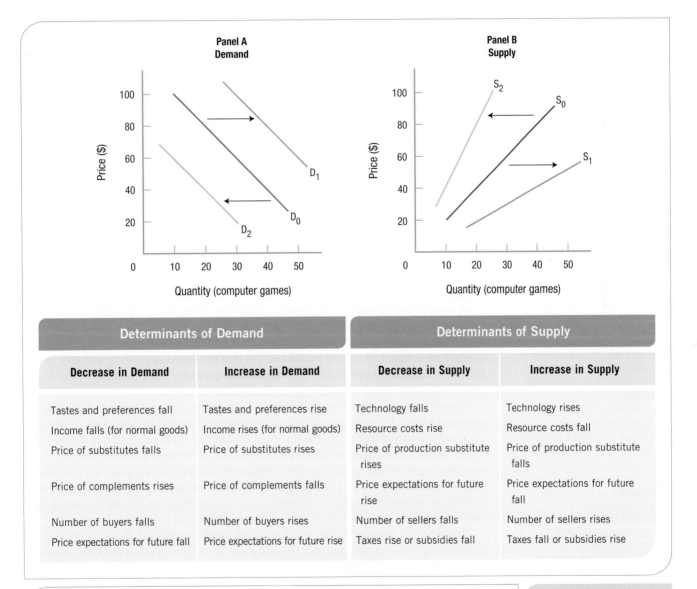

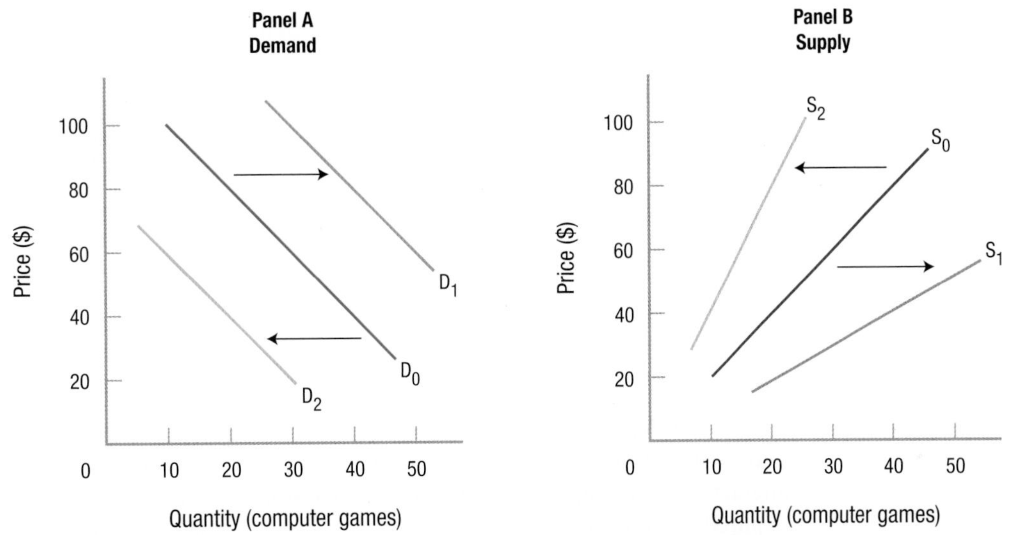

Determinants of Demand		Determinants of Supply	
Decrease in Demand	**Increase in Demand**	**Decrease in Supply**	**Increase in Supply**
Tastes and preferences fall	Tastes and preferences rise	Technology falls	Technology rises
Income falls (for normal goods)	Income rises (for normal goods)	Resource costs rise	Resource costs fall
Price of substitutes falls	Price of substitutes rises	Price of production substitute rises	Price of production substitute falls
Price of complements rises	Price of complements falls	Price expectations for future rise	Price expectations for future fall
Number of buyers falls	Number of buyers rises	Number of sellers falls	Number of sellers rises
Price expectations for future fall	Price expectations for future rise	Taxes rise or subsidies fall	Taxes fall or subsidies rise

FIGURE 8

Summary of Changes in Demand and Supply and Their Determinants

Various factors cause a market demand curve to shift to the left (decrease in demand) or shift to the right (increase in demand) in panel A. Similarly, various factors cause a market supply curve to shift to the left (decrease in supply) or shift to the right (increase in supply) in panel B. The table summarizes the factors influencing demand and supply shifts.

CHECKPOINT

SUPPLY

- Supply is the quantity of a product producers are willing and able to put on the market at various prices, all other relevant factors being held constant.
- The law of supply reflects the positive relationship between price and quantity supplied: the higher the market price, the more goods supplied, and the lower the market price, the fewer goods supplied.
- As with demand, market supply is arrived at by horizontally summing the individual supplies of all of the firms in the market.
- A change in supply occurs when one or more of the determinants of supply change.
- The determinants of supply are production technology, the cost of resources, prices of other commodities, expectations, the numbers of sellers or producers in the market, and taxes and subsidies.
- A *change in supply* is a shift in the supply curve. A shift to the right reflects an increase in supply, while a shift to the left represents a decrease in supply.
- A *change in quantity supplied* is only caused by a change in the price of the product; it results in a movement along the existing supply curve.

QUESTIONS: At the end of the term, bookstores often increase the prices offered to students for their used textbooks in order to stock their shelves for the following term. Would an increase in the buyback price affect the supply or the quantity supplied of used textbooks? Suppose an unusually difficult professor leads to many students having to retake the course the next term. How might this affect the supply for used textbooks?

Answers to the Checkpoint questions can be found at the end of this chapter.

Market Equilibrium

Supply and demand together determine the prices and quantities of goods bought and sold. Neither factor alone is sufficient to determine price and quantity. It is through their interaction that supply and demand do their work, just as two blades of a scissors are required to cut paper.

A market will determine the price at which the quantity of a product demanded is equal to the quantity supplied. At this price, the market is said to be cleared or to be in **equilibrium,** meaning that the amount of the product that consumers are willing and able to purchase is matched exactly by the amount that producers are willing and able to sell. This is the **equilibrium price** and the **equilibrium quantity.** The equilibrium price is also called the market-clearing price.

equilibrium Market forces are in balance when the quantities demanded by consumers just equal the quantities supplied by producers.

equilibrium price Market equilibrium price is the price that results when quantity demanded is just equal to quantity supplied.

equilibrium quantity Market equilibrium quantity is the output that results when quantity demanded is just equal to quantity supplied.

Figure 9 puts together Figures 2 and 5, showing the market supply and demand for computer games. It illustrates how supply and demand interact to determine equilibrium price and quantity. Clearly, the quantities demanded and supplied equal one another only where the supply and demand curves cross, at point *e*. Alternatively, you can see this in the table that is part of the figure: Quantity demanded and quantity supplied are the same at only one particular point. At $60 per game, sellers are willing to provide exactly the same quantity as consumers would like to purchase. Hence, at this price, the market clears, since buyers and sellers both want to transact the same number of units.

The beauty of a market is that it automatically works to establish the equilibrium price and quantity, without any guidance from anyone. To see how this happens, let us assume that computer games are initially priced at $80, a price above their equilibrium price. As we can see by comparing points *a* and *b*, sellers are willing to supply more games at this price than consumers are willing to buy. Economists characterize such a situation as one of excess supply, or **surplus.** In this case, at $80, sellers supply 40 games to the market (point *b*), yet buyers want to purchase only 20 (point *a*). This leaves an excess of 20 games overhanging the market; these unsold games ultimately become surplus inventories.

surplus Occurs when the price is above market equilibrium, and quantity supplied exceeds quantity demanded.

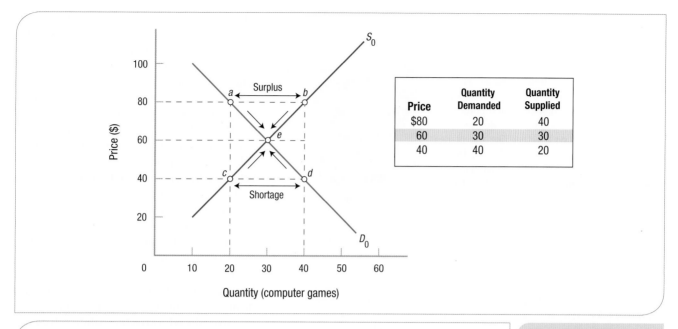

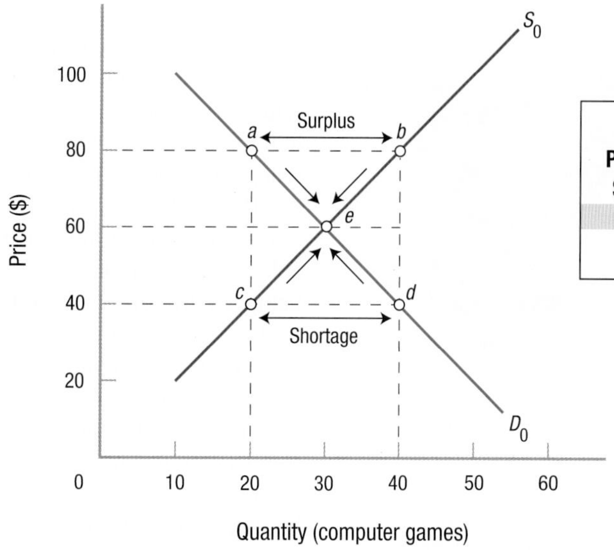

Price	Quantity Demanded	Quantity Supplied
$80	20	40
60	30	30
40	40	20

FIGURE 9

Equilibrium Price and Quantity of Computer Games

Market equilibrium is achieved when quantity demanded and quantity supplied are equal. In this graph, that equilibrium occurs at point *e*, at an equilibrium price of $60 and an equilibrium output of 30. If the market price is above equilibrium ($80), a surplus of 20 computer games will result (*b* – *a*), and market forces would drive the price back down to $60. When the market price is too low ($40), a shortage of 20 computer games will result (*d* – *c*), and businesses will raise the offering prices until equilibrium is again restored.

Here is where the market kicks in to restore equilibrium. As inventories rise, most firms cut production. Some firms, moreover, start reducing their prices to increase sales. Other firms must then cut their own prices to remain competitive. This process continues, with firms cutting their prices and production, until most firms have managed to exhaust their surplus inventories. This happens when prices reach $60 and quantity supplied equals 30, because consumers are once again willing to buy up the entire quantity supplied at this price, and the market is restored to equilibrium.

In general, therefore, when prices are set too high, surpluses result, which drive prices back down to their equilibrium levels. If, conversely, a price is initially set too low, say at $40, a **shortage** results. In this case, buyers want to purchase 40 games (point *d*), but sellers are only providing 20 (point *c*), creating a shortage of 20 games. Because consumers are willing to pay more than $40 to obtain the few games available on the market, they will start bidding up the price of computer games. Sensing an opportunity to make some money, firms will start raising their prices and increasing production once again until equilibrium is restored. Hence, in general, excess demand causes firms to raise prices and increase production.

shortage Occurs when the price is below market equilibrium, and quantity demanded exceeds quantity supplied.

When there is a shortage in a market, economists speak of a tight market or a seller's market. Under these conditions, producers have no difficulty selling off all their output. When a surplus of goods floods the market, this gives rise to a buyer's market, because buyers can buy all the goods they want at attractive prices.

We have now seen how changing prices naturally works to clear up shortages and surpluses, thereby returning markets to equilibrium. Some markets, once disturbed, will return to equilibrium quickly. Examples include the stock, bond, and money markets, where trading is nearly instantaneous and extensive information abounds. Other markets react very slowly. Consider the labor market, for instance. When workers lose their jobs due to a plant closing, most will search for new jobs that pay at least as much as that at their previous jobs. Some

ALFRED MARSHALL (1842–1924)

British economist Alfred Marshall is considered the father of the modern theory of supply and demand—that price and output are determined by both supply *and* demand. He noted that the two go together like the blades of a scissors that cross at equilibrium. He assumed that changes in quantity demanded were only affected by changes in price, and that all other factors remained constant. Marshall also is credited with developing the ideas of the laws of demand and supply, and the concepts of consumer surplus and producer surplus—concepts we will study in the next chapter.

With financial help from this uncle, Marshall attended St. John's College, Cambridge, to study mathematics and physics. However after long walks through the poorest sections of several European cities and seeing their horrible conditions, he decided to focus his attention on political economy.

In 1890, he published *Principles of Economics.* In it he introduced many new ideas, though he would never boast about them as being novel. In hopes of appealing to the general public, Marshall buried his diagrams in footnotes. And, although he is credited with many economic theories, he would always clarify them with various exceptions and qualifications. He expected future economists to flesh out his ideas.

Above all, Marshall loved teaching and his students. His lectures were known to never be orderly or systematic because he tried to get students to think *with* him and ultimately think for themselves. At one point near the turn of the twentieth century, essentially all of the leading economists in England had been his students. More than anyone else, Marshall is given credit for establishing economics as a discipline of study. He died in 1924.

Sources: E. Ray Canterbery *A Brief History of Economics: Artful Approaches to the Dismal Science* (Hackensack, New Jersey: World Scientific), 2001; Robert Skidelsky, *John Maynard Keynes: Volume 2, The Economist as Saviour 1920–1937* (New York: Penguin Press), 1992; and John Maynard Keynes, *Essays in Biography* (New York: Norton), 1951.

will be successful, while others might struggle, having to settle for a lower paying position after a long job search. Similarly, real estate markets can be slow to adjust because sellers will often refuse to accept a price below what they are asking, until the lack of sales over time convinces sellers to adjust the price downward.

These automatic market adjustments can make some buyers and sellers feel uncomfortable: It seems as if prices and quantities are being set by forces beyond anyone's control. In fact, this phenomenon is precisely what makes market economies function so efficiently. Without anyone needing to be in control, prices and quantities naturally gravitate toward equilibrium levels. Adam Smith was so impressed by the workings of the market that he suggested that it is almost as if an "invisible hand" guides the market to equilibrium.

Given the self-correcting nature of the market, long-term shortages or surpluses are almost always the result of government intervention, as we will see in the next chapter. First, however, we turn to a discussion of how the market responds to changes in supply and demand, or to shifts of the supply and demand curves.

Moving to a New Equilibrium: Changes in Supply and Demand

Once a market is in equilibrium and the forces of supply and demand balance one another out, the market will remain there unless an external factor changes. But when the supply curve or demand curve shifts (some determinant changes), equilibrium also shifts, resulting in a new equilibrium price and/or output. The ability to predict new equilibrium points is one of the most useful aspects of supply and demand analysis.

Predicting the New Equilibrium When One Curve Shifts When only supply or only demand changes, the change in equilibrium price and equilibrium output can be predicted. We begin with changes in supply.

Changes in Supply Figure 10 shows what happens when supply changes. Equilibrium initially is at point *e,* with equilibrium price and quantity at \$9 and 30, respectively. But let us assume that a rise in wages or the bankruptcy of a key business in the market (the number of sellers falls) causes a decrease in supply. When supply declines (the supply curve shifts from S_0 to S_2), equilibrium price rises to \$12, while equilibrium output falls to 20 (point *a*).

If, on the other hand, supply increases (the supply curve shifts from S_0 to S_1), equilibrium price falls to \$6, while equilibrium output rises to 40 (point *b*). This is what has happened in the electronics industry: Falling production costs have resulted in more electronic products being sold at lower prices.

We can predict how equilibrium price and quantity will change when supply changes. When supply increases, equilibrium price will fall and output will rise; when supply decreases, equilibrium price will rise and output will fall.

Changes in Demand The effects of demand changes are shown in Figure 11. Again, equilibrium is initially at point *e,* with equilibrium price and quantity at \$9 and 30, respectively. But let us assume that the economy then enters a recession and incomes

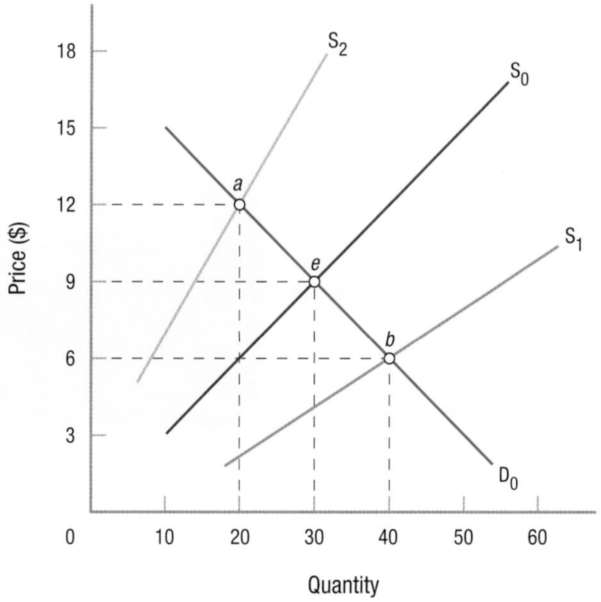

FIGURE 10

Equilibrium Price, Output, and Shifts in Supply

When supply alone shifts, the effects on both equilibrium price and output can be predicted. When supply grows (S_0 to S_1), equilibrium price will fall and output will rise. When supply declines (S_0 to S_2), the opposite happens: Equilibrium price will rise and output will fall.

sink, or perhaps the price of some complementary good soars; in either case, demand falls. As demand decreases (the demand curve shifts from D_0 to D_2), equilibrium price falls to \$6, while equilibrium output falls to 20 (point *a*).

During the same recession just described, the demand for inferior goods (beans and bologna) will rise, as falling incomes force people to switch to less expensive substitutes. For these products, as demand increases (shifting the demand curve from D_0 to D_1), equilibrium price rises to \$12, and equilibrium output grows to 40 (point *b*).

Like changes in supply, we can predict how equilibrium price and quantity will change when demand changes. When demand increases, both equilibrium price and output will rise; when demand decreases, both equilibrium price and output will fall.

Sergey Kashkin/iStockphoto

Truffles, a mushroom-like delicacy, can easily fetch over a \$1,000 per pound, due to their scarce supply. Truffles grow in the wild and generally are found using trained dogs. But along with limited supply, demand for truffles has increased among foodies, putting upward pressure on their prices.

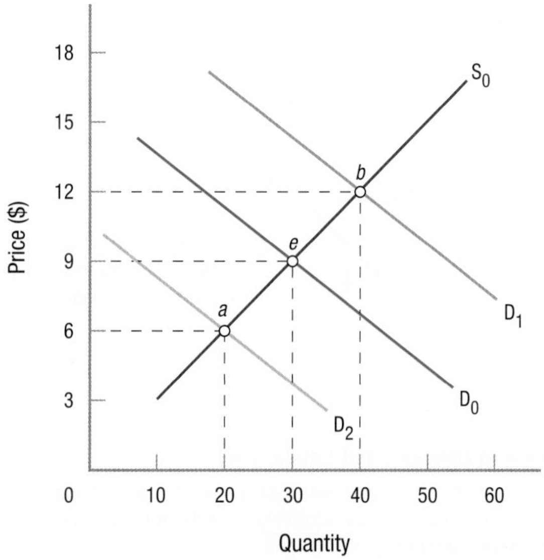

FIGURE 11

Equilibrium Price, Output, and Shifts in Demand

When demand alone changes, the effects on both equilibrium price and output can again be determined. When demand grows (D_0 to D_1), both price and output rise. Conversely, when demand falls (D_0 to D_2), both price and output fall.

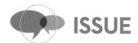

ISSUE

Two-Buck Chuck: Will People Drink $2-a-Bottle Wine?

The great California wines of the 1990s put California vineyards on the map. Demand, prices, and exports grew rapidly. Overplanting of new grapevines was a result. When driving along Interstate 5 or Highway 101 north of Los Angeles, one can see vineyards extending for miles, and most were planted in the mid- to late 1990s. The 2001 recession reduced the demand for California wine, and a rising dollar made imported wine relatively cheaper. The result was a sharp drop in demand for California wine and a huge surplus of grapes.

Bronco Wine Company president Fred Franzia made an exclusive deal with Trader Joe's, an unusual supermarket that features exotic food and wine products. He bought the excess grapes at distressed prices, and in his company's modern plant produced inexpensive wines—chardonnay, merlot, cabernet sauvignon, shiraz, and sauvignon blanc—under the Charles Shaw label. Consumers flocked to Trader Joe's for wine costing $1.99 a bottle and literally hauled cases of wine out by the carload. In less than a decade, 400 million bottles of Two-Buck Chuck, as it is known, have been sold. This is not rotgut: The 2002 shiraz beat out 2,300 other wines to win a double gold medal at the 28th Annual International Eastern Wine Competition in 2004. Still, to many Napa Valley vintners it is known as Two-Buck Upchuck.

Two-Buck Chuck was such a hit that other supermarkets were forced to offer their own discount wines. This good, low-priced wine has had the effect of opening up markets. People who previously avoided wine because of the cost have begun

joel zatz/Alamy

drinking more. However, the influence of Two-Buck Chuck, which sold 60 million bottles in 2012, may be waning. In January 2013, Trader Joe's announced an increase in the price of the Two-Buck Chuck from $1.99 to $2.49 due to a poor grape harvest that raised the cost of producing the wine. Although the new price is still a bargain, the product that changed the wine industry may soon need another name.

Predicting the New Equilibrium When Both Curves Shift When both supply and demand change, things get tricky. We can predict what will happen with price in some cases and output in other cases, but not what will happen with both.

Figure 12 portrays an increase in both demand and supply. Consider the market for corn. Suppose that an increase in corn-based ethanol production causes demand for corn

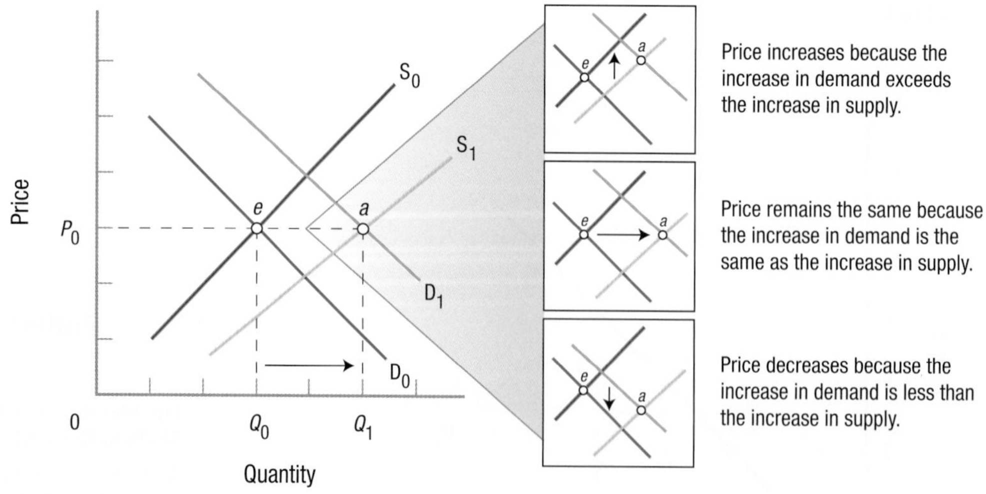

Price
P_0
0
Q_0
Q_1
Quantity
S_0
S_1
D_1
D_0
e
a
Price increases because the increase in demand exceeds the increase in supply.
Price remains the same because the increase in demand is the same as the increase in supply.
Price decreases because the increase in demand is less than the increase in supply.

FIGURE 12

Increase in Supply, Increase in Demand, and Equilibrium

When both demand and supply increase, output will clearly rise, but what happens to the new equilibrium price is uncertain. If demand grows relatively more than supply, price will rise, but if supply grows relatively more than demand, price will fall.

The Effect of Changes in Demand or Supply on Equilibrium Prices and Quantities **TABLE 1**

	Change in Demand	Change in Supply	Change in Equilibrium Price	Change in Equilibrium Quantity
One Curve Shifting	No change	Increase	Decrease	Increase
	No change	Decrease	Increase	Decrease
	Increase	No change	Increase	Increase
	Decrease	No change	Decrease	Decrease
Both Curves Shifting	Increase	Increase	Indeterminate	Increase
	Decrease	Decrease	Indeterminate	Decrease
	Increase	Decrease	Increase	Indeterminate
	Decrease	Increase	Decrease	Indeterminate

to increase. Meanwhile, suppose that bioengineering results in a new corn hybrid that uses less fertilizer and generates 50% higher yields, causing supply to also increase. When demand increases from D_0 to D_1 and supply increases from S_0 to S_1, output grows to Q_1 as shown in the left panel.

But what happens to the price of corn is not so clear. If demand and supply grow the same, output increases but price remains at P_0 (also captured in the middle panel to the right). If demand grows relatively more than supply, the new equilibrium price will be higher (top panel on the right). Conversely, if demand grows relatively less than supply, the new equilibrium price will be lower (bottom panel on the right). Figure 12 is just one of the four possibilities when both supply and demand change. The other three possibilities are shown in Table 1 along with the four possibilities when just one curve shifts. When only one curve shifts, the direction of change in equilibrium price and quantity is certain. But when both curves shift, the direction of change in either the equilibrium price or quantity will be indeterminate.

CHECKPOINT

MARKET EQUILIBRIUM

- Together, supply and demand determine market equilibrium, which occurs when the quantity supplied exactly equals quantity demanded.
- The equilibrium price is also called the market-clearing price.
- When quantity demanded exceeds quantity supplied, a shortage occurs and prices are bid up toward equilibrium. When quantity supplied exceeds quantity demanded, a surplus occurs and prices are pushed down toward equilibrium.
- When supply and demand change, equilibrium price and output change.
- When only one curve shifts, the resulting changes in equilibrium price and quantity can be predicted.
- When both curves shift, we can predict the change in equilibrium price in some cases or the change in equilibrium quantity in others, but never both. We have to determine the relative magnitudes of the shifts before we can predict both equilibrium price and quantity.

QUESTIONS: As China and India (both with huge populations and rapidly growing economies) continue to develop, what do you think will happen to their demand for energy, and specifically oil? What will suppliers of oil do in the face of this demand? Will this have an impact on world energy (oil) prices? What sort of policies or events could alter your forecast about the future price of oil?

Answers to the Checkpoint questions can be found at the end of this chapter.

chapter summary

Section 1: Markets

A **market** is an institution that enables buyers and sellers to interact and transact with one another.

Corbis/SuperStock

Stars and Stripes/Alamy

Markets can be as simple as a lemonade stand, as large as an automobile lot, as valuable as the stock market, as virtual as an Internet shopping site, or as illegal as a ticket scalping operation.

Buyers and sellers communicate their desires in a market through the prices at which goods and services are bought and sold. Hence, a market economy is called a **price system.**

Robert Harding World Imagery/Corbis

Section 2: Demand

Demand refers to the goods and services people are willing and able to buy during a period of time. It is a horizontal summation of individual demand curves in a defined market.

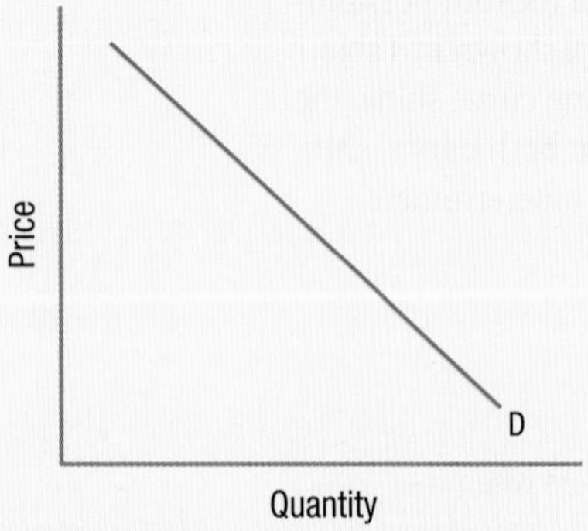

The **law of demand** states that as prices increase, quantity demanded falls, and vice versa, resulting in downward-sloping demand.

A Common Confusion in Terminology:

A "change in demand" is a shift of the entire demand curve and is caused by a change in a nonprice demand factor.

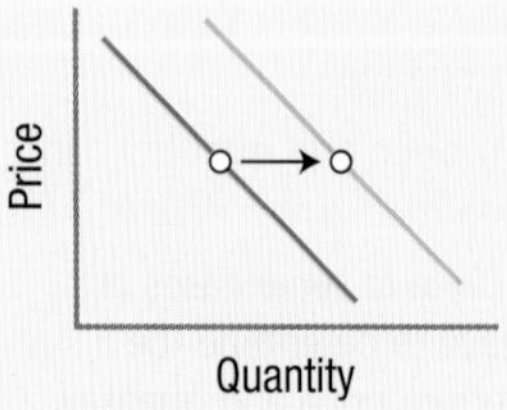

A "change in quantity demanded" is a movement from one point to another on the same demand curve, and is caused only by a change in price.

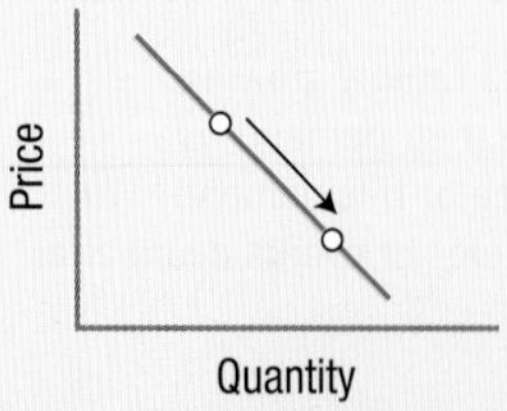

Alan Schein Photography/Corbis

Roller coasters are a lot of fun, but riding the same one over and over gives less satisfaction with each ride; therefore, willingness-to-pay falls with each ride.

Determinants of Demand: How Demand Curves Shift

- ↑ Tastes and preferences: Demand shifts right.
- ↑ Income: Demand for normal goods shifts right, while demand for inferior goods shifts left.
- ↑ Price of substitutes: Demand shifts right.
- ↑ Price of complements: Demand shifts left.
- ↑ Number of buyers: Demand shifts right.
- ↑ Price expectations: Demand shifts right.

Bryan Smith/ZUMA Press/Newscom

When investors expect stock prices to increase, demand for stock increases.

Section 3: **Supply**

Supply analysis works the same way as demand, but looking at the market from the firm's point of view.

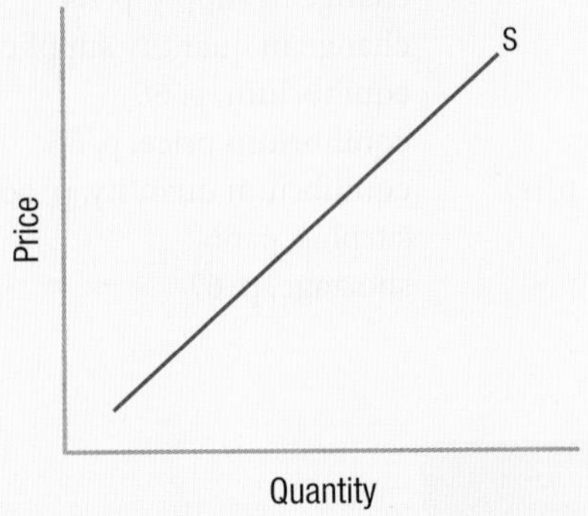

The **law of supply** states that as prices increase, firms want to supply more, and vice versa. It leads to an upward-sloping supply curve.

Philip Gostelow/Aurora Photos/Corbis

Determinants of Supply: How Supply Curves Shift

- ↑ Production technology: Supply shifts right.
- ↑ Cost of resources: Supply shifts left.
- ↑ Price of other commodities: Supply shifts left.
- ↑ Price expectations: Supply shifts left.
- ↑ Number of sellers: Supply shifts right.
- ↑ Taxes: Supply shifts left.
- ↑ Subsidies: Supply shifts right.

Section 4: **Market Equilibrium**

Market equilibrium occurs at the price at which the quantity supplied is equal to quantity demanded; in other words, where demand intersects supply.

How does equilibrium change?

Which curve slopes up and which slopes down? Two tricks to aid in memory:

- S"up"ply contains the word "up" for upward-sloping.
- Only the fingers on your right hand can make a "d" for demand. Hold that hand up in front of you!

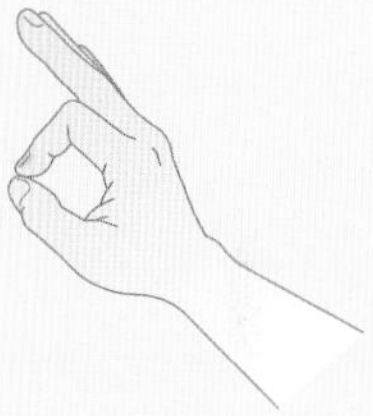

A shift in demand or supply will change equilibrium price and quantity.

Neil Emmerson/Robert Harding World Imagery/Corbis

Higher oil prices raise the cost of resins used to produce surfboards.

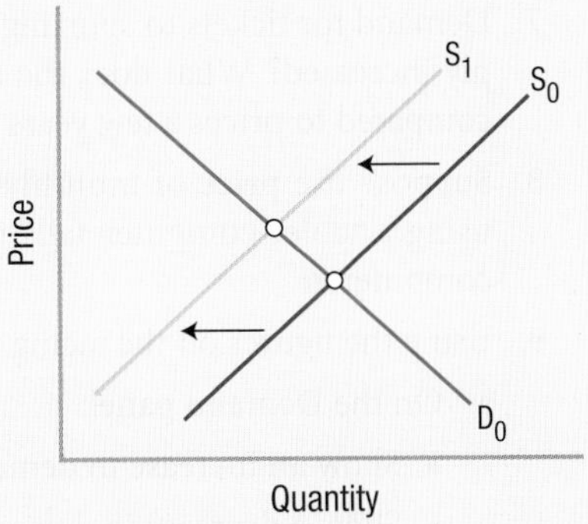

Supply of surfboards shifts left, raising equilibrium price and lowering equilibrium quantity.

Summary of Demand and Supply Shifts on Equilibrium Price and Quantity:

D shifts right:	P↑	Q↑
D shifts left:	P↓	Q↓
S shifts right:	P↓	Q↑
S shifts left:	P↑	Q↓

KEY CONCEPTS

markets, p. 52
price system, p. 54
willingness-to-pay, p. 55
demand, p. 56
law of demand, p. 56
demand curve, p. 57
demand schedule, p. 57
horizontal summation, p. 58
determinants of demand, p. 58
normal good, p. 58
inferior good, p. 59
substitute goods, p. 59
complementary goods, p. 59
change in demand, p. 60
change in quantity demanded, p. 60
supply, p. 61
law of supply, p. 62
supply curve, p. 62
determinants of supply, p. 62
change in supply, p. 64
change in quantity supplied, p. 64
equilibrium, p. 66
equilibrium price, p. 66
equilibrium quantity, p. 66
surplus, p. 66
shortage, p. 67

QUESTIONS AND PROBLEMS

Check Your Understanding

1. Product prices give consumers and businesses a lot of information besides just the price. What kinds of information?
2. Describe the determinants of demand. Why are they important?
3. As the world population ages, will the demand for cholesterol drugs increase, decrease, or remain the same? Assume there is a positive relationship between aging and cholesterol levels. Would this cause a change in demand or a change in quantity demanded?
4. Describe some of the reasons why supply changes. Improved technology typically results in lower prices for most products. Why do you think this is true? Describe the difference between a change in supply and a change in quantity supplied.
5. If a strong economic recovery boosts average incomes, what would happen to the equilibrium price and quantity for a normal good? How about an inferior good?
6. Suppose the market for tomatoes is in equilibrium, and events occur that simultaneously shift both the demand and supply curves to the right. Is it possible to determine how the equilibrium price and/or quantity would change?

Apply the Concepts

7. Demand for tickets to sporting events such as the Super Bowl has increased. Has supply increased? What does the answer to this tell you about the price of these tickets compared to prices a few years ago?
8. Suppose the price of monthly data plans required to access the Internet anywhere using a tablet computer falls in price. How would this affect the market for tablet computers?
9. Using the figures on the facing page, answer the following questions:
   a. On the Demand panel:
      - Show an increase in demand and label it D_1.
      - Show a decrease in demand and label it D_2.
      - Show an increase in quantity demanded.

- Show a decrease in quantity demanded.
- What causes demand to change?
- What causes quantity demanded to change?

b. On the Supply panel:

- Show an increase in supply and label it S_1.
- Show a decrease in supply and label it S_2.
- Show an increase in quantity supplied.
- Show a decrease in quantity supplied.
- What causes supply to change?
- What causes quantity supplied to change?

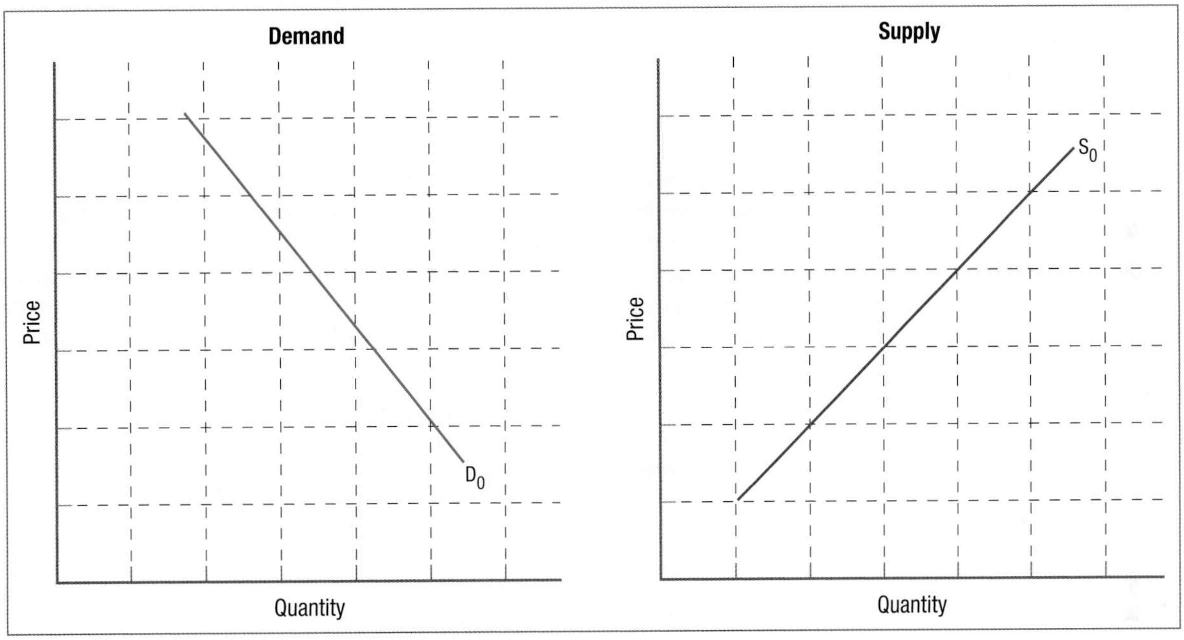

10. Several medical studies have shown that drinking red wine in moderation is good for the heart. How would such a study affect the public's demand for wine? Would it have an impact on the type of grapes planted in new vineyards?
11. Assume initially that the demand and supply for premium coffees (one-pound bags) are in equilibrium. Now assume Starbucks introduces the world to premium blends, and so demand rises substantially. Describe what will happen in this market as it moves to a new equilibrium. If a hard freeze eliminates Brazil's premium coffee crop, what will happen to the price of premium coffee?
12. Over the past decade, cruise ship companies have dramatically increased the number of mega-ships (those that carry 3,000 passengers or more), increasing the supply of cruises. At the same time, the popularity of cruising has increased among consumers, increasing demand. Explain how these two effects can coincide with a decrease in the average price of cruise travel.

In the News

13. In China, a small but increasing number of people are choosing to work as professional queuers, and exactly as it sounds, they are paid to wait in line for others. An NPR story in July 25, 2011, tells the story of a few professional queuers who earn about $3 an hour to wait in line, a wage that is about double that of the typical factory worker in China. Given that one can easily pay someone else to wait, what do you think will happen in the market for goods and services most prone to long waiting times, such as for concert tickets, the latest technology gadget, or low-cost apartments?
14. An August 12, 2011, article in *Time Magazine*, "As Regular Malls Struggle, Outlet Malls Are Booming," analyzed trends in how consumers shop, and found that more and more consumers are visiting outlet malls as a way to save money on name brand clothing and housewares. Given that most stores offer an outlet option, why would anyone choose to pay more at regular malls? Use supply and demand analysis to explain why prices differ between regular stores and outlet stores. Why would outlet stores be a strategic way for businesses to sell their unsold (surplus) goods instead of just offering a sale at their regular stores?

Solving Problems

15. The table below represents the world supply and demand for natural vanilla in thousands of pounds. A large portion of natural vanilla is grown in Madagascar and comes from orchids that require a lot of time to cultivate. The sequence of events described below actually happened, but the numbers have been altered to make the calculations easier. (See James Altucher, "Supply, Demand, and Edible Orchids," *Financial Times*, September 20, 2005, p. 12.) Assume the original supply and demand curves are represented in the table below.

Price ($/pound)	Quantity Demanded (thousands)	Quantity Supplied (thousands)
0	20	0
10	16	6
20	12	12
30	8	18
40	4	24
50	0	30

a. Graph both the supply (S_0) and demand (D_0) curves. What is the current equilibrium price? Label that point *a*.

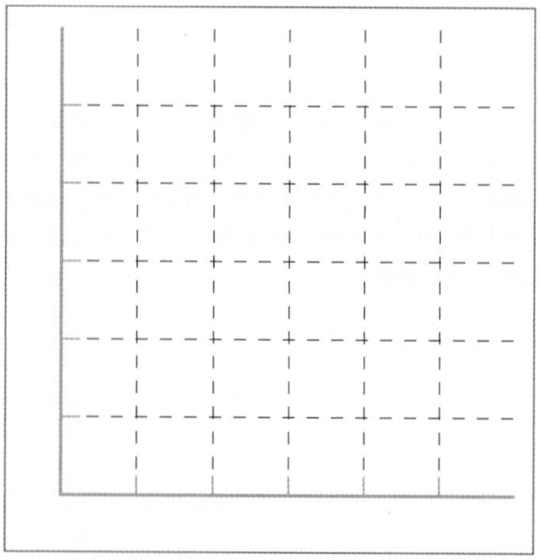

b. Assume that Madagascar is hit by a hurricane (which actually did happen in 2000), and the world's supply of vanilla is reduced by five-sixths, or 83%. Label the new supply curve (S_1). What will be the new equilibrium price in the market? Label that point *b*.

c. Now assume that Coca-Cola announces plans to introduce a new "Vanilla Coke," and this increases the demand for natural vanilla by 25%. Label the new demand curve (D_1). What will be the new equilibrium price? Label this new equilibrium point *c*. Remember that the supply of natural vanilla was reduced by the hurricane earlier.

d. Growing the orchids that produce natural vanilla requires a climate with roughly 80% humidity, and the possible grower countries generally fall within 20° north or south of the equator. A doubling of prices encouraged several other countries (e.g., Uganda and Indonesia) to begin growing orchids or increase their current production. Within several years, supply was back to normal (S_0), but by then, synthetic vanilla had replaced 80% of the original demand (D_0). Label this new demand curve (D_2). What is the new equilibrium price and output?

16. The following figure shows the supply and demand for strawberries. Answer the questions that follow.

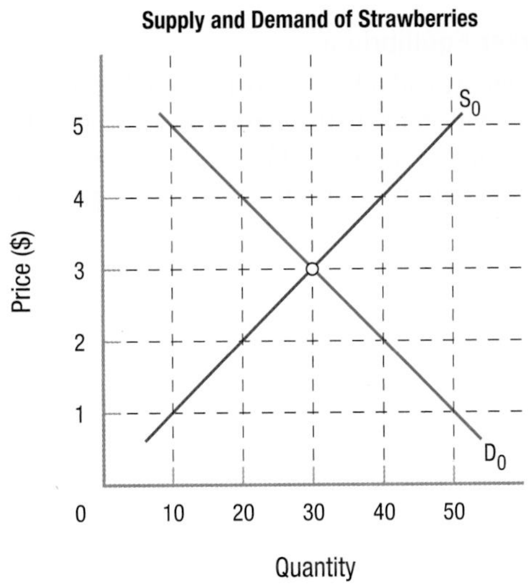

a. Indicate the equilibrium price and equilibrium quantity.

b. Suppose sellers try to sell strawberries at $4. How much of a shortage or a surplus of strawberries would result?

c. Now suppose that the demand for strawberries falls by ten units at every price. Draw the new demand curve in the figure, and estimate what the new equilibrium price and equilibrium quantity would be.

d. If sellers still try to sell strawberries at $4, would the shortage or the surplus increase or decrease?

USING THE NUMBERS

17. According to By the Numbers, about how many times larger is the bottled water market in the United States in the year 2012 compared to 1982?

18. According to By the Numbers, which of the following categories of college/university enrollment have risen from 1996 to 2012: public two year, public four year, private not-for-profit, private for-profit? Which of these categories have fallen in enrollment from 1996 to 2012?

ANSWERS TO QUESTIONS IN CHECKPOINTS

Checkpoint: Markets

The market for financial securities is a huge, well-organized, and regulated market compared to local farmer's markets. Trillions of dollars change hands each week in the financial markets, and products are standardized.

Checkpoint: Demand

Rising gasoline prices, a general rise in environmental consciousness, and incentives (such as preferred parking and reduced tolls offered by some states) have caused the demand for plug-in hybrids to swell. This is a change in demand, because factors other than the price of the car itself have led to an increase in demand for such cars.

Checkpoint: Supply

A higher textbook buyback price would entice more students to sell their textbooks instead of keeping them. Because the price of the offer has increased, it results in an increase in the quantity supplied of used textbooks. If, however, many students are forced to retake a class, they would likely not sell their textbooks, hence the supply of used textbooks would shift to the left.

Checkpoint: Market Equilibrium

Demand for both energy and oil will increase. Suppliers of oil will attempt to move up their supply curve and provide more to the market. Because all of the easy (cheap) oil has already been found, costs to add to supplies will rise, and oil prices will gradually rise; in the longer term, alternatives will become more attractive, keeping oil prices from rising too rapidly.

4 Markets and Government

Hamachi, Unagi, Ikura, Maguro, Toro. . . . Fish from an ocean halfway around the world to a dinner plate in a rural inland town highlights the ability of efficient markets to provide what consumers want.

After studying this chapter you should be able to:

- Define the concepts of consumer surplus and producer surplus and explain how they are used to measure the benefits and costs of market transactions.
- Use consumer surplus and producer surplus to describe the gains from trade.
- Explain the causes of deadweight loss and how markets can mitigate them.
- Understand why markets sometimes fail to provide an optimal outcome.
- Describe what an effective price ceiling or price floor does to a market and how it creates shortages or surpluses.
- Determine the winners and losers when price ceilings and price floors are used.

Once an exotic food from the orient eaten by few outside Asia, sushi has become part of the American diet in all parts of the country, available in sushi bars, cafés, buffets, and even grocery stores. The popularity of sushi stems largely from the known health benefits of eating fish, providing omega-3-rich, low-fat, and low-calorie meals. But to have sushi, one must have access to fresh fish, not easy for those not living near a coastline. Or is it?

To provide fresh sushi to inland consumers, fish must be caught, flash frozen (to kill bacteria), then flown to destinations in a short period of time in order to maintain the fish's freshness. In some cases, fish is flown around the world to meet the demand. At the Tsukiji fish market in Tokyo, Japan, the largest fish market in the world, over 6 million pounds of fish are auctioned off *each morning* and then flown to wholesalers and restaurants around the globe.

Why would fishermen, fish markets, wholesalers, and restaurants go through so much trouble just to provide fresh sushi to customers in faraway places whom they will never meet? Because the market provides incentives for each person to do so. Every person in the supply chain for sushi acts in his or her own best interest by supplying what the market wants (as determined by the prices received for their goods), and that leads to an efficiently functioning market. Adam Smith's notion of the *invisible hand* works to ensure that, in a market society, consumers get what they want.

Everywhere we look in the world there are markets, and not just the big markets for fish or other major industries. Countless smaller markets dot our local landscapes, and many new virtual markets are springing up on the Internet. All play a similar role in terms of providing what consumers want, using prices as a way to signal the values placed on goods and services.

The previous chapter considered how supply and demand work together to determine the quantities of various products sold and the equilibrium prices consumers must pay for them in a market economy. The markets we have studied thus far have been stylized versions of competitive markets: They have featured many buyers and sellers, a uniform product, consumers and sellers who have complete information about the market, and few barriers to market entry or exit.

In this chapter, we start with this stylized competitive market and introduce tools for measuring the efficiency of competitive markets. We then apply these tools to reveal the gains from trade. We briefly consider some of the complexities inherent to most markets. The typical market does not meet all the criteria of a truly competitive market. That does not mean that the supply and demand analysis you just absorbed will not be useful in analyzing

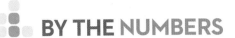

BY THE NUMBERS

Price Controls and Supports in the Economy Today

Efficient markets are an essential part of modern societies. However, sometimes governments intervene in markets to address equity concerns. The use of price controls and price supports is a common way of intervening in markets, as the following illustrates.

Average difference between rent-controlled housing prices and market prices:

1. New York City—43%
2. San Francisco—41%
3. Washington, D.C.—30%
4. Los Angeles—26%

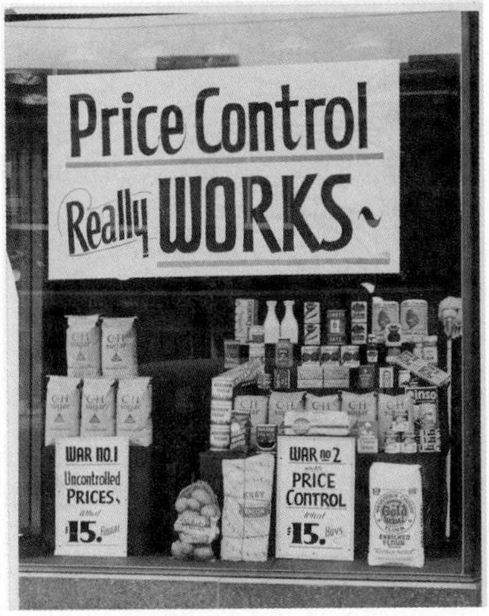

World War II price controls.

States receiving the most federal telephone support in 2011:

1. Alaska: $280 million
2. Oklahoma: $235 million
3. Mississippi: $232 million
4. Louisiana: $152 million
5. Kansas: $142 million

States paying the most federal telephone support in 2011:

1. California: $326 million
2. Florida: $290 million
3. New York: $230 million
4. New Jersey: $175 million
5. Pennsylvania: $169 million

Prices for telephone landlines in rural communities are capped below their cost, with the shortfall in revenues compensated for by a government program funded by all U.S. states, resulting in some states paying more than they receive in support and some states receiving more than they pay.

$7.25

The U.S. federal minimum wage (price floor) for workers over age 16 in 2013.

$11,176,000,000

Spending by the U.S. government in 2012 to maintain agricultural price floors.

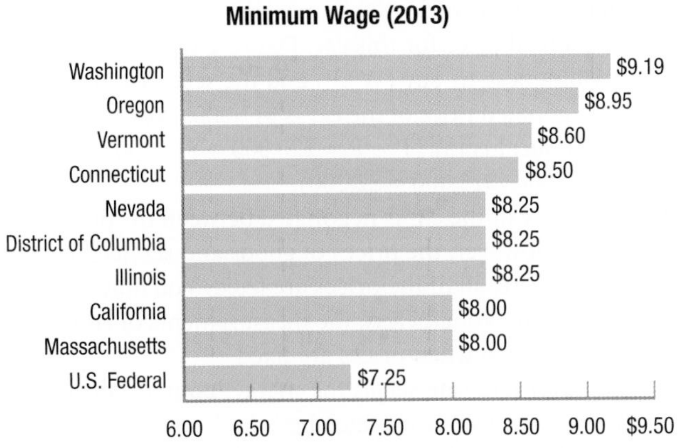

Nine U.S. states have a statewide minimum wage of $8.00 per hour or more, significantly higher than the federal minimum wage of $7.25 per hour.

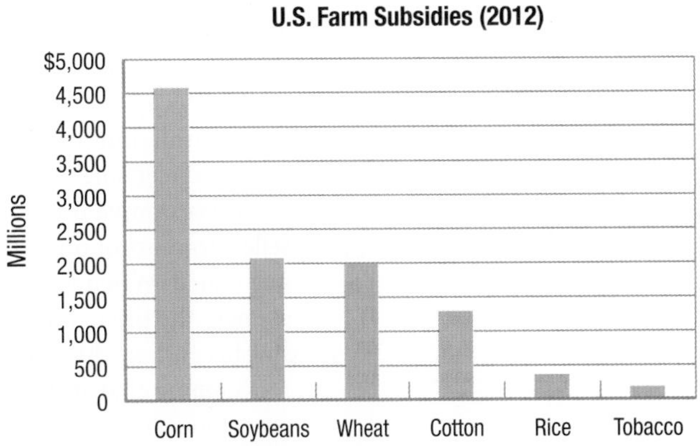

Certain agricultural crops are protected by price supports (price floors), with the difference from their market prices paid by the U.S. government.

economic events. Often, however, you will need to temper your analysis to fit the specific conditions of the markets you study. Finally, we will look at what happens when government intervenes in markets.

Consumer and Producer Surplus: A Tool for Measuring Economic Efficiency

Suppose you find a rare comic book on eBay that you believe is worth $100, and start putting in bids hoping to buy it. After a week, you get the comic book with the winning bid of $80. You are happy because not only will you get the comic book you've been looking for, but you have paid a price lower than what you were willing to pay. However, you're likely not the only one who is happy. The person who sold you that comic book found it in her granddad's old trunk that she inherited, and had hoped to get at least $60 for it. In fact she ended up receiving more money than the minimum amount she had hoped to receive. In this situation, the transaction took place, and both the buyer and seller are better off.

When consumers go about their everyday shopping or when they seek out their next major purchase, their objective typically is to find the lowest price relative to the perceived value of the product. It is the reason why consumers compare prices, shop online, or bargain with sellers. In other words, the general goal of consumers is to find the product at a price no greater than their willingness-to-pay (perceived value); if the price is less, consumers benefit more. These "savings," so to speak, are referred to as **consumer surplus,** and are a measure of the net benefits consumers receive in the market.

consumer surplus The difference between market price and what consumers (as individuals or the market) would be willing to pay. It is equal to the area above market price and below the demand curve.

Producers also have a corresponding objective. When an entrepreneur opens up a new business, her intention is to maximize its success by getting the highest price for a product relative to its cost for as large a quantity as possible. Sometimes this is achieved by selling fewer units at a higher markup (such as rare art), while other times it is achieved through the sale of mass quantities of products at relatively small markups (such as goods sold at Walmart). Regardless of the strategy used, the general goal of producers is to obtain a price at least equal to their willingness-to-sell; if the price is higher, producers benefit more. These gains are called **producer surplus,** and are a measure of the net benefits producers receive in the market.

producer surplus The difference between market price and the price at which firms are willing to supply the product. It is equal to the area below market price and above the supply curve.

Now that you have an intuitive sense of what consumer and producer surplus are, let's look more carefully into how they are measured. We begin with a single case of a buyer and a seller at a car dealership. Suppose you are the buyer, and you find a car that interests you. Let's assume that the most you would be willing to pay for that car is $20,000. In other words, you find the car to be worth $20,000, but paying that price would be the worst case scenario other than not buying the car at all. You would rather get a better deal by negotiating with the sales manager. But now let's look at the other side: Assume that the sales manager has a minimum price of $15,000 at which he is willing to sell the car. Selling the car at this price would be his worst case scenario other than not selling the car.

We have now determined a potential "gain" of $5,000 that can be shared by the buyer and seller depending on the final negotiated price for this car. Figure 1 shows this gain as the difference between the buyer's willingness-to-pay (WTP) and the seller's willingness-to-sell (WTS). Assume that the final negotiated price of the car is $17,200. We can now use this information to calculate consumer surplus (WTP – P = $20,000 – $17,200 = $2,800) and producer surplus (P – WTS = $17,200 – $15,000 = $2,200).

This example is unique in that the price of the car is negotiated between the buyer and seller. In most of our daily transactions, however, the prices of goods and services are not negotiated. When you go to the grocery store, all of the prices are fixed. You don't negotiate over the price of milk, bread, or chicken. Nonetheless, the measurements of consumer surplus and producer surplus remain the same when prices are fixed.

Suppose that instead of just one buyer and one seller, the market contains dozens or even thousands of buyers and sellers. What would change? Let's look at the market for Frisbees used in the popular intramural sport of Ultimate. First, each of the many buyers would have a different WTP, which would be represented as a downward-sloping demand curve (by definition, demand is just a collection of WTP of all consumers in a market).

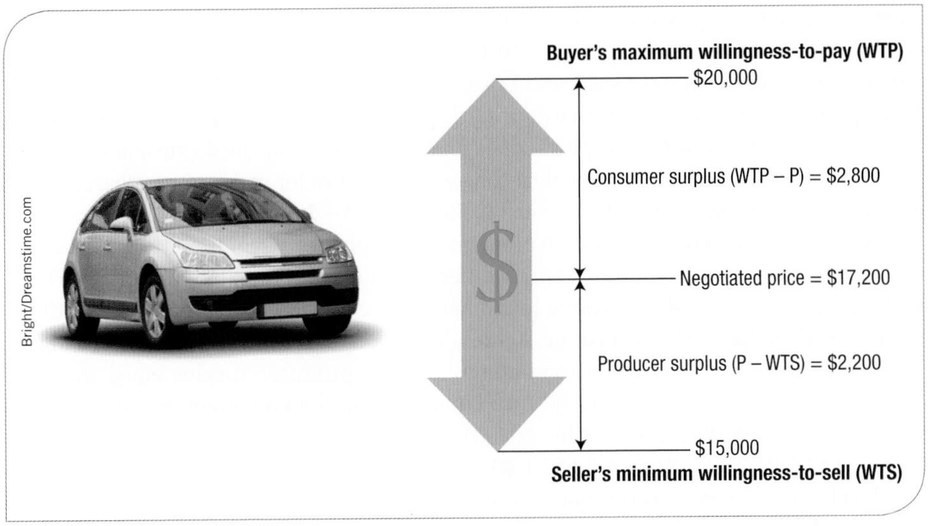

FIGURE 1

Willingness-to-Pay and Willingness-to-Sell

In a transaction with a single buyer and a single seller, consumer surplus ($2,800) is the difference between the maximum amount the buyer was willing to pay ($20,000) and the actual price paid ($17,200). Producer surplus ($2,200) is the difference between the actual price ($17,200) and the minimum amount the seller was willing to accept ($15,000).

Second, each of the many sellers would have a different WTS, which would be represented as an upward-sloping supply curve. But the definition of consumer surplus (WTP – P) and producer surplus (P – WTS) remains the same, except that now we apply it to the entire market. Figure 2 illustrates how consumer and producer surplus is determined in a small market for Frisbees with specific consumers and firms and for the overall market.

Panel A in Figure 2 represents a small market with 6 individual buyers and 6 individual sellers, with an equilibrium price of $6 (point *e*) at which 6 units of output are sold. In this market, Alanna has the highest willingness to pay, because she values a Frisbee to be worth $11. Because the market determines that $6 is the price everyone pays, Alanna clearly gets a

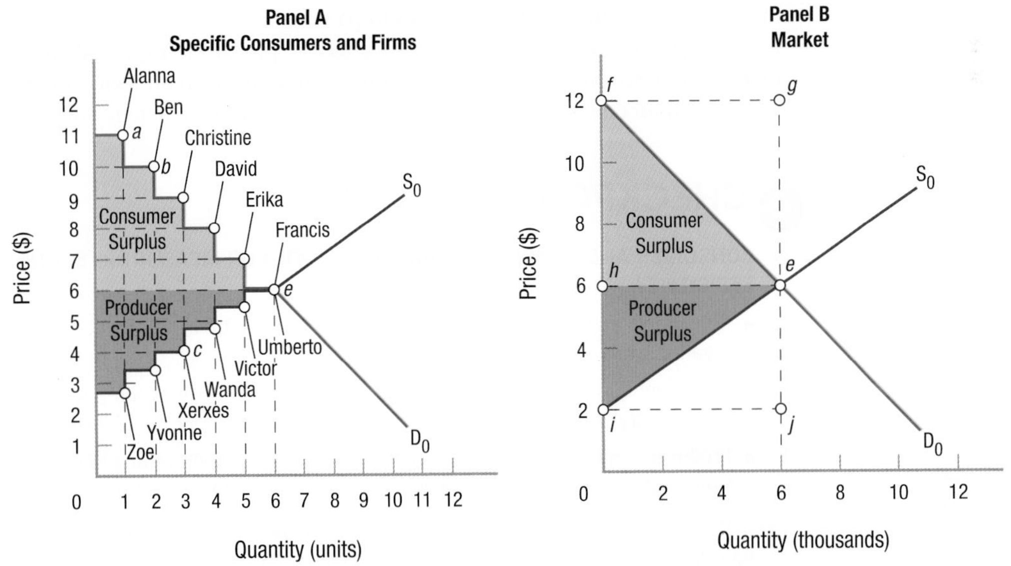

FIGURE 2

Consumer and Producer Surplus

Panel B shows a market consisting of many more of the specific consumers and firms shown in panel A. This market determines equilibrium price to be $6 (point *e*), and total sales for the market is 6,000 units. Consumer surplus is equal to the area under the demand curve but above the equilibrium price of $6. Producer surplus is the area under the equilibrium price but above the supply curve.

bargain by purchasing the unit and receiving a consumer surplus equal to \$5 (\$11 – \$6). Ben, however, values a Frisbee a little less at \$10, but still receives a consumer surplus of \$4 (\$10 – \$6). And so on for Christine, David, and Erika, who receive a consumer surplus of \$3, \$2, and \$1, respectively. Only Francis, who values a Frisbee to be worth exactly the same amount as the price, earns no consumer surplus. Total consumer surplus for the 6 consumers in panel A is found by adding all of the individual consumer surpluses for each unit purchased. Thus, total consumer surplus in panel A is equal to \$5 + \$4 + \$3 + \$2 + \$1 + \$0 = \$15.

In a similar way, assume that each point on the supply curve represents a specific seller, each with a Frisbee to sell but each with a different willingness to sell. Equilibrium price is still \$6, therefore Zoe, who is willing to sell her Frisbee for just \$2.67, receives a producer surplus of \$3.33 (\$6 – \$2.67). Yvonne, Xerxes, Wanda, and Victor, who each have a higher willingness-to-sell, receive a correspondingly smaller producer surplus equal to \$2.67, \$2.00, \$1.33, and \$0.67, respectively. And Umberto, who had a willingness-to-sell of \$6, receives no producer surplus for his sale. Total producer surplus in panel A is equal to \$3.33 + \$2.67 + \$2.00 + \$1.33 + \$0.67 + \$0 = \$10.

Panel B illustrates consumer and producer surplus for an entire market. For convenience we have assumed that the market is 1,000 times larger than that shown in panel A, so the *x* axis is output in thousands. Whereas in panel A we had discrete buyers and sellers, we now have one big market, therefore consumer surplus is equal to the area under the demand curve and above equilibrium price, or the area of the shaded triangle labeled "consumer surplus."

To put a number to the consumer surplus triangle (*feh*) in panel B, we can compute the value of the rectangle *fgeh* and divide it in half. Thus, total market consumer surplus in panel B is [(\$12 – \$6) × 6,000] ÷ 2 = (\$6 × 6,000) ÷ 2 = \$18,000. The shaded triangle labeled "producer surplus" (area *hei*) is found in the same way by computing the value of the rectangle *heji* and dividing it in half. Producer surplus is equal to [(\$6 – \$2) × 6,000] ÷ 2 = (\$4 × 6,000) ÷ 2 = \$12,000.

Although we simplify the calculation of consumer and producer surplus using the area of the triangle, remember that it is still the sum of the consumer and producer surpluses of many individual buyers and sellers. It is merely the fact that markets have thousands of buyers and sellers that the steps in panel A of Figure 2 become very small, thus resulting in smooth demand and supply curves in panel B.

We have now defined consumer surplus and producer surplus for individuals and for markets. But how do we know whether the market leads to an ideal outcome for consumers and producers? The next section goes on to reveal the efficiency of markets.

CHECKPOINT

CONSUMER AND PRODUCER SURPLUS: A TOOL FOR MEASURING ECONOMIC EFFICIENCY

- Consumers and producers both attempt to maximize their well-being by achieving the greatest gains in their market transactions.
- Consumer surplus occurs when consumers would have been willing to pay more for a good or service than the actual price paid. It represents a form of savings to consumers.
- Producer surplus occurs when businesses would have been willing to provide a good or service at prices lower than the going price. It represents a form of earnings to producers.

QUESTION: At the end of the semester, four college students list their economics textbooks for sale on the bulletin board in the student union. The minimum price Alex is willing to accept is \$20, Caroline wants at least \$25, Kira wants at least \$30, and Will wants at least \$35. Now assume that four college students taking an economics class next semester are searching for a deal on the textbook. Cole wishes to pay no more than \$50, Jacqueline no more than \$55, Sienna no more than \$60, and Tessa no more than \$65. Suppose that the actual sales price for each of the four textbooks is \$40. What is the total consumer surplus received by the four buyers and the total producer surplus received by the four sellers?

Answers to the Checkpoint question can be found at the end of the chapter.

Using Consumer and Producer Surplus: The Gains from Trade

Markets are efficient when they generate the largest possible amount of net benefits to all parties involved. When transactions between a buyer and a seller take place, each party is better off than before the transaction, leading to gains from trade. We had previously looked at gains from trade in an earlier chapter from the perspectives of individuals, firms, and countries specializing in activities and engaging in mutually beneficial transactions. This is no different than our present market examples, in which buyers and sellers mutually gain from transacting with one another.

At the equilibrium price, shortages and surpluses are nonexistent, and all consumers wanting to buy a good at that price are able to find a seller willing to sell at that price. The market efficiency that results maximizes the sum of consumer surplus and producer surplus, referred to as **total surplus,** gained in the market. Total surplus is a measure of the total net benefits a society achieves when both consumers and producers are valued components of an economy.

total surplus The sum of consumer surplus and producer surplus, and a measure of the overall net benefit gained from a market.

To see why markets are efficient at equilibrium, we need to analyze what happens to total surplus when markets deviate from equilibrium.

The Consequences of Deviating from Market Equilibrium

The market mechanism ensures that goods and services get to where they are most needed, because consumers desiring them bid up the price, while suppliers eager to make money supply them. Adam Smith termed this process the *invisible hand* to describe how resources are allocated efficiently through individual decisions made in markets.

But not all markets end up in equilibrium, especially if buyers or sellers hold inadequate information about products, or if buyers or sellers hold unrealistic or inaccurate expectations about market prices and behavior. Let's examine two scenarios in the market for video game consoles in which prices deviate from the equilibrium price.

When Prices Exceed Equilibrium Figure 3 illustrates a market for video game consoles with an equilibrium price of $300. Suppose that due to unrealistic expectations of demand, prices for video game consoles are set at $400, above the equilibrium price. We know from the previous chapter that a price above equilibrium leads to excess supply, because consumers only demand 10 thousand units while producers desire to sell 30 thousand units. Our tools of consumer surplus and producer surplus allow us to evaluate the effects on buyers and sellers in this market.

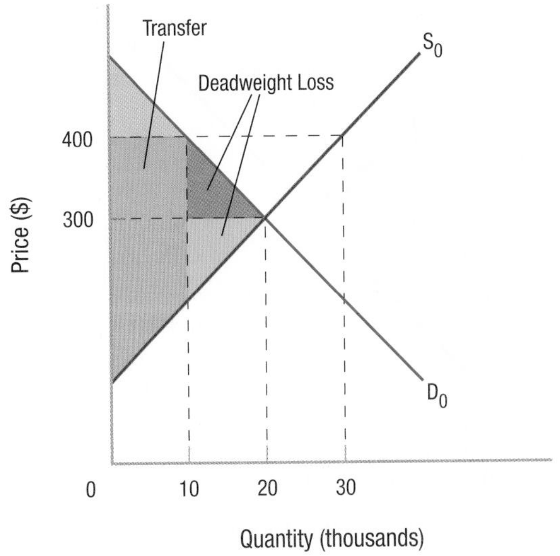

FIGURE 3

Consumer and Producer Surplus When Prices Exceed Equilibrium

Compared to the equilibrium price, a price of $400 would prevent some consumers from purchasing the product. A loss of consumer surplus equal to the blue region occurs. Further, consumers who still purchase the product pay $100 more than the equilibrium price, causing an additional loss of consumer surplus equal to the pink area. Producers, meanwhile, lose producer surplus equal to the yellow area resulting from the units that consumers no longer buy, but earn additional producer surplus equal to the pink area as a result of the higher price. Total lost surplus, called deadweight loss, is the blue and yellow areas (no one gets this because some trades are not made now). The pink area is surplus transferred from consumers to producers because of the higher price.

When prices are above equilibrium, consumer surplus shrinks due to two effects: First, a price of $400 causes some consumers to not make a purchase, because these consumers were only willing to pay between $300 and $400. The area shown in blue represents the lost consumer surplus from these forgone purchases. Second, the consumers who still are willing and able to purchase a unit pay $100 more, which represents a loss in consumer surplus equal to the pink area. In sum, the pink and blue regions represent the total reduction in consumer surplus from the higher price.

Producers, on the other hand, may or may not benefit from the higher price because of two opposing effects. First, the fact that the higher price causes some consumers to not purchase a unit causes a loss in producer surplus equal to the area shaded in yellow. However, this is offset by the additional money earned from the consumers who buy the unit at the higher price, which is represented by the pink area.

deadweight loss The reduction in total surplus that results from the inefficiency of a market not in equilibrium.

Therefore, the pink area represents a transfer of surplus from consumers to producers. The blue and yellow areas represent **deadweight loss,** the loss of consumer surplus and producer surplus caused by the inefficiency of a market not operating at equilibrium. Nobody gets the blue and yellow areas. Deadweight loss represents a loss in total surplus, because both buyers and sellers would have benefited from these transactions.

When Prices Fall Below Equilibrium When prices are below equilibrium, the opposite effects happen as a result of a shortage. Figure 4 shows the market for video game consoles in which the price of $200 is below the equilibrium price. At that price, sellers provide 10 thousand units for sale, while buyers demand 30 thousand units, causing a shortage.

At a price of $200, producers are clearly worse off. Some producers are unable to sell at that low price, causing a loss of producer surplus equal to the yellow area, while those who still sell the product earn $100 less per unit, resulting in a loss of producer surplus equal to the pink area.

At first, you might believe consumers are better off with the lower price, and some in fact are. But these gains, shown by the pink area, are limited to consumers lucky enough to purchase the good. The rest of the consumers who are affected by the shortage are worse off, because consumer surplus equal to the blue area is lost because of trades never made. In sum, deadweight loss equal to the blue and yellow areas results.

The two scenarios shown in Figures 3 and 4 demonstrate that whenever prices deviate from equilibrium, total surplus as measured by the sum of consumer surplus and producer surplus falls, resulting in a deadweight loss from mutually beneficial transactions between

FIGURE 4

Consumer and Producer Surplus When Prices are Below Equilibrium

Compared to the equilibrium price, a price of $200 causes some producers to not sell the product, resulting in a loss of producer surplus equal to the yellow area. Further, producers who still sell the product earn $100 less than before, causing an additional loss of producer surplus equal to the pink area. Consumers, meanwhile, lose consumer surplus equal to the blue area resulting from the shortage of units, but receive additional consumer surplus equal to the pink area as a result of the lower price for those lucky enough to find units for sale. Once again, deadweight loss is the blue and yellow areas, and the pink area is surplus transferred.

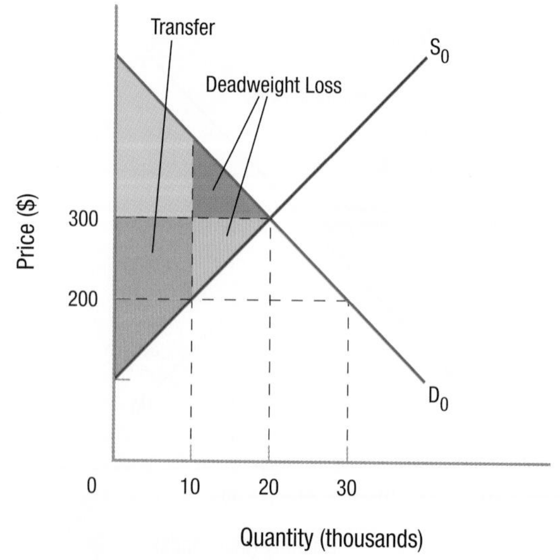

buyers and sellers not taking place. But why would markets not achieve equilibrium? Sometimes a market will fail to achieve equilibrium because it is prevented from doing so on its own.

market failure Occurs when a free market does not lead to a socially desirable outcome.

asymmetric information Occurs when one party to a transaction has significantly better information than another party.

Market Failure

Markets are inherently efficient mechanisms for allocating resources because of the incentives that drive consumers and firms to act in their own best interests. But like all things, exceptions occur when circumstances prevent the market from achieving the socially desirable outcome. When freely functioning markets fail to provide an optimal amount of goods and services, a **market failure** occurs.

There are four major reasons why markets fail: a lack of competition, a mismatch of information, external benefits or costs, and the existence of public goods, each of which causes total surplus to fall, resulting in deadweight loss.

Lack of Competition When a market has many buyers and sellers, no one seller has the ability to raise its price above that of its competitors. But when a market lacks competition, a firm can raise its price in the market without worrying that other firms will undercut its price. The local water provider is an example of a firm in a market that lacks competition, which can lead to inefficient production and higher prices unless the market failure is corrected using government regulation.

Information Is Not Shared by All Parties Adequate information about products by buyers and sellers is an important condition for efficient markets. Sometimes, one party knows more about a product than the other, a situation known as **asymmetric information.** For example, a seller of a used car knows more about the true condition of the car than a potential buyer. Conversely, an art or antique buyer may know more about the value of items than the seller at an estate sale. In these cases, a mismatch of information may lead to prices being set too high or too low.

The Existence of External Benefits or Costs When you drive your car on a crowded highway, you inflict external costs on other drivers by adding to congestion. When you receive a flu shot, you confer external benefits on the rest of us by reducing the chances of spreading an illness. Markets rarely produce the socially optimal output when external costs or benefits are present. When deciding whether to drive or obtain a flu shot, you tend not to think of the costs and benefits you impose on others. As a result, more people drive and fewer people receive flu shots than would be ideal to achieve the socially optimal outcome.

NOBEL PRIZE
PAUL A. SAMUELSON (1915–2009)

In 1970, Paul Samuelson became the first American to win the Nobel Prize in Economics. One could say that Paul Samuelson literally wrote the book on economics. In 1948, when he was a young professor at the Massachusetts Institute of Technology, the university asked him to write a text for the junior year course in economics. Sixty years later more than 4 million copies of his textbook, *Economics,* have been sold.

Samuelson's interests were wide ranging, and his contributions include everything from the highly technical and mathematical to a popular column for *Newsweek* magazine. He made breakthrough contributions to virtually all areas of economics.

Born in Gary, Indiana, in 1915, Samuelson attended the University of Chicago. He received the university's Social Science Medal and was awarded a graduate fellowship, which he used at Harvard, where he published eleven papers while in the graduate program.

He wanted to remain at Harvard, but was only offered an instructor's position. However, MIT soon made a better offer and, as he describes it, "On a fine October day in 1940 an *enfant terrible emeritus* packed up his pencil and moved three miles down the Charles River, where he lived happily ever after." He often remarked that a pencil was all he needed to theorize. Seven years later, he published his Ph.D. dissertation, *Foundations of Economic Analysis,* a major contribution to the area of mathematical economics. Robert Lucas, another Nobel winner, declared, "Here was a graduate student in his twenties reorganizing all of economics in four or five chapters right before your eyes . . ."

Harvard made several attempts to lure him back, but he spent his entire career at MIT and is often credited with developing a department as good as or better than Harvard's. Samuelson was an informal advisor to President John F. Kennedy. A prolific writer, he averaged one technical paper each month during his active career, and often said "a day spent in committee meetings [is] for me a day lost." He wrote that he "has always been incredibly lucky, throughout his lifetime overpaid and underworked." Quite a modest statement for a man whose *Collected Works* takes up five volumes and includes more than 350 articles. He was an active economist until his death in 2009 at the age of 93. As you read through this book, keep in mind that in virtually every chapter, Paul Samuelson has created or added to the analysis in substantial ways.

Sources: David Warsh, *Knowledge and the Wealth of Nations: A Story of Economic Discovery* (New York: Norton), 2006; Paul Samuelson, "Economics in My Time," in William Breit and Roger Spencer, *Lives of the Laureates: Seven Nobel Economists* (Cambridge, MA: The MIT Press), 1986.

ISSUE

Can Markets Accurately Predict the Future?

Can an online market predict the outcomes of political elections, wars, and other world events? A growing number of online betting exchanges think they can. These simple online markets have predicted major events and elections over the past decade with precision.

Traditionally, polls and other surveys are used to make predictions about the likelihood of future events. Although no one can truly predict the future, predictions markets gained significant attention by allowing real people to wager real money.

The first major online predictions market was the Iowa Electronic Markets established by the University of Iowa in 1988, allowing any individual to buy "shares" of various events ranging in price from $0.00 (0% probability of occurring) to $1.00 (100% probability of occurring). The value of these shares fluctuates as the perceived probability of the event occurring changes, allowing individuals to buy and sell shares at the current price until the event actually occurs (or not occurs).

The efficiency of this market lies in (1) the perpetual trading of shares and (2) the fact that people are motivated to make accurate predictions based on monetary incentives rather than personal opinions. For example, if one buys shares at $0.60 and something increases the perceived likelihood of the event occurring to 70% (or $0.70 a share), the shareholder can sell her shares at the new price, earning $0.10 per share without incurring any further risk.

The accuracy of predictions markets has been impressive. Intrade, one of the most popular predictions markets (established in 1999), accurately predicted the winner of the last four U.S. presidential elections, and with three exceptions it predicted the candidate winning the most votes in every state, even when various news polls showed opposing outcomes.

Although the power of predictions markets is potent, its legal status is not as certain. Intrade was shut down in 2013 after facing legal issues regarding its status as either an unregulated market exchange or an online betting site. To avoid legal troubles, other companies have found ways to harness the predictive power of markets by using incentives other than money, such as game points and prizes. Regardless of the incentives used, predictions markets remain a powerful tool that illustrates the efficiency of markets.

The Existence of Public Goods

Most goods we buy are private goods, such as meals and concert tickets; once we buy them, no one else can benefit from them. Public goods, however, are goods that one person can consume without diminishing what is left for others. Public television, for example, is a public good that illustrates nonrivalry (my watching of PBS does not mean there is less PBS for you to watch) and nonexclusivity (once a good is provided, others cannot be excluded from enjoying it). Because of these characteristics, public goods are difficult to provide in the private market.

Market Efficiency Versus Equity

Overcoming market failure is an important goal of government, which can enact policies to address markets in which private transactions do not lead to the optimal outcome. But the role of government extends beyond that of achieving social efficiency. It is also tasked with the goal of achieving equity in markets. For example, if a policy creates considerable unfairness, while spurring only a small gain in efficiency, some other policy might be better. One tool used by government to balance efficiency with equity is the use of price controls, which we turn to next.

CHECKPOINT

USING CONSUMER AND PRODUCER SURPLUS: THE GAINS FROM TRADE

- The sum of consumer surplus and producer surplus is total surplus, a measure of the overall net benefits for an economy.
- Markets are efficient when all buyers and all sellers willing to buy and sell at a market price are able to do so.
- When buyers and sellers engage in a market transaction, gains from trade are created from consumer surplus and producer surplus.
- Total surplus is maximized at a market equilibrium.
- When markets deviate from equilibrium, deadweight loss is created, an inefficiency caused by the loss of total surplus.
- Markets are typically efficient, although sometimes they can fail by not providing the socially optimal amount of goods and services.
- Market failure is caused by a lack of competition, mismatched information, external costs and external benefits, and the existence of public goods.

QUESTION: Waiting for an organ transplant is an ordeal for patients. Some wait years for an available donor organ that is compatible. Some economists have suggested that offering monetary compensation to organ donors would increase the supply of available organs. Would such a system lead to gains from trade? Why are such incentives difficult to implement?

Answers to the Checkpoint questions can be found at the end of this chapter.

Price Ceilings and Price Floors

To this point, we have assumed that competitive markets are allowed to operate freely, without any government intervention. Economists refer to freely functioning markets as **laissez-faire,** a French term meaning "let it be." The justification for this type of economic policy is that when competitive markets are left to determine equilibrium price and output, they clear. Businesses provide consumers with the quantity of goods they want to purchase at the established prices; there are no shortages or surpluses. Consumer and producer surplus together, or total surplus, is maximized.

laissez-faire A market that is allowed to function without any government intervention.

However, as we saw at the end of the previous section, sometimes freely functioning markets fail to achieve the optimal quantity of goods and services. This is an equilibrium price in a free market that leads to what many people consider an unfair price. Because of these economic (*efficiency*) or political (*equity*) reasons, governments will sometimes intervene in the market by setting limits on the prices of various goods and services. Governments use price ceilings and price floors to keep prices below or above market equilibrium. What really happens when government sets prices below or above market equilibrium? The previous section hinted at the answer. Let's look at price ceilings and floors more closely.

Price Ceilings

When the government sets a **price ceiling,** it is legally mandating the maximum price that can be charged for a product or service. This is a legal maximum; regardless of market forces, price cannot exceed this level. An historical example of a price ceiling is the establishment of rent-controlled apartment buildings in New York City during World War II, many of which still exist today. However, more common examples of price ceilings include limits on what insurance companies can charge customers, price caps on telecommunications and electric services to customers in rural or remote locations, and limits on tuition hikes at state public universities.

price ceiling A government-set maximum price that can be charged for a product or service. When the price ceiling is set below equilibrium, it leads to shortages.

Panel A in Figure 5 on the next page shows an *effective* price ceiling, or one in which the ceiling price is set below the equilibrium price. In this case, equilibrium price is at P_e, but the government has set a price ceiling at P_c. Quantity supplied at the ceiling price is Q_1, whereas consumers want Q_2, therefore the result is a shortage of $Q_2 - Q_1$ units of the product. As we saw in the previous section, setting a price below equilibrium alters consumer and producer surplus and results in a deadweight loss indicated by the shaded area. If the price ceiling is raised toward equilibrium, the shortage is reduced along with the deadweight loss. If the price ceiling is set above P_e (as shown in panel B), the market simply settles at P_e, and the price ceiling has no impact; it is nonbinding, and no deadweight loss occurs. A price ceiling can also *become* nonbinding if market factors cause supply to rise or demand to fall, pushing the equilibrium price below the ceiling.

A common mistake when analyzing the effect of price ceilings is assuming that effective price ceilings appear above the market equilibrium, because the word *ceiling* refers to something *above you*. Instead, think of ceilings as something that keep you from moving higher. Suppose you build a makeshift skateboarding ramp in your apartment hallway, and tempt your friends to test it out. If the ceiling is too low, some of your friends might end up with a severe headache. In other words, an effective (binding) ceiling is one that is kept lower than normal. If the ceiling can be raised by 5 feet, then all of your friends would achieve their jumps without bumping their heads. In sum, price ceilings have their strongest effects when kept very low; as the ceiling is

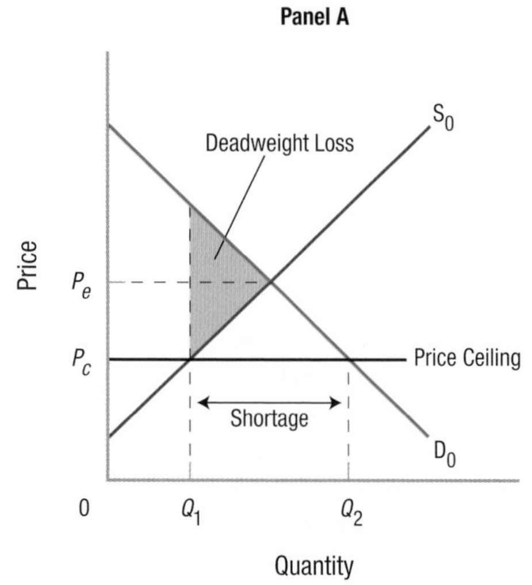

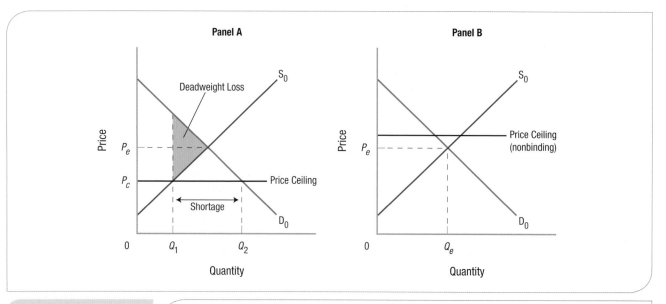

FIGURE 5

A Price Ceiling Below Equilibrium Creates Shortages

When the government enacts a price ceiling below equilibrium (panel A), consumers will demand Q_2 and businesses will supply only Q_1, creating a shortage equal to $Q_2 - Q_1$, and causing deadweight loss equal to the shaded area. If the price ceiling is set above equilibrium (panel B), the price ceiling has no effect, and the market price and quantity prevail with no deadweight loss created.

raised, the effect of the policy goes away, and becomes nonbinding once it reaches the equilibrium price.

Given the price ceiling, one might argue that although shortages might exist, at least prices will be kept lower and therefore more "fair." The question is, fairer to whom? Suppose your university places a new price ceiling on the rents of all existing apartments located on campus, one that is below the rents of similar apartments off campus. This might sound like a great idea, but often what sounds like a great idea comes with costs.

A price ceiling creates a much higher demand for on-campus apartments than the available supply, creating a shortage. Those lucky enough to obtain an on-campus

Low ceilings have a greater impact than high ceilings; similarly, price ceilings below equilibrium (rather than above equilibrium) lead to shortages in the market.

apartment benefit from the lower rents. But what about those who couldn't? Because some students who really could have benefited from lower rents (those with lower incomes or without cars) cannot find an on-campus apartment, while other students who could have easily afforded a higher priced off-campus apartment managed to snatch one up, this creates a **misallocation of resources.** Further, when on-campus apartments do open up, students eager to obtain one might spend a lot of time and resources trying. These resources (an opportunity cost) end up offsetting some or all of the savings from finding an on-campus apartment.

misallocation of resources Occurs when a good or service is not consumed by the person who values it the most, and typically results when a price ceiling creates an artificial shortage in the market.

Besides the misallocation of resources and potential opportunity costs of long waits and search costs, price ceilings also lead to some unintended long-term consequences. For example, if a landlord owns some apartments on campus (where rents are controlled) and some apartments off campus (where rents are higher), on which apartments is she likely to spend more money for upgrades and/or maintenance? The quality of goods and services subjected to price ceilings tends to deteriorate over time, as the incentives shift toward products with higher prices. Further, when it comes time to invest in new apartments, where do you think they are likely to be built—on campus or off?

The key point to remember here is that price ceilings are intended to keep the price of a product below its market or equilibrium level. When this happens, consumer surplus increases for those able to purchase the good, while producer surplus falls. The ultimate effect of a price ceiling, however, is that the quantity of the product demanded exceeds the quantity supplied, thereby producing a shortage of the product in the market. When shortages occur, deadweight losses are created because some mutually beneficial transactions do not take place, causing a reduction in total surplus.

Price Floors

A **price floor** is a government-mandated minimum price that can be charged for a product or service. Regardless of market forces, product price cannot legally fall below this level.

price floor A government-set minimum price that can be charged for a product or service. When the price floor is set above equilibrium, it leads to surpluses.

Figure 6 shows the economic impact of price floors. In panel A, the price floor, P_f, is set above equilibrium, P_e, resulting in a surplus of $Q_2 - Q_1$ units. At price P_f, businesses

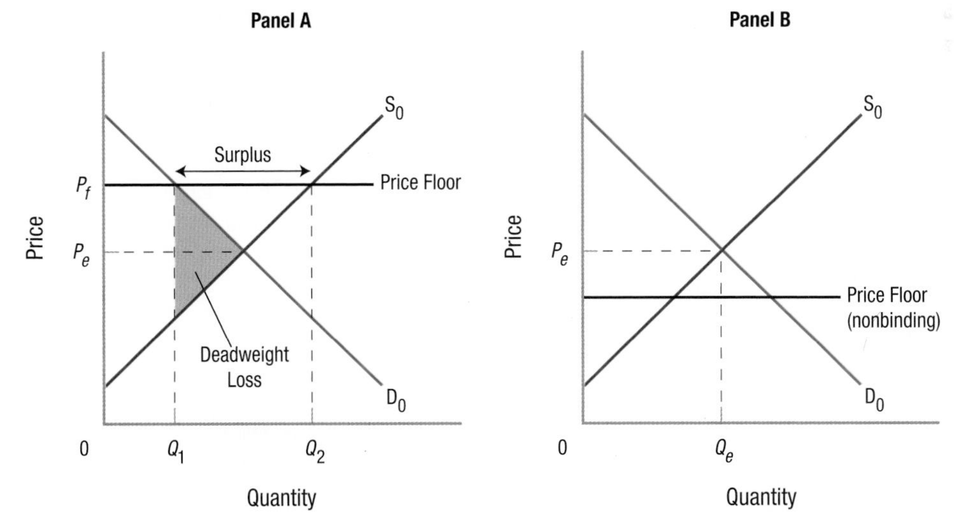

FIGURE 6

A Price Floor Above Equilibrium Creates Surpluses

When the government sets a price floor above equilibrium (panel A), businesses try to sell Q_2 at a price of P_f, but consumers are willing to purchase only Q_1 at that price, resulting in a surplus equal to $Q_2 - Q_1$, and causing deadweight loss equal to the shaded area. If the price floor is set below equilibrium (panel B), the price floor has no effect, and the market price and quantity prevail with no deadweight loss created.

want to supply more of the product (Q_2) than consumers are willing to buy (Q_1), thus generating a surplus. Because only Q_1 is transacted in the market, a deadweight loss equal to the shaded area is created. If the price floor is set below equilibrium (as shown in panel B), the market will move toward the equilibrium price, P_e. Therefore, a price floor set below P_e has no impact on the market and no deadweight loss occurs. Likewise, a price floor can *become* nonbinding if market factors push the equilibrium price above the price floor.

Throughout much of the past century, the U.S. government has used agricultural price supports (price floors) in order to smooth out the income of farmers, which often fluctuates due to wide annual variations in crop prices. This approach is not limited to the United States. Many developed countries, including members of the European Union and Japan, have long protected their agricultural industries by ensuring a minimum price level for many types of crops.

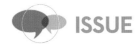

ISSUE

Are Price Gouging Laws Good for Consumers?

During the summer hurricane season, residents along the Atlantic and Gulf Coasts brace for hurricanes that can wreak havoc on the unprepared. The routine is well known: buy plywood and shutters to protect windows; fill up gas tanks in cars and buy extra gas for generators; and stock up on batteries, bottled water, and nonperishable foods. Because of the huge spike in demand, numerous states have introduced price gouging laws, which prevent stores from raising prices above the average price of the past 30 days. Penalties for violating such laws are severe.

Price gouging laws generally pass with huge majority votes from both major political parties. The logic seems clear—to prevent businesses from exploiting a bad situation to their benefit by raising prices. Passing such laws always appears to be a victory for the consumer. But is it really?

Price gouging laws are price ceilings placed at the price last existing when times were normal. But during a natural disaster, the market is far from normal—demand is higher, and supplies are often restricted due to plant closures. The figure shows what happens when these two effects come together—the market price spikes upward. But price gouging laws require that prices remain at the *original* level, resulting in a shortage when demand increases to D_1 and supply falls to S_1.

Thomas Frey/imagebroker/age fotostock

AP Photo/David Caruso

The inside of a jumbo jet cargo plane, a spacious solution to supply shortages, as long as an incentive exists to use that plane for this purpose.

What happens during a shortage? Huge lines form at home improvement stores, gas stations, and grocery stores. Time spent waiting in line is time that can be spent completing other tasks in preparation for the storm. What might be a better solution?

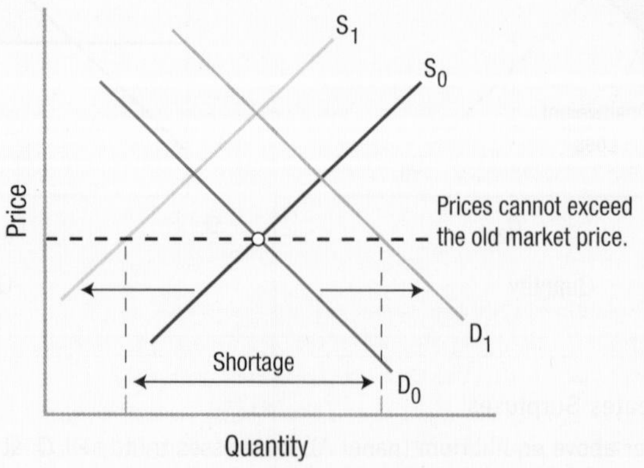

Instead of capping prices and causing a shortage, efforts can be made to provide incentives to businesses to generate more supply. If supply shifts enough to the right to compensate for the increase in demand, then prices need not increase, regardless of the price ceiling. But the question is, How do we incentivize supply? Subsidies to offset increased transportation costs might be an example. Imagine how many supplies could be flown in on a single jumbo jet cargo plane from a non–hurricane-prone area. Quite a bit, but firms aren't willing to spend that money. If the incentive is provided, supply will increase, reducing shortages and costs to everyone.

These price supports act very much as they are intended. By ensuring a minimum price for a crop, farmers have an incentive to grow more of these crops relative to crops that aren't protected by price supports. Further, because the price supports typically are above market equilibrium prices, resulting in higher prices for consumers, demand for such crops is less than what it would be without the supports.

Thus, with greater supply and smaller demand, price supports lead to surpluses of crops. What happens to these surpluses? Because the government guarantees the price levels of the crops, it must purchase the excess supply, which is typically stored for use in the event of future shortages. But surpluses eventually rot, which means government must find other ways to use the surplus before it goes bad. One common use of surplus foods is in public school lunches, leading to some criticism that the types of foods being provided (wheat, grains, and corn) are not the most nutritious foods for children to eat.

Kelly Cline/iStockphoto

Surplus foods resulting from government price floors are often given away to public schools to be used in school lunches.

Another criticism of agricultural price supports comes from developing countries that depend on agricultural exports for their economic output. These countries claim that price supports hamper their economic development by preventing them from selling goods in which they have a comparative advantage. In other words, agricultural price supports restrict gains from trade.

Despite their questionable economic justification, political pressures have ensured that agricultural price supports and related programs still command a sizable share of the discretionary domestic federal budget.

Price floors are also used in regard to the minimum wage. To the extent that the minimum wage is set above the equilibrium wage, unemployment—a surplus of labor—may result if jobs go uncreated when employers are forced to pay the higher minimum wage. However, the minimum wage offers a potential positive effect of reducing income inequality by raising earnings among low-wage workers. This effect is stronger if increasing the minimum wage subsequently leads to higher wages for workers who are already earning slightly more than the minimum wage.

In sum, price ceilings and price floors often are policies aimed at promoting equity or fairness in a society, such as preventing rapid price increases for consumers or ensuring fair wages for workers. Still, governments must be careful when setting price ceilings and price floors to avoid meddling with markets.

CHECKPOINT

PRICE CEILINGS AND PRICE FLOORS

- Governments use price floors and price ceilings to intervene in markets.
- A price ceiling is a maximum legal price that can be charged for a product. Price ceilings set below equilibrium result in shortages.
- A price floor is the minimum legal price that can be charged for a product. Price floors set above market equilibrium result in surpluses.

QUESTION: The day after Thanksgiving, also known as *Black Friday*, is a day on which retailers advertise very steep discounts on selected items such as televisions or laptops. Assuming the number of units available at the discounted price is limited, in what ways are the effects of this pricing strategy similar to a price ceiling set by the government? In what ways do they differ?

Answers to the Checkpoint questions can be found at the end of the chapter.

chapter summary

Section 1: Consumer and Producer Surplus: A Tool for Measuring Economic Efficiency

Economic efficiency is measured by the gains that consumers and producers achieve when engaging in an economic transaction.

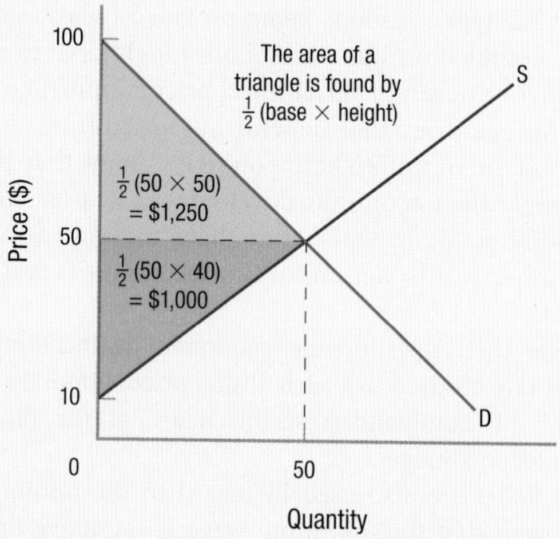

Consumer surplus is the difference between a person's willingness-to-pay and the price paid. For a market, consumer surplus is the area between the demand curve and the market price. In the figure, consumer surplus equals $1,250.

Producer surplus is the difference between the price a seller receives and its marginal cost. For a market, producer surplus is the area between the market price and the supply curve. In the figure, producer surplus equals $1,000.

Section 2: Using Consumer and Producer Surplus: The Gains from Trade

Markets exhibit efficiency when every buyer and every seller eager to buy and sell goods is able to do so, resulting in **gains from trade.** Gains from trade are measured by the **total surplus,** or the sum of consumer and producer surplus in a market. Total surplus is maximized when a market is at equilibrium.

Suppose the price of a good rises above equilibrium to $75. The higher price causes two effects on consumer surplus and two effects on producer surplus:

1. Consumers who are priced out of the market lose consumer surplus equal to the blue area.
2. Consumers who continue to buy the good pay more, and lose consumer surplus equal to the pink area.
3. Producers who want to sell more at $75 but cannot lose producer surplus equal to the yellow area.
4. Producers who do sell units earn $25 more per unit, equal to the pink area.

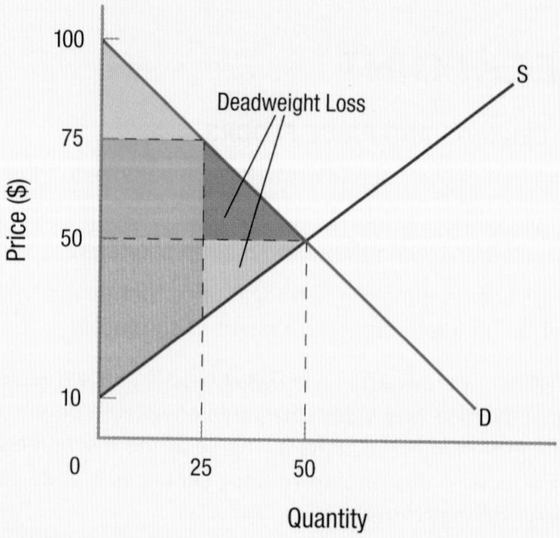

Deadweight loss occurs when prices deviate from equilibrium. In the above example, deadweight loss is shown by the blue and yellow areas.

Markets can sometimes fail to produce the socially optimal output. Reasons for **market failure** include:

Lack of competition

When a firm faces little to no competition, it has an incentive to raise prices.

Existence of external benefits or costs

Markets tend to provide too little of products that have external benefits, and too much of products with external costs.

Tim Pannell/Corbis

Planting trees creates external benefits.

Corbis

Talking loudly on your phone creates external costs.

A mismatch of information

Asymmetric information occurs when either a buyer or a seller knows more about a product than the other.

Existence of public goods

Public goods are nonrival and nonexclusive. This means:

- My consumption does not diminish your ability to consume.
- Once a good is provided for one person, others cannot be excluded from enjoying it.

Susan E. Degginger/Alamy

Ecological conservation is a public good. Once people devote time and resources to saving the environment, everybody benefits from it, even if one does not contribute to the costs of maintaining it.

Section 3: Price Ceilings and Price Floors

A **price floor** is a minimum price for a good. A binding price floor appears above equilibrium and causes a surplus.

A **price ceiling** is a maximum price for a good. A binding price ceiling appears below equilibrium and causes a shortage.

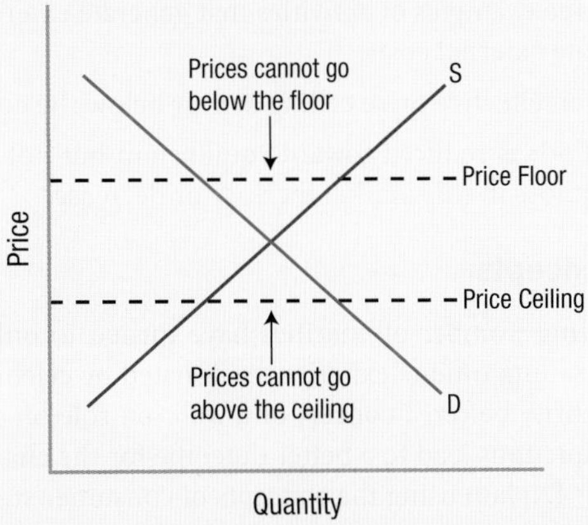

Phil Augustavo/iStockphoto

A literal mountain of surplus corn caused by agricultural price floors.

KEY CONCEPTS

consumer surplus, p. 82
producer surplus, p. 82
total surplus, p. 85
deadweight loss, p. 86
market failure, p. 87
asymmetric information, p. 87
laissez-faire, p. 89
price ceiling, p. 89
misallocation of resources, p. 91
price floor, p. 91

QUESTIONS AND PROBLEMS

Check Your Understanding

1. Describe how consumer surplus and producer surplus are measured.
2. Using the graph below, show what happens to consumer surplus when a new technology reduces the cost of production.

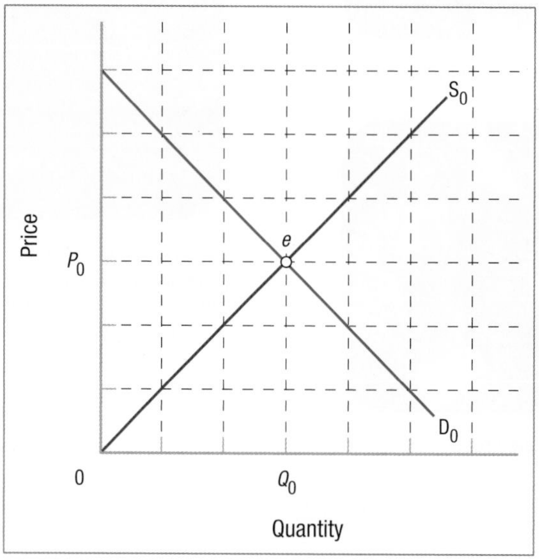

3. Explain why deadweight loss can occur with a price below equilibrium even when some consumers benefit from it.
4. Provide three examples of activities that generate external benefits and three activities that generate external costs.
5. Why does an effective price ceiling appear below the equilibrium rather than above it?
6. If a price floor is reduced toward equilibrium but not below it, does the surplus and deadweight loss in this market increase or decrease?

Apply the Concepts

7. An increasing number of charities have turned to online auctions as a way to raise money by selling unique experiences donated by celebrities (such as a *meet-and-greet* with a celebrity before a concert or a walk-on role on a television show). Why would the use of auctions lead to a better outcome for the charity as opposed to just setting a fixed price? Explain using the concepts of consumer surplus and producer surplus.

8. Luigi's is the only pizzeria in a small town in northern Alaska. It is constantly busy but there is never a wait for a table. One of Luigi's friends suggests that he would earn much more money if he raises his menu prices by 25%, because no one is likely to open a new pizzeria in the near future. If Luigi follows his friend's advice, what would happen to consumer and producer surplus, and efficiency, in this market?
9. "If millions of people are desperate to buy and millions more desperate to sell, the trades will happen, whether we like it or not." This quote from Martin Wolf[1] refers to trades in illicit goods such as narcotics, knockoffs (counterfeit goods), slaves, organs, and other goods we generally refer to as "bads." Wolf suggests that the only way to eliminate traffic in these illicit goods is to eliminate their profitability. Do you agree? Why or why not?
10. Academic studies suggest that the amount people tip in restaurants is only slightly related to the quality of service, and that tips are poor measures of how happy people are with the service. Is this another example of market failure? What might account for this situation?
11. In the 1940s, rent controls were widely used in New York City, and to this day, tenants in rent-controlled apartments continue to pay low rents as long as they do not move. As a result, some of New York's prime real estate is renting for a fraction of the true market value. Explain how the existence of rent controls affects the market prices for non-rent-controlled apartments. How are incentives by New York landlords affected in terms of maintaining rent-controlled and non-rent-controlled apartments?
12. The U.S. Department of Labor reports that of the roughly 155 million people employed, just over half are paid by the hour, but fewer than 5% earn the minimum wage or less; 95% of wage earners earn more. And of those earning the minimum wage or less, 25% are teenagers living at home. If so few people are affected by the minimum wage, why does it often seem to be such a contentious political issue?

In the News

13. In 2009, the Hershey Company of Pennsylvania became the latest company to open a candy factory in Mexico (*USA Today,* February 13, 2009), joining other American candy companies including Brach's Confections and Ferrara Pan Candy, which had opened plants there earlier. The reason for Hershey's move was more than just lower wages; it was also because of lower sugar prices. Sugar prices in the United States have for many decades been supported in order to protect the American sugar industry and the thousands of farmers it employs. Using the tools of consumer and producer surplus, explain how the events described may have resulted from price supports for sugar.
14. Professor Donald Boudreaux wrote (*Wall Street Journal,* August 23, 2006, p. A11) that "there are heaps of bad arguments for raising the minimum wage. Perhaps the worst . . . is that a minimum wage increase is justified if a full-time worker earning the current minimum wage cannot afford to live in a city such as Chicago." He then asked, "why settle for enabling workers to live only in the likes of Chicago? Why not raise the minimum wage so that everyone can afford to live in, say, Nantucket, Hyannis Port or Beverly Hills, within walking distance of Rodeo Drive?" Should the minimum wage be a "living wage," so a full-time worker can live comfortably in a given locale? What would be the impact if minimum wages were structured this way?

---

[1] Martin Wolf, "The Profit Motive May Be Universal but Virtue Is Not," *Financial Times,* November 16, 2005, p. 13.

Solving Problems

15. Consider the market shown in the graph below.

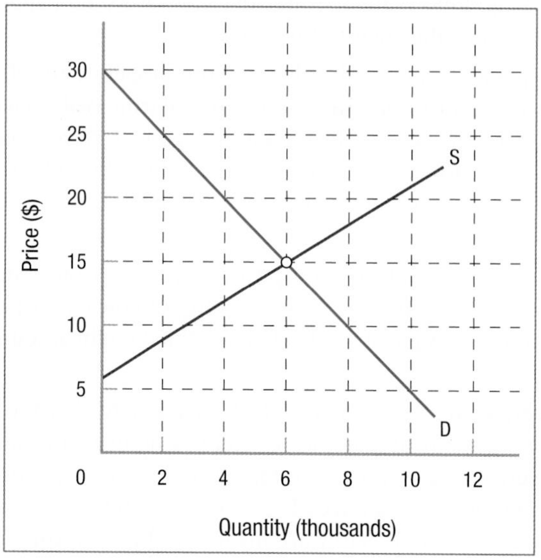

a. Compute the consumer surplus.

b. Compute the producer surplus.

Now assume that government puts a price floor on this product at $20 a unit.

c. Compute the new consumer surplus.

d. Compute the new producer surplus.

e. What group would tend to have their advocates or lobbyists support price floors?

16. Suppose the U.S. government places a price ceiling on the sale of gasoline at $3 per gallon in the figure below.

a. How much of a shortage or surplus of gasoline would result?

b. Calculate the effects of this policy in terms of the changes in consumer surplus and producer surplus.

c. How much deadweight loss is created?

d. What would happen if the price ceiling is raised to $6 per gallon?

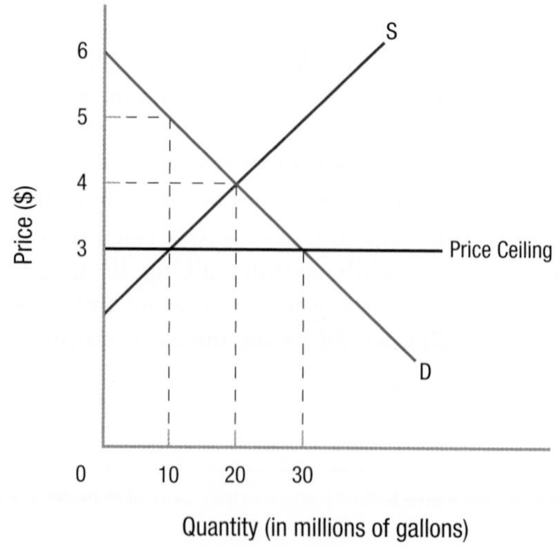

USING THE NUMBERS

17. According to By the Numbers, how much would you earn in one year if you worked 2,000 hours (50 weeks × 40 hours) at the federal minimum wage? How much more would you earn per year if you worked at the minimum wage rate in Washington state?
18. According to By the Numbers, which state received the highest average federal telephone support per capita in 2011? Approximately how much support did this state receive per resident? (Hint: search for the population of each state online to calculate the average support per person.)

ANSWERS TO QUESTIONS IN CHECKPOINTS

Checkpoint: Consumer and Producer Surplus: A Tool for Measuring Economic Efficiency

Cole's consumer surplus is ($50 – $40) = $10, Jacqueline's is ($55 – $40) = $15, Sienna's is ($60 – $40) = $20, and Tessa's is ($65 – $40) = $25. Total consumer surplus is $10 + $15 + $20 + $25 = $70. Alex's producer surplus is ($40 – $20) = $20, Caroline's is ($40 – $25) = $15, Kira's is ($40 – $30) = $10, and Will's is ($40 – $35) = $5. Total producer surplus is $20 + $15 + $10 + $5 = $50.

Checkpoint: Using Consumer and Producer Surplus: The Gains from Trade

Although many people voluntarily become organ donors because of the goodwill they feel knowing that their actions can potentially save a life, still many others choose not to become organ donors because they do not see any monetary benefit from doing so. Compensating individuals for becoming organ donors, thereby raising the "price" of organs, would be a way to increase the supply of organs, allowing the shortage to dissipate until equilibrium is reached. In doing so, organ donors and recipients both benefit, resulting in gains from trade. However, moral objections to selling body parts have led to many laws preventing organ donors from being compensated. As a result, shortages continue to be a problem.

Checkpoint: Price Ceilings and Price Floors

Black Friday specials are typically deeply discounted in order to attract customers into the store, which is why such specials are prominently shown on the first page of sales circulars. Like a price ceiling that is set below the equilibrium price, the quantity demanded for the discounted good increases, while stores limit the number of units available for sale, creating a shortage. Some buyers will be fortunate to find units available to purchase, while subsequent shoppers will find that the product has sold out. Deadweight loss is generated because some customers who would have been willing to pay a little more are unable to purchase the good. However, unlike with a price ceiling, stores strategically choose to advertise goods with many alternatives, such as different brands of televisions and laptops, so that when the discounted product sells out, customers may consider buying a nondiscounted product. Therefore, the pricing strategy leads to a strategic shortage that is designed to attract customers into the store to buy goods in addition to those that are advertised.

5 Elasticity

Trevor Smith/iStockphoto

Kris Tripplaar/TRIPPLAAR KRISTOFFER/SIPA/Newscom

From gas guzzlers to gas misers, auto manufacturers make what customers demand, which is influenced by the price of gasoline.

After studying this chapter you should be able to:

- Understand the concept of elasticity and why percentages are used to measure it.
- Describe the difference between elastic and inelastic demand.
- Compute price elasticities of supply and demand.
- Describe the relationship between total revenue and price elasticity of demand.
- Describe cross elasticity of demand and use this concept to define substitutes and complements.
- Use income elasticity of demand to define normal, inferior, and luxury goods.
- Describe the determinants of the elasticity of demand and the elasticity of supply.
- Use the concept of price elasticity of supply to measure the relationship between changes in product price and quantity supplied.
- Describe the time periods economists use to study elasticity, and describe the variables that companies can change during these periods.
- Describe the relationship between elasticity and the burden and incidence of taxes.

At the start of the new millennium, the price of gasoline hovered around $1.50 per gallon—a veritable bargain—with a tankful costing roughly $20. Encouraged by low gas prices and a healthy economy, consumer appetites for bigger vehicles grew, leading to a rapid increase in the market for sport utility vehicles (SUVs) and trucks. Not only did the quantity of large vehicles increase, but the size of SUVs and trucks grew as well. The Hummer H2, Ford Excursion, and Chevy Suburban were all designed for consumers who wanted cars with plenty of space and who were not too concerned about gas prices.

Over the decade that followed, the market for oil and gasoline changed dramatically. Increased tensions in the Middle East along with a huge spike in oil demand from emerging markets such as China and India pushed the prices of a gallon of gas in 2010 to over double what they were a decade ago, and prices have since remained elevated. How did consumers respond to the 100% increase in the average price of gasoline? They reduced consumption by driving less, carpooling, and using public transportation. But by *how much* did the quantity of gasoline demanded fall?

The rising price of oil not only reduced the amount of gasoline consumers demanded, consumers also changed their preferences for cars. SUVs and trucks became less desirable, while small cars, hybrids, and flex-fuel vehicles became popular. How responsive were consumers in terms of changing their vehicle preferences? Not only did consumers change their buying habits as a result of higher gasoline prices, but producers responded. As prices for oil rose, more companies found it worthwhile to drill for oil, leading countries in Africa, Northern Europe, and even the United States, Canada, and Mexico to increase production. By *how much* did oil producers respond?

Lastly, as demand for SUVs and trucks fell in response to higher gas prices, car manufacturers responded by reducing the quantity of SUVs and trucks produced. Hummers and Ford Excursions were phased out completely. Producers of vehicles that use gas inefficiently responded as well, but by *how much*?

We learned in Chapter 3 that consumers respond to higher prices by buying less, while producers respond to higher prices by producing more. We also know that as prices rise, demand for complements falls while demand for substitutes rises. However, we have not yet measured the extent of such responses. In other words, how responsive are consumers and producers to changes in prices in terms of what is purchased and what is produced?

We answer the important "how responsive" question in this chapter by studying how consumers and producers respond to changes in the price of goods and services.

Elasticity—the responsiveness of one variable to changes in another—is the term economists use to measure this change. In our example above, we know that the price of gasoline is one variable and the quantity of gasoline demanded is the other variable. The concept of elasticity lets us measure the relative change in quantity demanded corresponding to various changes in the price of gasoline.

But as our example shows, elasticity can be measured for many different items. If the price of gasoline changes, how will this affect sales of large cars? Small cars? How would demand for train and bus tickets change? And we not need limit our analysis to prices either. For example, income elasticity measures changes in consumer demand

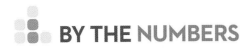

BY THE NUMBERS

Elasticity: How Markets React to Price Changes

Elasticity varies across goods and services, largely due to factors involving the price of the good, availability of substitutes, and whether a good is a necessity. Elasticity also varies across consumer groups and by country.

Roel Smart/iStockphoto

Salt (0.1)

Fancy/Alamy

Movies (0.9)

photo360/
Dreamstime.com

Foreign Travel (4.0)

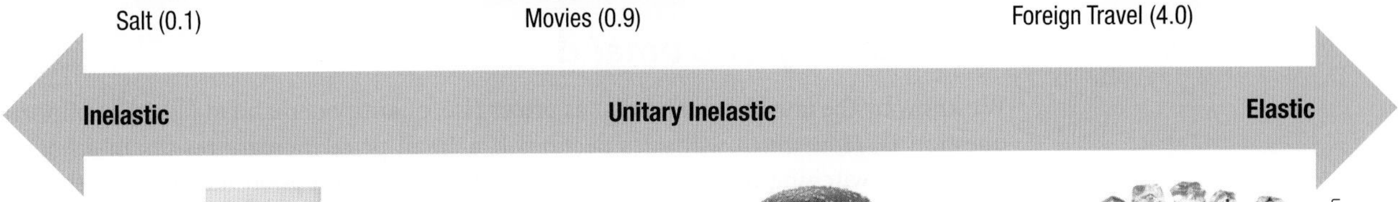

Hong Chan/
Dreamstime.com

Prescription
Medicine (0.3)

Johnfoto/
Dreamstime.com

Fast Food (1.3)

Daniel Gilbey/
Dreamstime.com

Diamonds (4.2)

Note: The numbers in parentheses refer to the price elasticity of demand.

Food is necessary for survival, and thus an inelastic good. Yet, elasticity varies by country; when the price of food rises, poorer countries reduce consumption more than rich countries.

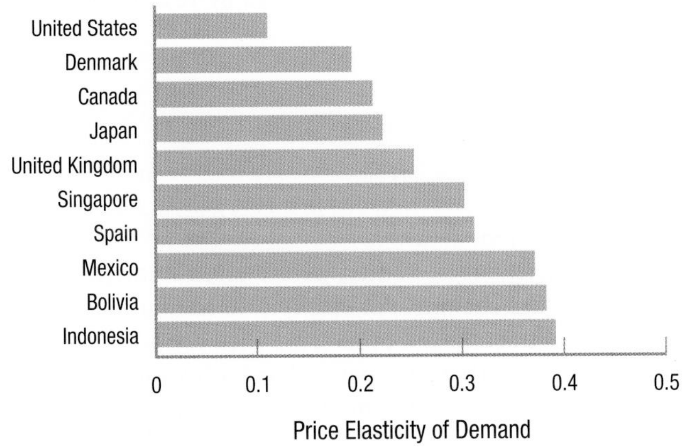

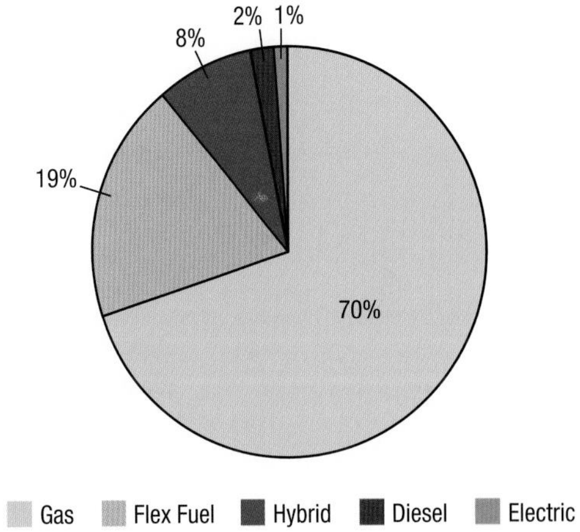

Alternative-fuel cars are growing in popularity. In 2012 they represented 30% of new vehicle sales.

Jennifer Pitiquen/Dreamstime.com

Don't like paying for parking? You're not alone. When the price of downtown parking in major cities increased 10%, people on average:

- Used that parking lot 5.4% less.
- Used farther parking lots 8.3% more.
- Used park & ride 3.6% more.
- Rode public transit 2.9% more.
- Reduced the number of trips downtown 4.6%.

71%
Average rise in public university tuition (a highly inelastic good) from 2000–2010.

68%
Average fall in international calling rates (a highly elastic good) from 2000–2010.

in response to changes in income. As incomes rise with a growing economy, will purchases of cars and trucks pick up? By how much? This is information automakers want to know.

Elasticity is a simple economic concept that nonetheless contains a tremendous amount of information about demand for specific products. If a firm raises its price by 50 cents, will it end up with more in revenue, or will the increase in price lead to a drop in quantity demanded that more than offsets the price increase? Knowing a product's price elasticity allows economists to predict the amount by which quantity demanded will drop in response to a price increase, or grow in response to a price decrease. The concept of elasticity helps you to put supply and demand concepts to work.

Elasticity of Demand

We know by the law of demand that as prices rise, quantity demanded falls. The important question is, *How much* will sales decline? If a small price increase results in *all* of your customers switching to your competitors, it is clearly not a good idea to raise the price; you will be out of business. And if a small price increase still results in a large reduction in quantity sold, then raising prices probably is not a good idea. However, if a large price increase elicits only a small loss in sales, then raising prices may make sense. As we shall see, the concept of elasticity and the impact of changing price on a firm's sales revenue help to determine the answer.

price elasticity of demand A measure of the responsiveness of quantity demanded to a change in price, equal to the percentage change in quantity demanded divided by the percentage change in price.

Price elasticity of demand (E_d) is a measure of how responsive quantity demanded is to a change in price and is defined as

$$E_d = \frac{\text{Percentage Change in Quantity Demanded}}{\text{Percentage Change in Price}}$$

For example, if prices of strawberries rise by 5% and sales fall by 10%, then the price elasticity of demand for strawberries is

$$E_d = \frac{-10\%}{+5\%} = -2$$

Alternatively, if a 5% reduction in strawberry prices results in a 10% gain in sales, the price elasticity of demand also is -2 ($E_d = 10 \div [-5] = -2$).

Often we are not given percentage changes. Rather, we are given numerical values and have to convert them into percentage changes. For example, to compute a change in price, take the new price (P_{new}) and subtract the old price (P_{old}), then divide this result by the old price (P_{old}). This approach to calculating percentage changes is known as the *base method*. Finally, to put this ratio in percentage terms, multiply by 100. In equation form:

$$\text{Percentage Change} = \frac{(P_{new} - P_{old})}{P_{old}} \times 100$$

For example, if the old price of gasoline (P_{old}) was \$2.00 per gallon and the new price goes up by \$1.00 to \$3.00 per gallon, then the percentage change is

$$\text{Percentage Change} = \frac{\$3.00 - \$2.00}{\$2.00} = \frac{\$1.00}{\$2.00} = 0.50 \times 100 = 50\%$$

Price Elasticity of Demand as an Absolute Value

The price elasticity of demand is always a negative number. This reflects the fact that the demand curve's slope is negative: As prices increase, quantity demanded falls. Price and quantity demanded stand in an inverse relationship to one another, resulting in a negative value for price elasticity. Economists nevertheless frequently refer to price elasticity of demand in positive terms. They simply use the *absolute value* of the computed price elasticity of demand. Recalling our examples, where $E_d = -2$, we can take the absolute value of -2, written as $|-2|$, and refer to E_d as 2. For most comparisons, we can use the absolute value of elasticity and ignore the minus sign.

What does this elasticity value of 2 tell us? Quite simply, that for every 1% increase in price, quantity demanded will decline by 2%. Conversely, for every 1% decline in price, quantity demanded will increase by 2%.

Measuring Elasticity with Percentages

Measuring elasticity in percentage terms rather than specific units enables economists to compare the characteristics of various unrelated products. Comparing price and sales changes for houses, cars, and hamburgers in dollar amounts would be so complex as to be meaningless. Because a dollar increase in the price of gasoline is different from a dollar increase in the price of a BMW, by using percentage change we can compare the sensitivity of demand curves of different products. Percentages allow us to compare changes in prices and sales for any two products, no matter how dissimilar they are; a 100% increase is the same percentage change for any product.

We have seen how to compute the elasticity of demand, and we have seen why working with percentage changes is so important. Elasticity is a relative measure giving us a way to compare products with widely different prices and output measures.

Elastic and Inelastic Demand

All products have some price elasticity of demand. When prices go up, quantity demanded will fall. That is the basis of the negative slope of the demand curve. But people are more responsive to changes in the prices of some products than others. Economists label goods as being *elastic, inelastic,* or *unitary elastic.*

Elastic When the absolute value of the computed price elasticity of demand is greater than 1, economists refer to this as **elastic demand.** An elastic demand curve is one that is responsive to price changes. At the extreme is the *perfectly elastic* demand curve shown in panel A of Figure 1 on the next page. Notice that it is horizontal, showing that the slightest increase in price will result in zero output being sold.

elastic demand The absolute value of the price elasticity of demand is greater than 1. Elastic demands are very responsive to changes in price. The percentage change in quantity demanded is greater than the percentage change in price.

In reality, no branded product—Coca-Cola, Apple iPhone, or Toyota Prius—ever has a perfectly elastic demand curve. Still, products with many close substitutes face highly elastic demand curves. One recent study of several brands of bath tissue found the price elasticities of demand for Scott, Kleenex, Charmin, Quilted Northern, and other brands ranged from 2.0 to 4.5—highly elastic.[1] Raise the price of Charmin, and watch how quickly sales fall as people switch to Quilted Northern or Scott. Canned peaches, nuts and bolts, cereal, and bottled water are all examples of products facing highly elastic demands. If one bottled water company were to raise its price by much, many consumers would switch to other brands, because all bottled water tastes pretty much the same. Demand curves for elastic goods are relatively flat, as shown in panel B in Figure 1.

Inelastic At the other extreme, what about products that see little change in sales even when prices change dramatically? The opposite of the perfectly elastic demand curve is the curve showing no response to changes in price. Economists call this a *perfectly inelastic* demand curve. An example appears in panel E of Figure 1. This curve is vertical, not horizontal as in panel A. For products with perfectly inelastic demands, quantity demanded does not change when price changes.

[1] Lawrence Wu, "Two Methods of Determining Elasticities of Demand and Their Use in Merger Simulation," in Lawrence Wu, Ed., *Economics of Antitrust: New Issues, Questions, and Insights* (New York: National Economic Research Associates), 2004, pp. 21–33.

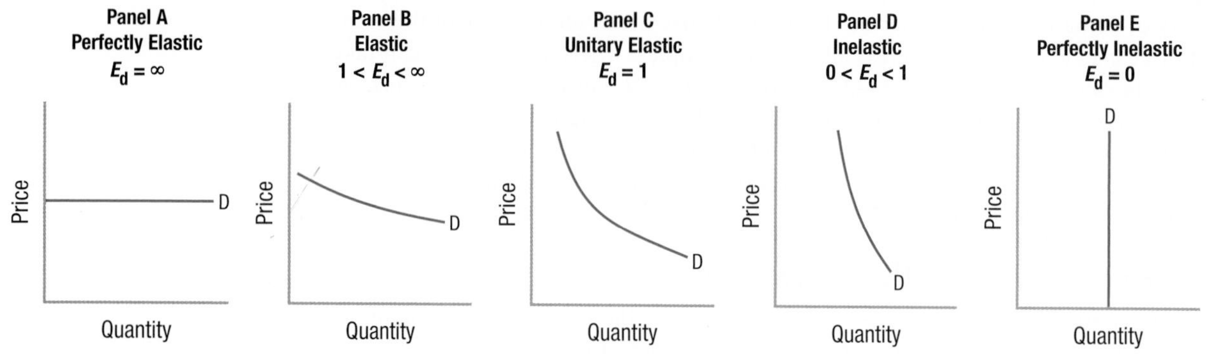

FIGURE 1

The Shape and Elasticity of Demand Curves

The horizontal demand curve in panel A represents perfectly elastic demand because when price increases, quantity demanded drops to zero. Panel E, on the other hand, illustrates a perfectly inelastic demand curve where quantity demanded does not change when the price changes. Panel B shows an elastic demand curve, which is relatively flat, and Panel D shows an inelastic demand curve, which is relatively steep. Panel C shows that if elasticity of demand is unitary, then a 1% increase in price will result in a 1% decrease in quantity demanded. Note that the unitary elastic demand curve is not a straight line.

What products might be inelastically demanded? Consider products that are immensely important to our lives but have few substitutes—for example, drugs that ameliorate life-threatening illnesses such as heart disease or stroke, and insulin for diabetics. If people who need these products have the money, they will buy them, no matter how high the price. Some products that are relatively, though not perfectly, inelastic include gasoline, tobacco, and most spices. If gasoline prices rise too sharply, some consumers will curtail their driving. Still, it takes a fairly drastic rise in gasoline prices before most people curtail their driving significantly. Doubling the price of cinnamon will probably not reduce our demand because it is such a small fraction of our overall food budget. Economists define **inelastic demand** as demand curves with elasticity coefficients that are less than 1. These demand curves are relatively steep, as shown in panel D in Figure 1.

inelastic demand The absolute value of the price elasticity of demand is less than 1. Inelastic demands are not very responsive to changes in price. The percentage change in quantity demanded is less than the percentage change in price.

Note that the demand for gasoline is inelastic, but the demand for specific brands of gasoline is elastic. Brand preferences for commodities that are nearly identical to one another, such as gasoline, are weak, and many different outlets exist for buying gas. If your local Shell station raises gasoline prices by a significant amount, you will probably go to the Exxon station down the street. Giving up using gasoline altogether, on the other hand, is much harder. Over time, public transportation or electric cars may be possible substitutes for gas-powered cars, but few people will be able to adopt these substitutes in the short run. On the contrary, many people are highly dependent on their gas-powered cars, therefore gas purchases do not drop substantially when prices rise. Thus, demand for a particular brand of gas (Exxon, Shell) is elastic, while the demand for gasoline as a commodity is inelastic.

Unitary Elasticity Elastic demand curves have an elasticity coefficient that is greater than 1, while inelastic demand curves have a coefficient of less than 1. That leaves those products with an elasticity coefficient just equal to 1. This condition is called **unitary elasticity of demand.** It means the percentage change in quantity demanded is precisely equal to the percentage change in price. Panel C of Figure 1 shows a demand curve where price elasticity equals 1. Note that this demand curve is not a straight line. The reasons for this will become clear in our discussion later in the chapter.

unitary elasticity of demand The absolute value of the price elasticity of demand is equal to 1. The percentage change in quantity demanded is just equal to the percentage change in price.

Determinants of Elasticity

Price elasticity of demand measures how sensitive sales are to price changes. But what determines elasticity itself? The four basic determinants of a product's elasticity of demand are (1) the availability of substitute products, (2) the percentage of income or household budget spent on the product, (3) the difference between luxuries and necessities, and (4) the time period being examined.

Substitutability The more close substitutes, or possible alternatives, a product has, the easier it is for consumers to switch to a competing product and the more elastic the demand. For many people, beef and chicken are substitutes, as are competing brands of cola, such as Coke and Pepsi. All have relatively elastic demands. Conversely, if a product has few close substitutes, such as insulin for diabetics or tobacco for heavy smokers, its elasticity of demand tends to be lower.

Proportion of Income Spent on a Product A second determinant of elasticity is the proportion (percentage) of household income spent on a product. In general, the smaller the percent of household income spent on a product, the lower the elasticity of demand. For example, you probably spend little of your income on salt, or on cinnamon or other spices. As a result, a hefty increase in the price of salt, say 25%, would not affect your salt consumption because the impact on your budget would be tiny. But if a product represents a significant part of household spending, elasticity of demand tends to be greater, or more elastic. A 10% increase in your rent upon renewing your lease, for example, would put a large dent in your budget, significantly reducing your purchasing power for many other products. Such a rent increase would likely lead you to look around earnestly for a less expensive apartment.

Luxuries Versus Necessities The third determinant of elasticity is whether the good is considered a luxury or a necessity. Luxuries tend to have demands that are more elastic than those of necessities. Necessities such as food, electricity, and health care are more important to everyday living, and quantity demanded does not change significantly when prices rise. Luxuries such as trips to Hawaii, yachts, and designer watches, on the other hand, can be given up when prices rise.

Time Period The fourth determinant of elasticity is the time period under consideration. When consumers have some time to adjust their consumption patterns, the elasticity of demand becomes more elastic. When they have little time to adjust, the elasticity of demand tends to be more inelastic. Thus, as we saw earlier, when gasoline prices rise suddenly, most consumers cannot immediately change their transportation patterns, therefore gasoline sales do not drop significantly. However, as gas prices continue to remain high, we see shifts in consumer behavior, to which automakers respond by producing smaller, more fuel-efficient cars.

Table 1 provides a sampling of estimates of elasticities for specific products. As we might expect, medical prescriptions and taxi service have relatively inelastic price elasticities of demand, while foreign travel and restaurant meals have relatively elastic demands.

Selected Estimates of Price Elasticities of Demand — **TABLE 1**

Inelastic		Roughly Unitary Elastic		Elastic	
Salt	0.1	Movies	0.9	Shrimp	1.3
Gasoline (short run)	0.2	Shoes	0.9	Furniture	1.5
Cigarettes	0.2	Tires	1.0	Commuter rail service (long run)	1.6
Medical care	0.3	Private education	1.1	Restaurant meals	2.3
Medical prescriptions	0.3	Automobiles	1.2	Air travel	2.4
Pesticides	0.4			Fresh vegetables	2.5
Taxi service	0.6			Foreign travel	4.0

Source: Compiled from numerous studies reporting estimates for price elasticity of demand.

FIGURE 2

Computing Elasticity of Demand Using Midpoints

A problem can occur when calculating elasticity over a range of prices. The calculated value can vary depending on whether price is increasing or decreasing. To avoid getting different results when approaching the same analysis from different directions, economists use midpoint price and midpoint quantity.

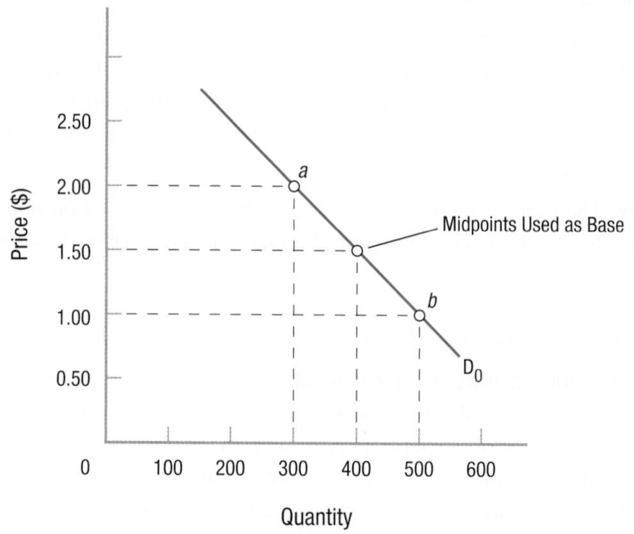

Computing Price Elasticities

When elasticity is computed between two points, the calculated value will differ depending on whether price is increasing or decreasing. For example, in Figure 2, if the price *increases* from \$1.00 to \$2.00, elasticity is equal to

$$\begin{aligned} E_d &= \frac{300 - 500}{500} \div \frac{2.00 - 1.00}{1.00} \\ &= \frac{-200}{500} \div \frac{1.00}{1.00} \\ &= -0.4 \div 1 \\ &= |-0.4| \\ &= 0.4 \end{aligned}$$

But when price *decreases* from \$2.00 to \$1.00, elasticity is equal to

$$\begin{aligned} E_d &= \frac{500 - 300}{300} \div \frac{1.00 - 2.00}{2.00} \\ &= \frac{200}{300} \div \frac{-1.00}{2.00} \\ &= 0.67 \div -0.5 \\ &= |-1.33| \\ &= 1.33 \end{aligned}$$

Using Midpoints to Compute Elasticity To avoid getting different results computing elasticity from different directions, economists compute price elasticity using the midpoints of price $[(P_0 + P_1)/2]$ and the midpoints of quantity demanded $[(Q_0 + Q_1)/2]$ as the base. This approach to calculating percentage changes is referred to as the *midpoint method.*

Therefore, the *price elasticity of demand* formula (assuming price falls from P_0 to P_1 and quantity demanded rises from Q_0 to Q_1) is

$$E_d = \frac{Q_1 - Q_0}{(Q_0 + Q_1)/2} \div \frac{P_1 - P_0}{(P_0 + P_1)/2}$$

Using the midpoints of price and quantity to compute the relevant percentage changes essentially gives us the average elasticity between point *a* and point *b*. Price elasticity of demand is the difference in quantity over the sum of the two quantities divided by 2, divided by the difference in price over the sum of the two prices divided by 2. In Figure 2, the price elasticity of demand between points *a* and *b* would equal

$$
\begin{aligned}
E_d &= \frac{500 - 300}{(300 + 500)/2} \div \frac{1.00 - 2.00}{(2.00 + 1.00)/2} \\
&= \frac{200}{400} \div \frac{-1.00}{1.50} \\
&= 0.50 \div -0.67 \\
&= |-0.75| \\
&= 0.75
\end{aligned}
$$

Check for yourself to see that this elasticity formula yields the same results whether you compute elasticity for a price increase from \$1.00 to \$2.00 or for a price decrease from \$2.00 to \$1.00.

Now that we have seen what price elasticity of demand is and how to calculate it, let's put this knowledge to work by looking at how elasticity affects total revenue.

CHECKPOINT

ELASTICITY OF DEMAND

- Elasticity summarizes how responsive one variable is to a change in another variable.
- Price elasticity of demand summarizes how responsive quantity demanded is to changes in price.
- Price elasticity of demand is defined as the percentage change in quantity demanded divided by the percentage change in price.
- Inelastic demands are relatively unresponsive to changes in price, while quantity demanded is more responsive with elastic demands.
- Elasticity is determined by a product's substitutability, its proportion of the budget, whether it is a luxury or a necessity, and the time period considered.
- Economists use midpoints to derive consistent estimates whether price rises or falls.

QUESTION: Using your knowledge of the determinants of elasticity, why is gasoline inelastic in the short-term but elastic in the long-term? Explain why automobiles tend to have the opposite effect, being elastic in the short-term but inelastic in the long-term?

Answers to the Checkpoint questions can be found at the end of this chapter.

Total Revenue and Other Measures of Elasticity

Elasticity is important to firms because elasticity measures the responsiveness of quantity sold to changes in price, which provides valuable information to firms in deciding whether to increase or decrease prices. Owners of a restaurant that is completely full each evening might ponder raising its prices, but only if it can retain most of its customers. Another restaurant, which has few customers, might wish to lower its prices to generate more business, but only if it generates enough business to offset the lower prices it charges.

Elasticity is also important because it allows firms to determine how a change in the price of one product might affect the demand for other items, or how changes in economic conditions might affect the market for their goods. If a supermarket discounts the price of sirloin steaks, how would this affect the demand for other cuts of beef, or other meats? Would it increase sales of steak sauce and potatoes? These are questions we address in this section using other measures of elasticity.

Elasticity and Total Revenue

total revenue Price × quantity demanded (sold). If demand is elastic and price rises, quantity demanded falls off significantly and total revenue declines, and vice versa. If demand is inelastic and price rises, quantity demanded does not decline much and total revenue rises, and vice versa.

The elasticity of demand, which we learned about in the previous section, has an important effect on the total revenues of the firm. **Total revenue** (TR) is equal to the number of units sold (Q) times the price of each unit (P), or

$$TR = Q \times P$$

The sensitivity of output sold to price changes greatly influences how much total revenue changes when price changes.

Inelastic Demand When consumers are so loyal to a product or so few substitutes exist that consumers continue to buy the product even when its price goes up, the product is inelastically demanded. Panel A of Figure 3 shows the impact such a price increase has on total revenue when the demand for a product is inelastic. Price rises from \$2.00 to \$4.00, and sales decline from 600 to 500 units. In this case, total revenue *rises*. We know this because the revenue gained from the price hike [(\$4.00 – \$2.00) × 500 = \$1,000] is greater than the revenue lost [(\$2.00 × (600 – 500) = \$200]. We can see this by comparing the size of the area labeled "Revenue Gained" with the area labeled "Revenue Lost" in the figure. What has happened here? The price hike has driven off only a few customers, but the firm's many remaining customers are paying a much higher price, thus driving up the firm's total revenue.

This may suggest that firms would always want the demand for their products to be inelastic. Unfortunately for them, inelastic demand has a flip side. Specifically, if supply increases (due to a technical advance, say), sales will rise only moderately, even as prices fall dramatically. This leads to a drop in total revenue: Consumers indeed buy more of the product at its new lower price, but not enough to offset the lower price per unit received by firms.

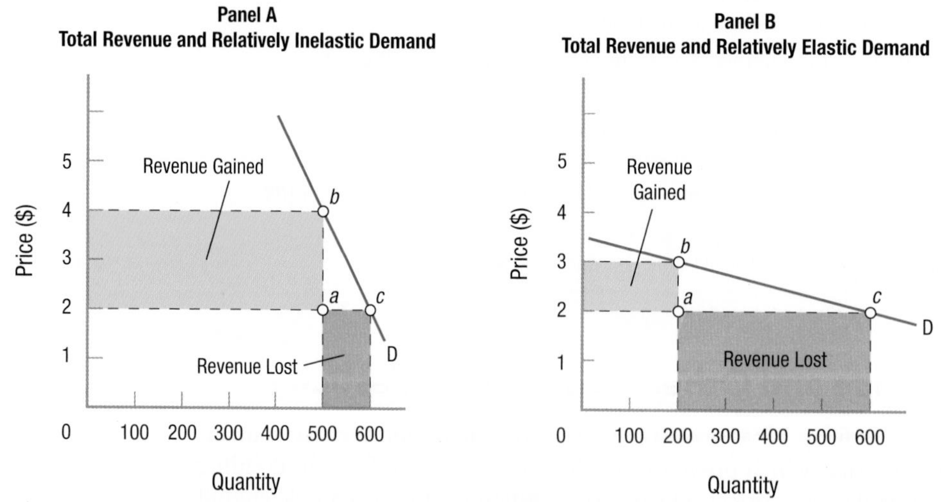

FIGURE 3

Total Revenue and Elasticity of Demand

Given inelastic demand in panel A, when price rises from \$2 to \$4, revenue rises because the revenue gained from the price hike (\$1,000) is greater than the revenue lost from fewer sales (\$200). The price hike may have driven off a few customers, but the firm's many remaining customers are paying a much higher price, thus increasing the firm's revenue. When products have elastic demands as shown in panel B, usually because many substitutes are available, firms feel a greater impact from changes in price. A small rise in price causes sales to fall off dramatically.

Elastic Demand Elastic demand is the opposite of inelastic demand. Firms with elastically demanded products will see their sales change dramatically in response to small price changes. Panel B of Figure 3 shows what happens to total revenue when a firm increases the price of a product with elastic demand. Although price does not increase much, sales fall significantly. Revenue lost greatly exceeds the revenue gained from the price increase, thus total revenue falls.

The opposite occurs when prices fall and demand is elastic. The high elasticity of demand faced by restaurants helps explain why so many of them offer "Happy Hour" specials and other discounts. As prices fall, sales have the potential to expand rapidly, thus increasing revenue.

Unitary Elasticity We have looked at the impact of changing prices on revenue when demand is elastic and inelastic. When the elasticity of demand is unitary ($E_d = 1$), a 10% increase in price results in a 10% reduction in quantity demanded. As a result, total revenue is unaffected.

Table 2 summarizes the effects price changes have on total revenue for different price elasticities of demand.

TABLE 2 Total Revenue, Price Changes, and Price Elasticity of Demand

	Elasticity		
Price Change	**Inelastic**	**Elastic**	**Unitary Elastic**
Price increases	TR increases	TR decreases	No change in TR
Price decreases	TR decreases	TR increases	No change in TR

Elasticity and Total Revenue Along a Straight-Line (Linear) Demand Curve Elasticity varies along a straight-line demand curve. Figure 4 on the next page shows a linear demand curve in panel A and graphs the corresponding total revenue points in panel B. In panel A, the elastic part of the curve is that portion above point *e*. Notice that when price falls from $11 to $10, the revenue gained ($100) is much larger than the revenue lost ($10), and thus total revenue rises. This is shown in panel B, where total revenue rises when output grows from 10 to 20 units.

As we move down the demand curve, elasticity will eventually equal 1 (at point *e*) where elasticity is unitary. Price was falling up to this point, while total revenue kept rising until the last price reduction just before $6, where revenue did not change. Revenue is at its maximum at point *e* or a price of $6 in both panels.

As price continues to fall below $6, the demand curve moves into an inelastic range because the percentage change in quantity demanded is less than the percentage change in price. Therefore, when price falls from $3 to $2, revenue declines. The revenue gained ($20) is less than the revenue lost ($90). This decline in revenue is shown in panel B, as total revenue falls as output rises from 90 to 100 units sold.

To summarize, elasticity changes along a negatively sloped linear demand curve because the *percentage* change in price and quantity varies along the curve. When the price of a product is low, a 1-unit change in price is a large percentage change while the percentage change in quantity demanded is small. When the price is high, a 1-unit change in price is a small percentage change but the percentage change in quantity is large.

FIGURE 4

Price Elasticity and Total Revenue Along a Straight Line (Linear) Demand Curve

Price elasticity varies along a straight line demand curve. In panel A, the elastic part of the curve lies above point *e*. Thus, when price falls from \$11 to \$10, revenue rises, as shown in panel B. As we move down the demand curve, elasticity equals 1 (at point *e*) where elasticity is unitary. Revenue is maximized at this point. As price continues to fall below \$6, demand moves into an inelastic range. When price falls from \$3 to \$2, revenue declines, as shown in panel B.

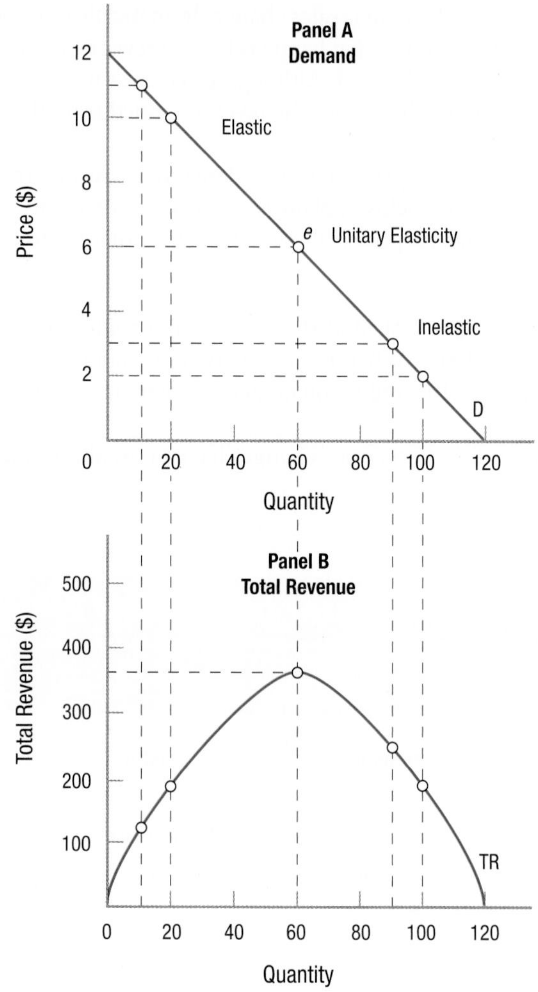

Other Elasticities of Demand

Besides the price elasticity of demand, two other elasticities of demand are important. The first, *cross elasticity of demand*, measures how changes in the price of one good affect the demand for other related goods. If Toyota is planning a price reduction, what impact will this have on the sale of Fords? Ford will want to estimate this to decide whether to ignore Toyota or lower its own automobile prices.

Another type of elasticity measures how responsive quantity demanded is to changes in income. This is called *income elasticity of demand.* Incomes vary as the economy expands and contracts. To plan their future employment and production, many industries want to know how the demand for their products will be affected when the economy changes. How much will airline travel be affected if the economy moves into a recession? What will happen to sales of lattes at Starbucks? Each business faces a different situation.

Let's consider these two elasticities of demand more closely, beginning with cross elasticity of demand.

cross elasticity of demand Measures how responsive the quantity demanded of one good is to changes in the price of another good. Substitute goods have positive cross elasticities: An increase in the price of one good leads consumers to substitute (buy more of) the other good whose price has not changed. Complementary goods have negative cross elasticities: An increase in the price of a complement leads to a reduction in sales of the other good whose price has not changed.

Cross Elasticity of Demand

Cross elasticity of demand (E_{ab}) measures how responsive the quantity demanded of one good (product a) is to changes in the price of another (product b):

$$E_{ab} = \frac{\text{Percentage Change in Quantity Demanded of Product a}}{\text{Percentage Change in Price of Product b}}$$

Using cross elasticity of demand, we can classify goods in two ways. Products a and b are **substitutes** if their cross elasticity of demand is positive ($E_{ab} > 0$). Common sense tells us that chicken and turkey are substitutes. Therefore, if the price of turkey rises, people will substitute away from turkey and toward chicken, thus the quantity demanded for chicken will grow. This illustrates a positive cross elasticity. Similar relationships exist between Toyota and Honda cars, wireless services provided by AT&T and Verizon, and the price of gas and public transportation.

Second, products a and b are **complements** if their cross elasticity of demand is negative ($E_{ab} < 0$). This is an instance in which a minus sign conveys important information. Complementary products are those goods and services that are consumed together, such as lift tickets and snowboard rentals. When the price of lift tickets rises, the result is that the quantity demanded for snowboard rentals falls as fewer people head to the mountains. Other complementary goods include coffee and cream, hamburgers and french fries, and hot dogs and hot dog buns. Finally, two goods are *not related* if a cross elasticity of demand is zero, or near zero.

substitutes Goods consumers substitute for one another depending on their relative prices, such as coffee and tea. Substitutes have a positive cross elasticity of demand.

complements Goods that are typically consumed together, such as coffee and sugar. Complements have a negative cross elasticity of demand.

income elasticity of demand Measures how responsive quantity demanded is to changes in consumer income.

normal goods Goods that have positive income elasticities of less than 1. When consumer income grows, quantity demanded rises for normal goods, but less than the rise in income.

luxury goods Goods that have income elasticities greater than 1. When consumer income grows, quantity demanded of luxury goods rises more than the rise in income.

inferior goods Goods that have income elasticities that are negative. When consumer income grows, quantity demanded falls for inferior goods.

Income Elasticity of Demand The **income elasticity of demand** (E_Y) measures how responsive quantity demanded is to changes in consumer income. We define the income elasticity of demand as

$$E_Y = \frac{\text{Percentage Change in Quantity Demanded}}{\text{Percentage Change in Income}}$$

Depending on the value of the income elasticity of demand, we can classify goods in three ways. First, a **normal good** is one whose income elasticity is positive, but less than 1 ($0 < E_Y < 1$). As income rises, quantity demanded rises as well, but not as fast as the rise in income. Most products are normal goods. If your income doubles, you will probably buy more sporting equipment and restaurant meals, but not twice as many.

A second category, *income superior goods* or **luxury goods,** includes products with an income elasticity greater than 1 ($E_Y > 1$). As income rises, quantity demanded grows faster than income. Goods and services such as Mercedes automobiles, caviar, fine wine, and visits to European spas are luxury or income superior goods.

Finally, **inferior goods** are those goods for which income elasticity is negative ($E_Y < 0$). When income rises, the quantity demanded for these goods falls. Inferior goods include potatoes, beans, cheap motels, and nosebleed section concert tickets. Get yourself a nice raise, and you will probably buy concert tickets that let you see the band up close and personal.

Keep in mind that inferior goods are not necessarily poor in quality; they simply describe goods that one buys fewer of as income increases, and vice versa. Therefore, inferior goods can vary from person to person. Nosebleed seats might be an inferior good for an avid concertgoer, but can be a normal good to a person who rarely goes to concerts.

Understanding how product sales are affected by changing incomes and economic conditions can help firms to diversify their product lines so that sales and employment can be stabilized to some extent over time. For example, firms that produce all three types of goods can try to switch production toward the good that current economic conditions favor: In boom times, production is shifted more toward the making of luxury goods. Chevrolet will produce more Corvettes in boom times, and more Chevy Sparks during economic slowdowns.

This is a good place to stop and reflect on what we have discovered so far. We have seen that elasticity measures the responsiveness of one variable to changes in another. Elasticity measures changes in percentage terms so that products of different magnitudes—a bottle of soda and an airplane—can be compared. Products that have a price elasticity of demand greater than 1 are elastic; products with price elasticity of demand less than 1 are inelastic; and products with a price elasticity

Ocean/Corbis

After college, incomes rise, which means fewer packed lunches on the lawn and more fancy lunches at the local bistro.

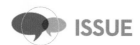

ISSUE

Using Loss Leaders to Generate Higher Total Revenue

At the start of each school year, office supply stores will often advertise items for as low as one cent. These items typically are essential school supplies such as paper, pencils, and folders that parents need to buy for their children. Because school supplies are necessities and generally low-priced, they are relatively inelastic goods. Why, then, would stores choose to reduce their prices, knowing that such actions would lead to a fall in total revenue?

The answer lies not in how prices for school supplies affect total revenue, but instead the effect that those remarkably low prices, known as *loss leaders*, has on the cross elasticity of demand for more pricier items, such as laptops, color printers, and office furniture, sold at the store. In other words, the practically free school supplies are used as an incentive to attract parents into the store.

Wouldn't some parents just buy the school supplies on sale and nothing else? Some actually do. However, most stores place limits on the quantity of the discounted items that can be purchased. Further, the inelastic nature of school supplies means that parents are not likely to hoard large quantities of school supplies because of the reduction in prices. More important, the potential gain from just one customer choosing to buy a high-priced computer or printer would offset the lost revenue from the loss leaders many times over. And because the start of the school year is when many high-priced school items are purchased, few parents end up buying just the advertised items.

Loss leaders are an effective advertising tool to increase total revenues from the sale of higher priced related goods. And loss leaders are not limited to office supply stores. Other examples of loss

Barbara Helgason/Dreamstime.com

leaders include convenience stores advertising a free soda or coffee on large banners visible to potential customers at the gas pump, fast-food restaurants featuring a 99 cent sandwich special on their marquee, or a campus sporting goods store offering a free T-shirt just for stopping by. In each case, stores are betting on consumers making decisions beyond that of the loss leader, thus illustrating the importance of cross elasticity of demand in business decisions.

of demand equal to 1 are unitary elastic. We saw how total revenue increases when price rises for an inelastic good but decreases when price rises for an elastic good. Finally, we saw that elasticity can be used to measure the effects of related goods using cross elasticity of demand, as well as changes in income using income elasticity of demand.

CHECKPOINT

TOTAL REVENUE AND OTHER MEASURES OF ELASTICITY

- When demand is inelastic and prices rise, total revenue rises. When demand is inelastic and prices fall, total revenue falls.
- When demand is elastic and prices rise, total revenue falls. When demand is elastic and prices fall, total revenue rises.
- Straight line demand curves have elastic (at higher prices) and inelastic (at lower prices) ranges.
- Cross elasticity of demand measures how responsive the quantity demanded of one product is to price changes of another. Substitutes have positive cross elasticities while complements have negative cross elasticities.
- Income elasticity of demand is a measure of how responsive quantity demanded is to changes in income. This determines whether a good is a luxury, normal, or inferior good.

QUESTION: Two clothing stores located in the same shopping center have a big sale: 20% off on everything in the store. After the sale, store 1 finds that its total revenue has increased, while store 2 finds that total revenue has decreased. What does this tell you about the price elasticity of demand for the clothes in stores 1 and 2?

Answers to the Checkpoint question can be found at the end of this chapter.

Elasticity of Supply

So far, we have looked at the consumer when we looked at the elasticity of demand. Now let us turn our attention to the producer, and look at elasticity of supply.

Price elasticity of supply (E_s) measures the responsiveness of quantity supplied to changes in the price of the product. Price elasticity of supply is defined as

$$E_s = \frac{\text{Percentage Change in Quantity Supplied}}{\text{Percentage Change in Price}}$$

price elasticity of supply A measure of the responsiveness of quantity supplied to changes in price. An elastic supply curve has elasticity greater than 1, whereas inelastic supplies have elasticities less than 1. Time is the most important determinant of the elasticity of supply.

Note that because the slope of the supply curve is positive, the price elasticity of supply will always be a positive number. Economists classify price elasticity of supply in the same way that they classify price elasticity of demand. Classification is based on whether the percentage change in quantity supplied is greater than, less than, or equal to the percentage change in price. When price rises just a little and quantity increases by much more, supply is elastic, and vice versa. The output of many commodities such as gold and seasonal vegetables cannot be quickly increased if their price increases, so they are inelastic. In summary:

Elastic supply: $E_s > 1$
Inelastic supply: $E_s < 1$
Unitary elastic supply: $E_s = 1$

elastic supply Price elasticity of supply is greater than 1. The percentage change in quantity supplied is greater than the percentage change in price.

inelastic supply Price elasticity of supply is less than 1. The percentage change in quantity supplied is less than the percentage change in price.

unitary elastic supply Price elasticity of supply is equal to 1. The percentage change in quantity supplied is equal to the percentage change in price.

Looking at the three supply curves in Figure 5, we can easily determine which curve is inelastic, which is elastic, and which is unitary elastic. First, note that all three curves go through point *a*. As we increase the price from P_0 to P_1, we see that the response in quantity supplied is different for all three curves. Consider supply curve S_1 first. When price changes to P_1 (point *b*), the change in output (Q_0 to Q_1) is the smallest for the three curves. Most important, the percentage change in quantity supplied is smaller than the percentage change in price, therefore S_1 is an inelastic supply curve.

Contrast this with S_3. In this case, when price rises to P_1 (point *d*), output climbs from Q_0 all the way to Q_3. Because the percentage change in output is larger than the percentage change in price, S_3 is elastic. And finally, curve S_2 is a unitary elastic curve because the percentage change in output is the same as the percentage change in price.

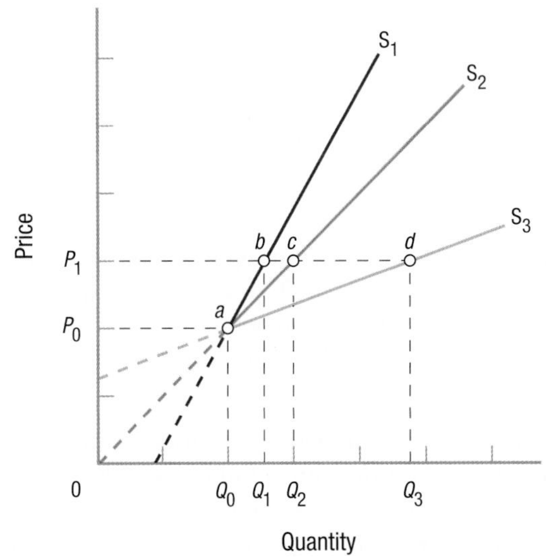

FIGURE 5

Price Elasticity of Supply

All three supply curves in this figure run through point *a*, but they respond differently when price changes from P_0 to P_1. Considering supply curve S_1 first, when price changes, the percentage change in quantity supplied is smaller than the percentage change in price, thus S_1 is an inelastic supply curve. Curve S_2 is a unitary elastic supply curve, because the percentage change in output is the same as the percentage change in price. For supply curve S_3, the percentage change in output is greater than the percentage change in price, so S_3 is elastic. Elastic linear supply curves cross the price axis, inelastic linear supply curves cross the quantity axis, and unitary elastic linear supply curves go through the origin.

Here is a simple rule of thumb. When the supply curve is linear, like those shown in Figure 5, you can always determine if the supply curve is elastic, inelastic, or unitary elastic by extending the curve to the axis and applying the following rules:

- Elastic supply curves always cross the price axis, as does curve S_3.
- Inelastic supply curves always cross the quantity axis, as does curve S_1.
- Unitary elastic supply curves always cross through the origin, as does curve S_2.

Time and Price Elasticity of Supply

The primary determinant of price elasticity of supply is time. To adjust output in response to changes in market prices, firms require time. Firms have both variable inputs, such as labor, and fixed inputs, such as plant capacity. To increase their labor force, firms must recruit, interview, and hire more workers. This can take as little time as a few hours—a call to a temp agency—or as long as a few months. On the other hand, building another plant or expanding the existing plant to increase output involves considerably more time and resources. In some instances, such as building a new oil refinery or computer chip plant, it can take as long as a decade, with environmental clearance alone often requiring years of study and costing millions of dollars. Finally, in some markets, such as that for original Rembrandt paintings, new supply will never be created (assuming that the dead cannot return). Economists typically distinguish among three types of time periods: the market period, the short run, and the long run.

market period Time period so short that the output and the number of firms are fixed. Agricultural products at harvest time face market periods. Products that unexpectedly become instant hits face market periods (there is a lag between when the firm realizes it has a hit on its hands and when inventory can be replaced).

The Market Period The **market period** is so short that the output and the number of firms in an industry are fixed; firms have no time to change their production levels in response to changes in product price. Consider a raspberry market in the summer. Even if consumers flock to the market, their tastes having shifted in favor of fresh raspberries, farmers can do little to increase the supply of raspberries until the next year. Figure 6 shows a market period supply curve (S_{MP}) for agricultural products such as raspberries. During the market period, the quantity of product available to the market is fixed at Q_0. If demand changes (shifting from D_0 to D_1), the only impact is on the price of the product. In Figure 6, price moves from P_0 (point *e*) to P_1 (point *a*). In summary, if demand grows over the market period, price will rise, and vice versa.

Changes in demand over the market period can be devastating for firms selling perishable goods. If demand falls, cantaloupes cannot be kept until demand grows; they must either be sold at a discount or trashed.

short run Time period when plant capacity and the number of firms in the industry cannot change. Firms can employ more people, have existing employees work overtime, or hire part-time employees to produce more, but this is done in an existing plant.

The Short Run The **short run** is defined as a period of time during which plant capacity and the number of firms in the industry cannot change. Firms can, however, change the amount of labor, raw materials, and other variable inputs they employ in the short run to adjust their output to changes in the market. Note that the short run does not imply a specific number of weeks, months, or years. It simply means a period short enough that firms cannot adjust their plant capacity, but long enough for them to hire more labor to increase their production. A restaurant with an outdoor seating area can hire additional staff and open this area in a relatively short timeframe when the weather gets warm, but manufacturing firms usually need more time to hire and train new people for their production lines. Clearly, the time associated with the short run differs depending on the industry.

This also is illustrated in Figure 6. The short-run supply curve, S_{SR}, is more elastic than the market period curve. If demand grows from D_0 to D_1, output expands from Q_0 to Q_2 and price increases to P_2 as equilibrium moves from point *e* to point *b*. Because output can expand in the short run in response to rising demand, the price increase is not as drastic as it was in the market period.

long run Time period long enough for firms to alter their plant capacities and for the number of firms in the industry to change. Existing firms can expand or build new plants, or firms can enter or exit the industry.

The Long Run Economists define the **long run** as a period of time long enough for firms to alter their plant capacity and for the number of firms in the industry to change. In the long run, some firms may decide to leave the industry if they think the market will be unfavorable. Alternatively, new firms may enter the market, or existing firms can

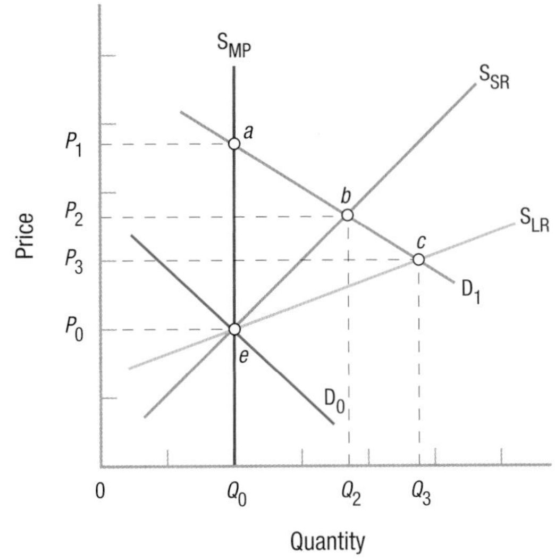

FIGURE 6

Time and Price Elasticity of Supply

During the market period, the quantity of output available to the market is fixed and the only impact will be on the price of the product, which will rise from P_0 to P_1 if demand increases. Over the short run, firms can change the amount of inputs they employ to adjust their output to market changes. Thus, the short-run supply curve (S_{SR}) is more elastic than the market period curve; and price increases are more moderate. In the long run, firms can change their plant capacity and enter or exit an industry. Long-run supply curve S_{LR} is elastic, and a rise in demand leads to only a small increase in price.

alter their production capacity. Because all these conceivable changes are possible in the long run, the long-run supply curve is more elastic, as illustrated in Figure 6 by supply curve S_{LR}. In this case, a rise in demand from D_0 to D_1 gives rise to a small increase in the price of the product, while generating a major increase in output, from Q_0 to Q_3 (point *c*).

In giving the long-run supply curve S_{LR} a small but positive slope, we are assuming that an industry's costs will increase slightly as it increases its output. Firms must compete with other industries to expand production. Wages and other input prices rise in the industry as firms attempt to draw resources away from their immediate competitors and other industries.

Some industries may not face added costs as they expand. Fast-food chains, copy centers, and coffee shops seem to be able to reproduce at will without incurring increasing costs. Therefore, their long-run supply curves may be nearly horizontal.

At this point, we have seen how elasticity measures the responsiveness of demand to a change in price and how total revenue is affected by different demand elasticities. We have also seen that supply elasticities are mainly a function of the time needed to adjust to price change signals. Next, let's apply our findings about elasticity to a subject that concerns all of us: taxes.

Eastphoto/age fotostock

A crowded restaurant might encourage its owner to expand. In the market period (i.e., same day), little can be done to accommodate more diners. In the short run, the restaurant can rearrange tables and hire more waitstaff. In the long run, it can expand the restaurant or open a second location.

CHECKPOINT

ELASTICITY OF SUPPLY

- Elasticity of supply measures the responsiveness of quantity supplied to changes in price.
- Elastic supplies are very responsive to price changes. With inelastic supply, quantity supplied is not very responsive to changing prices.

- Supplies are highly inelastic in the market period, but can expand (become more elastic) in the short run because firms can hire additional resources to raise output levels.
- In the long run, supplies are relatively elastic because firms can enter or exit the industry, and existing firms can expand their plant capacity.

QUESTION: A number of products are made in preparation for the annual flu season, although the types of goods vary in terms of their elasticity of supply. Rank the following goods from most elastic to least elastic: (a) over-the-counter flu remedies, (b) flu shots, (c) chicken soup, and (d) boxes of tissue.

Answers to the Checkpoint question can be found at the end of this chapter.

Taxes and Elasticity

On average, families pay more than 40% of their income in taxes, including income, property, estate, sales, and excise taxes. (An excise tax is a sales tax applied to a specific product, such as gasoline or tobacco.) Add to this the taxes that are embedded into the goods and services we buy, such as tariffs (taxes) on imports, tourism taxes, and airport security taxes, and it's no wonder that taxes are a perennial issue of debate among policymakers and their constituents.

Nobody likes paying taxes, but they are necessary to provide many of the public goods and services (such as roads, national defense, police protection, public education, clean air, and parks) from which everybody receives some benefit. The questions economists deal with are how to determine the efficient level of taxation and what is the most efficient way to reach that level?

Taxes can be separated into two general categories: taxes on income sources and taxes on spending. We now study how the economic burden of both categories of taxes can vary depending on how the tax policy is designed (in the case of income) and on the elasticity of the good or service being purchased (in the case of spending).

We begin by studying the various ways taxes are collected on income.

Taxes on Income Sources and Their Economic Burden

Taxes on income sources constitute the largest source of revenues for the federal government and many state governments. The most common types of taxes include individual income tax, payroll tax (i.e., Social Security tax), corporate income tax, dividend tax (taxes on earnings from financial assets), and capital gains tax (taxes on the rising values of assets such as property and financial instruments when sold).

Much of the debate on the economic burden of income taxes focuses on whether taxes are progressive, flat, or regressive with respect to income earned. **Progressive taxes** are those that rise in burden as income increases. **Flat taxes** take a constant percentage of one's income. **Regressive taxes** fall in burden as income increases, which means that individuals with lower incomes pay a greater percentage of their income in taxes than individuals with higher incomes. A type of regressive tax is called a **lump-sum tax,** which takes a fixed amount of tax regardless of income earned, and therefore falls in percentage as income rises. Table 3 lists the three categories of taxes and provides an example of an actual tax that falls within each category.

progressive tax A tax that rises in percentage of income as income increases.

flat tax A tax that is a constant proportion of one's income.

regressive tax A tax that falls in percentage of income as income increases.

lump-sum tax A fixed amount of tax regardless of income, and is a type of regressive tax.

TABLE 3 Types of Taxes and Their Economic Burden

Type of Tax	Example	Description of Tax Burden
Progressive	Individual income tax	As income rises, income is taxed at a higher percentage rate when a higher tax bracket is reached.
Flat	Medicare tax	Medicare tax is 2.9% of all income earned (half of which is paid by employees and half paid by employers).
Regressive	Payroll tax	Payroll taxes are a flat tax of 6.2% paid by both employees and employers up to an income cap. Therefore, those earning above the cap will pay a lower overall percentage of income in payroll taxes.

Taxes on Spending and the Incidence of Taxation

The typical household pays a substantial amount of taxes on goods and services. Almost everybody pays sales taxes on goods and services purchased, homeowners pay property taxes each year on the value of their homes, and all sorts of excise taxes exist on everything from car rentals and hotel stays to gasoline purchases.

Although income taxes typically represent the largest burden on most households, taxes on spending are sometimes larger for certain groups of people. For example, households with very low incomes often pay little to no income taxes, but pay a sizeable portion of their income in sales and excise taxes. Similarly, wealthy households often receive most of their income by way of investment earnings, which are taxed at a lower rate than traditional income earnings; for these households, taxes paid on property (often on multiple homes) and luxury taxes (on yachts and other expensive toys) may constitute a larger portion of their tax burden.

In sum, taxes on spending are not trivial, and elasticity plays an important role in determining the impact of these various taxes on individuals, families, and businesses. Economists studying taxes are interested in the **incidence of taxation** and in *shifts* in the tax burden. The incidence of a tax refers to who bears its economic burden. Statutes determine what is taxed, who must pay various taxes, and what agencies are responsible for collecting taxes and remitting the revenue collected. Even so, the individuals, firms, or groups paying a tax may not be the ones bearing its economic burden. This burden can be shifted onto others. Considering the elasticities of demand and supply will help us determine the incidence of various taxes—who really bears the tax burden—and thus the ultimate impact of various tax policies.

incidence of taxation Refers to who bears the economic burden of a tax. The economic entity bearing the burden of a particular tax will depend on the price elasticities of demand and supply.

Let's now analyze how the elasticity of a good or service can affect the incidence of taxation. To simplify the analysis, we will focus on excise taxes for the remainder of this section.

Elasticity of Demand and Tax Burdens

Let us consider what happens when an excise tax is levied on a product with elastic demand, such as strawberries. Panel A of Figure 7 shows the market before an excise tax is imposed. The initial supply curve (S_0) is supply before the tax and demand curve D_0 reflects

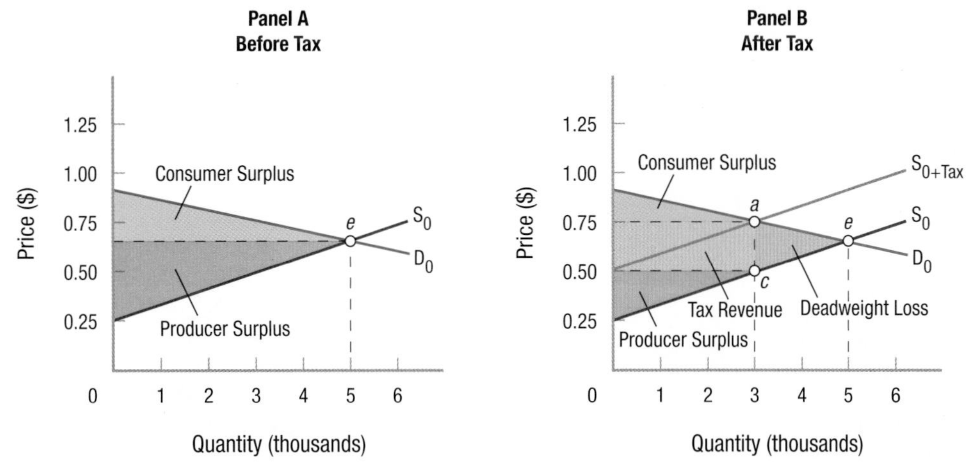

FIGURE 7

Tax Burden with Relatively Elastic Demand

S_0 is the initial supply curve for a product with elastic demand (panel A). When a 25 cent excise tax is placed on the product, the supply curve shifts upward by the amount of the tax, S_{0+Tax} (panel B). With demand remaining constant at D_0, equilibrium moves to point *a* (3,000 units). In this case, output falls substantially when the tax is imposed because elastic demand means extreme price sensitivity. As a result, sellers end up bearing most of the burden of this tax, and the deadweight loss is relatively large (area *cae*).

demand. Originally, the market is in equilibrium at point *e*, at which 5,000 baskets are sold for 65 cents each.

In panel B, we now add a per unit tax—say, 25 cents a basket—paid by the grower. This, in effect, adds 25 cents to the cost for each basket and adds a wedge between what consumers pay and what growers receive. Supply curve S_0 therefore shifts upward by this amount, to S_{0+Tax}. The new supply curve runs parallel to S_0, with the distance the curve has shifted (*ac*) equaling the 25 cent tax per basket collected by the government.

Assuming demand remains constant at D_0, the new equilibrium is at point *a*, with 3,000 baskets sold for a price of 75 cents each. The producer receives 75 cents per basket, of which it must send 25 cents to the government, keeping 50 cents for itself. Keep in mind that, because this demand is elastic, many consumers are not really willing to pay a higher price for the product; this is why output declines so much and why sellers bear most of the burden of this tax.

Before the tax, both consumer and producer surplus (discussed in Chapter 4) in panel A were substantial. After the tax, the government collects revenue equal to the tax (25 cents) times the number of baskets sold (3,000), or $750 (the blue area), consumer surplus now equals the area above the blue section, and producer surplus equals the area below it. Note that consumers and producers lose surplus equal not only to the revenue gained by the government but also to area *cae*, which represents a deadweight loss. Although this area is lost to society as a result of the tax, how the tax revenues are used to benefit society determines whether society is better or worse off with the tax.

Contrast this situation with the impact of an excise tax when the demand is inelastic (e.g., cigarettes), as in Figure 8. Initially, 23,000 packs are sold at $3.00 per pack. With a $1.25 tax, supply shifts to S_{0+Tax}, market equilibrium moves to point *g*, price increases from $3.00 to $4.00 per pack, and output declines from 23,000 to 20,000. Inelastic demands are price insensitive, therefore output declines much less when this tax is imposed. The $1.25 tax in this case is *gh*, with consumers paying *gi* (a dollar), sellers paying *ih* (25 cents), and a deadweight loss equal to area *hge*. In general, deadweight losses are small when demand is inelastic. A small quantity reduction given a higher price means that nearly all the excise tax is shifted forward to consumers. In this case, consumers pay an additional $1.00 for each unit, but manufacturers end up bearing only a small burden (25 cents).

We can generalize about the effects of elasticity of demand on the tax burden. For a given supply of some product, the greater the price elasticity of demand, the lower the share of the total tax burden shifted to consumers and the greater the share borne by sellers, and vice versa.

FIGURE 8

Tax Burden with Relatively Inelastic Demand

S_0 is the initial supply curve for a product with inelastic demand. When a $1.25 excise tax is placed on the product, the supply curve shifts upward by the amount of the tax, to S_{0+Tax}. Assuming demand remains constant at D_0, the new equilibrium will be at point *g*. Because this demand curve is inelastic, consumers are willing to pay a higher price for the product, and bear nearly all the burden of the tax. The deadweight loss (area *hge*) is relatively small when demand is inelastic.

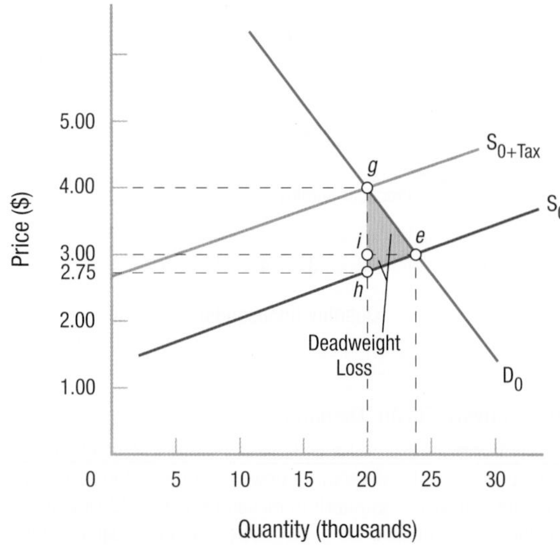

This analysis shows why proposals to raise excise taxes usually focus on such inelastically demanded commodities as tobacco, gasoline, and alcohol. For products with inelastic demands, the reduction in output is lower when prices rise because of the tax—most smokers keep smoking even when the tobacco tax goes up. Therefore, these taxes generate more revenue than would excise taxes on elastically demanded products. Proposals to raise excise taxes are often cloaked in public health and welfare rhetoric, politicians finding it easier to sell the idea of taxes that punish "sins" such as smoking and drinking. However, if the products in question did not have inelastic demands, the tax revenues generated by such taxes would be small. Because consumers substantially reduce their purchases when demand is elastic, many workers in the industries with such elastically demanded products would become unemployed. As a result, such taxes are rarely enacted on products with elastic demands.

Elasticity of Supply and Tax Burdens

In a similar way, the elasticity of supply is an important determinant of who bears the ultimate burden of taxation. In panel A of Figure 9, demand is held constant at D_0 and equilibrium is initially at point *e*. Supply curve S_0 is perfectly elastic, or horizontal. When a per unit tax is added to the product, supply shifts vertically to S_{0+Tax} and the new market equilibrium moves to point *d*, with Q_1 units sold at price P_1. Notice that in this limiting situation of perfectly elastic supply, the full monetary burden of the tax ($P_1 - P_0$) is borne by consumers in the form of higher prices, although industry bears an indirect burden of reduced output and employment. The deadweight loss, area *cde*, is relatively large with elastically supplied products.

Now consider the case in which the supply curve is inelastic, as with S_0 in panel B of Figure 9. When we add the same tax as before to this supply curve, market equilibrium

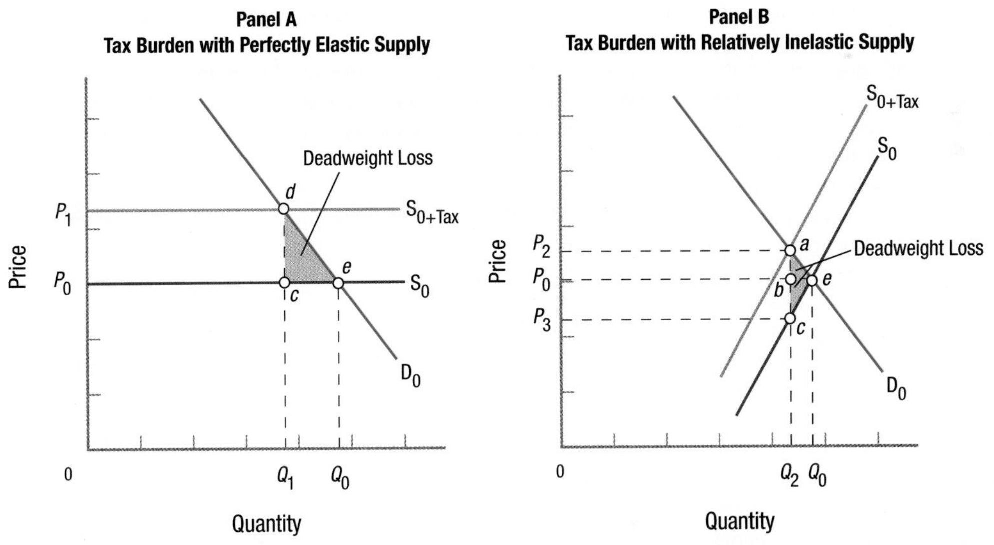

FIGURE 9

Tax Burden and Supply Elasticities

When supply curve S_0 is perfectly elastic as shown in panel A, a per unit excise tax added to the product shifts supply vertically to S_{0+Tax}. In this limiting case of perfectly elastic supply, the full burden of the tax ($P_1 - P_0$) is borne by consumers through higher prices. The deadweight loss is relatively large with elastic supply curves and equal to area *cde*. When supply is inelastic as in panel B, with the same excise tax (*ac* in panel B = *cd* in panel A), price increases are less, and the reduction in output is also less than before. Consumers pay only part of the tax, *ab*, and the deadweight loss to society is equal to area *cae*, less than with the elastic supply shown in panel A.

moves to point *a*. Price increases less than before (P_2 in panel B is lower than P_1 in panel A) and the reduction in output is also less than before ($Q_0 - Q_2$ in panel B is less than $Q_0 - Q_1$ in panel A). Consumers pay only part of the tax, *ab*, while sellers must absorb *bc*, and the deadweight loss *cae* is relatively small.

Note what happens in all of these tax cases. Figures 7 to 9 show that whenever a tax is added, the tax moves the market away from its equilibrium point, regardless of whether the tax is borne by consumers, producers, or both. All taxes generate a tax wedge, resulting in a deadweight loss to society. The more elastic the demand or supply, the greater this deadweight loss. Table 4 summarizes these general results.

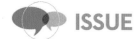

ISSUE

Are Sales Taxes Fair to Low-Income Households?

Image Source/Getty Images

With few exceptions, sales taxes are added to the price of nearly everything we buy. Sales taxes vary by state, and can also vary by cities or counties within states. Unlike income taxes, for which the tax rate changes as income rises, sales taxes are a fixed percentage of one's total purchase. For example, in the state of New Jersey, with a sales tax rate of 7%, you would pay $3.50 in sales tax if you bought a watch that sells for $50. Because of this fixed percentage, sales taxes are often referred to as a flat (or proportional) tax, because the tax rate remains constant regardless of the amount purchased. But is this an accurate depiction of the economic burden of sales taxes?

Many economists argue that sales taxes are *regressive* in nature, meaning that households with lower incomes pay a greater share of their income in sales taxes than households with higher incomes. Such claims have led some economists to vehemently oppose legislation that proposes higher sales taxes as a way to increase state tax revenues.

To measure the burden of sales taxes, one must first analyze how households spend their money. For example, a household earning $25,000 a year spends approximately $5,500 on items subject to the sales tax. These expenditures include most goods (except groceries in many states), car payments, and many services. Major items not subjected to sales taxes include rent and mortgage payments, tuition payments, and most financial instruments. Using an average sales tax rate of 7%, this household would spend $385 a year on sales taxes, or 1.54% of total income. A household earning $100,000 a year, however, spends approximately $18,000 on taxable items. This amounts to $1,260 a year in sales tax, or 1.26% of total income. Therefore, sales taxes *are* regressive.

How do states compare in terms of the average sales tax rate? The following table shows the ten states with the highest average sales tax rate and the ten states with the lowest. Surprisingly, a number of states with the highest sales tax rates are those with lower average incomes, such as Tennessee, Louisiana, Arkansas, and Alabama. This creates a double whammy—income tends to be lower in these states, and being poor takes an even greater toll with high sales taxes.

In sum, when municipalities and states need to raise revenue, the sales tax is the type of tax that hurts the poor the most. Therefore, a few states have opted not to use sales taxes at all, and instead rely on state income taxes, corporate taxes, or property taxes that are *progressive*, meaning that those with higher incomes pay a greater percentage in taxes. But for most states, sales taxes remain an important source of revenues.

Highest Average Sales Tax Rate	Lowest Average Sales Tax Rate
1. Tennessee (9.44%)	41. Wisconsin (5.43%)
2. Arizona (9.16%)	42. Wyoming (5.34%)
3. Louisiana (8.87%)	43 (tied). Virginia (5.00%)
4. Washington (8.86%)	43 (tied). Maine (5.00%)
5. Oklahoma (8.67%)	45. Hawaii (4.35%)
6. Arkansas (8.61%)	46. Alaska (1.69%)
7. New York (8.48%)	47 (tied). Delaware (0.00%)
8. Alabama (8.45%)	47 (tied). Montana (0.00%)
9. Kansas (8.38%)	47 (tied). New Hampshire (0.00%)
10. Illinois (8.25%)	47 (tied). Oregon (0.00%)

Source: Tax Foundation, 2013. (Percentages are state sales tax rate + average local sales tax rate.)

Summary of Elasticity and Taxes — TABLE 4

Elasticity		Tax Burdens			
Demand	**Supply**	**On Consumers**	**Businesses**	**Deadweight Loss**	**Figure Where Shown**
Elastic	No change	Lower	Higher	Large	7
Inelastic	No change	Higher	Lower	Small	8
No change	Elastic	Higher	Lower	Large	9A
No change	Inelastic	Lower	Higher	Small	9B

These last three chapters have given us the powerful tools of supply and demand analysis. Elasticity is important because it encapsulates the complex relationships among prices, quantity demanded, and total revenues in just two words: elastic and inelastic. When demands are inelastic and some incident marginally reduces supply, policymakers (and now you) know that price will go up substantially, although consumers will continue to purchase the product. Again, this is what happens when gasoline prices rise—consumers continue to purchase roughly the same amount as before, thus oil industry revenue and profits rise substantially in the short run.

If, however, demand is elastic and the same incident reduces supply, prices will rise, but by a smaller amount, and output and employment will fall a lot more. If weather conditions in California and Florida ruin the orange crop, reducing the supply and increasing the price of orange juice, consumers will readily substitute other juices. As a result, output, employment, revenues, and profits will decline in the orange industry.

CHECKPOINT

TAXES AND ELASTICITY

- Taxes on income can be progressive, flat, or regressive based on the percentage of income that becomes taxes. Most income taxes are progressive, but certain forms of flat and regressive taxes exist.
- When price elasticity of demand is elastic, consumers bear a smaller burden of taxes while more is borne by sellers. When demands are inelastic, a higher share of the total tax burden is shifted to consumers.
- When the price elasticity of supply is elastic, buyers bear a larger burden of taxes. Elastic supplies also lead to a larger deadweight loss. When supply is inelastic, more of the tax burden is shifted to sellers, but the deadweight loss is lower.

QUESTION: Excise taxes were the principal taxes levied in the United States for the first 100 years or so after the Revolutionary War. Today, excise taxes fall mainly on cigarettes, liquor, luxury cars and boats, telephones, gasoline, diesel fuel, aviation fuel, gas-guzzling vehicles, and vaccines. What do all of these products seem to have in common?

Answers to the Checkpoint question can be found at the end of this chapter.

chapter summary

Section 1: Elasticity of Demand

The **price elasticity of demand** measures how sensitive consumers are to changes in price.

What Do the E_D Numbers Mean?

$E_D > 1$: Elastic Demand (many substitutes, high-priced goods, longer time horizon, luxury goods)

$E_D < 1$: Inelastic Demand (few substitutes, low-priced goods, shorter time horizon, necessities)

$E_D = 1$: Unitary Elastic Demand (a change in price results in an equal % change in quantity demanded)

Tatiana Nikolaevna Kalashnikova/Getty Images

Your textbook is an **inelastic** good because few alternatives to it exist for your class and it may be required (a necessity).

Fancy/Alamy

A Spring Break trip is **elastic** because many choices of destinations exist, it is expensive, and it is not really a necessity.

The formula for price elasticity of demand is:

E_D = % change in quantity demanded/% change in price

Since all E_D must be negative according to the law of demand, the convention is to drop the negative sign.

Calculating % changes: **base method** versus **midpoint method**

base method: $\%\Delta$ in P = Δ in P/old P

The base method is simple because it is how one normally calculates percentages in everyday life, such as for store discounts or restaurant tips. For example, adding a 15% tip to a $20 bill is $3, or taking 25% off of a $40 shirt makes the shirt $30 using the base method.

midpoint method: $\%\Delta$ in P = Δ in P/[(old P + new P)/2]

The midpoint method is slightly more difficult to calculate; however, the advantage is that the percentage change stays the same whether a value increases or decreases. For example, using the midpoint method, going from 10 to 20 or from 20 to 10 is a 66.7% change in either direction.

How Do You Remember Which Diagram Is Elastic?

Think of a pair of shorts: You can easily pull them **side-to-side** because the waistband is very elastic!

John Lund/Paula Zacharias/Getty Images

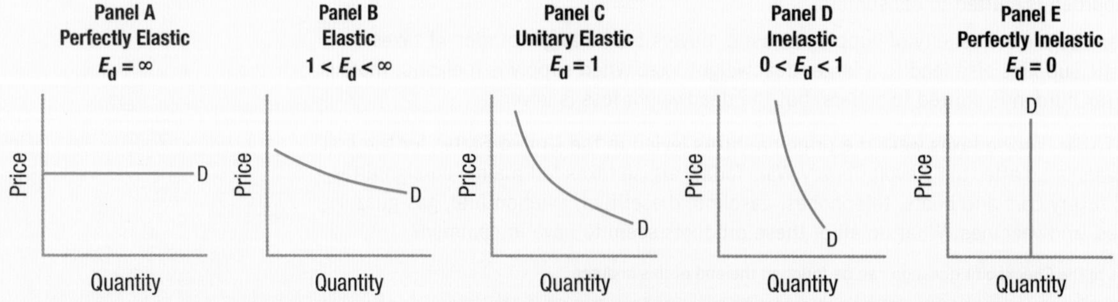

The flatter the demand curve, the more elastic the good or service; the steeper the demand curve, the more inelastic the good or service. Because elasticity changes along a linear demand curve, unitary elastic demand has a curved shape.

Section 2: Total Revenue and Other Measures of Elasticity

Total revenue is calculated as price × quantity demanded.

Total revenue increases when price rises on an inelastic good or is lowered on an elastic good.

Total revenue decreases when price rises on an elastic good or is lowered on an inelastic good.

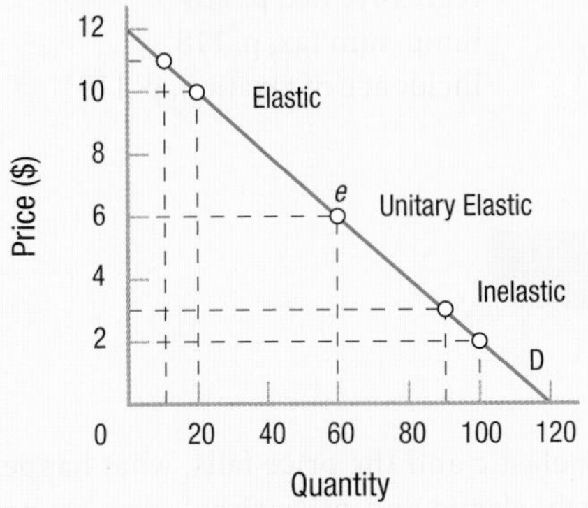

Elasticity and total revenue vary along a straight-line demand curve. Total revenue is maximized at the point where demand is unitary elastic.

When competition is nearly nonexistent, sellers can raise prices and increase total revenue because the good is inelastic.

Income elasticity of demand measures how quantity demand responds to changes in income: $E_Y = \%\Delta Q/\%\Delta\text{Income}$

$0 < E_Y < 1$: normal good

$E_Y > 1$: luxury good

$E_Y < 0$: inferior good

Cross elasticity of demand measures how responsive quantity demand for one good is to a change in the price of another good: $E_{ab} = \%\Delta Q_a/\%\Delta P_b$

$E_{ab} > 0$: Goods a and b are substitutes

$E_{ab} < 0$: Goods a and b are complements

$E_{ab} = 0$: Goods a and b are unrelated

Section 3: Elasticity of Supply

The **elasticity of supply** measures the extent to which businesses react to price changes.

The **elasticity of supply** formula is virtually identical to that of demand:

$E_S = \%\Delta\text{Quantity Supplied} / \%\Delta\text{Price}$

The base and midpoint methods both are still used to calculate % changes.

The **time horizon** affects the elasticity of supply: the longer the period, the more a firm is able to adjust to changing prices, and therefore the more elastic the good.

Short run: a time period in which plant capacity is fixed and the number of firms in an industry does not change.

Long run: a time period long enough for firms to alter their plant capacity or for firms to enter or leave the industry.

Section 4: Taxes and Elasticity

The **incidence of taxation** refers to who bears the economic burden of a tax.

The more elastic the demand or inelastic the supply, the greater the incidence of a tax on sellers. The more inelastic the demand or elastic the supply, the greater the incidence of a tax on consumers.

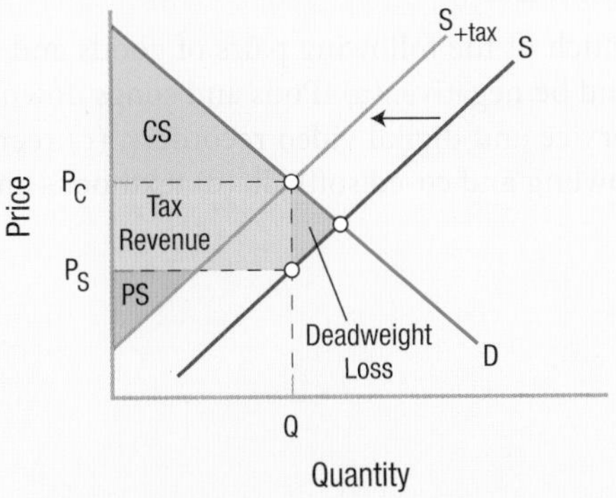

The tax created a deadweight loss shown in gray, along with a reduction in consumer surplus (CS) and producer surplus (PS). The government collects tax revenue shown as the area in blue.

A new tax collected on sellers shifts the supply curve to the left. The intersection of S_{+tax} and D is the price consumers pay, P_C. P_S is the price sellers receive. The difference between P_C and P_S is the tax per unit.

KEY CONCEPTS

price elasticity of demand, p. 104
elastic demand, p. 105
inelastic demand, p. 106
unitary elasticity of demand, p. 106
total revenue, p. 110
cross elasticity of demand, p. 112
substitutes, p. 113
complements, p. 113
income elasticity of demand, p. 113
normal goods, p. 113
luxury goods, p. 113
inferior goods, p. 113
price elasticity of supply, p. 115
elastic supply, p. 115
inelastic supply, p. 115
unitary elastic supply, p. 115
market period, p. 116
short run, p. 116
long run, p. 116
progressive tax, p. 118
flat tax, p. 118
regressive tax, p. 118
lump-sum tax, p. 118
incidence of taxation, p. 119

QUESTIONS AND PROBLEMS

Check Your Understanding

1. When the demand curve is relatively inelastic and the price falls, what happens to total revenue? If the demand is relatively elastic and price rises, what happens to total revenue?
2. Why is the demand for gasoline relatively inelastic, while the demand for Exxon's gasoline is relatively elastic?
3. Describe cross elasticity of demand. Why do substitutes have positive cross elasticities? Describe income elasticity of demand. What is the difference between normal and inferior goods?
4. Describe the impact of time on the price elasticity of supply.
5. Why would the demand for business airline travel be less elastic than the demand for vacation airline travel by retirees?
6. Would an excise tax placed on cereal be more likely or less likely to be passed on to consumers than an excise tax on wireless phone and data services? Why or why not?

Apply the Concepts

7. One major rationale for farm price supports is that rapidly improving technology, better crop strains, improved fertilizer, and better farming methods increased supply so significantly that farm incomes were severely depressed. Explain how the elasticity of demand for these crops influences this rationale.
8. If the price of chicken rises by 15% and the sales of turkey breasts expand by 10%, what is the cross elasticity of demand for these two products? Are they complements or substitutes?
9. For which of the following pairs of goods and services would the cross elasticity of demand be negative: (a) iPods and songs downloaded from iTunes, (b) digital satellite service and digital video recorders, (c) recreational vehicles and camping tents, (d) bowling and co-ed softball, (e) textbooks and study guides.

10. Consider chip plants: potato and computer. Assume there is a large rise in the demand for computer chips and potato chips.
    a. How responsive to demand is each in the market period?
    b. Describe what a manufacturer of each product might do in the short run to increase production.
    c. How does the long run differ for these products?
11. If one automobile brand has an income elasticity of demand of 1.5 and another has an income elasticity equal to –0.3, what would account for the difference? Give an example of a specific brand for each type of car.
12. Suppose you estimated the cross elasticities of demand for three pairs of products and came up with the following three values: 2.3, 0.1, –1.7. What could you conclude about these three pairs of products? If you wanted to know if two products from two different firms competed with each other in the marketplace, what would you look for?

In The News

13. A February 24, 2012, *New York Times* article titled "Access to the Car Pool Lane Can Be Yours, for a Price" describes the growing number of cities implementing express toll lanes alongside free lanes, allowing drivers to pay to avoid traffic (with higher tolls during times of greater traffic). However, when Atlanta introduced its express tolls lanes in October 2011, hardly anyone used them, causing even greater gridlock on the free lanes. Within a week and after much criticism, Governor Nathan Deal slashed the maximum toll from $5.50 to $3.05. When the express toll lanes were put in, what did the policymakers in Atlanta believe about the elasticity of demand for using the express toll lanes? Given the evidence, were they correct? By reducing the maximum toll, how would total revenues change given the elasticity of demand of Atlanta motorists?
14. According to a report from the Federal Trade Commission (FTC), in the first three weeks of August 2003, gas prices in Phoenix, Arizona, jumped from $1.52 to $2.11 a gallon, roughly a 40% increase, due to a ruptured pipeline between Tucson and Phoenix. The pipeline normally brought 30% of Phoenix's fuel from a Texas refinery. During this period, Phoenix gas stations were able to buy gas from West Coast refineries at higher prices. By the end of the month, the rupture was repaired and prices returned to normal. During this three-week period of supply disruption, gasoline sales fell by 8%. What was the approximate price elasticity of demand for gasoline during this period? If the gas stations were unable to get additional gas from the West Coast and supplies fell by the full 30%, how high might have prices risen during that three-week period?

Solving Problems

15. Rising world wholesale fair-trade coffee bean prices force the local Dunkin' Donuts franchise to raise its price of coffee from 89 cents to 99 cents a cup. As a result, management notices that donut sales fall from 950 to 850 a day. Shortly after the coffee price spike, the local Cinnabon franchise reduced its price on cinnamon rolls from $1.89 to $1.69. This resulted in a further decline in Dunkin' Donuts donut sales to 750 a day.
    a. What is the cross elasticity of demand for coffee and donuts? Are these two products complements or substitutes?
    b. What is the cross elasticity of demand for Dunkin' Donuts donuts and Cinnabon cinnamon rolls? Are these two products complements or substitutes?

16. Suppose the demand and supply for imported Kobe beef is as shown in the figure below. Now assume that the U.S. government imposes an import tax of $10 per pound on Kobe beef.

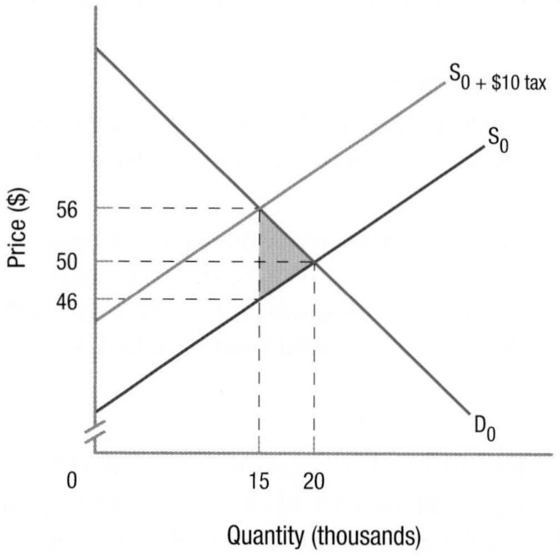

a. How does the market price change with the imposition of the $10 per pound tax?
b. Do the buyers or the sellers of Kobe beef bear the greater burden of the tax?
c. How much tax revenue does the government collect from this market?
d. Calculate the approximate value of deadweight loss created in this market from the tax.

USING THE NUMBERS

17. According to By the Numbers, how much greater is the elasticity of demand for food in Canada than in the United States? How about Mexico compared to the United States?
18. According to By the Numbers, what type of alternative-fuel car generated the highest sales in the year 2012? Which type of alternative-fuel car generated the second highest sales?

ANSWERS TO QUESTIONS IN CHECKPOINTS

Checkpoint: Elasticity of Demand

Gasoline is inelastic in the short-term because it is difficult to switch quickly to more fuel-efficient options. In the long-term, one can buy a more fuel-efficient car or move closer to work or to public transportation, allowing one to be more responsive to prices. Automobiles, however, tend to have the opposite effect. When prices of cars increase, consumers might keep their existing cars longer (an elastic response). In the long-term, however, older cars become more costly to maintain, and consumers would more likely buy a new car despite the higher prices (an inelastic response).

Checkpoint: Total Revenue and Other Measures of Elasticity

Store 1 has an elastic demand for its clothes, while store 2 faces an inelastic demand. Look back at Table 2.

Checkpoint: Elasticity of Supply

Although these rankings can be subjective, the most likely rank from most elastic to least elastic is: chicken soup, boxes of tissue, over-the-counter flu remedies, flu shots (generally requires over six months to produce, giving it the least flexibility in response to a price change for the current flu season).

Checkpoint: Taxes and Elasticity

They all appear to have relatively inelastic demands. This reduces the impact of taxes on the industries and leads to higher tax revenues.

6 Consumer Choice and Demand

After studying this chapter you should be able to:

- Use a budget line to determine the constraints on consumer choices.
- Determine how budget lines change when prices or income changes.
- Describe the difference between total and marginal utility.
- Describe the law of diminishing marginal utility.
- Use marginal utility analysis to derive demand curves.
- Explain why individuals sometimes make irrational decisions in predictable ways.
- Describe five psychological factors that influence economic decision making.

Each day, virtually every person makes consumption choices, whether that means going to the mall to buy a new outfit, to a restaurant to dine with friends, or to the supermarket to stock up on groceries for the week. The consumption choices that people make form what we have described as demand. But how do consumers make these choices? One of the important lessons from prior chapters is that individuals aim to maximize their well-being given a limited amount of resources.

In order to make consumption choices, individuals must first determine what is affordable; in other words, what choices of goods and services one's budget can afford. Although we naturally think of income as the primary determinant of what can be afforded, prices also play a key role. Think of how a sale at a department store increases the amount of goods we can buy, or how higher gas prices restrict what we can spend on other goods. Once we know what we can afford, the next question is then how to allocate budgets to maximize our well-being.

The process by which individuals choose goods and services to maximize their overall happiness can be tricky to analyze. The main reason is that demand analysis rests on an important assumption: People are rational decision makers. Do people always act rationally? Of course not. You might spend more money at an expensive restaurant than you had wanted because your friends convinced you to go, which then caused you to give up buying an outfit on sale that would have given you more satisfaction. In these situations, individuals often come to realize that money is not always spent in the optimal manner; if it were, we would never regret the spontaneous purchases we make.

The fact that individuals sometimes make irrational decisions makes the analysis of consumer choice difficult to predict. However, a number of economists, called behavioralists, have been studying certain situations in which people make irrational decisions. What these economists have found is that although the decisions we make may sometimes appear irrational, they are irrational in *predictable* ways. For example, having paid a nonrefundable deposit on a wedding dress, a bride is more likely to purchase the dress even if her preferences change, because she had already committed to part of the purchase. Or, a person attempting to start a diet program may purchase a long-term plan given an optimistic anticipation of completing the program, only to give up after a few months. These examples illustrate how psychological factors influence our consumption choices in ways that lead to decisions economists would view as irrational.

Important though this work on the irrational is, it does not invalidate the assumption that people choose rationally. If there were a preponderance of irrationality, society would come to a halt because we could not predict anything. What pedestrian would cross the street even if the light said "walk" if there was a modicum of fear that many drivers would act irrationally and ignore a red light? People *do* miss or ignore red lights, but not often.

So we are left with an underlying assumption of rational decision making that is not bedrock, but is reasonable and powerful nonetheless. In this chapter, we are going to see what lies behind demand curves by looking at how consumers choose. In the next chapter, we will examine what lies behind supply curves by looking at how producers choose to produce what they do.

There are two major ways to approach consumer choice. The first theory explaining what people choose to buy, given their limited incomes, is known as *utility theory* or *utilitarianism*, and owes its roots to the work of 18th century philosopher Jeremy Bentham. This theory holds that rational consumers will allocate their limited incomes so as to maximize their happiness or satisfaction.

The second approach, *indifference curve analysis,* is covered in the Appendix. Developed by Francis Ysidro Edgeworth in the late 19th century, it added analytical rigor to utility analysis by developing *indifference curves,* which portray combinations of two

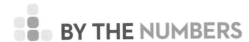

BY THE NUMBERS

How Do We Decide What to Buy?

Each day, we make economic decisions on what to buy, what to eat, and how to allocate our limited time. Although marginal utility analysis can guide us into making rational decisions, behavioral economic factors play an important role as well.

The average distribution of U.S. household budgets on various expenditure components in 2011, along with trends in selected components from 2009 to 2011.

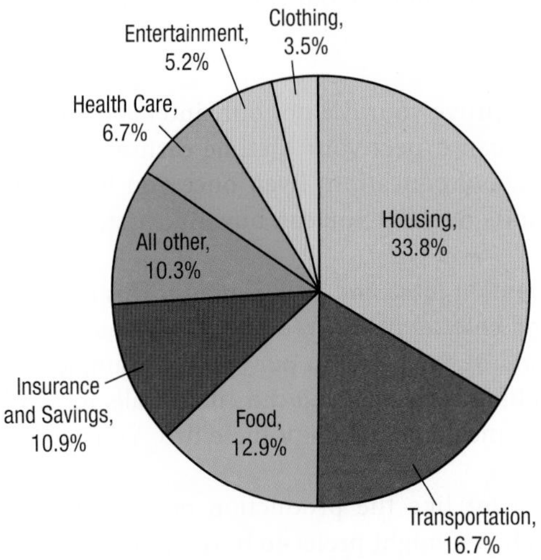

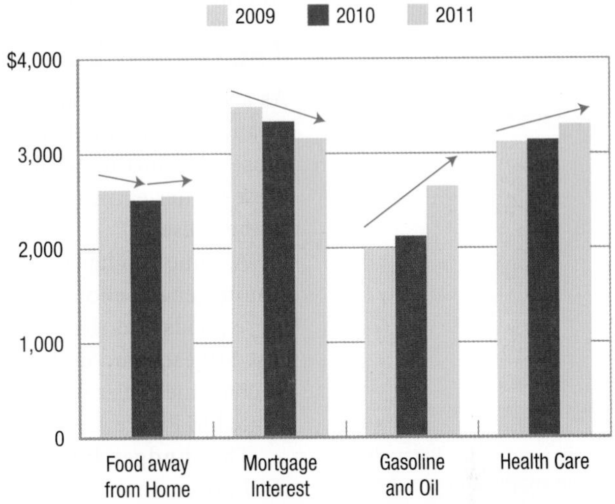

254,212,610
Total number of passenger vehicles registered in the United States in 2011 (1 car for every 1.2 persons).

$346,170,000,000
Total amount of charitable giving by Americans in 2011 (over $1,100 per person).

As preferences for organic foods increase, more supermarket chains respond, leading to rising sales of organic foods.

UpperCut Images/Alamy

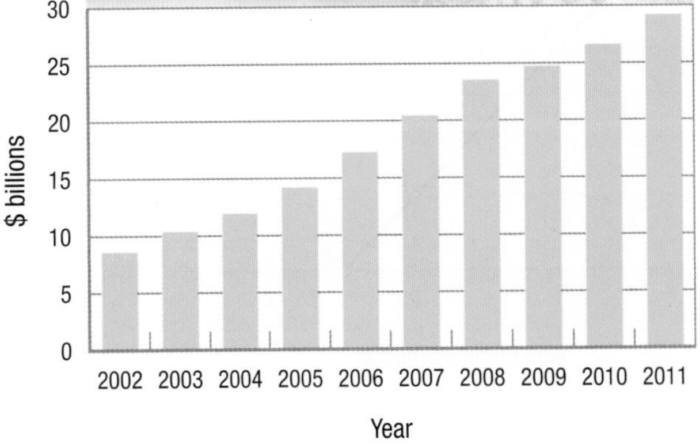

Player jerseys represent the largest component of the $3 billion annual NBA product market. The top selling jerseys in the 2011–2012 season were:

1. Derrick Rose, Chicago Bulls
2. Jeremy Lin, New York Knicks
3. Kobe Bryant, Los Angeles Lakers
4. LeBron James, Miami Heat
5. Carmelo Anthony, New York Knicks

Copyright 2010 NBAE (Photo by Noah Graham/NBAE via Getty Images)

goods of equal total utility. Edgeworth, a shy man who studied in public libraries because he saw material possessions as a burden, brought the precision of mathematics to bear on utility theory.

The Budget Line and Choices

To begin an analysis of consumption choices, we first must consider how a limited income and the prices of goods and services put constraints on our choices.

The Budget Line

As a student, you came to college to improve your life not only intellectually but also financially. As a college graduate, you can expect your lifetime earnings to be triple those of someone with only a high school education. Even once you have achieved these higher earnings, there will be limits on what you can buy. But first, let us return to the present.

Assume you have \$50 a week to spend on pizza and wall climbing. This is a proxy for a more general choice between food and entertainment. We could use different goods or more goods, but the principle would still be the same. In our specific example, if pizzas cost \$10 each and an hour of wall climbing costs \$20, you can climb walls for 2.5 hours or consume 5 pizzas each week, or do some combination of these two. Your options are plotted in Figure 1.

budget line Graphically illustrates the possible combinations of two goods that can be purchased with a given income, given the prices of both goods.

This **budget line** (constraint) is a lot like the production possibilities frontier (PPF) discussed in Chapter 2. Although you might prefer to have more of both goods, you are limited to consumption choices lying on the budget line, or inside the budget line if you want to save any part of your \$50 weekly budget. As with the PPF curve, however, any points to the right of the line are unattainable for you—they exceed your available income.

In this example, the budget line makes clear that many different combinations of wall climbing and pizzas will exhaust your \$50 budget. But which of these possible combinations will you select? That depends on your personal preferences. If you love pizza, you will probably make different choices than if you are a fitness fanatic who rarely consumes fatty foods. Your own preferences determine how much pleasure you can expect to get from the various possible options. We study how optimal choices are made in the next section of this chapter.

FIGURE 1

The Budget Constraint or Line

When pizzas cost \$10 each, wall climbing costs \$20 per hour, and you have \$50 a week to spend, you could buy 5 pizzas per week, 2.5 hours of wall climbing, or some combination of the two. The budget line makes clear all of the possible purchasing combinations of two products on a particular budget.

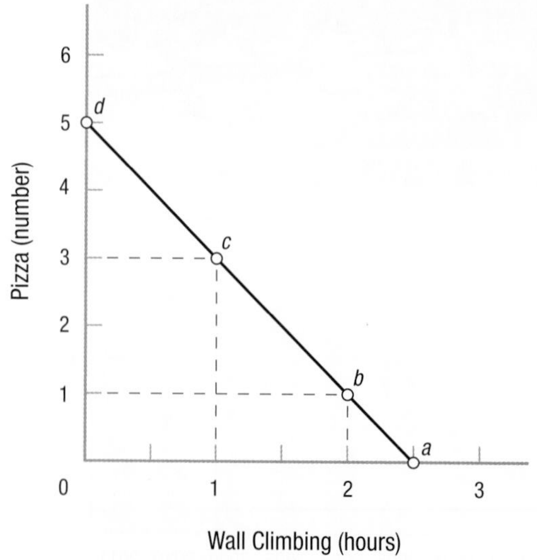

Changes to the Budget Line

The budget line, like most money matters, is subject to changes in the prices of goods or changes in income. When the price of a good or income changes, the combinations of goods that become affordable change as well. Let's look at how the budget line changes.

Changes to the Price of a Good Suppose the wall-climbing establishment offers a half-price discount to college students, reducing the price of wall climbing from $20 to $10 per hour. Figure 2 illustrates what happens when the price of wall climbing changes as the price of pizza stays the same. Notice that the vertical intercept remains at 5 pizzas; because the price of pizza did not change, the total number of pizzas that can be purchased for $50 is still 5. However, the reduction in the price of wall climbing allows the total number of hours that can be purchased to increase from 2.5 to 5. In Figure 2, the budget line pivots outward to budget line *b*, which opens up many more combinations of pizza and wall climbing that previously were unaffordable.

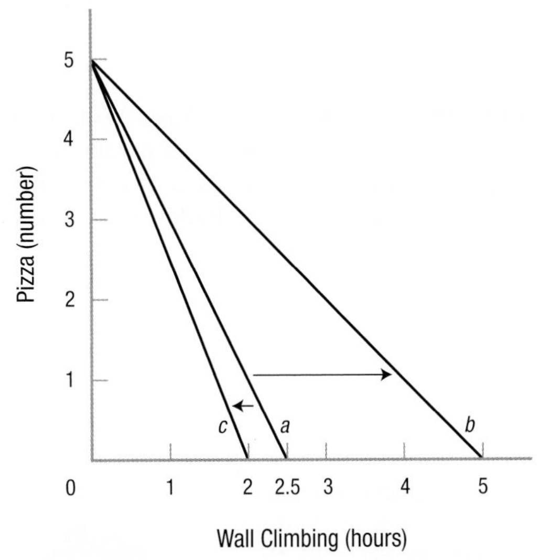

FIGURE 2

Changes in Price on a Budget Line

Budget line *a* shows the consumption choices available with a budget of $50 and prices of pizza and wall climbing at $10 and $20, respectively. When the price of wall climbing decreases to $10, the budget line pivots outward to budget line *b*. The combinations of pizza and wall climbing that can be purchased increases. When the price of wall climbing increases to $25, the budget line pivots inward to budget line *c*, reducing the amounts that can be purchased.

Notice that in this case it is possible for a person to actually consume *more* of both pizza and wall climbing, even though the price of pizza did not change, nor did the income of $50. Suppose that originally you would spend the entire $50 on wall climbing, purchasing 2.5 hours. Because the price is now $10, the new cost of maintaining the same purchase of 2.5 hours is $25, leaving $25 to use on *either* more wall climbing or pizza, or both. By virtue of the price of wall climbing decreasing to $10, what this income can buy increases, even though the actual income stays the same. This is true for any point along the original budget line except for the one point at which the entire budget was spent on pizza. Only in this case does the fall in price of wall climbing not increase the number of pizzas that can be purchased.

Now suppose that instead of a discount on wall climbing, the gym decides to raise the price to $25. How would this affect the budget line? It pivots inward. In Figure 2, budget line *c* shows the maximum quantity of wall climbing decreasing to two hours. The increase in price reduces the combinations of both pizza and wall climbing that can be purchased with $50.

Changes to Income We now know that changes in the price of a good will pivot the budget line inward or outward along the axis for that good. But what if income itself changes? Suppose that prices of pizza and wall climbing remain at $10 and $20, respectively, but you are given extra money by your parents, allowing you to increase your

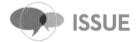

FIGURE 3

Changes in Income on a Budget Line

Budget line *a* shows the consumption choices available with a budget of $50 and prices of pizza and wall climbing at $10 and $20, respectively. When the budget increases to $100, the budget line shifts parallel outward to budget line *b,* doubling the quantities that can be purchased. When the budget falls to $20, the budget line shifts inward to budget line *c,* reducing the amounts that can be purchased.

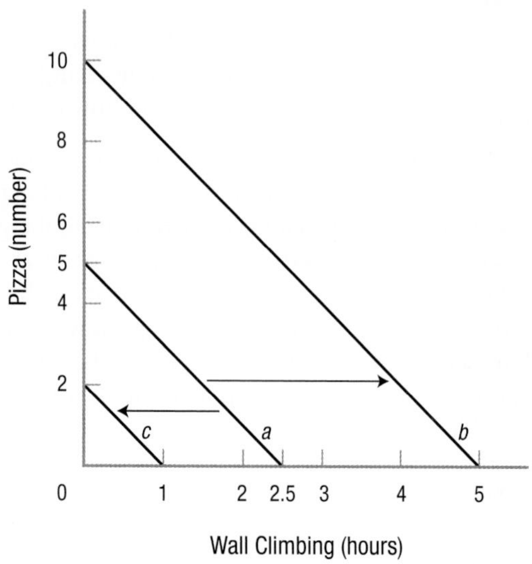

entertainment budget to $100 per week. Figure 3 illustrates how an increase in income shifts your budget line outward to budget line *b* in a parallel fashion. Because $100 is double the original income, you can now afford twice as many pizzas and wall climbing hours as before as long as prices do not change. Budget line *b* shows that the maximum

ISSUE

Smaller Cars and Larger Homes: A Permanent Trend?

Housing and auto transportation are the two largest monthly expenditures of a typical American household. As the prices of homes and cars change, along with the costs associated with their maintenance, the types of homes and cars consumers buy change as well.

The average home price in the United States fell by nearly 20% from 2006 to 2012, while the average price of a new car rose by nearly 20% over this same period. Although the effect of these price changes on consumption is predictable, other factors influence consumption patterns as well.

Unlike most consumer goods, individuals rarely buy homes and cars outright, but instead lease them or borrow money to pay them off over time. Therefore, an important factor influencing how homes and autos affect one's budget is the interest rate for borrowing. Further, maintaining a house or a car is not limited to the monthly payment. Complementary items, such as property taxes, utility bills, and furniture expenses affect the cost of home ownership, while gas prices and auto insurance premiums affect auto purchases.

Has there been a change in the costs of home and auto ownership?

From 2006 to 2012, mortgage interest rates declined significantly, from an average of 6% to 3%. As mortgage interest rates fell, housing payments fell, allowing people to seek larger homes that are now affordable with the same budget. The opposite occurred in the auto industry, as gas prices rose from an average of $2.50 per gallon in 2006 to $3.60 per gallon in 2012. As gasoline prices increased, transportation costs rose significantly, causing people to seek smaller and more fuel-efficient cars.

Kimimasa Mayama/Bloomberg via Getty Images

Changes in the costs of home and automobile ownership lead individuals to adjust their consumption habits as their budgets adjust. As a result, smaller cars and larger homes have been a trend for much of the past decade. Whether this trend continues depends on how prices, which play a critical role in the budget line, adjust in the future.

quantity of pizza that can be purchased increases to 10 and the maximum quantity of climbing hours increases to 5.

Like prices, we can analyze the effect of a decrease in income on the budget line as well. Suppose increased expenses elsewhere force you to cut back on entertainment spending from $50 to $20 per week. Figure 3 shows how the reduced income shifts the budget line parallel inward to budget line *c*.

Now that we have analyzed how budget lines determine what we can afford, we must now answer the important question of what combination of goods and services achieves the highest satisfaction. One approach is to use marginal utility analysis, which we turn to next.

Ron Zmiri/age fotostock

A decrease in the price of a good that you typically buy has the same effect as an increase in income. In both cases, your budget line expands outward, allowing for more consumption choices.

CHECKPOINT

THE BUDGET LINE AND CHOICES

- The budget line graphically illustrates the limits on purchases for a given income (budget).
- Changes in the price of a good cause the budget line to pivot inward or outward, affecting the combinations of goods that can be afforded.
- When the price of one good decreases, perceived income increases, allowing one to purchase more of both goods.
- Changes in income (budget) cause a parallel shift in the budget line.

QUESTION: Suppose that each week you eat ten meals on campus at $7.50 each and five meals off campus at $15 each. What is your total spending on meals? Suppose the price of off-campus meals decreases to $10. Explain how you can eat more meals in both locations (on campus and off campus), even though the price of on-campus meals stayed the same.

Answers to the Checkpoint question can be found at the end of this chapter.

Marginal Utility Analysis

The previous section showed how our choices of goods and services are limited to what we can afford given a budget. Similar to how PPFs showed the maximum output an economy can produce, budget lines show the maximum quantity of goods (in various combinations) that can be purchased. And like PPF analysis, an individual is able to select a point on the budget line that would maximize one's satisfaction. But which point would accomplish this goal?

To answer this question, we need to determine which combination of goods and services results in the highest level of satisfaction. Solving this riddle of consumer behavior can be accomplished using **marginal utility analysis.** Let's begin by defining preferences and utility, and then discuss how marginal utility analysis allows a person to maximize his or her well-being.

marginal utility analysis A theoretical framework underlying consumer decision making. This approach assumes that satisfaction can be measured and that consumers maximize satisfaction when the marginal utilities per dollar are equal for all products and services.

utility A hypothetical measure of consumer satisfaction.

Preferences and Utility

Utility is a hypothetical measure of consumer satisfaction. It was introduced by early economists attempting to explain how consumers make decisions. The utilitarian theory of consumer behavior assumes, first of all, that utility is something that *can* be

JEREMY BENTHAM (1748–1832)

Jeremy Bentham was a social philosopher, legal reformer, and writer who founded the philosophy known as utilitarianism. As an economic theorist, his most valuable contribution was the idea of *utility,* which explained consumer choices in terms of maximizing pleasure and minimizing pain.

Born in 1748, Bentham was the son of a wealthy lawyer. At age 12 he entered Oxford University, then studied for the bar although he decided not to practice law. Instead, he pursued a life of writing and thinking, with his primary contribution analyzing the notion of utility as a driving force in social and economic behavior. Bentham believed that the aim of society and government should be to maximize utility or to promote the "greatest happiness for the greatest number." In 1789, he published his most famous work, *Introduction to the Principles of Morals,* which laid out his utilitarian philosophy. Bentham believed it was possible to derive a "Felicific Calculus" to compare the various pleasures or pains.

Although modern economists have cast doubt on the notion that utility could be measured or calculated, Bentham had many ideas that were ahead of his time, including the notion of cost-benefit analysis, which logically followed from his utilitarian views on government policies. Bentham also formulated the contemporary notion of marginal utility. After reading this chapter, it will be hard for you to avoid thinking in Bentham's terms about your own consumption choices, and you'll find yourself asking questions such as, "Do I really get $12 worth of satisfaction out of a Coke and popcorn at the movies, or do I have better alternatives for that money?"

measured. Returning to our example from the previous section, the theory assumes that we can quantifiably determine how much utility (satisfaction) you derive from consuming one or more pizzas, and how much utility you derive from spending one or more hours on the climbing wall. Table 1 provides estimates of the utility you derive from both pizzas and wall climbing, measured in *utils,* hypothetical units of satisfaction or utility. Compare columns (1) and (2) with columns (4) and (5).

At first glance, it might seem that if you wanted to maximize your utility given your $50 budget, you would simply go wall climbing for 2.5 hours, thereby maximizing your total utility at 270 utils. If you spent a little time analyzing the table, you would notice that combinations give you more total utility. If you went wall climbing for 2 hours and had 1 pizza (again spending your entire $50 budget), your total utility would be 330 utils (260 + 70 = 330), much more than concentrating on one item alone.

Other than trial and error, how do we determine the best combination? Before we can see just which combination of these two goods would actually bring you the most happiness, we need to distinguish between *total utility* and *marginal utility.*

total utility The total satisfaction that a person receives from consuming a given amount of goods and services.

Total and Marginal Utility **Total utility** is the total satisfaction that a person receives from consuming a given quantity of goods and services. In Table 1, for example, the total utility received from consuming 3 pizzas is 180 utils, whereas the total utility from 4 pizzas is 220 utils. Marginal utility is something different.

TABLE 1 Total and Marginal Utility from Pizzas and Wall Climbing

Pizza			Wall Climbing		
(1) Quantity	(2) Total Utility	(3) Marginal Utility	(4) Quantity	(5) Total Utility	(6) Marginal Utility
0	0	0	0.0	0	0
1	70	70	0.5	90	90
2	130	60	1.0	170	80
3	180	50	1.5	230	60
4	220	40	2.0	260	30
5	250	30	2.5	270	10

Marginal utility is the satisfaction derived from consuming an *additional* unit of a given product or service. It is determined by taking the difference between the total utility derived from, say, consuming 4 pizzas and consuming 3 pizzas. The total utility derived from 4 pizzas is 220 utils, and that from 3 pizzas is 180 utils. Therefore, consuming the fourth pizza yields only an additional 40 utils of satisfaction (220 – 180 = 40 utils).

marginal utility The satisfaction received from consuming an additional unit of a given product or service.

The marginal utility for both pizza eating and wall climbing is listed in Table 1. Notice that as we move from one quantity of pizza to the next, total utility rises by an amount exactly equal to marginal utility. This is no coincidence. Marginal utility is nothing but the change in total utility obtained from consuming one more pizza (the marginal pizza), therefore as pizza eating increases by 1 pizza, total utility will rise by the amount of additional satisfaction derived from consuming that additional pizza. Also note that, for both pizzas and wall climbing, marginal utility declines the more a particular product or activity is consumed.

The Law of Diminishing Marginal Utility Why does marginal utility decline as the consumption of one product or activity increases? No matter our personal tastes and preferences, we eventually become sated once we have consumed a certain amount of any given commodity. Most of us love ice cream. As youngsters, some of us imagined a world in which meals consisted of nothing but ice cream—no casseroles, no vegetables, just ice cream. To children this might sound heavenly, but as adults, we recognize that we would quickly grow sick of ice cream. Human beings simply crave diversity; we quickly tire of the same product or service if we consume it day after day.

law of diminishing marginal utility As we consume more of a given product, the added satisfaction we get from consuming an additional unit declines.

This fact of human nature led early economists to formulate the **law of diminishing marginal utility.** This law states that as we consume more of a product, the rate at which our total satisfaction increases with the consumption of each additional unit will decline. And if we continue to consume still more of the product after that, our total satisfaction will eventually begin to decline.

This principle is illustrated by Figure 4 on the next page, which graphs the total utility and marginal utility for pizza eating, as listed in Table 1. Notice that total utility, charted in panel A, rises continually as we move from 1 pizza per week to 5 pizzas. Nevertheless, the rate of this increase declines as more pizzas are consumed. Accordingly, panel B shows that marginal utility declines with more pizzas eaten. On your student budget, you could not afford any more than 5 pizzas a week, but we can imagine that if you were to keep eating pizzas—20 pizzas in a week—your total utility would actually start to drop with each additional pizza. At some point, it simply hurts to stuff down any more pizzas.

Eric Chiang

Mega buffets in Las Vegas draw millions of diners each year. Diminishing marginal utility from each additional plate of food keeps the amount of food consumed by each diner at a reasonable level.

It is one thing to grasp the obvious fact that consumers have limited budgets and that the products they can choose among provide them increasing satisfaction but are subject to diminishing marginal utility. It is another thing to figure out exactly how consumers allocate their limited funds so as to maximize their total level of satisfaction or utility. We now turn our attention to how early economists solved the problem of maximizing utility and the analytic methods that flowed out of their work.

Maximizing Utility Let's take a moment to review everything we need to know to plot the budget line in Figure 1: your total income and the prices of all the products you could purchase. In our example, the weekly budget is \$50, pizzas cost \$10 apiece, and wall climbing is \$20 per hour or \$10 per half-hour. This is enough information to plot all of the options open to you.

Given these options, how do individuals maximize the total utility from the various combinations of goods? Knowing the marginal utility of each unit of a good consumed is

FIGURE 4

Total and Marginal Utility for Pizza

Total utility, charted in panel A, rises continually as we move from 1 pizza per week to 5. Nevertheless, the rate of this increase declines as more pizzas are consumed. Accordingly, panel B shows that marginal utility declines with more pizzas eaten.

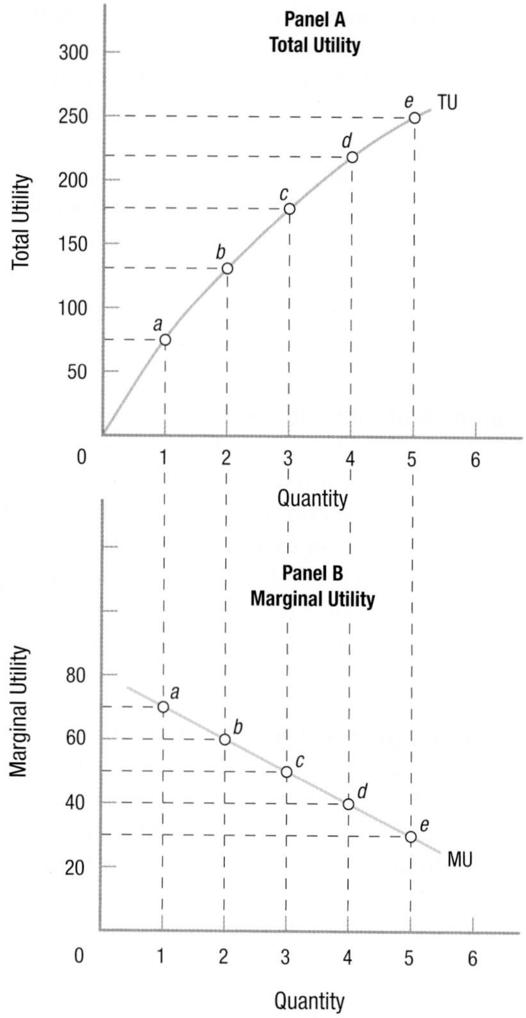

not enough. Surely the marginal utility of a new car is greater than the marginal utility of a cup of coffee. But the price of the car is also much greater than the price of coffee. The ability to maximize utility given a fixed budget requires us to compare the marginal utilities *per dollar* spent on each good.

Take a look at columns (4) and (8) of Table 2. These two columns express the marginal utilities of pizzas and wall climbing, respectively, in terms of marginal utility per dollar; these amounts are computed by dividing the marginal utility of each product by the product's price.

To see the importance of computing marginal utility per dollar, consider the following. Given the figures in columns (4) and (8), and assuming you want to get the most for your money, on which activity would you spend the first $10 of your weekly budget? You can spend the first $10 on a pizza or on a half-hour of wall climbing. A pizza returns 70 utils of satisfaction, whereas a half-hour of wall climbing yields 90 utils. Since 90 is greater than 70, clearly the first $10 would be better spent on wall climbing.

Now, for the sake of simplicity, let's keep your spending increments constant. On what will you spend your next $10—pizza or climbing? Look again at the table. Your first pizza still gives you 70 utils, while the second half-hour of wall climbing returns 80 utils. Wall climbing again is the obvious choice. If your total budget had only been $20 per week, you would have been inclined to give up pizzas completely.

Total and Marginal Utility per Dollar from Pizzas and Wall Climbing — **TABLE 2**

Pizza				Wall Climbing			
(1) Quantity (units of pizza)	(2) Total Utility	(3) Marginal Utility	(4) Marginal Utility per Dollar (price = $10)	(5) Quantity (hours of wall climbing)	(6) Total Utility	(7) Marginal Utility	(8) Marginal Utility per Dollar (price = $10 per half-hour)
0	0	0	0	0.0	0	0	0
1	70	70	7	0.5	90	90	9
2	130	60	6	1.0	170	80	8
3	180	50	5	1.5	230	60	6
4	220	40	4	2.0	260	30	3
5	250	30	3	2.5	270	10	1

Proceeding in the same way, using your third $10 to buy your first pizza will yield an additional 70 utils of satisfaction, whereas using this money to purchase a third half-hour of wall climbing will bring only 60 utils. (Wall climbing is starting to get a bit boring.) Thus, because 70 is greater than 60, with your third $10 you buy your first pizza.

The next $10 provides the same amount of utility (60 utils) regardless of whether you buy another pizza or another half-hour of wall climbing. Therefore, you split the remaining $20 of your budget evenly between these two activities. When the consumption of additional units of two products provides equal satisfaction, economists say consumers are *indifferent* to which product they consume first.

By following this incremental process, therefore, we have determined that you will spend your $50 on 2 pizzas ($20) and 1.5 hours of wall climbing ($30). This results in a total utility of 360 utils (130 for pizza and 230 for wall climbing). *No other combination of pizzas and wall climbing will result in total satisfaction this high,* as you can prove to yourself by trying to spend the $50 differently.

Note also that for the last two units of each product consumed, the marginal utilities per dollar were equal at 6. This result is to be expected. Simple logic tells us that if one activity yields more satisfaction per dollar than some other, you will continue to pursue the activity with the higher satisfaction per dollar until some other activity starts yielding more satisfaction. This observation leads to a simple rule for maximizing utility: You should allocate your budget so that the marginal utilities per dollar are equal for the last units of the products consumed. This **utility maximizing rule,** in turn, leads to the following equation, where MU = marginal utility and P = price.

utility maximizing rule Utility is maximized where the marginal utility per dollar is equal for all products, or $MU_a/P_a = MU_b/P_b = \ldots = MU_n/P_n$.

$$\frac{MU_{\text{Pizza}}}{P_{\text{Pizza}}} = \frac{MU_{\text{Wall Climbing}}}{P_{\text{Wall Climbing}}}$$

This equation and the analyses described earlier can be generalized to cover numerous goods and services. For all goods and services $a, b, \ldots n$:

$$\frac{MU_a}{P_a} = \frac{MU_b}{P_b} = \ldots = \frac{MU_n}{P_n}$$

The important point to remember is that, according to this theory of consumer behavior, consumers approach every purchase by asking themselves which of all possible additional acts of consumption would bring them the most satisfaction per dollar.

You have seen how the marginal utility analysis of consumer behavior works when we assume that satisfaction or well-being can be measured directly (in utils). We can now use this theory of consumer behavior to derive the demand curve for wall climbing.

Deriving Demand Curves

We know that consumers will maximize their utility by spending each dollar of their limited budgets on the goods and services yielding the highest marginal utility per dollar. In our previous example, with pizzas costing \$10 each and an hour of wall climbing costing \$20, this meant you bought 2 pizzas and 1.5 hours of wall climbing. Would your consumption choices change if these prices changed? Let us consider what happens when the cost of wall climbing rises to \$30 per hour.

Now that wall climbing costs \$30 per hour or \$15 per half-hour, column (8) of Table 3 has been altered to reflect this new rate for wall climbing. The first half-hour of climbing yields 90 utils and now costs \$15, so each dollar yields 6 utils. Now your first \$10 will be spent on a pizza ($MU/P = 7$ for pizza versus $MU/P = 6$ for wall climbing).

TABLE 3 Total and Marginal Utility per Dollar from Pizzas and Wall Climbing (Price of Wall Climbing Increases to \$30 per Hour or \$15 per Half-Hour)

Pizza				Wall Climbing			
(1) Quantity (units of pizza)	(2) Total Utility	(3) Marginal Utility	(4) Marginal Utility per Dollar (price = \$10)	(5) Quantity (hours of wall climbing)	(6) Total Utility	(7) Marginal Utility	(8) Marginal Utility per Dollar (price = \$15 per half-hour)
0	0	0	0	0.0	0	0	0.00
1	70	70	7	0.5	90	90	6.00
2	130	60	6	1.0	170	80	5.33
3	180	50	5	1.5	230	60	4.00
4	220	40	4	2.0	260	30	2.00
5	250	30	3	2.5	270	10	0.67

The next \$25 is split between another pizza and a half-hour of wall climbing because $MU/P = 6$ for both. Your final \$15 is spent on wall climbing because its marginal utility per dollar (5.33) is higher than for a third pizza (5).

Thus, your final allocation is 2 pizzas and 1 hour of wall climbing. Clearly, consumer choices respond to changes in product prices. With wall climbing at \$20 per hour, you consumed 1.5 hours of climbing and 2 pizzas. When the price of wall climbing rose to \$30 per hour you altered your consumption. Now, instead of 1.5 hours and 2 pizzas, you consume 1 hour and 2 pizzas. This new level is shown in the shaded row of Table 3.

Figure 5 plots both your budget constraint and your demand for wall climbing based on the results of Tables 2 and 3. Panel A shows the effect of increasing the

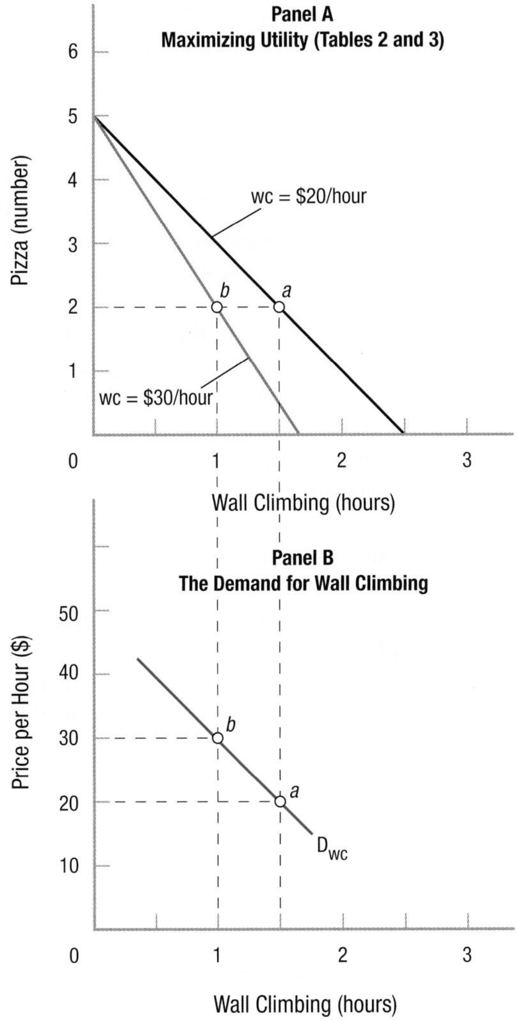

FIGURE 5

Deriving the Demand for Wall Climbing Using Marginal Utility Analysis

With the price of wall climbing at $20 per hour, you climb for 1.5 hours (point *a* in both panels). When the price increases to $30 per hour, you reduce your consumption of wall climbing to 1 hour (point *b* in both panels). Connecting these points in panel B yields the demand curve for wall climbing.

price of wall climbing from $20 to $30 per hour. At the increased price of wall climbing, if you were to spend your entire budget on this activity, you could only climb for 1.67 hours ($50/$30 = 1.67). This price increase rotates the budget line leftward, reducing your consumption opportunities, as the figure illustrates.

When the price of wall climbing was $20 per hour, you climbed for 1.5 hours (points *a* in both panels of Figure 5). When the price was increased to $30 per hour, marginal utility analysis led you to reduce your consumption of wall climbing to 1 hour (point *b* in both panels). Connecting these points in panel B of Figure 5 yields the demand curve for wall climbing.

Thus, the marginal utility theory of consumer behavior helps explain both how consumers allocate their income according to their personal preferences and the law of demand. Remember that the law of demand posited an inverse (negative) relationship between price and quantity demanded. This negative relationship is shown in panel B.

Limitations of Marginal Utility Analysis

Marginal utility analysis explains not only how consumers purchase goods and services but also how all household choices are made. We can analyze the decision of whether or not to get a job, for example, by comparing the marginal utility of work versus the marginal utility of leisure. As a college student, you are familiar with having many demands made on your time. More work means more money but less time for leisure, and vice versa. Marginal utility theory helps us to identify that point at which work and leisure (and hopefully study) balance out.

Although marginal utility theory is an elegant and logically consistent theory that helps us to understand how consumers behave, it does have some limitations. First, it assumes that consumers are able to measure the utility they derive from various sorts of consumption. Yet, this is virtually impossible in everyday life—how many utils do you get out of eating a bowl of ice cream? This is not to suggest that marginal utility theory is invalid. It simply requires one very restrictive assumption, namely, that people are able to measure their satisfaction for every purchase.

Others have argued that it is absurd to think that we could carry out the mental calculus required to compare the ratios of marginal utility to price for all possible goods and services. This is no doubt true, but even if we do not compare all possible goods and services in this way, we do draw some comparisons. After all, we somehow need to be able to distinguish between the desirability of going to a movie or going to a concert, because we cannot do both at the same time. Marginal utility theory is still a good way of approaching this choice, in a general way.

Lastly, marginal utility analysis has been criticized for not fully explaining why individuals sometimes act irrationally, at least according to what economic models predict. Indeed, human psychology often plays games with rational thinking, leading individuals to make decisions that would seem to go against the goal of maximizing utility. This topic of behavioral economics, which studies how human psychology enters into economic behavior, is one that has become increasingly popular among economists in recent decades, and is the focus of the next section.

CHECKPOINT

MARGINAL UTILITY ANALYSIS

- Utility is a hypothetical measure of consumer satisfaction.
- Total utility is the total satisfaction a person gets from consuming a certain amount of goods.
- Marginal utility is the additional satisfaction a consumer gets from consuming one more unit of the good or service.
- The law of diminishing marginal utility states that as consumption of a specific good increases, the increase in total satisfaction will decline.
- Consumers maximize satisfaction by purchasing goods up to the point at which the marginal utility per dollar is equal for all goods.
- Demand curves for products can be derived from marginal utility analysis by changing the price of one good and plotting the resulting changes in consumption.

QUESTIONS: Even though convenience stores have significantly higher prices than normal grocery stores such as Safeway, they seem to do well, judging by their numbers. Why are people willing to pay these higher prices? If a Safeway began to operate 24/7, would this affect the sales of a nearby convenience store?

Answers to the Checkpoint questions can be found at the end of this chapter.

Behavioral Economics

Up to this point, we generally have assumed that individuals make rational decisions that maximize their well-being. Yet, an increasing number of economists have devoted their attention to studying situations in which individuals *do not* appear to follow rational economic thinking, at least the behavior that economic models predict will result. This section turns our attention to the study of behavioral economics. **Behavioral economics** is the study of how human psychology enters into economic behavior as a way to explain why individuals sometimes act counter to how economic models predict.

behavioral economics The study of how human psychology enters into economic behavior as a way to explain why individuals sometimes act in predictable ways counter to economic models.

All individuals from time to time make irrational decisions; that is part of human nature. An important point to keep in mind is that we are not analyzing random behavior. Instead, behavioral economics looks at situations in which people act irrationally in *predictable* ways. This could be a big deal because it challenges the notion of economic rationality that we have assumed in our models. The fact that irrational behavior can occur in predictable ways means that clever people try to take advantage of this behavior. What psychological factors influence irrational behavior, and how do these factors translate into clever opportunism?

This section presents five important psychological factors influencing economic behavior: (1) sunk cost fallacy, (2) framing bias, (3) overconfidence, (4) overvaluing the present relative to the future, and (5) altruism. Each of these factors influences decisions we make every day. In fact, marketers of goods and services often exploit these factors in order to attract consumers to make purchases they otherwise might not make. Let's look at each factor and some common examples illustrating each concept.

Sunk Cost Fallacy

Suppose a few months ago you had paid a nonrefundable registration fee of $200 to attend your favorite annual collector's convention in town to be held this weekend. The fee is not refundable or transferable to another person. Therefore, the $200 fee you paid is a **sunk cost,** a cost that has been paid and cannot be recovered. As the weekend approaches, you realize that you are extremely behind in your studies, so much so that going to the convention would likely take away the last bit of time to prepare for upcoming midterm exams.

sunk cost A cost that has been paid and cannot be recovered; therefore, it should not enter into decision making affecting the present or future.

You think to yourself, "If I would have known I'd be so busy with school, I wouldn't have paid $200 to register for the convention. But since I've already paid it, I'm certainly not going to let my money go to waste, so I'm going to go despite the potential consequences to my grades." Does this seem logical?

According to economic theory, it does not. Sunk costs are costs that cannot be undone. Therefore, the decision whether to attend should not hinge upon past payments, because the registration fee has already been paid. By incorporating sunk costs into present and future decisions, a **sunk cost fallacy** occurs as people make decisions based on how much was already spent rather than how the decision might affect their current well-being. In this case, because going to the convention may have consequences on your grades, the wise decision would be to forgo the convention. Either way, the money is already gone.

sunk cost fallacy Occurs when people make decisions based on how much was already spent rather than how the decision might affect their current well-being.

The sunk cost fallacy often appears in situations in which people feel that they have invested too much time or money into a project to quit. Another common example is the tuition paid for school, a sunk cost. Often, students who fail the midterm and have little hope of raising their grades are reluctant to withdraw from a class because they are unwilling to give up a class that is already paid for, instead hoping for a miracle (or a sympathetic professor) that the final grade will be a passing one. But often the result is a failing grade, which means not only do they need to retake the class (and pay for it once more), but worse, a failing grade appears on their transcript.

Framing Bias

Does a price of $9.99 seem a lot different from $10.00? It really shouldn't, given the difference is one-tenth of 1%. Even more startling are prices displayed at most gas stations, which often show prices in tenths of a cent, such as $3.99^9 (the next time you pass by a gas

fred hall/iStockphoto

The not-so-noticeable nine-tenths of a cent added to the price of a gallon of gasoline adds up to over $1 billion in revenue for gas stations each year.

station, notice the extra nine-tenths of a cent). Compared to $4.00, $3.99⁹ is a difference of just one-fortieth of 1%. Finally, does "Buy One Get One Half-Off" sound like a better deal than "25% off"? It might; however, if you buy two items with the same price, the total cost is the same under each deal.

In each of the above examples, the percentage difference between the two prices is zero or virtually zero. Yet, consumers tend to react differently to these prices, with the former being interpreted as a lower price than the latter, enough to influence buying decisions. This ability to influence consumer decisions by how prices are displayed is an example of a **framing bias,** which occurs when individuals are steered toward one choice over another by how those choices are portrayed. Framing techniques are used by marketers to increase sales of products without actually lowering the price.

framing bias Describes when individuals are steered into making one decision over another or are convinced they are receiving a higher value for a product than what was paid for it.

Framing biases are not limited to pricing strategies. Much in the same way that firms steer consumers toward buying products using prices, a broad range of framing effects can be used to steer individuals toward one political candidate or one political issue over another, toward one product over another in advertising campaigns, and toward one policy over another in legislative debates.

Framing biases also occur when firms convince buyers that what they purchased is worth much more than what they paid. This type of strategy attempts to alter the perceptions of buyers into believing they are always receiving a great deal. Ever notice that some stores perpetually have sales of 10% to 20% off everything, or give money back in the form of gift cards for future visits? Wouldn't it be the same if a store just marks down the sticker prices of everything? Perhaps, but consumers tend to respond more positively to sales and other seemingly good offers.

Overconfidence

Feeling confident about one's abilities, attractiveness, or intellectual capacity is a trait often instilled from one's childhood. No doubt self-esteem plays an important role in the success of many people. But overconfidence in one's abilities can have the opposite effect.

Watch the auditions of any reality talent show, and notice the pitchy, off-key singers who belt their hearts out as if they were on stage at the Grammy Awards, only to be brought back to reality by the harsh criticism of the judges. Being overconfident can lead to decisions that have consequences, such as picking the wrong stock in which to invest, spending too much time and effort applying to only the very top graduate school or law school, or turning down potential respectable boyfriends or girlfriends in hopes of a dream mate.

Wanting to feel confident about one's abilities and choices sometimes leads to decisions that run counter to economic theory, and marketers often take advantage of this factor. One- and two-year gym memberships offered for an attractive upfront prepaid price is a great deal for someone eager to lose weight and get in shape. But often such ambitions fall short, leading many gym memberships to go unused (with the money comfortably in the gym's bank account).

Overvaluing the Present Relative to the Future

It is often difficult to plan for the future. Money saved today can earn interest, and money invested in financial instruments and assets can increase in value over time. Despite the higher value of money in the future, it is still money one must give up using *today*. Therefore, people sometimes are reluctant to save for the future despite lucrative incentives such as retirement fund matching programs offered by employers.

The same is true for paying off debt. Paying the minimum payment on credit card balances seems easy, but accruing finance charges of 15% or more can put a severe crunch on finances in the future. Although differences in time preferences themselves are not irrational per se, because the future often appears so distant, it can blur the reasoning behind sound economic decisions. For example, a society's unwillingness to fully tackle climate change results from overvaluing present benefits relative to future costs.

Altruism

The last factor to be discussed is **altruism,** or actions undertaken merely out of goodwill or generosity. Buying a sandwich for a homeless person you will likely not see again, donating money to a charitable organization, or helping a tourist find his or her way to a hotel all are friendly gestures that do not provide any reward except for the positive feeling one gets from helping others.

altruism Actions undertaken merely out of goodwill or generosity.

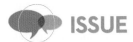

ISSUE

Tipping and Consumer Behavior

If consumers maximize their utility with a given (limited) budget, why would they ever tip? Consider that tips come at the end of a meal. How can tips affect the quality of service already given?

Many reasons might explain tipping. First, if it is a restaurant you frequent, tips might assure better service in the future. Second, you might consider tips to be rewards for higher quality service. Third, tipping is a custom and is part of the income for several dozen occupations.

What would happen if many people refused or neglected to tip? Would people in various occupations seek to make tipping legally binding? It is likely this would be the result, if a recent case in New York is any guide.

Jacobs Stock Photography/Exactostock/ SuperStock

If you have ever gone to a restaurant with a large party, you will notice that menus and bills often state that a set tip will be added for large parties. One large party gave a very small tip after what they considered to be inadequate service. The restaurant sued, claiming that an 18% tip was mandatory. The court's decision for the tipper turned on the phrasing in the menu. This could be viewed as a first shot: If too many people refuse to tip or tip poorly, we can expect legal redress.

We can establish, then, that tipping is a custom that leads to better service, and so is followed even though the tip comes after the service is performed. In this way, it seems to run counter to the idea of people tipping based on a calculation of marginal utility. And how much we tip raises questions about how we calculate marginal utility.

Economists have found only a weak statistical link between quality of service and size of the tip. Tipping also appears to be unrelated to the number of courses in the meal, and whether or not people intend to return to the restaurant. The accompanying table shows some of the things that do affect the size of the tip.

Obviously, a waiter or waitress cannot do all of these things and expect to see tips increase by the sum of all the percentages, but we all have experienced many of these techniques in restaurants. Interestingly, if a waitress draws a smiley face on the bill, her tips go up, but if a waiter does the same, his tips go down. Suggestive selling raises the tip because people tend to tip based on the size of the bill. After having read about this study, you probably will find yourself being a little cynical when some of these techniques are used the next time you dine out.

Percentage Increase in Tips from Specific Behavior by Waitstaff

Tip Enhancing Action	Change in Tip
Wearing a flower in hair	17%
Introducing yourself by name	53%
Squatting down next to the table	20%–25%
Repeat order back to customers	100%
Suggestive selling	23%
Touching customer	22%–42%
Using tip trays with credit card insignia	22%–25%
Waitress drawing a smiley face on check	18%
Writing "thank you" on the check	13%

See Michael Lynn, *Mega Tips: Scientifically Tested Techniques to Increase Your Tips,* 2004, p. 25.

Source: Based on Raj Persaud, "What's the tipping point?" *Financial Times,* April 9, 2005, p. w3.

Hill Street Studios/E/Blend Images/SuperStock

Helping the community by volunteering one's time provides satisfaction that is not measured by monetary gains.

Thus, altruistic behavior provides utility in the sense of feeling good about one's actions, even though the actions may cost money, time, and effort, resources that will reduce one's ability to consume other items. Although altruism is generally not viewed as a *mistake,* it nonetheless represents a limitation of the rational choice model. And because altruistic behavior is so commonplace (such as the generosity of individuals in times of natural disasters, both within the country and abroad), economic models need to account for the utility gained from being generous. Yet, such feelings of goodwill are difficult to measure in economic models, which makes it a factor left to behavioral economists to take into account.

Each of the five factors described in this section add to the discussion in the previous section that marginal utility analysis does not capture all circumstances of individual economic behavior. But it is important to note that these limitations and the behavioral factors are the exceptions to the rule; marginal utility analysis still plays an important role in how we live our daily lives.

Recognizing the validity of these criticisms, economists have tried to limit themselves to working with the sorts of data they can collect, in this case purchases by individuals. By formulating hypotheses about what consumers purchase and what this says about their preferences, economists have managed to develop a theory of consumer behavior that does not require that utility be measured. This more modern approach to analyzing consumer behavior that reaches the same conclusions as marginal utility theory is known as *indifference curve analysis.* Because indifference curve analysis extends the discussion of consumer behavior beyond the principles of consumer choice, it is discussed in the Appendix.

CHECKPOINT

BEHAVIORAL ECONOMICS

- Behavioral economics involves incorporating human psychology into economic decision making to explain why individuals sometimes do not act according to what economic models predict.
- Behavioral economics studies *predictable* deviations from rational behavior.
- The sunk cost fallacy is a common mistake when individuals feel obligated to take sunk cost expenditures into account when making present and future decisions.
- Framing biases occur when marketers present prices in a way that makes them appear lower than what they actually are.
- Overconfidence, overvaluing the present relative to the future, and altruistic actions are other factors influencing economic behavior.

QUESTIONS: A common practice in some supermarkets is to hang signs in the soup section that read "limit 12 per customer." Would our previous economic models predict that consumer behavior would change at all? How about behavioral economics? If it did, what deviation would this be?

Answers to the Checkpoint questions can be found at the end of this chapter.

chapter summary

Section 1: The Budget Line and Choices

A **budget line** shows all the combinations of two goods that can be purchased with a given income and given the prices of each good.

Example: Monthly workout budget = $100; price per wall climbing session = $20; price per racquetball session = $10.

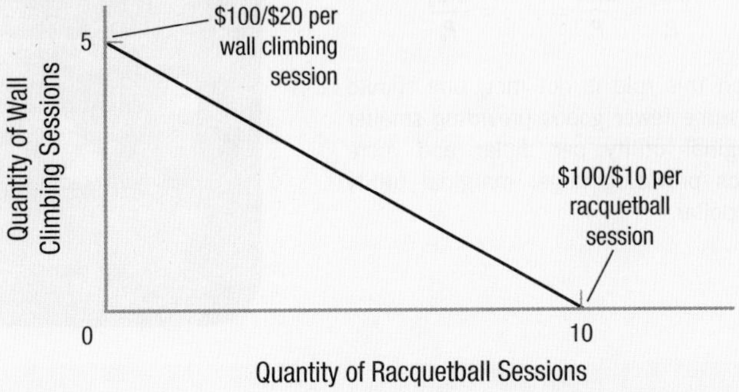

Changes in Prices and Income (initial budget = $30; initial price of movie ticket and cover charge = $10 each)

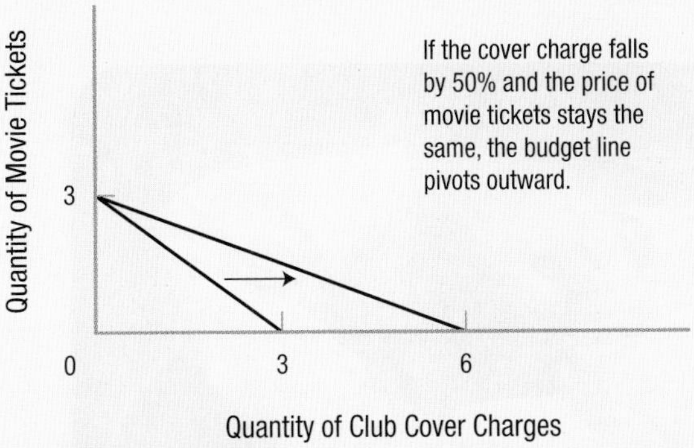

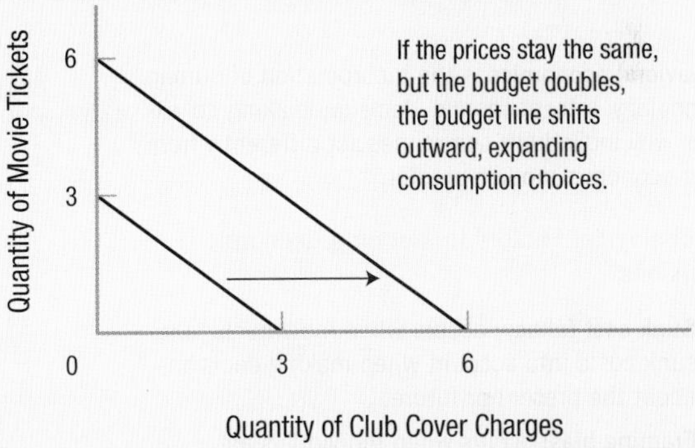

Section 2: Marginal Utility Analysis

Utility is a hypothetical measure of satisfaction.

Total utility is the satisfaction a person receives from consuming a quantity of a good, while **marginal utility** is the satisfaction received from consuming *one more unit* of a good.

Where should one consume on the budget?

The budget line shows what combinations are affordable, but not which point maximizes utility. This is determined using the **utility maximization rule,** which says that utility is maximized when the marginal utility per dollar is equal across all goods.

Aurora Photos/Alamy

Wall climbing is fun, but climbing the same rock wall every time might make the experience less exciting over time due to the **law of diminishing marginal utility.**

Section 2: Marginal Utility Analysis (continued)

The **utility maximization rule** states that total utility is maximized when the marginal utility per dollar is equal for all products purchased:

$$\frac{MU_a}{P_a} = \frac{MU_b}{P_b} = \ldots = \frac{MU_n}{P_n}$$

When this rule is not met, one should consume fewer goods providing smaller marginal utility per dollar and more goods providing larger marginal utility per dollar.

Lucas Tange/cultura/Corbis

Watching a boring movie is likely to provide very little utility, resulting in even smaller marginal utility per dollar spent at the cinema. Money in this case ought to have been spent on an activity providing greater marginal utility per dollar in order to maximize total utility.

Section 3: Behavioral Economics

Behavioral economics is the incorporation of human psychology into economic decision making to explain why individuals sometimes act differently from what economic models predict.

Psychological Factors Influencing Economic Decisions

- **Sunk cost fallacy:** occurs when individuals take sunk costs into account when making decisions about the present or future.
- **Framing bias:** occurs when individuals are steered toward making one decision over another, or when individuals are led to believe that they are getting a better deal than they actually are.
- **Overconfidence:** occurs when strong feelings of one's abilities lead to irrational decisions.
- **Overvaluing the present relative to the future:** occurs when future decisions appear too distant to be concerned about in the present, leading to irrational decisions.
- **Altruism:** occurs when feelings of goodwill lead individuals to make decisions that benefit others at the expense of their own consumption.

Image Source/Corbis

Overconfidence in one's ability to select stocks may cause some to lose significant sums of money. Further, once losses in the stock market occur, traders are often reluctant to sell, and instead hold onto stocks as they potentially fall further in price, an example of the sunk cost fallacy.

KEY CONCEPTS

budget line, p. 134
marginal utility analysis, p. 137
utility, p. 137
total utility, p. 138
marginal utility, p. 139
law of diminishing marginal utility, p. 139
utility maximizing rule, p. 141
behavioral economics, p. 145
sunk cost, p. 145
sunk cost fallacy, p. 145
framing bias, p. 146
altruism, p. 147

QUESTIONS AND PROBLEMS

Check Your Understanding

1. Using a budget line, why does a decrease in the price of a good allow one to potentially consume more of both goods?
2. Why do price changes cause a budget line to pivot while income changes cause a budget line to shift in a parallel manner?
3. Describe the utility-maximizing condition in words. Explain why it makes sense.
4. What conditions are necessary for total utility to be positive while marginal utility is negative?
5. Why should sunk costs not be taken into consideration when making decisions about the present or the future?
6. Why do the prices of many goods and services end in 99 cents? Why don't businesses just round to the nearest whole dollar?

Apply the Concepts

7. Scruffie the cat has $15 to spend each month on cat toys, which cost $3 each, and cat treats, which cost $1.50 each. Draw a budget line to show the combinations of each good that Scruffie can afford if she spends her entire budget. Now suppose that cat treats go on sale for $1 each. How does this change in price affect the budget line (show on a graph)?
8. Eric enjoys having sushi and sashimi for lunch every day. Suppose the marginal utility of the last sushi roll Eric eats is 40 and the marginal utility of the last piece of sashimi Eric eats is 20. If the price of a roll of sushi is $8 and the price per piece of sashimi is $2, did Eric maximize his utility? Explain.
9. One luxury goods manufacturer noted that, "Our customers do not want to pay less. If we halved the price of all our products, we would double our sales for six months, and then we would sell nothing." Is there something about luxury goods that suggests consumers are irrational? Do luxury goods not follow the law of demand?
10. Advertisements on television both inform consumers and persuade them to purchase products in differing proportions, depending on the ad. But today, because digital video recorders can be found in virtually all households, much of what these households watch is recorded, and the vast bulk of the ads are skipped. If this trend continues, where will consumers find out about new products?

11. Critics of marginal utility analysis argue that it is unrealistic to assume that people make the mental calculus of marginal utility per dollar for large numbers of products. But when you are making a decision to either go to a first-run movie or to buy a used DVD of last summer's blockbuster, does this analysis seem so complex? Is it a reasonable representation of your thought process?
12. A common practice at many supermarkets is to show the customer's total "savings" on their purchase at the bottom of the receipt. Such savings include the total discounts from goods purchased along with savings from coupons used. How would listing the total savings on a receipt influence an individual's consumption habits? Of what type of behavioral factor does this strategy take advantage?

In the News

13. Richard Layard, in his book *Happiness: Lessons from a New Science,* states that once a country's annual income exceeds $20,000 per capita, there is little relationship between happiness and income. But if you are poor, more money does make you happier. Does this fact suggest that the marginal utility from more income above $20,000 per capita is small?
14. In the summer of 2009, Chrysler announced that beginning with its 2010 models it was dropping the current lifetime powertrain (engine and transmission parts) warranty and replacing it with a five-year, 100,000-mile guarantee. *The Wall Street Journal* (August 20, 2009) reported that "Chrysler spokesman Rick Deneau said that the decision was driven by market research that showed customers prefer warranties with a fixed time period." The new five-year warranty was transferable if the vehicle was sold, while the prior lifetime warranty applied only to the original owner.

    Given marginal utility analysis, does it seem reasonable that consumers really prefer a five-year, 100,000-mile warranty to a lifetime warranty? What customers actually benefit from this new warranty?

Solving Problems

15. Assume a consumer has $20 to spend and for both products the marginal utilities are shown in the table below:

Quantity	MU_A	MU_B
1	20	30
2	10	10
3	5	2

Assume that each product sells for $5 per unit.

a. How many units of each product will the consumer purchase?
b. Assume the price of product B rises to $10 per unit. How will this consumer allocate her budget now?
c. If the prices of both products rise to $10 per unit, what will be the budget allocation?

16. Answer the questions following the table below.

First-Run Movies			Bottles of Wine		
Quantity	**Total Utility**	**Marginal Utility**	**Quantity**	**Total Utility**	**Marginal Utility**
0	0	—	0	0	—
1	140	_____	1	180	_____
2	260	_____	2	340	_____
3	360	_____	3	460	_____
4	440	_____	4	510	_____
5	500	_____	5	540	_____

a. Complete the table.

b. Assume that you have \$50 a month to devote to entertainment (column labeled First-Run Movies) and wine with dinner (column labeled Bottles of Wine). What will be your equilibrium allocation if the price to see a movie is \$10 and a bottle of wine cost \$10 as well?

c. A grape glut in California results in Napa Valley wine dropping in price to \$5 per bottle, and you view this wine as a perfect substitute for what you were drinking earlier. Now what will be your equilibrium allocation between movies and wine?

d. Given this data, calculate your elasticity of demand for wine over these two prices (see the midpoint method in Chapter 5).

USING THE NUMBERS

17. Using By the Numbers, list the top five categories that the average American household spent their incomes on in the year 2011 (start with the largest expenditure and proceed downward in terms of percentage of household budget).

18. According to By the Numbers, what category or categories of goods and services have increased in price (on average) every year from 2009 to 2011? What category or categories have fallen in price every year from 2009 to 2011?

ANSWERS TO QUESTIONS IN CHECKPOINTS

Checkpoint: The Budget Line and Choices

The total amount spent on meals each week is $(10 \times \$7.50) + (5 \times \$15) = \$150$. If the price of off-campus meals decreases to \$10, the cost of maintaining the same routine as before (10 meals on campus and 5 meals off campus) falls to \$125, leaving \$25 left over. This extra money (savings from the price decrease) can be used to purchase more meals at either location, including more meals on campus.

Checkpoint: Marginal Utility Analysis

Convenience stores offer a small set of products at high prices nearer to home and have extended hours of operation. They also provide quicker service in that customers are in and out of the store quickly with what they need. The marginal utility of convenience overcomes the higher prices, thus people shop there because time is money. A 24/7 Safeway would have an impact on convenience store sales. At off-hours, supermarkets might be as fast as convenience stores, but cheaper.

Checkpoint: Behavioral Economics

According to marginal utility analysis, putting up a sign indicating a limit of 12 cans of soup per customer should not affect buying behavior, unless the shopper actually planned to buy more than 12 cans, in which case the sign puts a restriction on the purchase. However, in behavioral economics, putting up this sign represents a framing technique: by putting a limit of 12 cans, the supermarket is implying that the soup is so good that customers have a habit of buying large quantities (which may not be likely at all). By suggesting the soup is "popular," it draws customers into buying the soup that they otherwise might overlook, creating a framing bias.

Appendix

Indifference Curve Analysis

After studying this Appendix you should be able to:

- Understand the properties of indifference curves and preference maps.
- Use indifference curves to derive demand curves and measure income and substitution effects.

Marginal utility analysis provides a good theoretical glimpse into the consumer decision-making process, yet it requires that utility be measured and that marginal utility per dollar be computed for innumerable possible consumption choices. In reality, measuring utility is impossible, as is mentally computing the marginal utility of thousands of products. To get around these difficulties, economists have developed a modern explanation of consumer decisions that does not require measuring utility. The foundation of this analysis is the indifference curve.

Indifference Curves and Consumer Preferences

If consumers cannot precisely measure the exact satisfaction they receive from specific products, economists reason that people can distinguish between different bundles of goods and decide whether they prefer one bundle over another. This analysis eliminates the idea of measuring consumer satisfaction. It instead assumes that consumers will either be able to choose between any two bundles, or else be *indifferent* to which bundle is chosen. An **indifference curve** shows all points at which consumers' choices are indifferent—points at which consumers express no preference between combinations of two products.

indifference curve Shows all the combinations of two goods where the consumer is indifferent (gets the same level of satisfaction).

To illustrate how an indifference curve works, let us return to our original example of pizzas and wall climbing, now graphed in Figure APX-1. Compare the combination represented by point *b* (2 pizzas and 1.5 hours of climbing) and the combination at point *e* (2 pizzas and 0.5 hour of wall climbing). Which would you prefer, assuming you enjoy both of these? Clearly, the combination at point *b* is preferable to the combination at point *e* because you get the same amount of pizza but more wall climbing. By the same logic, bundle *f* is preferable to bundle *b* because you get the same amount of climbing, but 3 more pizzas.

These choices have all been easy enough to make. But now assume you are offered bundles *d* and *b*. Bundle *d* contains more pizzas than bundle *b*, but bundle *b* has more climbing time. Given this choice, you may well conclude that you do not care which

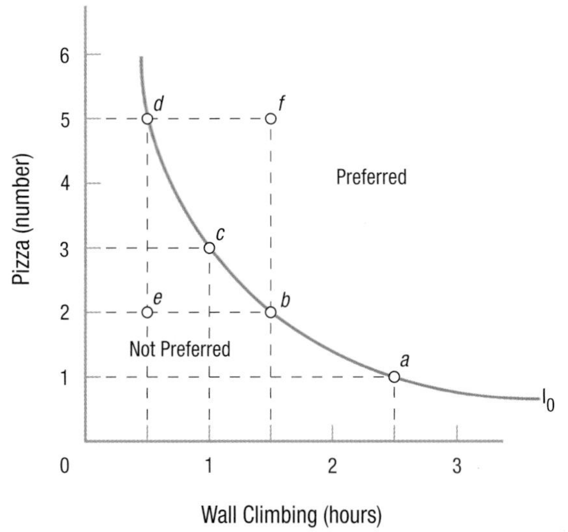

FIGURE APX-1

An Indifference Curve

All of the different possible combinations lying on the indifference curve I_0 represent bundles of goods to which you are indifferent—you would just as soon have any one of these combinations as any other. But compare the combination represented by point *b* and the combination at point *e*. Which would you prefer? Point *b*, of course, because you get more. All points upward and to the right are preferred to all points on indifference curve I_0.

bundle you get—you are indifferent. In fact, all of the different possible combinations lying on the indifference curve I_0 represent bundles to which you are indifferent, such that you would just as soon have any one of these combinations as any other. And this tells us what an indifference curve is: It identifies all possible combinations of two products that offer consumers the same level of satisfaction or utility. Notice that this mode of analysis does not require us to consider the precise quantity of utility that various bundles yield, but only whether one bundle would be preferable to another.

Properties of Indifference Curves

Indifference curves have negative slopes and are convex to the origin; they bow inward, that is. They have negative slopes because we assume consumers will generally prefer to have more, rather than less, of each product. Yet, to obtain more of one product and maintain the same level of satisfaction, consumers must give up some quantity of the other product. Hence, the negative slope.

Indifference curves are bowed inward toward the origin because of the law of diminishing marginal utility discussed earlier. When you have a lot of pizzas (point *d* in Figure APX-1), you are willing to give up 2 pizzas to obtain another half-hour of climbing (moving from point *d* to point *c*). But once you have plenty of wall time, yet few pizzas (point *b*), you are unwilling to give up as many pizzas to get more climbing time. This is the law of diminishing marginal utility at work: As we consume more of any particular product, the satisfaction we derive from consuming additional units of this product falls.

Indifference (or Preference) Maps

indifference map An infinite set of indifference curves in which each curve represents a different level of utility or satisfaction.

An indifference curve is a curve that represents a set of product bundles to which a consumer is indifferent. An **indifference map,** or *preference map,* is an infinite set of indifference curves, each representing a different level of satisfaction. Three possible indifference curves, forming part of a preference map, are shown in Figure APX-2.

Indifference curve I_0 is the same curve shown in Figure APX-1. Indifference curve I_1 provides consumers with greater satisfaction than I_0 because it is located farther from the origin. In general, utility rises as curves move outward from the origin, because these curves represent larger quantities of both goods. Conversely, indifference curve I_2 offers consumers less total satisfaction because it is located closer to the origin and represents smaller amounts of both products than I_0.

To confirm the observations just made, compare point *a* on indifference curve I_2 with point *b* on indifference curve I_0. Points *a* and *b* contain the same amount of pizza, but point *b* contains more climbing time. Hence, point *b* offers a higher level of satisfaction than

FIGURE APX-2

Three Indifference Curves for Pizza and Wall Climbing (An Indifference Map)

An indifference map, or preference map, contains an infinite set of indifference curves, each representing a different level of satisfaction. Three possible indifference curves for pizzas and wall climbing, forming part of a preference map, are shown here.

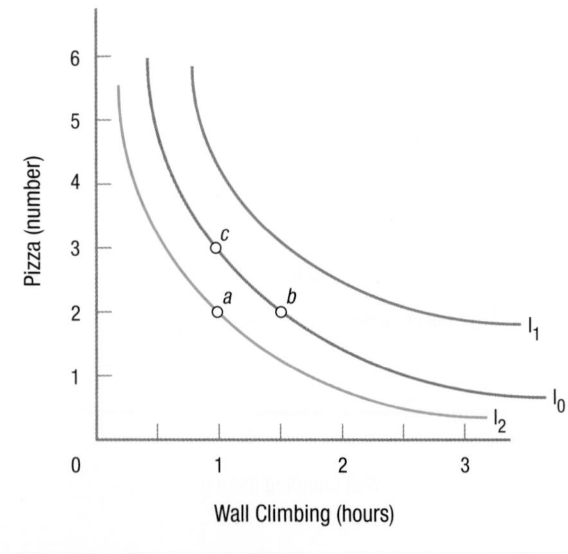

point *a*. An analysis of points *a* and *c* yields a similar conclusion. Because both points *c* and *b* on indifference curve I_0 are preferred to point *a* on I_2, indifference curve I_0 must generally offer higher levels of satisfaction than the points on indifference curve I_2.

This result leads us to one final property of indifference curves: They do not intersect. Because all of the points on any indifference curve represent bundles of goods to which consumers are indifferent, if two indifference curves were to cross, this would mean that some of the bundles they represent offered the same level of satisfaction (where the curves meet), but others did not (where the curves do not touch). Yet, this is a logical impossibility, because each indifference curve is defined as a set of bundles offering exactly the same level of satisfaction.

We now turn to the question of how consumers use such preference maps to optimize their satisfaction within their budget constraints.

Optimal Consumer Choice

Figure APX-3 superimposes a budget line of $50 per week onto a preference map that assumes pizzas cost $10 each and wall climbing costs $20 per hour. Maximizing your satisfaction on your limited income requires that you purchase some bundle of goods on the highest possible indifference curve. In this example, the best you can do is indicated by point *b:* 2 pizzas and 1.5 hours of wall climbing. Clearly, if you were to pick any other point on the budget line, your satisfaction would be diminished because you would end up on a lower indifference curve (points *a* or *c* in Figure APX-3). It follows that the indifference curve running tangent to the budget line identifies your best option, in this case the indifference curve that just touches the budget line at point *b*.

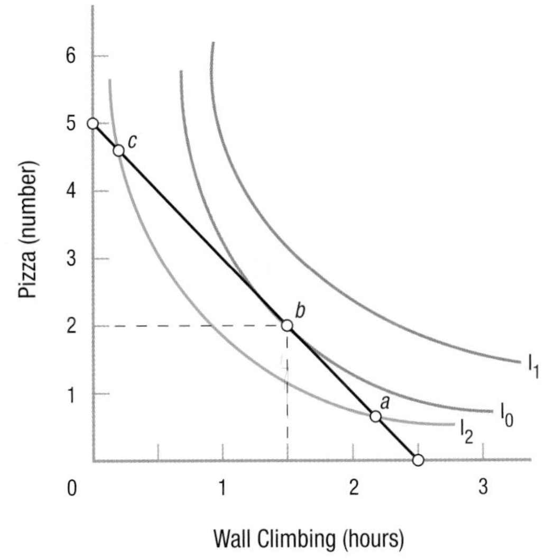

FIGURE APX-3

Optimal Consumer Choice

Maximizing your satisfaction on your limited income requires purchasing some bundle of goods on the highest possible indifference curve. The best you can do in this situation is indicated by point *b:* 2 pizzas and 1.5 hours of wall climbing. Indifference curve I_0 is the highest indifference curve that can be reached with the budget line shown.

Of course, this is the same result we reached earlier using marginal utility analysis, specifically in Table 2. Notice, however, that using indifference curve analysis, we did not have to assume that utility can be measured. We were able to understand how you would allocate your budget between two goods so as to achieve the highest possible level of satisfaction, even without knowing exactly how high that level might be.

Using Indifference Curves

Indifference curves are a useful device to help us understand consumer demand. Economists use indifference curves, for instance, to shed light on the impact of changes in consumer income and product substitution resulting from a change in product price. Indifference curve analysis, moreover, provides some insight into how households determine their supply of labor (this analysis, however, is left to a later chapter). Before we move on to applications of indifference curve analysis, however, we first need to derive a demand curve from an indifference map.

Deriving Demand Curves

We derive the demand curve using indifference curve analysis in much the same way we did using marginal utility analysis. Panel A of Figure APX-4 restates the results of Figure APX-3: When you have a budget of $50 per week, the price of pizza is $10, and climbing is $20 per hour, your optimal choice is found at point *a*. In panel B, we want to plot the demand curve for wall climbing. We know that when wall climbing costs $20 per hour, you will climb for 1.5 hours, so let us indicate this on panel B by marking point *a*.

To fill out the demand curve, let us now increase the price of wall climbing to $30 per hour. This produces a new budget line, *cd*. (Point *d* is located at 1.67 hours because $50/$30 = 1.67 hours of possible wall climbing.) This shift in the budget line yields a new optimal choice at point *b* on indifference curve I_2, now indicating the highest level of satisfaction you can attain. As panel A shows, the ultimate result of this hike in the price of wall climbing to $30 an hour is a reduction in your climbing to 1 hour per week. Transferring this result to panel B, we mark point *b* where price = $30 and climbing hours = 1. Now connecting points *a* and *b* in panel B, we are left with the demand curve for wall climbing.

Once again, therefore, we arrive at the same conclusion using indifference curve analysis as we did earlier using marginal utility analysis. Both approaches are logical and elegant,

FIGURE APX-4

Deriving the Demand for Wall Climbing Using Indifference Curve Analysis

In panel A, when wall climbing costs $20 per hour, your optimal choice is found at point *a*. When the price of wall climbing rises to $30 per hour, this produces a new budget line, *cd*, shifting the optimal choice to point *b*. Transferring points *a* and *b* down to panel B and connecting the points generates the demand curve for wall climbing.

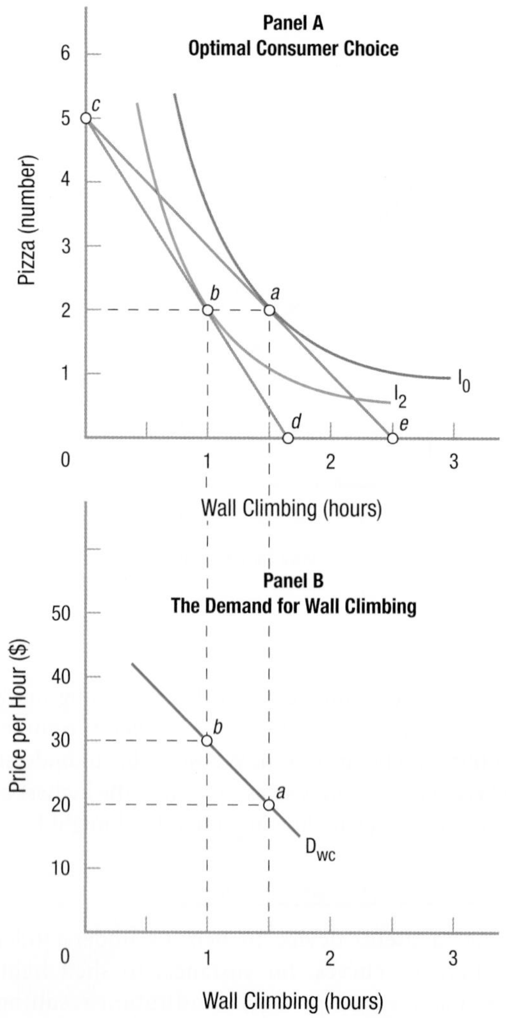

and both approaches tell us something about the thought processes consumers must use as they make their spending decisions. Indifference curve analysis, however, arrives at its conclusion without requiring that utility be measurable or that consumers perform complex arithmetic computations.

Income and Substitution Effects

Another way economists use indifference curves is to separate income and substitution effects when product prices change. First we need to distinguish between these two effects.

When the price of some product you regularly purchase goes up, your spendable income is thereby essentially reduced. If you always buy a latte a day, for instance, and you continue to do so even when the price of lattes goes up, you must then reduce your consumption of other goods. This essentially amounts to a reduction in your income. And we know that when income falls, the consumption of normal goods likewise declines. Hence, when higher prices essentially reduce consumer incomes, the quantity demanded for normal goods generally falls. Economists call this the **income effect.**

income effect When higher prices essentially reduce consumer income, the quantity demanded for normal goods falls.

When the price of a particular good rises, meanwhile, the quantity demanded of that good will fall simply because consumers substitute lower priced goods for it. This is called the **substitution effect.** Thus, when the price of wall climbing rises from \$20 to \$30, you cut back on your climbing, in part because you decide to dedicate more of your money to pizza eating. The challenge for us now is to determine just how much of this reduction in your climbing is due to the substitution effect (more pizzas mean less climbing) and how much is due to the income effect (the rise in price effectively leaves you with less money to spend).

substitution effect When the price of one good rises, consumers will substitute other goods for that good, therefore the quantity demanded for the higher priced good falls.

Figure APX-5 reproduces panel A of Figure APX-4, adding one line (*gh*) to divide the total change in purchases into the income and substitution effects. To see how this line is derived, let us begin by reviewing what has happened thus far. At point *a* you split your \$50 budget into 2 pizzas at \$10 each and 1.5 hours of wall climbing at \$20 per hour. When the price of wall climbing rose to \$30 per hour, you reduced your climbing time to 1 hour.

Consider now what happens when we evaluate what you are getting for your *current* allocation of money, but using the *old* price of wall climbing (\$20 per hour). You are now getting 2 pizzas, worth \$10 apiece, plus 1 hour of wall climbing, formerly valued at \$20. This means that your budget has effectively been cut to \$40. The ultimate effect of the rise in the price of climbing, in other words, has been to reduce your income by \$10. In Figure APX-5, the hypothetical budget line *gh* represents this new budget of \$40, though again reflecting the old price of climbing.

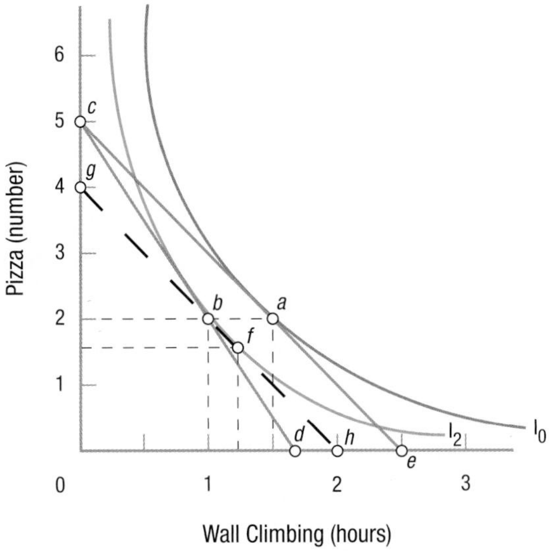

FIGURE APX-5

Income and Substitution Effects

Panel A of Figure APX-4 is reproduced in this figure. The price of climbing having risen to \$30 per hour, this effectively reduces your budget to \$40 per week, assuming you continue climbing as much as you did before. Line *gh* represents a new budget of \$40, though reflecting the old price of climbing. This new budget line *gh* allows us to divide the total change in purchases into the income and substitution effects. Increasing the price of wall climbing from \$20 to \$30 an hour would mean a reduction in wall climbing (holding income constant at \$40) from point *f* to point *b*. This is the substitution effect. The income effect is thus the reduction in consumption from point *a* to point *f*. Adding both effects together yields the total reduction.

Compare the original equilibrium point *a* on budget line *ce* with the new equilibrium point *f* on budget line *gh*. This new budget line *gh* reflects a budget of $40 with the old price of climbing ($20 per hour). Had your income previously been $40, you would have reduced your climbing by 15 minutes (to point *f*). This is the *income effect* associated with the rise in the price of wall climbing from $20 to $30 per hour. The rising price essentially reduced your income, causing you to consume 15 minutes less of wall climbing and 0.5 fewer pizzas due to this income reduction alone.

The change in price is the only thing that differentiates equilibrium point *b* from point *f*, income having been held constant. This difference of 15 minutes between point *f* and point *b* therefore represents a *substitution effect.* By changing the price of climbing while holding income constant, you consume 0.5 more pizza and 15 minutes less wall climbing.

Combined, the substitution and income effects constitute the entire change in quantity demanded when the price of wall climbing rises by $10 per hour. The income effect (movement from point *a* to point *f*) is a movement from one budget line to another. The substitution effect (movement from point *f* to point *b*) is a movement along the new budget line. Together, they represent the total change in quantity demanded. In this case the income and substitution effects were the same, 15 minutes, but this will not always be the case.

This chapter examined how consumers and households make decisions. Households attempt to maximize their well-being or satisfaction within the constraints of limited incomes. We have seen that the analysis of consumer decisions can be approached in two different ways, using marginal utility analysis or indifference curve analysis.

Marginal utility analysis assumes that consumers can readily measure utility and make complex calculations regarding the utility of various possible consumption choices. Both of these assumptions are empirically rather dubious. This does not, however, invalidate marginal utility analysis; it just makes it difficult to use and test in an empirical context. Indifference curve analysis gives us a more powerful set of analytical tools without these restrictive assumptions.

CHECKPOINT

INDIFFERENCE CURVE ANALYSIS

- Indifference curve analysis does not require utility measurement. All it requires is that consumers can choose between different bundles of goods.
- An indifference curve shows all the combinations of two goods where the consumer has the same level of satisfaction.
- Indifference curves have negative slopes, are convex to the origin due to the law of diminishing marginal utility, and do not intersect with one another.
- An indifference map is an infinite set of indifference curves.
- Consumer equilibrium occurs where the budget line is tangent to the highest indifference curve.
- When the price of one product rises, not only will your consumption of that product fall (the substitution effect), but also your relative income will be reduced as well, and for normal goods you will consume less (the income effect). The opposite occurs when price falls.

QUESTION: Consumers face a set of goods called "credence goods." Consumers of such goods must "take it on faith that the supplier has given them what they need and no more."[1] Examples include surgeons, auto mechanics, and taxi drivers. These experts tell us what medical procedures, repairs, and routes we require to satisfy our needs, and very often we don't know the price until the work is done. If we do not know the price and cannot establish whether we actually need some of these goods, how does this square with our indifference curve analysis?

Answers to the Checkpoint question can be found at the end of this chapter.

[1] "Economic Focus: Sawbones, Cowboys and Cheats," *Economist,* April 15, 2006.

APPENDIX KEY CONCEPTS

indifference curve, p. 155
indifference map, p. 156
income effect, p. 159
substitution effect, p. 159

APPENDIX QUESTIONS AND PROBLEMS

Check Your Understanding

1. Indifference curves cannot intersect. Why not?
2. Explain why the following bundles of apples (A) and bananas (B) cannot be on the same indifference curve: (4A, 2B); (1A, 5B); (4A, 3B).
3. Answer the following questions using the figure below:

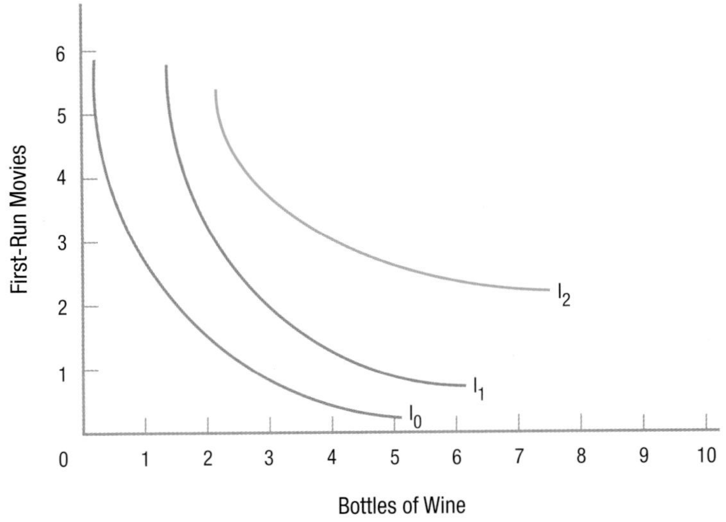

   a. Assume that you have \$50 a month to devote to entertainment (First-Run Movies) and wine with dinner (Bottles of Wine). What will be your equilibrium allocation if the price to see a movie or buy a bottle of wine is \$10? Graph the equilibrium on the figure and label it point *a*.
   b. A grape glut in California results in Napa Valley wine dropping in price to \$5 a bottle, and you view this wine as a perfect substitute for what you were drinking. Now what will be your equilibrium allocation between movies and wine? Graph that on the figure and label the new equilibrium as point *b*.

4. Research by Walter Enders and Todd Sandler, *The Political Economy of Terrorism* (New York: Cambridge University Press), 2006, and David Wessel, "Princeton Economist Says Lack of Civil Liberties, Not Poverty, Breeds Terrorism," *Wall Street Journal*, July 5, 2007, p. A2, suggests that terrorists are not spurred by poverty, but rather often are educated individuals who live in countries with a lack of civil liberties. These researchers treat terrorists as rational actors who maximize a set of goals subject to constrained resources.

   Assume that terrorists can choose between nonviolent acts and violent acts. Draw a budget line and indifference curves that show where a utility maximizing combination of these activities would occur. Now suppose that the U.S. government can choose between two types of antiterrorism policies: (1) a defensive approach such as increased airport screenings, and (2) a proactive approach, which includes activities such as infiltrating terrorist cells and freezing bank assets. Analyze how these policies affect the budget line of terrorists and how it affects the utility-maximizing combination of terrorist activities.

ANSWERS TO APPENDIX CHECKPOINT QUESTION

Checkpoint: Indifference Curve Analysis

Not very well. They are largely a problem of incomplete information and a challenging problem for consumers. If doctors make more money performing complex operations, they will be inclined to prescribe them more often. One study found that doctors elect surgery for themselves less often than nondoctors. As long as consumers are aware of the incentive structure of these transactions, they can build this into the decision calculus, but ultimately, information asymmetries are not adequately represented in this model.

7 Production and Costs

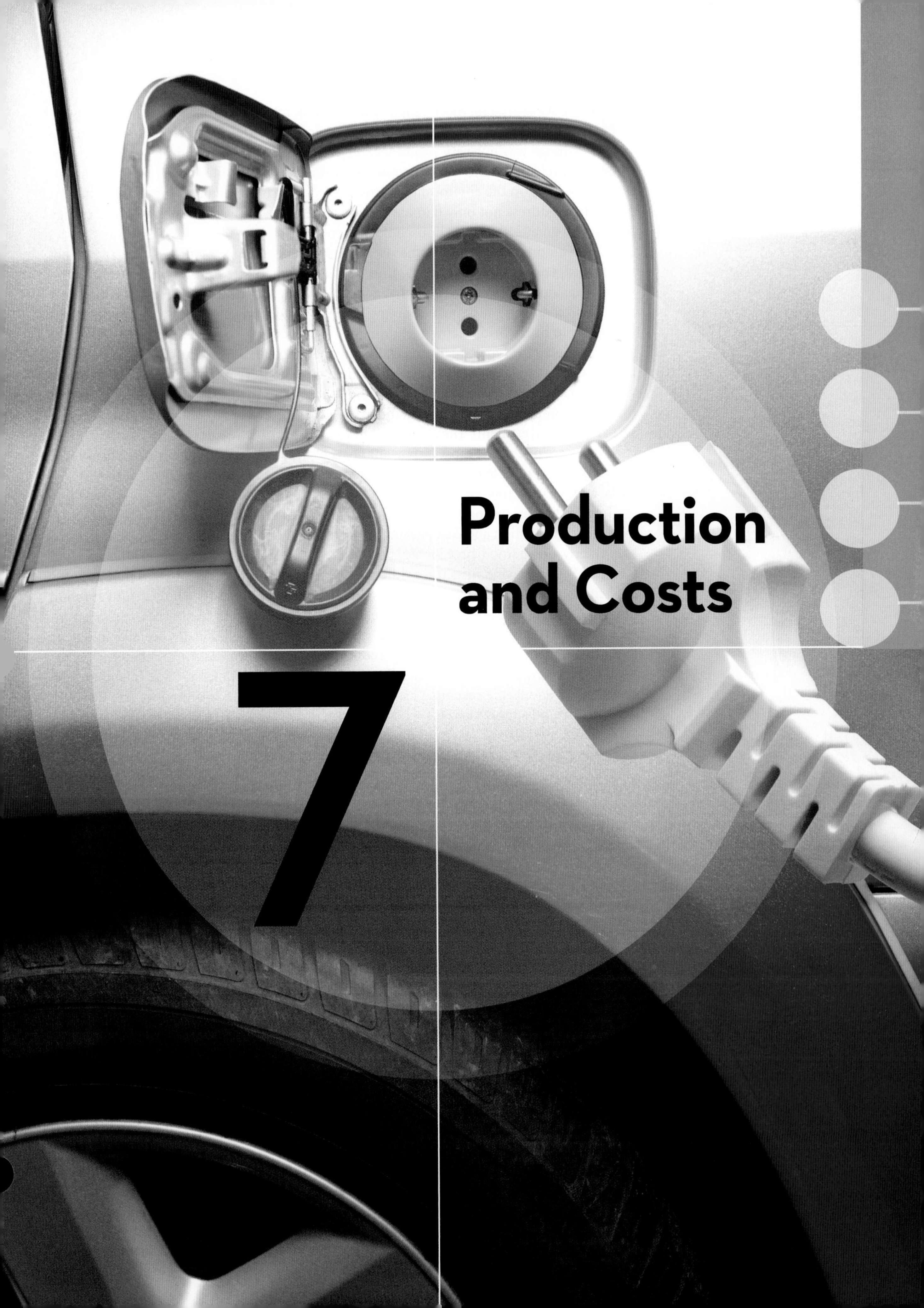

After studying this chapter you should be able to:

- Describe the nature of firms and markets.
- Explain the difference between accounting and economic costs and how they affect the determination of profits.
- Differentiate between the short run and long run.
- Describe the nature of short-run production, total product, marginal product, and average product.
- Differentiate among increasing, constant, and decreasing returns.
- Describe and compare the differences among fixed costs, variable costs, marginal costs, and average costs.
- Explain the importance of marginal costs in a firm's production decision.
- Use graphs to show the relationships among short-run average variable cost, average total cost, and marginal cost curves.
- Describe long-run costs.
- Describe the reasons for economies and diseconomies of scale.

Twenty years ago, most people did not think much about what they could do with sustainable products. Energy and gas prices were low, and the problem of climate change was not very prominent in everyday discussions and news reports. This has changed, and many people today do think about the impact their consumption habits have on the environment. This has led to a rise in demand for energy-efficient products to address not only climate change issues but also wallet issues as rising energy costs take a greater share of a household's budget.

In the automobile industry, the use of sustainable energy resources such as ethanol remains expensive. However, in the mid-1990s manufacturers foresaw an opportunity to satisfy consumer demand for cars that achieve much greater fuel efficiency, resulting in a similar effect as using sustainable energy. In 1997, Toyota unveiled the Prius, the first well-selling car to use hybrid electric technology.

Creating a new type of car, especially one that runs on a new source of energy, is not like creating a new type of pizza. It costs much more to develop, design, and produce the very first car. Toyota invested over $1 billion to develop the Prius, a great deal of money for a new compact car in an untested market. What motivated Toyota to undertake such an expensive investment? The answer is profits.

Profits are one of the most important goals of firms. To determine profits, a firm must calculate its revenues from sales and subtract all of its costs. How does a firm measure these costs, and what do these costs include?

In this chapter, we look at what motivates firms to do what they do—profits. We then look at the production and cost part of the profit equation. We discuss the concept of profit as properly understood by economists. Unlike an accountant or agents of the Internal Revenue Service, economists use a different measure of profit, one that takes into account explicit (out-of-pocket) costs and then adds the opportunity costs (the value of forgone opportunities) of a business decision. We then go on to discuss the production process and how output is determined based on the amount of inputs used. Finally, we take a look at the measurement of costs. Specifically, economists break down costs into different categories in order to create decision rules that firms follow to maximize profits. In subsequent chapters, we add in the revenue part to the production part. In this way, we will discover what lies behind supply curves.

Firms, Profits, and Economic Costs

We just read that Toyota had to make a decision about producing a product. Who makes such decisions? It's the firms and entrepreneurs who choose to take on the risk and effort to launch a new product. They are motivated by the profits that can be earned if the investment proves successful. But how do we measure profits, as properly understood by economists?

This section highlights the important role that firms and entrepreneurs play in producing the goods and services we enjoy as consumers. No matter how the organizational structure is set up, firms and entrepreneurs hold profits as their motivating force. To achieve profits, both revenues and costs must be considered. As we will see, profits can be measured using an accounting approach or an economics approach. These approaches differ in the way costs are measured.

Firms

firm An economic institution that transforms resources (factors of production) into outputs.

A **firm** is an economic institution that transforms inputs, or factors of production, into outputs, or products. Most firms begin as family enterprises or small partnerships. When successful, these firms can evolve into corporations of considerable size.

In the process of producing goods and services, firms must make numerous decisions. First, they have to determine a market need. Then, most broadly, firms must decide what quantity of output to produce, how to produce it, and what inputs to employ. The latter two decisions depend on the production technology that the firm selects.

Any given product can typically be produced in a wide variety of ways. Some businesses, like McDonald's franchises and Dunkin' Donuts shops, use considerable amounts of capital equipment, whereas others, such as T-shirt shops and small eateries, require very little. Even among similar firms, the quality and quantity of resources available often

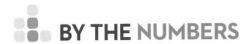

BY THE NUMBERS

Innovation, Productivity, and Costs Rule Business

To remain in business, firms must innovate not only by improving the products they make but also by controlling their costs. Controlling costs is done by introducing new technologies in production and increasing productivity. This holds for the service sector as well.

The cost of industrial robots has fallen over 70% since 1992.

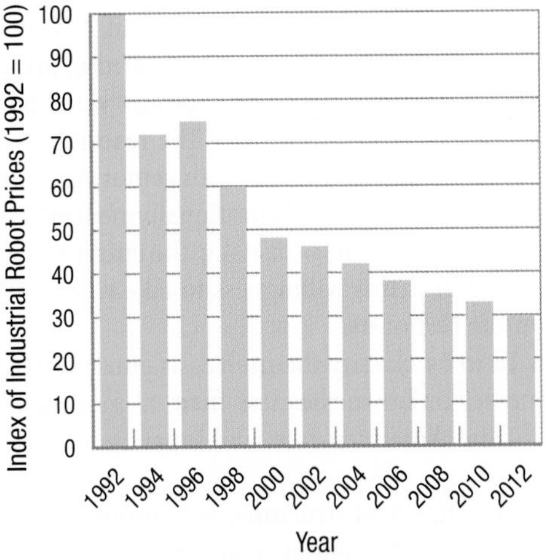

Christopher Honeywell/Alamy

Productivity has risen over 50% since 1992.

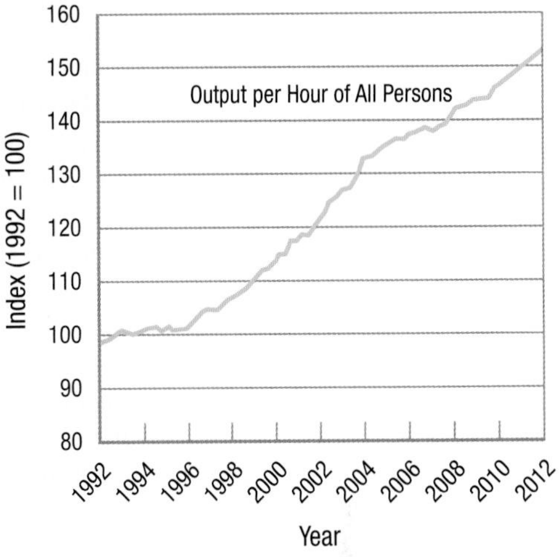

$9,000,000,000
Annual revenue needed to support a new semiconductor fabrication plant.

9.17 hours
Time spent by the average American on government paperwork each year.

"We've found the key to productivity. It's Fred, down in the shop. He makes the stuff."
From The Wall Street Journal, Permission Cartoon Features Syndicate

Cost Breakdown for an iPad

Retail Price	$399
Costs	
Touch display screen	85
Hard drive	52
Battery	22
Apps Processor	14
Misc. components	56
Assembly	10
Distribution costs	70
Profit for Apple	90

Businesses face a relentless need to lower costs, which has changed the way we live and travel. The percentage of travelers purchasing airline tickets and checking in online highlights this trend.

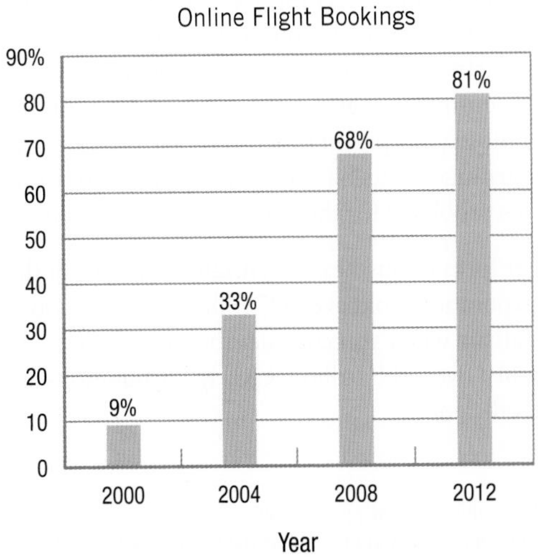

iStockphoto

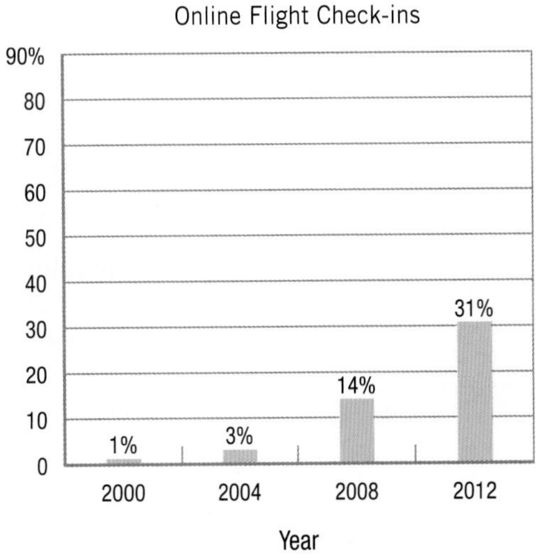

determine what technologies are used. Firms located in areas with an abundance of low-cost labor tend to use low-technology, labor-intensive production methods. In areas in which high-skill, high-wage labor is the norm, production is more often done using high-technology, capital-intensive processes.

Entrepreneurs

If a product or service is to be provided to the market, someone must first assume the risk of raising the required capital, assembling workers and raw materials, producing the product, and, finally, offering it for sale. Markets provide incentives and signals, but it is entrepreneurs who provide products and services by taking risks in the hopes of earning profits.

Recent research in neuroscience has shown that entrepreneurs' brains were more active in the region responsible for making risky or "hot" decisions.[1] The research compared entrepreneurs who had founded at least two high-tech firms with senior managers from the private and public sectors. When the decisions were "emotionally neutral," the groups performed the same, but when the decisions were "hot" or risky, the entrepreneurs were more impulsive and more mentally flexible. It is this willingness to take risk to earn profits that distinguishes entrepreneurs from the rest of us.

In the United States, 12% of people ages 18 to 64 classify themselves as entrepreneurs. This means they are running start-up businesses or businesses less than 42 months old. Entrepreneurial rates in Europe are only half the American rate, and Japanese entrepreneurship is less than 2%.[2]

Entrepreneurs can be divided into three basic business structures: sole proprietorships (one owner), partnerships (two or more owners), and corporations (many stockholders). The United States has more than 25 million businesses, over 70% of them sole proprietorships or small businesses. Only 20% of American businesses are corporations. Nevertheless, corporations sell nearly 90% of all products and services in the United States. Likewise, around the world, the corporate form of business has become the dominant form. To see why, we must first take a brief look at the advantages and disadvantages of each business structure.

sole proprietorship A type of business structure composed of a single owner who supervises and manages the business and is subject to unlimited liability.

Sole Proprietors The **sole proprietorship** represents the most basic form of business organization. A proprietorship is composed of one owner, who usually supervises the business operation. Local restaurants, dry cleaning businesses, and auto repair shops are often sole proprietorships. A sole proprietorship is easy to establish and manage, having much less paperwork associated with it than other forms of business organization. But the sole proprietorship has disadvantages. Single owners are often limited in their ability to raise capital. In many instances, all management responsibilities fall on this single individual. And most important, the personal assets of the owner are subject to unlimited liability. If you own a pizza shop as a sole proprietor and someone slips on the floor, he or she can sue you and you could lose your house and your life savings if you do not have sufficient insurance coverage.

partnership Similar to a sole proprietorship, but involves more than one owner who share the management of the business. Partnerships are also subject to unlimited liability.

Partnerships **Partnerships** are similar to sole proprietorships except that they have more than one owner. Establishing a partnership usually requires signing a legal partnership document. Partnerships find it easier to raise capital and spread around the management responsibilities. Like sole proprietors, however, partners are subject to unlimited liability, not only for their share of the business, but for the entire business. If your partner takes off for Bermuda, you are left to pay all the bills, even those your partner incurred. The death of one partner dissolves a partnership, unless other arrangements have been made ahead of time. In any case, the death of a partner often creates problems for the continuity of the business.

corporation A business structure that has most of the legal rights of individuals, and in addition, can issue stock to raise capital. Stockholders' liability is limited to the value of their stock.

Corporations The **corporation** is the premier form of business organization in most of the world. In 2012, roughly 5 million American corporations sold over $27 trillion worth of goods and services worldwide. This is an amazing statistic when you consider that the country's 23 million sole proprietorships had sales totaling just over $1.3 trillion. Clearly, corporations are structured in a way that enhances growth and efficiency.

---

[1] Andrew Lawrence et al., "The Innovative Brain," *Nature*, November 13, 2008, pp. 168–169.

[2] *Global Entrepreneurship Monitor*, "2011 Extended Report: Entrepreneurs and Entrepreneurial Employees Across the Globe," 2012.

Corporations have most of the legal rights of individuals; in addition, they are able to issue stock to raise capital, and most significant, the liability of individual owners (i.e., stockholders) is limited to the amount they have invested in (or paid for) the stock. This is what distinguishes corporations from the other forms of business organization: the ability to raise large amounts of capital because of limited liability.

Some scholars argue that corporations are the greatest engines of economic prosperity ever known.[3] Daniel Akst writes:

> When I worked for a big company, there was a miracle in the office every couple of weeks, just like clockwork. It happened every payday, when sizable checks were distributed to a small army of employees who also enjoyed health and retirement benefits. Few of us could have made as much on our own, and somehow there was always money left over for the shareholders as well.[4]

Without the corporate umbrella, most of the jobs we hold would not exist; most of the products we use would not have been invented; and our standard of living would be a fraction of what it is today.

dpa/Landov

Steve Wozniak (right) and Steve Jobs began their computer business in the Jobs family garage as a partnership before turning it into a public company, Apple, in 1980. Today, Apple is one of the largest companies in the world by market value.

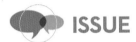

What is it that motivates business owners of all types to take on the risks of creating a product? Profits.

ISSUE

The Vast World of Corporate Offshoring and Profits

Most Americans are aware of the fact that corporations, particularly in manufacturing industries, often relocate factories to developing countries to take advantage of lower costs for labor and raw materials (in a process called offshoring) and to gain access to emerging markets for their products. Yet, another incentive exists for why companies choose to place important offices, even headquarters, abroad, and that is to avoid U.S. regulations and taxes.

One common example of corporate offshoring occurs in the cruise ship industry. Despite many cruise ships starting and ending trips at U.S. ports, virtually all large cruise vessels are registered outside of the United States, allowing cruise lines to circumvent, for example, U.S. labor laws (ever wonder how a room steward is able to legally work seven days a week, day and night, at less than minimum wage?).

The more egregious examples of offshoring occur when companies relocate headquarters to certain countries to take advantage of lower tax rates. And by relocating, this often does not mean moving to a shiny new skyscraper in a major European or Asian capital. On the contrary, it sometimes involves merely having a mailbox in an obscure town or island serving as the headquarters for a multimillion dollar enterprise.

Recent media attention exposing the abuse of corporate offshoring has led to new reforms being proposed in the United States and the European Union. Various proposed legislation, such as the 2011 Stop Tax Haven Abuse Act, aimed at curbing the use of corporate offshoring when the sole purpose is to avoid taxes (as opposed to traditional offshoring to take advantage of less expensive inputs of production). But like all new policies, tradeoffs exist, as companies affected by the new legislation claim such rules would reduce competition and raise consumer prices. The costs and benefits of any new policy are likely to be debated extensively before becoming law.

Prisma/SuperStock

At its height in 2011, Zug, Switzerland, was home to 30,000 corporate headquarters from around the world. Impressive for a quiet lakeside town with just 26,000 residents.

[3] John Micklethwait and Adrian Wooldridge, *The Company: A Short History of a Revolutionary Idea* (New York: The Modern Library), 2003.

[4] Daniel Akst, "Where Those Paychecks Come From," *Wall Street Journal*, February 3, 2004.

Profits

Entrepreneurs and firms employ resources and turn out products with the goal of making profits. This is not to say that firms put profit above all else (i.e., that they would do something immoral or socially irresponsible to increase profits), but instead that firms do not intentionally make decisions that would knowingly result in lower profit. **Profit** is the difference between total revenue and total cost.

profit Equal to the difference between total revenue and total cost.

total revenue Equal to price per unit times quantity sold.

total cost The sum of all costs to run a business. To an economist, this includes out-of-pocket expenses and opportunity costs.

Total revenue is the amount of money a firm receives from the sales of its products. It is equal to the price per unit times the number of units sold ($TR = p \times q$). Note that we use lower case p and q when we are dealing with an individual firm and use upper case when describing a market. **Total cost** includes both out-of-pocket expenses and opportunity costs; we will discuss this concept shortly.

Economists explicitly assume that firms proceed rationally and have the maximization of profits as their primary objective. Alternative behavioral assumptions for firms have been tested, including sales maximization, various goals for market share, and customer satisfaction. Although these more complex assumptions for firm behavior often predict different outcomes, economists have not been persuaded that any of them yield results superior to those of the profit maximization approach. Profit maximization has stood the test of time, and thus we will assume it is the primary economic goal of firms.

Economic Costs

When economists say "profit," they mean profits properly understood. Economists approach business costs and profits from the opportunity cost perspective discussed in Chapter 2. They separate costs into explicit costs, or out-of-pocket expenses, and implicit costs, or opportunity costs. **Economic costs** are the sum of explicit and implicit costs.

economic costs The sum of explicit (out-of-pocket) and implicit (opportunity) costs.

explicit costs Those expenses paid directly to another economic entity, including wages, lease payments, taxes, and utilities.

implicit costs The opportunity costs of using resources that belong to the firm, including depreciation, depletion of business assets, and the opportunity cost of the firm's capital employed in the business.

Explicit costs are those expenses paid directly to some other economic entity. These costs include wages, lease payments, expenditures for raw materials, taxes, utilities, and so on. A company can easily determine its explicit costs by summing all of the checks it has written during the normal course of doing business.

Implicit costs refer to all of the opportunity costs of using resources that belong to the firm. Recall that opportunity cost measures the value of the next best alternative use of resources, including that of time and capital. Implicit costs include depreciation, the depletion of business assets, and the opportunity cost of a firm's capital.

In any business, some assets are depleted over time. Machines, cars, and office equipment depreciate with use and time. Finite oil or mineral deposits are depleted as they are mined or pumped. Even though firms do not actually pay any cash as these assets are worn down or used up, these costs nonetheless represent real expenses to the firm.

Another major component of implicit costs is the capital firms have invested. Even small firms incur large implicit costs from their capital investment. Small entrepreneurs, for example, must invest both their own capital and labor into their businesses. Such people could normally be working for someone else, so their "lost salary" must be treated as an implicit cost when determining the true profitability of their businesses. Similarly, any capital invested in a business enterprise could just as well be earning interest in a bank account or returning dividends and capital gains through the purchase and sale of stock in other enterprises. Though not directly paid out as expenses, these forgone earnings nonetheless represent implicit costs for the firm.

Sunk Costs

sunk costs Those costs that have been incurred and cannot be recovered, including, for example, funds spent on existing technology that has become obsolete and past advertising that has run in the media.

The previous chapter introduced the concept of **sunk costs,** which are costs that have already been incurred and *cannot* be recovered. For example, should you leave in the middle of a movie because it stinks? The cost of admission has been paid, and staying until the end might add to the anguish of an already bad situation. Similarly, tuition is a sunk cost. Most colleges and universities do not provide refunds for dropped courses beyond the first week or two of the term. Because sunk costs are not recoverable, future decisions, such as whether to drop a course one is failing, should not depend on them. To a business, the decision to advertise a product in a new magazine depends on the benefits and costs of that advertising, not on how much has been spent on television ads in the past. You will hear the phrase that "sunk costs are sunk," meaning ignore them, they are gone.

Economic and Normal Profits

The primary goal of any firm is to earn a profit. However, how the Internal Revenue Service (IRS) measures profit for tax purposes is different from how an economist determines profit. Suppose that after graduating, you decide to open a new billiards hall on campus. After a year, counting all the revenues and subtracting all explicit costs (costs that you actually pay out), you end up with a profit of $20,000. Is your business a success? The IRS certainly thinks so, as it will collect taxes on these profits. And you might brag to friends that you turned a profit in your first year. But then you start thinking of all the time you spent on the business and the missed opportunities, such as the $40,000 a year job offer you turned down, and the money you could have earned had you invested your savings in stocks or bonds rather than in your business. Now, your business doesn't feel successful.

Economists include both explicit and implicit costs in their analysis of business profits. An **accounting profit** is calculated by including only explicit costs, while an **economic profit** is calculated using both explicit and implicit costs. Therefore, when a firm is earning economic profits, it is generating profits in excess of zero once implicit costs are factored in. This brings us to an important benchmark called **normal profits,** which occurs when economic profit equals zero. Economists refer to this level of profit as a *normal rate of return* on capital, a return just sufficient to keep investors satisfied and to keep capital in the business over the long run. If a firm's rate of return on capital falls below this rate, investors will put their capital to use elsewhere.

accounting profit The difference between total revenue and explicit costs. These are the profits that are taxed by the government.

economic profit Profit in excess of normal profits. These are profits in excess of both explicit and implicit costs.

normal profits The return on capital necessary to keep investors satisfied and keep capital in the business over the long run.

Although earning zero economic profit might sound dismal, this simply means that the firm is earning the same profit it would have earned had it chosen its next best alternative use of its capital, which can be quite substantial in terms of accounting profit. For example, if Mark Zuckerberg left Facebook and opened a new business, his new business (assuming he uses the same amount of capital and labor) would have to earn billions of dollars a year just to achieve normal profits. Not bad for *zero* economic profit. In other words, any profit less than what would be earned at Facebook under his leadership would be considered an *economic loss.* A firm earning normal profits means that it is earning just enough to cover the opportunity cost of its capital. Therefore, a firm may be earning *accounting profits* as defined by the IRS for tax purposes, yet still be suffering economic losses, because taxable income does not reflect all implicit costs.

Let's look at the difference between accounting profits and economic profits further in Table 1 on the next page, using our example of the billiards hall. Suppose your annual total revenue is $120,000. After subtracting out-of-pocket (explicit) costs of $100,000, you end up with an accounting profit of $20,000. However, if you could have earned $40,000 working elsewhere and $10,000 more by putting your savings into a stock or bond investment rather than into your business, you would incur a $30,000 economic loss.

Economists designate normal profits as economic profits equal to zero. To achieve normal profits, you would need to be just as well off operating the billiard hall as you would if you instead took another job and invested your savings elsewhere, which means earning $50,000 in accounting profits. Because you earned only $20,000 (or $30,000 less than the alternative), this results in an economic loss of $30,000. Normal profits are the profits necessary to keep a firm in business over the long run. This brings us to an important economic distinction, between the short run and the long run.

Short Run Versus Long Run

Although the short and the long run generally differ in their temporal spans, they are *not* defined in terms of time. Rather, economists define these periods by the ability of firms to adjust the quantities of various resources that they are employing.

As discussed in a previous chapter, the **short run** is a period of time over which at least one factor of production is fixed, or cannot be changed. For the sake of simplicity, economists typically assume that plant capacity is fixed in the short run. Output from a fixed plant can still vary depending on how much labor the firm employs. Firms can, for instance, hire more people, have existing employees work overtime, or run additional shifts. For discussion purposes, we focus here on labor as the variable factor, but changes in the raw materials used can also result in output changes.

short run A period of time over which at least one factor of production (resource) is fixed, or cannot be changed.

The **long run,** conversely, is a period of time sufficient for a firm to adjust all factors of production, including plant capacity. Since all factors can be altered in the long run,

long run A period of time sufficient for firms to adjust all factors of production, including plant capacity.

TABLE 1 Comparing Accounting Versus Economic Profits from Operating a Business

Fancy Collection/SuperStock

Item	Accountant	Economist
Annual revenue	$120,000	$120,000
***less* explicit costs**		
Wages	–$50,000	–$50,000
Lease payments	–$20,000	–$20,000
Cost of goods sold	–$15,000	–$15,000
Utilities	–$5,000	–$5,000
Insurance	–$5,000	–$5,000
Office supplies	–$5,000	–$5,000
Accounting Profit	**+$20,000**	
***less* implicit costs**		
Forgone earnings from job offer	—	–$40,000
Forgone earnings from money invested	—	–$10,000
Economic Profit		**–$30,000**

existing firms can even close and leave the industry, and new firms can build new plants and enter the market.

In the short run, therefore, with plant capacity and the number of firms in an industry being fixed, output varies only as a result of changes in employment. In the long run, as plant capacity and other factors are made variable, the industry may grow or shrink as firms enter or leave the business, or some firms alter their plant capacity.

Because all industries are unique, the time required for long-run adjustment varies by industry. Family-owned restaurants, lawn-mowing services, and roofing firms can come and go fairly rapidly. High-capital industries on the other hand, such as the chemical, petroleum, and semiconductor industries, face obstacles to change that require a long time to overcome, whether these be strenuous environmental regulation, immense research and development requirements, or huge capital costs for plant construction. Adding plant capacity in one of these industries can take a decade or more and cost billions of dollars.

The important point to note from this section is that firms seek economic profits and determine profits by first calculating their costs. These costs may differ over the short run versus the long run. Therefore, we look first at production basics, then consider costs in both the short run and the long run.

CHECKPOINT

FIRMS, PROFITS, AND ECONOMIC COSTS

- Firms are economic institutions that convert inputs (factors of production) into products and services.
- Entrepreneurs provide goods and services to markets. Entrepreneurs can be organized into three basic business structures: sole proprietorships, partnerships, and corporations.
- Corporations are the premier form of business organization because they give owners (shareholders) limited liability, unlike sole proprietorships and partnerships.
- Profit is the difference between total revenues and total costs.

- Explicit costs are those expenses, such as rent and the cost of raw materials, paid directly to some other economic entity. Implicit costs represent the opportunity costs of doing business, including depreciation and the firm's capital costs.
- Normal profits (or normal rates of return) are equal to zero economic profit. The firm is earning just enough to keep capital in the firm over the long run. Economic profits are those in *excess* of normal profits.
- The short run is a period of time during which one factor of production (usually plant capacity) is fixed. In the long run all factors can vary and the firm can enter or exit the industry.

QUESTION: Assume for a moment that you want to go into business for yourself and that you have a good idea. What are the pros and cons of setting up your company as a corporation as opposed to keeping it as a sole proprietorship?

Answers to the Checkpoint question can be found at the end of this chapter.

Production in the Short Run

Production is the process of turning inputs into outputs. Most products can be made using a variety of different technologies. As discussed earlier, these can be either capital-intensive or labor-intensive. The type of technology a firm chooses will depend on many things, including ease of implementation and the relative cost of each input into the process.

production The process of turning inputs into outputs.

Again, in the simplified model we are working with, firms can vary their output in the short run only by altering the amount of labor they employ, because plant capacity is fixed in the short run. The extent to which output will change from adding labor depends on the ability to specialize in tasks and use other resources efficiently. But like all resources, labor is eventually subject to diminishing returns. Therefore, an individual firm's production possibilities will follow the same general pattern as the production function for the entire economy introduced in Chapter 2. In the short run, output for an existing plant will vary by the amount of labor employed. This output is referred to as *total product.*

Total Product

Let's examine some production basics by assuming that you start your own firm. Imagine that you decide to begin manufacturing windsurfing sails in an old warehouse that you rent. Your physical plant is constrained in the short run by the size of the manufacturing facility. Table 2 lists your firm's total output (total product) as you hire more workers.

Panel A of Figure 1 on the next page displays your total product curve for windsurfing equipment, based on the data in columns (1) and (2) of Table 2. Output of sails varies with

TABLE 2 Production Data for Windsurfing Sail Firm

(1) L (labor)	(2) *Q* (total product)	(3) MP (marginal product)	(4) AP (average product)
0	0		—
		3	
1	3		3.00
		5	
2	8		4.00
		8	
3	16		5.33
		6	
4	22		5.50
		4	
5	26		5.20
		2	
6	28		4.67
		−2	
7	26		3.71
		−3	
8	23		2.88

FIGURE 1

Total Product Curve, Marginal Product, and Average Product

These two panels show the relationship between additional labor and productivity. Panel A shows how increasing labor increases productivity, up to a point. Panel B shows marginal and average product. Marginal product reaches its maximum as the third worker is hired, after which marginal product starts decreasing. Total product keeps increasing, however, until you hit 6 employees. At that point, marginal product becomes negative, meaning that each additional employee actually reduces production.

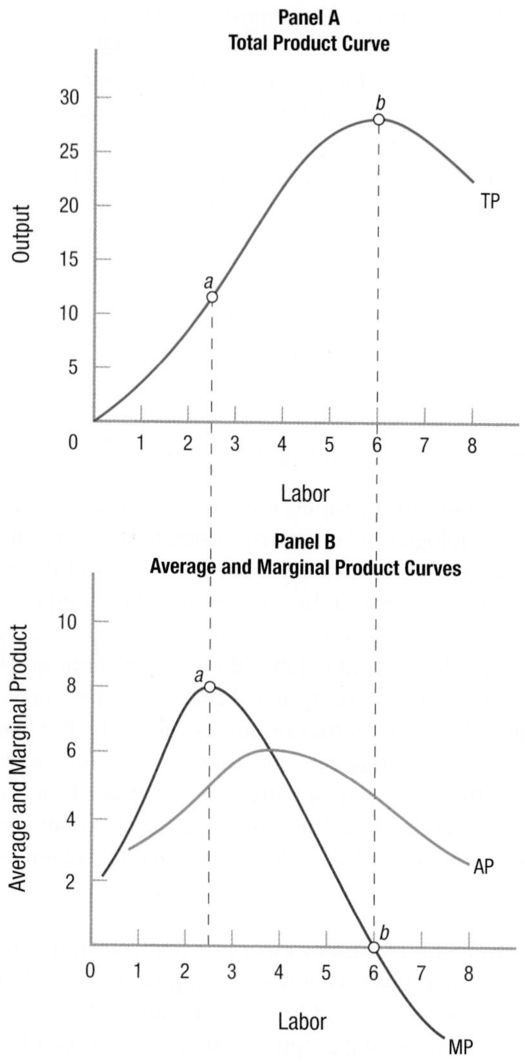

the number of people you employ. Output rises from 0 to 16 when 3 people are working to a maximum of 28 when 6 people are employed (point *b*). As you continue to hire employees beyond 6, you encounter *negative returns.* Total output actually begins to fall, possibly because the workplace has become overly crowded, confusing, hazardous, or noisy. Clearly, hiring any more than 6 employees would be counterproductive, because output falls but costs (such as the total wages of all the employees) rise.

Marginal and Average Product

marginal product The change in output that results from a change in labor ($\Delta Q/\Delta L$).

Marginal product [column (3) in Table 2] is the change in output that results from a change in labor input. Marginal product is computed by dividing the change in output (ΔQ) by the change in labor (ΔL). The delta (Δ) symbol is used to denote "change in." Thus, marginal product (MP) is equal to $\Delta Q/\Delta L$; it is the change in output that results from adding additional workers.

Notice that when employment rises from 2 workers to 3 workers, output grows from 8 to 16 sails. Marginal product is therefore 8 sails at this point (point *a* in panel B of Figure 1). This is shown graphically with a point placed between the second and third worker, because this represents the change in output going from 2 workers to 3 workers. Contrast this with a change in employment when 6 people are already employed. Adding another employee actually reduces the total output of windsurfing sails from 28 to 26, therefore marginal product is –2 from the sixth to the seventh worker.

Average product (AP) or output per worker is found by dividing total output by the number of workers employed to produce that output (Q/L). Average product is shown in panel B of Figure 1. When employment is 3 people and output is 16, for instance, average product is 5.33.

average product Output per worker, found by dividing total output by the number of workers employed to produce that output (*Q*/L).

Increasing and Diminishing Returns

In our example, each of the first three workers adds more to output than the previous worker hired. Therefore, the marginal product going from zero to one worker, one to two workers, and two to three workers increases. This is called the **increasing marginal returns** portion of the curve. In this range, output grows faster as you employ additional labor.

increasing marginal returns A new worker hired adds more to total output than the previous worker hired, so that both average and marginal products are rising.

diminishing marginal returns An additional worker adds to total output, but at a diminishing rate.

However, after you have employed three people, *marginal productivity* begins to trail off. Between three and six workers, you face **diminishing marginal returns** because each additional worker adds to total output, but at a diminishing rate.

Finally, once you have hired six employees, if you hire any more, this will result in negative marginal returns. Therefore, the marginal product curve crosses the horizontal axis at the sixth worker, which corresponds to the highest point on the total product curve (point *b* in Figure 1). Hiring additional people will actually reduce output, therefore rational firms never operate in this range.

Meanwhile, the average product curve follows a similar path as the marginal product curve, although there isn't as dramatic a change as each worker is added. Average product gives you a sense of the overall productivity of a firm. The relationship between marginal product and average product is an important one. When marginal product exceeds average product—when a new worker adds more to output than the average of the previous workers—hiring an additional worker increases average productivity. This might be because hiring more people allows you to establish more of a production line, thereby increasing specialization and raising productivity. The marginal product curve always crosses the average product curve at its highest point, because once marginal product falls below the average product, the average product must fall as well.

Firms hire workers to produce output based on available resources, many of which are fixed in the short run. By adding more workers, firms can increase productivity by allowing workers to specialize in tasks for which they are more suited. As more workers are hired, diminishing or even negative returns can set in. The typical production curves shown in Figure 1 embody the *law of diminishing returns.* All firms eventually face diminishing marginal returns, but this does not mean production should be avoided as long as the value of the additional output produced exceeds the additional costs.

This analysis is important because it shows how much output is generated based on the number of workers hired, which will eventually translate into revenues for the firm once the output is sold. Therefore, production is an important component of profits, but not enough to determine the optimal production output. To maximize profits, we must also evaluate the costs of production, to which we turn next.

CHECKPOINT

PRODUCTION IN THE SHORT RUN

- Production is the process of turning inputs into outputs.
- Total product is the total output produced by the production process.
- Marginal product (MP) is the change in output that results from a change in labor input and is equal to $\Delta Q/\Delta L$.
- Average product (AP) is output per worker and is equal to Q/L.
- Increasing marginal returns occur when adding a worker adds *more* to output than the previous worker hired.

- Diminishing marginal returns occur when adding a worker adds *less* to output than the previous worker hired.
- Negative marginal returns occur when adding a worker actually leads to less *total* output than with the previous worker hired.
- In most production processes, firms experience both increasing and then diminishing marginal returns to labor as workers are added.

QUESTION: Suppose a company has a policy to hire workers only when each additional worker hired is more productive than the previous worker hired. Using what you know about labor productivity, would this be a good policy?

Answers to the Checkpoint question can be found at the end of this chapter.

Costs of Production

Production tells only part of the story. We have to calculate how much it costs to produce this output in order to figure out if it is profitable to do so. Let's now bring resource prices, including labor costs, into our analysis to develop the typical cost curves for the firm, both in the short run and the long run.

Short-Run Costs

In a very straightforward way, production costs are determined by the productivity of workers. Ignoring all costs except wages, if you, by yourself, were to produce ten pizzas an hour and you were paid $8 an hour, then each pizza would cost an average of 80 cents to produce—the cost of your labor. Yet, to ignore any other costs would be to neglect a significant portion of business expenses known as *overhead.*

To begin developing the concept of overhead specifically, and production costs more generally, remember that production periods are split into the short run and the long run. In the short run, at least one factor is fixed, whereas in the long run, all factors are variable. This has led economists to define costs as fixed and variable.

fixed costs Costs that do not change as a firm's output expands or contracts, often called overhead. These include items such as lease payments, administrative expenses, property taxes, and insurance premiums.

variable costs Costs that vary with output fluctuations, including expenses such as labor and material costs.

Fixed and Variable Costs **Fixed costs,** or overhead, are those costs that do not change as a firm's output expands or contracts. Lease or rental payments, administrative overhead, and insurance premiums are examples of fixed costs—they do not rise or fall as a firm alters production to meet market demands. **Variable costs,** on the other hand, do fluctuate as output changes. Labor and material costs are examples of variable costs, because making more products requires hiring more workers and purchasing more raw materials.

Certain costs don't always fall so neatly into these two categories. For example, a new wireless communications tower can serve thousands of customers at the same cost as serving one (and resembles a fixed cost), but once capacity is reached, a new tower is needed (and resembles a variable cost). These types of costs are known as *incremental costs.* To

Ruth Peterkin/Dreamstime.com

Blaine Harrington/age fotostock

A cruise ship can cost hundreds of millions of dollars, a fixed cost that is spent regardless of how many passengers cruise. Food for meals, however, is a variable cost because it varies based on how many passengers are on board.

keep things simple, however, we will assume that all costs fit into either the fixed or variable cost categories, such that total cost (TC) is equal to total fixed cost (FC) plus total variable cost (VC), or

$$TC = FC + VC$$

Marginal Cost Although measuring total cost is important in determining the overall profitability of a business, the decision of whether to increase or decrease production largely depends on how total costs change when one increases or decreases the quantity produced. If the additional cost of producing one more unit of a good is greater than the additional revenue earned from that unit, then this unit would not be worth producing. Therefore, it is important to measure the change in costs with each additional unit of output produced.

Let's return to the windsurfing sail business example. Suppose your firm has orders for ten windsurfing sails this month, and you get an order for one more sail at the last minute. Just how much would this additional windsurfing sail cost to produce? Or, in the language of economics, what is the *marginal cost* of the next sail produced?

Marginal cost is the change in total cost arising from the production of additional units of output. Marginal cost (MC) is equal to the change in total cost (ΔTC) divided by the change in output (ΔQ), or

marginal cost The change in total costs arising from the production of additional units of output (ΔTC/ΔQ). Because fixed costs do not change with output, marginal costs are the change in variable costs associated with additional production (ΔVC/ΔQ).

$$MC = \Delta TC/\Delta Q = \Delta FC/\Delta Q + \Delta VC/\Delta Q$$

Note that, for simplicity, we have been discussing changes of one unit of output, but we can calculate MC for a change in output of any amount by plugging in the appropriate value for ΔQ. And because fixed costs do not vary with changes in output, $\Delta FC/\Delta Q = 0$, and thus marginal cost is also equal to just ΔVC/ΔQ.

Table 3 provides us with more complete cost data for your windsurfing sail business. Assuming that you pay $1,000 per month in rent for the warehouse, fixed costs equal $1,000 [column (2)]. Your variable costs (the wages you pay your employees plus the price of raw materials) vary depending on the number of sails produced, and is shown in column (3). The total cost, therefore, is the sum of fixed and variable cost and is shown in column (4). Marginal cost measures the change in total (or variable) cost with each additional sail produced, and is given in column (5).

Let's go through one row so that you can be sure of how we arrived at the numbers in columns (2) to (5). Looking at the row showing 4 sails, the fixed cost is $1,000 because this does not change based on the number of sails produced. Variable cost does change, because more work hours are needed to produce more sails; to produce 4 sails,

Cost Data for Windsurfing Sail Firm **TABLE 3**

(1) Q	(2) FC	(3) VC	(4) TC	(5) MC	(6) AFC	(7) AVC	(8) ATC
0	$1,000	$0	$1,000		—	—	—
				$500			
1	$1,000	$500	$1,500		$1,000.00	$500.00	$1,500.00
				$300			
2	$1,000	$800	$1,800		$500.00	$400.00	$900.00
				$200			
3	$1,000	$1,000	$2,000		$333.33	$333.33	$666.67
				$400			
4	$1,000	$1,400	$2,400		$250.00	$350.00	$600.00
				$500			
5	$1,000	$1,900	$2,900		$200.00	$380.00	$580.00
				$700			
6	$1,000	$2,600	$3,600		$166.67	$433.33	$600.00
				$1,000			
7	$1,000	$3,600	$4,600		$142.86	$514.29	$657.14

Senai Aksoy/Dreamstime.com

the variable cost is $1,400. Total cost is simply fixed cost plus variable cost, or $2,400 for 4 sails. Finally, the marginal cost of the fourth sail is the change in total cost from producing 3 sails ($2,000) to producing 4 sails ($2,400). Therefore, the marginal cost of the fourth sail is the change from $2,000 to $2,400, or $400, and is shown in column (5) between the third and fourth units. It is common for marginal costs to first fall and then rise, which gives the marginal cost curve the distinct shape, which we will see later.

Average Costs When a firm produces a product or service, it typically wants a breakdown of how much labor, raw material, plant overhead, and sales costs are imbedded in each unit of the product. Modern accounting systems permit a detailed breakdown of costs for each unit of production. For our purposes, however, that level of detail is not necessary. For us, cost per unit of output (or *average cost*), average fixed cost, and average variable cost are sufficient.

If we divide the total cost equation (TC) by total output Q, we get

$$TC/Q = FC/Q + VC/Q$$

Economists refer to total fixed costs divided by output (FC/Q) as **average fixed cost** (AFC). This represents the average amount of overhead for each unit of output. Total variable costs divided by output is known as **average variable cost** (AVC). It represents the labor and raw materials expenses that go into each unit of output. Adding AFC and AVC together results in **average total cost** (ATC), and thus the equation above can be rewritten as

average fixed cost Equal to total fixed cost divided by output (FC/Q).

average variable cost Equal to total variable cost divided by output (VC/Q).

average total cost Equal to total cost divided by output (TC/Q). Average total cost is also equal to AFC + AVC.

$$ATC = AFC + AVC$$

Hence, average cost per unit (ATC) is the sum of average fixed cost (AFC) and average variable cost (AVC).

Average total cost is an important piece of information for firms. Specifically, it provides a general measurement of productivity—how cost-efficient a firm is in producing a specified number of units. Further, it provides the firm guidance as to whether it is earning a profit or whether it should shut down the business and leave the industry altogether.

Returning to Table 3, columns (6), (7), and (8) provide the average fixed cost, average variable cost, and average total cost, respectively, for each quantity of windsurfing sails produced. Let's calculate the average costs of producing 4 sails. The average fixed cost is calculated by taking the fixed cost of $1,000 and dividing it by 4 to equal $250. Average variable cost takes the variable cost of $1,400 and divides by 4 to equal $350 in AVC. We can calculate average total cost in two ways. First, we can take total cost of $2,400 and divide by 4 sails to equal $600 in ATC. Second, we know that ATC = AFC + AVC, so if we know that AFC is $250 and AVC is $350, then $250 + $350 = $600.

Notice a few trends in the average cost data. First, the average fixed cost falls continuously as more output is produced; this is because your overhead expenses are getting spread out over more and more units of output (this is known as the *spreading effect*). Figure 2 shows the average fixed cost curve using the data from Table 3. If 2 sails are produced, the average fixed cost is $1,000 / 2 = $500 (point *a* on the AFC curve); if 4 sails are produced, the average fixed cost is $1,000 / 4 = $250 (point *b* on the AFC curve). Average fixed costs are important to entrepreneurs, who often seek out new businesses with low fixed costs, allowing them to recover these expenses quickly.

Second, average variable costs and average total costs typically fall initially before rising, just like marginal costs. In the short run, these costs initially fall as the costs of procuring variable inputs fall and due to the *spreading effect* (which affects the average total cost curve), but these costs eventually rise with greater output as access to available resources dries up, leading to diminishing returns (resulting in a *diminishing returns effect*). Finally, average variable cost will always be smaller than the average total cost according to the ATC = AFC + AVC equation. These trends will be important as we make greater use of average cost in the next three chapters.

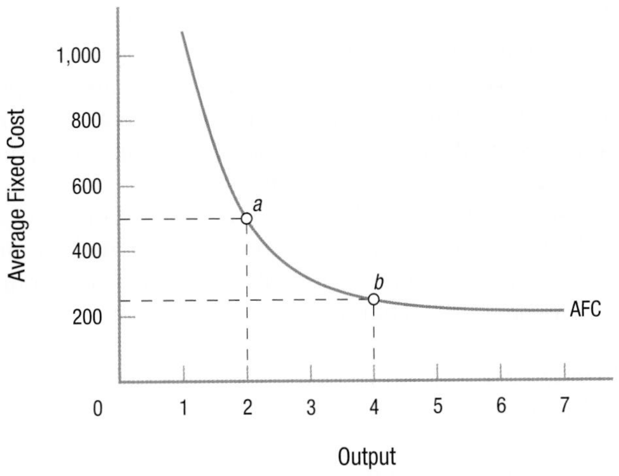

FIGURE 2

The Average Fixed Cost Curve

The average fixed cost (AFC) curve always decreases as production increases. This is because, in the short run, total fixed costs do not change, so that increasing production spreads the fixed costs over more units of output (the *spreading effect*).

Short-Run Cost Curves for Profit-Maximizing Decisions

Table 3 provides the numerical values for costs. Although all of the costs are important in their own way, we focus on three costs that will provide guidance to firms in their need to maximize profits. These are average variable cost, average total cost, and marginal cost. Let us now translate these costs into figures to make their analysis simpler. Figure 3 shows the three cost measures in graphical form, drawn using the data from Table 3.

Average Variable Cost (AVC) The AVC and ATC curves are U-shaped. At relatively low levels of output, the curves slope downward, reflecting an increase in returns as average costs drop. As production levels rise, however, diminishing returns set in, and average costs start to climb back up. We get some sense of this by examining Table 3, in which the numbers for AVC and ATC fall and then rise, but the figure makes it far easier to see.

In Figure 3, the average variable cost curve reaches its minimum where 3 sails are produced (point *c*). Since AVC = VC/Q, then VC = AVC × Q. Thus, at point *c*, VC is equal to the rectangular area 0*ace*, or $1,000 ($333.33 × 3).

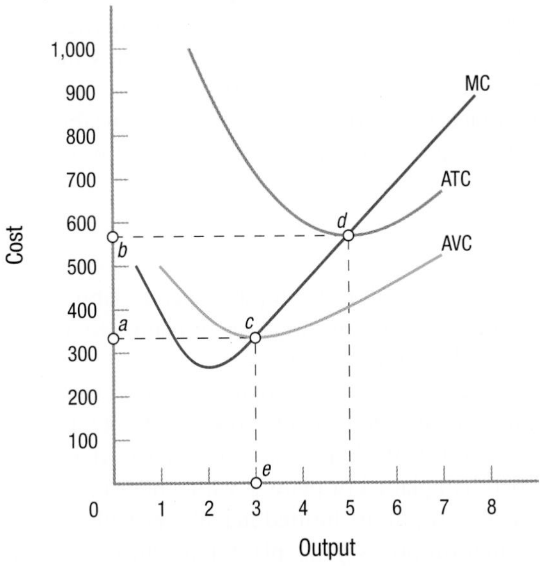

FIGURE 3

Average Total Cost, Average Variable Cost, and Marginal Cost

The average variable cost (AVC), average total cost (ATC), and marginal cost (MC) curves are shown. The bowl shape of the AVC and ATC curves demonstrates the law of diminishing returns: Beyond a certain level of output, average costs increase. Marginal costs represent the added cost of producing one more unit of output. Note that the marginal cost curve passes through the minimum points on both the AVC and ATC curves.

Average Total Cost (ATC) Average total cost equals total costs divided by output (ATC = TC / *Q*), or average fixed costs plus average variable cost (ATC = AFC + AVC). In Figure 3, the average total cost reaches its minimum where 5 sails are produced (point *d*). At this point, the average total cost is $580. As in the previous example, we can calculate the total cost of the firm at any point along the average total cost curve by multiplying the average total cost by the output produced. For example, the total cost of 5 sails would be $580 × 5 = $2,900, exactly as shown in Table 3.

Therefore, the use of cost curves allows us to determine both the total and average costs for a firm, which again is an important component in determining profits. Still, we cannot proceed until we examine marginal costs, a key determinant in whether firms should produce more or less output.

Marginal Cost (MC) Drawing our discussion of short-run costs to a close, Figure 3 plots the marginal cost curve, adding it to the AVC and ATC curves we have plotted already.

Notice that the marginal cost curve intersects the minimum points of both the AVC and ATC curves. This is not a coincidence. Marginal cost is the cost necessary to produce another unit of a given product. When the cost to produce another unit is *less* than the average of the previous units produced, average costs will *fall.* For the AVC curve in Figure 3, this happens at all output levels less than 3 units (*point c*); for the ATC curve, it happens at all output levels less than 5 units (*point d*). But when the cost to produce another unit *exceeds* the average cost for all previous output, average costs will *rise.*

In Figure 3, this happens at output levels greater than 3 units (point *c*) for AVC and greater than 5 units (point *d*) for ATC. Over these ranges, marginal cost exceeds AVC and ATC, respectively, and thus the two curves rise. At points *c* and *d*, marginal cost is precisely equal to average variable cost and average total cost, respectively, and thus the AVC and ATC curves are at their minimum values (where the slopes are zero).

The average variable cost, average total cost, and marginal cost curves will help us analyze the profit-maximizing equilibrium for each market structure in the next three chapters. We will see how marginal cost provides guidance to firms on the quantity of output to produce, and how average variable cost and average total cost inform firms whether to maintain or expand operations, shut down, or leave the industry.

We have now examined short-run costs for firms when one factor, in this case plant size, is fixed. When this occurs, firms face decisions about whether to operate or shut down given that the fixed costs are paid up front. As we analyze different types of markets in the next three chapters, we will examine how firms make short-run decisions when fixed and variable costs are taken into consideration. Let us now turn to costs in the long run, when all factors, including plant size, are variable. This means that fixed costs do not exist in the long run, because given enough time, a firm can expand or close its plant, and enter or leave an industry.

Long-Run Costs

In the long run, firms can adjust all factor inputs (such as labor and capital) to meet the needs of the market. Here we focus on variations in plant size, while recognizing that all other factors, including technology, can vary.

Figure 4 shows the short-run average total costs curves using three different production functions for three different plant sizes. Plant 1 (ATC_1) has fewer machines than either plant 2 or plant 3. With a smaller fixed cost, plant 1 can produce smaller quantities at lower cost than plant 2 or plant 3, which have higher fixed costs. However, if plant 1 tries to increase output, its limited machinery will cause average costs to rise very quickly. For a small output, say Q_0, plant 1 produces at an average cost of AC_0 (point *b*). Plant 2, with its additional overhead, can produce Q_0 output, but only for a

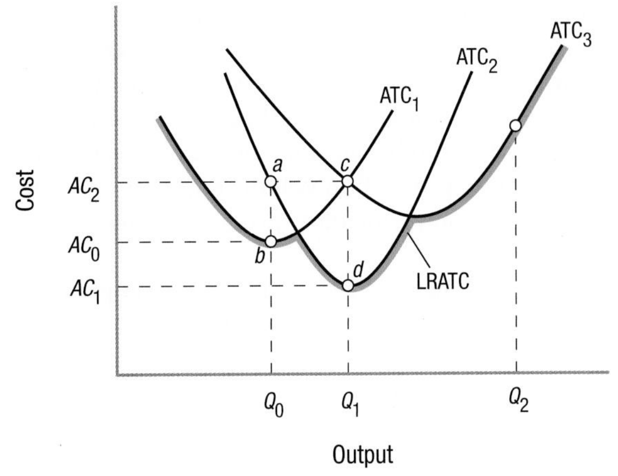

FIGURE 4

Various Short-Run Average Cost Curves and the Long-Run Average Total Cost Curve

This figure shows the average total cost curve for three plants of different sizes. The larger plants have relatively high average total costs at lower levels of output, but much lower average total costs at higher output levels. Firms are free to adjust plant size in the long run, therefore they can switch from one plant type to the next to minimize their costs at each production level. The green envelope curve represents the firm's lowest cost to produce any given output in the long run and represents the LRATC curve.

higher average cost of AC_2 (point *a*). And plant 3's average cost of producing Q_0 would be even higher.

Therefore, at lower levels of production, plant 1 is able to achieve the lowest average cost. However, plant 2 and plant 3 achieve greater cost savings at higher levels of production. Once output rises to Q_1, plant 2 begins to enjoy the benefits of a lower average cost of production. The additional machines mean that plant 2 can produce Q_1 for AC_1 (point *d*), whereas the machines in plant 1 become overwhelmed at this level of output, resulting in an average cost of AC_2 (point *c*). Similarly, if a firm expects market demand eventually to reach Q_2, it would want to build plant 3 because plant 1 and plant 2 are too small to accommodate that level of production efficiently.

Long-Run Average Total Cost The **long-run average total cost** (LRATC) curve represents the lowest unit cost at which any specific output can be produced in the long run, when a firm is able to adjust the size of its plant. In Figure 4, the LRATC curve is indicated by the green segments of the various short-run cost curves; these are the segments of each curve at which output can be produced at the lowest per unit cost (also known as the *envelope* curve, named after its telltale shape). In short, the LRATC assumes that, in the long run, firms will build plants of the size best fitting the levels of output they wish to produce.

long-run average total cost In the long run, firms can adjust their plant sizes so that LRATC is the lowest unit cost at which any particular output can be produced in the long run.

Although the LRATC curve in Figure 4 is relatively bumpy, it will tend to smooth out as more plant size options are considered. In some industries, such as agriculture and food service, the options for plant size and production methods are virtually unlimited. In other industries, such as semiconductors, however, sophisticated plants may cost several billion dollars to build and require being run at near capacity to be cost-effective.

These huge, sophisticated plants are so complex that Intel Corporation has dedicated teams of engineers that build new plants and operate them exactly as all others. These teams ensure that any new plant is a virtual clone of the firm's other operating facilities. Even small deviations from this standard have proven disastrous to cost control in the past.

Economies and Diseconomies of Scale As a firm's output increases, its LRATC tends to decrease. This is because, as the firm grows in size, **economies of scale** result from such items as specialization of labor and management, better use of capital, and increased possibilities for making several products that utilize complementary production techniques.

economies of scale As a firm's output increases, its LRATC tends to decline. This results from specialization of labor and management, and potentially a better use of capital and complementary production techniques.

A larger firm's ability to have workers specialize in particular tasks reduces the costs associated with shifting workers from one task to another. Similarly, management in larger operations can use technologies not available to smaller firms, for example computers to supervise workers remotely. It is true that today's powerful personal computer networks have begun to narrow the gap in this arena. Larger firms, though, can still afford to purchase larger, more specialized capital equipment, whereas smaller firms must often rely on more labor-intensive methods. This equipment typically requires large production runs in order to be efficient, and only larger firms can generate the sales necessary to satisfy these production volume requirements. Finally, larger firms are better able to engage in complementary production and use by-products more effectively.

The area for *economies of scale* is shown in Figure 5 at levels of output below Q_0 (average costs are falling).

FIGURE 5

Economies, Diseconomies, and Constant Returns to Scale

The curve in this figure shows how increasing production affects long-run average total cost (LRATC). Up to Q_0, economies of scale reduce LRATC as production increases. Over the range Q_0 to Q_1, the firm enjoys constant returns to scale, meaning that it can expand without affecting LRATC. Past Q_1, however, diseconomies of scale kick in, such that any further expansion causes an increase in LRATC.

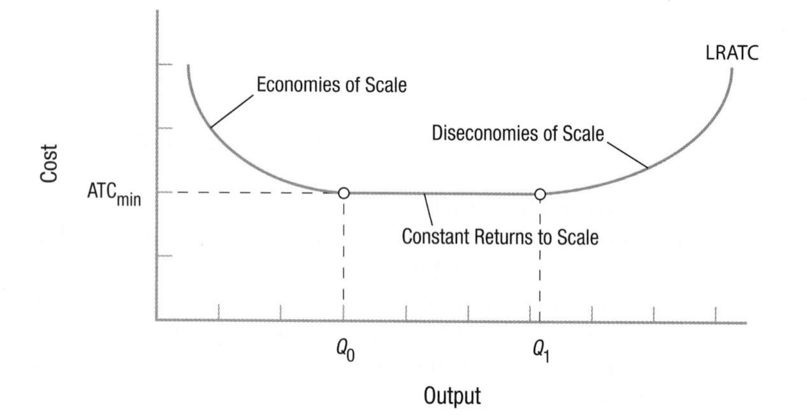

In many industries, there is a wide range of output wherein average total costs are relatively constant. Examples include fast-food restaurants, family restaurants such as Outback Steakhouse, and automotive service operations such as Jiffy Lube. Such businesses tend to have steady average costs because the cost to replicate their business in any community is relatively constant. Constructing and running a Dairy Queen franchise, for example, costs roughly the same no matter where it is operated. In Figure 5, this area of **constant returns to scale** is represented by output levels between Q_0 and Q_1.

constant returns to scale A range of output where average total costs are relatively constant. The expansion of fast-food restaurant franchises and movie theaters, which are essentially replications of existing franchises and theaters, reflect this.

As firms continue to grow, they eventually encounter **diseconomies of scale.** At some point, the firm gets so big that management is unable to control its operations efficiently. Some firms become so big that they get bogged down in bureaucracy and cannot make decisions quickly. In the late 1980s, Apple fell into this trap—slow to react to changing market conditions for computers and software, the company was left behind by sleeker competition from Dell and Microsoft. Only through downsizing, reorganizing, refocusing, and a management change did Apple get back on track in the late 1990s. Diseconomies of scale—where increased output increases costs disproportionately—are shown at outputs above Q_1 in Figure 5.

diseconomies of scale A range of output where average total costs tend to increase. Firms often become so big that management becomes bureaucratic and unable to control its operations efficiently.

Economies of Scope When firms produce a number of products, it is often cheaper for them to produce another product when the production processes are interdependent. These economies are called **economies of scope.** For example, once a company has established a marketing department, it can take on the campaign of a new product at a lower cost. It has already developed the expertise and contacts necessary to sell the product. Book publishers can introduce a new book into the market more quickly and cheaply, and with more success than can a new firm starting in the business.

economies of scope By producing a number of products that are interdependent, firms are able to produce and market these goods at lower costs.

Some firms generate ideas for products, then send the production overseas. After they have been through this process, they become more efficient at it. Economists refer to this as *learning by doing.* Economies of scope often play a role in mergers as firms look for other firms with complementary products and skills.

Procter & Gamble makes hundreds of household products, taking advantage of large economies of scope by producing many products that use the same inputs and equipment. For example, some of the chemicals used to produce Tide detergent are also used to produce Cascade dishwasher tablets.

Eric Chiang

Procter & Gamble makes hundreds of household products, taking advantage of large economies of scope by producing many products that use the same inputs and equipment.

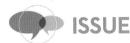

Role of Technology We know that technology creates products that were the domain of science fiction writers of the past. Dick Tracy's wrist radio, first introduced in the comics of 1940s, has now morphed into the many wireless products we see today.

But we should mention in passing the role technology plays in altering the shape of the LRATC curve. The output level at which diseconomies of scale are reached has significantly and continuously expanded since the beginning of the industrial revolution.

Enhanced production techniques, instantaneous global communication, and the use of computers in accounting and cost control are just a few recent examples of ways in which technology has permitted firms to increase their scale beyond what anyone had imagined possible 50 years earlier. Who would have imagined a century ago that one firm could have millions

ISSUE

How Large Are Fixed Costs? A Look at the Pharmaceutical and Software Industries

We show in this chapter that certain input costs are fixed in the short run, leading to U-shaped average variable and average total cost curves as economies of scale are realized and then exhausted. For most goods and services, economies of scale eventually disappear due to diminishing returns to production, causing average variable and average total costs to rise.

For certain industries, however, fixed costs represent the majority of the total cost of production. Consider the pharmaceutical industry: The cost of developing a successful new drug typically ranges from $100 million to over $1 billion, while the marginal cost of reproducing each pill costs just pennies. The same is true for the software industry; thousands of software engineers spend years writing code, costing the software company millions of dollars to produce the original copy, while the cost of disseminating the software to customers is virtually nothing (if purchased and downloaded online) or a few dollars if nicely packaged on a disc.

In both cases, the fixed cost of producing a new product far outweighs its variable cost, leading to marginal and average cost curves that differ from the typical U-shaped curves we have seen thus far. Because the marginal cost of reproduction is virtually nothing in these industries, the marginal cost curve for these goods will be horizontal and close to $0. As a result, the average total cost curve will be nearly identical to the average fixed cost curve, which slopes downward as more units are produced.

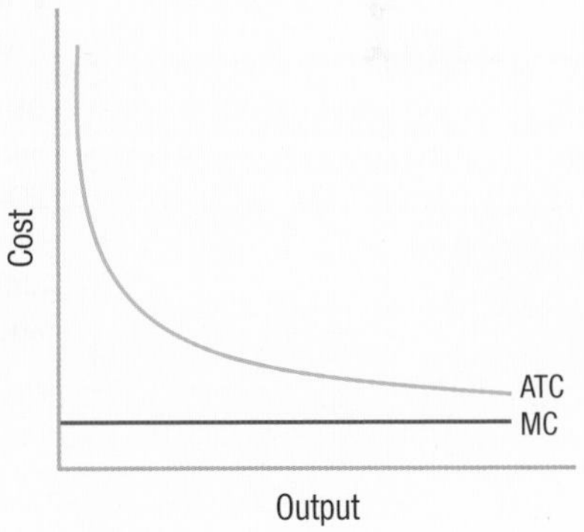

From this, we see that some products do not follow the typical shape of cost curves. However, these are the exceptions to the rule. Most products continue to show U-shaped marginal and average total cost curves, which are representative of goods that have both fixed and nonnegligible variable costs in their production.

of employees and billions of dollars in annual sales? Today, Wal-Mart has more than two million employees and annual sales of over $500 billion.

What spurs firms and entrepreneurs to develop new technologies and bring new products to market? Three things: profits, profits, and profits. In this chapter, we analyzed where profits come from by looking at what firms do, how they measure profits, and how they determine production and costs. In the next chapter, we will look at revenues, as well as examine how firms can maximize their profits by adjusting output to market demand.

CHECKPOINT

COSTS OF PRODUCTION

- Fixed costs (overhead) are those costs that do not vary with output, including lease payments and insurance. Fixed costs occur in the short run—in the long run, firms can change plant size or even exit an industry.
- Variable costs rise and fall as a firm produces more or less output. These variable costs include raw materials, labor, and utilities.
- Total cost equals fixed cost plus variable cost (TC = FC + VC).
- Average fixed cost, average variable cost, and average total cost provide a general measure of efficiency when looking at the total amount of output produced.
- Marginal cost is the change in total cost divided by the change in output ($MC = \Delta TC/\Delta Q$). Marginal cost provides important information to firms deciding whether to produce more or less output.
- The long-run average total cost curve (LRATC) represents the lowest unit cost at which specific output can be produced in the long run.
- As a firm grows in size, economies of scale result from specialization of labor and better use of capital, while diseconomies of scale occur because a firm gets so big that management loses control of its operations and the firm becomes bogged down in bureaucracy.
- Economies of scope result when firms produce a number of interdependent products, so it is cheaper for them to add another product to the line.
- Modern communications and computers have permitted firms to become huge before diseconomies are reached.

QUESTION: In the late 1990s, Boeing reported that it took roughly 12 years and $15 billion to bring a new aircraft from the design stage to a test flight. Boeing signed a 20-year exclusive agreement to supply aircraft to Delta, American, and Continental (now United) Airlines. The rationale for the agreement was that every time production of the plane doubled, the average production cost per plane would fall by about 20%.[5] Why would doubling production cut costs per unit by 20%?

Answers to the Checkpoint question can be found at the end of this chapter.

[5] "Peace in Our Time," *The Economist*, July 26, 1997.

chapter summary

Section 1: Firms, Profits, and Economic Costs

Firms are economic institutions that transform inputs (factors of production) into outputs (products and services).

© Rick Barrentine/Corbis

Nearly half of all businesses in the United States close within five years as new businesses take their place.

Types of Businesses

Sole proprietorship: unlimited liability, full control

Partnership: unlimited liability, shared control

Corporation: limited liability, ability to issue stock

Profit = Total Revenue – Total Cost

Accounting Costs	vs.	Economic Costs
Includes only explicit (out-of-pocket) costs		Includes explicit and implicit (opportunity) costs

Economic profit = **total revenue** – **economic costs**

Normal profit is an economic profit of $0.

Short run: period of time during which at least one factor of production is fixed.

Long run: a period long enough that firms can vary all factors, as well as leave and enter industries.

Section 2: Production in the Short Run

Total product is the quantity of output produced using a certain amount of labor inputs.

Marginal product is the change in output associated with hiring one additional worker, or $\Delta Q / \Delta L$.

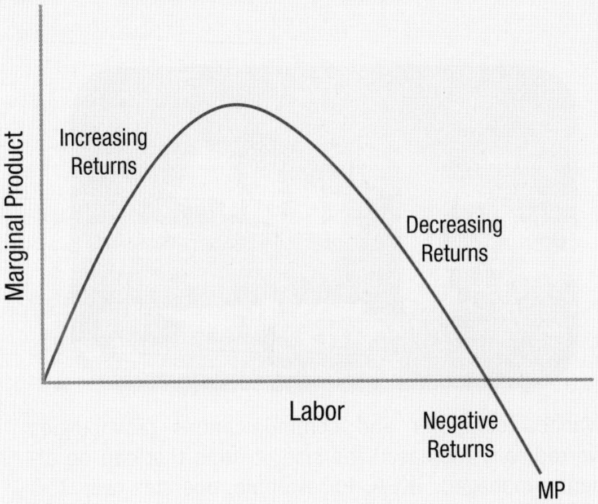

Increasing Versus Decreasing Returns to Labor

When *increasing returns* are present, each additional worker adds more to total output than previous workers.

Eventually, all production is subject to the *law of diminishing returns,* causing decreasing returns from adding more workers.

EIGHTFISH/Alamy

Having extra workers is very productive at first, but eventually everyone gets in each other's way, leading to decreasing returns to labor.

Section 3: Costs of Production

Short-Run Costs

In the short run, firms have **fixed costs** (FC) that do not vary with output and **variable costs** (VC) that do vary.

Total cost (TC) = fixed cost + variable cost

Marginal cost (MC) = change in total cost from producing one more unit

Average fixed cost (AFC) = fixed cost / quantity

Average variable cost (AVC) = variable cost / quantity

Average total cost (ATC) = total cost / quantity

Arnd Rockser/Dreamstime.com

Opening a personal training business involves fixed costs (equipment or gym membership) and variable costs (time spent with each client).

Abbreviated Cost Table for a Firm in the Short Run

Q	FC	VC	TC	MC	ATC
0	20	0	20		—
1	20	25	45	25	45
2	20	40	60	15	30
3	20	85	105	45	35

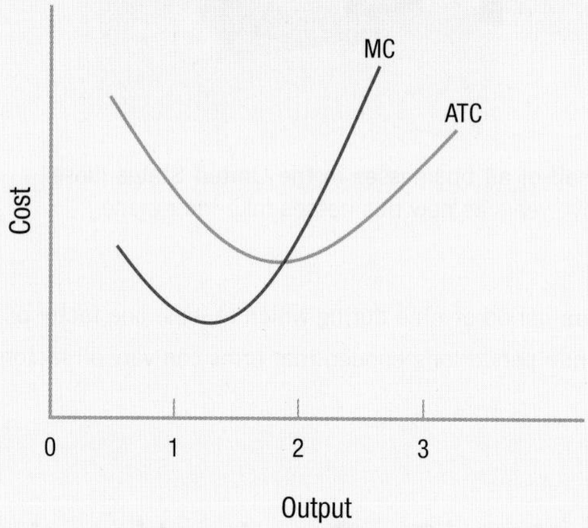

Why Does MC Cross ATC at Its Minimum Point?

When the next unit costs less than the average (MC < ATC), ATC falls. When the next unit costs more than the average (MC > ATC), ATC rises. For example, suppose your current course grade is 85%. If your grade on your next exam is 90%, your marginal exam score is greater than your average score, therefore your average rises. However, if your next exam grade (marginal score) is 70%, your average falls.

Long-Run Average Total Cost

In the long run, all factors of production are variable, and firms can enter or leave the industry. The **long-run average total cost** (LRATC) curve is the lowest unit cost for any specific output level in the long run.

Economies of scale occur when the average cost of production falls as a firm grows and cost savings from specialization in labor and management occur.

Eventually, **diseconomies of scale** occur when a firm's size becomes so large that efficient management becomes impossible.

Economies of scope are cost savings resulting from the ability of firms to produce many interdependent products.

© Lofik/Dreamstime.com

Advanced computer and communications technologies have radically increased the size of firms that can be efficiently managed. IKEA, for example, operates over 350 mega stores in 40 countries.

KEY CONCEPTS

firm, p. 164
sole proprietorship, p. 166
partnership, p. 166
corporation, p. 166
profit, p. 168
total revenue, p. 168
total cost, p. 168
economic costs, p. 168
explicit costs, p. 168
implicit costs, p. 168
sunk costs, p. 168
accounting profit, p. 169
economic profit, p. 169
normal profits, p. 169
short run, p. 169
long run, p. 169
production, p. 171
marginal product, p. 172
average product, p. 173
increasing marginal returns, p. 173
diminishing marginal returns, p. 173
fixed costs, p. 174
variable costs, p. 174
marginal cost, p. 175
average fixed cost, p. 176
average variable cost, p. 176
average total cost, p. 176
long-run average total cost, p. 179
economies of scale, p. 179
constant returns to scale, p. 180
diseconomies of scale, p. 180
economies of scope, p. 180

QUESTIONS AND PROBLEMS

Check Your Understanding

1. What is the difference between explicit and implicit costs? What is the difference between economic and accounting profits? Are these four concepts related? How?
2. Why should sunk costs be ignored for decision making?
3. How does the short run differ from the long run? Is the long run the same for all industries? Why or why not?
4. Why should a firm never hire a worker when negative marginal returns set in?
5. Why is the average fixed cost curve not U-shaped? Why does it not turn up as the average variable cost and average total cost curves do?
6. What is the difference between marginal cost and average total cost?

Apply the Concepts

7. If you work hard building your business and end up earning zero economic profit for the year, would this be considered a failed business to an economist? Why or why not?
8. In order to take this class, you had to pay tuition, buy the textbook, and buy a new laptop. Which of these items (if any) would be considered a sunk cost? Explain your reasoning.
9. Skype, the Internet phone company, uses peer-to-peer network principles to enable people to make free phone calls over the Internet to anywhere in the world. Skype forwards calls through users' computers without having any central infrastructure. Users agree to let their computer's excess capacity be used as transfer nodes. In this way, Skype does not have to invest in more infrastructure as it adds users, and the system is highly robust and scalable. What is the marginal cost to Skype to add another user to its system?
10. List some of the reasons why the long-run average total cost curve has sort of a flat bowl shape. It declines early on, then is rather flat over a portion, and finally slopes upward.

11. The Finger Lakes region in New York State produces wine. The climate favors white wines, but reds have been produced successfully in the past 15 years. Categorize the following costs incurred by one winery as either fixed or variable:
    a. the capital used to buy 60 acres of land on Lake Seneca
    b. the machine used to pick some varieties of grapes at the end of August and the beginning of September
    c. the salary of the chief vintner, who is employed year-round
    d. the wages paid to workers who bind the grape plants, usually in April, and usually over a period of three to four days
    e. the wages paid to the same workers who pick the grapes at the end of August or early September
    f. the costs of the chemicals sprayed on the grapes in July
    g. the wages of the wine expert who blends the wine in August and September, after the grapes have been picked
    h. the cost of the building where wine tastings take place from April to October
    i. the cost of the wine used in the wine tasting
12. If marginal cost is less than average total cost, are average total costs rising or falling? Alternatively, if marginal cost is more than average total cost, are average total costs rising or falling? Explain how this example might apply to a basketball player attempting to achieve a high average *points per game*.

In The News

13. Twenty-five years ago, coffee was a commodity product. Coffee brands such as Maxwell House ("good to the last drop") and Folger's advertised on television, but the difference between the brands was minimal. Not very satisfying, but no great pressure for change, either. In the 1990s, after touring coffeehouses in Rome, Howard Schultz brought the concept of upscale coffee to the United States and Starbucks was born ("Starbucks to Open 1,500 More Cafes in the U.S.," *The Seattle Times*, December 5, 2012). In 2012, over 13,000 Starbucks existed in the United States alone. How could a company such as Starbucks make any money in a highly competitive market like coffee? What factors did Howard Schultz need to consider before venturing into this business?
14. When J. P. Morgan Chase, one of the largest banks in the world, admitted to an embarrassing $9 billion trading loss in 2012, policymakers rushed to propose new regulations to prevent banks from taking risky bets ("J. P. Morgan Loss Spurs Scrutiny of Fed Governance," *Wall Street Journal*, May 14, 2012). Clearly, memories of bank bailouts by taxpayers in 2008 made the sentiment stronger. How do new regulations affect the costs of doing business? Do regulations represent a fixed or variable cost?

Solving Problems

15. Suppose you pay $10 to watch a movie at the local cineplex, and afterward you sneak into the next theater to watch a second movie without paying. What is your marginal cost of watching the second movie? What is the average cost of watching the two movies? After the movies, you go to the batting cages and stand in for two rounds of pitches, each round costing $2. What is your marginal cost of batting the second round? What is the average cost of batting two rounds?

16. Using the table below, answer the following questions.

Labor	Output	Marginal Product	Average Product
0	0		—
1	7		
2	15		
3	25		
4	33		
5	40		
6	45		

a. Complete the table, filling in the answers for marginal and average products.

b. Over how many workers is the firm enjoying increasing returns?

c. At what number of workers do diminishing returns set in?

d. Are negative returns shown in the table?

USING THE NUMBERS

17. According to By the Numbers, explain why a correlation exists between the costs of industrial robots and the productivity rate over the last 20 years.

18. According to By the Numbers, between which four years from 2000 to 2012 did Internet flight bookings increase the most (by percentage of overall sales)? Between which four years from 2000 to 2012 did Internet flight check-ins increase the most (by percentage of overall check-ins)?

ANSWERS TO QUESTIONS IN CHECKPOINTS

Checkpoint: Firms, Profits, and Economic Costs

Setting up your firm as a corporation has its benefits and its costs. One benefit of a corporation is limited liability, which means that if your company fails, the company can declare bankruptcy without it affecting your personal assets or credit. Another benefit is the ability to raise capital by issuing bonds or stocks. The downside of setting up a corporation is that profits are potentially shared by many shareholders. Also, corporations involve much more paperwork (such as setting up the firm and filing tax returns) than a sole proprietorship, which is much easier to set up and manage.

Checkpoint: Production in the Short Run

By hiring a worker only when she or he is more productive than the last worker hired means that a company insists on maintaining increasing marginal returns to labor. However, this generally occurs only for a limited number of workers. Eventually, all firms face diminishing marginal returns. This doesn't mean a firm should stop hiring, because the additional workers may still provide valuable productivity relative to their cost.

Checkpoint: Costs of Production

This immense $15 billion development cost is spread over more planes, and rising volume creates economies. Producing commercial aircraft has huge economies of scale and scope.

8 Perfect Competition

After studying this chapter you should be able to:

- Name the primary market structures and describe their characteristics.
- Define a perfectly competitive market and the assumptions that underlie it.
- Distinguish the differences between perfectly competitive markets in the short run and the long run.
- Analyze the conditions for profit maximization, loss minimization, and plant shutdown for a firm.
- Derive the firm's short-run supply curve.
- Use the short-run competitive model to determine long-run equilibrium.
- Describe why competition is in the public interest.

Visit your local farmer's market on a weekend morning, and you'll find dozens of individual stands offering the freshest fruits and vegetables, many of which are grown locally and delivered to the market directly by the grower. As you meander through the market you notice that the prices for any one type of fruit or vegetable are virtually the same from one stand to another. Further, the prices at the farmer's market often aren't much different from those that you might find in your grocery store's produce section.

With prices being nearly identical, shoppers are then left with the challenge of selecting the fruits and vegetables that look, feel, smell—and sometimes taste, if samples are available—the best, which for a food connoisseur is one of the pleasures of visiting a farmer's market. The rest of us, who do not have the skill to select the juiciest watermelon or peach, are often left to rely on our instincts. Even so, the difference in quality of the fruit across the various sellers is likely to be so small (because all are grown in the same area with the same climate) that typically one need not worry about making a bad choice.

This is the essence of a purely competitive market—the quality of a product is mostly indistinguishable, and hence the prices tend to be the same across sellers. In fact, each individual seller, being just one among thousands of sellers of fruit and vegetables, has little control over prices, another characteristic of a highly competitive market which forces sellers to be efficient. It's an example of the classic "survival of the fittest" problem—either produce high-quality produce at the lowest prices, or be sent packing.

The nature of intense competition extends well beyond farming, of course. Much of the goods we consume each day are produced in massive factories, often in Asia, where thousands of workers toil diligently in an often dreary environment to provide what we desire at the lowest cost. Before we debate the merits of whether this is good or bad for the factory workers, let's look at why many companies are using this form of production to stay competitive.

A firm's production function describes the manner in which inputs (resources such as labor and capital) are turned into outputs (goods). Since the cost of a set amount of inputs is fixed, being able to manufacture *more* with those inputs reduces the cost of production and increases productivity.

How does a firm increase productivity? First, it can hire better workers or offer training to make each worker more productive. Second, it can utilize better machinery (capital). And third, it can design the factory in a way to maximize the production given the workers and capital available. Choosing the production method by which inputs such as labor and capital are used is critical to productivity and the success of a firm. This is the role of the manager. If a firm uses inputs inefficiently, more efficient firms will drive it out of business.

The goal of any firm is to maximize profits given the market structure in which it exists. This is easier in some markets than in others. For example, if a company is the industry leader and has few competitors, earning profits is easier than it is for a struggling company facing intense competition.

This chapter focuses on market structure and the purest form of competition, which we call perfect competition. We explore some of the implications competition has for markets and consider why the competitive market structure is so central to the thinking of economists. When Adam Smith wrote his classic book, *The Wealth of Nations,* he wrote of a "hidden hand" that guides businesses in their pursuit of self-interest, or profits, allowing only the efficient to survive. Some observers have noted similarities between Smith's work, written in 1776, and Charles Darwin's *Origin of Species,* published in 1872. The late biologist and zoologist Stephen Jay Gould commented that "the theory of natural selection is, in essence, Adam Smith's economics transferred to nature."[1] Clearly, the notions of competition and the competitive market have played a prominent role in the history of ideas.

In this and the next two chapters, keep in mind the profitability equation developed in the previous chapter. Profits equal total revenues minus total costs. Total revenues equal

[1] Stephen Jay Gould, *The Structure of Evolutionary Theory* (Cambridge, MA: Belknap Press of Harvard University Press), 2002, pp. 121–125.

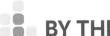

BY THE NUMBERS

Perfect Competition and Efficiency

Cost efficiency plays an important role in the survival of firms in perfectly competitive industries. Because each firm represents just one of many firms in the market, the actions of one firm do not affect any other firm.

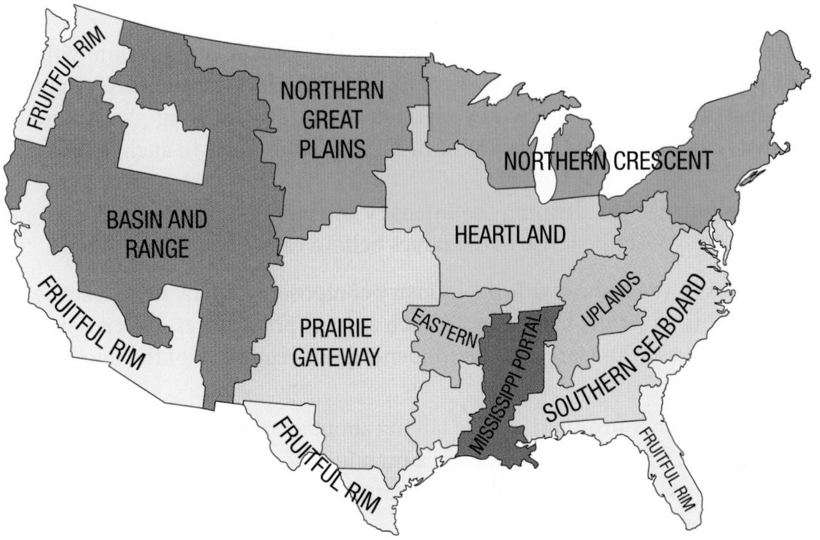

The United States Department of Agriculture divides the nation into regions for agricultural economic analysis. The number of farm workers varies significantly by region.

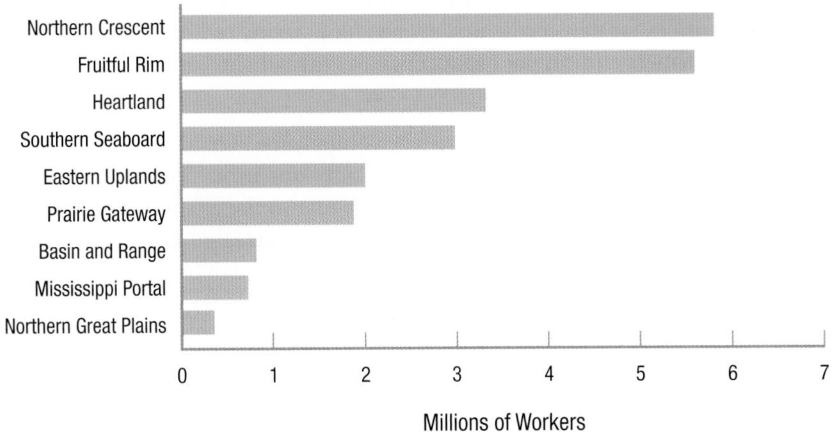

The average price per bushel of soybeans, wheat, and corn increased significantly in the past decade.

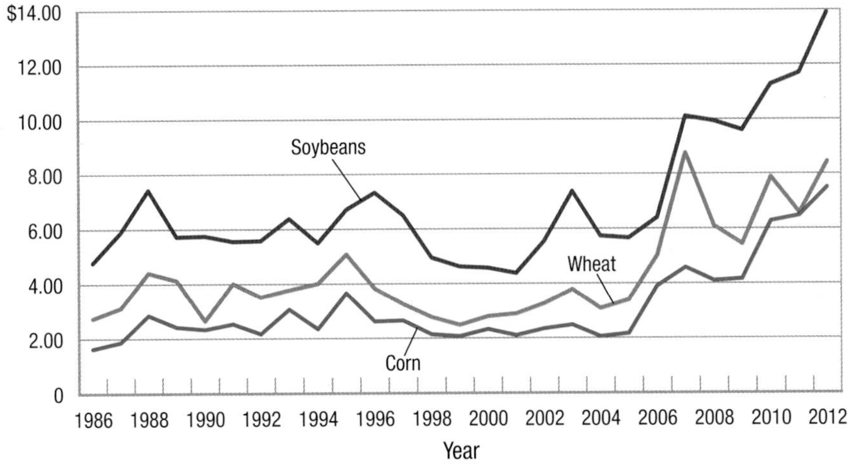

The world's top tea producers:

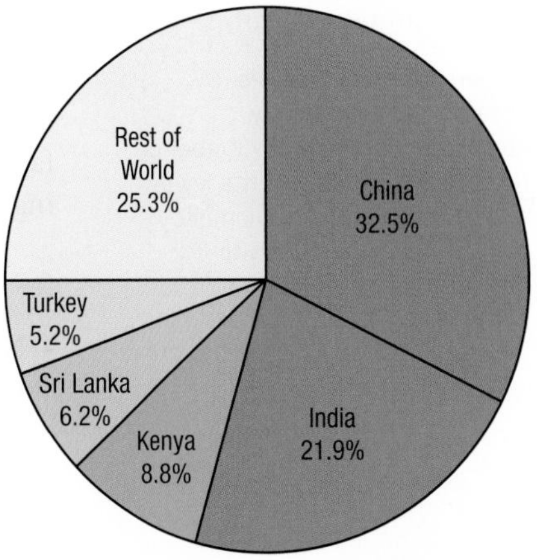

epa European Pressphoto Agency creative account/Alamy

9,980,823,315
Total world production of tea (in pounds) in 2012.

19,536,321,570
Total world production of coffee (in pounds) in 2012.

The legalization of marijuana in certain states has dramatically increased the number of growers in a highly competitive market, despite risk of federal prosecution.

AP Photo/Jeff Barnard, File

price times quantity sold. Keep in mind the three items that determine profitability: price, quantity, and cost. We will see how firms try to control each one of these. What you learn in this chapter will give you a benchmark to use when we consider the other market structures in the following chapters.

Market Structure Analysis

market structure analysis By observing a few industry characteristics such as number of firms in the industry or the level of barriers to entry, economists can use this information to predict pricing and output behavior of the firm in the industry.

To appreciate intensely competitive markets, we need to look at competition within the full range of possible market structures. Economists use **market structure analysis** to categorize industries based on a few key characteristics. By knowing simple industry facts, economists can predict the behavior of firms in that industry in such areas as pricing and sales.

Below are the four factors defining the intensity of competition in an industry and a few questions to give you some sense of the issues behind each one of these factors.

- **Number of firms in the industry:** Is the industry composed of many firms, each with limited or no ability to set the market price, such as local pizza places, or is it dominated by a large firm such as Wal-Mart that can influence price regardless of the number of other firms?
- **Nature of the industry's product:** Are we talking about a homogeneous product such as salt, for which no consumer will pay a premium or are we considering leather handbags, which consumers may think vary greatly, in that some firms (Coach, Gucci) produce better goods than others?
- **Barriers to entry:** Does the industry require low start-up and maintenance costs such as found at a roadside fruit and vegetable stand, or is it a computer-chip business that may require $1 billion to build a new chip plant?
- **Extent to which individual firms can control prices:** For example, pharmaceutical companies can set prices for new medicines, at least for a period of time, because of patent protection. Farmers and copper producers have virtually no control and get their prices from world markets.

Possible market structures range from perfect competition, characterized by many firms, to monopoly, where an industry is made up of only one firm. These market structures will make more sense to you as we consider each one in the chapters ahead. Right now, use this list and the descriptions below as reference points. You can always return here and put the discussion in context.

Primary Market Structures

The primary market structures economists have identified, along with their key characteristics, are as follows:

Perfect Competition

- Many buyers and sellers
- Homogeneous (standardized) products
- No barriers to market entry or exit
- No long-run economic profit
- No control over price

Monopolistic Competition

- Many buyers and sellers
- Differentiated products
- No barriers to market entry or exit
- No long-run economic profit
- Some control over price

Oligopoly

- Fewer firms (such as the auto industry)
- Mutually interdependent decisions
- Substantial barriers to market entry
- Potential for long-run economic profit
- Shared market power and considerable control over price

Monopoly

- One firm
- No close substitutes for product
- Nearly insuperable barriers to entry
- Potential for long-run economic profit
- Substantial market power and control over price

Putting off discussion of the other market structures for later chapters, we turn to an extended examination of the requirements for a perfectly competitive market. In the remainder of this chapter, we explore short-run pricing and output decisions, and also the importance of entry and exit in the long run. Moreover, we use the conditions of perfect competition to establish a benchmark for efficiency as we turn to evaluate other market structures in the following chapters.

Defining Perfectly Competitive Markets

The theory of **perfect competition** rests on the following assumptions:

perfect competition A market structure with many relatively small buyers and sellers who take the price as given, a standardized product, full information to both buyers and sellers, and no barriers to entry or exit.

1. Perfectly competitive markets have many buyers and sellers, each of them so small that none can individually influence product price.
2. Firms in the industry produce a homogeneous or standardized product.
3. Buyers and sellers have all the information about prices and product quality they need to make informed decisions.
4. Barriers to entry or exit are nonexistent in the long run; new firms are free to enter the industry if so doing appears profitable, while firms are free to exit if they anticipate losses.

One implication of these assumptions is that perfectly competitive firms are **price takers.** Market prices are determined by market forces beyond the control of individual firms. That is, firms must take what they can get for their products. Paper for copy machines, most agricultural products, basic computer memory chips, and many other goods are produced in highly competitive markets. The buyers or sellers in these markets are so small that their ability to influence market price is nonexistent. These firms must accept whatever price the market determines, leaving them to decide only how much of the product to produce or buy.

price taker Individual firms in perfectly competitive markets get their prices from the market because they are so small they cannot influence market price. For this reason, perfectly competitive firms are price takers and can produce and sell all the output they produce at market-determined prices.

Panel A of Figure 1 on the next page portrays the supply and demand for windsurfing sails in a perfectly competitive market; the market is in equilibrium at a price of $200 per sail and industry output Q_e. Remember that this product is a standardized sail (similar to 2 × 4 lumber, corn, or crude oil) and that the market contains many buyers and sellers, who collectively set the product price at $200.

Panel B shows the demand for a seller's products in this market. The firm can sell all it wants at $200 or below. Yet, what firm would set its price below $200 when it can sell everything it produces at $200? Were the firm to set its price above $200, however, it would sell nothing. What consumer, after all, would purchase a standardized sail at a higher price when it can be obtained elsewhere for $200? The individual firm's demand curve is horizontal at $200. The firm can still determine how much of its product to produce and sell, but this is the only choice it has. The firm cannot set its own price, therefore it is a *price taker*.

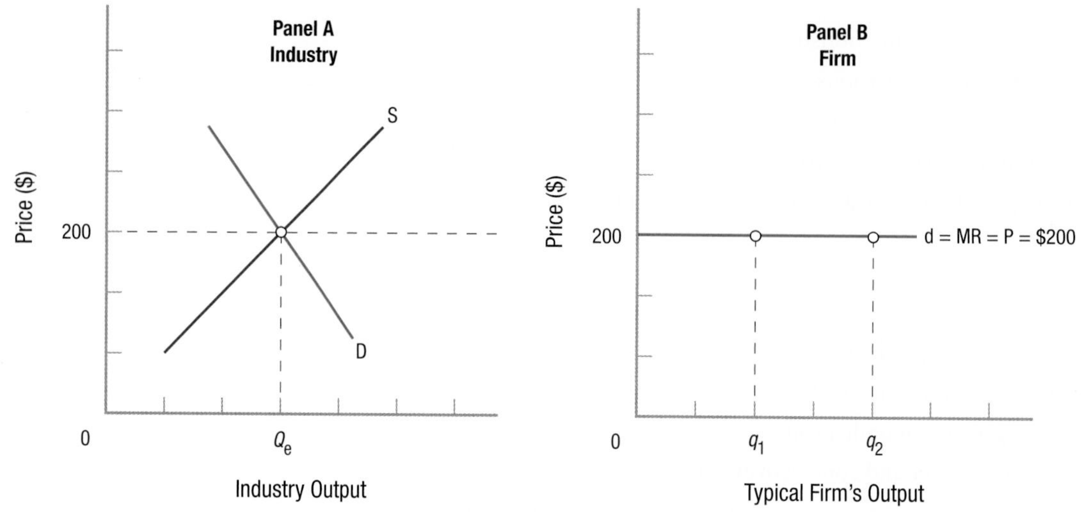

FIGURE 1

The Market for Competitive Products with an Equilibrium Price of $200

Panel A shows a market for standardized windsurfing sails in equilibrium at a price of $200 and industry output Q_e. This price is determined by the market's many buyers and sellers. Panel B illustrates product demand for an individual seller. The individual firm can sell all it wants to at $200 and has no reason to set its price below that. If it tries to sell at prices higher than $200, it sells nothing. The demand curve for the individual firm is horizontal at $200.

Recall the profitability equation. Profit equals total revenue minus total cost. Total revenue equals price times quantity sold. In perfectly competitive markets, a firm's profitability is based on a given market price, quantity sold, and its costs. So how does it determine how much to sell?

The Short Run and the Long Run (A Reminder)

Before turning to a more detailed examination of how firms decide how much output to produce in a perfectly competitive market, we need to recall a distinction introduced in the last chapter between the *short run* and the *long run.*

In the *short run,* one factor of production is fixed, usually the firm's plant size, and firms cannot enter or leave an industry. Thus, in the short run, the number of firms in a market is fixed. Firms may earn economic profits, break even, or suffer losses, but still they cannot exit the industry, nor can new firms enter.

In the *long run,* all factors are variable, and thus the level of profits induces entry or exit. When losses prevail, some firms will leave the industry and invest their capital elsewhere. When economic profits are positive, new firms will enter the industry. The long run is far more dynamic than the short run.

CHECKPOINT

MARKET STRUCTURE ANALYSIS

- Market structure analysis allows economists to categorize industries based on a few characteristics and use this analysis to predict pricing and output behavior.
- The intensity of competition is defined by the number of firms in the industry, the nature of the industry's product, the level of barriers to entry, and how much firms can control prices.
- Market structures range from perfect competition (many buyers and sellers), to monopolistic competition (differentiated product), to oligopoly (only a few firms that are interdependent), to monopoly (a one-firm industry).

- Perfect competition is defined by four attributes: Many buyers and sellers who are so small that none individually can influence price, firms that produce and sell a homogeneous (standardized) product, buyers and sellers who have all the information necessary to make informed decisions, and barriers to entry and exit that are nonexistent.
- Firms in perfectly competitive markets get the product price from national or global markets. In other words, firms are price takers.
- In the short run, one factor (usually plant size) is fixed. In the long run, all factors are variable, and firms can enter or leave the industry.

QUESTION: For the following firms, explain where in our market structure approach each firm best fits: Verizon (a wireless communications service provider), NFL (a professional football organization), Grandma's Southern Kitchen (a small café), Jack's Lumber (an independent lumber mill).

Answers to the Checkpoint question can be found at the end of this chapter.

Perfect Competition: Short-Run Decisions

Figure 1 in the previous section presented a perfectly competitive market with an equilibrium price of \$200. This translates into a horizontal demand curve for individual firms at that price. Individual firms are price takers in this competitive situation: They can sell as many units of their product as they wish at \$200 each.

Marginal Revenue

marginal revenue The change in total revenue from selling an additional unit of output. Because competitive firms are price takers, P = MR for competitive firms.

Economists define **marginal revenue** as the change in total revenue that results from the sale of one additional unit of a product. Marginal revenue (MR) is equal to the change in total revenue (ΔTR) divided by the change in quantity sold (Δq); thus,

$$MR = \Delta TR/\Delta q$$

Total revenue (TR), meanwhile, is equal to price per unit (p) times quantity sold (q); thus:

$$TR = p \times q$$

In a perfectly competitive market, we know that price will not change based on the output of any one firm. And because marginal revenue is defined as the change in revenue that comes from selling one more unit, marginal revenue is simply equal to price. To verify, suppose a firm sells ten units of a good at \$200 each, earning a total revenue of \$2,000. If the firm sells eleven units at \$200 each, total revenue becomes \$2,200. Using our marginal revenue equation, the added revenue a firm receives from selling the 11th unit is \$200, which is equal to the product price. Thus determining marginal revenue in a perfectly competitive market is easy. As we will see in later chapters, this gets more complicated in market structures in which firms have some control over price.

Profit-Maximizing Output

Suppose that you own a windsurfing sail manufacturing firm in a perfectly competitive market. Figure 2 on the next page shows the price and marginal cost curve that your firm faces while it seeks to maximize profits. As the price and cost curve show, you can sell all you want at \$200 a sail. Our first instinct might be to conclude that you will produce all that you can, but this is not the case. Given the marginal cost curve shown in Figure 2, if you produce 85 units, profit will be less than the maximum possible. This is because revenue from the sale is \$200, but the 85th sail costs \$210 to produce (point *b*). This means producing this last sail reduces profits by \$10.

Suppose instead that you produce 84 sails. The revenue from selling the 84th unit (MR) is \$200. This is precisely equal to the added cost (MC) of producing this unit, \$200

FIGURE 2

Profit Maximization in the Short Run in Perfectly Competitive Markets

If the firm produces 85 standardized windsurfing sails, the marginal cost to produce the last sail exceeds the revenue from its sale, thus reducing the firm's profits. For the 84th unit produced, marginal cost and price are both equal to \$200, therefore the firm earns a normal return from producing this unit. Producing only 83 units means relinquishing the normal return that could have been earned from the 84th sail. Hence, the firm maximizes profits at an output of 84 (point *e*), where MC = MR = P = \$200.

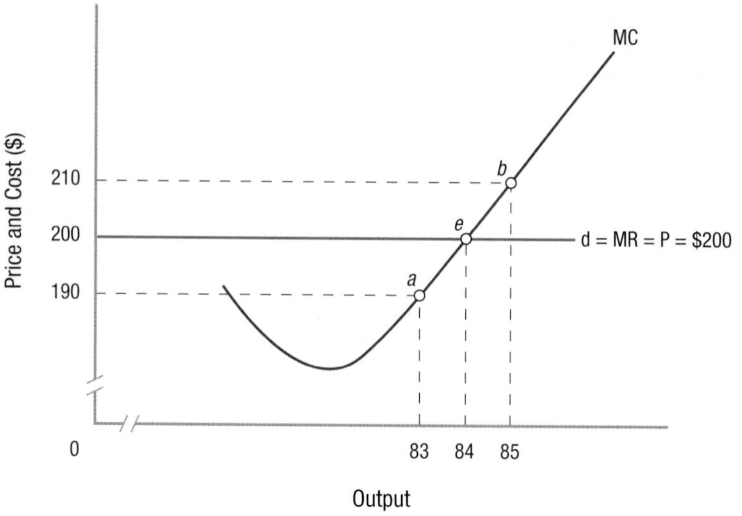

(point *e*). Therefore, your firm earns zero economic profit by producing and selling the 84th sail. Zero economic profit, or normal profits, mean that your firm is earning a normal return on its capital by selling this 84th sail. If you produce only 83 sails, however, the additional cost (point *a*) will be less than the price, and you will have to relinquish the normal return associated with the 84th sail. Profits from selling 83 sails will therefore be lower than if 84 sails are sold because the normal return on the 84th sail is lost.

profit maximizing rule Firms maximize profit by producing output where MR = MC. No other level of output produces higher profits.

These observations lead us to a **profit maximizing rule:** *A firm maximizes profit by continuing to produce and sell output until marginal revenue equals marginal cost (MR = MC).* As we will see in subsequent chapters, this rule applies to all firms, regardless of market structure.

Economic Profits

Continuing with the example of your windsurfing sail manufacturing firm, assume that the market has established a price of \$200 for each sail. Your marginal revenue and cost curves are shown in Figure 3 (the MR and MC curves are the same as those shown in Figure 2).

Earlier, we found that profits are maximized when your firm is producing output such that MR = MC, in this case, 84 sails. Looking at Figure 3, we see that profits are maximized at point *a*, because this is where MR = MC at \$200. We can compute the profit in this scenario by multiplying average profit (profit per unit) by output. Average profit equals price minus average total costs (P – ATC). In the figure, the average total cost of producing 84 sails is \$180 (point *b*). Thus, when 84 sails are produced, average profit is the distance *ab* in Figure 3, or \$200 – \$180 = \$20. Total profit, or average profit times output [(P – ATC) × Q], is \$20 × 84 = \$1,680; this is represented in the figure by area *cfab*. This area also is equivalent to total revenue minus total cost (TR – TC).

Note that there *is* a profit-maximizing point. The competitive firm cannot produce and produce—it has to take into consideration its costs. Therefore, for the price-taking competitive firm, its cost structure is crucial.

Five Steps to Maximizing Profit

Profit maximization is an important goal of any firm in any market structure. Yet, understanding revenue and cost curves can be frustrating given the many market structures and the different types of curves facing each market. Wouldn't it be useful to have a single approach when solving for a profit-maximizing outcome?

Let's review how we solved for the profit-maximizing equilibrium in the previous section, but this time using five simple steps that are illustrated in Figure 4.

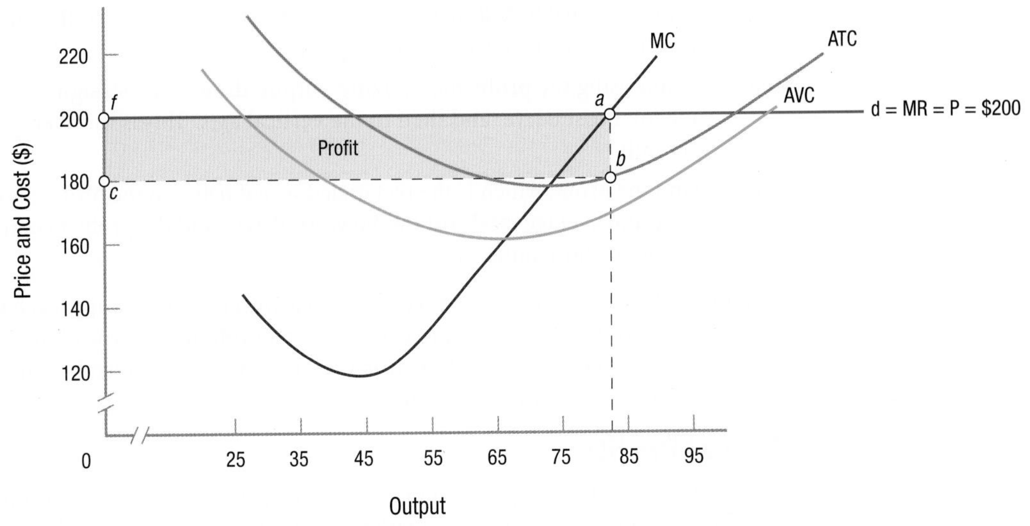

FIGURE 3

A Perfectly Competitive Firm Earning Economic Profits

Profits are maximized where marginal revenue equals marginal cost (MR = MC), or at an output of 84 and a price of $200. Price minus average total cost equals average profit per unit, represented by the distance *ab*. Average profit per unit times the number of units produced equals total profit; this is represented by area *cfab*.

Step 1: Find the point at which marginal revenue (MR) equals marginal cost (MC). Remember that in a perfectly competitive market, MR equals price.

Step 2: At the point at which MR = MC, find the corresponding point on the horizontal axis; this is the profit-maximizing output.

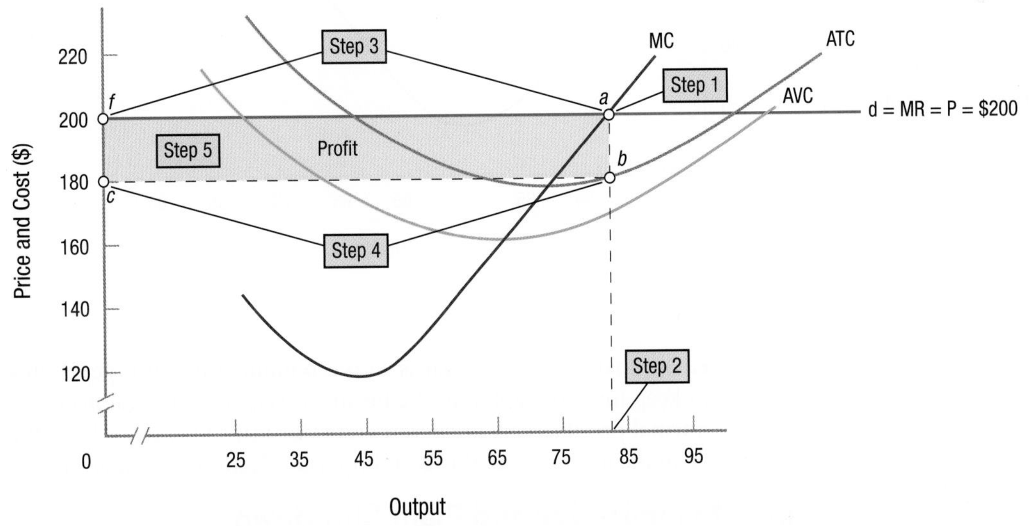

FIGURE 4

Five-Step Process to Determine Maximum Profit

The five steps shown provide a consistent approach to determining the profit-maximizing output and price and the area representing profit using revenue and cost curves in any market structure.

Step 3: At the profit-maximizing output, draw a line straight up to the demand curve (which is equal to MR in a perfectly competitive market) and then to the vertical axis. This is the profit-maximizing price.

Step 4: Again using the profit-maximizing output, draw a line straight up to the average total cost curve, and then to the vertical axis. This is the average total cost per unit.

Step 5: Find the profit, which is the rectangle formed between the profit-maximizing price and average total cost on the vertical axis, and the profit-maximizing output on the horizontal axis.

Some of these steps might seem redundant. However, using this approach will help you to identify the profit-maximizing price, output, and profit in any type of market structure, as we'll see in the next two chapters. It is therefore useful to remember these steps now when the diagrams are easier to follow.

Normal Profits

When the price of a windsurfing sail is $200, your firm earns economic profits. Consider what happens, however, when the market price falls to $175 a sail. This price happens to be the minimum point on the average total cost curve, corresponding to an output of 75 sails. Figure 5 shows that at the price of $175, the firm's demand curve is just tangent to the minimum point on the ATC curve (point *e*), which means that the distance between points *a* and *b* in Figure 3 has shrunk to zero. By producing 75 sails, your firm earns normal profits, or zero economic profit.

FIGURE 5

A Perfectly Competitive Firm Earning Normal Profits (Zero Economic Profit)

If the market sets a price of $175, the firm's demand curve is tangent to the minimum point on the ATC curve (point *e*). The best the firm can do under these circumstances is to earn normal profits on the sale of 75 windsurfing sails.

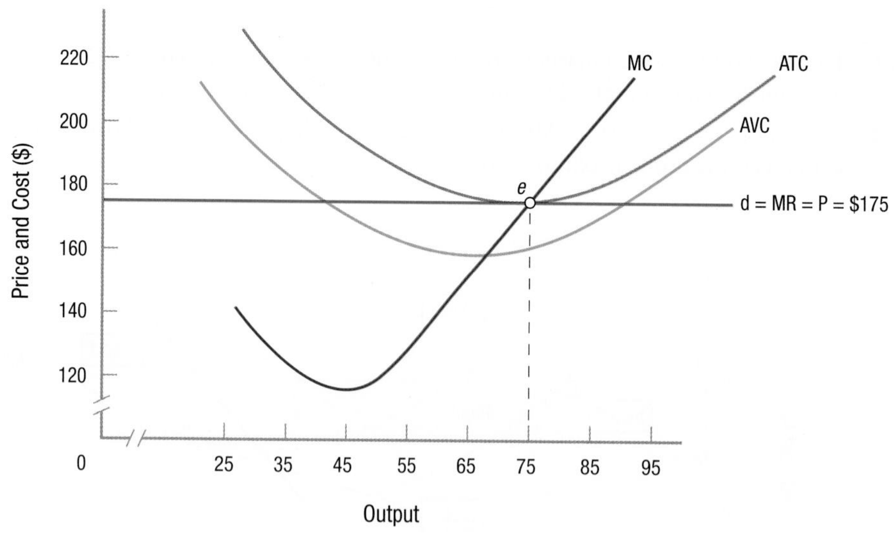

Remember that when a firm earns zero economic profit, it is generating just enough income to keep investor capital in the business. When the typical firm in an industry is earning **normal profits,** there are no pressures for firms to enter or leave the industry. As we will see in the next section, this is an important factor in the long run.

normal profits Equal to zero economic profits; where P = ATC.

Loss Minimization and Plant Shutdown

Assume for a moment that an especially calm summer with little wind leads to a decline in the demand for windsurfing sails. Assume also that, as a consequence, the price of windsurfing sails falls to $170. Figure 6 illustrates the impact on your firm. Market price has fallen below your average total cost of production (which takes into account the fixed cost, which in this case is $1,000, an amount determined in the previous chapter), but remains above your

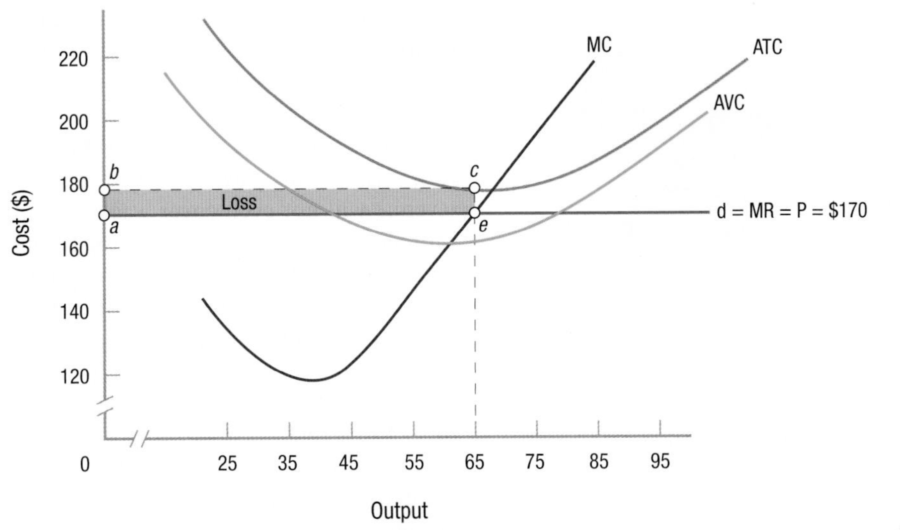

FIGURE 6

A Perfectly Competitive Firm Minimizing Losses

Assume that the price of windsurfing sails falls to $170 a sail. Loss minimization requires an output at which MR = MC, in this case at 65 units (point *e*). Average total cost is $178 (point *c*), therefore loss per unit is equal to $8. Total loss is equal to $8 × 65 = $520. Notice that this is less than the fixed costs ($1,000) that would have to be paid even if the plant was closed.

average variable cost. Profit maximization—or, in this case, *loss minimization*—requires that you produce output at the level at which MR = MC. That occurs at point *e*, where output falls to 65 units.

Using Figure 6, at 65 units the average total cost at this production level is $178, thus with a market price of $170, loss per unit is $8. The total loss on 65 units is $8 × 65 = $520, corresponding to area *abce*.

These results may look grim, but consider your alternatives. If you were to produce more or fewer sails, your losses would just mount. You could, for instance, furlough your employees. But you will still have to pay your fixed costs of $1,000. Without revenue, your losses would be $1,000. Therefore, it is better to produce and sell 65 sails, taking a loss of $520, thereby cutting your losses nearly in half.

But what happens if the price of windsurfing sails falls to $160? Such a scenario is shown in Figure 7. Your revenue from the sale of sails has fallen to a level just equal to variable costs. If you produce and sell 60 units of output (where MR = MC), you will be able to pay your employees their wages, but have nothing left over to pay your

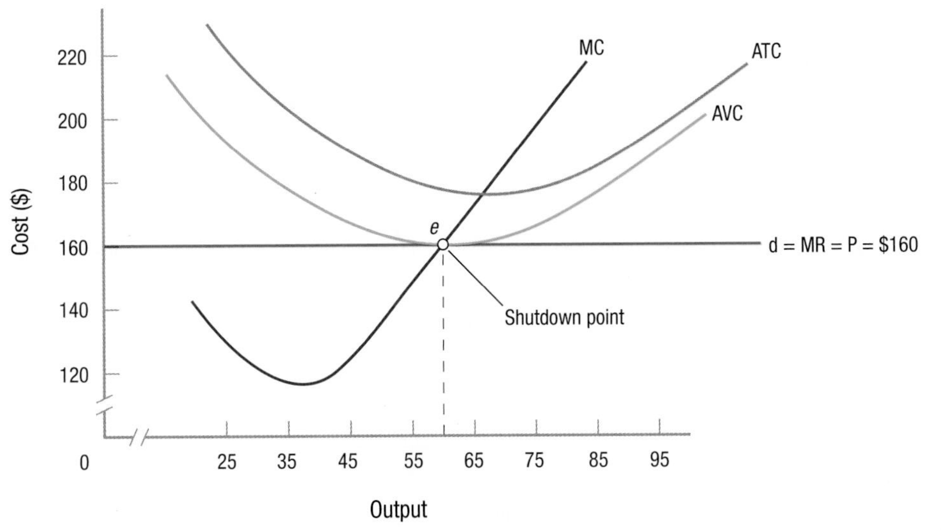

FIGURE 7

Plant Shutdown in a Perfectly Competitive Industry

When prices fall below $160, or below the minimum point of the AVC curve, losses begin to exceed fixed costs. The firm will close if price falls below this minimum point (point *e*); this is the firm's shutdown point.

NOBEL PRIZE HERBERT SIMON (1916–2001)

When he was awarded the Nobel Prize for Economics in 1978, Herbert Simon (1916–2001) was an unusual choice on two fronts. First, he wasn't an economist by trade; he was a professor of computer science and psychology at the time of his award. Second, Simon's major contribution to economics was a direct challenge to one of the basic tenets of economics: Firms, in fact, do not always act to maximize profits.

In his book *Administrative Behavior,* Simon approached economics and the behavior of firms from his outsider's perspective. Simon thought real-world experience showed that firms are not always perfectly rational, in possession of perfect information, or striving to maximize profits. Rather, he proposed, as firms grow larger and larger, the access to perfect information becomes a fiction and that firms are run by individuals whose decisions are altered by their inability to remain perfectly and completely rational.

To Simon, the reality is not that firms tilt at the mythical windmill of maximizing profits, but that, as he said in his Nobel Prize acceptance speech, they recognize their limitations and instead try to come up with an "acceptable solution to acute problems" by setting realistic goals and making reasonable assessments of their successes or failures.

Simon's views provided a new approach to analyzing market structure models. Simon brought data, theories, and knowledge from other disciplines and paved the way for behavioral economics (discussed in Chapter 6) to eventually become a prominent field of economics by broadening its scope and applying more realistic conditions found in the marketplace.

overhead; thus your loss will be $1,000. Point *e* in Figure 7 represents a **shutdown point,** because your firm will be indifferent to whether it operates or shuts down—you lose $1,000 either way.

If prices continue to fall below $160 a sail, your losses will grow still further, because revenue will not even cover wages and other variable expenses. Once prices drop below the minimum point on the AVC curve (point *e* in Figure 7), losses will exceed total fixed costs and your loss minimizing strategy must be to close the plant. It follows that the greatest loss a firm is willing to suffer in the short term is equal to its total fixed costs. Remember that the firm cannot leave the industry at this point, because market participation is fixed in the short run, but it can shut down its plant and stop production.

How practical is it to shut down production? That depends on the size of the firm and whether short-run losses are temporary or indicative of a permanent trend. The owner of a small kiosk selling decorative baskets might shut down and lay off the staff if losses mount and prospects for future profits are grim, while the owner of a fishing boat might furlough her employees during the off-season, with the expectation of resuming operations later on when prices recover and profits return.

The Short-Run Supply Curve

A glance at Figure 8 will help to summarize what we have learned so far. As we have seen, when a competitive firm is presented with a market price of P_0, corresponding to the minimum point on the AVC curve, the firm will produce output of q_0. If prices

FIGURE 8

The Short-Run Supply Curve for a Perfectly Competitive Firm

If prices fall below P_0, the firm will shut its doors and produce nothing. For prices between P_0 and P_1, the firm will incur losses, but these losses will be less than fixed costs, thus the firm will remain in operation and produce where MR = MC. At a price of P_1, the firm earns a normal return. If price should rise above P_1 (e.g., to P_2), the firm will earn economic profits by selling an output of q_2. The portion of the MC curve above the minimum point on the AVC curve, here thickened, is the firm's short-run supply curve.

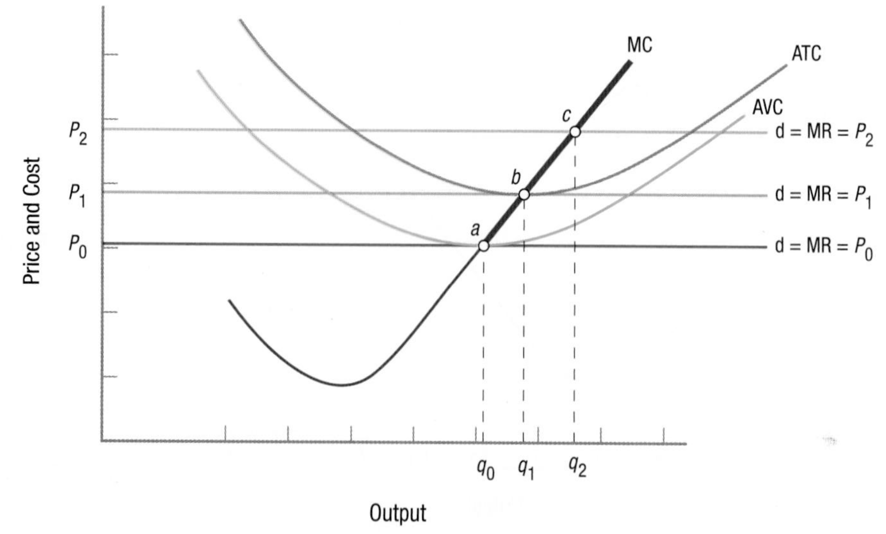

should fall below P_0, the firm will shut its doors and produce nothing. If, on the other hand, prices should rise to P_1, the firm will sell q_1 and earn normal profits (zero economic profits). And if prices continue climbing above P_1, say, to P_2, the firm will earn economic profits by selling q_2. In each instance, the firm produces and sells output where MR = MC.

From this quick summary, we can see that a firm's **short-run supply curve** is equivalent to the MC curve above the minimum point on the AVC curve. This curve, shown as the thickened portion of the MC curve in Figure 8, shows how much the firm will supply to the market at various prices, keeping in mind that it will supply no output at prices below the shutdown point.

Keep in mind also that the short-run supply curve for an industry is the horizontal summation of the supply curves of the industry's individual firms. To obtain industry supply, in other words, we add together the output of every firm at various price levels.

shutdown point When price in the short run falls below the minimum point on the AVC curve, the firm will minimize losses by closing its doors and stopping production. Because P < AVC, the firm's variable costs are not covered, therefore by shutting the plant, losses are reduced to fixed costs only.

short-run supply curve The marginal cost curve above the minimum point on the average variable cost curve.

CHECKPOINT

PERFECT COMPETITION: SHORT-RUN DECISIONS

- Marginal revenue is the change in total revenue from selling an additional unit of a product.
- Perfectly competitive firms are price takers, getting their price from markets, enabling them to sell all they want at the going market price. As a result, their marginal revenue is equal to product price and the demand curve facing the perfectly competitive firm is a horizontal straight line at market price.
- Perfectly competitive firms maximize profit by producing that output where marginal revenue equals marginal cost (MR = MC).
- When price is greater than the minimum point of the average total cost curve, firms earn economic profits.
- When price is just equal to the minimum point of the average total cost curve, firms earn normal profits.
- When price is below the minimum point of the average total cost curve, but above the minimum point of the average variable cost curve, the firm continues to operate, but earns an economic loss.
- When price falls below the minimum point on the average variable cost curve, the firm will shut down and incur a loss equal to total fixed costs.
- The short-run supply curve of the firm is the marginal cost curve above the minimum point on the average variable cost curve.

QUESTION: Describe why profit-maximizing output occurs where MR = MC. Does this explain why perfectly competitive firms do not sell "all they can produce"?

Answers to the Checkpoint question can be found at the end of this chapter.

Perfect Competition: Long-Run Adjustments

We have seen that perfectly competitive firms can earn economic profits, normal profits, or losses in the short run because their plant size is fixed, and they cannot exit the industry. We now turn our attention to the long run. In the long run, firms can adjust all factors, even to the point of leaving an industry. And if the industry looks attractive, other firms can enter it in the long run. Why are some industries (such as medical marijuana) thriving while others (such as photo developing) declining? The answer is tied to economic profits and losses.

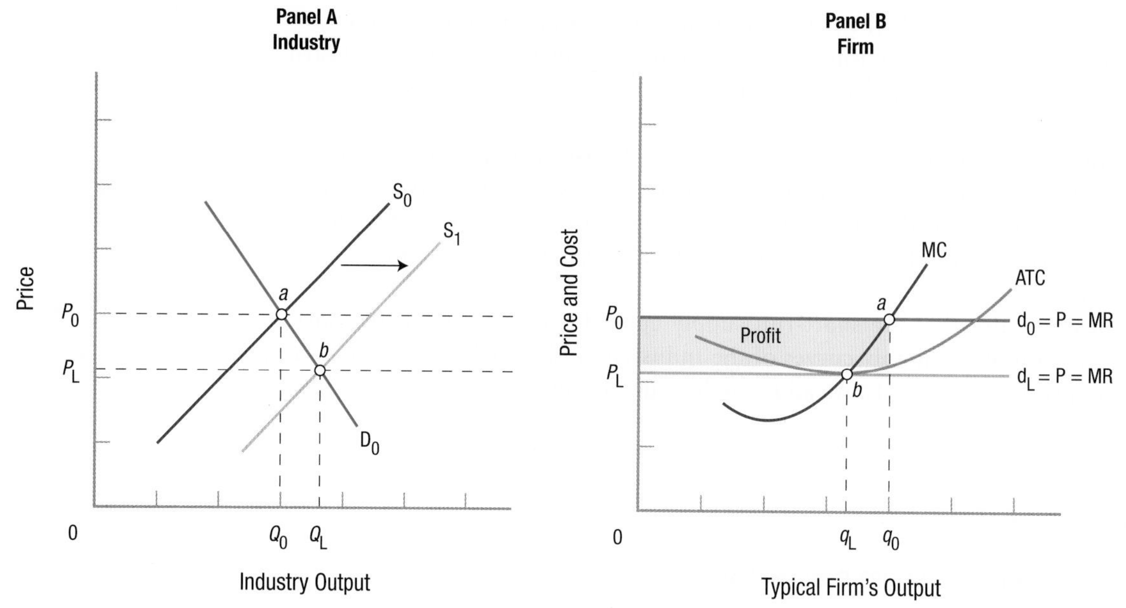

FIGURE 9

Long-Run Adjustment with Short-Run Economic Profits

Panel A shows a market initially in equilibrium at point *a*. Industry supply and demand equal S_0 and D_0, and equilibrium price is P_0. This equilibrium leads to the short-run economic profits shown in the shaded area in panel B. Short-run economic profits lead other firms to enter the industry, thus raising industry output to Q_L in panel A, while forcing prices down to P_L. The output for individual firms declines as the industry moves to long-run equilibrium at point *b*. In the long run, firms in perfectly competitive markets can earn only normal profits, as shown by point *b* in panel B.

Adjusting to Profits and Losses in the Short Run

If firms in the industry are earning short-run economic profits, new firms can be expected to enter the industry in the long run, or existing firms may increase the scale of their operations. Figure 9 illustrates one such possible adjustment path when the firms in an industry are earning short-run economic profits. To simplify the discussion, we will assume there are no economies of scale in the long run.

In panel A, the market is initially in equilibrium at point *a,* with industry supply and demand equal to S_0 and D_0, and equilibrium price equal to P_0. For the typical firm shown in panel B, this translates into a short-run equilibrium at point *a*. Notice that, at this price, the firm produces output exceeding the minimum point of the ATC curve. The shaded area represents economic profits.

These economic profits (sometimes called supernormal profits) will attract other firms into the industry. Remember that in a perfectly competitive market, entry and exit are easy in the long run; therefore, many firms decide to get in on the action when they see these profits. As a result, industry supply will shift to the right, to S_1, where equilibrium is at point *b,* resulting in a new long-run industry price of P_L. For each firm in the industry, output declines to q_L and is just tangent to the minimum point on the ATC curve. Thus, all firms are now earning normal profits and keeping their investors satisfied. There are no pressures at this point for more firms to enter or exit the industry.

Consider the opposite situation—that is, firms in an industry that are incurring economic losses. Figure 10 depicts such a scenario. In panel A, market supply and demand

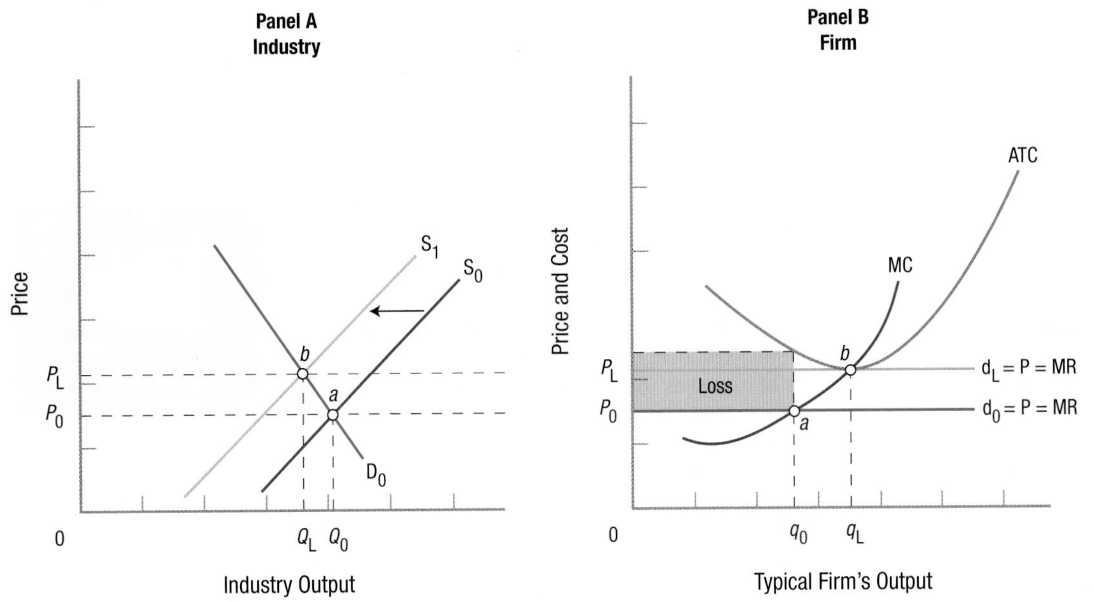

FIGURE 10

Long-Run Adjustment with Short-Run Losses

Panel A shows a market initially in equilibrium at point *a*. Industry supply and demand equal S_0 and D_0, and equilibrium price is P_0. This equilibrium leads to the short-run economic losses shown in the shaded area in panel B, thus inducing some firms to exit the industry. Industry output contracts to Q_L in panel A, raising prices to P_L and expanding output for the individual firms remaining in the industry, as the industry moves to long-run equilibrium at point *b*. Again, in the long run, firms in perfectly competitive markets will earn normal profits, as shown by point *b* in panel B.

are S_0 and D_0, with equilibrium price at P_0. In panel B, firms suffer economic losses equal to the shaded area. These losses cause some firms to reevaluate their situations and some decide to leave the industry, thus shifting the industry supply curve to S_1 in panel A, generating a new equilibrium price of P_L. This new price is just tangent to the minimum point of the ATC curve in panel B, expanding output for those individual firms remaining in the industry. Firms in the industry are now earning normal profits, therefore the pressures to leave the industry dissipate.

Notice that in Figures 9 and 10, the final equilibrium in the long run is the point at which industry price is just tangent to the minimum point on the ATC curve. At this point, there are no net incentives for firms to enter or leave the industry.

If industry price rises above this point, the economic profits being earned will induce other firms to enter the industry; the opposite is true if price falls below this point. A simple way to remember this is with the *elimination principle*: In a competitive industry in the long run with easy entry and exit, profits are eliminated by firm entry, and losses are eliminated by firm exit.

Competition and the Public Interest

Competitive processes dominate modern life. You and your friends compete for grades, concert tickets, spouses, jobs, and many other benefits. Competitive markets are simply an extension of the competition inherent in daily life. Figure 11 on page 205 illustrates the long-run equilibrium for a firm in a competitive market. Market price in the long run is P_{LR}; it is equal to the minimum point on both the short-run average total cost

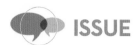

ISSUE

Can Businesses Survive in an Open-Source World?

Open-source software can be downloaded free, used free, and altered by anyone, provided that any changes made can also be freely used and altered by anyone else. Open-source systems such as Linux and Apache server software are used to run many of the Internet's biggest sites. Other types of software, including word processing, spreadsheets, and photo manipulation programs, are now becoming open source. Digital formats allow the cost of downloading, using, and duplicating this software to approach zero. Making a profit selling open-source software, even with enhanced features, is therefore a difficult process.

But now there is a movement to open-source *hardware*: products and plans that are available free, which anyone can duplicate, alter if they wish, and sell. What happens when open-source software is followed by open-source hardware?

Cory Doctorow, in his novel *Makers*, imagines a world in which the "system makes it hard to sell anything above the marginal cost of goods unless you have a really innovative idea, which can't stay innovative for long, so you need continuous invention and reinvention, too." This sounds eerily similar to the battles going on today with smart phones, televisions, video games, eBooks, and other high-tech products. As soon as one company presents a game-changing product (think iPod, iPhone, and iPad), other firms work feverishly to clone it and competition pushes prices and margins down to lower levels. Imagine what would happen if these products were both hardware and software open source.

Makers presents a world in which two engineers make three-dimensional (3D) desktop printers that can produce any product consumers want from inexpensive "goop." In *Makers*, the economy collapses, department stores vanish, and unemployment approaches depression levels of more than 20%. Coming up with a continuous stream of clever innovative ideas that initially make high short-run profits is the only way to stay ahead, because the transition to the long run happens so fast. Worse, people use their own 3D printers to duplicate products or designs for virtually nothing (just the cost of the goop).

Technology of the kind we are seeing now has the possibility of driving markets to these kinds of levels at which marginal cost and profit margins are

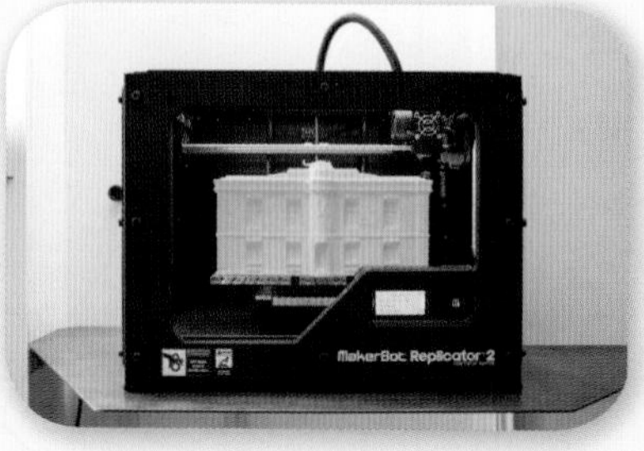

James Leynse/Corbis

low. Many companies have thousands of employees that make products from toothbrushes to plasticware to nearly everything you see at dollar stores. If households had the capability to produce their own products from some inexpensive substance, many companies we know today would disappear. Cory Doctorow explores what happens when the printers can produce other printers and other open-source machines. Although *Makers* is science fiction, the prototypes of 3D printers available today suggest it is not so far-fetched.

Sources: Cory Doctorow, *Makers* (New York: Tom Doherty Associates), 2009; L. Gordon Crovitz, "Technology Is Stranger Than Fiction," *Wall Street Journal,* November 23, 2009, p. A19; and Justin Lahart, "Taking an Open-Source Approach to Hardware," *Wall Street Journal,* November 27, 2009, p. B8.

(SRATC) curve and the long-run average total cost (LRATC) curve. At point *e,* the following is true:

$$P = MR = MC = SRATC_{min} = LRATC_{min}$$

This equation illustrates why competitive markets are the standard (benchmark) by which all other market structures are evaluated. First, competitive markets exhibit *productive efficiency*. Products are produced and sold to consumers at their lowest possible opportunity cost. For consumers, this is an excellent situation: They pay no more than minimum production costs plus a profit sufficient to keep producers in business, and consumer surplus shown in panel A is maximized. When we look at monopoly firms in the next chapter, consumers do not get such a good deal.

Second, competitive markets demonstrate *allocative efficiency*. The price that consumers pay for a given product is equal to marginal cost. Because price represents the value consumers place on a product, and marginal cost represents the

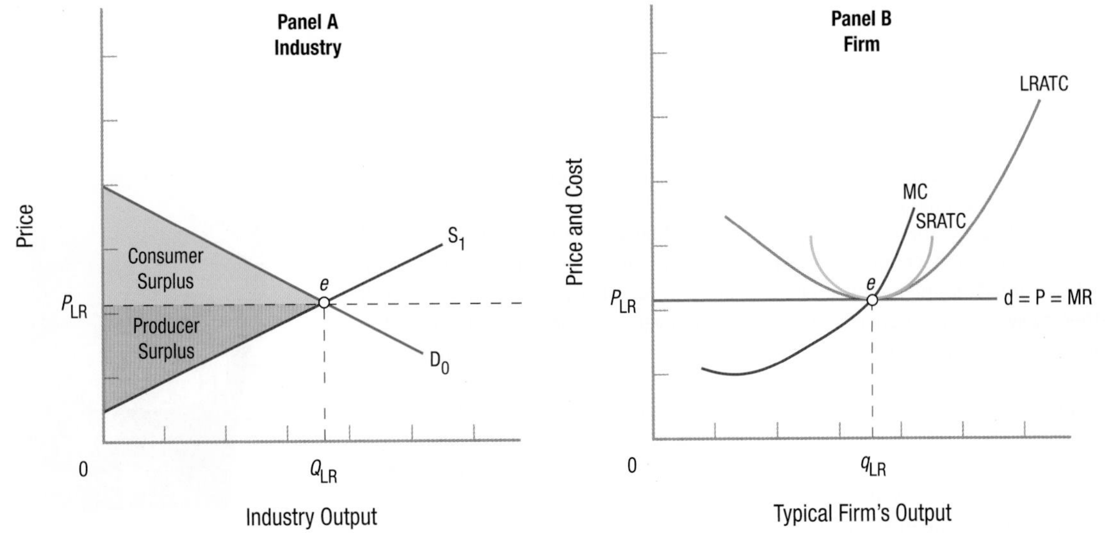

FIGURE 11

Long-Run Equilibrium for the Perfectly Competitive Firm

Market price in the long run is P_{LR}, corresponding to the minimum point on the SRATC and LRATC curves. At point *e*, P = MR = MC = $SRATC_{min}$ = $LRATC_{min}$. This is why economists use perfectly competitive markets as the benchmark when comparing the performance of other market structures. With competition, consumers get just what they want because price reflects their desires, and they get these products at the lowest possible price ($LRATC_{min}$). Further, as panel A illustrates, the sum of consumer and producer surplus is maximized. Any reduction in output reduces the sum of consumer and producer surplus.

opportunity cost to society to produce that product, when these two values are equal, the market is allocating the production of various goods according to consumer wants.

The flip side of these observations is that if a market falls out of equilibrium, the public interest will suffer. If, for instance, output falls below equilibrium, marginal cost will be less than price. Therefore, consumers place a higher value on that product than it is costing firms to produce. Society would be better off if more of the product were put on the market. Conversely, if output rises above the equilibrium level, marginal cost will exceed price. This excess output costs firms more to produce than the value placed on it by consumers. We would be better off if those resources were used to produce another commodity more highly valued by society.

Long-Run Industry Supply

Economies or diseconomies of scale determine the shape of the long-run average total cost (LRATC) curve for individual firms. A firm that enjoys significant economies of scale will see its LRATC curve slope down for a wide range of output. Firms facing diseconomies of scale will see their average costs rise as output rises. The nature of these economies and diseconomies of scale determines the size of the competitive firm.

Long-run industry supply is related to the degree to which increases and decreases in industry output influence the prices firms must pay for resources. For example, when all firms in an industry expand or new firms enter the market, this new demand for raw materials and labor may push up the price of some inputs. When this happens, it gives rise to an **increasing cost industry** in the long run.

increasing cost industry An industry that, in the long run, faces higher prices and costs as industry output expands. Industry expansion puts upward pressure on resources (inputs), causing higher costs in the long run.

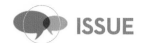

ISSUE

Globalization and "The Box"

When we think of disruptive technologies that radically changed an entire market, we typically think of computers, the Internet, and cellular phones. Competitors must adapt to the change or wither away. One disruptive technology we take for granted today, but one that changed our world, is "the box"—the standardized shipping container. As Dirk Steenken reported, "Today 60% of the world's deep-sea general cargo is transported in containers, whereas some routes, especially between economically strong and stable countries, are containerized up to 100%."

Before containers, shipping costs added about 25% to the cost of some goods and represented over 10% of U.S. exports. The process was cumbersome; hundreds of longshoremen would remove boxes of all sizes, dimensions, and weight from a ship and load them individually onto trucks (or from trucks to a ship if they were going the other way). This process took a lot of time, was subject to damage and theft, and was costly and inconvenient for business.

In 1955, Malcom McLean, a North Carolina trucking entrepreneur, got the idea to standardize shipping containers. He originally thought he would drive a truck right onto a ship, drop a trailer, and drive off. Realizing that the wheels would consume a lot of space, he soon settled on standard containers that would stack together, but would also load directly onto a truck trailer. Containers are 20 or 40 feet long, 8 feet wide, and 8 or 8½ feet tall. This standardization greatly reduced the costs of handling cargo. McLean bought a small shipping company, called it Sea-Land, and converted some ships to handle the containers. In 1956 he converted an oil tanker and shipped 58 containers from Newark, New Jersey, to Houston, Texas. It took roughly a decade of union bargaining and capital investment by firms for containers to catch on, but the rest is history.

Youssouf Cader

Longshoremen and other port operators thought he was nuts, but as the idea took hold, the West Coast longshoremen went on strike to prevent the introduction of containers. They received some concessions, but containerization was inevitable. Containerization was so cost effective that it could not be stopped. It set in motion the long-run adjustments we see in competitive markets. Ports that didn't adjust went out of business, and trucking firms that failed to add containers couldn't compete. The same was true for oceanic shipping companies.

Much of what we call globalization today can be traced to "the box." Firms producing products in foreign countries can fill a container, deliver it to a port, and send it directly to the customer or wholesaler in the United States. The efficiency, originally seen by McLean, was that the manufacturer and the customer would be the only ones to load and unload the container, keeping the product safer, more secure, and cutting huge chunks off the cost of shipping. Today, a 40-foot container with 32 tons of cargo shipped from China to the United States costs roughly $5,000 to ship, or 7 cents a pound! This efficient technology has facilitated the expansion of trade worldwide and increased the competitiveness of many industries.

Sources: Based on Tim Ferguson, "The Real Shipping News," *Wall Street Journal,* April 12, 2006, p. D12, and on Mark Levinson, *The Box* (Princeton, NJ: Princeton University Press), 2006. Dirk Steenken et al., "Container Terminal Operation and Operations Research," in Hans-Otto Gunther and Kap Hwan Kim, *Container Terminals and Automated Transport Systems* (New York: Springer), 2005, p. 4. Christian Caryl, "The Box Is King," *Newsweek International,* April 10–17, 2006. Larry Rather, "Shipping Costs Start to Crimp Globalization," *New York Times,* August 3, 2008, p. 10.

To illustrate, panel A of Figure 12 shows two sets of short-run supply and demand curves. Initially, demand and supply are D_0 and S_0, and equilibrium is at point *a.* Assume demand increases, shifting to D_1. In the short run, price and output will rise to point *b.* As we have seen earlier, economic profits will result and existing firms will expand or new firms will enter the industry, causing product supply to shift to S_1 in the long run. Note that at the new equilibrium (point *c*), prices are higher than at the initial equilibrium (point *a*). This is caused by the upward pressure on the prices of industry inputs, notably raw materials and labor that resulted from industry expansion. Industry output has expanded, but prices and costs are higher. This is an *increasing cost industry.*

Alternatively, an industry might enjoy economies of scale as it expands, as suggested by panel C of Figure 12. In this case, price and output initially rise as the short-run

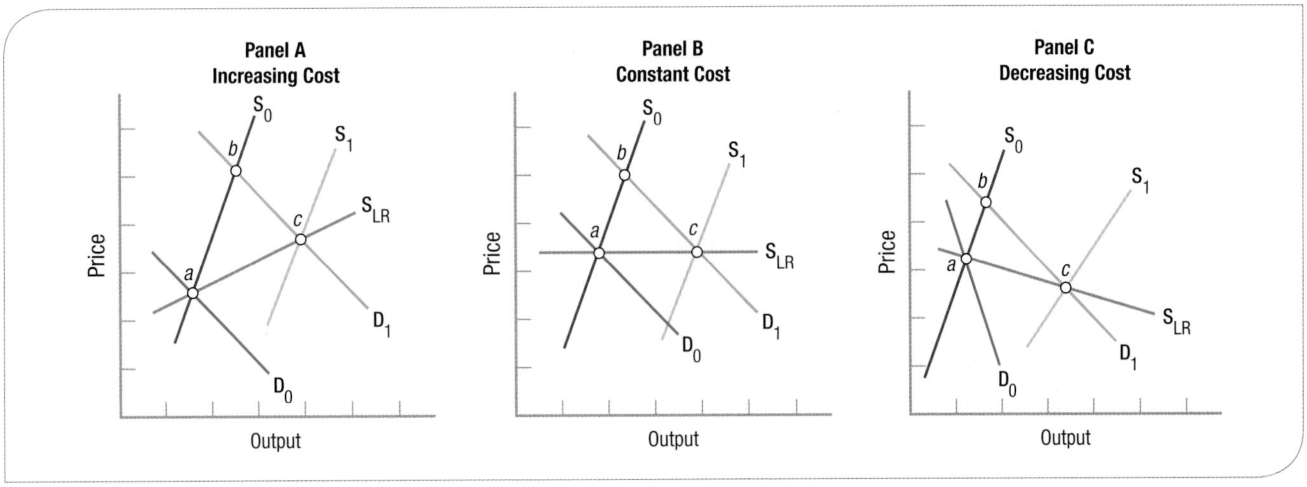

FIGURE 12

Long-Run Industry Supply Curves

Panel A shows an increasing cost industry. Demand and supply are initially D_0 and S_0, with equilibrium at point *a*. When demand increases, price and output rise in the short run to point *b*. As new firms enter the industry, they drive up the cost of resources. Supply increases in the long run to S_1 and the new equilibrium point *c* reflects these higher resource costs. In constant cost industries (panel B), firms can expand in the long run without economies or diseconomies, therefore costs remain constant in the long run. In decreasing cost industries (panel C), expansion leads to external economies and thus to a long-run equilibrium at point *c*, with lower prices and a higher output than before.

equilibrium moves to point *b*. Eventually, however, this industry expansion leads to lower prices; perhaps suppliers enjoy economies of scale as this industry's demand for their product increases. The semiconductor industry seems to fit this profile: As the demand for semiconductors has risen over the past few decades, their price has fallen dramatically. In the long run, therefore, a new equilibrium is established at point *c*, where prices are lower and output is higher than was initially the case. This illustrates what happens in a **decreasing cost industry.**

Finally, some industries seem to expand in the long run without significant change in average cost. These are known as **constant cost industries** and are shown in panel B in Figure 12. Some fast-food restaurants and retail stores, such as Wal-Mart, seem to be able to clone their operations from market to market without a noticeable rise in costs.

decreasing cost industry An industry that, in the long run, faces lower prices and costs as industry output expands. Some industries enjoy economies of scale as they expand in the long run, typically the result of technological advances.

constant cost industry An industry that, in the long run, faces roughly the same prices and costs as industry output expands. Some industries can virtually clone their operations in other areas without putting undue pressure on resource prices, resulting in constant operating costs as they expand in the long run.

Summing Up

This chapter has focused on markets in which there is perfect competition—that is, in which industries contain many sellers and buyers, each so small that they ignore the others' behavior and sell a homogeneous product. Sellers are assumed to maximize the profits they earn through the sale of their products, and buyers are assumed to maximize the satisfaction they receive from the products they buy. Further, we assume that buyers and sellers have all the information necessary for informed transactions, and that sellers can sell as much of their products as they want at market equilibrium prices.

These assumptions allow us to reach some clear conclusions about how firms operate in competitive markets. In the long run, firms will produce the efficient level of output at which LRATC is minimized, and profits are enough to keep capital in the industry. This output level is efficient because it gives consumers just the goods they want and provides these goods at the lowest possible opportunity costs. Competitive market efficiency represents the benchmark for comparing other market structures.

Competitive markets as we have described them might seem to have such restrictive assumptions that this model only applies to a few industries, such as agriculture, minerals, and lumber. Most businesses you deal with don't look like the assumptions of these competitive markets. This is true, but most businesses you encounter, such as bars, restaurants, coffee shops, fast-food franchises, cleaners, grocery stores, and shoe and clothing stores, do share some of the characteristics of perfectly competitive markets such as earning normal profits over the long run. In the chapter after next, we examine those markets where consumers see products as differentiated and see how that industry's behavior is different from a perfectly competitive market.

Because perfect competition is so clearly in the public interest and is the benchmark for comparing other market structures, we can ponder the answer to the following question: Do firms seek the competitive market structure? The answer is: Generally, no. Why? Recall the profit equation. In perfectly competitive markets, firms are price takers. They can achieve economic profits in the short run but find it almost impossible to have long-run economic profits. Most firms instead want to achieve long-run economic profits. To do so, they must have some ability to control price. In the next chapter, we will see what firms do to achieve this market power.

CHECKPOINT

PERFECT COMPETITION: LONG-RUN ADJUSTMENTS

- When perfectly competitive firms are earning short-run economic profits, these profits attract firms into the industry. Supply increases and market price falls until firms are just earning normal profits.
- The opposite occurs when firms are making losses in the short run. Losses mean some firms will leave the industry. This reduces supply, thus increasing prices until profits return to normal.
- Competitive markets are efficient because products are produced at their lowest possible opportunity cost, and the sum of consumer and producer surplus is at a maximum.
- An industry in which prices rise as the industry grows is an increasing cost industry, and increased costs may be caused by rising prices of raw materials or labor as the industry expands.
- Decreasing cost industries see their prices fall as the industry expands, possibly due to huge economies of scale or rapidly improving technology.
- Constant cost industries seem to be able to expand without facing higher or lower prices.

QUESTION: Most of the markets and industries in the world are highly competitive, and presumably most CEOs of businesses know that competition will mean that they will only earn normal profits in the long run. Given this analysis, why do they bother to stay in business, when any economic profits will vanish in the long run?

Answers to the Checkpoint question can be found at the end of this chapter.

chapter summary

Section 1: Market Structure Analysis

A **market structure** describes an industry based on several characteristics, including the number of firms, nature of the industry's product, barriers to entry, and the extent to which individual firms can control prices.

AgStock Images, Inc./Alamy

Types of Market Structure

Perfect competition: Many price-taking firms producing a nearly identical product.

Monopolistic competition: Many firms producing a differentiated product.

Oligopoly: Few large firms producing a standardized product.

Monopoly: One firm producing a unique product protected by barriers to entry.

Soybeans are produced in a perfectly competitive market. Because each soybean farmer produces a small portion of total soybean production, each farmer has no influence on price, and is therefore a **price taker.**

In a perfectly competitive market, the price of a good is determined by ordinary industry supply and demand curves, and that price becomes the horizontal demand curve for the price-taking firm. Any shift in demand or supply (such as the demand shift from D_0 to D_1) causes price to change for the firm.

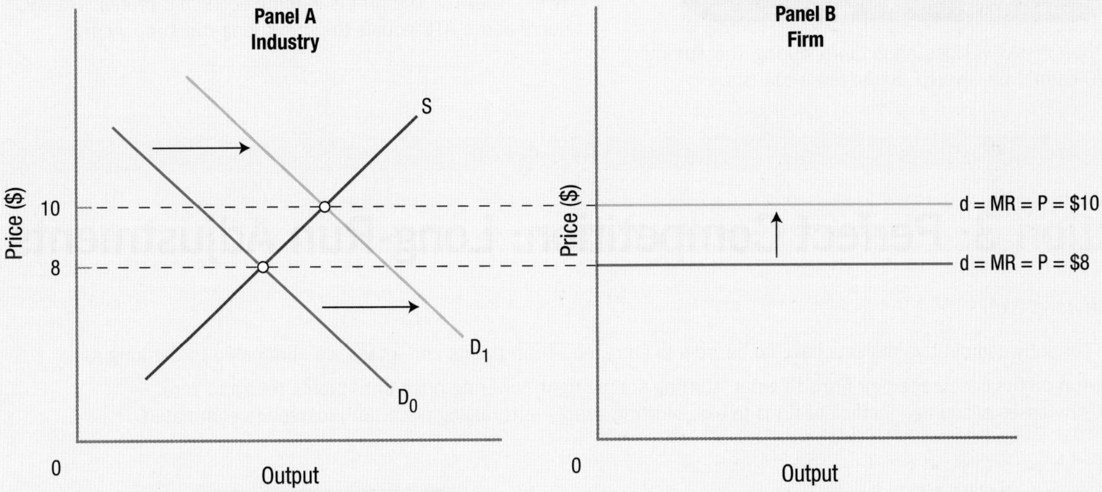

Section 2: Perfect Competition: Short-Run Decisions

Marginal revenue is the change in total revenue from producing one more unit, or $\Delta TR/\Delta Q$. In a perfectly competitive market, price does not change, therefore P = MR.

The **profit maximizing rule** says that firms maximize profit at an output where marginal revenue equals marginal cost.

When price (MR) > MC, the firm should increase production. When price (MR) < MC, the firm should decrease production.

Five Steps to Maximizing Profits in a Competitive Market:

1. Find MR = MC
2. Find optimal quantity where MR = MC
3. Find optimal price (Hint: It's already given!)
4. Find the average total cost at the optimal *Q*
5. Find the profit = $Q \times (P - ATC)$

In the graph to the right, this competitive firm is earning economic profits equal to the blue shaded area.

All Canada Photos/Alamy

Many shops in ski villages shut down during the summer when AVC cannot be covered due to fewer tourists.

Economic Versus Normal Profits

Economic profits take into account all explicit costs AND implicit costs such as the value of the next best use of time and money (opportunity cost).

Normal profits occur when economic profits are zero. But remember, zero economic profits can still represent substantial normal profits on paper.

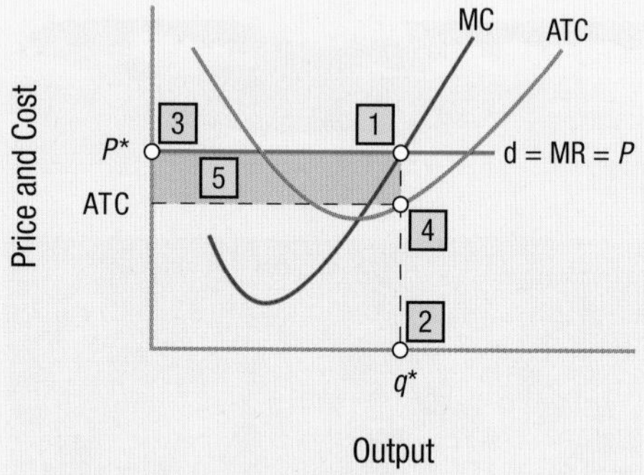

The Short-Run Supply Curve for a Competitive Firm

When P < AVC: The firm shuts down immediately.

When AVC < P < ATC: The firm operates in the short run to minimize losses, but exits the industry in the long run. The MC curve above AVC equals the firm's short-run supply curve.

When P > ATC: The firm is earning economic profits. The MC curve above ATC equals the firm's long-run supply curve.

Section 3: Perfect Competition: Long-Run Adjustments

Firm Entry and Exit

Because perfectly competitive markets have no barriers to entry, short-run profits and losses are eliminated in the long run.

Short-run profits encourage new firms to enter, shifting supply right, lowering price until profits return to zero.
Short-run losses encourage inefficient firms to exit, shifting supply left, raising price until losses are eliminated.

Productive and Allocative Efficiency

In the long run, the price of goods in a perfectly competitive market equals the minimum point on the LRATC curve. This demonstrates productive efficiency (goods are produced at their lowest possible cost) and allocative efficiency (goods are produced according to what society desires).

A **long-run industry supply curve** is flatter than a short-run industry supply curve, and can slope upward (increasing cost industry), downward (decreasing cost industry), or can be horizontal (constant cost industry). Costs are determined by industry structure, technology, and economies of scale.

Allison Joyce/Getty Images

Technology goods are a decreasing cost industry. Over time, the cost of production falls due to economies of scale. Further, costs fall as new technologies enable firms to produce the product at a much lower cost.

KEY CONCEPTS

market structure analysis, p. 192
perfect competition, p. 193
price taker, p. 193
marginal revenue, p. 195
profit maximizing rule, p. 196
normal profits, p. 198
shutdown point, p. 200
short-run supply curve, p. 201
increasing cost industry, p. 205
decreasing cost industry, p. 207
constant cost industry, p. 207

QUESTIONS AND PROBLEMS

Check Your Understanding

1. Why must price cover average variable costs if the firm is to continue operating?
2. Why do perfectly competitive firms sell their products only at the market price? Why not try to raise prices to make more profit or lower them to garner more sales?
3. Describe the role that easy entry and exit play in competitive markets over the long run.
4. Why are marginal revenue and price equal for the perfectly competitive firm?
5. Why, if competitive firms are earning economic profits in the short run, are they unable to earn them in the long run?
6. Describe the reasons why an industry's costs might increase in the long run. Why might they decrease over the long run?

Apply the Concepts

7. When a sports team consistently struggles, one strategy is to replace the coach. But when this happens, the new coach initially has the same players (its primary input). How can a new coach improve the team's record when the players are mostly the same?
8. How is the short-run supply curve for the competitive firm determined?
9. Suppose you master the art of growing herbs in your garden and selling them for profit at the local farmer's market. Your neighbor sees your profitable business and decides to do the same, however with less experience he faces a much higher marginal cost curve. How is it possible for both you and your neighbor to sell herbs at the same price?
10. Assume a competitive industry is in long-run equilibrium and firms in the industry are earning normal profits. Now assume that production technology improves such that average total cost declines by $5 per unit. Describe the process this industry will go through as it moves to a new long-run equilibrium.
11. When a competitive firm is earning economic profits, is it also maximizing profit per unit? Why or why not?

12. In this chapter we suggested that whenever market price fell below average variable costs, the firm would shut down. At that point revenue is not covering its variable costs and the firm is losing more money than if it just shut down and lost fixed costs. Clearly, shutting the firm is more complicated than that. Under what circumstances might the firm continue to operate even though prices are below average variable costs?

In The News

13. A January 25, 2012, article in *The New York Times* describes how more states are attempting to pass legislation to collect sales tax on Internet sales (sometimes dubbed the *Amazon Tax*) even when the seller does not have a physical presence in that state. Given the intense competition between online retailers and physical (brick-and-mortar) stores, how would such laws affect competition? Would brick-and-mortar stores be better off? How about customers? Why or why not?
14. An April 19, 2012, article by Art Carden in *Forbes* entitled "Let's Be Blunt: It's Time to End the Drug War" argues that legalizing marijuana is a key solution to ending the drug war. He argues that turning the industry into a competitive market would force cost-inefficient drug cartels to exit the market. Using what you know about competitive markets and firm entry and exit, explain the economics behind the author's theory.

Solving Problems

15. Use the following figure for a firm in a perfectly competitive market.

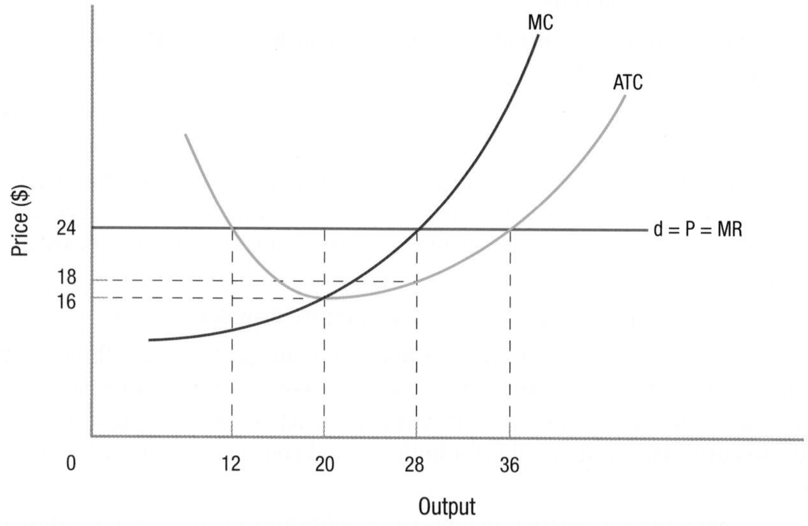

a. What is the output that maximizes the firm's profit?
b. At the profit-maximizing output, calculate total revenue and total cost.
c. If the firm maximizes profit, how much profit does it earn?
d. What will likely happen to market demand or market supply in the long run?
e. What will likely happen to the market price in the long run?

16. Use the figure below to answer the following true/false questions:
    a. If market price is $25, the firm earns economic profits.
    b. If market price is $20, the firm earns economic profit equal to roughly $100.
    c. If market price is $9, the firm produces roughly 55 units.
    d. If market price is $12.50, the firm produces roughly 70 units and makes an economic loss equal to roughly $210.
    e. Total fixed costs for this firm are roughly $100.
    f. If market price is $15, the firm sells 80 units and makes a normal profit.

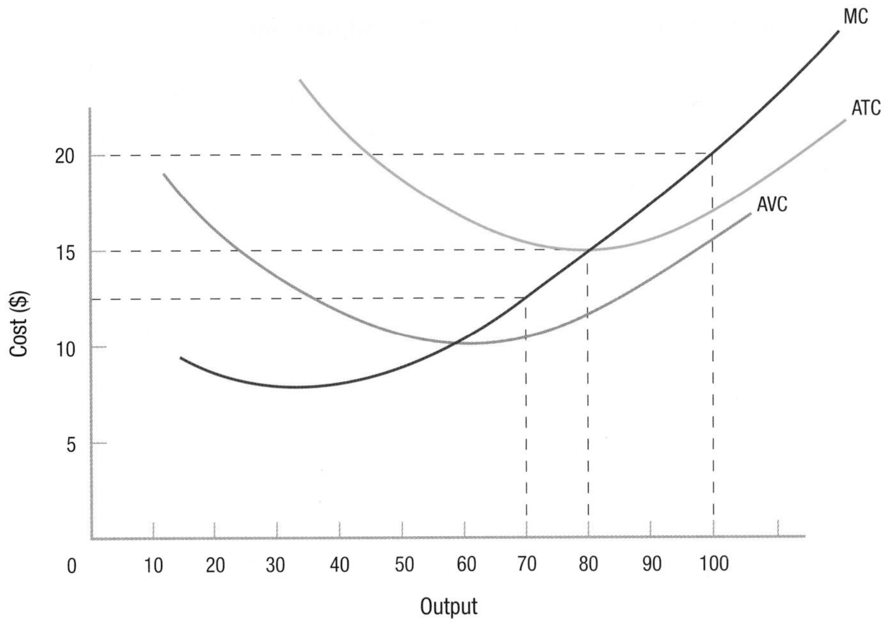

USING THE NUMBERS

17. According to By the Numbers, which two regions employ the highest number of people in the farm and farm-related industries? Approximately how many total persons are employed in the farm and farm-related industries in these two regions combined?
18. According to By the Numbers, in which year (since 1986) did the following crops reach their highest and lowest prices per bushel: corn, wheat, soybeans?

ANSWERS TO QUESTIONS IN CHECKPOINTS

Checkpoint: Market Structure Analysis

Verizon is one of a few major wireless providers in the U.S. market (others include AT&T, T-Mobile, and Sprint). The industry has considerable barriers to entry (e.g., the costs of cellular towers) and is therefore an oligopoly. The NFL is the only major organization for professional football teams, having complete control over all NFL teams nationwide. It also has exclusive contracts with advertisers and television networks. The NFL is best described as a monopoly. Grandma's Southern Kitchen is one of many restaurants serving southern food, and is differentiated by its location, menu, and quality of food. It is therefore a monopolistically competitive firm. Finally, Jack's Lumber is one of thousands of lumber mills across the country, each producing a standardized product. It is therefore in a perfectly competitive industry.

Checkpoint: Perfect Competition: Short-Run Decisions

Keep in mind that marginal cost is the additional cost to produce another unit of output, and price equals marginal revenue and is the additional revenue from selling one more unit of the product. If MR is greater than MC, the firm earns more revenue than cost by selling that next unit, therefore the firm will sell up to the point at which MR = MC. At that last unit at which MR = MC, the firm is earning a normal profit on that unit (a positive accounting profit). When MC > MR, the firm is spending more to produce that unit than it receives in revenue and is losing money on that last unit, lowering overall profits. Thus, firms will not produce and sell all they can produce: They will produce and sell up to the point at which MR = MC.

Checkpoint: Perfect Competition: Long-Run Adjustments

All businesses are looking for the "next new thing" that will generate economic profits and propel them to monopoly status. Even normal profits are not trivial. Remember, normal profits are sufficient to keep investors happy in the long run. When firms do find the right innovation, such as the iPad, Windows operating system, or a blockbuster drug, the short-run returns are huge.

9 Monopoly

After studying this chapter you should be able to:

- Describe the characteristics of a monopoly and market power.
- Describe the ways in which firms maximize market power using barriers to entry.
- Use monopoly market analysis to determine the equilibrium level of output and price for a monopoly.
- Describe the differences between monopoly and competition.
- Describe the different forms of price discrimination.
- Describe the different approaches to regulating a natural monopoly.
- Relate the history and purpose of antitrust legislation to monopoly analysis.
- Apply concentration ratios and the Herfindahl-Hirschman index to analyze the likelihood of regulation in a given market.
- Describe the conditions of a contestable market and its significance.

When was the last time you used Google to search for information? How about YouTube, Gmail, Google+, Google Docs, Chrome, or any Android application (app)? If you have used any of these services within the past 24 hours, you're in the majority of Americans who rely on at least one of over one hundred Web-based services offered by Google. And the best part is . . . it's all free. Or is it?

Although Google users rarely pay to use any of its Web services, the market value of the company as of June 2013 was over $250 billion, or approximately the same total market value of McDonald's (with its 35,000 restaurants) and Coca-Cola (which sells 1.7 billion servings each day) combined. How can Google be worth so much if it doesn't *sell* any physical products?

The answer is that Google sells advertising services, and lots of them (over $35 billion in sales in 2012), to companies worldwide that pay to have their Web sites show up on the first page of Web search results, or along the top and sides of Google's "free" services. Incredibly, Google charges some companies as much as $50 every time someone clicks on their ad links, although the average price is closer to $1. But with over 1 billion Google users worldwide, it doesn't take much to bring in a significant amount of revenue.

How is Google so profitable? In the previous chapter, we constructed a model of perfectly competitive markets in which many sellers compete against one another for the business of many buyers. This model assumed that different firms sell almost identical products, produce at the point where price equals marginal cost, and face no barriers to entry, entering or exiting industries when they see profit opportunities. Keep in mind that firms in perfectly competitive markets have no pricing power. They are price takers, accepting the market price as given—they have no ability to change prices.

Although Google has competitors, such as Yahoo!, Bing, and others, Google commands a dominant share (over 70%) of the search engine market. Unlike perfectly competitive firms, Google has a lot of market power. By market power, we mean the ability to have some control over price.

In reality, most firms have some market power. You see this every day. The cleaners located at the train station is more convenient than the cleaners located in town, at least for those taking the train, and therefore can get away with charging a little more for cleaning and pressing shirts or skirts. A gas station located near a highway can charge a little more than a gas station a mile away.

As we move down the market structure spectrum from the perfectly competitive firms on one end to the monopolistically competitive firms, and then to the oligopolies, finally ending up with monopolies at the other end, we will see that firms obtain more and more market power. We will see why firms want to be monopolies.

What is a monopoly? When a single company is the only firm in the industry, the company is a pure monopoly. Google is not a pure monopoly because it has some competitors, but it is so dominant that it comes close. In both situations, the economic analysis is similar, and for simplicity we refer to these firms as monopolies, even if they are not in the purest sense.

This chapter studies the theory of monopoly, which is at the other market-structure extreme from the competitive model. Whereas the competitive model is in the public interest, we can guess at the outset that monopolies generally are not. We will see why monopolies exist and how they act. Then we will see what it means to have market power, the ability to set price, and why monopolies have maximum market power. After that, we will see what can be done to mitigate the powers of monopolies that must exist, and how the United States tries to prevent monopolies from arising in the first place.

We also study how monopolies can be beneficial. Some monopolies create economies of scale or provide product innovation and creativity. Many of today's new technologies and pharmaceuticals would never have been created if firms with complete market power did not exist. These products create benefits to users that offset some of the inefficiencies firms with market power pass on to consumers through higher prices. As with all economic analysis, costs and benefits must be weighed to determine the effect on consumers and producers, and the study of monopoly is no different.

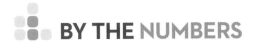

BY THE NUMBERS

Monopoly and Market Power

Monopolies achieve market power by establishing barriers to entry preventing competition. These barriers include prohibitive fixed costs, control of a key resource, and government protection.

Professional sports leagues exhibit market power by establishing exclusive relationships with players, teams, and television networks. U.S. television viewers by championship series:

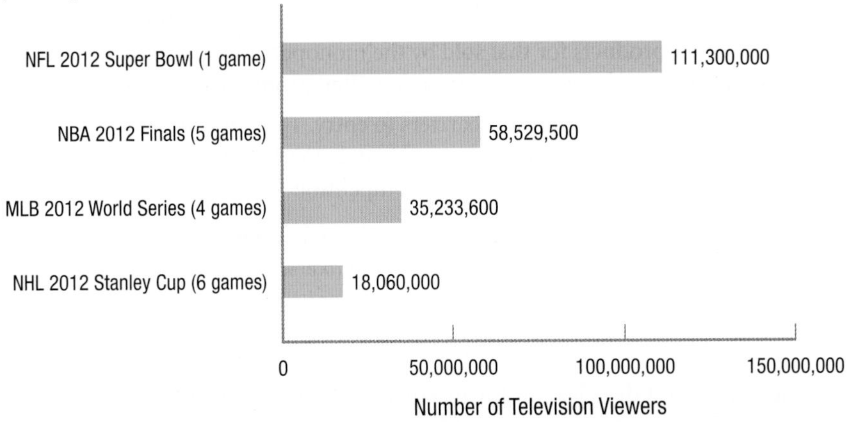

Facebook maintains a dominant market share in social media despite attempts by competitors to wrestle this power away.

AP Photo/Paul Sakuma

Pharmaceutical companies spend billions of dollars developing successful drugs. Government patents allow companies to recoup their investment by preventing competition for a fixed period of time, allowing drugs to be priced high when they cost pennies to reproduce (marginal cost is very low). The world's most expensive drugs by annual cost of treatment:

1. Soliris (to treat a rare immune system disease): $409,500
2. Naglazyme (to treat a rare metabolic disorder): $365,000
3. Elaprase (to treat Hunter's syndrome): $350,000
4. Cynryze (to prevent dangerous face swelling): $350,000

Pictac/Dreamstime.com

$250,000
Published price (in 2013) for one ride on Virgin Galactic into space.

91.6%
Global desktop market share of Microsoft Windows in March 2013.

Many electric companies are natural monopolies protected from competition by the government. However, the annual percentage growth in electricity demand has fallen at the same time as competition from renewable energy increases.

John Kroetch/Dreamstime.com

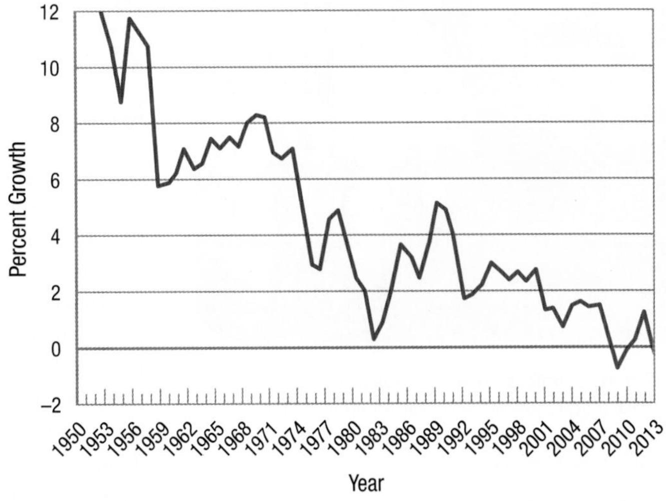

Monopoly Markets

The very word *monopoly* almost defines the subject matter: a market in which there is only one seller. For example, if you pay an electric bill every month, it's likely that you do not have a choice of which electric company services your apartment or house. Economists define a **monopoly** as a market sharing the following characteristics:

monopoly A one-firm industry with no close product substitutes and with substantial barriers to entry.

- The market has just one seller—one firm *is* the industry. This contrasts sharply with the competitive market, where many sellers comprise the industry.
- No close substitutes exist for the monopolist's product. Consequently, buyers cannot easily substitute other products for that sold by the monopolist. In the case of electricity, you could install solar panels, but such options are often prohibitively expensive.
- A monopolistic industry has significant barriers to entry. Though competitive firms can enter or leave industries in the long run, monopoly markets are considered nearly impossible to enter. Thus monopolists face no competition, even in the long run.

market power A firm's ability to set prices for goods and services in a market.

This gives pure monopolists what economists call **market power.** Unlike competitive firms, which are price takers, monopolists are *price makers.* Their market power allows monopolists to adjust their output in ways that give them significant control over product price.

As we noted already, nearly every firm has some market power, or some control over price. Your neighborhood dry cleaner, for instance, has some control over price because it is located close to you, and you are probably not going to want to drive 5 miles just to save a few cents. This control over price reaches its maximum in the case of monopolies, and becomes minor as markets approach more competitive conditions at the other end of the market structure spectrum.

Sources of Market Power

Monopoly is defined as one firm serving a market in which there are no close substitutes and entry is nearly impossible. Market power means that a firm has some control over price. As a market structure approaches monopoly, one firm gains the maximum market power possible for that industry. The key to the market power of monopolies is significant **barriers to entry.** These barriers can be of several forms.

barriers to entry Any obstacle that makes it more difficult for a firm to enter an industry, and includes control of a key resource, prohibitive fixed costs, and government protection.

economies of scale As the firm expands in size, average total costs decline.

Control Over a Significant Factor of Production If a firm owns or has control over an important input into the production process, that firm can keep potential rivals out of the market. This was the case with Alcoa Aluminum 70 years ago. Alcoa owned nearly all the world's bauxite ore, a key ingredient in aluminum production, before the company was eventually broken up by the government.

A contemporary example would be the National Football League (NFL), which has negotiated exclusive rights with colleges to draft top players (the most important input), along with exclusive rights with television networks and sponsors to broadcast games. Such control over key components of football entertainment makes entry into the industry very difficult.

Chris Chambers/Getty Images

The NFL draft is an annual event at which the best players are offered multi-million dollar contracts. The exclusivity of the event gives the NFL maximum market power.

Economies of Scale The **economies of scale** in an industry (when average total costs decline with increased production) give an existing firm a competitive advantage over potential entrants. By establishing economies of scale early, an existing firm has the ability to underprice new competitors, thereby discouraging their entry into the market. By doing so, a firm increases its market power.

In some industries, economies of scale can be so large that demand supports only one firm. Figure 1 illustrates this case. Here the long-run average total cost curve (LRATC) shows extremely large economies of scale. With industry demand at D_0, one firm can earn economic profits by producing between Q_0 and Q_1. If the industry were to contain two firms, however, demand for each would be D_1, and neither firm could remain in business without suffering losses. Economists refer to such cases as *natural monopolies.*

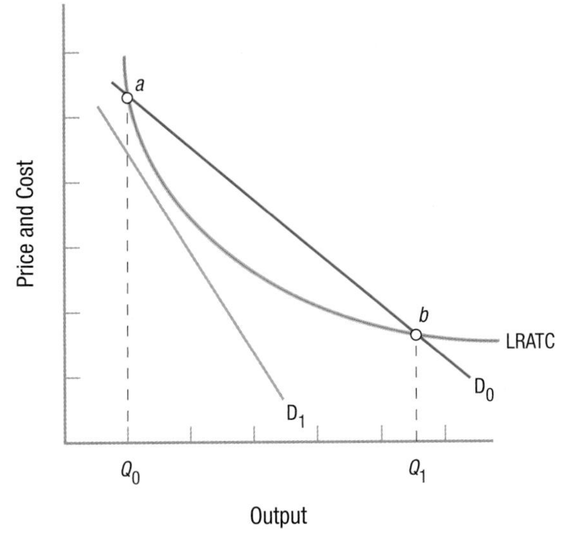

FIGURE 1

Economies of Scale Leading to Monopoly

The economies of scale in an industry can be so large that demand supports only one firm. In the industry portrayed here, one firm could earn economic profits (by producing output between Q_0 and Q_1 when faced with demand curve D_0). If the industry consisted of two firms, however, demand for each would be D_1, and neither firm could remain in business without suffering losses.

Utility industries have traditionally been considered natural monopolists because of the high fixed costs associated with power plants and the inefficiency of several different electric companies stringing their wires throughout a city. Recent technology, however, is slowly changing the utilities industry, as smaller plants, solar units, and wind generators permit a smaller yet efficient scale of operations. Smaller plants can be quickly turned on and off, and the energy from the sun and wind is beginning to be stored and transported to where it is needed in the system.

Government Franchises, Patents, and Copyrights The government is the source of some barriers to market entry. A government franchise grants a firm permission to provide specific goods or services, while prohibiting others from doing so, thereby eliminating potential competition. The United States Postal Service, for example, has an exclusive franchise for the delivery of mail to your mailbox. Similarly, water companies typically are granted special franchises by state or local governments.

Patents provide legal protection to individuals who invent new products and processes, allowing the patent holder to reap the benefits from the creation for a limited period, usually 20 years. Patents are immensely important to many industries, including pharmaceuticals, technology, and automobile manufacturing. Many firms in these industries spend huge sums of money each year on research and development—money they might not spend if they could not protect their investments through patenting. Similarly, a copyright protects ideas created by individuals or firms in the form of books, music, art, or software code, allowing these innovators to benefit from their creativity.

AP Photo/Chris Pizzello

Copyrights allow Matt Stone and Trey Parker, creators of *South Park,* to earn royalties on every episode (new and repeated) shown on television.

Some firms guard trade secrets to protect their assets for even longer periods than the limited timeframes provided by patents and copyrights. Only a handful of the top executives at Coca-Cola, for instance, know the secret to blending Coke.

Monopoly Pricing and Output Decisions

Monopolies gain market power because of their barriers to entry. Shortly we will discuss some ways in which this power is maintained. First, however, let us consider the basics of monopoly pricing and output decisions. In the previous chapter, we saw that competitive firms maximize profits by producing at a level of output where MR = MC, selling this output at the established market price. The monopolist, however, *is* the market. It has the ability to set the price by adjusting output.

MR < P for Monopoly A monopolist faces a demand curve, just like a perfectly competitive firm. But there is a big difference. For the monopolist, marginal revenue is less than price (MR < P). To see why, look at Figure 2. Panel A shows the demand curve for a perfectly competitive firm. At a price of $10, the competitive firm can sell all it wants. For each unit sold, total revenue rises by $10. Recalling that marginal revenue is equal to the change in total revenue from selling an added unit of the product, marginal revenue is also $10.

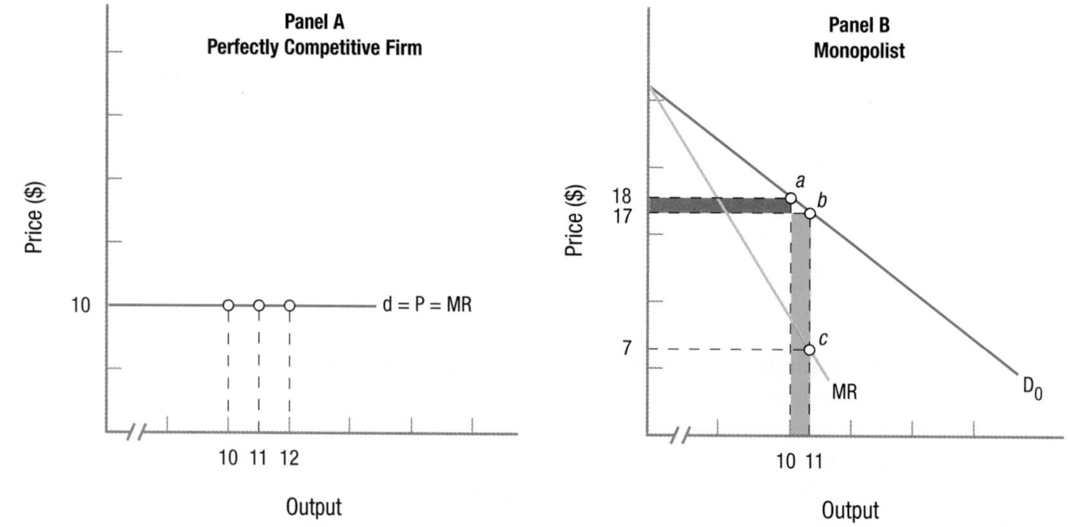

FIGURE 2

Marginal Revenue for Monopolies and Perfectly Competitive Firms

Panel A shows the demand curve for a perfectly competitive firm. At a price of $10, the competitive firm can sell all it wants. For each unit sold, revenue rises by $10; hence, marginal revenue is $10. Panel B shows the demand curve for a monopolist. Because the monopolist constitutes the entire industry, it faces a downward sloping demand curve (D_0). If the monopolist decides to sell 10 units at $18 each (point *a*), total revenue is $180. Alternatively, if the monopolist wants to sell 11 units, the price must be dropped to $17 (point *b*). This raises total revenue to $187 (11 × $17), but marginal revenue falls to $7 ($187 – $180, point *c*). Gaining the added $17 in revenue from the sale of the 11th unit requires the monopolist to give up $10 in additional revenue that would have come from selling the previous 10 units for an extra $1, or $18 each.

Contrast this with the situation of the monopolist in panel B. Because the monopolist constitutes the entire industry, it faces the downward sloping demand curve (D_0). If the monopolist decides to produce and sell 10 units, they can be sold in the market for the highest price the market would pay for 10 units (based on the demand curve), which is $18 each (point *a*), generating total revenue of $180. Alternatively, if the monopolist wants to sell 11 units, the price must be dropped to $17 (point *b*). This raises total revenue to $187 (11 × $17). Notice, however, that marginal revenue, or the revenue gained from selling this added unit, is only $7 ($187 – $180). In other words, the $17 in revenue (shown in green) gained from the sale of the 11th unit requires that the monopolist give up $10 in revenue (shown in red) that would have come from selling the previous 10 units for $1 more, or $18 each. Marginal revenue for the 11th unit is shown as $7 (point *c*) in panel B, which is also the difference between the green and red areas.

Notice that we are assuming that the monopolist cannot sell the 10th unit for $18 and then sell the 11th unit for $17; rather, the monopolist must offer to sell a given quantity to the market at a single price per unit. We are assuming, in other words, that there is no way for the monopolist to separate the market by specific individuals who are willing to pay different prices for the product. Later in this chapter, we will relax this assumption and discuss *price discrimination.*

In summary, we can see from panel B of Figure 2 that MR < P, and the marginal revenue curve is always plotted below the demand curve for the monopolist. This contrasts with the situation of the perfectly competitive firm, for which price and marginal revenue are always the same. We should also note that marginal revenue can be negative. In such an instance, total revenue falls as the monopolist tries to sell more output. However, no profit maximizing monopolist would knowingly produce in this range because costs are rising even as total revenue is declining, thus reducing profits.

Equilibrium Price and Output As noted earlier, product price is determined in a monopoly by how much the monopolist wishes to produce. This contrasts with the perfectly competitive firm that can sell all it wishes, but only at the *market-determined price.* Both types of firms wish to make profits. Finding the monopolist's profit maximizing price and output is a little more complicated, however, because competitive firms have only output to consider.

Like competitive firms, the profit maximizing output for the monopolist is found where MR = MC. Turning to Figure 3, we find that marginal revenue equals marginal cost at point *e,* where output is 120 units. Now we must determine how much the monopolist will charge for this output. This is done by looking to the demand curve. An output of 120 units can be sold for a price of $30 (point *a*).

Profit for each unit is equal to $8, the difference between price ($30) and average total cost ($22). Profit per unit times output equals total profit ($8 × 120 = $960), as indicated by the shaded area in Figure 3. Following the MR = MC rule, profits are maximized by selling 120 units of the product at $30 each.

Using the Five Steps to Maximizing Profit We can use the same five-step approach to analyzing equilibrium for a profit maximizing monopolist as we used for a perfectly competitive firm in the previous chapter. The main difference is that for a monopolist, the

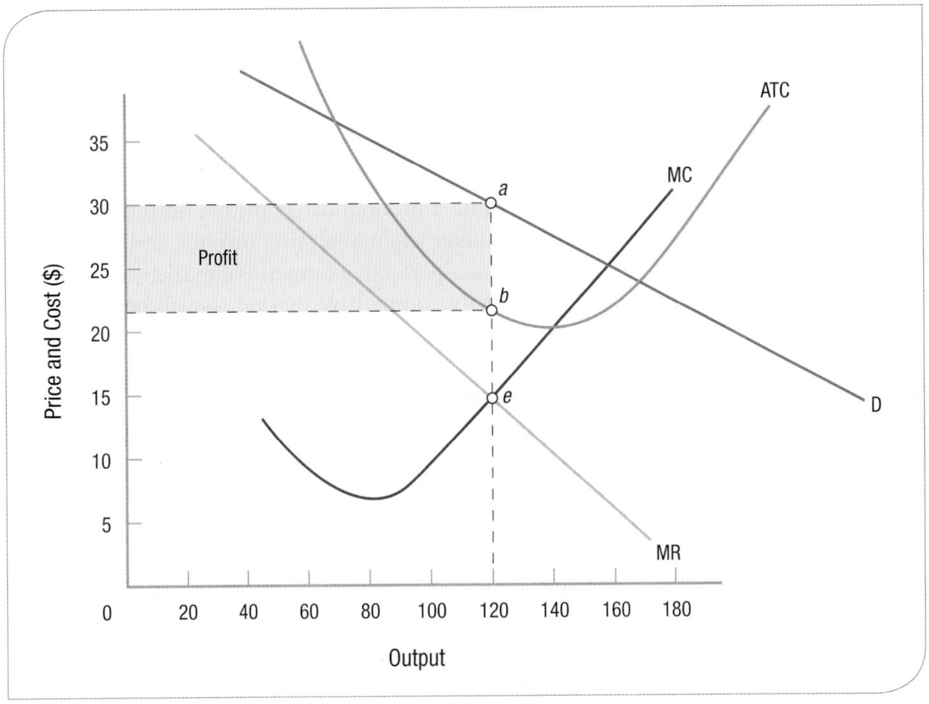

FIGURE 3

Monopolist Earning Economic Profits

Profit maximizing output is found for monopolists, as for competitive firms, at the point where MR = MC. In this figure, marginal revenue equals marginal cost at point *e,* where output is 120 units. These 120 units are sold for $30 each (point *a*). Profit is equal to average profit per unit times units sold: Profit = (P − ATC) × *Q* = ($30 − $22) × 120 = $8 × 120 = $960. The shaded area represents profit.

FIGURE 4

Five-Step Process to Determine a Monopolist's Optimal Output, Price, and Profit

The same five steps that were used to determine the profit maximizing output, price, and profit in a perfectly competitive market can be used in a monopoly market. The process begins by finding MR = MC, and then locating the optimal output and price, average total cost, and finally profit.

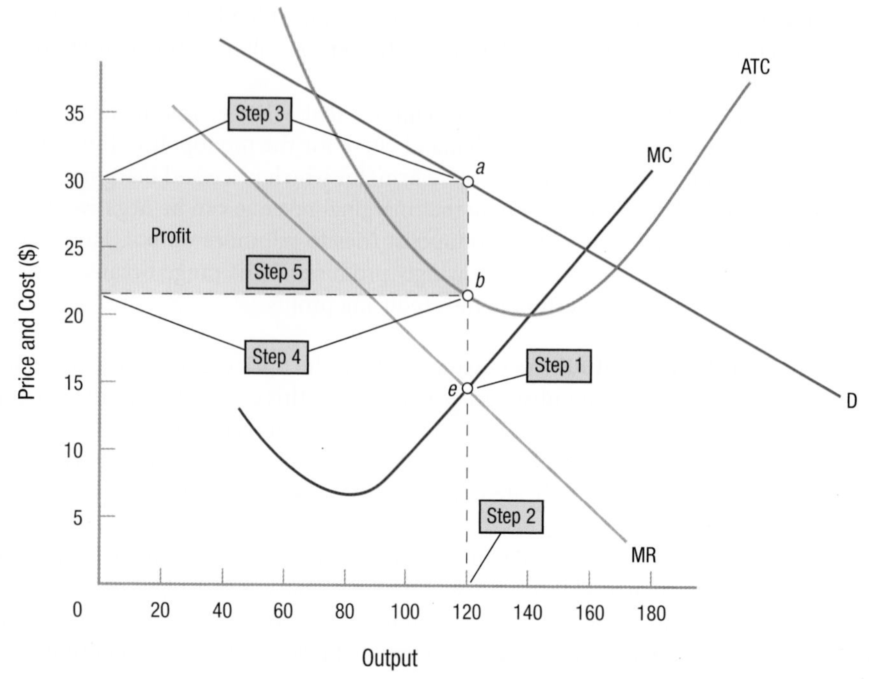

demand and marginal revenue curves are downward sloping, but that does not change the procedure, as shown in Figure 4.

Step 1: Find the point at which MR = MC.

Step 2: At that point, look down and determine the profit maximizing output on the horizontal axis.

Step 3: At this output, extend a vertical line upward to the demand curve and follow it to the left to determine the equilibrium price on the vertical axis.

Step 4: Using the same vertical line, find the point on the ATC curve to determine the average total cost per unit on the vertical axis.

Step 5: Find total profit by taking P – ATC, and multiply by output.

Using the five-step process to determine a monopolist's optimal output, price, and profit is a useful way to avoid making mistakes when analyzing revenue and cost curves. The same five steps can be used to analyze a perfectly competitive market, as shown in the previous chapter, and a monopolistically competitive market, as will be seen in the next chapter.

Monopoly Does Not Guarantee Economic Profits We have seen that competitive firms may or may not be profitable in the short run, but in the long run, they must earn at least normal profits to remain in business. Is the same true for monopolists? Yes. Consider the monopolist in Figure 5. This firm maximizes profits by producing where MR = MC (point *e*) and selling 80 units of output for a price of $25.

In this case, however, price ($25) is lower than average total cost ($28), and thus the monopolist suffers the loss of $240 (–$3 × 80 = –$240) indicated by the shaded area. Because price nonetheless exceeds average variable costs, the monopolist will minimize its losses in the short run by continuing to produce. But if price should fall below AVC, the monopolist, just like any competitive firm, will minimize its losses at its fixed costs by shutting down its plant. If these losses persist, the monopolist will exit the industry in the long run.

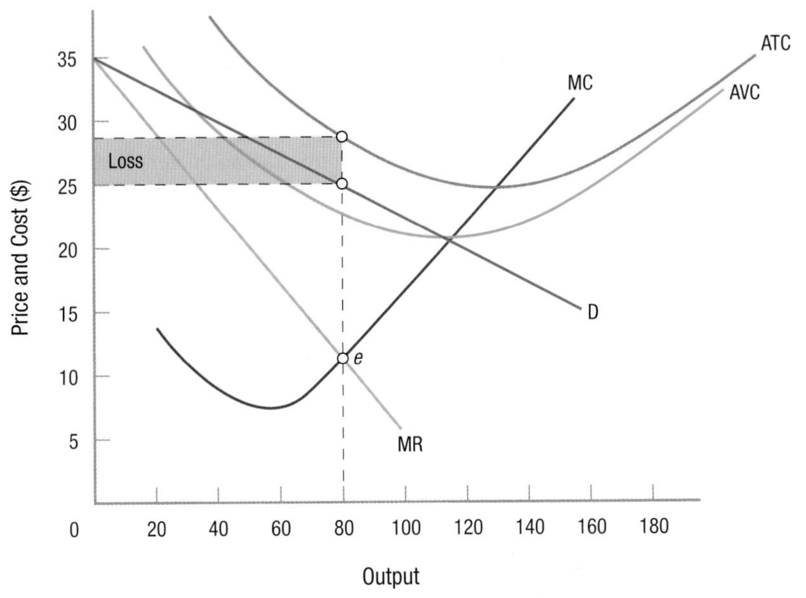

FIGURE 5

Monopolist Firm Making Economic Losses

Like perfectly competitive firms, monopolists may or may not be profitable in the short run, but in the long run, they must at least earn normal profits to remain in business. The monopolist shown here maximizes profits (minimizes losses) by producing at point *e*, selling 80 units of output at $25 each. Price is lower than average total cost, so the monopolist suffers the loss indicated by the shaded area. Because price still exceeds average variable cost (AVC), in the short run the monopolist will minimize its losses by continuing to produce.

This is an important point to remember. Being a monopolist does not automatically mean that there will be monopoly profits to haul in. Even monopolies face *some* cost and price pressures, and they face a demand curve, which ultimately limits their price making.

ISSUE

"But Wait . . . There's More!" The Success and Failure of Infomercials

"But wait . . . there's more!" is a familiar phrase to anyone who has watched an infomercial selling unique products that generally are not sold in retail stores. The size of the infomercial industry is significant and growing. In 2012, infomercials generated over $150 billion in sales. What do infomercials sell? Why are they successful and why do many infomercial products fail?

Unlike regular television commercials, which air for 30 seconds or one minute during daytime and primetime shows, infomercials typically are longer, ranging from one minute to 30 minutes or longer. The longest infomercials typically air in the middle of the night when television advertising rates are much lower.

Infomercials typically sell newly invented products that are not well known. Most infomercial products fit the monopoly market structure because although the product may have similarities to other products, infomercials advertise them as one-of-a-kind products. Examples include new types of knives, towels, beauty products, and workout equipment. However, because not all infomercials are able to convince prospective buyers of the distinction from existing products, many infomercial products fail.

Eric Chiang

Infomercials focus on the product characteristics that make the product completely different from anything on the market. Because the target market of infomercials is consumers who buy on impulse, even in the middle of the night, they use various techniques to increase sales. First, many infomercials show a high "retail" price (such as $100) and then reduce it rapidly until it becomes $19.99. Second, infomercials will offer something extra with the tag line "But wait . . . there's more!" Third, many infomercials show a fixed time period in which to buy, often within hours, even if the deadline is not actually enforced. And last, infomercials tend to offer return policies and often lifetime warranties (which is attractive but not that valuable if the company fails).

Some infomercials have become remarkably successful, with the product even becoming sold in stores. One example of a successful product that started from an infomercial is the Ped Egg, a cheese-grater-like device that removes dead skin from one's feet, which has sold over 50 million units and is now available through retailers such as Walgreens and Amazon.com.

CHECKPOINT

MONOPOLY MARKETS

- Monopoly is a market with no close substitutes, high barriers to entry, and one seller; the firm is the industry. Hence, monopolists are price makers.
- Monopolies gain maximum market power from control over an important input, economies of scale, or from government franchises, patents, and copyrights.
- For the monopolist, MR < P because the industry's demand is the monopolist's demand.
- Profit is maximized by producing that output where MR = MC and setting the price off the demand curve.
- Being a monopolist does not guarantee economic profits if demand is insufficient to cover costs.

QUESTIONS: When legendary country singer Dolly Parton goes on tour, sometimes she will perform in a relatively small (< 1,500 seats) venue when she could easily fill much larger arenas. Why would music artists intentionally choose a smaller venue? Wouldn't they make more money if they performed in a larger arena?

Answers to the Checkpoint questions can be found at the end of this chapter.

Comparing Monopoly and Competition

We have seen that perfectly competitive firms are price takers and produce as much as they can where MR = MC. In contrast, monopolies are price makers: They have the market power to set price and quantity, constrained only by their demand curve.

Would our economy be better off with more or fewer monopolies? This question almost answers itself. Who would want more monopolies—except the few lucky monopolists? The answer is, consumers are better off when competition is strong and monopolies are limited to certain industries. The reasons for this have to do with the losses associated with monopoly markets and market power. Losses directly attributed to monopolies include reduced output at higher prices, deadweight losses, rent-seeking behavior of monopolists, and x-inefficiency losses. But as we'll see later in this section, part (but not all) of these losses can be at least partially offset by some benefits that monopolies provide.

Higher Prices and Lower Output from Monopoly

Imagine for a moment that a competitive industry is monopolized, and the monopolist's marginal cost curve happens to be the same as the competitive industry's supply curve. Figure 6 illustrates such a scenario. In panel A, the competitive industry produces where supply equals demand, and thus where price and output are P_C and Q_C (point *a*). In panel B, monopoly price and output, as previously determined, are P_M and Q_M (point *b*).

Clearly, monopoly output is lower, and monopoly price is higher, than the corresponding values for competitive industries. How does this translate into the welfare of consumers and producers? Recall that we measure consumer surplus as the difference between market demand and price, as shown by the green areas in each panel. Producer surplus is the difference between price and market supply (marginal cost) as shown by the orange areas in each panel. The higher price charged by a monopolist results in part of the consumer surplus from Panel A being transferred into producer surplus in Panel B. Panel B shows a smaller consumer surplus and a larger producer surplus under a monopoly compared to a competitive market in Panel A. But this is not the end of the story.

Notice that at monopoly output Q_M, consumers value the Q_Mth unit of the product at P_M (point *b*), even though the cost to produce this last unit of output is considerably less (point *c*). This difference creates inefficiency because additional beneficial transactions could take place if output were expanded. The *deadweight loss,* otherwise known as the *welfare loss,* is comprised of consumer surplus and producer surplus that is lost from producing less than the efficient output. In panel B, deadweight loss from monopoly is

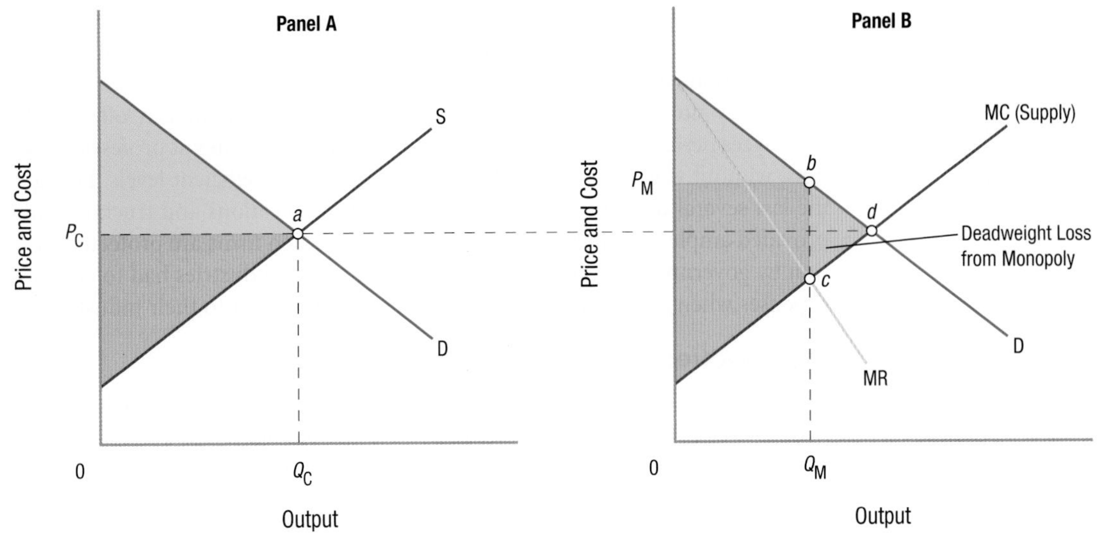

FIGURE 6

Monopoly Inefficiency

This figure shows what would happen if a competitive industry were monopolized and the new monopolist's marginal cost curve was the same as the competitive industry's supply curve. When the industry was competitive, it produced where S = D, and thus where price and output are P_c and Q_c (point *a* in panel A). Monopoly price and output, however, are P_M and Q_M (point *b* in panel B); output is lower and price is higher than the corresponding values for competitive firms. As a result, part of consumer surplus (shown in green) is transferred into producer surplus (shown in orange) in a monopoly, and in the process, inefficiency is created in the form of deadweight loss (shaded area *bcd*).

shown as the shaded area *bcd*. This area represents the deadweight loss to society from a monopoly market.

Even though deadweight loss derives partly from lost producer surplus, monopoly firms willingly forgo this portion of producer surplus in order to transfer a larger portion of consumer surplus into producer surplus (the orange rectangular area above the P_c line in Panel B). Therefore, monopoly firms use their market power to gain producer surplus at the expense of consumers and create inefficiency in the form of deadweight loss. But this is not the only source of inefficiency caused by firms with complete market power.

Rent Seeking and X-Inefficiency

Monopolies earn economic profits by producing less and charging more than competitive firms. Although these actions generate deadweight loss, monopolists are protective of the profits they earn. If barriers to entry to the market were eased, economic profit would evaporate as price falls, as it does in competitive markets. How, then, can a monopolist protect itself from potential competition? One way is to spend resources that could have been used to expand its production on efforts to protect its monopoly position.

Economists call this behavior **rent seeking**—behavior directed toward avoiding competition. Firms hire lawyers and other professionals to lobby governments, extend patents, and engage in a host of other activities intended solely to protect their monopoly position. For example, in order to pick up passengers on the street, taxis in New York City require a medallion registered with the Taxi and Limousine Commission; restricting the number of medallions drives up their price and gives medallion holders a further incentive to restrict the number of new medallions issued, by lobbying and other means. Many industries spend significant resources lobbying Congress for tariff protection to reduce foreign competition. All these activities are inefficient, in that they use resources and shift income

rent seeking Resources expended to protect a monopoly position. These are used for such activities as lobbying, extending patents, and restricting the number of licenses permitted.

from one group to another without producing a useful good or service. Rent seeking thus represents an added loss to society from monopoly.

x-inefficiency Protected from competitive pressures, monopolies do not have to act efficiently. Spending on corporate jets, travel, and other perks of business represents x-inefficiency.

Another area in which society might lose from monopolies is called **x-inefficiency.** Some economists suggest that because monopolies are protected from competitive pressures, they do not have to operate efficiently. Management can offer itself and their employees perks, such as elaborate corporate retreats or suites at professional sports stadiums, without worrying about whether costs are kept at efficient levels. Deregulation over the last several decades, particularly in the communications and trucking industries, has provided ample evidence of inefficiencies arising when firms are protected from competition by government regulations. Many firms in these industries had to cut back on lavish expenses when competitive pressures were reintroduced into their industries.

Monopolies and Innovation

Much of our analysis of monopolies has focused on the inefficiencies created and the detrimental effects on consumers. However, monopolies do create some benefits that are shared among all of society. For example, monopolies provide new products, technologies, and medical breakthroughs that benefit many consumers. The incentives to earn monopoly profits created by patents and copyrights encourage firms to invest in developing these new products. Otherwise, what firm would be willing to spend hundreds of millions of dollars inventing a product only to have it copied and sold by other firms?

Similarly, much of the entertainment industry, including music, television shows, books, and movies would not exist to such a great extent if copyrights did not provide singers, authors, and other media creators the monetary incentive to create such products for our enjoyment. Therefore, the ability to achieve market power through innovation provides an incentive to individuals and firms to invest time and money to create new products and other creative works that could generate substantial profits over time.

Benefits Versus Costs of Monopolies

Are there any other benefits to monopolies aside from innovation? The answer to this question is, "Possibly yes, though generally no." If the economies of scale associated with an industry are so large that many small competitors would face substantially higher marginal costs than a monopolist, a monopolist would produce and sell more output at a lower price than could competitive firms. This is the case of natural monopolies, and the justification for why monopolies are allowed to exist in industries such as the provision of water or electricity in many communities.

Imagine what might happen if a storm knocks out power to your neighborhood, and instead of one electric company restoring power to your street, each household needed to wait for its specific electricity provider to show up.

Larger firms, moreover, can allocate more resources to research and development than smaller firms, and the possibility of economic profits may be the incentive monopolists require to invest.

Still, economists tend to doubt that monopolies are beneficial enough to outweigh their disadvantages.

In actuality, pure monopolies are rare, in part because of public policy and antitrust laws—more about this later in this chapter—and in part because rapidly changing technologies limit most monopolies to short-run economic profits—witness the battle between Facebook and Google+ for domination of social media services, and Sony, Amazon.com, Apple, and several other firms to dominate the eBook market. Even so, firms seek to increase their market power by trying to become monopolies and gain the ability to influence price.

We have seen what monopolies are and how they arise. We also saw why a monopolist produces less than the socially optimal quantity at a higher than socially necessary price, and witnessed how monopoly compares unfavorably to the competitive model. Furthermore, we looked at an expensive drawback of monopolies: the amount of resources wasted in maintaining a monopolist's position. In the next section, we relax the assumption of one price, revealing what monopolies are always trying to do.

Rachel Epstein/The Image Works

Although often criticized for inefficient operations, the U.S. Postal Service still offers the ability to send a letter to any address in the country, including far places such as Hawaii, Alaska, or Guam, for the price of a single stamp.

CHECKPOINT

COMPARING MONOPOLY AND COMPETITION

- Monopoly output is lower and price is higher when compared to competition, resulting in a deadweight loss.
- Monopolies are subject to rent-seeking behavior directed toward avoiding competition (lobbying and other activities to extend the monopoly).
- Because monopolies are protected from competitive pressures, they often engage in x-inefficiency behavior—extending perks to management and other inefficient activities.
- Monopolies can provide benefits in the form of economies of scale and incentives to innovate. However, these benefits are outweighed by the costs resulting from the lack of competition.

QUESTIONS: Google has over 70% of the search business on the Internet and generates a great deal of advertising revenue. Microsoft has 85% of the operating system business, 55% of the Internet browsers in use, and a growing search engine market. In late 2012, Microsoft accused Google of engaging in dishonest searches in the online shopping market (which Google denied) by listing search results based on how much merchants are willing to pay in ads. Microsoft even launched a Web site and campaign called "Scroogled" whose main purpose was to attack Google. Do these actions by Microsoft feel a little like monopolistic rent-seeking? Should the government step in, or is this just competition between giants?

Answers to the Checkpoint questions can be found at the end of this chapter.

Price Discrimination

When firms have some market power, they will try to charge different customers different prices for the same product. For example, senior citizens might pay less for a movie ticket than you do. This is called **price discrimination** and it is used to increase the firm's profits by converting part or all of consumer surplus into producer surplus. If a product costs $100 in a competitive market but you are willing to pay $150, a monopolist wants to grab as much of your $50 consumer surplus as possible.

price discrimination Charging different consumer groups different prices for the same product.

Remember that unlike monopolies, competitive firms cannot price discriminate because they get their prices from the market (they are price takers). Several conditions are required for successful price discrimination:

- Sellers must have some market power.
- Sellers must be able to separate the market into different consumer groups based on their elasticities of demand.
- Sellers must be able to prevent arbitrage; that is, it must be able to keep low-price buyers from reselling to higher-price buyers.

There are three major types of price discrimination. The first is known as **perfect (first-degree) price discrimination.** It involves charging each customer the *maximum price* each is willing to pay. Because firms cannot always determine individual willingness-to-pay, other forms of price discrimination exist. **Second-degree price discrimination** involves charging different customers different prices based on the *quantities* of the product they purchase. The final and most common form of price discrimination is **third-degree price discrimination,** which occurs when firms *charge different groups of people different prices.* This is an everyday occurrence with airline, bus, and movie theater tickets.

perfect (first-degree) price discrimination Charging each customer the maximum price each is willing to pay, thereby expropriating all consumer surplus.

second-degree price discrimination Charging different customers different prices based on the quantities of the product they purchase.

third-degree price discrimination Charging different groups of people different prices based on varying elasticities of demand.

Perfect (First-Degree) Price Discrimination

When perfect price discrimination can be employed, a firm will charge each customer the maximum price each is willing to pay. This type of price discrimination is perhaps best exemplified by an online auction, where buyers often bid up the price of a good to their maximum willingness to pay. Figure 7 on the next page portrays such a scenario for a market with constant cost conditions (assumed for simplicity) and where one unit of the good

FIGURE 7

Perfect Price Discrimination

With perfect price discrimination, firms charge each customer the maximum price each is willing to pay in order to extract all consumer surplus. Thus, every point on the demand curve in this figure represents a price. The first few customers—those who value the product most—are charged a high price. The next customers are charged a slightly lower price, and so on, until the last unit is sold for P_C (point *b*). As a result, a perfectly discriminating monopolist earns profits represented by the shaded area P_CP_Tb. This is considerably more profit than the monopolist would earn by selling Q_M units at price P_M, represented by area P_CP_Mac.

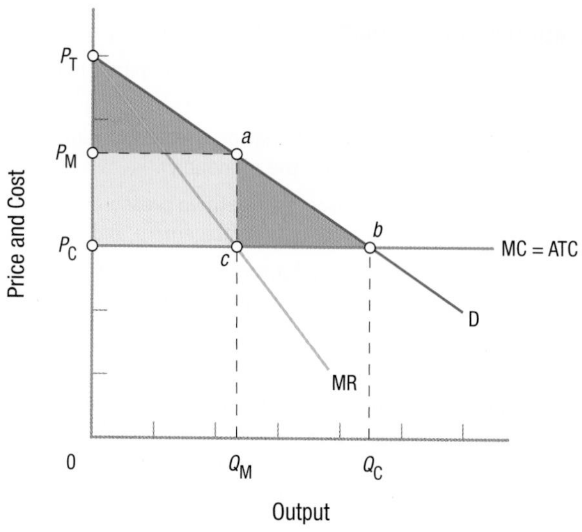

is offered to the highest bidder each day. Every point on the demand curve represents a price. The first few customers—those who value the product the most—are charged a high price. The next customers are charged slightly lower prices, the Q_Mth customer is charged P_M (point *a*), and so on, until the last unit is sold to the Q_Cth customer for P_C (point *b*). As a result, a perfectly discriminating monopolist earns profits equal to the shaded area P_CP_Tb.

Figure 7 shows why firms would want to price discriminate. Typical monopoly profits in this case, assuming the monopolist sells Q_M units at price P_M, would be the rectangle area P_CP_Mac (the lighter shaded area). This area is considerably smaller than the triangle P_CP_Tb, earned by the perfectly price discriminating monopolist. That is why price discrimination exists—it is profitable. Note also that the *last* unit of the product sold by this monopolist is priced at P_C, the competitive price. In this limited sense, then, the monopolist who can perfectly price discriminate is as efficient as a competitive firm. Notice that perfectly price discriminating monopolists manage to expropriate the entire consumer surplus.

Second-Degree Price Discrimination

Second-degree price discrimination involves charging consumers different prices for different blocks of consumption. For example, by purchasing items in bulk (such as a pack of six tubes of toothpaste) at Costco or Sam's Club, the cost per unit is typically less than buying just one tube at the local store. Similarly, producers of electric, gas, and water utilities often incorporate block pricing. You pay one rate for the first so many kilowatt-hours of electricity and a lower rate for more, and so on.

The rationale for second-degree price discrimination is twofold. First, the cost of selling many units of a good to one customer is often less than that of selling a single unit to many customers due to overhead costs such as cashiers and accounting expenses. Second, if stores convince consumers to buy more than they had intended by offering discounts, profits can be earned as long as the discounted price exceeds marginal cost.

An illustration of second-degree price discrimination is shown in Figure 8 using the block pricing scheme example.

For the first Q_0 units of the product, consumers are charged P_0; between Q_0 and Q_1, the price falls to P_1; and after that, the price is reduced to P_C. This results in profit to the firm equal to the shaded area. The shaded profit area for the price discriminating monopolist is greater than that of the monopolist charging just one price P_M (area P_CP_Mac). The most common price discrimination scheme, however, is third-degree, in which *groups* of consumers are charged different prices.

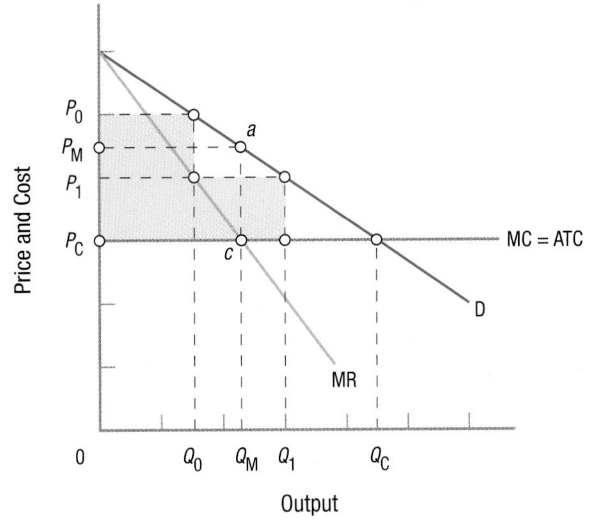

FIGURE 8

Second-Degree Price Discrimination

Second-degree price discrimination involves charging different customers different prices based on the quantities of the product they purchase. A single-price monopolist would earn economic profits equal to P_CP_Mac, but by charging three different prices—P_0, P_1, and P_C—profits increase, as shown by comparing the shaded area with area P_CP_Mac.

Third-Degree Price Discrimination

Third-degree, or imperfect, price discrimination involves charging different groups of people different prices. An obvious example would be the various fares charged for airline flights. Business travelers have much lower elasticities of demand for flights than do vacationers, therefore airlines place all sorts of restrictions on their tickets to separate people into distinct categories. Purchasing a ticket several weeks in advance, for instance—which vacationers can usually do, but businesspeople may not be able to—often results in a significantly lower fare. Arbitrage (the ability of low-price buyers to sell to higher-price buyers) is prevented, meanwhile, by rules stipulating that passengers can only travel on tickets purchased in their name. Other examples of third-degree price discrimination include different ticket prices for children, adults, and seniors at movie theaters; student discounts for many services; and even ladies' night at clubs.

Firms engage in third-degree price discrimination in order to increase their producer surplus from serving more customers. For example, if a software firm is restricted to offering their product at one price, it would choose the profit maximizing monopoly price, which means customers with lower willingness-to-pay would be priced out of a purchase. However, by offering a discounted price to these customers (and only these customers who otherwise would not have made a purchase), firms can gain more producer surplus as long as the discounted price exceeds the marginal cost of providing the extra units.

Third-degree price discrimination is illustrated in Figure 9 on the next page. The two demand curves, D_0 and D_1, represent two segments of a market with different demand elasticities. The less elastic market, D_1, is offered price P_1. This is higher than price P_0 offered to the more elastic market, D_0. Profits are maximized for both markets. For market D_0, profits are P_CP_0bc, and for less elastic market D_1, they are P_CP_1ad. Like the perfectly discriminating monopolist, the third-degree price-discriminating monopolist earns profits that exceed those that would come from a normal one-price policy.

We can look at price discrimination in an intuitive way by focusing on a restaurant. Most dinner customers frequent the restaurant after 6:30 P.M. However, the restaurant is still open from 4:30 to 6:30 P.M. and incurs costs (if workers start their shifts before the 6:30 rush). It is in the restaurant's interest to offer early bird specials, discounting dinners purchased before 6:30, as long as this policy attracts new customers and does not pull in too many of its later-appearing regular diners. In this way, the restaurant

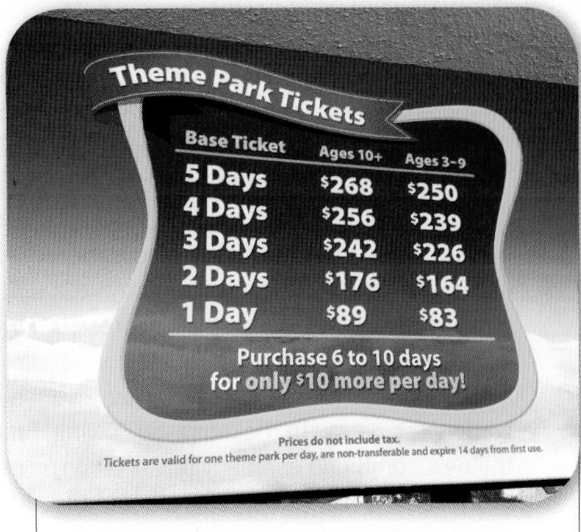

Eric Chiang

Theme park pricing shows both second-degree price discrimination (the more days you buy, the lower the average price per day) and third-degree price discrimination (lower prices for guests under age 10).

FIGURE 9

Third-Degree Price Discrimination

This figure illustrates third-degree price discrimination, in which firms segment markets based on consumers' willingness-to-pay in order to maximize producer surplus. The two demand curves, D_0 and D_1, represent two segments of a market with different demand elasticities. The less elastic market, D_1, is offered price P_1, which is higher than price P_0, offered to the more elastic market, D_0, thus maximizing the profits in both markets.

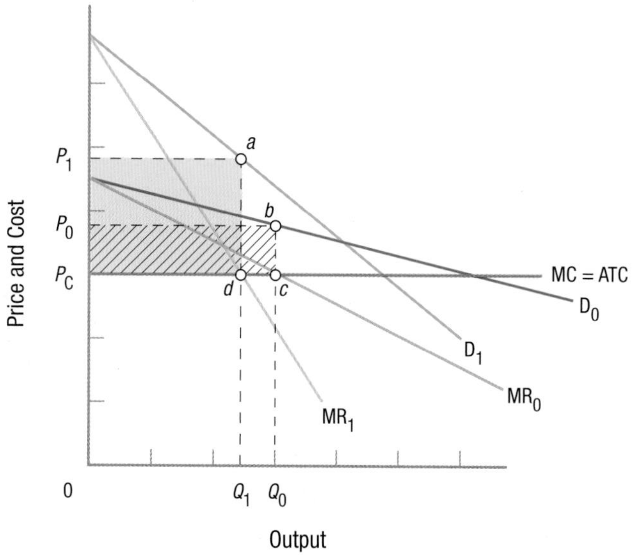

generates profits from two separate groups, while charging two separate prices. As long as the restaurant has some market power—it can offer these two prices without driving its regular customers from higher-priced meals to lower-priced meals—it makes sense for it to act this way. Therefore, we can conclude that firms with market power will always try to price discriminate.

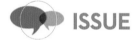

ISSUE

Is Flexible Ticket Pricing the New Form of Price Discrimination?

Ticketmaster has long held market power in the entertainment and sports ticket-selling industry. Although Ticketmaster faces competition from other ticket sellers, its market power stems from the exclusivity contracts it establishes with concert promoters, artists, and sports teams.

When an agreement is made with Ticketmaster, it becomes the only site through which consumers can purchase tickets other than the ticket resale market. This gives ticket sellers and the entertainers and shows they represent considerable market power to set prices.

In early 2010, concert promoter Live Nation merged with Ticketmaster, giving the new combined company (Live Nation) even more market power. This allowed the new company to implement new strategies to correct problems with their original pricing model. Specifically, Ticketmaster typically offered several ticket tiers with different prices based on seating location. These prices, however, often are printed on the tickets and do not change.

However, setting prices too low results in a quick sellout, leading to a resale market in which tickets initially sold at one price are resold at much higher prices, with the profits going to the reseller instead of Ticketmaster. Setting prices too high, on the other hand, leaves many tickets unsold and results in many tickets being given away in radio promotions and other deals.

In 2011, Live Nation announced a new flexible pricing model (to be implemented in phases) that has been successfully used in the airline industry. With flexible pricing, concert tickets do not have a fixed price. Instead, ticket prices are set and changed based on demand—if tickets sell too fast, prices would rise; if tickets sell too slowly, prices would fall. This form of price discrimination allows ticket sellers to reap more consumer surplus that otherwise might go to the resale market. This new approach to ticket sales is another example of how firms use strategies to maximize their market power.

ANDREW GOMBERT/epa/Corbis

In all three types of price discrimination, monopoly firms use their market power to increase their producer surplus. Although part of this increase in producer surplus comes from consumers in the form of higher prices, the rest comes from the reduction in deadweight loss. Unlike a single-price monopolist, efficiency is improved in multiple-price scenarios because more output is being produced, allowing more consumers to purchase the good. Still, all forms of monopoly pricing (single-price or multiple-price through price discrimination) create concerns about the welfare of consumers. Therefore, regulations and rules are sometimes used to reduce the market power firms exert. We turn to these topics in the next section.

CHECKPOINT

PRICE DISCRIMINATION

- Firms with market power price discriminate to increase profits.
- To price discriminate, firms must have some market power (control over price) and must be able to separate the market into different consumer groups based on their elasticity of demand, and firms (sellers) must be able to prevent arbitrage.
- With perfect price discrimination the firm can charge each customer a different price and expropriate the entire consumer surplus for itself.
- Second-degree price discrimination involves charging customers different prices for different quantities of the product.
- Third-degree price discrimination (the most common) involves charging different groups of people different prices.
- Price discrimination may lead to higher prices for some consumers, but it also improves efficiency by allowing more consumers to purchase the good, reducing deadweight loss.

QUESTIONS: Researchers at Yale University and the University of California, Berkeley, found that minorities and women pay about $500 more on average for a car than white men when bargaining directly with car dealers. However, when minorities and women used online auto retailers such as Autobytel.com to purchase a car, the price discrimination disappeared. Is this price discrimination the same as that discussed in this section? Why or why not?

Answers to the Checkpoint questions can be found at the end of this chapter.

Regulation and Antitrust

We have seen that monopolies have the ability to raise prices and restrict quantities, putting them at the other end of the spectrum from the competitive market price-taker ideal. Thus, monopolies are price makers. Also, we have just seen that firms use their market power to price discriminate, attempting to achieve as much producer surplus as they can even if it comes by way of reducing consumer surplus. In an attempt to mitigate the maximum market power of monopolies, government has used two approaches: regulation and antitrust.

Regulating the Natural Monopolist

As we saw when we discussed barriers to entry, there are some instances when natural monopolies occur. A **natural monopoly** exists when economies of scale are so large that the minimum efficient scale of operation is roughly equal to market demand. In this case, efficient production can only be accomplished if the industry lies in the hands of one firm—a monopolist. Public utilities and water departments are examples.

natural monopoly An industry exhibiting large economies of scale such that the minimum efficient scale of operations is roughly equal to market demand.

How can policymakers prevent natural monopolists from abusing their positions of market dominance? There are various approaches to dealing with natural monopolies: (1) They can be publicly owned, (2) they can be privately owned but subjected to price and quantity constraints, or (3) their right to operate could be auctioned to the firm agreeing to the most competitive price and quantity conditions.

A market representing a natural monopoly is shown in Figure 10. Notice that the average cost and marginal cost curves decline continually because of large economies of scale.

If the monopolist were a purely private firm, it would produce only output Q_M and sell this for price P_M (point *a*). Accordingly, the monopolist would earn economic or monopoly profits, and consumers would be harmed, receiving a lower output at a higher price. This is the major argument for regulation.

marginal cost pricing rule Regulators would prefer to have natural monopolists price where P = MC, but this would result in losses (long term) because ATC > MC. Thus, regulators often must use an average cost pricing rule.

Marginal Cost Pricing Rule Ideally, regulators would like to invoke the P = MC rule of competitive markets and force the firm to sell Q_C units for a price of P_C. This is the **marginal cost pricing rule** and would be the optimal resource allocation solution. Yet, because price P_C is below the average total cost of production for output Q_C, this would force the firm to sustain losses of *cd* per unit, ultimately driving it out of business. The public sector could subsidize the firm by an amount equal to area P_CC_Cdc; this subsidy allows the firm to supply the socially optimal output at the socially optimal price, while earning a normal return. This approach has not been used often in the United States. Amtrak, with its history of heavy subsidies for maintaining rail service, may be the one major exception.

average cost pricing rule Requires a regulated monopolist to produce and sell output where price equals average total cost. This permits the regulated monopolist to earn a normal return on investment over the long term and therefore remain in business.

Average Cost Pricing Rule The more common approach to regulation in the United States has been to insist on an **average cost pricing rule.** Such a rule requires that the monopolist produce and sell output where price equals average total costs. This is illustrated by point *b* in Figure 10, where the demand curve intersects the ATC curve and the firm produces output Q_R and sells it for price P_R. The result is that the firm earns a normal return. Consumers do lose something, in that they must pay a higher price for less output than they would under ideal competitive conditions. Still, the normal profits keep the firm in business, and the losses to consumers are significantly less than if the firm were left unregulated.

FIGURE 10

Regulating a Natural Monopoly

A natural monopoly exists when economies of scale are so large that the minimum efficient scale of operation is roughly equal to market demand. In this case, efficient production can only be accomplished if the industry lies in the hands of one firm—a monopolist. Yet, if the monopolist is a purely private firm, it will produce only output Q_M, selling it for price P_M (point *a*). This is the principal rationale for regulating natural monopolies to produce output Q_R for a price of P_R (point *b*).

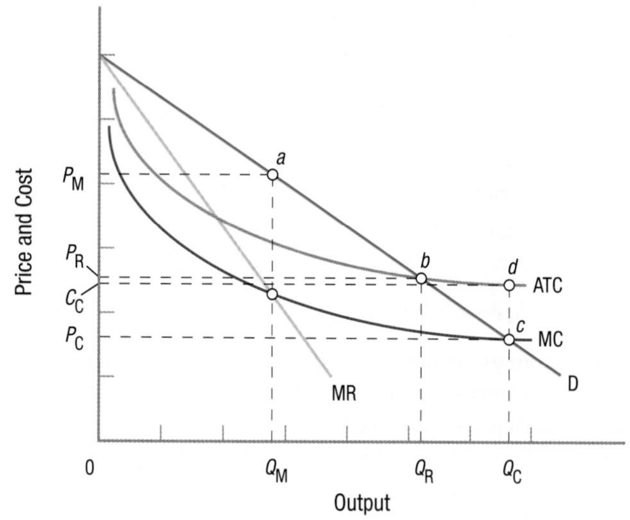

Regulation in Practice America has a long history of public utility regulation. For most of this history, regulation has been accepted as the lesser of two evils. Monopolists have long been viewed with distrust, but regulators have just as often been portrayed as incompetent and ineffectual, if not lapdogs of the industries they regulate.[1] Although this characterization is probably unfair, a number of economists, including Nobel Prize–laureate George Stigler, viewed regulation with skepticism and proposed changes on improving the efficiency of regulation.

[1] See George Stigler, "The Theory of Economic Regulation," *Bell Journal of Economics,* 1971, pp. 3–21.

Regulating a large enterprise always presents immense difficulties and tradeoffs. For one thing, finding a point like *b* in Figure 10 is difficult in practice, given that estimating demand and cost curves is an inexact science, at best, and markets are always changing. In practice, regulators must often turn to *rate of return* or *price cap* regulation.

Rate of return regulation allows a firm to price its product in such a way that it can earn a normal return on capital invested. This leads to added regulations about the acceptable items that can be included in costs and capital expenditures. Can the country club memberships of top executives be counted as capital investments? Predictably, firms always want to include more expenses as legitimate business expenses, and regulators want to include fewer. Regulatory commissions and regulated firms often have large staffs to deal with such issues, and protracted court battles are not uncommon.

Alternatively, regulators can impose **price caps** on regulated firms, which place maximum limits on the prices firms can charge for products. These caps can be adjusted in response to changing cost conditions, including changes in labor costs, productivity, technology, and raw material prices. When a large part of a regulated firm's output is not self-produced but purchased on the open market, price caps can have disastrous results. This was seen in the California energy market, when wholesale prices for energy went through the roof, but price caps prevented private utilities from raising the retail price of electricity. Several firms had to file for bankruptcy.

NOBEL PRIZE
GEORGE STIGLER (1911–1991)

Few modern economists have broken ground in so many different areas as George Stigler, described by some admirers as the "ultimate empirical economist." His 1982 Nobel Prize cited seminal work in industrial structure, the functioning of markets, and the causes and effects of public regulation.

Born in 1911 in the Seattle suburb of Renton, Washington, Stigler attended graduate school at the University of Chicago with fellow students and eventual Nobel Prize winners Milton Friedman and Paul Samuelson. Stigler later became a professor at the University of Chicago where he stayed until his death in 1991.

Exploring the relationship between size and efficiency led him to the "Darwinian" conclusion that by observing competition in an industry, he could determine the most efficient sizes for firms, a method he called "the survivor technique." In the 1960s, Stigler studied the impacts of government regulation on the economy with skepticism, arguing that government interventions were often designed to optimize market conditions for producers instead of protecting the public interest. This work opened up a new field known as "regulation economics" and kindled greater interest in the relationship between law and economics.

Stigler considered his work on information theory his greatest contribution to economics. Conventional wisdom suggested that prices for perfectly competitive industries should be uniform, but in the real world, prices often varied. His research suggested that the variation could be explained by the costs of gathering and diffusing information about goods and prices. The Internet was supposed to bring a convergence of prices for nearly every product because the Internet's low information costs and competition would force firms to quickly meet the lowest seller's price. The fact that there are still widely varying prices for many products suggests that Stigler's insights are still important.

Today, the pace of technological change is so rapid that regulation has lost some of its earlier luster and is not used as often. Rather than regulate the few natural monopolies that do arise, government has sought to prevent monopolies and monopolistic practices from arising at all—what is called antitrust policy.

Antitrust Policy

Rather than regulatory tinkering, governments have tried a broader approach to deal with monopolies and their market power. The goal of **antitrust law** is to preserve competition and prevent monopolies with their maximum market power from arising in the first place.

The origin of antitrust policy came in the late 1800s, when many large trusts were established, which brought many firms under one organizational structure allowing them to act as monopolists. Massive wealth accumulations by such "robber barons" as John D. Rockefeller (Standard Oil) and Jay Gould (railroads and stock manipulation) sparked resentment and fear against trusts and the growing inequity of income and wealth. Trusts had become so powerful—and so hated—that Congress passed the first antitrust act, the Sherman Act, in 1890. Antitrust laws and policies thus had their origins in trust-busting activity. Many of these laws still are in existence today with their primary role of preventing the inefficiencies associated with monopoly behavior.

rate of return regulation Permits product pricing that allows the firm to earn a normal return on capital invested in the firm.

price caps Maximum price at which a regulated firm can sell its product. They are often flexible enough to allow for changing cost conditions.

antitrust law Laws designed to maintain competition and prevent monopolies from developing.

The Major Antitrust Laws

Several major statutes form the core of the country's antitrust laws. The most important provisions of these laws (as amended) are described in Table 1.

TABLE 1 **Major Antitrust Laws**

I. The Sherman Act (1890)
  A. Activity in "restraint of trade" is made a felony.
  B. Monopolization or attempt to monopolize is made a felony.
  C. Conviction in either carries a fine of up to $10,000,000 for corporations and $350,000 for individuals, and/or a prison sentence of up to 3 years.
  D. Congress purposefully left "restraint of trade" and "monopolization" undefined, thus requiring the courts to flesh them out.

II. The Clayton Act (1914)
  A. Unlawful to price discriminate if such discrimination substantially lessons competition. This rule was strengthened by the Robinson-Patman Act in 1936, although today the federal government rarely enforces its provisions, viewing them as outdated.
  B. Companies cannot acquire all or part of another where the effect may be to substantially lessen competition or create a monopoly. This rule was strengthened by the 1950 Celler-Kefauver Act by preventing mergers via asset acquisition and setting up elaborate premerger notification requirements for mergers exceeding a certain size.

III. The Federal Trade Commission Act (1914)
  A. Unfair methods of competition and deceptive acts are made illegal.
  B. Established an independent regulatory body, the Federal Trade Commission (FTC).

This Act is the centerpiece of federal consumer protection. The Supreme Court has given the FTC the power to enforce antitrust laws, except the Sherman Act.

The intensity of antitrust enforcement has varied over the past century, from an early focus on monopolies, then on mergers, and more recently on price fixing—conspiracies by firms to agree on industry prices to suppress or eliminate competition. Although price-fixing cases have been prominent, it is merger policy developed in the 1950s that has really stood the test of time. Economists and judges generally agree that the reason for antitrust enforcement is to prevent the inefficiencies associated with significant market power. Premerger notification for approval or challenge by the Department of Justice is designed to prevent mergers that have a reasonable likelihood of creating market power. This is easier said than done.

Defining the Relevant Market and Market Power

The first problem involves defining market power. What is the relevant product market? Some markets can be severely limited geographically, such as concrete, with its extremely high transport costs, and dry cleaning, limited by the unwillingness of consumers to travel far for this service. Other markets are national in scope, like airlines, breakfast cereals, and electronics. Still others extend beyond the borders of a country, with the forces of global competition increasingly reducing domestic market power.

The second problem is determining the proper measuring device of market power. As an industry moves from competition to monopoly, pricing power rises from zero to total. One of the challenges economists have faced is developing one measure that accurately reflects market power or concentration for all these market structures.

Industries that become more concentrated increase the losses to society. Therefore, any measure of concentration should accurately reflect the ability of firms to increase prices above that point which would prevail under competitive conditions.

Concentration Ratios The most widely used measure of industry concentration is the **concentration ratio.** The n-firm concentration ratio is the share of industry sales accounted for by the industry's n largest firms. Typically, four- and eight-firm concentration ratios (CR-4 and CR-8) are reported.

concentration ratio The share of industry shipments or sales accounted for by the top four or eight firms.

Although useful in giving a quick snapshot of an industry, concentration ratios express only one piece of the market power distribution picture: the market share enjoyed by the industry's four or eight largest firms. Table 2 shows the market shares of the four largest firms in two different industries. Industry 1 contains a dominant firm with 65% of the market, followed by a bunch of smaller firms. Industry 2 consists of four fairly equal-sized firms, followed by a bunch of smaller firms. In both industries, however, the four-firm concentration ratio is 85; that is, the top four firms control 85% of industry sales. But do the two industries exhibit the same level of monopoly power? Hardly! The second industry, whose top four firms are roughly equal in size, would be expected to be more competitive than the first, in which 65% of the market is controlled by one firm.

Four-firm Concentration Ratio — TABLE 2

	Industry 1	Industry 2
Firm 1's market share	65%	25%
Firm 2's market share	10%	20%
Firm 3's market share	5%	20%
Firm 4's market share	5%	20%
All other firms' market share combined	15%	15%
Four-firm concentration ratio	**85**	**85**

Industry 1 is dominated by a large firm with 65% of market share, whereas Industry 2 contains four fairly equal-sized firms, with smaller firms making up the rest of both industries. The CR-4 is the same in both industries, although Industry 2 would be expected to be much more competitive.

Without more information about each industry, concentration ratios are not overly informative, except to point out extreme contrasts. If one industry's four-firm concentration ratio is 85, for instance, and another's is 15, the first industry has considerably more monopoly power than the second.

Economists and antitrust enforcers, however, need finer distinctions than concentration ratios permit. For this reason, the profession has developed the Herfindahl-Hirschman index.

Herfindahl-Hirschman Index The **Herfindahl-Hirschman index (HHI)** is the principal measure of concentration used by the Department of Justice to evaluate mergers and judge monopoly power. The HHI is defined by the equation:

Herfindahl-Hirschman index (HHI) A way of measuring industry concentration, equal to the sum of the squares of market shares for all firms in the industry.

$$HHI = (S_1)^2 + (S_2)^2 + (S_3)^2 + \ldots + (S_n)^2,$$

where $S_1, S_2, \ldots S_n$ are the percentage market shares of each firm in the industry. Thus, the HHI is the sum of the squares of each market share. In a five-firm industry, for instance, in which each firm enjoys a 20% market share, the HHI is

$$\begin{aligned} HHI &= 20^2 + 20^2 + 20^2 + 20^2 + 20^2 \\ &= 400 + 400 + 400 + 400 + 400 \\ &= 2{,}000 \end{aligned}$$

The HHI ranges from roughly zero (a huge number of small firms) to 10,000 (a one-firm monopoly: $100^2 = 10{,}000$). By squaring market shares, the HHI gives greater weight to those firms with large market shares. Thus, a five-firm industry with market shares equal to 65, 15, 10, 5, and 5 would have an HHI equal to

$$\begin{aligned} HHI &= 65^2 + 15^2 + 10^2 + 5^2 + 5^2 \\ &= 4{,}225 + 225 + 100 + 25 + 25 \\ &= 4{,}600 \end{aligned}$$

The HHI is consistent with our intuitive notion of market power. It seems clear that an industry with several competitors of roughly equal size will be more competitive than an industry in which one firm controls a substantial share of the market.

Applying the HHI The Hart-Scott-Rodino Act (1976) requires prenotification of large proposed mergers to the FTC and the antitrust division of the Department of Justice. Prenotification gives federal agencies a chance to review proposed mergers for anticompetitive impacts. This approach prevents some mergers from taking place that would ultimately have to be challenged by Sherman Act litigation, a far more costly alternative for the government and for the firms involved.

The Department of Justice and the FTC in 2010 issued revised merger guidelines based on the HHI. These guidelines classify industries as follows:

- HHI < 1,500: Industry is not concentrated.
- 1,500 < HHI < 2,500: Industry is moderately concentrated.
- HHI > 2,500: Industry is highly concentrated.

Mergers where the resulting HHI is below 1,000 will often be approved. Mergers with postmerger HHIs between 1,000 and 1,800 will be closely evaluated; they are often challenged if the proposed merger raises the HHI by 100 points or more. When the HHI for the industry exceeds 1,800, a postmerger rise in the HHI of 50 points is enough to spark a challenge.

These guidelines have worked well, giving businesses a good idea of when the government will challenge mergers. Most mergers are rapidly approved; the remainder often require only minor adjustments or more information to satisfy government agencies. In the end, only a few proposed mergers are seriously challenged.

Contestable Markets

contestable markets Markets that look monopolistic but where entry costs are so low that the sheer threat of entry keeps prices low.

Sometimes what looks like a monopolist does not act like a monopolist. Markets that are contestable fit this description. **Contestable markets** are those markets with entry costs so low that the sheer threat of entry keeps prices in contestable markets low. Potential competition constrains firm behavior. For example, Microsoft might charge more for its latest version of Windows if Linux were not nipping at its heels.

Another common example of a contestable market is the airline industry. Small regional carriers often fly unique routes from small airports to major tourist destinations such as Las Vegas and several spots in Florida. Although many of these routes are unique (in that only one airline serves the route), airlines tend to keep fares reasonable rather than exploit their market power for that route. Airlines realize that if fares are priced at the monopoly level, another airline might enter and compete. The ability to change airline service routes quickly forces airlines to keep prices at a competitive level, even if they are the only airline providing service between two cities.

The Future of Antitrust Policy

Today's economy differs from the old economy in many ways. The old economy was grounded in manufacturing and distributing physical goods such as steel, automobiles, appliances, and shoes. These old economy industries enjoyed economies of scale in production, often requiring huge capital requirements and modest rates of innovation.

Much of what new economy firms produce is intellectual property. In large measure, it is computer code of one form or another. Most of the costs to produce the programs are fixed, already sunk once the product is completed. To produce and distribute the product costs only a fraction of the product's value; if the Internet is used, distribution costs can approach zero. This means markups and profits are high, which creates a strong incentive to clone successful products. Monopolies, therefore, tend to be transitory in the new economy. The travails of Lotus 123, WordPerfect, Myspace, and Netscape all testify to the vulnerability of temporary monopolists in the media industry. All were industry leaders at one point, only to be rapidly displaced.

Antitrust laws and policy need to be adjusted to new market realities. In our global information and service economy, many of the old rules are irrelevant. One federal judge and economist, Richard Posner, argues that we should repeal all the old antitrust laws and replace them with a simple statute that prohibits "unreasonably anti-competitive practices."[2]

When a firm's market share approaches monopoly levels, turning to antitrust laws is the obvious response.

This and the last chapter looked at the polar opposites of market structures, competition and monopoly, with characteristics of each shown in Table 3. The next chapter looks at the market structures in the middle and also looks at a more modern approach to analyzing firm behavior, game theory.

Comparison Between Perfect Competition and Monopoly — **TABLE 3**

Perfect Competition	Monopoly
Many firms	One firm
Price-taking	Price-making
No barriers to entry	Significant barriers to entry
Marginal revenue = Price	Marginal revenue < Price
Zero economic profit in the long run	Potential economic profits in the long run
No deadweight loss (efficiency)	Deadweight loss (inefficiency)

Perfectly competitive firms and monopoly firms differ in the number of firms in the industry, the ability to set prices, the barriers to enter the industry, the ability to earn long-run economic profits, and the likelihood of achieving a socially efficient output.

CHECKPOINT

REGULATION AND ANTITRUST

- Regulating monopolies may involve a marginal cost pricing rule (have the monopolist set price equal to marginal cost) or an average cost pricing rule (have the monopolist set price equal to average total cost).
- In practice, regulation often involves setting an acceptable rate of return on capital or setting price caps on charges.
- The Sherman Act (1890) prohibited monopolization and attempts to monopolize.
- The Clayton Act (1914) prohibited price discrimination that lessened competition.
- The Federal Trade Commission Act (1914) prohibited unfair or deceptive business practices and established the Federal Trade Commission.
- Concentration ratios measure market concentration by looking at the share of industry sales accounted for by the top *n* firms.
- The Herfindahl-Hirschman index (HHI) measures concentration by computing the sum of the squares of market shares for all firms in the industry.
- The Department of Justice uses the HHI to set premerger guidelines.
- Contestable markets are markets with entry costs so low that the potential threat of entry keeps prices low.

QUESTION: In September 2011, AT&T attempted to buy one of its major competitors, T-Mobile, in a $39 billion acquisition that the U.S. Department of Justice eventually blocked. Explain why the Department of Justice would block such a merger from taking place. Assume that the wireless communications industry contains four equal-sized firms (AT&T, Verizon, Sprint, and T-Mobile); how would the HHI be used to justify the government's decision?

Answers to the Checkpoint question can be found at the end of this chapter.

[2] Richard A. Posner, *Antitrust Law*, 2nd ed. (Chicago: University of Chicago Press), 2001, p. 260.

chapter summary

Section 1: Monopoly Markets

A **monopoly** is a one-firm industry with no close product substitutes and with substantial barriers to entry.

Types of Barriers to Entry

Control over a significant factor of production: occurs when a company owns a significant share of its key ingredient or input in production

Economies of scale: occurs when firms must incur large fixed costs before production can begin

Government protection: patents and copyrights that provide an exclusive right to sell a product

5 Steps to Maximizing Profits for a Monopolist:

1. Find MR = MC
2. Find optimal quantity where MR = MC
3. Find optimal price where quantity meets the demand curve
4. Find average total cost at the optimal Q
5. Find the profit = $Q \times (P - ATC)$

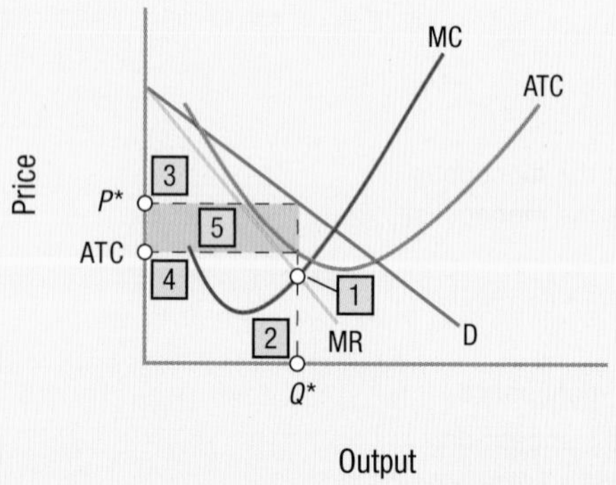

The firm's demand and supply curve is the same as the industry's demand and supply curve.

Marginal revenue is less than price for a monopoly: If a firm can sell 4 units at $10 but must drop price to $9 to sell 5 units, marginal revenue equals $5 because the seller loses a dollar from each of the previous 4 units (red area) but gains $9 from the sale (green area).

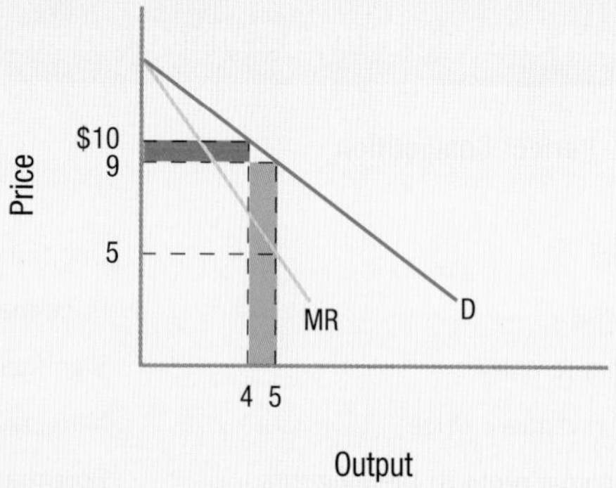

Just because a monopolist has no competitors doesn't mean it always earns profits. Think of late-night infomercials selling, at times, bizarre products. Some are successful but others fail.

Eric Chiang

Mop slippers were a unique invention that really never took off. Not all monopolies are profitable.

Section 2: Comparing Monopoly and Competition

In a monopoly market, output is lower and price is higher compared to a competitive market due to the lack of competitors to the monopoly firm.

A firm with market power is more likely to engage in **rent-seeking** behavior (spending resources to protect market power) and **x-inefficiency** (wasting resources because competition doesn't exist).

Joe Robbins/Getty Images

Without competition from another football league, the NFL likely produces fewer games and charges higher prices than it would in a competitive market.

Section 3: Price Discrimination

Price discrimination is charging different prices for the same product in the attempt to grab more surplus from consumers.

Conditions for Price Discrimination to Work Best

1. Firm must have market power (i.e., cannot be a price taker).
2. Market can be segmented into different consumer groups.
3. Seller must be able to prevent arbitrage.

Three Forms of Price Discrimination

Perfect (first-degree) price discrimination: Seller charges exactly what consumers are willing to pay, and extracts all consumer surplus.

Second-degree price discrimination: Prices differ based on the quantity being purchased.

Third-degree price discrimination: Prices differ based on consumer characteristics, such as age (e.g., kids and senior discounts), status (e.g., student or military discounts), or flexibility (e.g., airline pricing).

Francis Dean/Corbis

Shopping at Costco might save you money, but you often need to buy in bulk, an example of second-degree price discrimination.

Section 4: Regulation and Antitrust

A **natural monopoly** has large economies of scale such that one firm is more efficient than multiple firms. The profit maximizing point occurs where MC (and ATC) is falling. To prevent exploitation of market power, natural monopolies are often regulated.

mood/board/Corbis

Besides economies of scale, most people prefer just one electric company as a monopolist, rather than multiple electric companies each with its own power lines.

Antitrust laws are designed to promote competition and prevent monopolies from developing.

Two Major Antitrust Laws

Sherman Act of 1890: outlawed trusts and cartels—restraint of trade and monopolization.

Clayton Act of 1914: outlawed some forms of price discrimination and mergers that would significantly reduce competition.

Ways to Measure Market Power

Concentration ratios: adding up the market shares of the 4 or 8 largest firms in an industry, and ranges from 0 to 100.

HHI index: sum of the square of market shares of all firms in an industry, and ranges from 0 (perfect competition) to 10,000 (monopoly). HHI values over 1,800 are concentrated industries where mergers are likely to be challenged.

James Leynse/Corbis

A **contestable market** looks like a monopoly but does not act like one because the threat of entry keeps prices low. Low-fare airlines that serve unique routes still offer low prices if they fear new entrants.

KEY CONCEPTS

monopoly, p. 218
market power, p. 218
barriers to entry, p. 218
economies of scale, p. 218
rent seeking, p. 225
x-inefficiency, p. 226
price discrimination, p. 227
perfect (first-degree) price discrimination, p. 227
second-degree price discrimination, p. 227
third-degree price discrimination, p. 227
natural monopoly, p. 231
marginal cost pricing rule, p. 232
average cost pricing rule, p. 232
rate of return regulation, p. 233
price caps, p. 233
antitrust law, p. 233
concentration ratio, p. 235
Herfindahl-Hirschman index (HHI), p. 235
contestable markets, p. 236

QUESTIONS AND PROBLEMS

Check Your Understanding

1. Are McDonald's and Starbucks monopolies? Why or why not?
2. Explain why MR < P for the monopolist, but MR = P for perfectly competitive firms.
3. What do economists mean when they call monopolies inefficient? What is the deadweight loss of monopoly?
4. Why are monopoly firms able to earn long-run economic profits while perfectly competitive firms cannot?
5. Under what market conditions would a firm find it easier to engage in price discrimination?
6. What is a natural monopoly and why is such a monopoly often regulated by government?

Apply the Concepts

7. How important is the existence of a significant barrier to entry to maintaining a monopoly? What would be the result if a monopoly market could easily be entered? Why might a monopoly in a high-tech field such as computers, the Internet, and consumer electronics be rather short-lived?
8. My dentist recently recommended that I have a tooth replaced with a titanium pin inserted in my jaw and capped with a crown. I went to an oral surgeon to have the tooth removed and the pin inserted. The bill for the procedure was $300 to remove the tooth and $1,500 to insert the titanium pin. Removing the tooth and inserting the pin each took roughly the same amount of time. Because the cost of the pin is negligible and both parts of the procedure took the same amount of time, why would the oral surgeon charge 5 times as much to set the pin as to pull the tooth? (Hint: Market power and level of competition underlies the answer.)
9. The taxi industry in many large cities spends millions of dollars lobbying local policymakers not to build rail links connecting airports to the city center, even if such mass transportation infrastructure would benefit many consumers traveling to and from the airport. Explain why such actions by the taxi industry are taken. Then, explain why taxi owners in cities without airport rail links are less likely to invest in fuel-efficient cars and in-taxi technologies such as televisions and Internet access.
10. If the Miami Heat can sell five courtside seats for $2,000 each or six courtside seats if it reduces the price to $1,600 each, what is the marginal revenue of the sixth seat? Should the owner make this sixth seat available? If all six seats can be sold for $1,800 each, would this make the sixth seat worth selling? (Hint: What costs are involved with selling the sixth seat?)

11. Sally owns the only cake shop in town (she is a monopolist). At a quantity of five, the marginal cost of producing one more cake is $12, while the marginal revenue from selling one more cake is $10. In order for Sally to maximize profits, should she increase or decrease output? Should she increase or decrease prices? Explain.
12. Airlines that compete against one another have at times merged with each other to create a larger airline. What are some factors that would determine whether such a merger would constitute an uncompetitive environment according to antitrust law?

In the News

13. In July 2012, a court found several electronics manufacturers guilty of price-fixing LCD television and computer panels in one of the largest price-fixing cases in history ("What the $1.1 Billion LCD Price-Fixing Settlement Means for You," *CNN Money*, July 16, 2012). The alleged actions involved many major manufacturers, including Toshiba, Samsung, and Sharp. The total settlement that manufacturers paid to compensate victims of the scheme came to an astounding $1.12 billion. What potential benefits do companies gain by working together to fix prices on a good? Why do companies choose to engage in such unlawful behavior despite the risk of being caught and having to pay significant fines?
14. Being number one in any business attracts a lot of attention. As *The Economist* (December 17, 2005) noted,

    > *As soon as a firm climbs above the sharp elbows of its rivals, it starts getting pelted with the eggs of anti-business activities. People who hate big business aim high. So while big, bad Wal-Mart is pilloried, Target has in the past couple of years blithely cut the benefits of its non-union workers. And when was the last time you saw an anti-globalization mob destroy a Burger King outlet?*

    Describe some of the benefits of being number two in a large industry. In terms of total revenues (sales), name the number one and two firms in the following industries: major auto manufacturers, major drug manufacturers, and major integrated oil and gas.

Solving Problems

15. Using the figure for a monopoly firm below, answer the following questions.
    a. What will be the monopoly price, output, and profit for this firm?

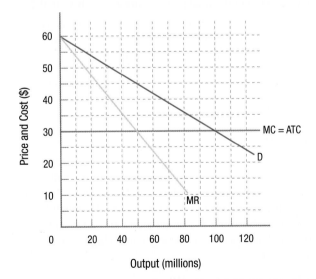

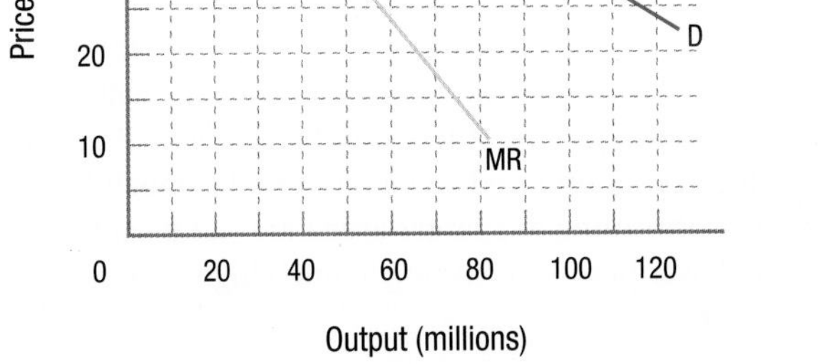

    b. If this monopolist could perfectly price discriminate, what would profit equal?
    c. If this industry were competitive, what would be the price, output, and profit?
    d. How large (in dollars) is the deadweight loss from this monopolist?

16. Assume the following table represents the sales figures for the eight largest firms in the auto industry in the United States:

Company	Sales (billions of dollars)
General Motors	2.063
Toyota	1.77
Ford	1.616
Honda	1.151
Chrysler	0.931
Nissan	0.77
Hyundai	0.435
Mazda	0.208
Total	**8.944**

a. Compute the four-firm concentration ratio for the industry.

b. Compute the HHI for the industry (assuming the industry contains just these eight firms).

c. Assuming the industry is represented by these eight firms, if Toyota and Ford wanted to merge, and you were the head of the Department of Justice, would you permit the merger? Why or why not? (Hint: Calculate the new values from parts a and b assuming the merger takes place.) How about if Hyundai and Mazda wanted to merge?

USING THE NUMBERS

17. According to By the Numbers, assuming that the number of viewers for each of the five games in the 2012 NBA Finals were the same, approximately how many more people watched the 2012 Super Bowl than the final game of the 2012 NBA Finals?

18. According to By the Numbers, the annual growth in demand for electricity has fallen over the past half-century but remained positive nearly every year. In what years did actual electricity demand fall (negative growth in demand)?

ANSWERS TO QUESTIONS IN CHECKPOINTS

Checkpoint: Monopoly Markets

By performing in a smaller venue (such as a performing arts hall with 1,500 seats instead of an arena with 10,000 or more seats), the artist can target the core fans willing to pay high prices for tickets. With market power in pricing (there is only one Dolly Parton), nearly all seats would be sold at the high price, as opposed to having to offer much lower prices to fill a larger arena. If the costs of performing at a larger arena are significant, artists can do better by producing less (selling fewer tickets), charging a much higher price, and reducing the costs of putting on the concert.

Checkpoint: Comparing Monopoly and Competition

Although Microsoft's actions in this case do not involve lobbying for special privileges (the traditional definition of rent seeking), its tactics nonetheless resemble rent seeking in that costly (even wasteful) actions are being used to protect one's market share. Microsoft has a huge capital base and cash flow, and could compete with Google in the search market without the need to make accusations regarding its business practices.

Checkpoint: Price Discrimination

No, this is not the same type of price discrimination discussed in this section. This type of discrimination occurs because of information problems, gender discrimination, racism, or other factors. The authors conclude that a large part of the price differences between buying online and bargaining in the showroom comes from the fact that online consumers have better information. Price discrimination in this section of the chapter is based on consumers with different elasticities of demand, not information problems or racism. Examples include student, senior, and adult pricing in movie theaters.

Checkpoint: Regulation and Antitrust

The government aims to prevent powerful monopolies, which can restrict competition and lead to fewer choices and higher prices, from forming. The Sherman Antitrust Act of 1890 and the Clayton Act of 1914 provide the legal basis for such action. The government uses concentration ratios or the HHI as a gauge to determine whether a pending merger would harm competition. If each of four firms controls 25% of the market, the HHI is 2,500, already a very concentrated industry. By allowing AT&T and T-Mobile to merge, the HHI would increase from 2,500 to 3,750, making the industry even more concentrated.

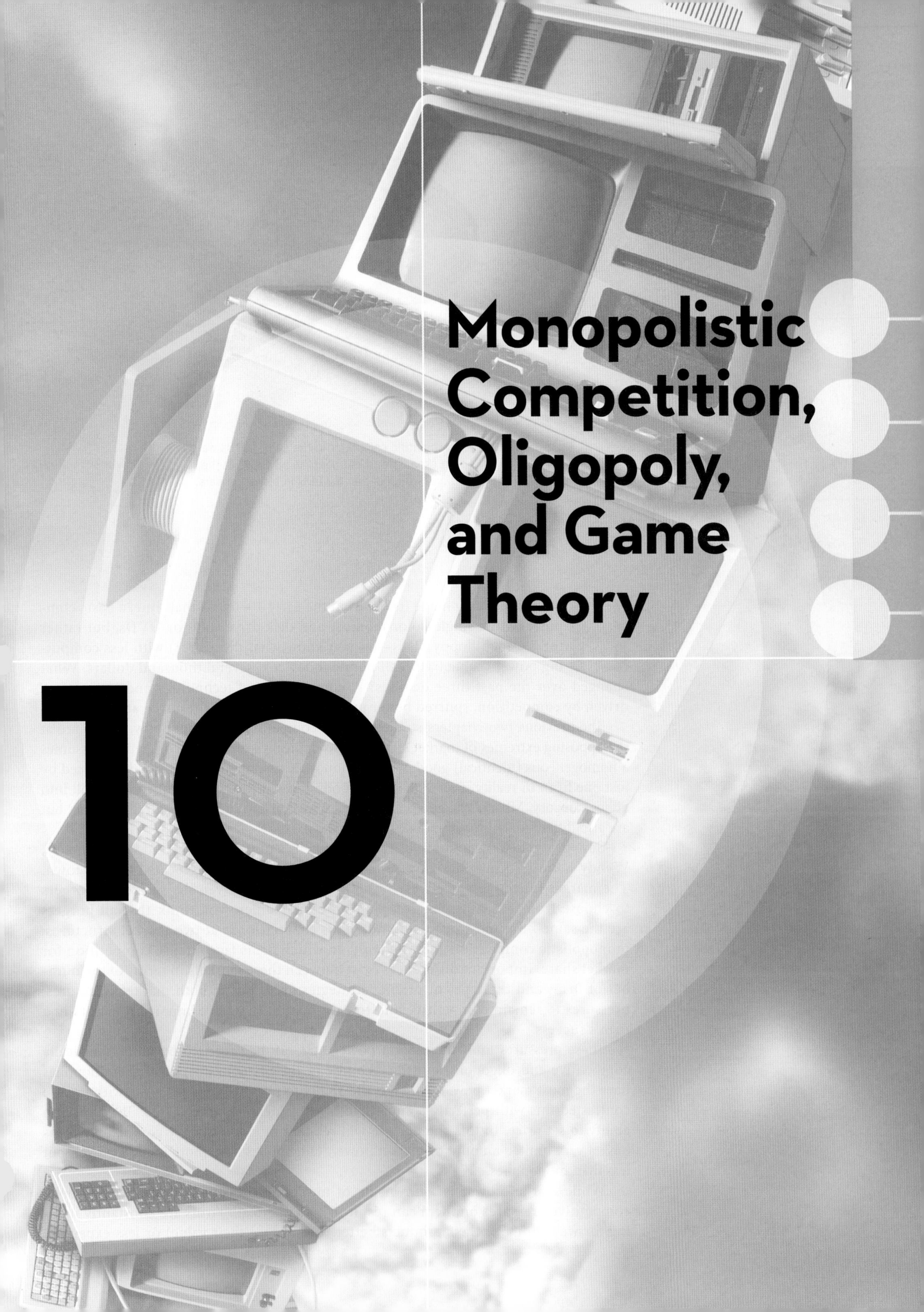

10

Monopolistic Competition, Oligopoly, and Game Theory

Gareth Byrne/Alamy

A scientific calculator in the early 1970s was an expensive investment, about $400 at the time, which is over $2,000 in today's dollars.

After studying this chapter you should be able to:

- Describe product differentiation and its impact on the firm's demand curve, and how it determines the market power that a monopolistically competitive firm can exercise.
- Compare pricing and output decisions for monopolistically competitive firms in the short run and long run, and explain why firms earn only normal profits in the long run.
- Compare the efficiency of monopolistic competition to perfect competition.
- Describe cartels and the reasons for their instability.
- Describe the kinked demand curve model and why prices can be relatively stable in oligopoly industries.
- Describe the benefits of using game theory to understand oligopoly and strategic interdependence.
- Describe the basic components of a game and explain the difference between simultaneous-move and sequential-move games.
- Solve for Nash equilibria using a best-response analysis and understand their importance to economists.
- Recognize why Prisoner's Dilemma outcomes occur and provide real-life examples of such situations.
- Explain how firms can overcome the Prisoner's Dilemma using cooperative strategies and repeated actions.

Home computing made its debut in the early 1980s. At that time, a basic computer with a single-color monitor and disk drive (not for DVDs, but rather for 5¼-inch floppy disks—do you know what those are?) with less computing power than a basic cell phone today cost several thousand dollars. What changed over the past three decades? A combination of technology and innovation, driven by competition, spurred better products that could be produced at lower costs.

The previous two chapters studied perfect competition and monopoly, which are at the opposing extremes of market structures we typically see. Perfect competition assumes a homogeneous (identical) good, while a monopoly assumes a unique good produced by just one firm. In reality, over 90% of the goods and services we consume do not fall into either category. Most of the goods and services we consume are competitive in nature but are also differentiated (or branded) in some way.

Suppose you want a quick burger for lunch. Your choices include McDonald's, Wendy's, Burger King, Five Guys, and many other burger joints located in your town. The market for burgers is clearly not a monopoly. Yet, given the variety of burgers to choose from, it's not pure competition either, unless you think that all burgers are the same—but most people do not. This chapter looks at two market structures, monopolistic competition and oligopoly, in which firms face intense competition for market share. Important differences exist between these markets in terms of the number of firms and the types of pricing strategies used. But in both market structures, pressures to remain competitive and to gain market share are important factors in a firm's success.

These pressures limit the market power that can be exercised by monopolistically competitive and oligopolistic firms. We saw in the previous chapter that monopolies have the most market power, which is the ability to set price (and get away with it). We contrasted this with perfectly competitive firms, which are price takers: They have no ability to set price. In this chapter, we will see that monopolistically competitive firms have a very limited amount of market power. Oligopolies have more market power, but less than monopolies.

While market power is a downside of monopolistic competition and oligopoly, competitive pressures on them can result in benefits to all. Firms are constantly looking for ways to make their products better (to increase their value) or less expensive

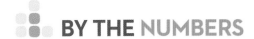

BY THE NUMBERS

Product Differentiation and Market Share

For nearly all goods and services we buy, we are faced with numerous choices: brands, features, quality, style, and more. Product differentiation is a signature characteristic of monopolistically competitive markets, and to a lesser extent oligopoly markets.

Claver Carroll/age fotostock

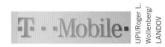

The largest fast-food chains in the United States (numbers of stores as of May 2012).

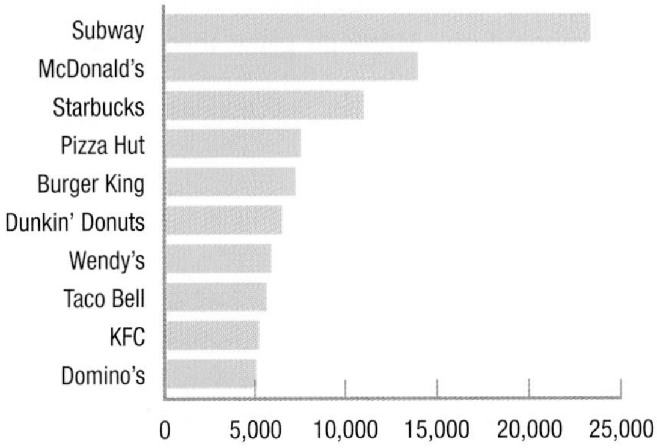

PSL Images/Alamy

PSL Images/Alamy

PR NEWSWIRE/AP

UPI/Roger L. Wollenberg/ LANDOV

The wireless communications market is an oligopoly dominated by four large firms, controlling 93% of total market share.

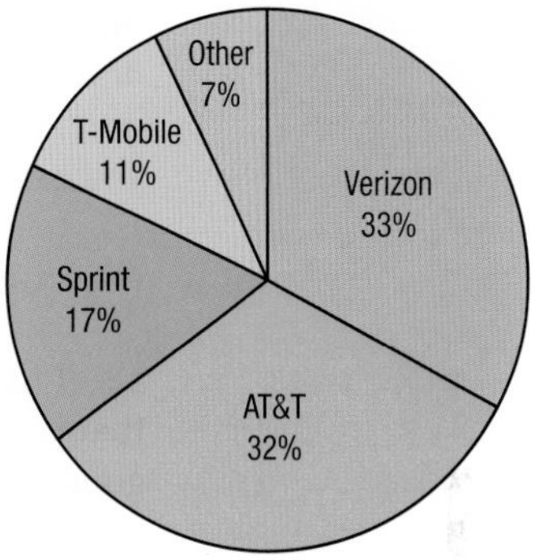

655

Total marathons in the United States in 2012 (differentiated by location, size, elevation change, and scenery).

Sports Illustrated/Getty Images

1,500+

Total number of shoe models produced by Nike Corporation since 1972.

Bill Cobb/Superstock

Colleges and universities are differentiated by size, location, athletic prowess, and academic reputation.

Largest Universities in the United States
(on a single campus in the Fall of 2012)

Arizona State University; Tempe, AZ: 60,169 students
University of Central Florida; Orlando, FL: 59,767
The Ohio State University; Columbus, OH: 56,387

Smallest Colleges in the United States

Alaska Bible College; Glennalen, AK: 38
Shimer College; Chicago, IL: 81
Sterling College; Craftsbury Common, VT: 105

to produce. By doing so, this has led to a number of important changes in the global competitive market:

1. Increase in technological development
2. Increase in variety of goods and services
3. Reduction in the price of inputs and resources (with economies of scale or offshoring of production)
4. Reduction in transportation costs
5. Reduction in trade barriers

Recall from Chapter 3 that when supply increases (shifts to the right), the market price falls and the market quantity rises. For each of the factors listed above, a corresponding increase in supply results, helping to explain why last year's computers and smartphones cost so much less than today's—even if the suppliers of computers and smartphones are oligopolies with some degree of market power.

The key to understanding monopolistic competition is product differentiation, as we saw in the burger example, and the key to understanding oligopolies is interdependence. By interdependence, economists mean that pricing and other decisions have to be made by taking into consideration what other firms might do. If Delta Airlines raises its prices, will United and American follow suit, or will they freeze their prices in the hope of luring Delta customers to their airlines?

To best explain interdependence, the chapter concludes by studying game theory, a modern way to examine strategy and competition. Although game theory was initially developed to analyze the behavior of interdependent oligopolistic firms, it has countless uses and applications in our daily lives. We will touch on a few of these many uses so that you can see the richness of taking a game theory approach.

Monopolistic Competition

Until the 1920s, competition and monopoly were the only models of market structure that economists had in their toolbox. As consumerism expanded and more varieties of goods and services became available, economists found that these two models were inadequate to explain the vast markets for many goods. In other words, some markets were considered imperfect, or not fitting the mold of the traditional competitive structure. This led to the study of imperfect markets, which included monopolistic competition and oligopoly.

monopolistic competition A market structure with a large number of firms producing differentiated products. This differentiation is either real or imagined by consumers and involves innovations, advertising, location, or other ways of making one firm's product different from that of its competitors.

Monopolistic competition is nearer to the competitive end of the spectrum and is defined by the following:

- A large number of small firms. Similar to perfect competition, each firm has a very small share of the overall market. They and their competitors cannot appreciably affect the market and, therefore, mostly ignore the reactions of their rivals.
- Entry and exit are easy.
- Unlike perfect competition, products are different. Each firm produces a product that is different from its competitors or is perceived to be different by consumers. What distinguishes monopolistic competition from perfectly competitive markets is product differentiation.

Product Differentiation and the Firm's Demand Curve

Most firms sell products that are in some way differentiated from their competitors. For example, this differentiation can take the form of a superior location. Your local dry cleaner, restaurant, grocery, and gas station can have slightly higher prices, but you will not abandon them altogether. Other companies have branded products that give them some ability to increase price without losing all of their customers, as would happen under perfect competition.

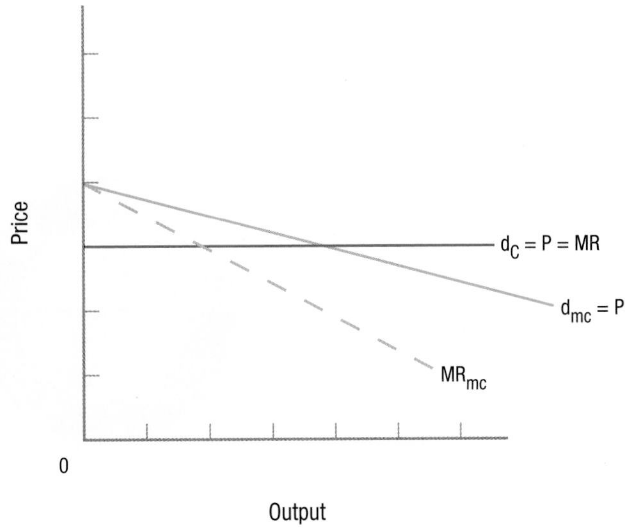

FIGURE 1

Product Differentiation and Demand

Product differentiation gives the firm some market power to raise prices. Demand curve d_{mc} is the demand curve for a monopolistically competitive firm with modest price-making ability. Marginal revenue curve MR_{mc} also slopes downward, reflecting the weak negative slope of the demand curve.

Product differentiation gives the firm some (however modest) control over prices (market power). This is illustrated in Figure 1. Demand curve d_c is the competitive demand curve, and d_{mc} is the demand faced by a monopolistic competitor. This is similar to the monopolist's demand, but the demand curve is considerably more elastic. Because a monopolistic competitor is small relative to the market, there are still a lot of substitutes. Thus, any increase in price is accompanied by a substantial decrease in output demanded. But unlike the perfectly competitive firm that faces a horizontal demand curve with no power to raise price, a monopolistically competitive firm has some market power with its not quite horizontal demand curve.

Like a monopolist, the monopolistically competitive firm faces a downward sloping marginal revenue curve, shown in Figure 1 as MR_{mc}.

Product differentiation can be the result of a superior product, a better location, superior service, clever packaging, or advertising. All of these factors are intended to increase demand or reduce the elasticity of demand and generate loyalty to the product or service. Therefore, the demand curve for monopolistically competitive firms can vary. Although demand curves tend to be elastic (flat), firms that are able to differentiate their products the most can achieve greater market power, which makes their demand curves steeper, allowing them to charge higher prices.

product differentiation One firm's product is distinguished from another's through advertising, innovation, location, and so on.

The Role of Advertising An important way to differentiate products is through advertising. Economists generally classify advertising in two ways: informational and persuasive. The informational aspects of advertising let consumers know about products and reduce search costs. Advertising is a relatively inexpensive way to let customers know about the quality and price of a company's products. It can also enhance competition by making consumers aware of substitute or competitive products. Advertising also has the potential to reduce average costs by increasing sales, bringing about economies of scale.

But advertising does have a negative side as well. Because so much of advertising is persuasive (ads containing little informational content but designed to shift buyers among competitors of similar products), the result is that the cost of advertising drives up the price of many products. With all the advertising we see, a significant portion probably cancels each other out.

Advertising is another area in which technology has transformed the medium: Digital video recorders permit ad-skipping and have significantly reduced the impact of TV ads. A lot of advertising dollars are shifting away from conventional media (newspapers, magazines, and television) and moving to the Internet, where consumers can be targeted more inexpensively and efficiently.

Mikael Damkier/Dreamstime.com

Product differentiation counts. Although hundreds of brands of blue jeans compete in the same general market, product differentiation in style and comfort allows some brands to achieve substantial market power, resulting in higher prices.

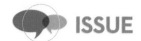

ISSUE

Do Brands Really Represent Pricing Power?

What is a brand? All of us know brands through their names and logos. Nike has the swoosh, Intel has a logo and the four-note jingle that sounds whenever its processors are advertised, Coca-Cola has a distinctive way of spelling its name. Names and logos are communication devices, but brands are more than this. They are a promise of performance. A branded product or service raises expectations in a consumer's mind. If these expectations are met, consumers pay a price premium. If expectations are not met, the value of the brand falls as consumers seek alternatives.

Brand names start with the company that makes the product or provides the service. In the past, this meant that brand names came from a limited number of sources. Some companies were named after their founders, such as Walt Disney; some companies were named after what they supplied, such as IBM (International Business Machines); and some have also been named by their main product, such as the Coca-Cola Company. Sometimes the company name has a tenuous link with the product but is strong nevertheless, such as the Starbucks name for coffee products: Master Starbuck was first mate to Captain Ahab in *Moby-Dick* and did drink coffee in the book, but who remembers that?

Whatever their origins, these brands have recognizable brand names, and they command price premiums. According to the annual BrandZ study by Millward Brown, Apple was the most valuable brand in 2012, valued at nearly $182 billion, followed by IBM, Google, McDonald's, and Microsoft. Nine of the top ten brands were American, with the only non-American brand being China Mobile, coming in at number ten and worth $47 billion. Brands this valuable must convey some considerable pricing power, or what we called market power in the previous chapter. Market power is what companies want.

In the auto industry, Toyota was knocked out of its position as the highest valued brand by BMW, whose brand is worth $25 billion. This was not the result of a lack of an efficient production system by Toyota, but rather a case of bad luck in recent years. First, in 2010, Toyota recalled over 7 million cars due to an accelerator issue that ultimately was determined to have been caused by driver error. Then, in 2011, an earthquake and tsunami in Japan caused severe supply disruptions to car manufacturers, which caused further deterioration of Toyota's reputation. Despite these setbacks, Toyota maintained its concentration on consistent high quality, a commitment to customer service, and continuous improvement of the product line.

Peter Probst/Alamy

The Toyota brand has cachet: At the California plant that until 2009 Toyota shared with General Motors, *identical* cars came off the production line. Some were branded as GM cars, others Toyotas. When the cars were traded in, the Toyotas had a much higher trade-in value. The Toyota brand conveys quality, which gives Toyota its pricing power. As Toyota rebuilds its reputation from the recent setbacks, it may potentially re-emerge as the top auto brand.

Sources: BrandZ Top 100 Most Valuable Global Brands 2012, Millward Brown, WPP Companies.

All of these ways to differentiate their products give monopolistically competitive firms some control over price. This market power means that their profit maximizing decisions will be a little different from those of perfectly competitive firms.

Price and Output Under Monopolistic Competition

Profit maximization in the short run for the monopolistically competitive firm is a lot like that for a monopolist, but given the firm's size, profit will tend to be less. Short-run profit maximizing behavior is shown in Figure 2. The firm maximizes profit where MR = MC (point *c*) by selling output q_0 for a price of P_0. Total profits are the shaded area C_0P_0ab. All of this should look very familiar from the last chapter (review the five-step approach to maximizing profit). The difference is that the monopolistically competitive demand curve is quite elastic, and economic profits are diminished. The level of profits is dependent on the strength of demand, but in any event will be considerably lower than that of a monopolist.

This does not mean that profits are trivial. Many huge global firms sell their products in even larger global markets, and their profits are significant. They are large firms, but do not

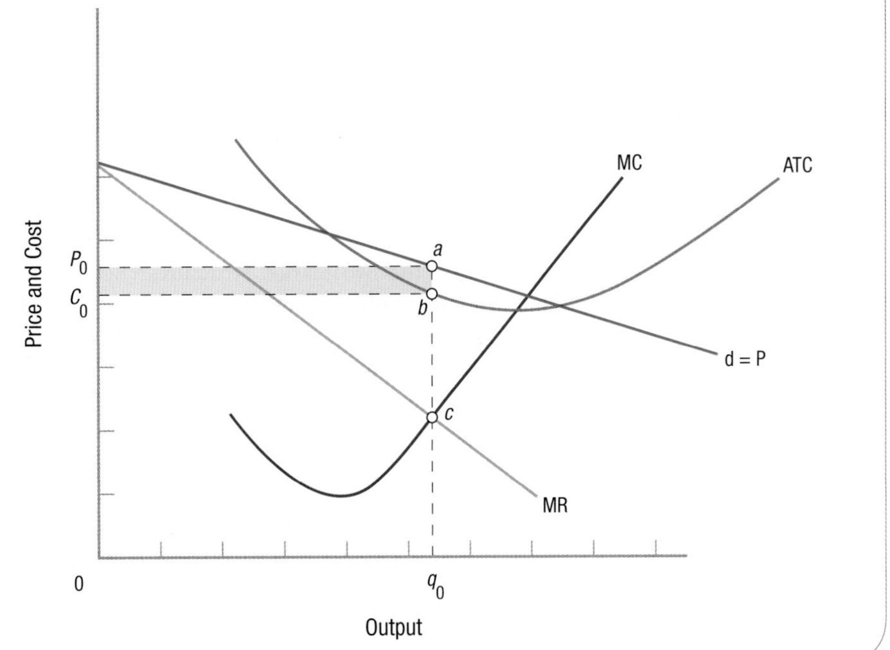

FIGURE 2

Short-Run Equilibrium for Monopolistic Competition

This monopolistically competitive firm will maximize profits in the short run by producing where MR = MC (point *c*). Profits are equal to the shaded area.

have significant market power. Many companies—such as Armani, Nike, and Sony—are all quite large but relative to their markets face daunting competition.

If firms in the industry are earning economic profits like those of the firm shown in Figure 2, new firms will want to enter. Since there are no restrictions on entry or exit, new firms will enter, soaking up some industry demand and reducing the demand to each firm in the market. Demand will continue to decline as long as economic profits exist. At equilibrium in the long run, the typical firm in the industry will look like the one shown in Figure 3.

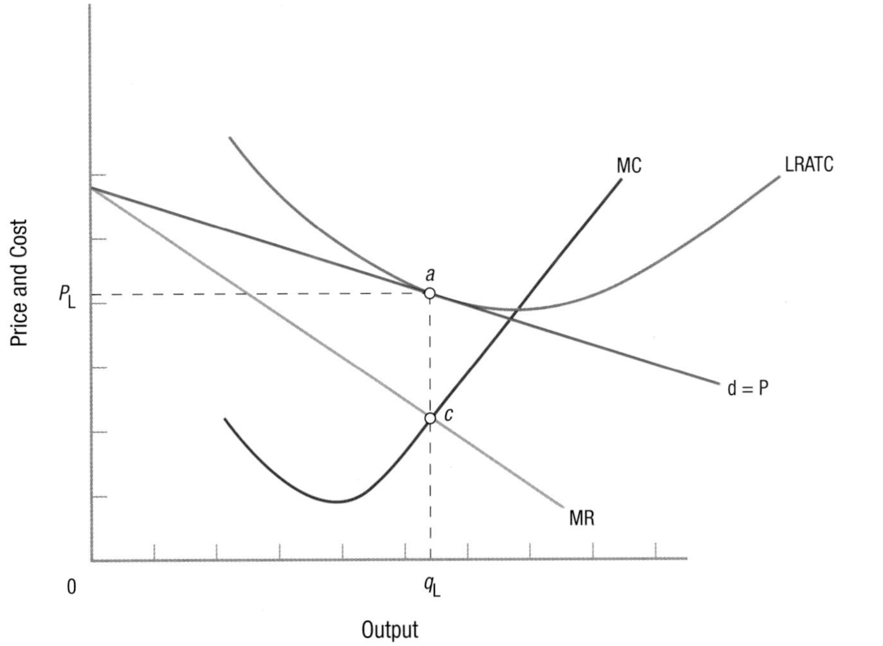

FIGURE 3

Long-Run Equilibrium for Monopolistic Competition

In the long run, easy entry and exit will adjust the demand for each firm so that the demand curve will be tangent (at point *a* in this case) to the long-run average total cost curve. This is long-run equilibrium because existing firms are earning normal profits and there is no incentive for further entry or exit. Compared to perfect competition, this long-run output does not minimize LRATC, which means prices are higher in a monopolistically competitive industry.

Notice that the demand curve is just tangent to the long-run average total cost (LRATC) curve, resulting in the firm earning normal profits in the long run. The firm produces and sells q_L output at a price of P_L (point *a*). Note that price P_L is not at the minimum point of the LRATC, which shows that prices in monopolistically competitive markets are higher than prices in perfectly competitive markets. Once the typical firm reaches this point, there is no longer any incentive for other firms to enter the industry. Like perfectly competitive firms, monopolistically competitive firms earn normal profits in the long run.

Comparing Monopolistic Competition to Competition

How does allocative efficiency compare for the two market structures? Because firms in both earn normal profits, you might think that both market structures are equally efficient. Unfortunately, this is not the case. Differentiated products create minimarkets within each industry. For example, Wrangler and True Religion are both brands of blue jeans, but each caters to a different set of customers, allowing True Religion to charge more than Wrangler. By differentiating products, economies of scale for monopolistically competitive firms are likely to be smaller compared to a perfectly competitive firm whose product is essentially identical, resulting in slightly higher prices and lower output.

These relatively small differences in price and output represent the costs we pay for product differentiation and innovation. To the extent that these differences are real, the costs are justified. When advertising provides accurate information that helps us select products, or if the products are sufficiently distinct that they provide real choices, then the additional costs can be worth it. Plus, competitive pressures will keep prices significantly lower than if a monopoly emerges in the market.

Firms differentiate their products through style and features that matter. Coca-Cola offers Cherry, Vanilla, and Black Cherry Vanilla Coke, as well as diet versions. Watches offer everything from the time and date to temperature, stopwatch capabilities, Global Positioning System (GPS) capability, altitude, and, most recently, Internet access. Product differentiation is important and for most of us valuable, but not free.

From this discussion, you might get some sense of the pressures firms face to differentiate their products. The more they can move away from the competitive model, the better chance they have of using their market power to make more profit. But because market power evaporates over the long run for monopolistically competitive firms, these firms have to try to sustain the value in the differentiated product. This is hard to do. The price premium charged by Hollister will not be paid when Hollister becomes less fashionable, or more like everyone else. Yet, it is in the firm's interest to product differentiate as long as it can. When you see firms trying to differentiate their products, ask yourself if the products really are so different after all.

CHECKPOINT

MONOPOLISTIC COMPETITION

- Monopolistically competitive firms look like perfectly competitive firms (large number of small firms in a market in which entry and exit is unrestricted) but have differentiated products.
- Monopolistically competitive firms have downward-sloping demand curves and elastic demands.
- Short-run equilibrium output for the monopolistic competitor (like the monopolist) is at an output where MR = MC, and can result in positive or negative profits.
- In the long run, easy entry and exit result in monopolistically competitive firms earning only normal profits.
- Output is lower and price is higher for monopolistically competitive firms when compared to price and output for perfectly competitive firms. Monopolistically competitive firms have some market power.

QUESTION: At Disney World in Florida, you can stay at the Disney Grand Floridian Resort for $350/night or at the Disney All-Star Resort for $125/night. Both hotels are located within the park boundaries and are owned by Disney. How does product differentiation explain the significant price difference? Search and browse the hotels' Web sites to provide examples of product differentiation between the hotels.

Answers to the Checkpoint question can be found at the end of this chapter.

Oligopoly

Oligopoly markets are those in which a large market share is controlled by just a few firms. What constitutes a few firms controlling a large market share is not rigidly defined. Further, these firms can sell either a homogeneous product (e.g., gasoline, sugar) or a differentiated product (e.g., automobiles, pharmaceuticals).

oligopoly A market with just a few firms dominating the industry, where (1) each firm recognizes that it must consider its competitors' reactions when making its own decisions (mutual interdependence), and (2) there are significant barriers to entry into the market.

Industries can be composed of a dominant firm with a few smaller firms making up the rest of the industry (e.g., computer operating systems), or the industry can be composed of a few similarly sized firms (e.g., automobiles, tobacco). The point of this discussion is that oligopoly models are numerous and varied, and we will explore only a few. Oligopoly models do, however, have several common characteristics.

Defining Oligopoly

All oligopoly models share several common assumptions:

- There are only a few large firms in the industry.
- Each firm recognizes that it must take into account the behavior of its competitors when it makes decisions. Economists refer to this as **mutual interdependence.**
- There are significant barriers to entry into the market.

mutual interdependence When only a few firms constitute an industry, each firm must consider the reactions of its competitors to its decisions.

Because there are only a few firms, each firm possesses substantial market power. However, because the products sold by oligopolists are similar to each other, the actions of one will affect the ability of the others to sell or price their output successfully. If one firm changes the specifications of its product or increases its advertising budget, this will have an impact on its rivals, and they can be expected to respond in kind. Thus, one firm cannot forecast its change in sales for a new promotion without first making some assumption about the reaction of its rivals.

In an industry composed of just a few firms, entry scale is often huge. Plus, with just a few firms, typically brand preferences are quite strong on the part of consumers, and a new firm may need a substantial marketing program just to get a foot in the door. For example, the investment in a plant for a new automaker is huge, and the marketing effort also must be large to get people to even consider a new auto brand.

Cartels: Joint Profit Maximization and the Instability of Oligopolies

Cartels are theft—usually by well-dressed thieves.

GRAEME SAMUEL, HEAD OF AUSTRALIA'S ANTITRUST OFFICE

The first oligopoly model we examine is *collusive* joint profit maximization, or a **cartel** model. Here we assume that a few firms collude (combine secretly) to operate like a monopoly, using maximum market power to set the monopoly price and output and share the monopoly profits. Cartels are illegal in the United States and in the European Union, although international laws do not ban them.

cartel An agreement between firms (or countries) in an industry to formally collude on price and output, then agree on the distribution of production.

The most famous cartel operating today is OPEC, the Organization of Petroleum Exporting Countries. OPEC countries meet to establish an output level that each individual member can produce, thus pushing up prices and carving up shares of the profits. OPEC, formed principally of Middle Eastern countries in the early 1960s, really didn't become effective until 1973 when member countries took greater control of their domestic oil industries. Today, however, competition from non-OPEC countries in Africa, Northern Europe, and Canada is slowly reducing the power of OPEC.

FIGURE 4

Cartels and the Incentive to Cheat

A cartel consisting of five firms collectively agrees to restrict total output to the monopoly output of 100 units and charges $10 per unit. If one firm chooses to cheat by increasing its output by an additional 20 units, total output increases to 120 units and price falls to $8. This results in a loss of revenue of $200, which is shared equally among the five cartel members ($40 loss per member, equal to one share of the yellow area). However, the cheating member gains $160 from the additional 20 units sold at $8 each (green area). The marginal revenue for the cheating member is therefore $160 – $40 = $120.

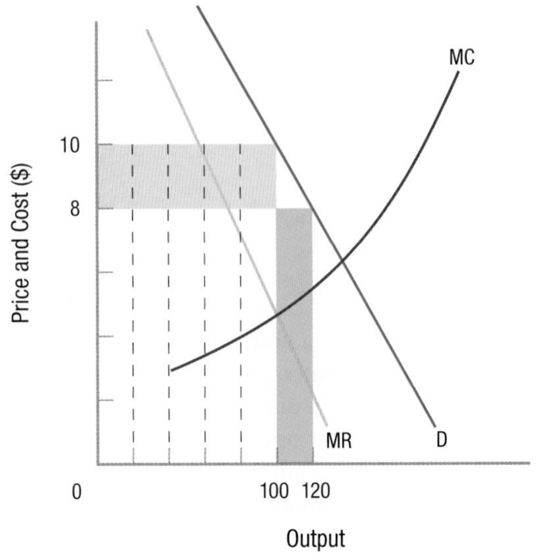

Figure 4 illustrates a hypothetical cartel consisting of five firms. By forming a cartel, these five firms agree to fix their overall output equal to the profit maximizing output of a monopolist, which is 100. At this restricted output, each cartel member produces its fixed quota of output (20 units per firm, assuming the cartel divides total output equally), and shares the resulting profit. Under this scenario, the cartel exhibits maximum market power equal to a single-firm monopolist.

However, cartels are inherently unstable because of the incentive to cheat by individual members. Although the cartel as a whole is maximizing profits, each individual member can potentially earn more profits by producing more than its output quota. As illustrated in Figure 4, if one firm exceeds its quota by doubling output from 20 to 40, the overall output of the cartel increases from 100 to 120 units. By expanding production, the market price falls from $10 to $8, causing revenues to fall by $200 ($2 × 100 units), shown as the yellow area. This reduction in revenues is *shared* by all five firms, with each firm losing $40 (or one share of the yellow area). Despite this loss, the cheating firm benefits because the extra 20 units it produces earns the firm $160 in additional revenue ($8 × 20 units), shown as the green area. The marginal revenue from cheating is therefore $160 – $40 = $120. As long as the marginal cost of producing the extra 20 units is less than $120, the firm benefits from cheating on the cartel agreement.

However, when one firm cheats, this often leads to other firms cheating. As more and more cartel members cheat, the price continues to fall toward the competitive price, greatly hurting the noncheating members. Over time, the cartel falls apart when all members increase their output, resulting in a competitive outcome. Therefore, market power in a cartel can range from the monopoly case (if all members adhere to their quotas) to the competitive case when cartels completely break down.

One reason that cartels are inherently unstable is because increasing output by one member can be undetected. However, once quotas are breached, the effects on all other members expand, increasing the likelihood of more cheating, especially if the marginal cost of production is low. For oil-producing countries, additional production is particularly profitable because a $100 barrel of oil may only cost $10 to $20 to produce. Each firm in the cartel faces these incentives, and if many attempt to sell additional output, the cartel agreement will break down. This analysis has led some economists to lose interest in cartels, because cartels are likely to fail in the long run.

Although cartels are inherently unstable, certain factors can enhance the likelihood of the cartel's survival. First, cartel stability is enhanced with fewer members with similar goals. With fewer members, any action that breaches the cartel agreement is more easily noticed and punishable. Second, stability is improved if the cartel is maintained with legal provisions (such as government protection). Third, stability is improved if firms are unable to differentiate their products (such as providing enhanced service or some other product as an inducement to purchase). Fourth, stability is improved when each firm's cost structure is similar, thereby not giving any firm a cost advantage over another. Finally, a cartel is more stable when there are significant barriers to entry preventing new firms from competing against existing cartel members.

These factors do not bode well for the future of the twelve member countries of OPEC. Although OPEC members produce a uniform product (crude oil) and have similar cost structures, enforcement of the quotas has at times been shaky with politically unstable countries. Further, OPEC's total share of world oil production has been surpassed by non-OPEC countries, led by Russia, the United States, Mexico, Canada, China, and Brazil. Maintaining an effective oil cartel will become more difficult as more countries enter the industry and as new alternative fuels are developed.

The Kinked Demand Curve Model and the Stability of Oligopolies

Oligopoly industries share a characteristic that prices tend to be stable for extended periods of time. For example, prices for wireless data plans are often \$39.99 per month, and prices of unlimited texting plans are usually \$19.99 per month. Why do these prices tend to stay the same when the underlying costs of providing the services change?

A study by Sweezy, Hall, and Hitch in the 1930s recognized that prices tended to be stable for extended periods in oligopolistic industries. It was in an effort to model this price stability that they settled on the idea of a kinked demand curve.

Demand curve d in Figure 5 represents the demand for one firm when all other firms in the industry *do not follow* its price changes. Demand curve D represents demand when all other firms raise or lower prices *in concert.* Demand curve d is relatively more elastic than demand curve D because when the firm raises prices and others do not follow, quantity demanded declines rapidly as customers substitute to the now lower priced products from competitors. Similarly, when one firm's prices fall and the others ignore this change, demand for the lower priced products grows rapidly. Hence, demand curve d is relatively elastic.

Demand curve D, on the other hand, is more like the industry demand. When all firms raise and lower their prices together, demand will be less elastic than demand curve d.

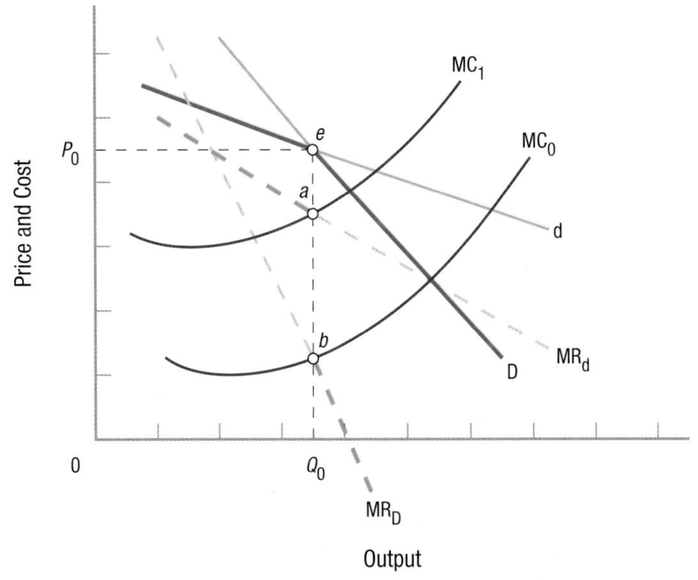

FIGURE 5

The Kinked Demand Curve Model of Oligopoly

The kinked demand curve model of oligopoly shows why oligopoly prices appear stable. The model assumes that if the firm raised its price, competitors will not react and raise their prices, but if the firm lowers its price, other firms will lower theirs in response. These reactions create a "kink" in the firm's demand curve at point *e*, and a discontinuity in the MR curve equal to the distance between points *a* and *b*. This discontinuity permits marginal costs to vary from MC_0 to MC_1 before the firm will change its price.

kinked demand curve An oligopoly model that assumes that if a firm raises its price, competitors will not raise theirs; but if the firm lowers its price, all of its competitors will lower their price to match the reduction. This leads to a kink in the demand curve and relatively stable market prices.

The **kinked demand curve** model assumes the following:

- If a firm raises prices for its products, its competitors will not react by raising prices, expecting to see their market share rise.
- If a firm lowers its prices, its competitors will meet the new prices with lower ones of their own to make sure that they do not lose market share.

As a result, the relevant demand curve facing the firm is the darkened portion of demand curves d and D that is kinked at point *e*. The relevant portion of the marginal revenue curve is the darkened dashed curve MR with the discontinuity between points *a* and *b*. Notice, we are just using the relevant portions of MR_d and MR_D. As shown, marginal cost crosses through the discontinuity, resulting in an equilibrium price and output of P_0 and Q_0.

It is, of course, the discontinuity in the MR curve that gives this model its price stability. The marginal cost curve can vary anywhere between points *a* and *b* before the firm will have any incentive to change prices to maximize profits.

The analysis of unstable and stable oligopoly models underscores the importance of the mutual interdependence of firms. How one firm reacts to a competitor's market strategy determines the nature of competition in the industry. These ideas led to game theory, which we consider in the next section.

CHECKPOINT

OLIGOPOLY

- Oligopolies are markets (a) with only a few firms, (b) where each firm takes into account the reaction of rivals to its policies or firms recognize their mutual interdependence, and (c) where there are significant barriers to entry.
- The market power for an oligopoly can be substantial, although the ability of a firm to utilize its market power fully depends on its interdependence with competing firms.
- Cartels result when several firms collude to set market price and output. Cartels typically use their market power to act like monopolists and share the economic profits that result.
- Cartels are inherently unstable because individual firms can earn higher profits by selling more than their allotted quota. As more firms in the cartel cheat, prices fall, defeating the agreement.
- The observation that prices are stable in oligopoly industries (other than in cartels) gave rise to the kinked demand curve model. The model assumes that competitors will follow price reductions but not price increases. This leads to a discontinuity in MR, permitting cost to vary substantially before prices are changed.

QUESTION: The major drug cartels operating along the U.S.–Mexico border have become increasingly violent in recent years as cartels try to protect their trafficking routes to the U.S. market from competitors. But in addition to conflicts with external competition, cartel members have been murdered for exceeding their distribution quotas. Given the nature of how cartels function, explain why cartel leaders have become increasingly violent as a result of the above events.

Answers to the Checkpoint question can be found at the end of this chapter.

Game Theory

game theory The study of how individuals and firms make strategic decisions to achieve their goals when other parties or factors can influence that outcome.

Technology standards are constantly changing. Compare your current smartphone with your previous one and notice the features that have become standard, such as voice recognition typing and advanced GPS applications. Behind the scenes, technology firms such as Apple and Samsung engage in fierce competition in the development of the next technological feature. But developing a new feature itself is not enough; to become the industry standard, all firms must adopt compatible features. Meanwhile, competing firms strive to improve upon existing features to avoid becoming obsolete and losing market power. The study of how oligopoly firms use strategies to gain market power and their effects on competing firms and on consumers form the foundation of game theory.

Reuters/CORBIS

Jacob Andrzejczak/Getty Images

Dan Kelly Photo/Corbis

What do Warren Buffett, Bill Gates, Annie Duke, and Mike McCarthy have in common? They are all experts in strategic thinking.

Game theory is the study of how individuals and firms make strategic decisions to achieve their goals when other parties or factors can influence that outcome. In short, it is the study of strategy and strategic behavior and is used in any situation in which one must predict the actions of others and respond by choosing among more than one strategy, each resulting in a potentially different outcome. Although game theory was first developed from the analysis of imperfect competition, particularly in explaining the actions of firms that are oligopolies, today it is used to study situations that extend well beyond the typical economic problems we have seen thus far in this book.

Real-life applications of game theory are abundant, and include situations common in sports coaching, business pricing, management, politics and elections, law and courtroom proceedings, military strategy, and even literal games such as poker. In 1995, Johnnie Cochran successfully defended O. J. Simpson against a murder charge when the evidence seemed to be stacked against him. In 2004, Annie Duke became the world's top female poker player by winning the World Series of Poker Tournament of Champions. In 2005, Bill Belichick took his New England Patriots to an unprecedented third Super Bowl win in four years. In 2008, Barack Obama surpassed favored Hillary Clinton to become his party's presidential nominee and eventually the president. As these events suggest, the importance of strategic thinking is a reason why game theory is an interdisciplinary topic that extends well beyond economics.

This section highlights key concepts of game theory, beginning with the important concept of a Nash equilibrium, named after famous mathematician-turned-economist and eventual Nobel Prize winner John Nash. In the next section, we extend this analysis to realistic cases and applications to illustrate how game theory is a part of our lives. We will show how game theory helps explain the actions of oligopolies.

NOBEL PRIZE
JOHN NASH

No person arguably has had more influence on strategic economic analysis than John Nash, a mathematician turned economist whose theories led to the development of modern game theory. Born in 1928 to well-educated parents in Bluefield, West Virginia, John Nash was encouraged to pursue educational interests at a young age. As his aptitude for math developed, he enrolled in advanced mathematics classes at a local college while still in high school.

At age 16, he attended the Carnegie Institute of Technology (now Carnegie Mellon University), where by age 20 he earned both his bachelor's and master's degrees in mathematics. His advisor wrote a one-line letter of recommendation for his graduate school applications: "This man is a genius." Nash continued his education at Princeton University where he earned his Ph.D. at age 22, completing what remains one of the shortest yet most influential dissertations: a 28-page study of noncooperative games whose conclusion would eventually be coined the Nash equilibrium.

John Nash worked as a professor at the Massachusetts Institute of Technology and also for the U.S. government as an expert code breaker. It was during these early adult years when mental illness began to set in, and he eventually was diagnosed with paranoid schizophrenia. His battles with severe disillusions consumed much of his life, and he was often seen talking to imaginary figures. Yet, his ability to make new contributions to game theory, a relatively new topic at the time, earned him a permanent faculty position at Princeton, where he remains a professor to this day.

In 1994, John Nash was recognized with the Nobel Prize in economics for his contributions to game theory. His life would be the subject of several books, including Sylvia Nasar's *A Beautiful Mind*, published in 1998. The book was adapted into the 2001 blockbuster movie by the same name, starring Russell Crowe, that would go on to win four Academy Awards, including Best Picture.

Basic Game Setup and Assumptions

A basic setup of a "game" requires players, information, strategies, outcomes, and payoffs. This game setup applies to virtually all situations in which strategy (game theory) is used to analyze a real-life scenario. Let's look at each component.

- **Players:** Players can be firms competing for customers, a plaintiff and a defendant in a courtroom, two or more countries at war, or actual *players* in the literal sense in a sporting match or card game.
- **Information:** Each player holds information that is either known to others or is private. Having private information changes the way in which a game is played and the outcomes it produces.
- **Strategies:** Players make choices based on strategies devised from the information they have and the information they suspect other players hold. Players use strategies to improve the likelihood of achieving their best outcome.
- **Outcomes:** Outcomes refer to all possibilities, good and bad, that can occur given the strategies employed by players. In zero-sum games, outcomes are a "win" or a "loss." In any given hand in poker, for example, one person wins the pot of money while everyone else loses. In other games, there may be no losers per se, but firms compete for market share, or job applicants compete for various types of jobs.
- **Payoffs:** The payoff is the value players attach to each outcome. Each player has his or her own perception of each outcome, because rarely do players in a game have exactly the same objective. Payoffs are what players ultimately try to maximize.

In addition to identifying the setup described above, analyses of situations involving game theory typically make two general assumptions:

1. *Preferences are clearly defined.* The objectives of each player must be known. For example, a firm's objective might be to maximize its profits, while a golfer's objective is to achieve a low score.
2. *Players rationally choose strategies to achieve objectives.* Players make consistent decisions that improve their chances of achieving their goals. Sometimes, however, people make decisions that seem irrational. Game theory does have something to say about irrational behavior, but this is beyond the scope of this section.

Simultaneous Versus Sequential-Move Games

simultaneous-move games Games in which players' actions occur at the same time, forcing players to make decisions without knowing how the other players will act. These games are analyzed using diagrams called game tables.

sequential-move games Games in which players make moves one at a time, allowing players to view the progression of the game and to make decisions based on previous moves.

Game theory moves can be simultaneous or sequential. **Simultaneous-move games** involve actions by players that occur at the same time. Examples include sporting matches such as a soccer game with offensive and defensive players, and business pricing where firms must decide on prices to be placed in ads without knowing what prices their competitors will choose. **Sequential-move games** are situations in which one player at a time makes a move. Examples include games such as chess or tic-tac-toe, but also extend to examples such as negotiations (where offers are made back-and-forth), golf, or reality show competitions.

The way in which simultaneous-move and sequential-move games are analyzed differs. We focus primarily on simultaneous-move games, leaving the discussion of sequential-move games to later in the chapter.

Simultaneous-Move Games

Figure 6 illustrates a two-player simultaneous-move game in a diagram called a game table (also known as a payoff matrix or normal form analysis). In our example, Lowe's and Home Depot must choose one of two policies: advertise in the local paper or don't advertise. Lowe's strategies are listed in rows, while Home Depot's strategies are listed in columns. Because players (firms) move at the same time, outcomes are determined by the interaction of strategies chosen by each player. In this case, four potential outcomes exist, with Lowe's payoff shown before Home Depot's in each outcome. The outcome depends on which strategy each player actually chooses.

Let's go through each outcome, to show you how to read the figure. If Lowe's and Home Depot both advertise, each will earn a profit of $100,000. The advertising will induce some customers to buy now, but won't much affect whether they will buy at Lowe's or at Home Depot. There is a cost to advertising, which is why profits are lower when both firms advertise than when both do not. When both do not advertise, each earns a profit of $200,000. Customers continue to go to Lowe's and Home Depot about equally, and both firms do not bear the cost of the advertising.

What happens if one advertises while the other does not? The one that advertises increases profits. If Lowe's advertises while Home Depot does not, it earns a profit of $300,000 compared to Home Depot's $50,000. Why this result? Lowe's has to pay the cost of advertising but more than makes up for it by taking customers away from Home Depot. By not advertising, Home Depot saves on this cost, but it does not make up for the lost customer sales. This result is the same, but reversed, if Lowe's does not advertise while Home Depot does: Home Depot sees $300,000 in profits while Lowe's profit is only $50,000.

		Home Depot: Advertise		Home Depot: Don't advertise	
Lowe's	Advertise	$100,000 (underlined)	$100,000 (underlined)	$300,000 (underlined)	$50,000
	Don't advertise	$50,000	$300,000 (underlined)	$200,000	$200,000

FIGURE 6

Simultaneous-Move Game Illustrated in a Game Table

A simultaneous-move game between Lowe's and Home Depot is shown in which both firms must choose whether to advertise in the local paper or not, without knowing what the other will do. The choice made by each firm results in a different payoff for each.

Strategically, what is the best thing for each to do: advertise or not advertise? Let's first look at the best possible outcome for Lowe's. Its best outcome would be to advertise when Home Depot does not, allowing Lowe's to earn $300,000 while Home Depot ends up with $50,000, its worst outcome. Alternatively, the best collective outcome for Lowe's and Home Depot occurs when both do not advertise and each earns $200,000. Is either of these outcomes likely?

Let's approach this question by looking at the best response of one firm to the other's action. Suppose Home Depot strives for its highest possible outcome of $300,000 by advertising. What would be Lowe's best response? Clearly, Lowe's does not want to bear the minuscule profits of $50,000 if it does not advertise and Home Depot does advertise, therefore it advertises and earns $100,000. Therefore, choosing to advertise is a best response if competitors advertise. In Figure 6, this payoff is underlined.

Looking at it from Home Depot's point of view, it also advertises in response to Lowe's advertising, because it too would not want Lowe's to grab too many of its customers. Advertising is a best response for Home Depot because it results in a payoff of $100,000 (underlined) instead of $50,000. If both Lowe's and Home Depot act strategically by advertising to avoid the worst possible outcome, then the best case scenario of earning $300,000 is not possible.

If the best outcome is not possible, then how about the best collective outcome in which both firms choose not to advertise and each earns $200,000? Clearly, this outcome is better than if both firms advertise. But they cannot call each other up and say "I will not advertise if you do not advertise." This is collusion, prevented by law in the United States and in many other countries. Each firm has to make a decision without knowing what the other will do.

Again using the best-response approach, if Home Depot chooses not to advertise, Lowe's would still be better off advertising, because (1) it eliminates the worst-case outcome if Home Depot does in fact advertise, and (2) if Home Depot does not advertise, advertising would allow Lowe's to achieve its highest payoff of $300,000. Therefore, Lowe's best response to Home Depot not advertising is still to advertise (the corresponding payoff is underlined in Figure 6). From Home Depot's perspective, its best response if Lowe's does not advertise would be to advertise as well.

In sum, the best action each firm can take, *considering each of the possible actions the other might take*, is to bear the cost of advertising. This outcome is what economists call a Nash equilibrium.

Nash Equilibrium

Nash equilibrium An outcome that occurs when all players choose their optimal strategy in response to all other players' potential moves. At a Nash equilibrium, no player can be better off by unilaterally deviating from the noncooperative outcome.

A **Nash equilibrium** occurs when all players in a game use an optimal strategy in response to all other players' strategies. It is the outcome that maximizes all players' expected payoffs (the value of each potential outcome times the probability of that outcome occurring) given the information they have. In other words, aiming for the outcome with the highest payoff is not always prudent if the likelihood of achieving that outcome is small. Solving for Nash equilibrium is therefore valuable because it represents a player's best payoff taking into account the self-interested actions of all other players affecting the outcome. Once a Nash equilibrium is achieved, no individual player can do better by changing his or her mind.

For example, it is possible that Lowe's or Home Depot could see higher profits if it chose not to advertise, but there's a higher probability of it leading to lower profits. Nash equilibrium guides players to choose strategies that result in the best expected payoff. In the Lowe's–Home Depot example, the Nash equilibrium is for each to advertise when neither knows what the other will do.

An outcome is a Nash equilibrium if it results from all players acting strategically (using a best response) to each other's actions. In some cases, players choose the same action regardless of what others do, while in other cases, players choose different actions in response to other players' actions. In the Home Depot–Lowe's example, each firm's best response is to advertise regardless of what the other firm does, and is known as a dominant strategy. A **dominant strategy** occurs when one player chooses the same action regardless of what the other player chooses. When both players have a dominant strategy, a single Nash equilibrium will result. For Lowe's and Home Depot, both advertising is the Nash equilibrium. But not all Nash equilibria are the result of dominant strategies. In fact, games need not be limited to one Nash equilibrium. When dominant strategies do not exist, games can have no Nash equilibrium while others might have more than one, as we'll soon see.

dominant strategy Occurs when a player chooses the same strategy regardless of what his or her opponent chooses.

Also, a Nash equilibrium outcome is not always obvious. In Figure 6, it might seem that Lowe's and Home Depot not advertising would be a Nash equilibrium; besides, the profits for both are higher than the profits with advertising. But such a quick conclusion does not take into account the fact that one firm could do even better by advertising if the other does not. And because neither firm wishes to risk the worst-case scenario, they both engage in advertising as their best response action. Fortunately, not all Nash equilibrium outcomes are so pessimistic. In many cases, acting in response to another player's actions can lead to a good outcome for all players, as we'll see next.

Nash Equilibrium: A Personal Example Let's look at a personal example to make sure that the idea of a Nash equilibrium is clear. Suppose you are talking with a friend on the phone, and the line suddenly goes dead. Does this scenario sound familiar? Perhaps it is because it happens so often. This very moment often creates a quick but annoying dilemma: Do you immediately call your friend back, or do you wait for your friend to call you back?

For simplicity, assume you are given just one opportunity to make a decision. If both you and your friend immediately call each other back, chances are you might end up reaching each other's voicemail. If instead, you both wait for each other to call back, then you end up waiting anxiously wondering why your friend didn't call you back. In each situation, players did not accurately select the best response to the other player's action. Therefore, a Nash equilibrium occurs when one person calls and the other responds by waiting.

		Friend	
		Call back	Wait
You	Call back	Voicemail	Connected call
	Wait	Connected call	Silence

Tim Pannell/Corbis

FIGURE 7

Dropped Call Dilemma: Who Should Call Back First?

The two cases in which the call is successfully connected each represent a Nash equilibrium.

Figure 7 illustrates each of the four possible outcomes. Two outcomes meet the criteria for a Nash equilibrium, which is common for coordination-type games when players are attempting to achieve a mutually beneficial outcome. For each Nash equilibrium, both you and you friend used a best-response action that led to a completed call; in other words, if your friend calls, you wait. If your friend waits, you call.

To review, a Nash equilibrium describes any outcome when all players respond optimally to all possible actions by other players. At that outcome, no player would choose to deviate unilaterally from that outcome; this doesn't mean that a better outcome might prevail with some cooperation, but rather that no player would change her position by herself. Finding a Nash equilibrium is therefore useful because it represents the best outcome given the self-interested actions of all other players.

We have seen two situations with different Nash equilibrium outcomes. For Lowe's and Home Depot, the Nash equilibrium was an outcome that neither firm truly desired. In the next section, we will classify these outcomes as a Prisoner's Dilemma and show what can be done to overcome such outcomes. For the dropped call example, we found more than one Nash equilibrium in which both players would be happy. But we need not stop here. The next section will highlight other Nash equilibrium outcomes that can result depending on the circumstances facing each player.

ISSUE

Mission ~~Im~~possible: The Power of Focal Points in a Simulated Mission

Barry Nalebuff is a respected economist who has published several books on game theory, and is known for constructing unorthodox methods of using game theory to solve life's problems. In 2006, Barry Nalebuff teamed up with the show *PrimeTime* to create a unique game theory experiment dealing with Nash equilibria and focal points. They took six pairs of people who did not know one another and placed them in different locations in New York City's Manhattan. The objective of this game was to have at least one pair find one of the other five pairs within a day, not knowing where they would be or what they looked like. It's a true needle in a haystack problem trying to locate an unfamiliar person among millions in Manhattan. Sound impossible? Perhaps. But game theory teaches us to use clues effectively to solve such problems. In this case, when players have the same goal, strategies can be employed to maximize the chances of achieving it.

Recall the concepts of Nash equilibrium in the dropped call problem. Unlike that situation, which contained four potential outcomes and two Nash equilibria, the present example contains infinite outcomes and infinite Nash equilibria (since pairs could meet at any of millions of locations at any time of the day). When many possible solutions exist, players must use focal points to reach an equilibrium solution. Focal points are solutions that seem more obvious based on clues and past experience.

In the present example, focal points rely on three dimensions: where, when, and who. Where would pairs go to facilitate spotting others? Common answers might include Times Square, the Empire State Building, the Statue of Liberty, and Grand Central Terminal, among others. By listing these likely locations, we reduce the number of likely outcomes from millions of locations to fewer than a dozen. Next is the timing issue. Two pairs could be at the same location but at different times. Thus, a focal point in time is necessary; obvious times might be noon (the strongest focal point), 9 A.M., 3 P.M., or 5 P.M. Lastly, two pairs could be at the same location at the same time, but still not recognize one another. Thus, a focal point on recognizing another pair is necessary, and can be achieved through costumes, posters and signs, and noisemaking devices. Would the combination of each of the dimensions of focal points turn a seemingly impossible task into a successful one?

On the show, the six teams had resounding success. Three teams found each other at the top of the Empire State Building at noon wearing signs, while another three teams found each other in Times Square at noon also holding signs and using whistles and other noisemakers. Clearly, the use of game theory is a powerful and effective tool when confronted with some of life's biggest challenges.

Because the Nash equilibrium in each situation is not automatically obvious, it's important to use the best-response method to solve for Nash equilibrium to ensure that each player's expected payoff is maximized.

CHECKPOINT

GAME THEORY

- Game theory uses sophisticated mathematical analysis to help explain the actions of oligopolies, as well as develop optimal strategies for life's everyday situations.
- Game theory characteristics include the number of players and strategies, information completeness, and the value of potential outcomes (payoffs).
- Simultaneous-move games occur when players make decisions without knowing what other players will choose, and are analyzed using diagrams called game tables.
- Nash equilibrium analysis describes outcomes in which all players respond optimally to all possible actions by other players to achieve the highest expected payoff.
- It is possible to have zero, one, two, or more Nash equilibria in a game.

QUESTION: In the dropped call example presented earlier, two Nash equilibria existed in which one person calls back and the other person waits. However, this does not completely resolve the situation because each player must still figure out what his or her role will be: to call back or to wait. Using your own personal experiences with this type of situation, what strategies would you use to determine who would call and who would wait? Assume that you have just one opportunity to choose (either to call or wait) and that you cannot communicate using any other method (such as texting).

Answers to the Checkpoint question can be found at the end of this chapter.

Applications of Game Theory

This section focuses on four common categories of games: Prisoner's Dilemma, repeated games, leadership games, and chicken games. In each of the examples within each category, we solve for a Nash equilibrium using the best-response method introduced in the previous section, and discuss the characteristics of these outcomes that are found in real-life examples. In doing this, you should get a sense of how game theory helps explain many oligopoly behaviors.

The Prisoner's Dilemma

Ever notice how competing stores pay very close attention to what their competitors do? When Office Depot offers back-to-school specials, Staples is sure to do the same. When one airline offers a summer fare sale, other airlines tend to follow. In our example of Lowe's and Home Depot in the previous section, each firm chooses to advertise even if it results in lower profits than if neither advertises. If you were a manager of one of these firms, shouldn't you immediately cease advertising? Not necessarily. Game theory helps to explain this seemingly counterintuitive outcome. In each of these situations, the Nash equilibrium that results is an outcome that is inferior to another outcome that can be achieved through cooperation, and is referred to as a **Prisoner's Dilemma.**

Prisoner's Dilemma A noncooperative game in which players cannot communicate or collaborate in making their decisions, which results in inferior outcomes for both players. Many oligopoly decisions can be framed as a Prisoner's Dilemma.

Given the similarities of products sold by monopolistically competitive and oligopoly firms, Prisoner's Dilemma outcomes occur frequently as firms compete for market share, such as AT&T and Verizon in wireless communications, Carnival and Royal Caribbean in cruise vacations, and Target and Wal-Mart in discount retailing.

For consumers, however, Prisoner's Dilemma outcomes are beneficial because they result in lower prices for goods. As competing firms lower their prices to gain market share, they earn a smaller profit from each customer. In some cases, competition becomes so intense that a competitor is forced out of business. Just ask Circuit City, Borders, Sharper Image, and Linens-N-Things, just to name a few. Why would firms compete to the point of nearly zero profit margins? Wouldn't it make sense for competing firms to utilize their collective market power by all raising their prices to make more money?

Alas, here's the dilemma: Firms cannot openly collude to raise prices (that is illegal under antitrust laws). However, firms *can* silently collude by raising prices unilaterally and hoping that others will follow. But will the others follow?

Suppose two shoe stores operate near campus, Shoe Carnival and Shoe Festival. Assume, for simplicity, that each has two pricing strategies: a high markup and a low markup. If both stores choose the same strategy, they each attract the same number of customers. But if one store is less expensive than the other, it takes most of the customers and profits (despite earning less profit per customer at the lower price). Figure 8 shows a game table with presumed profits under the four outcomes.

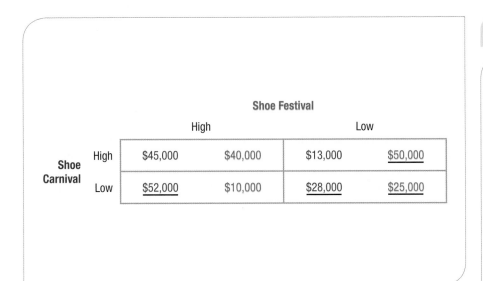

		Shoe Festival: High		Shoe Festival: Low	
Shoe Carnival	High	$45,000	$40,000	$13,000	$50,000
Shoe Carnival	Low	$52,000	$10,000	$28,000	$25,000

FIGURE 8

Prisoner's Dilemma Game Between Two Firms

Intense competition between Shoe Carnival and Shoe Festival results in both stores pricing their products low, resulting in a Nash equilibrium payoff of $28,000 for Shoe Carnival and $25,000 for Shoe Festival. However, another outcome provides a greater profit for *both* stores, that is, if both stores price high. But because the two stores cannot openly collude, and neither trusts the other to maintain high prices, both stores end up pricing their products low, resulting in lower profits.

Using the best-response method to solve for Nash equilibrium, Shoe Carnival's best response to a high price by Shoe Festival is to price low, thereby stealing most of Shoe Festival's customers and earning a higher profit. And to prevent the same from happening if Shoe Festival prices low, Shoe Carnival's best response is also to price low. Therefore, Shoe Carnival has a dominant strategy to keep its prices low regardless of what Shoe Festival does. In Figure 8, the strategies selected by Shoe Carnival in response to each strategy by Shoe Festival are underlined. If we conduct the same analysis for Shoe Festival, we also find that Shoe Festival has a dominant strategy to price low, resulting in a Nash equilibrium when both stores price low, resulting in a payoff of $28,000 for Shoe Carnival and $25,000 for Shoe Festival.

Does this equilibrium seem odd? It might because another outcome (where both stores price high) provides greater profit to *both* stores. Yet, that outcome is *not* a Nash equilibrium. A Prisoner's Dilemma therefore results because players are unable to cooperate effectively with one another. Why don't the stores just agree to price their products high? They can't do it by colluding; that is illegal. And if one store raises its prices unilaterally, there is no guarantee the other store will follow, thus risking a loss of customers and profit.

The Classic Prisoner's Dilemma How did the Prisoner's Dilemma get its name? Two criminal suspects (Matthew and Chris) are apprehended on a charge of robbery. They are separated, put in solitary confinement, and are unable to speak to each other. Each prisoner is offered the same bargain: Confess that you and your partner both committed the crime and you will go free while your non-confessing partner will go to prison for three years. If neither confesses, the state likely will convict them both on lesser charges resulting in a one-year sentence for each. Finally, if both confess, they each will go to prison for two years.

Figure 9 on the next page illustrates this game in which payoffs represent the number of years in prison. The prisoners must make a decision without knowing what the

FIGURE 9

The Classic Prisoner's Dilemma

Matthew and Chris are two suspects held in separate cells. Each is given an opportunity to confess to the crime, with the resulting jail sentences shown for each outcome. Under this payoff structure, the optimal response by each player is to confess, resulting in a single Nash equilibrium where each receives two years of jail time. This Nash equilibrium is a Prisoner's Dilemma because a better outcome (not confessing) exists for both players.

		Chris: Do not confess		Chris: Confess	
Matthew	Do not confess	1 year	1 year	3 years	<u>0 years</u>
	Confess	<u>0 years</u>	3 years	<u>2 years</u>	<u>2 years</u>

other chose, and decisions are irrevocable. Each prisoner is only concerned with his own welfare—minimizing his time in prison. Is there a unique solution?

Using the best-response method, Matthew and Chris both have a dominant strategy to confess! This outcome results despite the fact that both would be better off by not confessing: one year served in prison versus two. The Prisoner's Dilemma results because neither player trusts the other not to confess given the structure of the payoffs.

Other Examples of Prisoner's Dilemma Outcomes Now that you have an idea of what a Prisoner's Dilemma entails, particularly when oligopoly firms compete, let's mention a few other examples in which a Prisoner's Dilemma might occur.

- **Political Campaigns:** Politicians spend immense amounts of time, effort, and money to win elections. Some members of Congress in swing districts spend half of their two-year terms in office campaigning, leaving little time to get anything else done, like passing laws. If competing candidates have roughly equal amounts of time and money, the result is likely to be similar if the candidates agree not to campaign at all; but that requires each candidate to trust the other not to break that promise, which is not an easy proposition.
- **Legal Disputes:** When individuals or firms end up in litigation, plaintiffs and defendants often will spend large amounts of money in legal fees and for consultants merely to offset what the other side spends. For high-profile cases, add the costs of media coverage and the costs incurred by family, friends, and curious onlookers, and the outcome often is more costly for all parties involved.
- **Trade Disputes:** When one country restricts imported goods to protect domestic producers from foreign competition, other countries have an incentive to do the same, making it difficult for domestic producers to sell their goods abroad. When countries restrict trade against each other, a Prisoner's Dilemma outcome occurs because trade barriers cause a reduction in the gains from specialization and trade, harming all countries.

Resolving the Prisoner's Dilemma Prisoner's Dilemma type of situations are difficult to resolve in a noncooperative framework when the players are not able to coordinate their strategies, whether as a result of antitrust laws or an inability to retaliate against other players if the cooperative action is not played. Although Prisoner's Dilemma outcomes might be bad for firms in a pricing game or for litigants in a trial, they surely are beneficial to consumers who enjoy lower prices and for lawyers who might earn a lot of money in a high-profile case.

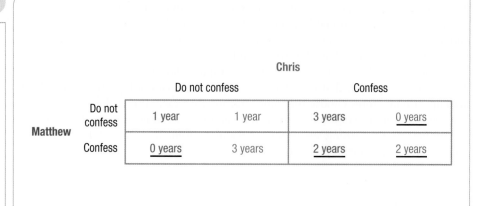

Let's consider a case of trade protection in which a Prisoner's Dilemma might be resolved successfully. A Prisoner's Dilemma occurs when countries enact trade barriers, causing the gains from trade to be restricted. Free trade agreements are a way for countries to overcome the Prisoner's Dilemma by agreeing to promote free trade among members. And unlike collusive agreements between firms, free trade agreements are legal and have been implemented extensively in recent decades.

Another way to overcome the Prisoner's Dilemma is by ensuring that the game is repeated over time. When games are played just once, players have an incentive to maximize their payoffs in the game without worrying about long-term consequences. However, when a game is repeated indefinitely, incentives change, and players worry about retaliation.

Repeated Games

Pick up a Sunday newspaper and notice the large selection of circulars included. Many retailers advertise their products using a Sunday ad without knowing what their competitors' ads look like. But because this game is repeated every Sunday, no firm would risk retaliation by advertising prices that are *too* low relative to other firms. Thus, repeated games provide a way for competing players to check how other players are behaving, and to provide a way of punishing unfair players.

Olivier Le Queinec/Dreamstime.com

Sunday ads: an example of a repeated game by retailers.

Games can be endlessly (infinitely) repeated or repeated for a specific number of rounds. In either case, repeating opens the game to different types of strategies that are unavailable for a game played only once. These strategies can take into account the past behavior of rivals. This section briefly explores these strategies and some of their implications for understanding oligopoly behavior.

One possibility is simply to cooperate or defect from the beginning. These strategies, however, leave you at the mercy of your opponent, or lead to unfavorable outcomes where both firms earn less or suffer losses. A more robust set of strategies are **trigger strategies:** action is taken contingent on your opponent's past decisions. Here are a few of them.

trigger strategies Action is taken contingent on your opponent's past decisions.

Grim Trigger Let's start by considering an industry that is earning oligopoly profits. Suppose that all of a sudden, one firm lowers its price, maybe because it is in financial trouble and wants to increase sales right away. Under the grim trigger rule, the other firms lower their prices—but they do not stop there. They permanently lower their prices, making the financial condition of the original firm that reduced prices even more severe.

The grim trigger rule, thus, is this: Any decision by your opponent to defect (choose an unfavorable outcome) is met by a permanent retaliatory decision forever. This is a harsh decision rule. Its negative aspect is that it is subject to misreading. For example, has your competition lowered its price in an attempt to gain market share at your expense, or has the market softened for the product in general? This strategy can quickly lead to the unfavorable Prisoner's Dilemma result. To avoid this problem, oligopoly firms might use other trigger strategies.

Trembling Hand Trigger A trembling hand trigger strategy allows for a mistake by your opponent before you retaliate. This gives your opponent a chance to make a mistake and reduces misreads that are a problem for the grim trigger strategy. This approach can be extended to accept two nonsequential defects, and so on, but they can be exploited by clever opponents who figure out that they can get away with a few "mistakes" before their opponent retaliates.

Tit-for-Tat A **tit-for-tat** strategy is one that repeats the prior move of competitors. If one firm lowers its price, its rivals follow suit one time. If the same firm offers rebates or special offers, rivals do exactly the same in the next time period. This strategy has the efficient qualities that it rewards cooperation and punishes defection.

tit-for-tat strategies A trigger strategy that rewards cooperation and punishes defections. If your opponent lowers its price, you do the same. If your opponent returns to a cooperative strategy, you do the same.

This short list of strategies illustrates the richness of repeated games. Strategies tend to be more successful if they are relatively simple and easy to understand by competitors, tend to foster cooperation, have some credible punishment to reduce defections, and provide for forgiveness to avoid the costly mistakes associated with misreading opponents.[1]

Using Sequential-Move Analysis to Model Repeated Games Because repeated games involve multiple iterations of the same game, it can be shown in sequential-move game diagrams called game trees, also called decision trees or extensive form analysis. In Figure 10, a game tree is shown between two hardware firms that advertise each week in the Sunday ads. To avoid the Prisoner's Dilemma, both firms must choose to advertise lightly. They continue to do so unless one firm chooses to advertise heavily, which would lead to a trigger strategy in the next stage. Suppose Tool Shack contemplates advertising heavily this week: Tool Kingdom can respond to this action by advertising heavily next week, or choose not to. In the figure, Tool Shack makes the first decision whether to advertise lightly or heavily. If Tool Shack chooses to advertise heavily, Tool Kingdom then chooses whether to respond.

FIGURE 10

Sequential-Move Game Illustrated in a Game Tree

A sequential-move game is illustrated between Tool Shack and Tool Kingdom. Tool Shack makes the first move by choosing whether to advertise heavily. After seeing Tool Shack's decision, Tool Kingdom responds by choosing to retaliate (by also advertising heavily) or not. For each possible outcome, a payoff results for each firm.

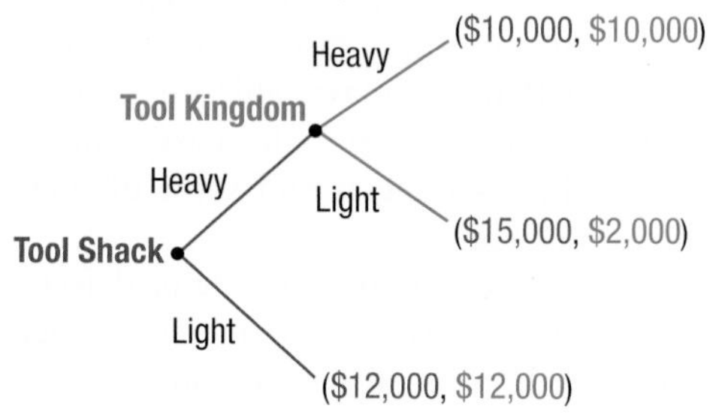

Looking at Tool Kingdom's payoffs, it is in its best interest to advertise heavily if Tool Shack chooses to advertise heavily. Tool Shack, knowing that advertising heavily would be Tool Kingdom's best response in the next stage, would likely choose to maintain its light advertising to avoid the Prisoner's Dilemma outcome. The sequential nature of game trees allows players to see the progression of moves across time from start to finish.

Resolving the Prisoner's Dilemma is an important outcome of cooperative strategies. But not all competitive games lead to a Prisoner's Dilemma to begin with. One example is called a leadership game, where an industry is dominated by a market leader.

Leadership Games

Facebook is the world's largest social media provider, which earns its revenues primarily through advertising and sets prices to maximize its profits. Yet, other smaller social networks also compete for revenues. Unlike earlier examples, in which competing firms are of similar size, Facebook's market dominance allows it to ignore the pricing actions of its smaller competitors. In other words, if Facebook loses a few advertisers due to lower prices on other networks, the loss in revenues is smaller than what it would lose if Facebook lowers its own prices.

[1] Nick Wilkinson, *Managerial Economics: A Problem Solving Approach* (Cambridge: Cambridge University Press), 2005, p. 373.

Another example of a leadership game occurs when a small low-fare airline competes against a larger airline. Frontier Airlines is a relatively small airline based in Denver; it competes on many routes that United Airlines serves. But because United is a significantly larger airline with greater market power, it does not always match Frontier's lower fares because United believes it would not lose many customers.

Chicken Games

Another category of game that does not result in a Prisoner's Dilemma can be seen if you belong to a union at work, or enjoy watching professional sports or television shows, situations where collective bargaining (organized labor) is powerful. Every once in a while, a labor dispute boils over to a point where a strike is either threatened or sometimes carried out. Although we discuss labor disputes in the next chapter, this is an example of an important class of games called chicken.

A chicken game is portrayed in the classic movie *Rebel Without a Cause*, in which James Dean's character is challenged by a rival to a stunt challenge. Both players race their cars toward a cliff, and the first person to jump out is the "chicken." The winner is the person who stays in the car longer. Of course, if neither player leaves his car, they both plunge to their deaths.

Chicken games describe games of holdouts or brinkmanship. Players involved in chicken games want to hold out as long as they can to win, trying to get the other side to give in. If neither side does, the worst outcome occurs. Examples of brinkmanship occur regularly in Congress. Neither Democrats nor Republicans wish to concede anything up to the very end, when some catastrophic consequence threatens the economy such as a government default (from failing to raise the debt ceiling) or a *fiscal cliff* of higher taxes and severe spending cuts (from failing to agree on a budget). Brinkmanship often ties one's hands.

Figure 11 illustrates a chicken game using the 2012 NHL labor dispute as an example. Suppose the players union and the team owners are in a dispute over salaries. Each side can remain tough, or loosen their position. The worst outcome occurs when both sides refuse to give in, resulting in a lockout or strike that is devastating to both sides, not to mention all the fans, who are not able to watch their favorite teams play.

		NHL Owners: Tough		NHL Owners: Loose	
NHL Players	Tough	0	0	_4_	_1_
	Loose	_1_	_4_	2	2

FIGURE 11

A Chicken Game Between NHL players and NHL Owners

Neither side wishes to give in to the other side in a labor dispute, but if neither gives in, the worst outcome of 0, 0 results (i.e., a lockout or strike). In chicken games, two Nash equilibria exist, each with one player achieving his ideal result while the other side settles.

Using the best-response method, we find that chicken games have two Nash equilibria, where one side ultimately *gives in* to the other. Specifically, if NHL owners choose the tough strategy by refusing to compromise, the best response of players would be to loosen their position and earn a payoff of 1 instead of 0. If NHL owners are willing to compromise, the best response of players would be to maintain a tough position and earn a payoff of 4 instead of 2. The same best-response strategies can be determined by the NHL owners in response to the NHL players' strategies.

Thus, in a chicken game, one party is much happier with a Nash equilibrium result than the other. Yet, the *loser* still would not have wanted to change its strategy, for doing so unilaterally would result in an even worse outcome. Unfortunately for the NHL, a Nash equilibrium did not occur as both sides refused to give in, resulting in a lockout and a severely compromised 2012–2013 season. This is an outcome that occasionally occurs in chicken games, one that had clear consequences for both players and owners, not to mention many disappointed fans.

As seen in the many applications in this and the last section, game theory is a powerful tool to analyze market competition when firms each have the ability to influence price and the market share of their competitors. The ability to anticipate another player's actions and respond optimally is the key to achieving a Nash equilibrium. Nash equilibrium is the outcome that maximizes all players' expected payoffs. Recognizing such outcomes allows all players to achieve the best outcome given the self-interested motives of all other players involved. Game theory has applications that extend beyond oligopoly competition and economics in general.

Summary of Market Structures

In this and the previous two chapters, we have studied the four major market structures: perfect competition, monopolistic competition, oligopoly, and monopoly. As we move through this list, market power becomes greater, and the ability of the firm to earn economic profits in the long run grows.

Table 1 summarizes the important distinctions among these four market structures. Keep in mind that market structure analysis allows you to look at the overall characteristics of the market and predict the pricing and profit behavior of the firms. The outcomes for perfect competition and monopolistic competition are particularly attractive for consumers because firms price their products equal to average total costs and earn just enough to keep them in the business over the long haul.

TABLE 1 Summary of Market Structures

	Perfect Competition	Monopolistic Competition	Oligopoly	Monopoly
Number of Firms	Many	Many	Few	One
Product	Homogeneous	Differentiated	Homogeneous or differentiated	Unique
Barriers to Entry or Exit?	No	No	Yes	Yes
Strategic Interdependence?	No	No	Yes	Not applicable
Market Power	None	Limited	Some	Absolute
Long-Run Price Decision	P = ATC	P = ATC	P > ATC	P > ATC
Long-Run Profits	Zero	Zero	Usually economic	Economic
Key Summary Characteristic	Price taker	Product differentiation	Mutual interdependence	One-firm industry

In contrast, the outcomes for oligopoly and monopoly industries are not as favorable to consumers. Concentrated markets have considerable market power, which shows up in pricing and output decisions. However, keep in mind that markets with market power (oligopolies) often involve giants competing with giants. Even though there is a mutual interdependence in their decisions and they may not always compete vigorously over prices, they often are innovative because of some competitive pressures. We see this today especially in the electronics and automobile markets.

CHECKPOINT

APPLICATIONS OF GAME THEORY

- The Prisoner's Dilemma is a noncooperative game in which players minimize their maximum prison time by both confessing, a strategy that neither would have taken had they been able to communicate with one another.
- Applications of Prisoner's Dilemma games extend well beyond criminal cases, and can involve firm pricing strategies, legal disputes, international trade protection, and political campaigns.
- Resolving the Prisoner's Dilemma is not easy because of antitrust laws preventing firms from colluding. However, when games are repeated, the threat of retaliation encourages players to use a cooperative strategy.
- Games that are repeated lead to more nuanced trigger strategies, including grim trigger, trembling hand trigger, and tit-for-tat.
- Leadership games describe competitive games in which one player is dominant in size relative to the rest of the players.
- Chicken games involve players who try to hold out for the optimal outcome; however, if neither side gives in, the worst outcome occurs. Labor disputes that often end up in strikes or lockouts are examples of chicken games.

QUESTIONS: Suppose your economics professor grades the class on a curve, such that exactly 25% of the class receives an A, 25% receives a B, 25% receives a C, and 25% receives a D, regardless of how the class actually performs. One of your classmates comes up with an idea: Instead of having the entire class study for hours and hours for each exam, everyone in the class agrees *not* to study, with the presumption that everyone would likely receive the same grade as if they did study given the grade distribution. Would this strategy work? Why or why not? What type of game does this best represent, a chicken game or a Prisoner's Dilemma? Explain.

Answers to the Checkpoint questions can be found at the end of this chapter.

chapter summary

Section 1: Monopolistic Competition

A **monopolistically competitive** industry has the following characteristics:

- Large number of firms with insignificant market share.
- No barriers to entry and exit.
- Products sold by firms are similar but differentiated (has a brand).
- Limited market power.

Short-run profit maximization for a monopolistically competitive industry looks identical to a monopoly. In the long run, however, the demand curve is tangent to the average total cost curve, signaling zero economic profit.

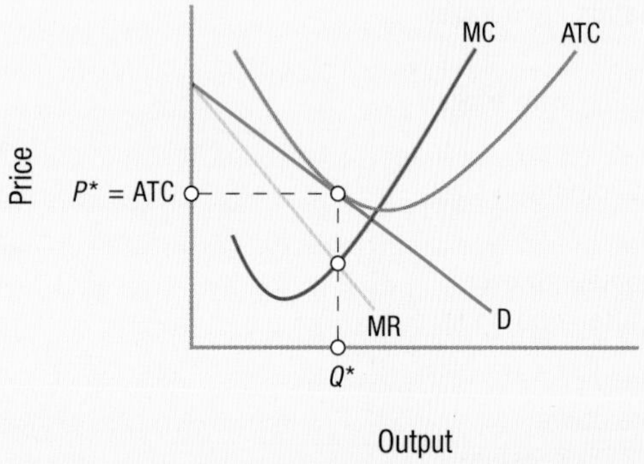

Because of product differentiation, a firm's demand curve is downward sloping. However, it is highly elastic due to the competitive nature of the industry.

Antonchalakov/Dreamstime.com

A shopping mall offers dozens of stores at which to buy clothing, each of which is differentiated.

Types of Product Differentiation

Location

Quality

Style, Design, and Features

Advertising

Section 2: Oligopoly

Oligopoly industries are controlled by a few large firms. Barriers to entry are significant, the product is less differentiated than in monopolistically competitive industries, and pricing decisions by one firm directly impact other firms (mutual interdependence). Oligopoly firms possess market power but not as much as a monopoly.

Cartels are agreements to restrict output to push prices higher, but are inherently unstable because cheating is profitable.

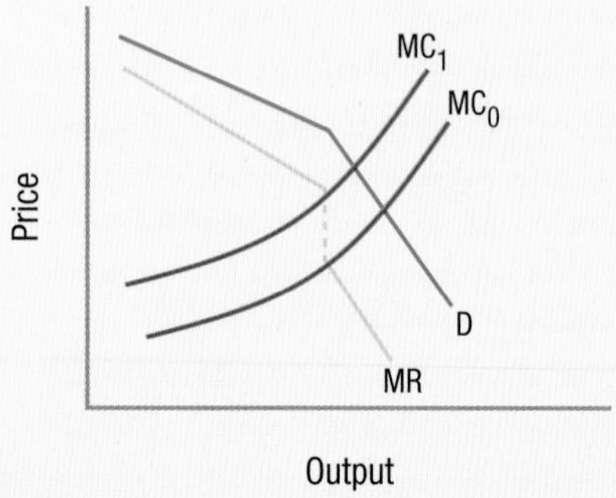

A **kinked demand curve** occurs because firms are reluctant to match price increases but not price decreases. The kink creates a discontinuity in the marginal revenue curve, allowing marginal cost to vary (from MC_0 to MC_1) while prices remain stable.

Kevork Djansezian/Getty Images

Competing gas stations keep their prices close to one another's.

Section 3: Game Theory

Game theory is the study of strategic decision making when multiple players each act in their own interests.

Components of a Game

Players

Information

Strategy choices

Outcomes and payoffs

Dave Reede/First Light/Corbis

Golf is a sequential-move game, in which players take their shots one at a time.

Nash equilibrium is an outcome that results from all players responding optimally to all other players' actions to maximize their expected payoffs. In a Nash equilibrium, no player wishes to deviate unilaterally from that outcome.

Solving for a Nash equilibrium requires analyzing a game table for best responses to the other player's possible actions.

		Player 2: Left	Player 2: Right
Player 1	Top	8 4	2 6
	Down	6 3	7 5

Player 1's best response to "Left" is "Top" = 8.

Player 1's best response to "Right" is "Down" = 7.

Player 2's best response to "Top" is "Right" = 6.

Player 2's best response to "Down" is "Right" = 5.

One Nash equilibrium = "Down", "Right" = (7, 5).

Section 4: Applications of Game Theory

A **Prisoner's Dilemma** occurs when optimal noncooperative play results in an outcome that is inferior to another for both players.

Ways to Overcome the Prisoner's Dilemma

Collusion: This is illegal in most cases, although international cartels exist, such as the OPEC oil cartel and the De Beers diamond cartel. Also, free trade agreements are a legal form of cooperation between countries.

Tacit collusion: Occurs when one player takes the lead, and everyone else follows. This strategy is more effective when games are repeated, allowing for the possibility of retaliation should other players not cooperate.

Richard Baker/In Pictures/Corbis

American Airlines was the first major airline to charge for checked baggage. Almost all other airlines followed, allowing the airlines to achieve a mutually beneficial outcome.

Trigger Strategies Used in Repeated Games

Grim trigger: When one player defects, the other refuses to cooperate again (no forgiveness).

Trembling hand trigger: Players forgive certain instances of defection as "mistakes" before retaliation is taken.

Tit-for-tat trigger: Essentially an eye-for-an-eye: If one player defects, the other player punishes this player until cooperation resumes.

Chicken games occur when opposing players have an incentive to maintain a tough stance; however, if neither player refuses to back down, the worst outcome for both players occurs.

KEY CONCEPTS

monopolistic competition, p. 248
product differentiation, p. 249
oligopoly, p. 253
mutual interdependence, p. 253
cartel, p. 253
kinked demand curve, p. 256
game theory, p. 256
simultaneous-move games, p. 258
sequential-move games, p. 258
Nash equilibrium, p. 260
dominant strategy, p. 260
Prisoner's Dilemma, p. 262
trigger strategies, p. 265
tit-for-tat strategies, p. 265

QUESTIONS AND PROBLEMS

Check Your Understanding

1. How do monopolistically competitive markets differ from perfectly competitive markets? If monopolistically competitive firms are making economic profits in the short run, what happens in the long run?
2. How do monopolistically competitive firms exhibit market power? In what ways can a firm increase market power?
3. Explain what strategic interdependence means and how it applies to oligopoly markets.
4. Why is it difficult for cartels to maintain high prices effectively over the longer term?
5. Why would the use of repeated games make overcoming the Prisoner's Dilemma easier compared to a game that is played only once?
6. What is the difference between a tit-for-tat trigger strategy and a grim trigger strategy?

Apply the Concepts

7. "Monopolistic competition has a little of monopoly and a little of competition, hence its name." Do you agree? Why or why not?
8. We saw in the last chapter that the HHI (Herfindahl-Hirschman index) is used by the Department of Justice to measure industry concentration. Because domestically we have very few monopolies, some would argue that the HHI is really used to measure the degree of oligopoly. However, the HHI represents domestic concentration, and many of the products we purchase are made globally and sold in the United States by foreign firms. Has global competition made these HHI estimates less meaningful? Are old-line American oligopolies (autos, steel, and airlines) more like monopolistic competitors today? Why or why not?
9. In both competitive and monopolistically competitive markets, firms earn normal profits in the long run. What enables oligopoly firms to have the opportunity to earn economic profits in the long run?
10. Poker players are known to *bluff* once in a while, meaning that they will make a large bet despite holding bad cards in an effort to pressure other players to *fold* their hands. Would bluffing be considered a dominant strategy to be used in poker?
11. Suppose you choose to pledge for your top choice of sorority or fraternity at your university. Despite the tiny odds of getting accepted into your top choice, that does not deter you from spending all of rush week focusing on your top choice. Would this strategy coincide with a best-response strategy in a Nash equilibrium?
12. Suppose two competing stores each announce a "low price guarantee," meaning that each store would match the prices of the other store if they were lower. Does providing this guarantee make it easier or more difficult to overcome the Prisoner's Dilemma facing the two firms?

In the News

13. The *Wall Street Journal* reported on April 25, 2012, that Pakistan launched a test missile in response to India launching a missile of its own the previous week. Both countries want to prove that they are the dominant military power in South Asia. Explain how this ongoing game between nuclear powers represents a game of chicken, and what might happen if neither side chooses to back down.
14. "Bank of America Faces Outrage over Debit Card Charge" was the headline in the *Washington Post* on September 30, 2011. Bank of America attempted to institute a new fee on debit card accounts by charging its debit card users $5 per month, in hopes that other banks would follow its lead. However, no other major bank did, and Bank of America was pummeled in the media and by customers who closed their accounts until Bank of America relented and dropped the new fee. Explain how Bank of America was attempting to overcome the Prisoner's Dilemma. Provide reasons why this attempt was unsuccessful.

Solving Problems

15. Suppose each member of a diamond cartel consisting of five producers agrees to sell 100 carats of diamonds a day. With 500 total carats being sold, the market price is $1,000/carat, and each firm earns $100,000. Now assume that one producer cheats by producing 110 carats, causing the market price for 510 total carats to drop to $980/carat. How does this action affect the revenues of the cheating firm and the noncheating firms? Suppose the four noncheating firms change course and all produce 110 carats, and the market price for 550 total carats drops to $850/carat. How much does each firm earn now? How important is loyalty to maintaining an effective cartel?
16. The following shows a pricing game between JetBlue and Delta. Each airline has a choice between engaging in a fare sale or not. The resulting profits of each airline are provided, where the first number in each payoff box equals JetBlue's profit and the second number is Delta's profit.

		Delta: Fare sale		Delta: No fare sale	
JetBlue	Fare sale	80	500	200	800
	No fare sale	50	700	100	1200

What is the Nash equilibrium of this game? Does this game resemble a Prisoner's Dilemma? Explain.

USING THE NUMBERS

17. According to By the Numbers, in terms of number of restaurants, what percentage of all restaurants among the top ten chains is a Subway, McDonald's, or a Starbucks? (Hint: First calculate the total number of Subways, McDonald's, and Starbucks combined and compare with the total restaurants among all top ten chains.)
18. According to By the Numbers, if the third and fourth largest wireless providers merged into one new company, would the combined company surpass the market share of either of the largest two firms prior to the merge?

ANSWERS TO QUESTIONS IN CHECKPOINTS

Checkpoint: Monopolistic Competition

Although both hotels are located on Disney property, the Grand Floridian Resort is much closer to the theme parks, and is located on the Monorail for easy transportation throughout the park. Also, the Grand Floridian is an upscale hotel with many fine restaurants and shops, and offers luxurious room amenities. The All-Star Resort, on the other hand, caters to budget conscious families that are willing to forgo some convenience and amenities in exchange for significant savings. Disney differentiates its hotels to cater to different groups of customers with varying willingness-to-pay. The result is a significant price difference between the two hotels.

Checkpoint: Oligopoly

A cartel functions best when its members adhere to the established quotas (which keep prices for drugs high) and also when no external competition exists (allowing the cartel to operate as if it were a monopoly). Competition from noncartel drug traffickers as well as cartel members exceeding their production quotas poses a threat to the cartel's existence, and hence cartels will often use violence to prevent those activities from occurring. When the drug trade is dominated by several large and powerful organizations, the actions of one organization have a significant effect on the others, an example of the mutual interdependence of firms in an oligopoly.

Checkpoint: Game Theory

This is a situation in which each player must develop a coordination strategy to achieve a Nash equilibrium (a connected call). No rule exists for coordination strategies. Instead, such strategies often are formed by experience. For example, the person who calls back might be the one who made the initial call, or the one who typically calls. Or, it might be the one who has more at stake in the call (such as a pesky friend asking to borrow money). With more experience, coordination strategies become easier to implement.

Checkpoint: Applications of Game Theory

This strategy might work in theory if everybody in the class is committed to it. Practically speaking, it's highly unlikely that everyone would stick to the agreement. For example, if you were someone destined to receive a C or a D, and you know that the A and B students promised not to study if you don't study, you would have a strong incentive to break your promise and study hard knowing that an A or a B is now within easier reach. At the same time, those destined for an A or a B might want to insure themselves against the plan by studying to secure the high grade. In the end, the cooperative agreement does not hold, because each player has a dominant strategy to study. This represents a Prisoner's Dilemma because, in the end, everyone studies and the scheme falls apart.

11

The Labor Market

After studying this chapter you should be able to:

- Define and describe competitive labor markets.
- Derive a supply curve for labor.
- Describe the factors that can change labor supply.
- Describe the factors that can change labor demand.
- Determine the elasticity of demand for labor.
- Determine the competitive market equilibrium for labor.
- Describe Becker's theory of economic discrimination.
- Describe the concept of segmented labor markets and how they affect wage levels.
- Describe federal laws and policies regarding discrimination.
- Describe the history, costs, and benefits of trade unions.

Andy Hayt/San Diego Padres/Getty Images

Mark Cunningham/MLB Photos via Getty Images

Why are Kyle Blanks and Ramiro Peña making more than the president of the United States? Have you ever heard of these guys?

Did you see where some baseball player just signed a contract for $50,000 a year just to play ball? It wouldn't surprise me if someday they'll be making more than the President.

QUOTE FROM 1955

Some professions, such as baseball, try to maintain their traditions, but salaries for Major League Baseball players certainly have not remained the same. The average professional athlete did not used to be a multimillionaire. In 1964, the average salary in Major League Baseball was a mere $14,000 (about $100,000 in current inflation-adjusted dollars), suggesting that professional athletes back then chose their careers for the love of the game rather than as a way to become rich. Today, the labor market for professional athletes has changed. With lucrative advertising revenue and broadcasting rights, professional sport has become big business. In 2012, companies spent $28.6 billion for advertising in all U.S. sports. The World Series between the San Francisco Giants and the Detroit Tigers alone generated over $150 million, impressive considering only four of seven games were played, as the Giants swept the series.

Because the labor market demand for athletes is so great, professional sports leagues need to pay much higher salaries than they did 50 years ago in order to encourage the very best athletes to seek a career in sports. The result of this increase in demand in the labor market is a dramatic rise in salaries. In 2012, the average salary for a Major League Baseball player was $3,440,000, with the top earning player, Alex Rodriguez, earning $29 million. Even relatively unknown players, such as Kyle Blanks and Ramiro Peña, made over $480,000, the minimum salary in Major League Baseball in 2012. The president of the United States makes $400,000 a year. Indeed, the prediction from 1955 came true . . . for every player in the major leagues!

This chapter and the next begin our analysis of input markets, also called factor markets. Up to this point in the book, we have focused on product markets, mentioning input markets only incidentally. Sitting behind the production of goods and services, however, are inputs: workers, machinery, and manufacturing plants. Few firms can operate without employees or capital. Similarly, few households could survive without the income that work provides. Fortunately, many of the tools we introduced for the product market, such as demand and supply analysis, apply the same way in input markets. The main difference, however, is that in input markets, firms demand inputs whereas in product markets, firms supply goods and services.

This chapter focuses on the analysis of labor markets. The first two sections look at competitive labor markets, where the participants—firms and employees—are price takers. We then take a closer look at several situations in which wages are not set by competitive markets: instances of economic discrimination, and the economic effects of labor unions.

BY THE NUMBERS

Your Wages and Your Job After College

College students face important career decisions once they graduate. Some choose to pursue a professional or graduate degree, while others choose to venture into the labor force. One of the key factors influencing this decision is the wages offered to college graduates.

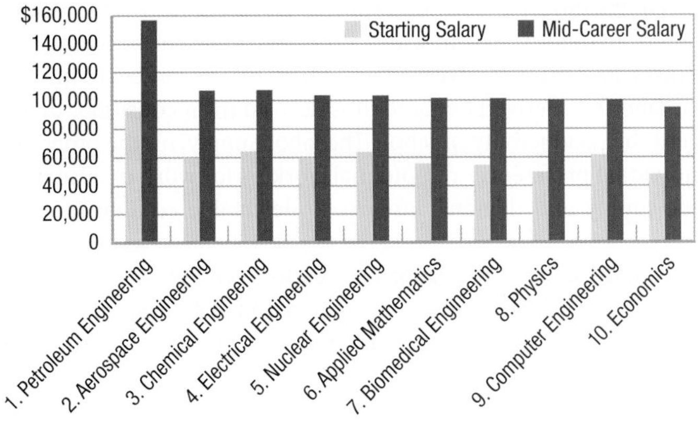

Choosing the right major in college can lead to a higher paying job. Economics is among the top 10 highest earning undergraduate majors out of a total of 128 majors surveyed. Studying economics can be interesting *and* lucrative!

Randy Faris/Corbis

82.2%

Average salary for women as a percent of men's salaries for the same occupation in 2012.

41.3%

Average cost of full-time employee benefits (paid vacation, sick leave, health insurance, retirement benefits, and employer tax contributions) as a percent of wages.

Average Starting Salaries for Jobs Out-of-College in 2011.

Journalist:	$35,527
Counselor:	$37,392
Public school teacher:	$37,881
Architect:	$39,561
Marketing coordinator:	$43,628
Registered nurse:	$44,104
Hotel manager:	$46,106
Web designer:	$48,160
Accountant:	$50,708
Financial analyst:	$52,689
Computer technician:	$54,667
Electrical engineer:	$58,247

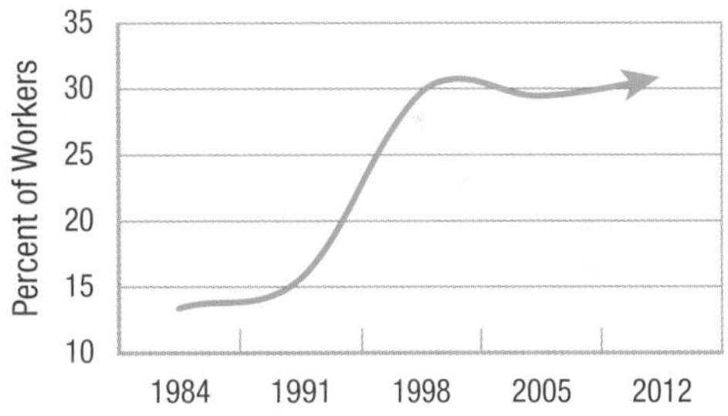

Careers with flexible working hours ("flextime") increased in the 1980s and 1990s and have since leveled off. Today, three in ten full-time workers in the United States have flexible work schedules.

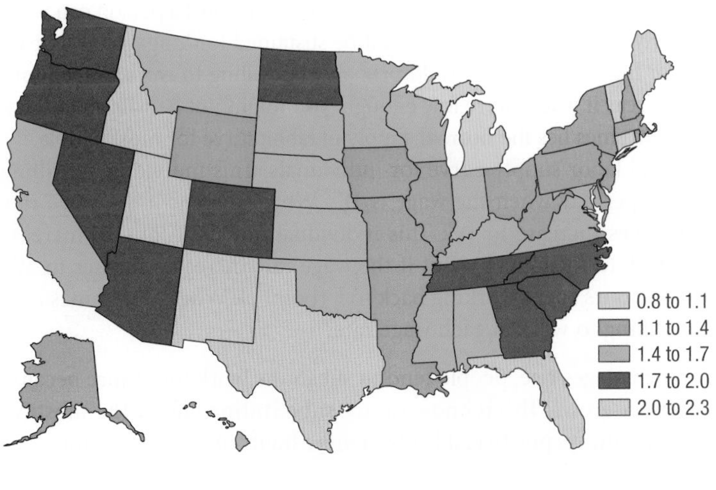

Projected annual job growth (in percent) through 2017 is shown by state. States with the highest projected job growth include Idaho, Texas, Utah, New Mexico, and Florida.

Competitive labor markets are similar to competitive product markets. We make several key assumptions. First, we assume that firms operate in competitive industries with many buyers and sellers, a homogeneous product, and easy entry and exit. A second assumption of competitive labor markets is that workers are regarded as equally productive, such that firms have no preference for one employee over another. Inhumane as it sounds, labor is treated as a homogeneous commodity. Third, a competitive labor market assumes that information in the industry is widely available and accurate. Everyone knows what the going wage rate is, therefore well-informed decisions about how much labor to supply are made by workers, and firms can wisely decide how many workers to hire.

A firm's demand for labor is a derived demand; it is derived from consumer demand for the firm's product and the productivity of labor. The labor supply, on the other hand, is determined by the individual preferences of potential workers for work or leisure. Like all competitive markets, supply and demand interact to determine equilibrium wages and employment.

Following the analysis of the competitive labor market, we then ask why some people make more than others. Although differences in occupation and skill levels play a dominant role in determining wages, how often are wage differences the result of discrimination against people of a certain race, ethnicity, or gender?

Another reason for differences in wages is the role of unions. Unions are legal associations of employees that bargain with employers over terms and conditions of work. Unions use strikes and the threat of strikes to achieve their goals. The Major League Baseball Players Association is a powerful union, which negotiates salaries and benefits on behalf of its members. Sometimes disputes between the players union and team owners have resulted in strikes. In 1994–1995, a long strike led to a very short baseball season. Without the union, today's baseball players might not all be making more than the president of the United States.

Competitive Labor Supply

Economists divide your activities into two categories: work and leisure. When you decide to work, you are giving up leisure, understood broadly as nonwork activity, in exchange for the income that work brings. Economists assume people prefer leisure activities to work. This may not be entirely true, as work can be a source of personal satisfaction and a network of social connections, as well as provide many other benefits. For our discussion, however, we follow the practice of economists in dividing individual or household time into just work and leisure. Note that the term *leisure* encompasses all activities that do not involve paid work, including caring for children, doing household chores, and activities that are truly leisurely.

Individual Labor Supply

supply of labor The amount of time an individual is willing to work at various wage rates.

The **supply of labor** represents the time an individual is willing to work—the labor the individual is willing to supply—at various wage rates. On a given day, the most a person can work is 24 hours, although clearly such a schedule could not be sustained for long, given that we all need rest and sleep. For high wages, you would probably be willing to work horrendous hours for a short time, whereas if wages were low enough, you might not be willing to work at all. Between these two extremes lies the normal supply of labor curve for most people.

Figure 1 shows a typical labor supply curve for individuals. This individual is willing to supply l_1 hours of work per day when the wage is W_1. What happens if the wage rate increases? Assume that wages increase to W_2: This individual now is willing to increase hours spent working from l_1 to l_2 (point *b*). But if the wage rate increases further to W_3, this individual reduces the hours spent working back to l_1 (point *c*). What determines how many hours a person is willing to work at each wage rate?

substitution effect Higher wages mean that the value of work has increased, and the opportunity costs of leisure are higher, hence work is substituted for leisure.

Substitution Effect When wages rise, people tend to substitute work for leisure because the opportunity cost of leisure grows. This is known as the **substitution effect.** The substitution effect for labor supply is always positive; it leads to more hours of work when the wage rate increases.

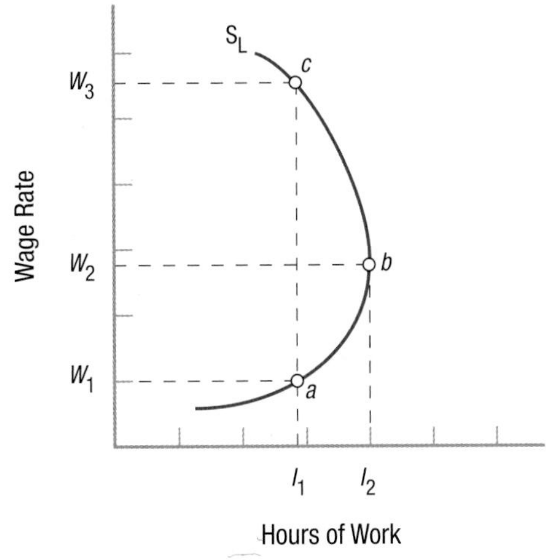

FIGURE 1

Individual Supply of Labor

When wages are W_1, this individual will work l_1 hours, but when the wage rate rises to W_2, her willingness to work rises to l_2. Over these two wage rates she is substituting work for leisure. Once the wage rises above W_2, the income effect begins to dominate, since she now has sufficient income that leisure is now more important and her labor supply curve is backward bending.

Note that this effect is similar to the substitution effect consumers experience when the price of a product declines. When the price of one product falls, consumers substitute that product for others. The substitution effect for consumer products, however, is negative (price falls and consumption rises), while it is always positive for labor (wages rise and the supply of labor increases).

Income Effect When wages rise, if you continue to work the same hours as before, your income will rise. As income rises, you have an ability to purchase more goods, *including leisure.* Thus, as wages rise to a level high enough to live the lifestyle you wish, you might desire to reduce the hours you work (besides, if you work too much you won't have time to enjoy spending the money you earned). This notion of working less (and consuming more leisure) as wages rise is known as the **income effect.** The income effect on labor supply is normally negative—higher wages and income lead to fewer hours worked as individuals desire more leisure. This effect counteracts the substitution effect, which encourages individuals to work more as wages rise.

income effect Higher wages mean that you can maintain the same standard of living by working fewer hours. The impact on labor supply is generally negative.

Both the substitution and income effects are present for all individuals, but at varying levels. The individual supply of labor, therefore, depends on which effect is stronger at each wage rate, and the individual labor supply curve is *backward bending* as shown in Figure 1.

When the labor supply curve is positively sloped, as it is below W_2 in Figure 1, the substitution effect is stronger than the income effect; income is more important than leisure at these wage levels, thus, higher wages lead to more hours worked. Conversely, when the supply of labor curve bends backward, as it does above W_2, the income effect overpowers the substitution effect. In this case, higher wages mean fewer hours worked.

Backward bending labor supply curves have been observed empirically in developed and developing countries. Still, it takes rather high income levels before the income effect begins to overpower the substitution effect. People like to have incomes well beyond what is required to satisfy their basic needs before they select more leisure over work as wages rise.

Market Labor Supply Curves

The labor supply for any occupation or industry is upward sloping; higher wages for a job mean more inquiries and job applications. Thus, although an individual's labor supply curve may be backward bending, market labor supply curves are normally positively sloped as shown in Figure 2 on the next page. Note that this is true for all other inputs to the production process, including raw materials such as copper, steel, and silicon, as well as for capital and land: Higher prices mean higher quantities supplied.

FIGURE 2

Market Labor Supply

Market labor supply is positively related to the wage rate. Increasing wages in one industry attract labor from other industries (a movement from point *d* to point *e* as the wage rises from W_1 to W_2). In contrast, market labor supply curves *shift* in response to demographic changes, changes in the nonwage benefits of jobs, wages paid in other occupations, and nonwage income.

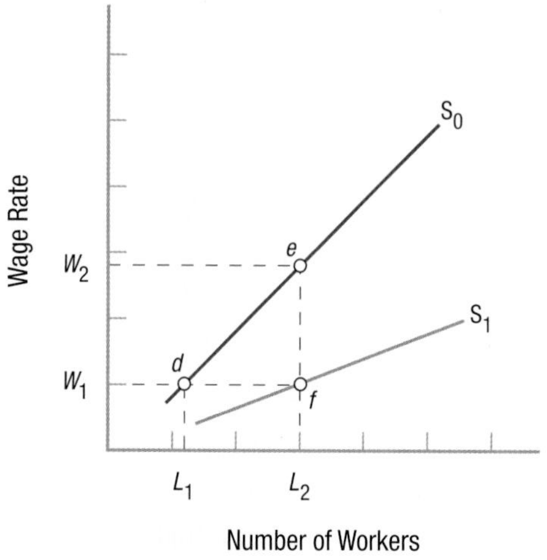

Changes in wage rates change the quantity of labor supplied. For example, increasing wages in one industry attract labor from other industries. This is a movement along the market labor supply curve, shown as a movement along S_0 from points *d* to *e* as wages (input prices) rise from W_1 to W_2.

Factors That Change Labor Supply

What factors will cause the entire market labor supply curve to shift from, say, S_0 to S_1 in Figure 2 so that L_2 workers are willing to work for a wage of W_1 (point *f*)? These include demographic changes, nonwage benefits of jobs, wages paid in other occupations, and nonwage income.

Demographic Changes Changes in population, immigration patterns, and labor force participation rates (the percentage of individuals in a group who enter the labor force) all change labor supplies by altering the number of qualified people available for work.

Over the past three decades, labor force participation rates among women have steadily risen, continually adding workers to the expanding American labor force; dual-earner households are increasingly the norm. Today, both parents work in about 60% of all married-couple households with children.

Another demographic change is the increasing portion of population growth in the United States resulting from immigration (both legal and illegal). Over 80% of net population growth over the next four decades will result from immigrants and their U.S.-born descendants.[1] This will have a significant effect on the labor supply.

Finally, other demographic changes have shifted the labor supply curve by modifying the labor–leisure preferences among workers. Health improvements, for example, have lengthened the typical working life, thereby increasing the supply of labor.

Nonmoney Aspects of Jobs Changes in the nonwage benefits of an occupation will similarly shift the supply of labor in that market. If employers can manage to increase the pleasantness, safety, or status of a job, labor supply will increase. Other nonmoney perks also help. The airline industry, for example, has greatly increased the number of people willing to work in mundane positions by allowing employees to fly anywhere free.

Wages in Alternative Jobs When worker skills in one industry are readily transferable to other jobs or industries, the wages paid in those other markets will affect wage rates and the labor supply in the first industry. For example, Web site designers and computer

[1] Jeffrey Passel and D'Vera Cohn, "Immigration to Play Lead Role in Future U.S. Growth," Pew Research Center Publications, February 11, 2008.

technicians are useful in all industries, and their wages in one industry affect all industries. Because at least some of the skills that all workers possess will benefit other employers, all labor markets have some influence over each other. Rising wages in growth industries will shrink the supply of labor available to firms in other industries.

Nonwage Income Changes in income from sources other than working (such as income from a trust) will change the supply of labor. As nonwage income rises, hours of work supplied declines. If you have enough income from nonwork sources, after all, the retirement urge will set in no matter what your age.

The key thing to remember here is that market labor supply curves are normally positively sloped, even though an individual's labor supply curve may be backward bending. In the next section, we put this together with the other blade of the scissors: the demand for labor in competitive labor markets.

CHECKPOINT

COMPETITIVE LABOR SUPPLY

- Competitive labor markets assume that firms operate in competitive product markets and purchase homogeneous labor, and that information is widely available and accurate.
- The supply of labor represents the time an individual is willing to work.
- The substitution effect occurs when wages rise, as people tend to substitute work for leisure because the opportunity cost of leisure is higher, or vice versa when wages fall.
- When wages rise and you continue to work the same number of hours, your income rises. When wages rise high enough, an income effect occurs in which income is traded for leisure, and the supply of labor curve for individuals is backward bending.
- Industry or occupation labor supply curves are upward sloping.
- The labor supply curve shifts with demographic changes, changes in the nonwage aspects of an occupation, changes in the wages of alternative jobs, and changes in nonwage income.

QUESTIONS: Assume that you take a job with flexible hours, but initially your salary is based on a 40-hour week. Your salary begins at $15 an hour, or $30,000 a year. Assuming your salary rises, at what salary (hourly wage) would you begin to work fewer than 40 hours a week (remember, the job permits flexible hours)? If your rich aunt dies and leaves you $500,000, would this alter the wage rate at which you cut your work hours? Do you think this wage rate will be the same when you are 35 and have two children?

Answers to the Checkpoint questions can be found at the end of this chapter.

Competitive Labor Demand

The competitive firm's **demand for labor** is derived from the demand for the firm's product and the productive capabilities of a unit of labor.

demand for labor Demand for labor is derived from the demand for the firm's product and the productivity of labor.

Marginal Revenue Product

Assume that a firm wants to hire an additional worker, and that worker is able to produce 15 units of the firm's product. Further, assume that the product sells for $10 a unit, and labor is the only input cost (such as blackberry picking in Oregon), with this cost including a normal return on the investment. The last worker hired is therefore worth $150 to the firm (15 × $10 = $150). If the cost of hiring this worker is $150 or less (remember, a normal profit is included in the wage), then the firm will hire this person. If the wage rate for labor exceeds $150, a competitive firm will not hire this marginal worker.

MRP differs from worker to worker. As we saw in Chapter 7, production is subject to diminishing marginal returns. In the example of blackberry picking, the first blackberry picker takes the nearest low-hanging fruit. The next picker takes low-hanging fruit farther away. The third has to do a little more work to harvest the same amount of fruit. Because each additional worker is able to pick less fruit per day, the MRP of each additional worker will correspondingly fall. This decrease in MRP represents the same diminishing marginal returns concept introduced in the product market.

To see how this works in greater detail, look at Table 1. The production function here is similar to the one used earlier in the chapter on production. Column (1) is labor input (L), column (2) is total output (Q), and column (3) is the **marginal physical product of labor** (MPP_L). This last value is the additional output a firm receives from employing an added unit of labor ($MPP_L = \Delta Q \div \Delta L$). For example, adding a fourth worker raises output from 25 to 40 units, thus the marginal physical product of labor for this additional worker is 15 units.

marginal physical product of labor The additional output a firm receives from employing an added unit of labor ($MPP_L = \Delta Q \div \Delta L$).

TABLE 1 Competitive Labor Market

(1) L	(2) *Q*	(3) MPP_L	(4) MRP_L (P = $10)	(5) *W*
0	0			$100
		7	$70	
1	7			$100
		8	$80	
2	15			$100
		10	$100	
3	25			$100
		15	$150	
4	40			$100
		14	$140	
5	54			$100
		11	$110	
6	65			$100
		10	$100	
7	75			$100
		9	$90	
8	84			$100
		6	$60	
9	90			$100
		5	$50	
10	95			$100

In this example, the firm is operating in a competitive market, therefore it can sell all the output it produces at the prevailing market price of $10. The value of another worker to the firm, called the **marginal revenue product** (MRP_L), is equal to the marginal physical product of labor times marginal revenue:

marginal revenue product The value of another worker to the firm is equal to the marginal physical product of labor (MPP_L) times marginal revenue (MR).

$$MRP_L = MPP_L \times MR$$

In our example, adding a fourth worker leads to a marginal revenue product of $150; we multiply the marginal physical product of labor of 15 units by the marginal revenue—or price in this competitive market—of $10 per unit.

A related term to marginal revenue product is the **value of the marginal product,** defined as $VMP_L = MPP_L \times P$. Because competitive firms are price takers for whom marginal revenue is equal to the price of the product (MR = P), $VMP_L = MRP_L$ in the competitive case.

value of the marginal product The value of the marginal product of labor (VMP_L) is equal to marginal physical product of labor times price, or $MPP_L \times P$.

Column (4) contains the firm's MRP_L. Additional workers add this value to the firm. Thus, the marginal revenue product curve is the firm's demand for labor, which is graphed

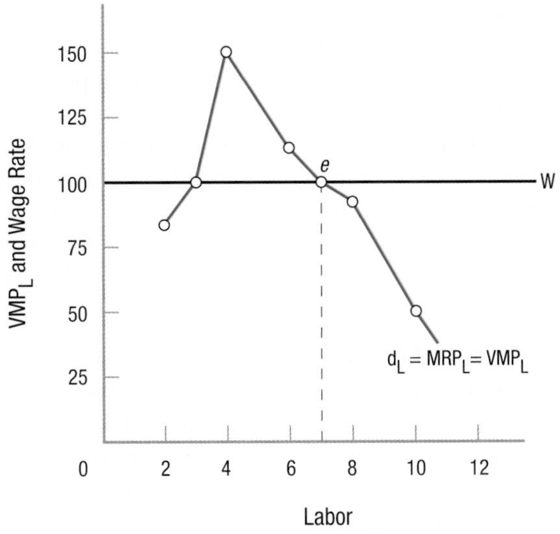

FIGURE 3

The Competitive Firm's Demand for Labor

This figure reflects the data from columns (4) and (5) of Table 1. In this example, the firm is operating in a competitive market, therefore it can sell all the output it produces at the prevailing market price. The value of the additional worker to the firm, the marginal revenue product (MRP_L), is equal to the marginal physical product of labor times marginal revenue (or price in this case). MRP_L is the competitive firm's demand for labor. If wages are equal to \$100, the firm will hire 7 workers (point *e*).

in Figure 3. Note how the marginal revenue product reaches a maximum at 4 workers, as shown in column (4) of the table and in the figure.

Competitive firms hire labor from competitive labor markets. Because each firm is too small to affect the larger market, it can hire all the labor it wants at the market-determined wage.

Table 1 and Figure 3 assume that the going wage for labor (W) is \$100. For our firm, this results in 7 workers being hired at \$100 (point *e*), because this is the employment level at which $W = MRP_L$. Note that $W = MRP_L$ at 3 workers as well, but because the marginal revenue product is greater than the wage rate for workers 4 to 6, the firm would hire 7 workers, not 3, to maximize its gains. The value to the firm of hiring the seventh worker is just equal to what the firm must pay this worker. Profits are maximized for the competitive firm when workers are hired out to the point at which $MRP_L = W$.

However, if market wages were to fall to \$90, the firm would hire an eighth worker to maximize profits, because with 8 employees, MRP_L is also equal to \$90.

In a competitive labor market, the prevailing wage (\$90 in this case) would be paid to each worker regardless of the actual MRP. Thus, firms maximize gains from hiring workers in the labor market similar to how consumers maximize consumer surplus when buying goods and services in the product market.

Factors That Change Labor Demand

The demand for labor is derived from product demand and labor productivity—how much people will pay for the product and how much each unit of labor can produce. It follows that changes in labor demand can arise from changes in either product demand or labor productivity. Because most production also requires other inputs, changes in the price of these other inputs also change the demand for labor.

Changes in Product Demand A decline in the demand for a firm's product will lead to lower market prices, reducing MRP_L, and vice versa. As MRP_L for all workers declines, labor demand will shift to the left. Anything that changes the price of the product in competitive markets will shift the firm's demand for labor.

A recent trend in the movie industry is for people to download movies directly to their computers or to order movies directly from their televisions. This has decreased demand for movies on DVDs, and subsequently led to a reduction in prices. As a result, labor demand by DVD movie manufacturers has shifted to the left.

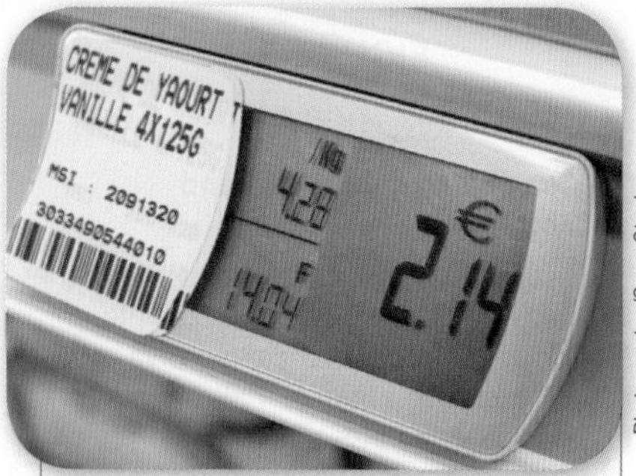

Photononstop/SuperStock

Digital price tags, such as the one found in this European supermarket, make workers more productive.

Changes in Productivity Changes in worker productivity (usually increases) can come about from improving technology or because a firm uses more capital or land along with its workforce. For example, some supermarkets have introduced digital price tags on their store shelves, allowing prices to be changed remotely instead of having a store clerk physically replace each tag on the shelf as prices change. Such improvements in productivity raise MPP_L. The demand for the marginal worker rises, shifting the demand for labor to the right as firms are willing to pay higher wages. To be sure, the number of workers hired may fall due to digitalization, but the workers programming the price codes, as in any capital-intensive industry, are generally more highly skilled and hence earn higher wages.

Changes in the Prices of Other Inputs Changes in input prices can affect the demand for labor through their effect on capital prices. For example, rising steel and glass prices can dramatically raise the costs of equipment such that firms are unable to replace aging equipment. Without the ability to afford the rising costs of new capital equipment, firms are forced to substitute labor for capital in new projects, thus increasing the demand for labor. Relative costs of capital and labor will therefore affect the capital and labor mix firms choose for their production.

At this point, we know that more labor will be hired when wages fall, but how much more? The answer depends on the elasticity of demand for labor.

Elasticity of Demand for Labor

elasticity of demand for labor The percentage change in the quantity of labor demanded divided by the percentage change in the wage rate.

The **elasticity of demand for labor** (E_L) is the percentage change in the quantity of labor demanded (Q_L) divided by the percentage change in the wage rate (W). This elasticity is found the same way we calculated the price elasticity of demand for products, except that we substitute the wage rate for the price of the product:

$$E_L = \frac{\%\Delta Q_L}{\%\Delta W}$$

The elasticity of demand for labor measures how responsive the quantity of labor demanded is to changes in wages. An inelastic demand for labor is one in which the absolute value of the elasticity is less than 1. Conversely, an elastic curve's computed elasticity is greater than 1.

The time firms have to adjust to changing wages will affect elasticity. In the short run, when labor is the only truly variable factor of production, elasticity of demand for labor is more inelastic. In the long run, when all production factors can be adjusted, elasticity of demand for labor tends to be more elastic.

Factors That Affect the Elasticity of Demand for Labor

Although time affects elasticity, three other factors also affect the elasticity of demand for labor: elasticity of product demand, ease of substituting other inputs, and labor's share of the production costs. Let's briefly consider each of these.

Elasticity of Demand for the Product The more price elastic the demand for a product, the greater the elasticity of demand for labor. Higher wages result in higher product prices, and the more easily consumers can substitute away from the firm's product, the greater the number of workers who will become unemployed. An elastic demand for labor means that employment is more responsive to wage rates. The opposite is true for products with inelastic demands.

Ease of Input Substitutability The more difficult it is to substitute capital for labor, the more inelastic the demand for labor will be. At this point, computers cannot yet substitute for pilots in commercial airplanes, which results in an inelastic demand for pilots. As a result, pilots have been able to secure high wages from airlines. The easier it is to substitute capital for labor, the less bargaining power workers have, and labor demand tends to be more elastic.

Labor's Share of Total Production Costs The share of total costs associated with labor is another factor determining the elasticity of demand for labor. If labor's share of total costs is small, the demand for labor will tend to be rather inelastic. In the example of airline pilots, the percentage of costs going to pilot wages is small, perhaps 10%. Thus, a large increase in pilot wages would have a relatively small effect on ticket prices and demand, resulting in little change in demand for pilot labor. The opposite is true when labor's share of costs is large.

Competitive Labor Market Equilibrium

Generalized market equilibrium in competitive labor markets requires that we take into account the industry supply and demand for labor. The market supply for labor (S_L) is the horizontal sum of the individual labor supply curves in the market.

The market demand for labor, however, is not simply a summation of the demand for labor by all the firms in the market. When wages fall, for instance, this affects all firms—all want to hire more labor and produce more output. This added production reduces market prices for their output and negatively affects the demand for labor. For our purposes it is enough to be aware that market demands for labor are not the horizontal summation of individual firm demands.

Turning to Figure 4, we have put both sides of the market together. In panel A, the competitive labor market determines equilibrium wage ($100 per day) and employment (300 workers) based on market supply and demand. Individual firms, in light of their own situation, hire 6 workers at the point where this equilibrium wage is equal to marginal revenue product (MRP_L), point *e* in panel B. Much like the product markets we discussed in earlier chapters, the invisible hand of the marketplace sets wages and in the end determines employment.

To this point we have assumed that labor markets are competitive and that firms are able to hire as many workers as they desire at the prevailing wage rate. This analysis of competitive labor markets goes a long way but just as with product markets, it does not tell the whole story. We are going to look at two familiar cases in which the competitive

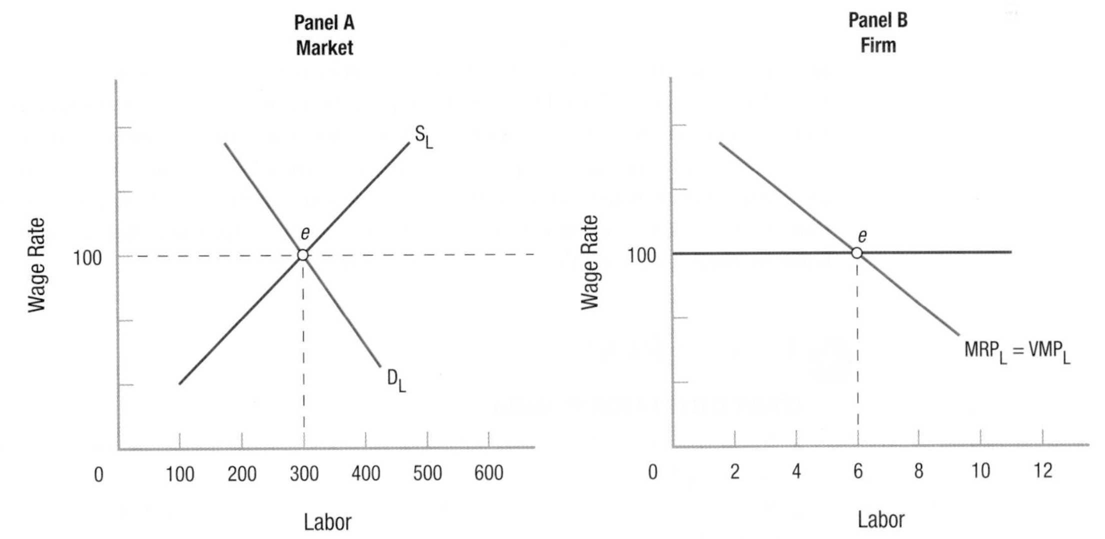

FIGURE 4

Competitive Labor Markets

In panel A, the competitive labor market determines equilibrium wages ($100 per day) and employment (300 workers). Individual firms hire 6 workers, where this equilibrium wage is equal to marginal revenue product (MRP_L), point *e* in panel B.

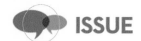

ISSUE

Reality TV and the Labor Market for Entertainers

Before the onslaught of reality shows that are today a ubiquitous presence on our television schedules, becoming a "TV star" was a much more arduous endeavor. One would need to find an agent and audition for specific roles, and then wait until a producer found an appropriate role for the aspiring actress or actor. The labor market for TV entertainment was considerably smaller at that time.

That all changed in 1992, when MTV debuted *The Real World* as an experiment bringing unknown people without any acting experience (but with unique personalities or traits) together to live in a house with cameras rolling. For the rest of the decade, *The Real World* continued to launch new seasons with new participants, but the idea of reality TV did not truly catch on until a major network, CBS, debuted *Survivor*, in 2000. Again produced as an experiment to fill a slow summer schedule, it became an instant hit.

Moreover, *Survivor* started a global phenomenon, which led to hundreds of reality shows including the top-rated series *The Amazing Race*, *The Apprentice*, and *Big Brother*, among others. Further, it led to the creation of new talent competitions including *American Idol* and *America's Got Talent*, which again turned unknowns into stars, even if just for one season.

CBS/Monty Brinton/Landov

The cast of the first season of *Survivor* started a global phenomenon of reality TV.

How does reality TV affect the labor market for TV entertainers? With reality TV, almost anyone can audition for a show, with the eventual "star" being determined as the shows progress in front of television audiences. As a result, the supply of labor in the entertainment labor market has increased as more people seek to become the newest star.

But perhaps a greater effect is the new demand for labor. Traditional programs such as situation comedies and soap operas require networks to secure long-term contracts with their casts to ensure they return each season. Because reality TV stars generally appear for just one season, producers are constantly looking to cast new people each season. Although the success of reality TV has perhaps reduced the demand for traditional acting roles, it has created huge labor demand (opportunities), and subsequently higher wages, to the benefit of many aspiring entertainers.

model is clearly not the case. The first case is economic discrimination in the labor market in which the personal preferences of employers, employees, or consumers cause some workers to be preferred over others, creating wage differentials. The second case involves unions, which restrict labor supply in certain industries to raise wages relative to nonunion industries. When wage differentials exist for workers performing the same tasks, we say that labor markets are imperfect. There are other, more technical instances of imperfect labor markets—we hold these until the Appendix.

CHECKPOINT

COMPETITIVE LABOR DEMAND

- The firm's demand for labor is a derived demand—derived from consumer demand for the product and the productivity of labor.
- Marginal revenue product is equal to the marginal physical product of labor times marginal revenue.
- The demand for labor is equal to the marginal revenue product of labor for competitive firms.
- The demand for labor curve will change if there is a change in the demand for the product, if there is a change in labor productivity, or if there is a change in the price of other inputs.

- The elasticity of demand for labor is equal to the percentage change in quantity of labor demanded divided by the percentage change in the wage rate.
- The elasticity of demand for labor will be *more* elastic the greater the elasticity of demand for the product, the easier it is to substitute other factors for labor, and the larger the share of total production costs attributed to labor.
- Market equilibrium occurs at the point at which the labor demand and supply curves intersect.

QUESTIONS: Individuals are different in terms of ability, attitude, and willingness to work. Given this fact, does it make sense to assume labor is homogeneous? Does this model better fit firms such as Wal-Mart that hire 800+ employees at each store at roughly standardized wages than, say, firms such as Google, which look for highly skilled computer geeks?

Answers to the Checkpoint questions can be found at the end of this chapter.

Economic Discrimination

We have seen that all workers are paid the same wage in competitive labor markets. This is seen in real life in low-skilled industries (such as fast-food restaurants) in which workers earn close to the minimum wage, or even in some occupations that require high-skilled workers whose wages are determined by contract based on market conditions. For example, public elementary school teachers in a district might all earn a starting salary set by a county school board. However, in industries in which managers are given discretion to set the wages of their employees, different wages may be given to employees doing the same work. Although these wage differentials may be due to differences in training or work experience, some differentials may be due to economic discrimination.

Economic discrimination takes place whenever workers of equal ability and productivity are paid different wages or are otherwise discriminated against in the workplace because of their race, color, religion, gender, age, national origin, sexual orientation, or disability. This can mean that one group is paid lower wages than another for doing the same job, or that members of different groups are segregated into occupations that pay different wages.

economic discrimination When workers of equal ability are paid different wages or in any other way discriminated against because of race, color, religion, gender, age, national origin, or disability.

The U.S. Bureau of Labor Statistics (BLS) measures wages for persons of various races and ethnicities as well as by gender in the labor force. Each year, it collects data on the gender wage gap, the salary that women make as a percentage of what men earn in the same occupation. The trend has been a narrowing of the wage gap, indicating that gender discrimination has diminished over time. Less certain based on the data is whether discrimination based on race or ethnicity has seen similar improvements. Data from the BLS continue to show that African Americans and Latinos earn substantially less than Caucasians and Asians; however, these data are not separated by occupation, thus it is uncertain the extent these differences in earnings are due to discrimination as opposed to occupational choices.

Economic theories of discrimination generally take one of two approaches. The first, developed by Gary Becker, rests on the notion that bias is articulated in the *discriminatory tastes* of employers, workers, and consumers. The second approach, the *segmented markets approach,* maintains that labor markets are divided into segments based on race, gender, or some other category. This approach is often referred to as the *job crowding hypothesis,* or the *dual labor market hypothesis.*

Becker's Theory of Economic Discrimination

Gary Becker's main contribution to economics is that he vastly broadened the issues that economists study. This was no small feat. Before Becker's influence, economists focused almost exclusively on the production and exchange of material goods and services. One early example shows the difficulties Becker faced in broadening this focus.

In 1955, Becker was asked to speak at Harvard about his dissertation on the economics of discrimination. Becker noted that his audience was perplexed. "They thought I

NOBEL PRIZE GARY BECKER

The 1992 winner of the Nobel Prize in Economic Sciences, Gary Becker, applied the theory of "rational choice" to areas of human behavior not ordinarily associated with economic analysis and research. He has offered provocative insights on a broad array of subjects, including family relations, racial discrimination, and the criminal justice system.

Born in Pottsville, Pennsylvania in 1930, Becker completed his undergraduate degree at Princeton before entering the University of Chicago, where he studied under economist Milton Friedman. In 1957, he published his dissertation, *The Economics of Discrimination,* an analysis of the effects of racial prejudice on earnings and employment among minorities.

In 1981, he published his book, *A Treatise on the Family.* According to his theory, rising wages led to changes in the family, including more women working outside the home instead of "specializing" in child care and housework. On questions of crime and punishment, Becker suggested that most criminals react in predictable ways to the costs and benefits of illegal activity; namely, that the probability of being caught and punished was a greater deterrent than the harsh nature of the punishment. On the question of race, Becker viewed discrimination as a "tax wedge" between social and private returns, concluding that prejudice tends to be economically detrimental to all parties concerned.

would discuss price discrimination"—that is, the analysis of why businesses charge different prices for the same goods. "No one conceived that an economist would talk about race discrimination in those days."[2]

Published in 1957, *The Economics of Discrimination* was not warmly received by the profession. Not until the mid-1960s, when the civil rights movement gained momentum, did the book receive the recognition it deserved. Surprisingly enough, Becker challenged the conventional view that discrimination benefits the person who discriminates. Let's see why he thought the conventional wisdom was wrong.

Becker argued that employers who discriminate against women will lose market share and profit opportunities, both because they do not always hire the best employees available, and because they must pay mostly high-wage male employees. Nondiscriminating firms, in contrast, will have lower labor costs, having more women earning lower wages on the payroll. Nondiscriminating firms will attract the most productive managers and employees, many of whom will be women. Profits for the nondiscriminating firm should therefore be higher. Becker concluded that the cost of wage differentials and the pressures of the marketplace should drive discrimination down to zero in the long run.

In practice, we know that wage discrimination still exists. According to the Bureau of Labor Statistics, women in 2012 earned 82.2% of what men earned in the same occupation. Why might competition fail to erase wage differentials? For one thing, the adjustment costs of firing unproductive workers, giving them severance pay, then recruiting and training new workers can be extremely high, especially considering the protections unions and the legal system offer workers. Second, women may be less mobile than men when it comes to work. They may be less willing to move to accommodate employer preferences, and thus be forced to accept lower wage positions. Third, if women continue to choose occupations with more flexible career paths that do not heavily penalize extended absences from the labor market, wage differentials between men and women may always exist. Note, however, that such differentials could also be caused by discrimination that precedes labor market entry, as when social norms direct girls toward lower-wage occupations such as elementary education or social work.

Segmented Labor Markets

segmented labor markets Labor markets split into separate parts. This leads to different wages paid to different sectors even though both markets are highly competitive.

Economists who advocate **segmented labor market** theories argue that discrimination does not arise due to a lack of competitive labor markets, but rather because these markets, although competitive, are segmented into a variety of constituent parts. And these different parts, while interacting, are noncompeting sectors. Segmented labor market theories have been developed along several different lines.

- The *dual labor market hypothesis* splits the labor market into primary and secondary sectors. The primary market consists of jobs that offer high wages, good working conditions, job stability, and advancement opportunities, while jobs in the secondary

[2] Peter Passell, "New Nobel Laureate Takes Economics Far Afield," *The New York Times,* October 14, 1992, p. D1.

market tend to have low wages and benefits, poor working conditions, high labor turnover, and little chance of advancement.

- The *job crowding hypothesis* breaks occupations into predominately male and female jobs. In 1922, Edgeworth recognized this problem when he wrote, "The pressure of male trade unions appears to be largely responsible for that crowding of women into a comparatively few occupations, which is universally recognized as a main factor in the depression of their wages."[3]
- The *insider-outsider theory* maintains that workers are segregated into those who belong to unions and those who are unemployed or are nonunion workers. Alternatively, economists have recognized that large firms use internal promotion and job security to inspire loyalty to the firm; however, such practices can also become an indirect method of segregating the labor market.

These hypotheses all predict that separate job markets will emerge for different groups. Figure 5 shows how segregated markets can lead to significant wage differentials, such as those we see for men and women.

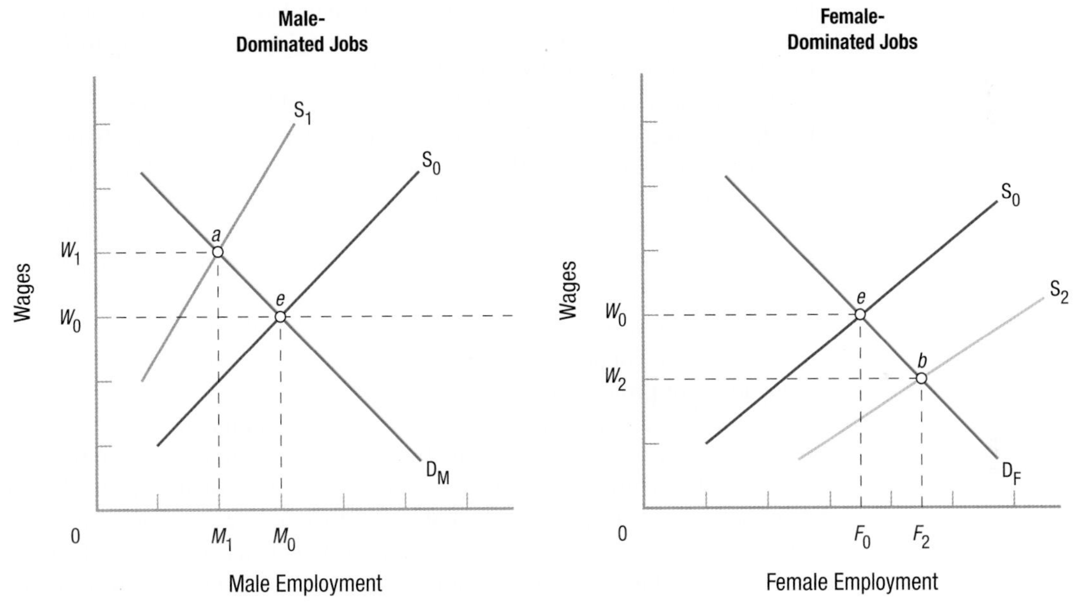

FIGURE 5

Job Crowding and a Dual Labor Market

Segregated markets can lead to significant wage differentials between men and women. Without discrimination, equilibrium wages will be W_0 for everyone, with total employment at $M_0 + F_0$. If, however, there is some form of discrimination in male-dominated jobs, the supply of labor to that segment will decline to S_1, wages will rise to W_1, and employment will fall to M_1 (point *a*). Those women who are excluded from jobs in this sector will have to move to available jobs in the female-dominated sector, thus increasing the labor supplied for these jobs to S_2, raising employment to F_2, but reducing wages to W_2 (point *b*). The result is a wage differential equal to $W_1 - W_2$.

In a world without discrimination, equilibrium wages for everyone would be W_0, with total employment at $M_0 + F_0$. If some form of discrimination in male-dominated jobs is present, labor supply to that segment will decline to S_1, wages will rise to W_1, and hiring will fall to M_1 (point *a*). Those women who are excluded from jobs in this sector will have

[3] F. Y. Edgeworth, "Equal Pay to Men and Women for Equal Work" (1922), p. 439, cited in Stephen Smith, *Labour Economics* (New York: Routledge), 1994, p. 102.

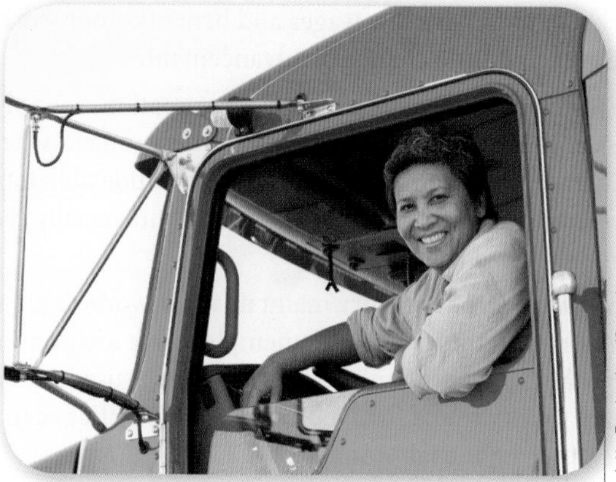

Traditional female-dominated and male-dominated professions are becoming less prevalent as gender discrimination and the gender wage gap continue to narrow.

to move to jobs available in the female-dominated sector, thus increasing the supply of labor there to S_2 and reducing wages to W_2, employment climbing to F_2 (point *b*). The result is a wage differential equal to $W_1 - W_2$.

Notice that once such a wage differential is established, the firms in competitive markets have no real incentive to eliminate the gap. Men and women are both being paid their marginal revenue products, therefore no profits are gained by substituting workers.

Wage differentials can arise for a variety of reasons. Some people may simply prefer one occupation to another. If such preferences have their roots in specific social groups, group-wide wage differentials can be expected to arise. Wages will vary between occupations, moreover, because of differences in their attractiveness, difficulty, riskiness, social status, and the human capital investments required. Still, lingering wage differentials today may be the result of past discriminatory practices that barred women from entering some occupations or professional schools.

Do wage differentials necessarily mean that discrimination exists in the market? Job crowding and wage differentials could just reflect different levels of human capital investment or different professional choices. Many women, for instance, may truly prefer occupations that are complementary to parenting. Further, female labor force participation is often interrupted when women take a break from working to have children. Therefore, jobs such as nursing, teaching, and administrative work may look attractive as women can leave their jobs, later returning or finding a new employer, with little loss in salary or benefits.

Public Policy to Combat Discrimination

For the first half of the last century, the inequities associated with various forms of discrimination were mostly accepted as a part of life in the United States. Gradually, however, a groundswell developed to end racial segregation and other forms of discrimination, culminating in passage of the Civil Rights Act in 1964. In what follows, we briefly outline the major acts and public policies that have been implemented with the goal of ending discrimination. Because of these policies, discrimination, wage differentials, and segmented labor markets have declined markedly over the past five decades.

The Equal Pay Act of 1963 The Equal Pay Act of 1963 amended the Fair Labor Standards Act of 1938. It requires that men and women receive equal pay for equal work. Equal work is defined as work performed under similar circumstances requiring equal effort, skill, and responsibility. Some argue that the Equal Pay Act was a hollow victory because occupational segregation forced women into specific occupations, causing them to earn less than men for essentially comparable work. Further, the law provided a limited time during which a worker must file a case against an employer for wage discrimination. This prevented many women from filing cases out of fear that they would lose their jobs.

In 2009, the Lily Ledbetter Fair Pay Act was signed into law, providing employees more flexibility to file cases asserting that they have been discriminated against with respect to pay. Specifically, it allowed the 180-day statute of limitations for filing a case to be reset with each discriminating paycheck received. Thus, a worker could file a case long after the discriminatory action began, as long as the worker had worked at the company within the last 180 days.

Civil Rights Act of 1964 Title VII of the Civil Rights Act of 1964 makes it unlawful to

> refuse to hire or to discharge any individual, or otherwise to discriminate against any individual with respect to his [her] compensation, terms, conditions, or privileges of employment, because of such individual's race, color, religion, sex, or national origin.

To date, most of the litigation brought under this statute has focused on the meaning of the phrase *to discriminate*, requiring a plaintiff to show that an employment practice inflicts a "disparate" or unequal impact on members of a minority group, as compared to its impact on others. Once this has been demonstrated, the burden shifts to the defendant (the employer) to show that its employment practices are related to employee performance or are otherwise a matter of "business necessity." Plaintiffs may sue for a full range of remedies, including back pay, reinstatement, court costs, attorney's fees, and punitive damages.

Executive Order 11246—Affirmative Action In 1965, President Lyndon Johnson issued Executive Order 11246. A key provision of this order required that firms doing at least $50,000 in business with the federal government submit an affirmative action program that includes a detailed analysis of their labor force.

Affirmative action programs have been controversial from the outset. Critics see such programs as "enforced quotas," whereas supporters see them as a way of breaking down discriminatory hiring barriers. Further, affirmative action has extended to other selection criteria such as college admissions.

In the summer of 2003, the U.S. Supreme Court ruled in the University of Michigan case (*Gratz v. Bollinger*) that adding a large specific numerical adjustment for minority group status to university admission criteria was unacceptable. The Law School at Michigan, on the other hand, simply took race into account in a nuanced approach to improving diversity of the class. The Supreme Court found this approach acceptable (*Grutter v. Bollinger*).

Age, Disabilities, and Sexual Orientation Two other acts were designed to reduce discrimination based on age and physical or mental disabilities. The Age Discrimination in Employment Act of 1967 protects workers over age 40 from discrimination based on age. The Americans with Disabilities Act of 1990 prohibits discrimination against people with a physical or mental disability who could still perform a job with reasonable accommodation by an employer. What constitutes "reasonable accommodation" has been a point of contention in many recent court cases. Lastly, the proposed Employment Non-Discrimination Act would prohibit discrimination against employees on the basis of sexual orientation or gender identity by civilian, nonreligious employers with at least 15 employees.

CHECKPOINT

ECONOMIC DISCRIMINATION

- Economic discrimination occurs whenever workers of equal ability and productivity are paid different wages or otherwise discriminated against because of their race, color, religion, gender, age, national origin, sexual orientation, or disability.
- Becker's analysis of discrimination assumed that employers had a taste for discrimination, and he showed that both parties were harmed by discrimination.

- Segmented labor markets assume that separate markets lead to wage differentials that represent discrimination.
- Public policy to eliminate discrimination has included the Equal Pay Act of 1963, Civil Rights Act of 1964, Executive Order 11246 (Affirmative Action), Age Discrimination in Employment Act of 1967, Americans with Disabilities Act of 1990, and the Lily Ledbetter Fair Pay Act of 2009.

QUESTION: Some types of labor discrimination are more likely to be eroded by market forces than others. Provide an example of a type of discrimination that is likely to dissipate through the labor market and one that is likely to persist over time.

Answers to the Checkpoint question can be found at the end of this chapter.

Labor Unions and Collective Bargaining

Suppose Max, an engineer and project coordinator, has worked at a large construction company for eight years. He had been training new employees on various aspects of cost estimating and job specification, and he noticed that these new people were being hired at salaries approaching his own. He requested a raise several times, but was essentially ignored. Exasperated, he refused to go to work one day, informing his boss that he would not return without a raise. He did not quit; he simply staged a walkout and refused to return until given a raise. In other words, Max staged a one-man strike. He was out for two weeks before his supervisor called and asked him how much he wanted. They settled on a raise of over 20%.

This story is unique in that one-person strikes are rarely successful; more often they are career busters. In most instances, individual employees have little control over wages or job conditions, essentially being at the mercy of employers and the market. This is the primary reason that unions exist: Collective action is more powerful than the action of one individual. As individuals, we can easily be replaced (except in rare occasions like for Max in the story above). To replace an entire workforce, on the other hand, imposes serious costs to an employer.

This section looks at the role unions play in our economy, their history, and their effects on the labor market. We show how unions create wage differentials that work against the assumptions of the competitive labor market in which all workers earn the same wage. We will see that although unions have been successful in some industries, their influence has faded in other industries.

Types of Unions

Labor unions are legal associations of employees that bargain with employers over terms and conditions of work, including wages, benefits, and working conditions. They use strikes and threats of strikes, as well as other tactics, to try to achieve their goals.

Unions are usually defined by industry, or by craft or occupation. A *craft* union represents members of a specific craft or occupation, such as air traffic controllers (PATCO), truck drivers (Teamsters), and teachers (AFT). An *industrial* union represents all workers employed in a specific industry. Examples include auto workers (UAW) and public employees (AFSCME).

Benefits and Costs of Union Membership

Without a union, each individual employee would have to bargain with management over his or her own wages, benefits, and working conditions. Unions bring collective power to this bargaining arrangement. The source of this power is ultimately the willingness of the union to strike if no agreement is reached during negotiations. Collective bargaining often leads to a more equitable pay schedule than individual negotiation. It also provides workers with greater job security by protecting them against arbitrary or vindictive decisions by management.

Union membership, like everything else, has its price. First, union members must pay monthly dues. Then, if negotiations break down and a strike is called, wages are lost and the possibility exists, however remote, that management will refuse to settle with the union and replace the entire workforce. Finally, union workers must give up some individual flexibility because their work rules are more rigid.

Brief History of American Unionism

Labor unions date from the late 18th century in England. In the United States, public attitudes toward unions were highly unfavorable until the Great Depression. In the early part of the 20th century, employers could easily secure legal injunctions against union organization by arguing that unions behaved like monopolies, in violation of antitrust laws. Employers often required employees to sign enforceable *yellow dog contracts,* in which they agreed not to join a union as a condition of employment.

Figure 6 shows union membership as a percentage of total employment since 1930. Going into the 1930s, unions represented just over 7% of workers because of public attitudes and legal restrictions. With the onset of the Depression, attitudes about collective bargaining began to change. In 1932, Congress passed the Norris–LaGuardia Act, which outlawed yellow dog contracts and prohibited injunctions against union organizing. Then, in 1935, Congress enacted the Wagner Act, or the National Labor Relations Act (NLRA). It prohibited a variety of unfair labor practices by employers, including firing employees for engaging in union activities. The act also required employers to "bargain in good faith" with those unions that had won recognition through a majority vote of the firm's workers.

The NLRA also established the National Labor Relations Board (NLRB) to oversee union certification elections. These elections were to be held to determine which union, if any, would represent employees.

As Figure 6 illustrates, union membership grew dramatically from the mid-1930s until after World War II. Following the war, union membership covered over one-quarter of American workers. It was concentrated in a few major industries.

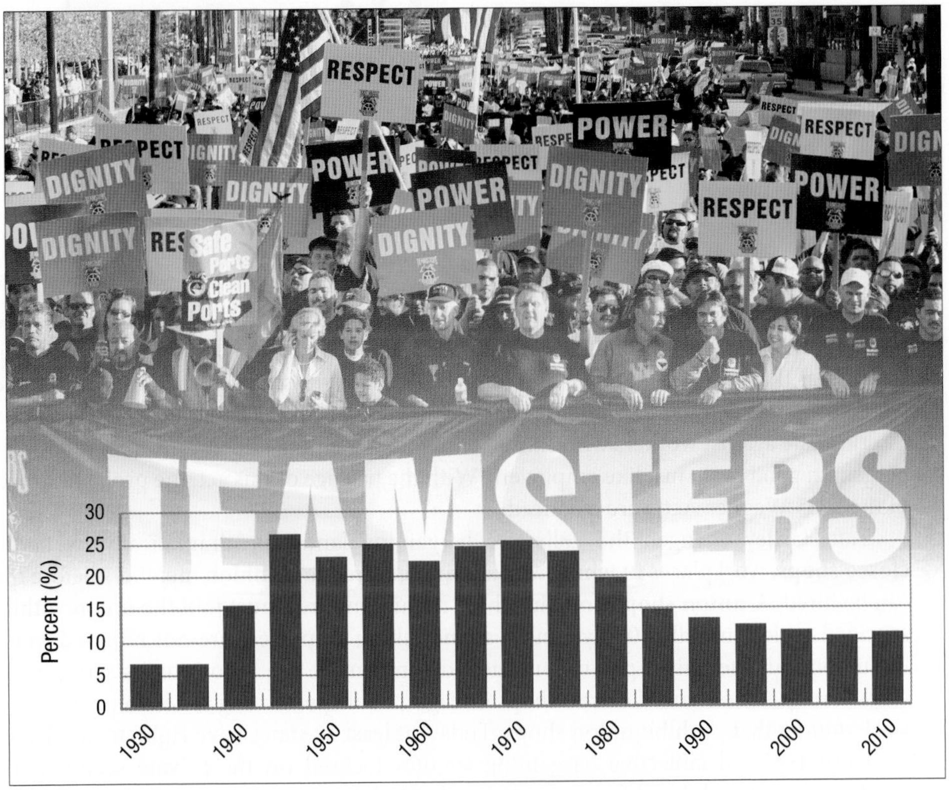

AP Photo/Kevork Djansezian

FIGURE 6

Union Membership as a Percent of Employment

Union membership grew dramatically from the mid-1930s until after World War II. Following the war, over one-quarter of American workers were unionized. Union membership has fallen because benefits obtained by unions for union members spread throughout the wider workforce, making the benefits of joining a union less valuable. Also, the changing economy led to faster growth in the service sector, which has traditionally been less unionized.

AP Photo/Elaine Thompson

FIGURE 7

Work Stoppages (Strikes)

This figure shows work stoppages, or strikes, since 1950. In 1946, numerous strikes turned public opinion against unions. In 1947, Congress reacted by passing the Taft-Hartley Act, seeking a balance between unions and management. After this, the use of work stoppages by unions gradually began to decline.

Figure 7 shows work stoppages, or strikes, since 1950. In 1946 a rash of strikes turned public opinion against the unions; many people felt unions had become too powerful. Because of this swing in popular opinion, in 1947 Congress passed the Taft-Hartley Act, which prohibits some unfair labor practices by unions. Unions could no longer coerce or discriminate against workers who chose not to join the union, and unions were required to bargain in good faith, just like employers. With the passage of this act, the prolabor aspects of the 1935 Wagner Act were balanced.

Taft-Hartley changed the collective bargaining landscape dramatically by ending **closed shops,** workplaces in which workers are required to be union members before they can be hired. A **union shop** is one in which nonunion hires must join the union within a specified period, usually 30 days. In an **agency shop,** employees are not required to join the union, but they must pay union dues to compensate the union for its services. The Taft-Hartley Act outlawed closed shops outright, while permitting states to pass *right-to-work statutes* that prohibit union shops. Today, at least 24 states have **right-to-work laws.**

Until 1962, all collective bargaining statutes focused on the private sector; public employees were prohibited from organizing. In 1962, however, President John F. Kennedy signed Executive Order 10988, giving federal workers the right to bargain collectively. Still, public employees are not permitted to strike. Rather, when an impasse is reached, both sides must submit to binding arbitration in which a neutral arbitrator resolves the dispute. In 2011, the collective bargaining rights of public employees came to the forefront of public debate as many state legislatures considered bills to reverse these rights. This is discussed further in the Issue box on page 296.

closed shop Workers must belong to the union before they can be hired.

union shop Nonunion hires must join the union within a specified period of time.

agency shop Employees are not required to join the union, but must pay dues to compensate the union for its services.

right-to-work laws Laws created by the Taft-Hartley Act that permitted states to outlaw union shops.

Why has union membership declined as a percentage of wage and salary workers since World War II? The answer lies partly in the changes in labor laws just discussed, the country's changing economy—notably, a larger service sector—and ironically, the very success of labor at pushing its agenda of promoting rules that protect workers (such as minimum wage laws, antidiscrimination statues, and restrictions on firing employees) through Congress and the courts has resulted in union membership being a little less valuable. As a result, union membership may continue to shrink as a percentage of the workforce.

Union Versus Nonunion Wage Differentials

Why join a union? The primary benefit to unionization should be higher wages, given the union's collective bargaining power. The general theoretical argument for union–nonunion wage differentials is illustrated in Figure 8.

This figure shows how unions are able to increase the wages in their sectors by restricting entry into union jobs. The markets for both unionized and nonunion labor begin at equilibrium, at point *e* in both panels of Figure 8. Thus, union and nonunion wages are initially equal, at W_0. If the union successfully restricts supply to S_1 in panel A, union wages will rise to W_1, but employment will fall to L_1 (point *a*). Those workers who are released have no choice but to move over to the nonunion sector represented in panel B, thus shifting its supply to S_2. Equilibrium in the nonunion sector moves to point *b*, where more workers (L_2) are employed at lower wages (W_2). The resulting wage differential, $W_1 - W_2$, is caused by successful collective bargaining in the union sector. Notice that this analysis is substantially the same as that for discrimination in the segmented labor force described in Figure 5 earlier.

Union–nonunion wage differentials vary by the union, occupation, industry, and historical period. In general, average union wages are 10% to 20% higher than the average

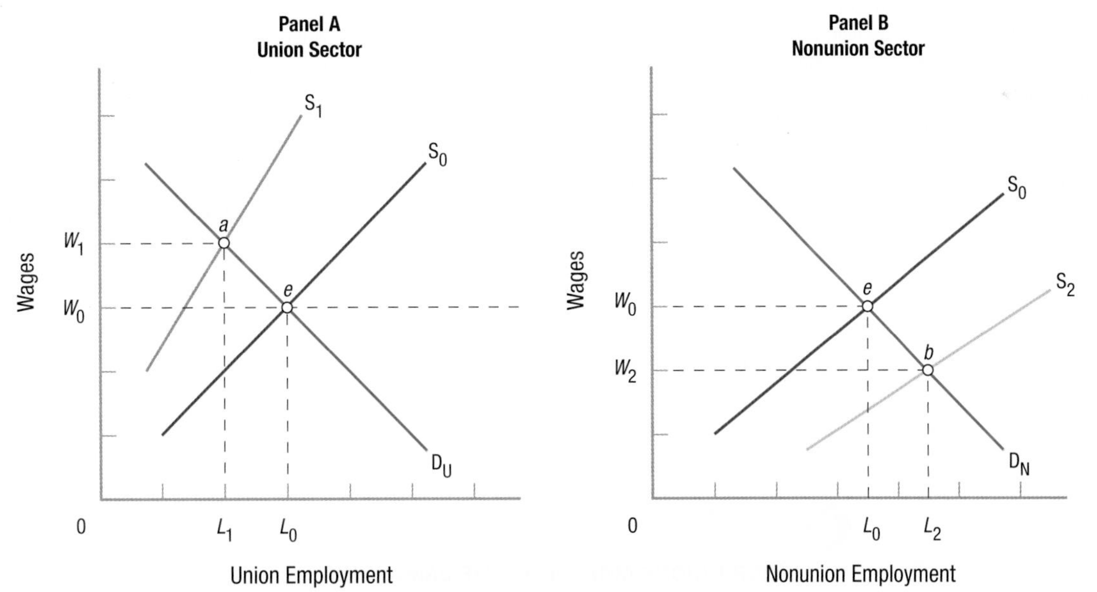

FIGURE 8

Union Versus Nonunion Wage Differentials

This figure illustrates the analysis of union–nonunion wage differentials. Unions increase wages in their sectors by restricting entry into union jobs. Assuming the markets for unionized and nonunionized jobs begin at equilibrium, at point *e* in both panels, union and nonunion wages are initially W_0. If the union successfully restricts supply to S_1 in panel A, union wages will rise to W_1, but employment will fall to L_1 (point a). Those workers released will have no choice but to move to the nonunion sector represented in panel B, thus increasing its supply to S_2. Equilibrium in the nonunion sector thus moves to point *b*, where more workers (L_2) are employed at a lower wage (W_2). The result is a wage differential equal to $W_1 - W_2$.

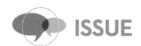

ISSUE

Will Public Unions Become an Endangered Species?

Scott Olson/Getty Images

"I love teachers—I just can't stand your union."

—New Jersey Governor Chris Christie (Feb. 24, 2011, *New York Times* Magazine)

For nearly a month in February 2011, thousands of union workers staged a round-the-clock protest at the Wisconsin state capital as state legislators debated whether to prohibit collective bargaining among state employees including teachers, state agency employees, and others (though policemen and firemen were exempt from this legislation). The act effectively ended the long-standing ability of state workers to form unions within their professions.

As the quote from New Jersey Governor Christie suggests, Wisconsin was hardly alone. Attempts by other states to eliminate collective bargaining for public unions or otherwise reduce their powers subsequently arose. For example, Ohio passed a law abolishing collective bargaining for public unions; however, unlike Wisconsin, voters successfully overturned the law at the ballot box.

Still, why has there been hostility toward public unions? There is a simple answer: Public unions have an important difference from private unions such as the automobile workers union or the steelworkers union.

Collective bargaining between private unions and private firms rests on three things. First, unions have the ability to strike. Second, while this threat of a strike can bring management to the negotiating table, management is constrained in what it can offer because of the need for the firm to generate profits. Third, the ultimate arbiter of what can be asked for by unions and acceded to by management is the market: The firm has to stay in business.

What is different about public unions? Many public unions are legally prevented from striking (teachers' unions are often an exception to this)—but this should make public unions more acceptable to state government, not less.

Public unions have a potent weapon that private unions do not have: the ballot box. Public unions can threaten state officeholders with something private unions cannot: votes, and getting out the votes to remove people from office. State officeholders have an incentive to placate large public unions if they want to keep their jobs.

Critics of public unions say the result of this political power has been higher wages and benefits unseen in the private sector. For example, private businesses generally make workers contribute toward their health insurance premiums. Public union workers often do not have to make such contributions.

Who pays for these public union benefits? The taxpayers. What became particularly galling to harried taxpayers who had suffered through their own wage freezes or wage rollbacks were public unions that demanded large pay raises even during the depths of the last recession. Rather than just say no, politicians in some states sought more radical solutions such as abolishing collective bargaining for public unions.

nonunion wage. Union wage effects are most pronounced among blue-collar workers and service employees. These differentials suggest that unionization may tend to reduce the inequities inherent in labor markets.

CHECKPOINT

LABOR UNIONS AND COLLECTIVE BARGAINING

- Unions are typically organized around a craft or an industry.
- Unions and the managers of firms must bargain "in good faith."
- In a closed shop, only union members are hired. This was outlawed by the Taft-Hartley Act. In a union shop, nonunion workers can be hired, but they must join the union within a specified period. An agency shop permits both union and nonunion workers, but the nonunion workers must pay union dues.
- Union wage differentials are between 10% and 20% higher.

QUESTION: Union negotiations always seem to run up against a "strike deadline." Are there incentives for both sides to put off a settlement until the very last moment?

Answers to the Checkpoint question can be found at the end of this chapter.

The Changing World of Work

Labor markets, like all other markets, change with time and the wishes of their participants. Over the last three decades, the entry of women into the labor force has been a major factor spurring economic growth. Over this same period, two-earner families increased so that today about 60% of all families with small children are two-earner households.

These demographic changes have shifted the focus of labor politics from union bargaining to issues such as telecommuting, family leave policies, affirmative action, and the question of how much employers should pay for medical benefits. As Social Security begins to look more fragile and the baby boomers begin flooding the retirement ranks, employer retirement packages will undoubtedly receive even more attention.

Immigration, legal and illegal, has caught the attention of labor economists. The United States has relatively open borders. Some argue that we need new immigrants to do the work that most Americans are unwilling to do. Other economists suggest that, in the absence of such inflows, salaries in these low-skill occupations would be high enough to attract the needed labor. This great tide of immigrants into lower wage jobs, together with the growth of high-skilled, high-wage jobs and the rise in dual-earner households, has resulted in a significant change in the types of jobs available today.

Jobs of the Past Versus the Present

Ask your parents or grandparents about the job opportunities they had when they completed school and you're likely to receive a description much different from the opportunities you have today. Prior to the Internet revolution and the globalization of manufacturing, the United States produced many of its own goods, including clothing, electronics, and household goods. As a result, work in factory plants was plentiful, and an individual with a high school diploma could find a well-paying job that led to a comfortable standard of living. What has changed over the past 25 to 50 years?

First, a shift from manufacturing to service industries occurred in the United States. Rather than producing physical products, considerable growth in the health care, computer programming, transportation, telecommunications, and technology industries led to greater production of services than goods. Service industries generally require a higher level of training as well as interpersonal and communications skills that one generally acquires with greater education.

Second, significant growth in international trade and foreign direct investment, components of globalization, changed labor demand. In addition to trading goods between countries, which reduces the need to produce certain goods in our own country, many industries have outsourced labor-intensive jobs to other countries, where wages are much lower than in the United States. At the same time, significant growth in high-skilled jobs in the United States has resulted from globalization, as the world demands better cell phone connectivity, health care services, and technology goods, which the United States is a leader in providing.

Third, the Internet has transformed the manufacturing process. With the ability to manage production in real time, many companies have moved away from producing and storing goods and now can source goods quickly from a variety of companies. For example, Amazon.com is a company that sells just about everything one can think of through their Web site, yet it hardly produces anything that it sells, but rather relies on thousands of individual manufacturers to provide ordered goods on demand. Similarly, for a small manufacturer, there are now thousands of Internet sites through which they can sell their goods. These changes have made the labor needs of firms much more flexible. Firms need not always rely on their own production to fill their customers' orders, and thus do not require an abundance of labor on their payrolls.

Future Jobs in the U.S. Economy

The future growth of jobs in the United States will likely continue to focus on those requiring increasingly higher levels of education and training, which we refer to as human capital and will be discussed in the next chapter. Growing professions such as health care professionals, financial services analysts, Web designers, social media managers, telecommunications technicians, and others will continue to exert increasing pressure to achieve greater levels of education. Projections from the Bureau of Labor Statistics *Occupational Outlook Handbook* show that the industries that are expected to generate the most new jobs over the next 10 years are health care, scientific and technical services, and education.

chapter summary

Section 1: Competitive Labor Supply

Work Versus Leisure: The Relationship Between Wages and Hours Worked

- Substitution effect: higher wages lead to more hours worked, and vice versa
- Income effect: higher wages lead to fewer hours worked, and vice versa

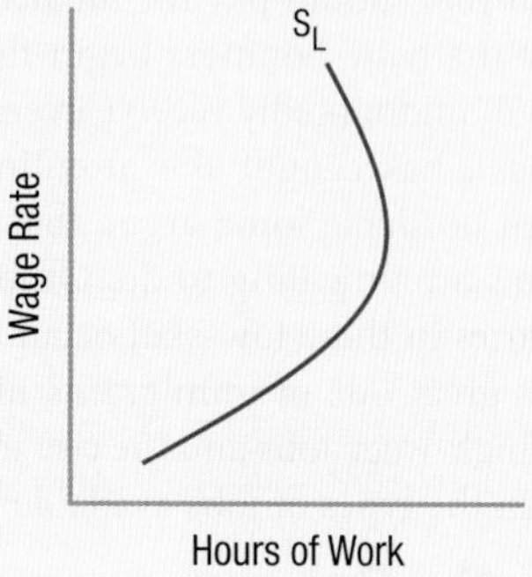

Stefanie Grewel/Corbis

A strong **income effect** means that a worker chooses to work fewer hours as wages increase to pursue other activities (such as studying). This leads to a backward-bending *individual* labor supply curve.

Factors That Change Labor Supply

- Demographic changes (population growth, immigration, labor force participation)
- Nonmoney aspects of jobs
- Wages in alternative jobs
- Nonwage income

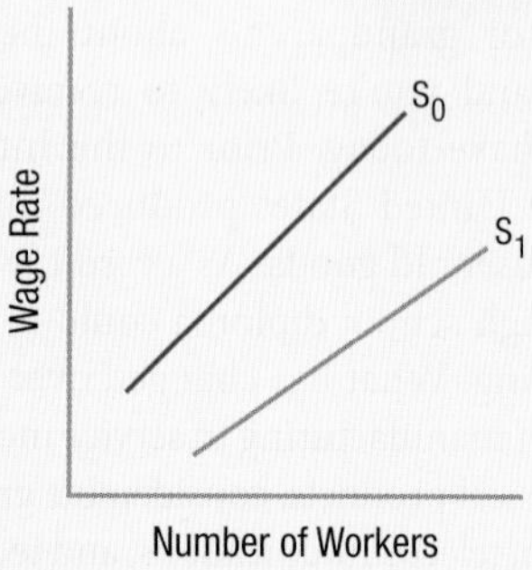

Market labor supply curves are upward sloping and can shift due to the factors listed above.

Section 2: Competitive Labor Demand

A firm's demand for labor is a derived demand: It depends on the productivity of labor and the demand for the good or service workers produce.

Factors That Change Labor Demand

- Change in product demand (affecting MR)
- Changes in productivity (affecting MPP_L)
- Changes in prices of other inputs

In a competitive labor market, wages are determined by the intersection of labor supply and labor demand. For an individual firm, they take wages as given (firms are price takers) and hire workers until its MRP equals the wage.

Marginal Revenue Product (MRP) = $MPP_L \times MR$

- MPP_L is the marginal physical product.
- MR is the marginal revenue from the product.
- MRP is the value provided by the last worker.
- Firms hire workers until MRP = wage.

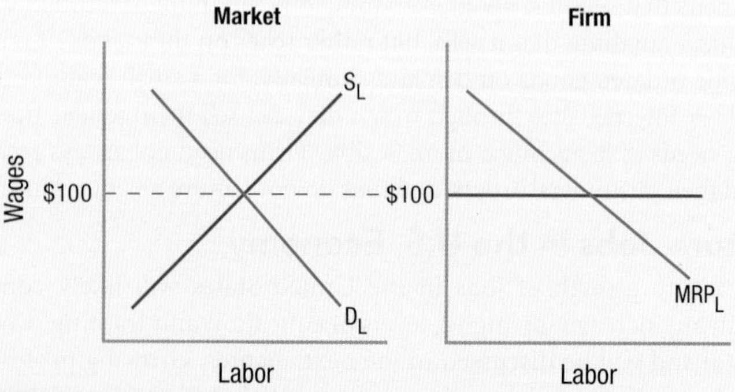

Section 3: Economic Discrimination

Economic discrimination occurs whenever workers of equal ability and productivity are paid different wages or otherwise discriminated against because of their:

- race or color
- religion
- gender
- age
- national origin
- sexual orientation
- disability

Laws Banning Labor Discrimination

- On gender: Equal Pay Act of 1963
- On race/ethnicity: Civil Rights Act of 1964
- On age: Age Discrimination in Employment Act of 1967
- On disabilities: Americans with Disabilities Act of 1990

Firms That Discriminate Must Pay More for Labor

- The supply of "preferred" workers decreases in a segmented market, increasing their wage.
- "Nonpreferred" workers enter a different market, increasing the labor supply and decreasing their wage.
- Firms that hire "nonpreferred" workers enjoy greater profits from a lower cost of labor.

Wavebreakmedia Ltd/Dreamstime.com

Employers choosing not to discriminate have access to a greater pool of talented labor.

Section 4: Labor Unions and Collective Bargaining

Labor unions are legal associations of employees formed to bargain collectively with employers over the terms and conditions of employment. They use:

- Strikes
- Threats of strikes
- Other tactics

Unions restrict labor supply, shifting the labor supply to the left, raising wages. Those not in the union are forced to find nonunion jobs, increasing the labor supply in those markets and lowering wages, creating a wage gap of $W_1 - W_2$.

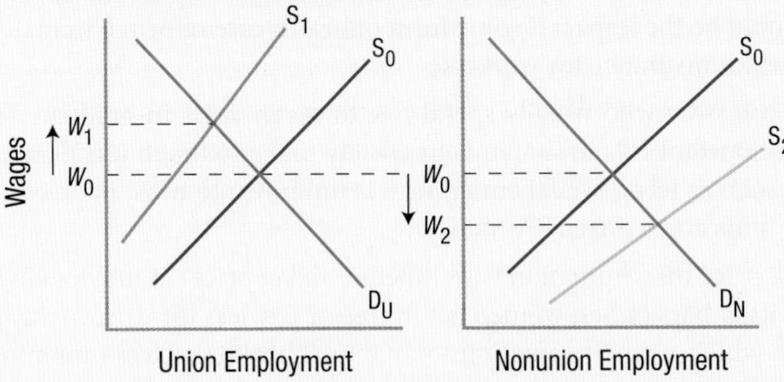

Major Laws Affecting Unions in the United States

- Wagner Act (National Labor Relations Act): protected union workers and their rights
- Taft-Hartley Act: Placed rules on unions to prevent them from becoming too powerful

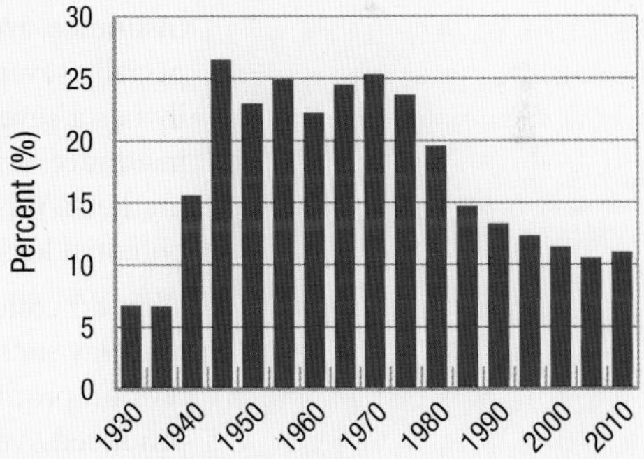

Union membership has declined since the 1970s. Recent state laws banning collective bargaining among public workers may further reduce union membership.

Section 5: The Changing World of Work

Changes in the U.S. Labor Force

- Two-earner families: more women in labor force
- Immigration growth filling low-wage jobs
- Increase in flex-time workers: workers that are able to set their own work hours

Significant Changes in Careers in the Past 50 Years

- Shift from manufacturing to service industries
- Significant growth in international trade and foreign direct investment
- The introduction of the Internet, which has transformed the manufacturing process

KEY CONCEPTS

supply of labor, p. 278
substitution effect, p. 278
income effect, p. 279
demand for labor, p. 281
marginal physical product of labor, p. 282
marginal revenue product, p. 282
value of the marginal product, p. 282
elasticity of demand for labor, p. 284
economic discrimination, p. 287
segmented labor markets, p. 288
closed shop, p. 294
union shop, p. 294
agency shop, p. 294
right-to-work laws, p. 294

QUESTIONS AND PROBLEMS

Check Your Understanding

1. Why are individual supply curves of labor potentially backward bending, but market and industry supply curves are always positively sloped?
2. What factors will increase the demand for labor?
3. When there is discrimination in the labor market, who loses? Why? Why is it harder to discriminate when both labor and product markets are competitive?
4. What are the important laws in place in the United States to prevent discrimination in the workplace based on race or gender?
5. How do unions exert their influence in the labor market?
6. What are some changes in the types of jobs available in the United States over the past 50 years and what are some trends for future labor employment?

Apply the Concepts

7. Some employees feel locked into their jobs because employer benefits, such as health insurance, are not transferrable to other companies. This "job lock" phenomenon is especially severe with health insurance coverage for employees if someone in their family has a severe pre-existing condition that prevents them from getting private health insurance at reasonable rates. What are the effects of this type of inflexibility on labor markets? What would be the impact if some form of health care reform eliminated the potential loss of health insurance for workers?
8. Why do college professors who usually spend five to seven years in graduate school and play such an important role in shaping our society make so much less than a Hollywood producer such as Jerry Bruckheimer, who is unknown to most people (he has produced over 40 films and a dozen TV shows)?
9. Why do we permit price discrimination with different ticket prices at movies based on age, or ladies' nights at bars (when women get in free or pay less for drinks), or insurance coverage, for which women sometimes pay more (health) or less (automobile), but we do not permit discrimination in wage rates?
10. Has globalization made it more difficult for unions to negotiate higher wages? Why or why not?
11. The airline pilots union has been very successful in negotiating six-figure salaries for pilots. The unions representing flight attendants have not been nearly as successful. What probably accounts for the difference?
12. Fifty years ago, married women ages 35 to 44 worked for pay only 10 hours per week on average; today they work over 26 hours on average. During the same period, the workweek for married men of the same age has been relatively constant, between 42 and 44 hours. Can you think of reasons why women's working hours have nearly tripled in the last half-century?

In the News

13. Tightened visa rules since September 11 have reduced the number of high-skill legal immigrants. Stiffer security rules and insufficient personnel have substantially increased the waiting time (and certainty) for visas. A *New York Times* article titled "Immigration and American Jobs" (October 19, 2012) reports a finding by economist Giovanni Peri that the wave of high-skilled legal immigrants from 1990 to 2007 increased the average wage of American workers by lifting the overall economy. Such findings have increased the pressure for immigration reform allowing more foreign graduates of American universities in the math, science, and technology fields to become permanent residents in the United States. Using the tools of labor demand and supply, evaluate the merits of the proposed immigration policy.
14. The National Bureau of Economic Research in December 2010 reported a study by Elizabeth Wilde, Lily Batchelder, and David Ellwood that a highly skilled woman loses anywhere from $230,000 to $349,000 in lifetime earnings by having children. What are the reasons that having children reduces women's earnings so much?

Solving Problems

15. Joe's Mechanic, which provides oil changes for $40 per car, decides to increase the number of mechanics on staff from four to five. As a result, the number of oil changes completed in a day increases from fifteen to seventeen. What is the marginal revenue product of the fifth worker?
16. In the following table, suppose the price of output is $10 per unit. What are the marginal physical product and the marginal revenue product of the sixth worker? If the wage of each worker is $150, should the sixth worker be hired?

Number of Workers	Units of Output
1	50
2	110
3	170
4	220
5	250
6	270

USING THE NUMBERS

17. According to By the Numbers, what is the average starting salary of workers with an undergraduate degree in economics? What is the average mid-career salary of workers with an undergraduate degree in economics?
18. According to By the Numbers, during which seven-year period did the percentage of Americans with flexible work schedules increase the most?

ANSWERS TO QUESTIONS IN CHECKPOINTS

Checkpoint: Competitive Labor Supply

Each person will have a different wage where their supply of labor curve bends backward. Getting a large inheritance will generate substantial nonwage income and typically lead to fewer hours worked. Having a family will probably raise the income required before you will cut your hours.

Checkpoint: Competitive Labor Demand

For many jobs, firms have standardized procedures that each employee follows. Therefore, the difference in productivity between individuals is relatively narrow. While homogeneous labor is a simplification, taking in everyone's difference would make analysis impractical. No, the model explains both since markets exist for each broad category of workers.

Checkpoint: Economic Discrimination

Discrimination in the workplace can be caused by preferences of employers, employees, or customers. If the discriminatory tastes are strictly due to employer preferences, then employers who discriminate will be forced to pay a higher wage for the "preferred" worker. Because employers who do not discriminate are able to hire an equally talented but less preferred worker at a lower wage, these employers will have a cost advantage in production. Over time, discriminating employers may need to reduce their discriminatory tastes or be forced out of business by lower cost competitors. Therefore, market forces tend to dissipate the extent of discrimination.

If the discriminatory tastes lie with the employees or customers, however, firms may be less able to reduce labor discrimination. For example, if employees refuse to work with a certain type of worker, or if customers refuse to buy goods and services from a particular type of worker, hiring these workers may negatively affect the firm's profit. Therefore, firms may choose to maintain segmented markets because the higher cost of labor is needed to prevent a potentially larger loss of revenues if their employees or customers act on their discriminatory tastes by refusing to work for or buy from the firm.

Checkpoint: Labor Unions and Collective Bargaining

Both sides work hard to get the best bargain for their constituents. There are incentives to continue negotiations up to the last moment to get the most and to appear to be driving a hard bargain. Strikes involve costs, and both sides use the threat of imposing these costs as a bargaining chip.

Appendix
Imperfect Labor Markets

After studying the appendix you should be able to:

- Explain why market power allows a firm to benefit from the labor market.
- Define a monopsony and explain how it affects wages in the labor market.
- Explain why imperfect labor markets are less efficient than competitive input (labor) markets.

In the world as we know it, markets are not perfectly competitive. Product markets and labor markets contain *monopolistic* and *oligopolistic* elements. In many product markets, a few firms control the bulk of market share. They may not be monopolies, but they do have some market power, through brand loyalty if nothing else.

Similarly, in most communities, there is only one government hiring firefighters and police officers. When the market contains only one buyer of a resource, economists refer to this lone buyer as a *monopsonist. Monopsony power,* meanwhile, is the control over input supply that the monopsonist enjoys. Before we look at the impact of **monopsony** on the labor market, let us first consider monopoly power in the product market.

monopsony A labor market with one employer.

Monopoly Power in Product Markets

As we know, firms that enjoy monopoly power in product markets are price makers, not price takers. Because P > MR, it follows that $VMP_L > MRP_L$. Figure APX-1 shows why. The firm depicted has monopoly power in the product market, but buys inputs in a competitive environment.

As Figure APX-1 shows, a competitive firm would equate the wage and the value of the marginal product (VMP_L), hiring L_C workers and paying the going wage of W_0 (point *c*). The firm with monopoly power, however, will equate the wage and marginal revenue product (MRP_L), thus hiring L_0 workers, though again paying the prevailing wage W_0 (point *a*). Therefore, although both firms hire workers at the same wage, the firm with monopoly power hires fewer workers.

This means that the value of the marginal product (VMP_L) of workers in the monopolistic firm is much higher than what they are paid. Their value to the firm

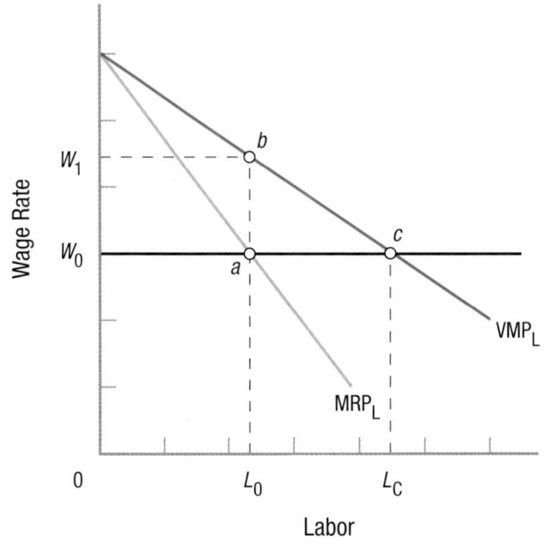

FIGURE APX-1

Monopoly Firm in Product Market Employing Labor from a Competitive Market

Firms with monopoly power in product markets are price makers. Because P > MR, it follows that $VMP_L > MRP_L$. A competitive firm would equate wages and value of the marginal product (VMP_L), hiring L_C workers and paying the going wage of W_0 (point *c*). A firm with monopoly power, however, will equate wages and marginal revenue product (MRP_L), thus hiring L_0 workers, although again paying the prevailing wage W_0 (point *a*). Hence, although both firms hire workers at the same wage, the firm with monopoly power hires fewer workers. Also, the value of the marginal product (VMP_L) of workers in the monopolistic firm is much higher than what they are paid; their value to the firm is W_1 (point *b*), although they are only paid W_0 (point *a*). This difference is called monopolistic exploitation of labor.

monopolistic exploitation of labor Occurs when workers are paid less than the value of their marginal product because the firm has monopoly power in the product market.

(point *b*) is W_1, even though they are only paid W_0. This difference is referred to as **monopolistic exploitation of labor.** The term is loaded, but what economists mean by it is that workers get paid less than the value of their marginal product when working for a monopolist. This is, as you might expect, a source of monopoly profits.

Monopsony

A monopsony is a market with one buyer or employer. The United States Postal Service, for instance, is the sole employer of mail carriers in this country, just as the armed forces are the only employers of military personnel. Single-employer towns used to dot the American landscape, and some occupations still face monopsony power regularly. Nurses and teachers, for example, often have only a few hospitals or local school districts for which they can work.

Because a monopsonist is the only buyer of some input, it will face a positively sloped supply curve for that input, such as supply curve S_L in Figure APX-2. This firm could hire 14 workers for \$10 (point *a*), or it could increase wages to \$11 and hire 15 workers (point *b*). Because the supply of labor is no longer flat, however, as it was in the competitive market, adding one more worker will cost the firm more than the new worker's higher wage. But just how much more?

marginal factor cost (MFC) The added cost associated with hiring one more unit of labor. For competitive firms, it is equal to the wage; but for monopsonists, it is higher than the new wage (*W*) because all existing workers must be paid this higher new wage, making MFC > *W*.

Marginal factor cost (MFC) is the added cost associated with hiring one more unit of labor. In Figure APX-2, assume that 14 workers earn \$10 an hour (point *a*), and hiring the 15th worker requires paying \$11 an hour (point *b*). Assume that you decide to go ahead and hire a 15th worker. When you employed 14 workers, total hourly wages were \$140 (\$10 × 14). But when 15 workers are employed at \$11 an hour, all workers must be paid the higher hourly wage, and thus the total wage bill rises to \$165 (\$11 × 15). The total wage bill has risen by \$25 an hour, not just the \$11 hourly wage the 15th worker demanded. The marginal factor cost of hiring the 15th worker, in other words, is \$25 per hour. This is shown as point *c*. Because the supply of labor curve is positively sloped, the MFC curve will always lie above the S_L curve.

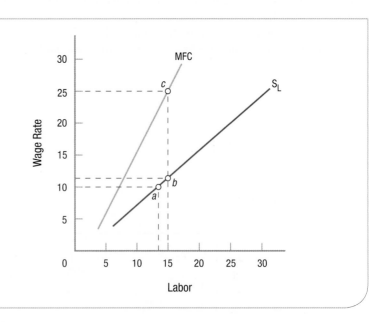

FIGURE APX-2

Marginal Factor Cost

This monopsonistic firm faces a positively sloped supply curve, S_L. The firm could hire 14 workers for \$10 an hour (point *a*), or it could increase wages to \$11 an hour and hire 15 workers (point *b*). Since the supply curve is positively sloped, however, adding one more worker will cost the firm more than the cost of a new worker. To hire an added worker requires a higher wage, and all current employees also must be paid the higher wage. Therefore, the total wage bill rises by more than just the added wages of the last worker hired. The marginal factor cost curve reflects these rising costs.

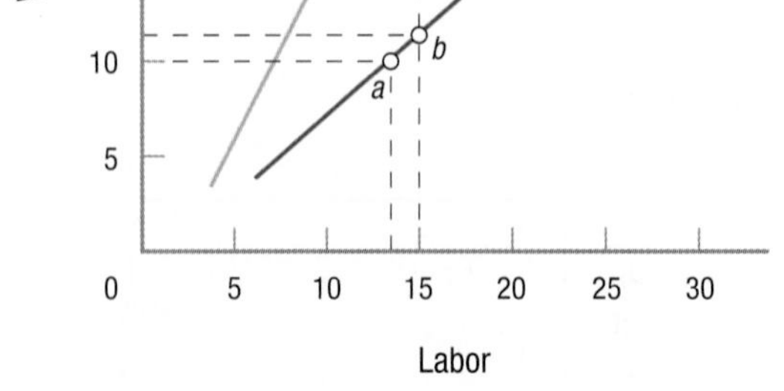

How does being a monopsonist in the labor market affect the hiring of a firm that is competitive in the product market? The monopsonist shown in Figure APX-3 is a competitor in the product market and has a demand for labor equal to its VMP_L.

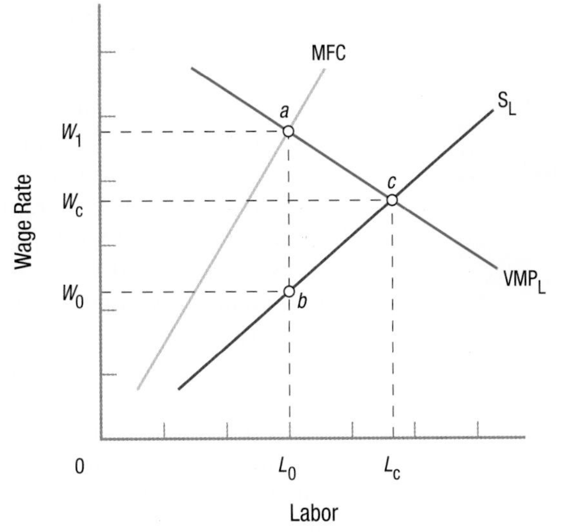

FIGURE APX-3

Competitive Firm in the Product Market That Is a Monopsonist in the Input Market

The monopsonist in this figure is a competitor in the product market and has a demand for labor equal to its VMP_L, while facing supply of labor, S_L. The firm will hire at the level where MFC = VMP_L (point *a*), hiring L_0 workers at wage W_0 (point *b*). Note that these L_0 workers, although paid W_0, are worth W_1. This is called the monopsonistic exploitation of labor. Note also that the wages paid in this monopsony situation (W_0) are less than those paid under competitive conditions (W_C), and that monopsony employment (L_0) is lower than competitive employment (L_C).

This firm faces the supply of labor, S_L. It will hire at the level where MFC = VMP_L (point *a*), thus hiring L_0 workers at wage W_0 (point *b*). Note that these L_0 workers, although paid W_0, are actually worth W_1. Economists refer to this disparity as the **monopsonistic exploitation of labor.** Again, the term is loaded, but to economists it describes a situation in which labor is paid less than the value of its marginal product.

monopsonistic exploitation of labor Occurs when workers are paid less than the value of their marginal product because the firm is a monopsonist in the labor market.

Note that the wages paid in the monopsony situation (W_0) are less than those paid under competitive conditions (W_C), and that monopsony employment (L_0) is similarly lower than competitive hiring (L_C). As was the case with monopoly power, monopsony power leads to results that are less than ideal when compared to competitive markets.

To draw together what we have just discussed, Figure APX-4 portrays a firm with both monopoly and monopsony power. The firm's equilibrium hiring will be at the

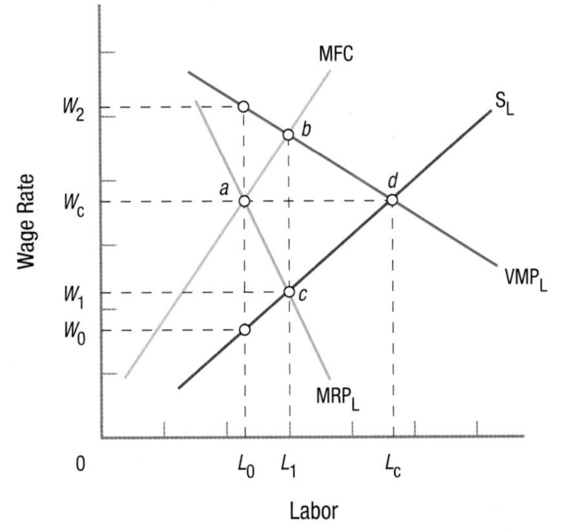

FIGURE APX-4

Monopolist Firm in the Product Market That Is a Monopsonist in the Input Market

This firm has both monopoly and monopsony power. The firm's equilibrium hiring will be at the point at which MFC = MRP_L (point *a*), and thus the firm will hire L_0 workers, although at wage W_0. Note that this is the lowest wage and employment level shown in the graph. If the firm only had monopsony power, it would hire L_1 workers (point *b*) at a wage of W_1. If the firm only had monopoly power, it would also hire L_1 workers for wage W_1 (point *c*). Both of these employment levels and wage rates are less than the competitive outcome of L_C and W_C (point *d*).

KARL MARX (1818–1883)

"Working men of all countries unite!" With this exhortation, Karl Marx ended his seminal *Communist Manifesto,* neatly summing up both his philosophy and his view of the world.

Karl Marx was born in Germany in 1818, but spent much of his adult life in England. By the time of his death in 1883, Marx and Friedrich Engels had crafted the essence of communism—the last ideology to seriously challenge capitalism in the 20th century. In their two major works, *The Communist Manifesto* (1848) and *Das Kapital* (1867), Marx and Engels offered a severe critique of capitalism and extolled the virtues of proletariat rebellion.

To preserve their privileges, the ruling class had always striven to oppress the underclasses. Marx saw a struggle between the bourgeoisie (or property owners) and the proletariat (the working class). This exploitation—the essence of capitalism—not only kept the bourgeoisie in power, but it also alienated the proletariat from its own labor, which to Marx was the true essence of all economic value. The only prescription to cure the monopolistic and monopsonistic exploitation of labor was proletariat revolution.

point where MFC = MRP_L (point *a*), and thus the firm will hire L_0 workers, although at wage W_0. Note that this is the lowest wage and employment level shown in the graph. If the firm only had monopsony power, it would hire L_1 workers (point *b*) at a wage of W_1, which is higher than W_0. If the firm only had monopoly power, it would also hire L_1 workers for wage W_1 (point *c*). Both of these employment levels and wage rates are less than the competitive outcome of L_C and W_C (point *d*).

The key lesson to remember here is that competitive input (factor) markets are the most efficient, because inputs in these markets are paid precisely the value of their marginal products, and the highest employment results. This translates into the lowest prices for consumers at the highest output, assuming efficient production. Thus, just as competition is good for product markets, so too is it good for labor and other input markets.

CHECKPOINT

IMPERFECT LABOR MARKETS

- When a firm is a monopolist in the product market and hires labor from competitive markets, the firm will hire labor at the point which the marginal revenue product is equal to the competitive wage.
- Monopolistic exploitation results because the monopolist pays less than the value of the marginal product of labor.
- Monopsony is a market with one employer. A monopsonist that sells its product in a competitive market hires labor at the point where the value of the marginal product is equal to the marginal factor cost.
- Monopsonistic exploitation occurs when the monopsonist pays labor less than the value of its marginal product.

QUESTIONS: Are public schools in rural areas a monopsony? Do they set wages in a way that is different from how wages are set in large urban areas?

Answers to the Checkpoint questions can be found at the end of this Appendix.

APPENDIX KEY CONCEPTS

monopsony, p. 303
monopolistic exploitation of labor, p. 304
marginal factor cost (MFC), p. 304
monopsonistic exploitation of labor, p. 305

APPENDIX SUMMARY

Imperfect Labor Markets

If wages are determined in a competitive market, a firm will hire labor until $MRP_L = W$. But if the firm enjoys some market power in the product market, marginal revenue product will be less than the value of the marginal product because MR < P. The difference between the value of the marginal product and marginal revenue product is known as monopolistic exploitation of labor.

A monopsony is a market with a single buyer or employer. Marginal factor cost (MFC) is the added cost associated with hiring one more unit of labor. For the monopsonist, the MFC curve lies above the supply of labor curve because the firm must increase the wages of all workers to attract added labor. A monopsonist, which is a competitor in the product market, hires labor up to the point at which $VMP_L = MFC > W$. At this point, the value of labor's marginal product exceeds the wage rate; economists refer to this as monopsonistic exploitation of labor.

APPENDIX QUESTIONS AND PROBLEMS

1. The figure below shows the supply of labor, marginal factor costs, and the demand for labor for a firm that is large enough that it is essentially a monopsonist in the community in which it operates. Assume that all workers are paid the same wage and that they work 2,000 hours per year (40 hours a week for 50 weeks).

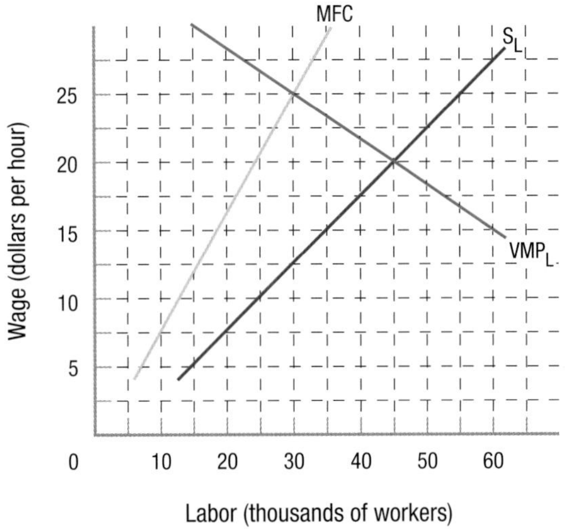

   a. What is the total wage bill (total wages paid by the firm) for this monopsonistic firm?

   b. If the firm was actually hiring from a competitive labor market, what would be the total wage bill for the firm?

c. What is the total value of the monopsonistic exploitation of labor by this firm?

d. Is the firm a competitor or a monopolist in the product market?

2. Would unions be more likely to organize successfully in highly competitive markets or in markets with monopsony power? Explain.

ANSWERS TO APPENDIX CHECKPOINT QUESTION

Checkpoint: Imperfect Labor Markets

Yes, they are monopsonists when it comes to hiring teachers. Generally, there is only one school district in rural areas. They probably act more like monopsonists when setting wages when compared to their urban counterparts, which have competition for teachers from other districts and private schools.

12

Land, Capital Markets, and Innovation

After studying this chapter you should be able to:

- Describe the impact of the supply of land on markets.
- Determine the present value of an investment.
- Compute the rate of return of an investment.
- Describe how businesses acquire financial capital.
- Understand how debt and equity instruments work and the differences between them.
- Describe the relationship between education and earnings.
- Know how market equilibrium levels for human capital are determined.
- Describe the different forms of on-the-job training and why both employers and employees benefit from it.
- Describe the impact of economic profits on entrepreneurs and markets.
- Explain the role of innovation in improving standards of living.

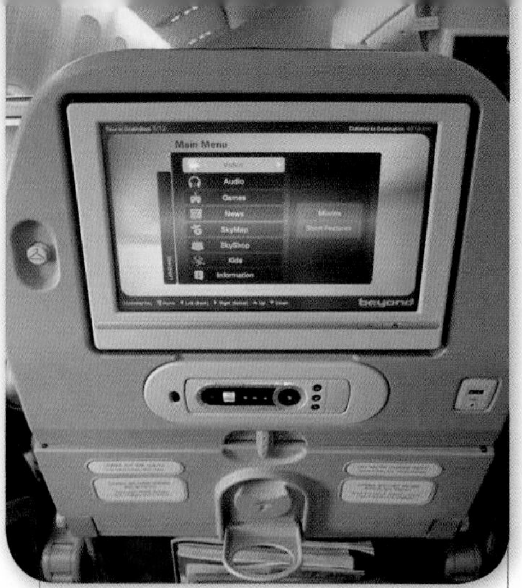

Patrick Smith www.askthepilot.com

Innovations in airplanes have made traveling more enjoyable. Korean Air's economy class seats feature a large personal video screen, satellite phone, USB charge port, cup holder, and coat hook.

Have you ever dreamed of venturing into space without having to undergo years of astronaut training? Richard Branson, the CEO of Virgin Group, wants to make that dream a reality with the launch of Virgin Galactic. Already an innovator in the aerospace industry, Branson's new space travel service will take six passengers at a time on a 3.5-hour suborbital flight 65 miles above the Earth's surface, allowing passengers to experience several minutes of weightlessness before the spacecraft returns to Earth. How does a business like Virgin Galactic go about creating its service and what resources would it need?

In the previous chapter, we studied how businesses rely on labor markets to acquire the workers needed to produce their products. To build a technologically advanced product such as a space plane, much more than labor is needed. First, the firm must buy abundant amounts of capital inputs, such as aluminum, glass, and engines, in addition to the massive machinery required to put the plane together. Second, the firm must obtain the financial resources to fund the operation until the planes are built, placed into service, and generate revenue. Third, the firm must find labor that has the knowledge to build airplanes. For Virgin Galactic, it would seek workers who studied aerospace engineering in college or those who have acquired skills from previous jobs, such as serving in the Air Force. Last, the firm must have the overall vision to provide the market with what it wants—or what it thinks the market will want in the immediate future.

Although space travel might be just a dream for those unable to afford the expensive ride, examples of innovation abound in the aerospace industry. If you have recently flown on a commercial airliner, you may have noticed the technological innovations that are becoming more prevalent on airplanes. In some aircraft, you can now watch live TV, view movies on demand, and even browse the Internet. Such features are just some of the amenities airlines are offering to make airline travel more enjoyable. Further, innovations in aircraft operation, such as lighter composite materials used in new aircraft, will allow significant savings in fuel, the largest cost component of airlines. Developing a plane that provides customers with new amenities while cutting operating costs is a major goal of the aerospace industry.

The necessary inputs (also called factors) for the production of commercial spaceships and airplanes require firms to use other resource markets, such as those for land and capital, in addition to the labor market. Land markets are used to obtain actual land along with natural resources. Capital markets are used to obtain physical capital, financial capital, and human capital.

BY THE NUMBERS

Innovation Is the Cornerstone of Growth

Innovation is the use of ideas and knowledge to produce new goods and services that raise a country's standard of living. Human capital and financial capital are important drivers of innovation that lead to economic growth.

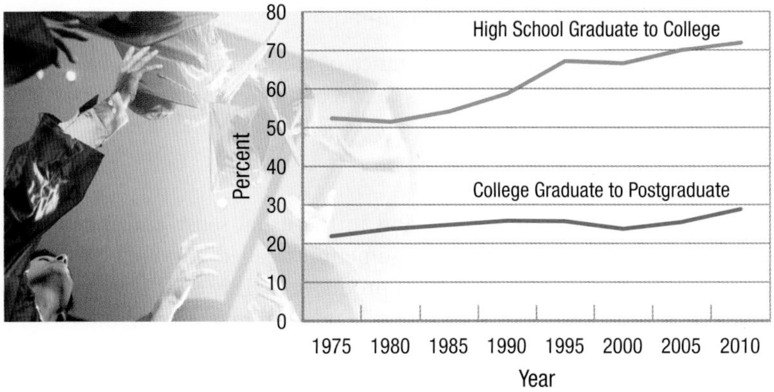

Simon Jarratt/Corbis

Human capital investment has grown over the past 35 years as the percent of high school graduates enrolling in college continues to increase. The percent of college graduates pursuing postgraduate degrees also has steadily increased.

253,155

Total number of patents granted in 2012 by the U.S. Patent and Trade Office.

66,170

Total number of patents granted in 1980 by the U.S. Patent and Trade Office.

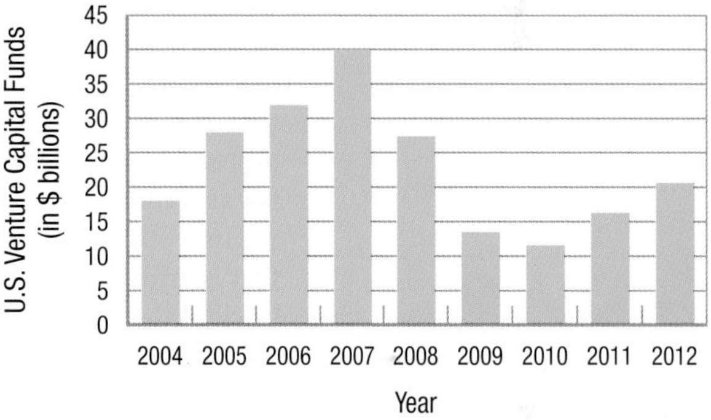

Venture capital firms provide financial capital to entrepreneurs to produce new products that lead to economic growth. The 2007–2009 recession dramatically reduced the amount of venture capital funds available.

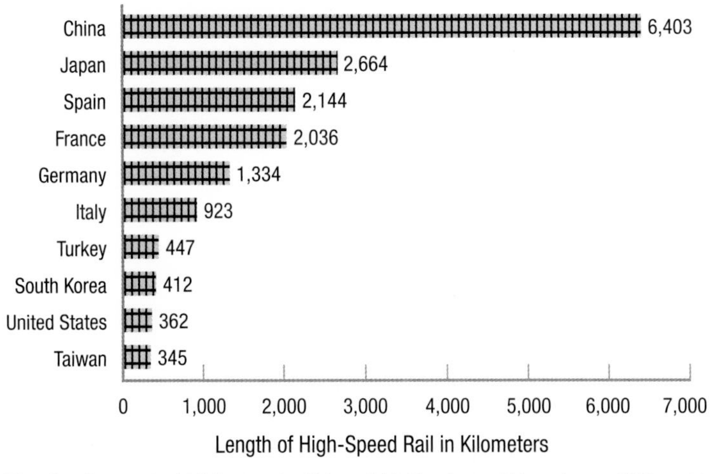

The development of high-speed rail travel (defined as rail travel over 150 mph) is an innovation that saves time and costs in transporting passengers and freight. As of January 2013, China led the world in total length of high-speed rail in kilometers currently in operation as well as the amount of planned new railways over the next decade.

Reuters/CORBIS

The Acela from Washington, D.C., to Boston is the only high-speed rail service currently in operation in the United States, with a top speed of 150 mph.

This chapter begins with an analysis of the land market, followed by a study of the three capital markets and the role that each plays in the economy. The chapter concludes with a discussion of entrepreneurship, the factor of production that brings all physical inputs together to generate profits and leads to innovation that increases economic growth.

Land and Physical Capital

In the previous chapter, we discussed the importance of labor in the production process. But certainly more is required than just workers to run a business and produce products. A business also needs land and physical capital.

Land

rent The return to land as a factor of production. Sometimes called economic rent.

For economists, the term *land* includes both land in the usual sense and other natural resources that are inelastically supplied. **Rent,** sometimes called *economic rent,* is any return or income that flows to land as a factor of production. This is a different meaning from when we speak of the rent on an apartment. Land is unique among the factors of production because of its inelasticity of supply.

In some instances, the supply of land is perfectly inelastic. Finding an empty lot on which to build in San Francisco is virtually impossible. The land available is fixed by the terrain; it cannot be added to nor moved from one place to another.

Figure 1 shows how rent is determined when the available supply of land is fixed. In this example, the number of acres of usable land is fixed at L_0 (or supply S_0). If the demand for land is D_0, the economic rent will be r_0 (point *a*). When demand rises to D_1, rent increases to r_1 (point *b*). Notice that because the supply of land in this example is perfectly inelastic, rent depends entirely on demand. If demand were to fall, rent would fall as well.

In a strict sense, land is not perfectly fixed in supply. Land can be improved. Land that is arid, like the deserts of Arizona, can be improved through irrigation. Jungles can be cleared, swamps can be drained, and mountains can be terraced, making land that was once worthless productive.

Even more ambitious are cities that have reclaimed land in the ocean by extending out from the coastline or creating new islands using large amounts of sand. Balboa Island off Newport Beach, California, and Star Island off Miami Beach, Florida, are examples of artificially made islands. Much larger projects are seen in Asia, where land is limited due to large populations and mountainous terrain. Still, even if the supply

FIGURE 1

Determination of Rent

This figure shows how rent is determined when the available supply of land is fixed. The acres of usable land are fixed at L_0 (supply S_0). If the demand for land is D_0, the economic rent is r_0 (point *a*). When demand rises to D_1, rent increases to r_1 (point *b*). Notice that because the supply of land in this example is perfectly inelastic, rent depends entirely on demand. If demand were to fall, rent would fall as well.

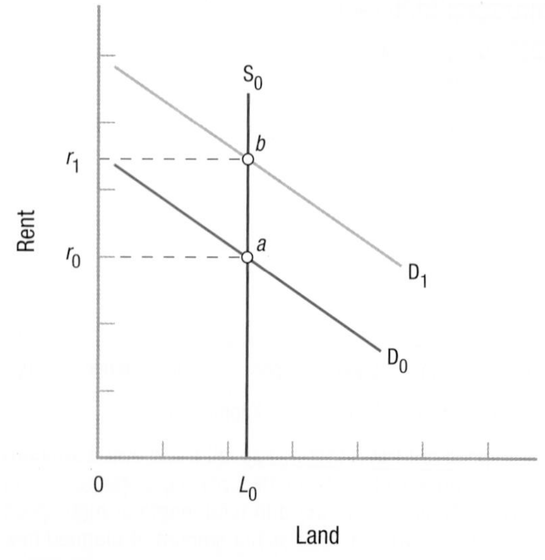

Bobby Yip/Reuters /Landov

ImageDB / Alamy

Reclaimed land was used to build Hong Kong Disneyland in 2005 in an area that used to be ocean. Although such methods have been used in coastal cities throughout the world, these expensive projects to increase the availability of land constitute a tiny portion of total land.

of land is not perfectly inelastic, it is quite inelastic when compared to other production inputs.

The price of land varies based on many factors, such as its terrain, its view, but most importantly, its location. Why are land prices so much higher in Manhattan and San Francisco than in Iowa? Land prices are driven by demand from households and firms choosing to build a home or a business. Because the supply of land in any single location is fixed (or the least inflexible), changes in demand will cause large fluctuations in land prices between more desirable and less desirable locations. But what determines a household or a firm's desire to locate in a particular place? The cost of land is an obvious factor, but other factors also influence a firm's potential profitability. For example, a business generally prefers to be close to its product market or its input suppliers.

Industrial agglomeration describes the geographical clusters of firms within an industry that choose to locate in close proximity with one another, such as Silicon Valley for the computer industry, Detroit for the auto industry, Dalton, Georgia, for the carpet industry, and Hollywood for the entertainment industry. By doing so, these firms benefit from external economies of scale. In a similar way, people of similar cultures sometimes choose to live near one another as well, leading to Chinatowns, Koreatowns, and Brazilian communities in various metropolitan areas throughout the country. Any time people choose a particular location for their home or business, demand for the land in that area increases, which will affect prices.

Physical Capital

Capital is the other important physical input in production. **Physical capital** includes all manufactured products that are used to produce goods and services. Examples of physical capital range from the massive cranes used to construct new skyscrapers to the espresso machine Starbucks uses to make your daily latte. Firms must determine what capital inputs are needed, and then calculate the value of adding additional capital to their production. When firms purchase capital inputs it is called investment. The investment decisions by firms involve calculating the marginal benefits and costs of each capital input.

physical capital All manufactured products that are used to produce goods and services.

In the previous chapter, we introduced the concept of the marginal revenue product of labor (MRP_L) and showed how firms choose to add additional units of labor if the cost of labor, or wage (W), is less than the MRP_L. In the capital market, we study a similar concept called the marginal revenue product of capital (MRP_K). Like MRP_L, MRP_K is downward sloping, showing that the returns a firm earns on its investments diminish as more capital is invested.

When firms choose which capital inputs in which to invest, they clearly would make their most productive investments first. For a fast-food burger joint, for example, a working deep-fryer would be more valuable than an automatic soda dispenser. Firms continue to invest until the cost of capital is equal to the MRP_K.

The cost of capital is the price of an additional unit of capital. Because the price of actual capital inputs varies significantly, we simplify things by measuring the cost of capital by their opportunity cost, or interest rate (i). In other words, to buy another capital input, firms must either borrow money and pay interest, or use savings and forgo interest. Thus, the interest rate can be used to measure the cost of capital.

Financial resources to pay for capital inputs come from the savings of households and other firms. Suppliers of funds and the demanders of these funds interact through what is called the *loanable funds market.* As with competitive labor markets, in which the market determines wages and each individual firm determines how many workers to employ, the loanable funds market determines interest rates, leaving individual firms to calculate how much they should borrow.

Through their interactions in the loanable funds market, suppliers and demanders determine the interest rates to be charged for funds. Individual firms then evaluate their investment opportunities to determine their own investment levels. Figure 2 shows how this process works. The demand and supply of loanable funds is shown in panel A, where equilibrium interest rates equal i_0. Note that the demand for loanable funds looks just like a normal demand curve. Its downward slope shows that, as the price of funds declines—as interest rates go down—the quantity of funds demanded rises. The supply of funds is positively sloped because individuals will be willing to supply more funds to the market when their price (interest rate) is higher.

Once the market has determined an equilibrium rate of interest, an individual firm like the one shown in panel B will take this rate of interest, or cost of capital, and determine how much to invest.

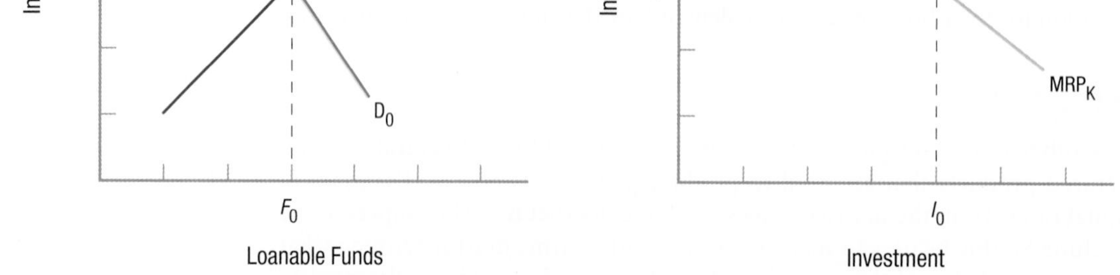

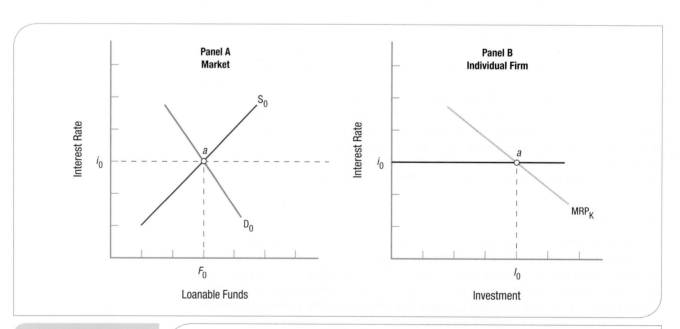

FIGURE 2

Loanable Funds Market and Individual Firm Investment

Panel A shows the market demand and supply of loanable funds, with equilibrium interest rates equal to i_0. Individual firms such as the one shown in panel B will take this rate of interest, or cost of capital, and determine how much to invest. Firms make their best investments first, and then continue investing (to I_0) until the cost of capital (i_0) is equal to the MRP_K.

This admittedly simplifies the investment process, but it is a good general model of investment decisions. Next, we turn to two more precise ways in which investment is determined, the present value approach and the rate of return approach.

Present Value Approach

When a firm considers upgrading its information system or purchasing a new piece of equipment, a building, or a manufacturing plant, it must evaluate the returns it can expect over time. Firms invest money today, but earn returns over years. To compare investments having different income streams and different levels of required investment, firms look at the *net* **present value** of the investment.

present value The value of an investment (future stream of income) today. The higher the discount rate, the lower the present value today, and vice versa.

The sum of $100 *a year from now* is worth *less* than $100 *today*. This is illustrated by the fact that you could put less than $100 in the bank today, earn interest on this money over the next year, and still end up with $100 at year's end. Yet, exactly how much less than $100 would you be willing to give up today for $100 received a year from today? To answer this question, let us begin by looking at a simple form of financial assets, annuities.

An annuity is a financial instrument that pays the bearer a certain dollar amount in perpetuity, or generally for the life of the annuity holder. Assume that the market rate of interest is 5%, and you are offered an annuity that pays you or the holder of the annuity $1,000 a year indefinitely. How much would you be willing to pay for this annuity? If you want to follow the market in earning 5% a year, then the question you must ask is this: On what amount of money does $1,000 a year in income represent a 5% return? The answer is found through the formula:

$$\text{PV} = X/i$$

where PV is the present value of the investment (what you are willing to pay for the annuity today), X is the annual income ($1,000 in this case), and i is the market interest rate. In this case, you would be willing to pay $20,000 for this annuity, since $20,000 = $1,000 / 0.05. We have thus reduced an infinite stream of income to the finite amount you would pay today. You would pay $20,000, and the annuity would give you $1,000 a year, for an annual return on your investment of 5%.

What happens to the value of this annuity if the market interest rate should rise to 10%? You will still receive $1,000 a year, but if you want to sell the annuity to someone else, the buyer will only be willing to pay $10,000 for it ($10,000 = $1,000 / 0.10). Interest rates doubled, and the value of your annuity has been halved. Higher interest rates mean that income in future years is not worth as much today.

Valuing future income today by this process is known as *discounting*. This principle applies not only to annuities, but computing for years less than perpetuity requires a more complex formula. For example, assume that someone agrees to pay you $500 in two years, and that the going interest rate is 5%. What would you be willing to pay today for this future payment of $500? The answer is found using the following formula:

$$\text{PV} = X/(1 + i)^n$$

Again, PV is the present value of the future payment, X is the future payment of $500, i is the interest rate (5%), and n is the number of years into the future before the payment is made. In this case the calculations are

$$\begin{aligned} \text{PV} &= \$500/(1 + 0.05)^2 \\ &= \$500/[(1.05)(1.05)] \\ &= \$500 / 1.1025 \\ &= \$453.51 \end{aligned}$$

Hence, you would be willing to pay only $453.51 for this $500 payment coming two years in the future. Again, the higher the interest or discount rate, the lower your price.

When only one future payment is at stake, computing the present value of that payment is fairly simple. When future streams of income are involved, however, things get more complicated. We must compute the present value of each individual future payment. The general formula looks nearly the same as before:

$$PV = \Sigma X_n/(1 + i)^n$$

Here, the Greek letter Σ (sigma) stands for "sum of," and X_n is the individual payment received at year *n*. Assume, then, that you are going to receive \$500, \$800, and \$1,200 over the next three years, and that the interest rate is still 5%. The present value of this income stream is therefore

$$\begin{aligned} PV &= \$500 / (1.05)^1 + \$800 / (1.05)^2 + \$1{,}200 / (1.05)^3 \\ &= \$500 / (1.05) + \$800 / (1.1025) + \$1{,}200 / (1.1576) \\ &= \$476.19 + \$725.62 + \$1{,}036.63 \\ &= \$2{,}238.44 \end{aligned}$$

Given the complexity of such computations, economists often use computers to solve for present value, especially when the annual income stream is complicated. When the annual income is constant, tables of discount factors are also available. In any case, the point to note is that payments to be made in the future are worth a lower dollar amount today.

Firms often use present value analysis to determine if potential investments are worthwhile. Turning back to our chapter opener, suppose that an airline is considering installing wireless Internet access in all of its planes. Assume that the service will yield a stream of income (from charging users a fee) exceeding operating costs over a given period. The present value of this income is then compared to the cost of installing the wireless Internet service. The service's *net present value* (NPV) is equal to the difference between the present value of the income stream and the cost of installing the service. If NPV is positive, the firm will invest; if it is negative, the firm will choose not to invest.

When interest rates are high, firms will find fewer investment opportunities where NPV is positive because the higher discount rate reduces the value of the income streams for investments. As interest rates fall, more investment is undertaken by firms.

Rate of Return Approach

An alternative approach to determining whether an investment is worthwhile involves computing the investment's rate of return. This rate of return is also known as a firm's *marginal efficiency of capital,* or its *internal* **rate of return.**

rate of return Uses the present value formula, but subtracts costs, then finds the interest rate (discount rate) at which this investment would break even.

Computing an investment's rate of return requires using essentially the same present value formula for income streams introduced above with a slight modification: You have to explicitly consider the cost of capital in the calculation. This new formula is

$$PV = [\Sigma X_n/(1 + i)^n] - C$$

where *C* represents the cost of capital. The question we must ask is: At what rate of interest (*i*) will the investment just break even? You would compute the present value of the income streams, then subtract the cost of the capital investment, and finally find the rate of interest (*i*) where the present value equals zero. This discount rate is the rate of return on the investment.

Suppose you find a rare vintage car for sale at \$20,000 that you believe will be worth \$25,000 next year. If you buy this car with the intention of selling it next year, the rate of return that would allow your investment to break even would be calculated as:

$$0 = [\$25{,}000 / (1 + i)^1] - \$20{,}000$$

Solving for *i* yields a rate of return of 25%.

The calculated rate of return can be compared to the firm's required rate of return on investments to determine whether the investment is worthwhile. The firm might require, say, a 20% yield on all projects based on the opportunity cost of the investment, in which case investments yielding returns of less than 20% are deemed not worthwhile. Risk in investment projects is usually managed by adding a risk premium to the required rate of return for risky projects. This risk premium can vary by project type or with the business cycle. Some investments, such as drilling for oil or researching innovative new drugs, are risky and require high rates of return if they are to be undertaken.

CHECKPOINT

LAND AND PHYSICAL CAPITAL

- Land includes both land and natural resources and is inelastically supplied. Returns on land are called rents (or economic rent).
- Because land is inelastically supplied, the rent on land is determined by demand.
- Firms weigh the benefits of investing in physical capital such as new buildings or machinery versus their costs.
- To compare investments with different investment streams over time, firms will use either the present value approach or the rate of return approach.

QUESTION: Suppose a good friend asks you to invest in some new equipment for her smoothie shop on campus in exchange for a share of the income earned at the end of the year. It will cost $10,000 to lease the new equipment for one year. What type of data and information would you be interested in estimating before you decide whether to pursue this investment?

Answers to the Checkpoint question can be found at the end of this chapter.

Financial Capital

To this point, we have introduced various physical inputs needed to produce a product, including labor, land, and physical capital. But how does a firm pay for these inputs? Most new businesses start out small, using personal savings or help from family to come up with the money to lease business space and rent or buy equipment. In fact, the founders of Apple, Steve Wozniak and Steve Jobs, started out in the Jobs family garage, and Mark Zuckerberg started Facebook out of his college dorm room. How does a relatively new business expand? Sometimes a business can expand using the profits earned and saved from its initial operation. But eventually, most if not all businesses require larger sources of **financial capital,** which is money required to purchase inputs for production. Firms use capital markets to acquire financial capital.

financial capital The money required by businesses to purchase inputs for production and to run their operations.

In the previous section, we described generally how firms calculate the cost of capital using the interest rate determined in the *loanable funds market*. Firms use the cost of capital to determine how many inputs to employ in their production process. But the loanable funds market is a general description of all sources of capital funding, whether that be borrowing from banks, or using more complex instruments such as bonds, stocks, or venture capital. In this section, we describe the specific mechanisms that firms can use to acquire financial capital to build, operate, and expand their businesses.

Banks and Borrowing

Let's start with the simplest means of acquiring financial capital other than self-financing. Suppose you wish to open a new sporting goods store and estimate that you will need $100,000 in financial capital. One way to obtain this money is through your local bank. Banks and other financial institutions offer small business loans (called commercial and industrial loans) based on your credit history, the potential success of the business, and the ability to resell collateral used to secure the loan. **Collateral** is an asset, such as a home or building, that a bank can sell if a borrower is unable to repay a loan. If you buy a car and take out a loan to pay for it, the car is the collateral for the loan.

collateral An asset used to secure a loan that can be sold if the borrower fails to repay a loan.

The ability to run a business with a bank loan is restricted to what the bank is willing to lend. This amount may not be enough to build a business and sustain its operation until a consistent cash flow is established to pay back the loan. Further, banks are more likely to address the inherent information problem between lenders and borrowers by scrutinizing the business plan and auditing files to ensure that a business is capable of paying back its loan. When bank borrowing is not feasible, the bond market may offer a more plentiful source of financial capital.

Bonds (Debt Capital)

Because bank loans are subject to credit restrictions and are usually limited in amount, it often is necessary for firms to borrow money by issuing bonds. A bond is an IOU certificate that promises to pay back a certain amount over time. The bond market offers firms an opportunity to acquire financial capital. The bond market is made up of firms that issue bonds and bondholders willing to invest by loaning money in exchange for an interest rate commensurate with the risk of that loan. Would you be willing to buy a bond issued by IBM or Coca-Cola? How about one issued by the Pep Boys—Manny, Moe, and Jack? This is an indication of what is meant by risk.

There are three main components to a bond: its face value, its coupon rate, and its maturity date. The **face value** of a bond is the amount that must be repaid to the bondholder upon its maturity. A **coupon rate** is a periodic fixed payment made to a bondholder expressed as a percent of the face value; some bonds do not have coupon payments, and instead are repaid in a single payment (these bonds are called zero-coupon bonds or more generally, discount bonds). A **maturity** date is the date when the face value of a bond must be paid to the bondholder. Maturity dates vary, and the length of time to maturity can range from a few months to up to 30 years. Some bonds even have no maturity dates (called perpetuity bonds).

face value The value of a bond that is paid upon maturity. This value is fixed, and therefore not the same as the market value of a bond, which is influenced by changes in interest rates and risk.

coupon rate A periodic fixed payment to the bond holder measured as an annual percent of the bond's face value.

maturity The date on which the face value of the bond must be repaid.

yield The annual return to a bond measured as the coupon payment as a percentage of the current price of a bond.

Many types of bonds exist, including corporate bonds, Treasury bonds, and municipal bonds, in addition to the many bond choices within each category. Corporate bonds are most likely to be used by firms to purchase productive inputs. In most cases, corporate bonds can be bought and resold in a bond market between investors. Because the price of a bond will vary based on the coupon rate, current market interest rates, and risk factors at the time of the transaction, a bond's yield is an important value for investors. The **yield** is the current annual return to a bond measured as the coupon payment as a percentage of the current price of a bond.

A bond's yield is positively related to its risk. In other words, the greater the risk that the company issuing the bond might default on its bond payments, the greater return an investor would demand for holding that bond. A bond's risk is measured by various bond agencies, including Moody's, Standard & Poor's (S&P), and Fitch. These agencies provide bond ratings that range from AAA (the safest bonds) to C (the riskiest rating by Moody's) or D (the riskiest by S&P and Fitch).

Figure 3 shows a corporate bond listing on January 2, 2013, showing the coupon rate, maturity date, bond ratings, the last price, and the yield. Looking at the first row, for JPMorgan Chase, this bond pays a coupon rate of 4.5% per year. However, because the bond's risk rating has improved since its initial issuance, the price has risen from its base price of 100 to 113.46. Because the face value of most corporate bonds is $1,000, this means one must pay $1,134.60 for this bond. Because the price exceeds the face value to earn the bond's fixed coupon payment, the yield falls to 2.809%, reflecting the reduced risk perceived by investors.

Looking at the last row, the Harrah's bond offers a coupon rate of 6.5%. In addition, you can buy the bond for $620 in January 2013, and cash this bond in for $1,000 at maturity in June 2016. The yield for this bond is significantly higher at 23.15%. Sounds like a

Issuer Name	Coupon	Maturity	Rating: Moody's/S&P/Fitch	Last Price	Yield
JPMorgan Chase	4.500%	Jan 2022	A2/A/A+	113.46	2.809
Microsoft	0.875%	Sept 2013	Aaa/AAA/AA+	100.48	0.228
IBM	7.125%	Dec 2096	Aa3/AA–/A+	159.80	4.415
Visant Corporation	10.000%	Oct 2017	Caa2/B–/___	90.50	12.709
Edison Mission Energy	7.000%	May 2017	Ca/D/C	53.25	20.357
Harrah's Operating Company, Inc.	6.500%	Jun 2016	Caa/CCC/C	62.00	23.150

FIGURE 3

Corporate Bond Listing in the *Wall Street Journal* on January 2, 2013

Corporate bond listings are shown with their current price in the "Last Price" column. Bond prices are standardized such that each bond is worth "100" percent of the $1,000 face value upon maturity. Bond prices higher than 100 means that the yield % is lower than the coupon %, which indicates that the bond is viewed as less risky relative to that suggested by the coupon rate. Conversely, bond prices lower than 100 suggest riskier bonds.

Data Source: FINRA and Wall Street Journal

great investment, but notice its risk rating of Caa/CCC/C, indicating a high likelihood of default. If Harrah's files for bankruptcy at any time up until June 2016, the expected 23.15% return will turn into a negative return after the bankruptcy filing. Indeed, high yields equal high risk.

Bonds provide advantages and disadvantages to acquiring financial capital compared to borrowing money from a bank. The benefits of bonds are that other investors share the risk of the business, and a business can generally raise more money through bonds by offering higher interest rates. The drawbacks are that bonds are a claim against a business, and the ability to issue future bonds depends on the ratings issued by ratings agencies and the overall demand and supply for its bonds in the market.

Although differences exist between bonds and bank loans, they still share similar characteristics. Both are IOUs to a lender, whether that be a bank or a bondholder. In both cases, the business maintains control over the management of the business. There is no risk of an outside investor or firm forcefully taking over the business, because the entire ownership is maintained by the company's owners. The disadvantage of relying on bonds and banks, however, is that the ability to raise large sums of capital may be difficult or expensive, and the burden of making debt payments may limit the performance of the business. An alternative approach is for a firm to acquire financial capital from the public in exchange for a share of ownership in the company. This involves stocks, which we discuss next.

Stocks (Equity Capital)

An alternative to using debt instruments such as a bank loan or the issuing of bonds to acquire financial capital is to offer partial ownership (also known as equity) in the company. The most common approach is to issue stock shares. Each **share of stock** issued represents one fraction (of the total shares issued) of ownership in the company, and subsequently one vote in shareholder meetings and one share of any dividends (periodic payments to shareholders).

share of stock A unit of ownership in a business that entitles the shareholder to one vote at shareholder meetings and one share of any dividends paid.

When a firm issues stock, it receives money in exchange for ownership in the company. This is handled in what is known as an initial public offering, or IPO. Typically, the founders of the company will retain a significant portion of the shares for themselves. However, the more shares that are issued, the smaller the value that each share will be. Therefore, when firms increase the number of shares issued without justifying their value to existing shareholders through actual or potential earnings, it is likely that the price per share will fall.

market cap The market value of a firm determined by the current price per share of its stock multiplied by the total number of shares issued.

The **market cap** of a firm is what a firm is estimated to be worth based on its stock value, calculated as the current price per share multiplied by the total number of shares issued. The price of a share of stock is determined by supply and demand just as in any other market, and for every buyer of a share of stock there must be a seller. Shares of stock generally are traded in stock exchanges (such as the New York Stock Exchange or NASDAQ).

An important point here is that firms receive money only once from issuing a share of stock. Once a share of stock is issued, the trading of that share among investors and the corresponding price fluctuations of that share do not provide any additional funds to the company, although company executives who hold significant number of shares clearly would benefit from a higher share price of their stock.

Like bonds, there are advantages and disadvantages to firms that raise financial capital from issuing stock. Advantages of issuing stock relative to bonds include the ability to raise substantial amounts of financial capital by sharing ownership in the business and its profits. In addition, businesses are not required to make repayments to stockholders, allowing them to reinvest their earnings as opposed to repaying lenders. Lastly, should the business fail, the losses are spread among all shareholders, not just to the business's founder, a concept known as *limited liability*. The main disadvantage of issuing stock is that partial ownership in the business is given up. In fact, with enough shareholder votes, an external investor can vote to replace a firm's management and/or board of directors, or even take over the company outright by buying all or a majority of the shares in the company.

Suppose that for your fifth birthday in 1998, instead of a shiny new bike, your parents bought you 50 shares of Apple Computer Inc. stock for $164 (each share of Apple stock was worth $3.28, adjusted for two stock splits, on January 1, 1998). Today, those 50 shares would be worth over $25,000. Would you rather have that bike or a brand new car today?

From an investor's point of view, why would people find stocks an attractive investment given the real risks of businesses failing? Some companies do fail, and stockholders in these cases often lose their entire investment as opposed to bondholders, who are able to make claims on a firm's remaining assets before shareholders. However, historical data have shown that investing in stocks, despite the higher risk, generates a much higher return over the long run than investing in bonds, buying certificates of deposit (CDs), or keeping money in a savings account. In other words, by owning a share of stock, one is entitled to a share of the company's future value. For many businesses that do succeed, this can result in a very profitable return. In some cases, owning shares in certain businesses over time has made investors very wealthy.

Venture Capital and Private Equity

An alternative approach to raising financial capital using equity instruments is to secure venture capital or private equity, both of which are large sums of money offered by financial investment firms eager to earn potentially large profits by investing a significant amount of money in a company.

The difference between venture capital firms and private equity firms lies primarily in the type of firms targeted. Venture capital firms typically invest in new start-up companies, providing seed money to entrepreneurs with potentially profitable ideas in exchange for a share of company ownership. Private equity firms typically target mature firms that are struggling to maximize profits or are on the verge of bankruptcy. By providing a substantial capital investment to a struggling firm in exchange for a large (often majority) share of company ownership, private equity firms can replace a firm's board of directors as well as management in an effort to turn a company's performance around.

How do venture capital and equity capital differ from financial capital acquired through the stock market? The key factors are timing, volume, and risk. A venture capital firm seeks out the next Fortune 500 company in its earliest stages, hoping to turn a relatively small amount of money into a huge return. Similarly, a private equity firm seeks large returns by reorganizing existing firms. In both cases, individual stock investors may be hesitant to invest, either because the company is too young (or has not established a product to generate revenues), or the company is nearing bankruptcy. By purchasing a large share of a company, venture capital and private equity firms take substantial risks in exchange for potential large returns to their own shareholders.

According to the National Venture Capital Association (NVCA), the largest trade association for venture capital firms, there were 526 venture capital investment firms in the United States in 2012. In 2012, a total of $20.6 billion in venture capital was invested in new businesses in many industries. According to the Private Equity Growth Capital Council, there were over 2,600 private equity firms in the United States in 2012. The amount of private equity investment is more difficult to measure, given the frequent buying and selling of shares in existing firms as opposed to the providing of start-up capital by venture capital firms, which is easier to measure.

Despite the year-to-year fluctuations in venture capital and private equity investments, these investments represent a large source of financial capital in the United States. While some investments have gone sour, some have turned into moneymaking machines. The following Issue box describes one of the most successful venture capital stories: Google. Yet, even today there are new firms that may potentially provide even bigger success stories, and investors are actively seeking these firms out.

ISSUE

Venture Capital: A Few Success Stories and One Big Missed Opportunity

Hardly a day goes by without most of us performing an Internet search using Google. Google has become one of the most successful Internet companies in history. How did Google get its start, and how did it find the financial capital to begin its remarkable climb to success? The story begins in 1996 with Larry Page and Sergey Brin.

Larry Page and Sergey Brin were Ph.D. candidates at Stanford University when in March 1996 they started a project called the Stanford Digital Library Project. It then became known as BackRub. Their first source of funding came in August 1998, when Andreas (Andy) von Bechtolsheim, co-founder of Sun Microsystems, and Professor David Cheriton of Stanford, provided $100,000 each in start-up capital in exchange for partial ownership of the still unincorporated company. The company was officially named Google as a play on the word *googol*, which is a number representing a 1 with 100 zeros after it.

The following year, in June of 1999, Google secured $25 million in venture capital from two venture capital firms (Sequoia Capital and Kleiner Perkins Caufield & Byers), which each received 10% ownership in the company. In the year prior to securing these funds, Page and Brin had made an offer to sell the entire company (albeit a much smaller company at the time) for as little as $750,000!

In 2004, Google made an initial public offering of stock shares, generating a huge infusion of cash, while Page, Brin, Bechtolsheim, Cheriton, the original venture capital firms, and Google's employees collectively retained nearly 90% of the shares for themselves. As of August 2013, Google was worth over $250 billion based on its stock value. For the venture capitalists who turned $12.5 million into $25 billion (10% ownership), that is a 200,000% return over 14 years. For Bechtolsheim and Cheriton, who each turned $100,000 into $2.5 billion, that is a 2,500,000% return over 15 years. Unfortunately, not all venture capitalists became billionaires. It was quite a missed opportunity for those who turned down Page and Brin's original offers.

CHECKPOINT

FINANCIAL CAPITAL

- Firms require financial capital to purchase inputs needed in their production.
- Financial capital can be obtained from bank loans, from the issuing of bonds or stock shares, or from venture capital or private equity firms.
- Bonds are IOU notes that provide a return based on their level of risk.
- Owning a share of stock entitles an investor to one share of ownership in a business, and can lead to substantial gains if the business is successful.
- Venture capital and private equity firms take on risk in exchange for potential large returns by investing in new or underperforming companies, respectively.

QUESTIONS: What is the difference between a bond and a share of stock? What are some advantages and disadvantages of acquiring financial capital by issuing bonds in the bond market instead of issuing shares in the stock market?

Answers to the Checkpoint questions can be found at the end of this chapter.

Investment in Human Capital

In the previous chapter, we discussed some of the reasons why some people are paid more than others, including discrimination in the labor market and the role of unions. But even if we put these important considerations aside, other factors may lead to wage differences, such as how much education one has. Previously, we had treated labor as a homogeneous input to simplify our analysis. In this section, we look at labor that has been enriched by training or education and how it affects the productivity of firms.

Is there a relationship between your earnings and your education? Let us first consider the role education and on-the-job-training (OJT) play in determining wage levels in labor markets. Workers, students, and firms all invest in themselves or their employees to increase productivity. This is called **investment in human capital.** Workers invest by accepting lower wages while they undertake apprenticeships. Students invest by paying for tuition and books, and by forgoing job opportunities, to learn new skills. Firms invest in their workers through OJT and in-house training programs that involve workers being paid to attend classes. These investments entail costs in the current period that are borne in the interest of raising future productivity.

investment in human capital Investments such as education and on-the-job training that improve the productivity of labor.

Education and Earnings

One of the surest ways to advance in the job world and increase your income is by investing in education. The old saying, "To get ahead, get an education," still holds true. Table 1 shows the age/earnings profiles for all Americans between 25 and 64 for 2009. It provides strong evidence that education and earnings are related.

TABLE 1 Average Earnings by Highest Degree Earned, 2009

Age Grouping	No HS Diploma	HS Diploma	Some College	Bachelor's Degree	Professional
25–34	$19,415	$27,511	$31,392	$45,692	$86,440
35–44	24,728	33,614	39,806	65,346	136,366
45–54	23,725	36,090	44,135	69,548	148,805
55–64	24,537	34,583	42,547	59,670	149,184

Source: U.S. Census Bureau, *Statistical Abstract of the United States, 2012* (Washington, DC: U.S. Government Printing Office), 2012, Table 232.

Average earnings for those without a high school diploma peaked at $24,728 a year, while those completing high school peaked at $36,090, a 45% increase. Getting a college degree bumped peak earnings up to $69,548, over a 180% rise. Going on to get a professional degree moved the peak all the way up to $149,184, over a 100% increase over a bachelor's degree alone. These figures represent average earnings. It is easy to see that earnings in all age groups were much higher for those with higher levels of education.

Table 1 suggests that education is a good investment. But like any investment, future earnings must be balanced against the cost of obtaining that education. The costs of education must be borne today, but the earnings benefits do not arrive until later. Making optimal educational decisions therefore requires some tools to help evaluate investments in human capital markets.

Education as Investment

To keep our analysis simple, we will focus on the decision to attend college for four years. The basic approach outlined in this section will nonetheless apply to other investments in education or training.

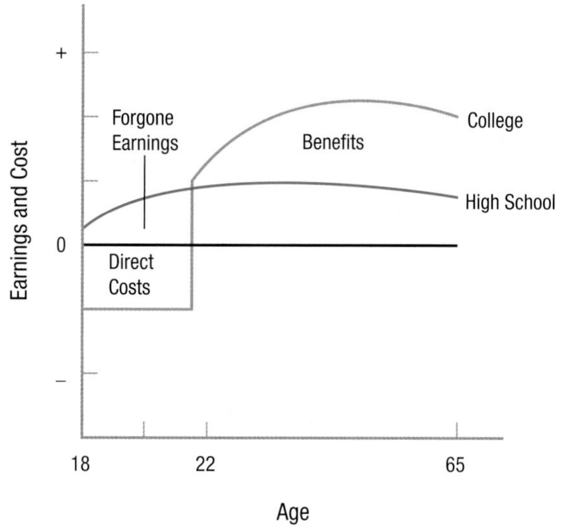

FIGURE 4

Benefits and Costs of a College Education

If an individual chooses not to go to college at age 18, he or she enters the labor market on leaving high school, and earnings rise and fall along the path labeled "High School." The college student incurs the direct costs of education, such as tuition and books, and the forgone earnings of not immediately entering the job market. The benefits of the college education show up as the difference in earnings from ages 22 to 65.

Figure 4 presents a stylized graph showing the benefits and costs of a college education. For simplicity, we will assume students go to college at age 18. If an individual chooses not to go to college, the high school earnings path applies: On leaving high school, the person enters the labor market immediately, and earnings begin rising along the path labeled "High School." Note that the earnings are positive throughout the individual's working life.

A college student immediately incurs costs in two forms. First, tuition, books, and other fees must be paid. These direct costs exclude living expenses, such as food and rent, because these must be paid whether one works or goes to college. Tuition varies substantially depending on whether one attends a private or public university.

Second, students give up earnings as they devote all their time to their studies (and to the occasional party). These costs can be substantial when compared to the direct costs of an education at a state-supported institution, because the average earnings for high school graduates range between $17,000 and $22,000 a year.

The benefits from a college degree show up as the difference in earnings from ages 22 to 65. If the return on a college degree is to be positive, this area must offset the direct costs of college and the forgone earnings. We must also keep in mind that a large part of the income high school and college graduates earn will not come until well into the future. For college graduates, this is especially important, because they will not see income for at least four years. How can we tell if this sacrifice is worth it? The fact that the median earnings of college graduates exceeded that of high school graduates by over 80% suggests a college education is worth it.[1]

An alternate way to decide which of the two career paths is best is by computing the rate of return on a college degree. If the annual return on a college education over the course of one's working life is 10% a year, the earnings of the college graduate in middle age will exceed those of the high school graduate by enough to generate a 10% return. A lower return would mean that the difference in earnings is smaller, while a higher return suggests the difference in earnings is greater. An extensive study[2] of rates of return to higher education in nearly 100 countries put the average return at nearly 20%. That is, college graduates around the world earn on average nearly 20% more per year over the course of their working lifetime than high school graduates, taking into consideration all of the costs of going to college.

[1] U.S. Census Bureau, *Statistical Abstract of the United States, 2012* (Washington D.C.: U.S. Government Printing Office), 2012.

[2] G. Psacharopoulos and H. Patrinos, "Returns to Investment in Education: A Further Update," *Education Economics,* 2004.

Equilibrium Levels of Human Capital

Each of us must decide how much to invest in ourselves. This decision, like so many in economics, ultimately depends on supply and demand, in this case, the supply of, and demand for, funds to be used for human capital investment. A hypothetical market for human capital is shown in Figure 5. In this scenario, "price" is the percentage rate of return on human capital investments and the interest cost of borrowing funds.

FIGURE 5

Equilibrium Levels of Investment in Human Capital

This graph portrays a hypothetical market for human capital; the percentage rates of return and the interest costs of borrowing funds are shown on the vertical axis. With demand D_0 and supply S_0, equilibrium will be at point *e*. If the supply of funds is reduced (S_1), interest rates and the cost of investment increase, resulting in less investment. Reduced demand for education (D_1) similarly reduces human capital investment.

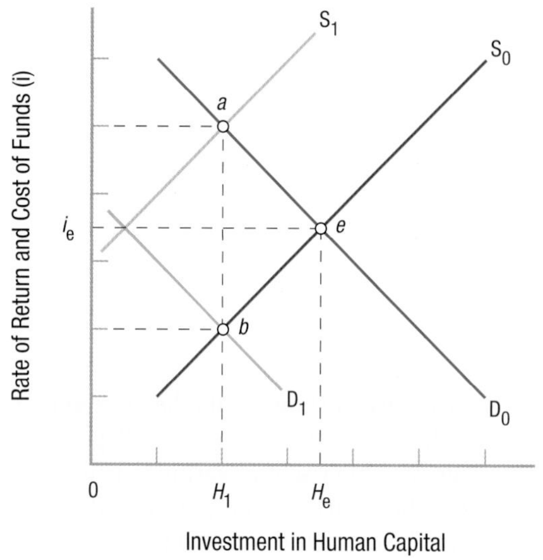

The demand for human capital investment slopes down and to the right, reflecting the diminishing returns of more education and that more time in school leaves you less time to earn back its costs. Students pursuing a Ph.D. or a medical degree are often into their thirties before they can begin paying back their student loans. As a result, they require higher salaries to bring their rates of return up above those of college-educated workers.

The supply of investable funds, meanwhile, is positively sloped, because students will use the lowest-cost funds first—mom and dad paying for college—then turn to government-subsidized funds, and finally use private market funds, if needed.

With demand (D_0) and supply (S_0), equilibrium in this market is at point *e*. Human capital investment is equal to H_e, with the rate of return equaling the interest rate (i_e). Notice that reducing the supply of funds, or shifting the supply curve to S_1, will increase interest rates and the cost of investment. This results in lower investments in education. Similarly, anything reducing the demand for funds, or shifting the demand curve to D_1, will result in reduced human capital investment. Let us briefly consider some of the factors that might cause these curves to shift.

The most important factor determining the supply of investable funds for students consists of family resources. Students from well-off families can draw on a pool of inexpensive funds, but students from poorer families must scratch together funds that are often expensive. At the aggregate level, reductions in federally subsidized low-interest student loans will result in a shift in the supply curve to S_1, meaning lower investments in human capital (H_1). Conversely, the GI Bills enacted after World War II and the Vietnam War, along with recent tax policies that allow certain individuals to deduct a portion of their tuition payments from their taxes, have made a college education easier to afford. These policies have shifted the supply curve to the right and have increased college enrollments and the stock of human capital in America.

Another factor influencing human capital investment is discrimination. Assume D_0 represents the demand for human capital investment for individuals facing no discrimination in the labor market. If these same people were to face a reduced wage in the market from wage discrimination, their demand for education would fall to D_1, reflecting the reduced return on investment in human capital. A similar decline in demand would result if the choice of jobs is limited by occupational discrimination.

The demand for human capital is also influenced by an individual's abilities and learning capacity: the more able the person, the larger the expected benefits of human capital investment.

Implications of Human Capital Theory

Individuals are more productive because of their investment in human capital, and thus they are capable of earning more during their working lives. Because younger people have longer earning horizons, they are more likely to invest in human capital and education. As workers get older and gain labor market experience and higher wages, their opportunity costs for attending college grow larger, while their potential post-college earning period shrinks. This explains why most students in college classrooms are young.

The greater the market earnings differential between high school and college graduates, the more people will attend college, because a higher earnings differential raises the return on college educations. Similarly, reductions in the cost of education lead to greater educational investment.

Further, the more an individual discounts the future—the more she or he values present earnings over future earnings—the less investment in human capital we would expect. People with high discount rates often are not willing to pursue doctoral or medical degrees because the time between the beginning of the training process and the point when earnings begin is simply too long.

Human Capital as Screening or Signaling

Human capital theorists see investments in human capital as improving the productivity of individuals. This higher productivity then translates into higher wages. There is another view of why higher educational levels lead to higher wages: Higher education acts as a **screening** or **signaling** device for employers.

screening or **signaling** The use of higher education as a way to let employers know that the prospective employee is intelligent and trainable and potentially has the discipline to be a good employee.

Economists who advocate this view concede that some education will undoubtedly lead to higher productivity. But these economists argue that higher education is largely an indicator to employers that the college graduate is trainable, has discipline, and is intelligent. In their view, the job market is one big competition in which entry-level workers compete for on-the-job training. As a result, earning a college degree does little more than give the college graduate a leg up in this competition.

Most economists, however, doubt the theory that screening is the only purpose served by higher education. If it were, the high costs of college education and the higher wages employers must pay college graduates would create tremendous incentives for workers and employers to develop an alternative, less expensive screening device.

On-the-Job Training

On-the-job training (OJT) is the investment by firms to increase the human capital of their workers, and can take many different forms. First, training can be as simple as receiving instructions from a supervisor on how to help customers, operate a machine, or retrieve items from inventory. Second, training can take place in a more formal setting away from the job, almost like a college course. Lastly, training can consist of a firm providing tuition reimbursement for college courses, professional certificates, or MBA degrees.

on-the-job training Training typically done by employers, ranging from suggestions at work to intensive workshops and seminars.

College internship programs are a good example of OJT that provide firms an extended look at potential employees while providing students with a look at several different firms and industries before graduating and entering the job market.

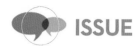

ISSUE

The Role of Educational Systems in Human Capital Accumulation

Countries use different strategies to promote human capital accumulation using their educational systems. For example, the educational system in the United States tends to emphasize a well-rounded curriculum by requiring most students to study subjects outside of their primary area of interest. Educational systems in Europe and Asia, however, tend to emphasize a more focused path of study, one in which students may select their area of study even before entering high school and take few courses outside of their major subject area. We can use anecdotal evidence to show how these differences translate into human capital outcomes.

For the United States, one can argue that emphasizing creativity and a diverse curriculum in the classroom has led to the development of world-renowned universities and research facilities, attracting students and researchers from around the world and leading to a huge boost in human capital. According to the annual *Times Higher Education's* World University Rankings, the United States is home to 15 of the top 20 universities in the world, and 47 of the top 100 universities in the world.

However, a tradeoff exists in that emphasizing one area means less emphasis on others. For example, the U.S. primary and secondary educational systems have lagged behind much of the developed world in the subjects of math, science, and foreign language skills. According to the OECD Programme for International Student Assessment, in 2009 the United States ranked 25th out of thirty-four developed countries in math proficiency, while faring somewhat better (17th) in science. Finland and South Korea ranked at the top of most subject rankings.

Lyngbyvej/Dreamstime.com

The United States consistently ranks first in the world in higher education, but lags behind most of the developed world in primary and secondary education.

What are other examples of policies aimed toward developing human capital through education? In Finland, which has one of the world's top primary education systems, teachers are highly paid and teaching is considered a prestigious job requiring many years of postgraduate education. Interestingly, the amount of time children spend in school is less than in most developed countries, using the philosophy that "less is more" by emphasizing quality over quantity.

Saudi Arabia offers all of its citizens the opportunity to study at any college in the world (based on acceptance at a college on the approved list) that is fully paid by the Saudi king (The King Abdullah Scholarship Program). Although there are no strings attached to the offer, a large majority of students graduating from foreign universities under this program returned to Saudi Arabia to work, a huge boost to human capital.

Regardless of how countries educate their citizens, investments in human capital lead to economic growth, making such investments among the most valuable in terms of the return on money spent.

Today, spending on OJT exceeds \$100 billion a year, including training costs and the wages paid to employees during training. The costs of OJT are usually borne by employers, but workers may bear some of the costs through reduced wages throughout the training period. Firms benefit from OJT by gaining more productive workers, and workers gain by becoming more versatile, and thus more competitive, in labor markets. Because all OJT entails present costs meant to yield future benefits, firms choose to provide OJT if the returns from this investment compare favorably to other investment alternatives.

Investments in human capital go a long way toward explaining why people are paid different wages. Education and earnings are closely related. Human capital theorists believe that this is because education and productivity are closely related. For this reason, firms are willing to pay higher wages to individuals with greater amounts of human capital. For industries that require advanced skills, such as in computer programming, aerospace, and biotechnology (just to name a few), human capital is difficult if not impossible to replace with ordinary labor. Therefore, human capital is considered a capital input in the factors of production.

CHECKPOINT

INVESTMENT IN HUMAN CAPITAL

- Investment in human capital includes all investments in human beings such as education and on-the-job training.
- There is a positive relationship between education and earnings.
- The rate of return to education is computed by comparing the streams of income from two different levels of education.
- The greater the wage differential between two levels of education, the more people will pursue that next level of education.
- Higher education may just be a screening or signaling device telling potential employers that this individual is trainable, has discipline, and is intelligent.
- Firms are willing to provide on-the-job training when the future returns to human capital investment in terms of increased productivity to the firm exceed the costs of that training.

QUESTIONS: If the United States decided, as part of an immigration reform package, to restrict immigration only to those with college degrees, and thus decided to allow only 500,000 foreigners a year to enter, what would happen to the rate of return on college education? Alternatively, if, as part of a reform package, 500,000 low-skilled workers were permitted to enter the United States, what would happen to the rate of return on college education?

Answers to the Checkpoint questions can be found at the end of this chapter.

Entrepreneurship and Innovation

We have now addressed the basic requirements of production—acquiring land, labor, physical and human capital, and finding financial capital to pay for it. Is that all that is required to operate a business? Not quite. Recall from Chapter 2 that the factors of production are land, labor, capital, and entrepreneurship.

What is entrepreneurship? Entrepreneurship is the willingness to take risks and to use ideas to convert physical inputs into final products that are appealing to consumers. One can argue that entrepreneurship is the most essential factor of production—without a great idea on how to use resources, the final products will likely be of little value or may not even be produced.

Entrepreneurship

Profits are the rewards entrepreneurs receive for (1) combining land, labor, and capital to produce goods and services, and (2) assuming the risks associated with producing these goods and services. Entrepreneurs must combine and manage all the inputs of production; make day-to-day production, finance, and marketing decisions; innovate constantly if they hope to remain in business over the long run; and simultaneously bear the risks of failure and bankruptcy.

As we have seen over the past decade, large firms that have become household names can implode quickly. Lehman Brothers, Circuit City, Blockbuster Video, and Borders are a few companies that have either closed or filed for bankruptcy protection.

Even for large firms, business is risky. Bankruptcy or business failure, meanwhile, can be exceedingly painful for business owners, stockholders, employees, and communities. Still, a free economy requires such failures. If firms were guaranteed never to fail, perhaps through government subsidies (bailouts), they would have little incentive to be efficient or to innovate, or to worry about what consumers want from them.

When a firm earns economic profits—profits exceeding normal profits—this is a signal to other firms and entrepreneurs that consumers want more of the good or service the

intellectual property rights A set of exclusive rights granted to a creator of an invention or creative work, allowing the owner to earn profits over a fixed period of time. The types of protection include patents, copyrights, trademarks, and industrial designs.

profitable firm provides, and that they are willing to pay for it. Profit signals shift resources from areas of lower demand to the products and services consumers desire more highly. It is entrepreneurs who are attuned to the profit signals.

Innovation and the Global Economy

Innovation describes both entrepreneurship, when individuals and firms develop something new, and the constant retooling of existing products. Innovation arguably is the most productive input in the production process. Many countries, such as those in Africa, have abundant natural resources and labor, yet have not been able to convert those inputs into substantial outputs. Meanwhile, such countries as Japan, Germany, and Sweden, with more limited physical resources, have compensated by generating high levels of human capital and innovation, and subsequently generate a very high standard of living for their citizens.

An important issue is that to encourage innovation, those who innovate must be provided with incentives to make the money and effort invested worthwhile. For example, an individual's or a firm's innovations can be protected using **intellectual property rights,** including patents, copyrights, trademarks, and industrial designs, allowing innovators an exclusive right to earn profits from their investments for a fixed amount of time.

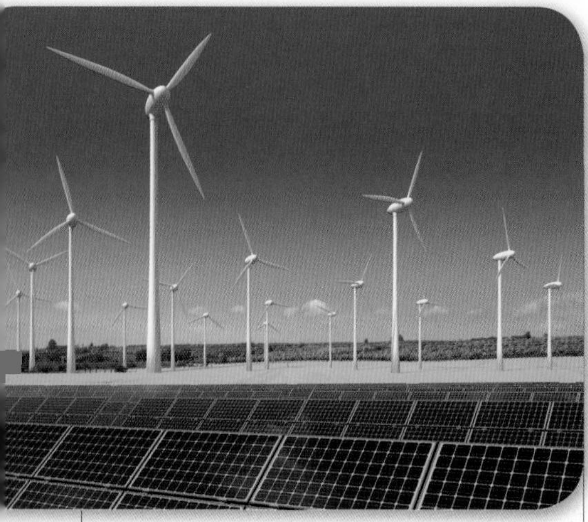
Visdia/Dreamstime.com

Investment in wind and solar energy technology has increased as more countries emphasize innovations in renewable energy.

The importance of innovation as a driver of economic growth will continue to increase as the economy becomes more globalized. Specifically, deficiencies in physical capital can easily be resolved through trade and foreign direct investment. But deficiencies in human capital and innovation are a much more difficult obstacle to overcome.

Therefore, the future of a country's economic growth will depend on its ability to generate new ideas and find more productive uses of its limited resources. At the start of this chapter, we discussed the aerospace industry and its goals of developing planes that provide more comfort to passengers, and reduce operating costs. Both objectives increase the productive use of limited resources, which will allow the industry to grow as people demand more travel.

But advances in innovative technology cannot be limited to just a few industries. All industries must avoid falling behind the trend of increasing productivity throughout the world. Emerging countries have begun to invest significant sums to improve physical infrastructure and human capital. This had led to innovations in all industries and an improvement in the standards of living in these countries. In order for the United States to continue increasing its standard of living, it must maintain its position as a leader in innovation.

CHECKPOINT

ENTREPRENEURSHIP AND INNOVATION

- Entrepreneurs earn profits for combining other inputs to create products and for assuming the risks of producing goods and services.
- Innovation includes the efforts by entrepreneurs to produce new products as well as efforts by firms to make existing products better.
- Entrepreneurship and innovation is arguably the most productive of the factors of production, allowing countries to use limited resources to produce valuable outputs that lead to a higher standard of living.

QUESTIONS: Why is entrepreneurship considered a factor of production despite the fact that it does not exist in physical form? Suppose a country has abundant amounts of natural resources and labor, would this automatically translate into a highly productive economy?

Answers to the Checkpoint questions can be found at the end of this chapter.

chapter summary

Section 1: Land and Physical Capital

Kuosumo/Dreamstime.com

Land prices are driven by a fixed supply and by demand factors such as the terrain, attributes, view, and location.

Timiskim/Dreamstime.com

Rent is the return or income that flows to land or physical capital as a factor of production.

MRP_K is the additional value that a unit of capital brings to the firm. It represents the maximum a firm is willing to pay for capital.

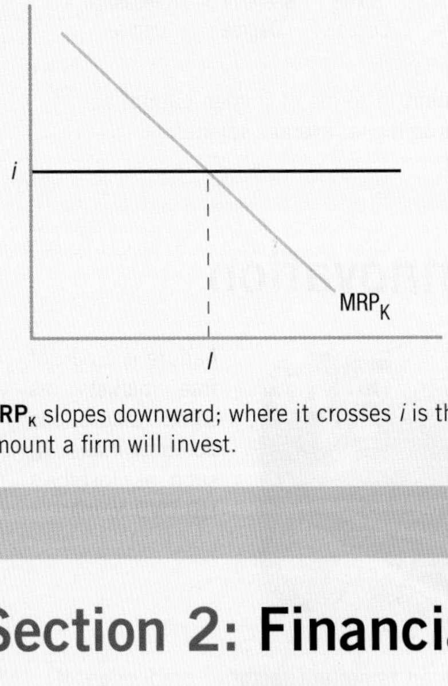

MRP_K slopes downward; where it crosses *i* is the amount a firm will invest.

Present Value Versus Rate of Return

- Present value measures the value today of money collected in the future.
- $PV = X/(1 + i)^n$, where i = discount rate and n = years.
- Rate of return is the interest rate that is required for a project to break even in the long run.
- Calculating the rate of return requires solving for the interest rate that makes the present value of all future income from a project equal to its cost of capital.

Section 2: Financial Capital

Four Sources of Financial Capital

Banks: Offer loans based on credit history and ability to produce collateral in case of default; the amount borrowed is usually limited.

Najlah Feanny/CORBIS SABA

Ptoone/Dreamstime.com

Bond market: Bonds are claims on a company's assets. A bond pays a fixed payment called a coupon rate and a face value upon maturity.

Stock market: Stocks give partial ownership in a company, entitling owners (shareholders) to a vote in company matters and a share of dividends.

Rudy Sulgan/Corbis

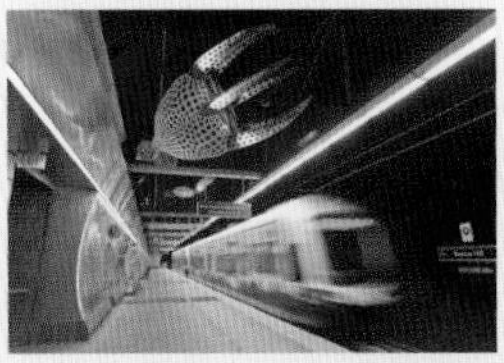

David Sailors/Corbis

Venture capital: Provides seed money to new businesses in exchange for partial ownership in the company.

Section 3: Human Capital

Investment in human capital can come from

- Education
- On-the-job-training

Nikolais/Dreamstime.com

Monkeybusinessimages/Dreamstime.com

The greater the wage differential between two levels of human capital investment, the more people will pursue that next level.

Is education just a signal or does it provide inherent productive value? Economists believe it's a little of both.

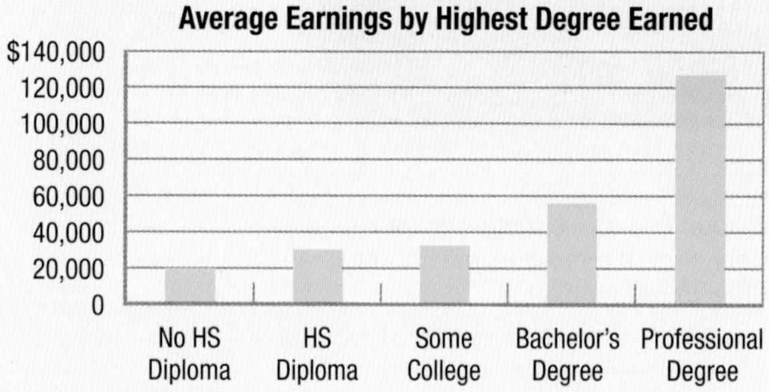

Education is a good investment in terms of human capital accumulation, which translates to higher average salaries.

Section 4: Entrepreneurship and Innovation

Entrepreneurs assume the risk of using capital and labor markets to create new goods and services and to make existing products better.

Franz-Marc Frei/Corbis

Success brings great rewards to entrepreneurs, many of whom have become very rich, such as the inventor of the Segway.

Yuriko Nakao/Reuters/Newscom

Failure is a part of free markets, as some innovations do not make it, such as Toshiba's HD DVD format.

Entrepreneurship is an important factor of production. It allows countries to turn limited resources into productive outputs and higher standards of living.

Irfannurd/Dreamstime.com

Intellectual property rights are needed to protect innovation and provide rewards for entrepreneurs. These include:

- Patents: to protect ideas and inventions
- Copyrights: to protect writings and artistic impression
- Trademarks: to protect names and symbols
- Industrial Designs: to protect product designs

KEY CONCEPTS

rent, p. 312
physical capital, p. 313
present value, p. 315
rate of return, p. 316
financial capital, p. 317
collateral, p. 318
face value, p. 318
coupon rate, p. 318
maturity, p. 318
yield, p. 318
share of stock, p. 319
market cap, p. 320
investment in human capital, p. 322
screening or signaling, p. 325
on-the-job training, p. 325
intellectual property rights, p. 328

QUESTIONS AND PROBLEMS

Check Your Understanding

1. What does the term *land* refer to in economics and why is it very inelastic in supply?
2. If the interest rate is 6% and you are offered a bond that will pay you $2,000 in two years, but no interest between now and then, what would you be willing to pay for this bond today?
3. What are the different ways in which businesses can acquire financial capital?
4. Why are colleges filled with young people rather than middle-aged individuals? If interest rates rose to over 10%, would this have any impact on the number of people attending college or its composition?
5. What is the difference between physical capital and human capital?
6. What do intellectual property rights protect and why is it important to entrepreneurship?

Apply the Concepts

7. How do times of growth in the general economy encourage capital investments? How do recessions discourage capital investments? What happens to the cost of capital in boom times when the economy is growing? What happens in recessionary times?
8. Cities such as London and Johannesburg spent billions in capital expenditures building new stadiums, roads, and public transportation to host the 2012 Summer Olympics and the 2010 World Cup, respectively, in hopes of generating a spike in future tourism and business investment. Explain how these cities would use a rate of return approach to determine whether the effort to host the sporting event was worthwhile.
9. Suppose you wish to purchase a corporate bond that offers a coupon rate of 10% in the bond market. On a particular day, you notice the price of the bond listed as greater than "100." Given this price, would the yield on this bond be greater than or less than 10%? List some possible reasons that would cause the price of the bond to exceed "100."
10. When a company uses resources to train staff or subsidize tuition for employees, it is clearly investing in human capital. However, this investment is treated as current spending (cost of selling or producing goods) rather than investment. Should these activities be treated as investments and be reflected in the investment statistics of the economy?
11. Does it seem reasonable that a certain portion of the benefits of a college education is essentially a way to show prospective employers that you are reasonably intelligent, trainable, and have a certain degree of discipline?
12. Some politicians during any election campaign offer proposals to make college more affordable by increasing subsidies through higher Pell grants and subsidizing reduced rate loans. If these policies come to pass, and college becomes less expensive, more people will attend college. What will this do to the rate of return on a college education?

In the News

13. A December 13, 2012, article in the *Los Angeles Times*, "Colorado River Water Supply to Fall Short of Demand . . . " highlighted the concern regarding the ability of the Colorado River, the primary source of water for the greater Los Angeles area residents, to fulfill the needs as the river continues to decrease in water flow. Using a market diagram, show what happens to water prices if the supply of water, a natural resource, is fixed each year while demand continues to increase due to population growth. If the article's predictions come true and the supply decreases, show what happens to the price of water.
14. Steve Wynn is a billionaire Las Vegas casino tycoon who built famous hotels such as the Mirage, Bellagio, Wynn, and Encore resorts. In 2012, he announced a plan to invest $4 billion to build his third hotel in Macao, a tiny former Portuguese colony near Hong Kong that has been returned to China ("Wynn Macao Plans to Invest $4 Billion for New Resort," Bloomberg.com, June 5, 2012). The size of the investment surprised analysts, because the gaming market in Macao, while still the world's largest in total revenue, has begun to slow in recent years. What are some market factors influencing the present value of Wynn's future earnings that might justify his decision to build such a lavish resort?

Solving Problems

15. Suppose you win the lottery and are given a choice to collect either the grand prize of $6 million in 20 annual installments of $300,000, or collect an immediate one-time payment of $4 million today. If the interest rate is 5% and that is what you use to discount future earnings, which option should you select to maximize the present value of the winnings?
16. The mayor of your city is considering building a new toll road to reduce congestion. The cost of the toll road is $10 million and is estimated to generate a profit (from tolls collected less expenses collecting the tolls and maintaining the road) of $1.5 million per year. If the discount rate is 10%, how many years would it take before the road is paid for? (Hint: Calculate the present value of the annual profit—for year 1, discount $1.5 million by 10%.)

USING THE NUMBERS

17. According to By the Numbers, in the year 2011 (the last year for which data are reported) approximately what percentage of high school graduates attended college? Approximately what percentage of college graduates attended a graduate program?
18. According to By the Numbers, by approximately what percentage did venture capital funding fall from its peak in 2007 to its lowest point in 2010?

ANSWERS TO QUESTIONS IN CHECKPOINTS

Checkpoint: Land and Physical Capital

To determine whether this investment is worthwhile, you would want to know how much income the store expects to generate over the year, as well as the current market interest rate. Using this information, you can estimate the net present value of the investment to determine whether it is a good idea or not. The higher the market interest rate, the greater the income stream you would require to invest.

Checkpoint: Financial Capital

Bonds are promises to pay back a lender (bondholder) a specific amount on a specific date, while stocks represent actual ownership (to the extent of the number of shares held) in a business. A bondholder does not own any part of the business, and therefore does not influence the day-to-day management of the firm.

An advantage of issuing bonds is that it allows a business to maintain control of its management. Another advantage is that the business is unlikely to be subjected to a forceful takeover by a large investor. A disadvantage of bonds is that a business must pay an interest rate that is sometimes high depending on how investors perceive their risk. Another disadvantage of bonds is that a business must make periodic coupon payments to bondholders, as well as pay back the bonds as they mature. This may restrict a business's ability to use available cash funds to invest in additional capital inputs.

Checkpoint: Investment in Human Capital

Letting in a large number of college-educated immigrants would drive the rate of return on college down as wages of college graduates would not grow very rapidly. The opposite would occur when unskilled immigrants enter, holding down the wages of those without college educations, leading to a growing gap between those with college degrees, increasing the rate of return to a college degree.

Checkpoint: Entrepreneurship and Innovation

Entrepreneurship is the idea and vision to turn physical inputs such as land, labor, and capital into valuable outputs that people demand. An economy cannot produce goods without someone willing and able to determine what the market wants. Therefore, entrepreneurship is a vital factor of production.

Although having abundant amounts of natural resources and labor may provide a country with an advantage in production, a country still requires entrepreneurship to turn those physical inputs into valuable products people desire. Thus, having abundant physical inputs does not automatically result in a productive economy. The reverse is also true—having few physical inputs does not preclude a country from being productive if it is able to use its limited resources effectively.

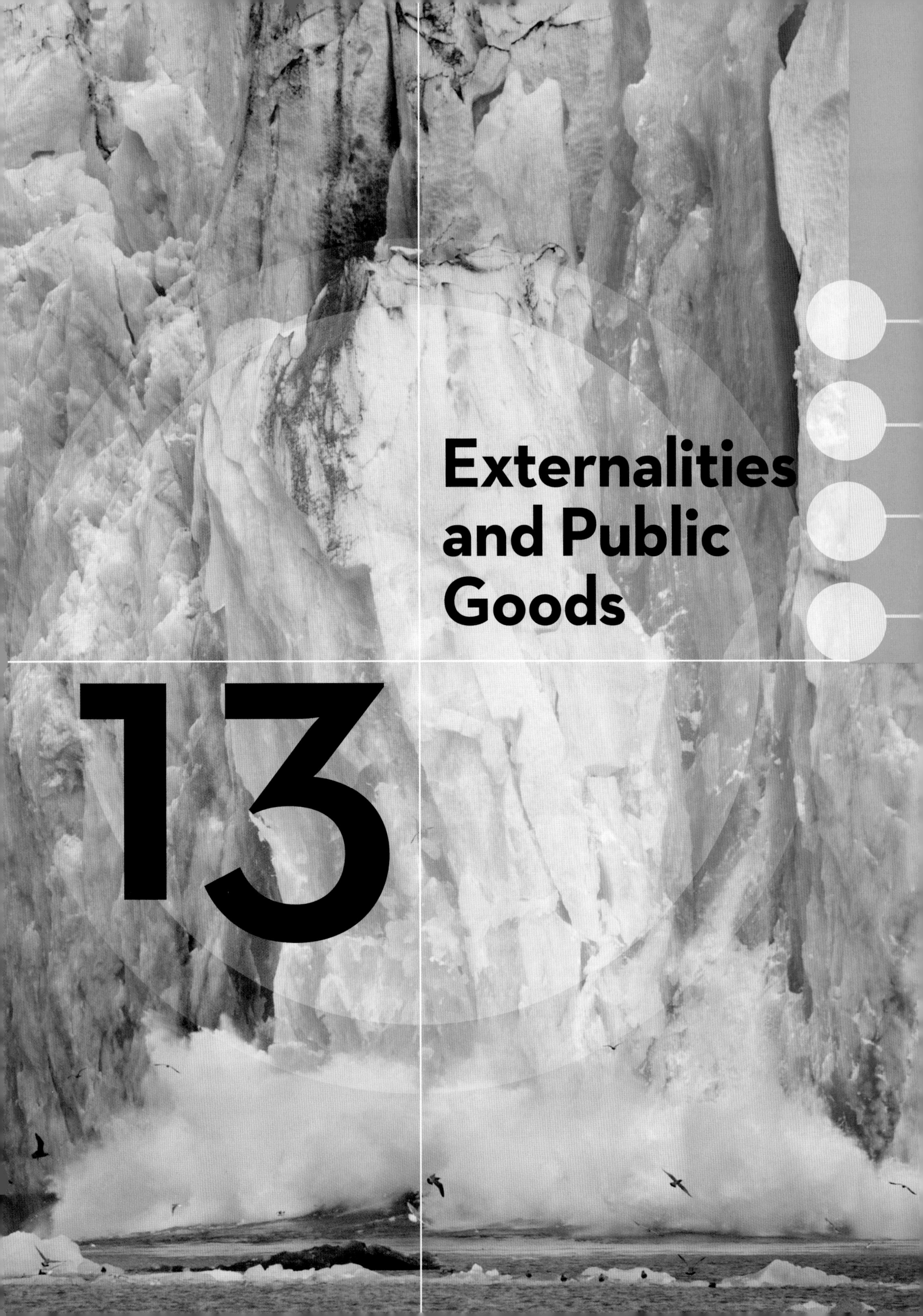

13

Externalities and Public Goods

After studying this chapter you should be able to:

- Describe the types of market failures.
- Describe the impact of negative and positive externalities on society.
- Describe the Coase theorem on social costs and the role transaction costs play in the optimal allocation of resources.
- Explain the nature of public goods and why they are difficult to provide in the market.
- Explain how common property resources can lead to resource degradation.
- Recognize the importance of the discount rate in assessing the costs and benefits of environmental policies.
- Use marginal analysis to determine the optimal level of pollution.
- Describe the differences between command and control policies and market-based approaches to environmental regulation.
- Understand the economic issues surrounding global climate change.

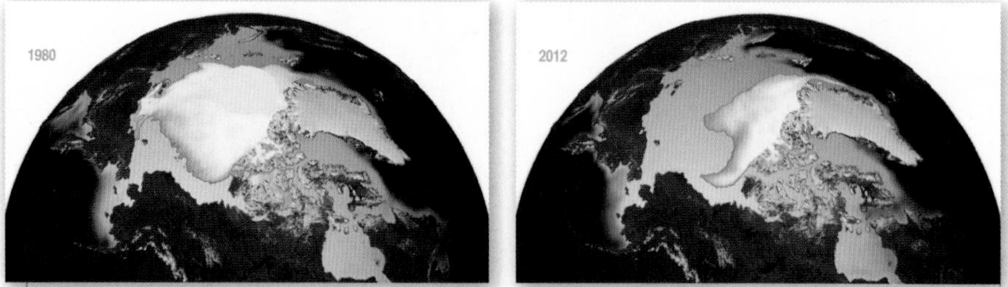

NASA/Goddard Scientific Visualization Studio

NASA/Goddard Scientific Visualization Studio

A computerized visualization of the Arctic ice caps showing the extent to which the area covered by the thickest ice, known as *multiyear ice*, has diminished from 1980 to 2012.

Each day, thousands of spectacular explosions occur in a process called calving, when ice breaks off from mountains of glaciers and falls into the ocean as icebergs, eventually melting away. The withering ice shelves and frozen tundra that constitute the vast wilderness of the arctic (and the Antarctic) have affected the landscape that hundreds of wildlife species, including the polar bear, call home.

According to a 2012 NASA study, the volume and area of the Arctic ice caps fluctuate from year to year based on atmospheric cycles, but the overall trend has been declining as average surface temperatures rise. Estimates show that the overall area covered by the thickest ice, known as multiyear ice, has been shrinking between 12% and 17% per decade over the last 30 years. Other ice caps and glaciers around the world are also melting, and the consequences extend beyond the wildlife affected. It also affects human lives as ocean levels rise. Despite widely varying estimates that ocean levels will rise between 7 inches and 63 inches by the end of the century, these statistics highlight the important idea that actions taken today, both positive and negative, will affect future generations.

The impact of human actions that contribute to global climate change is one that economic policy tries to address, although not without significant challenges and obstacles. An important issue is that the Earth's climate is shared: One country's efforts are not enough, while achieving consensus on environmental policy is difficult, if not impossible.

How environmental policies are set depends largely on the priorities placed by individual countries. For example, during much of the 20th century, the United States was a highly industrialized country; standards of living increased dramatically, but at the cost of greater pollution. However, many Americans now place a higher priority on maintaining a cleaner environment for future generations. This transformation from a polluting industrial society to a cleaner, energy-efficient society can be seen in many developed nations, such as the United States, the countries of the European Union, Japan, and Australia.

In contrast, much of the world remains very poor. In these poor countries, economic development to improve basic living conditions takes precedence over environmental concerns. In countries that have grown significantly in recent years, such as China and India, polluting factories are churning out goods as fast as they can, and consumers are buying more cars and air travel. China is now the largest market in the world for new cars. The ability of previously impoverished nations to experience economic prosperity often comes at the expense of the environment.

Because of differing environmental priorities among nations, it is difficult to achieve a consensus. In addition, any one country's efforts to improve the environment benefit the entire world, yet that country bears the full costs of these efforts. Meanwhile, other countries may exploit the environment for their economic gain, offsetting the environmental efforts made by others.

The actions affecting the environment extend beyond the national level. Individuals and firms make decisions that affect the environment, such as the type of cars we buy and

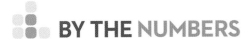

BY THE NUMBERS

The Environment and Sustainability

Having a sustainable economy will likely require a focus on energy other than fossil fuels, finding better methods to recycle waste, and developing methods to manage the natural environment.

Hybrid sales grew quickly from 2000 to 2007, then declined from 2008 to 2011 due to the last recession and slow economic recovery, before picking up again in 2012.

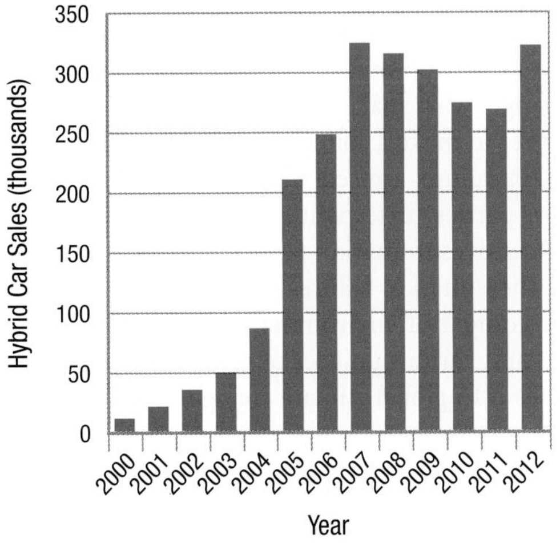

120 million

Number of electric bicycles in China.

301%

Increase in wind energy generated in the United States between 2007 and 2012.

$39

Annual savings from replacing five 60-watt bulbs with compact fluorescents.

1.4 (0.2)

Acres of arable land per person in the United States (and China).

Millions of tons of solid waste fill landfills, while some is recovered and recycled. To be sustainable, the United States must recover more in the future.

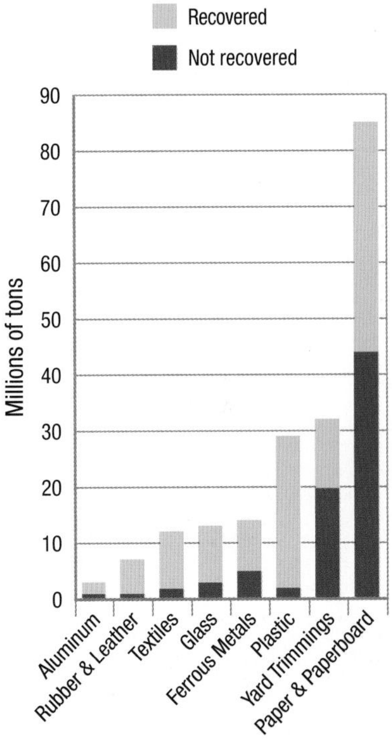

Over 80,000 European fishing boats are fishing out Atlantic cod using advanced technology.

Jeff Rotman/Alamy

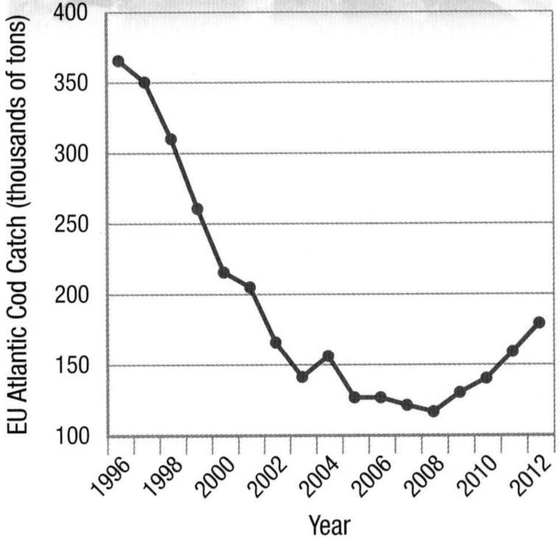

49¢

Average gasoline tax per gallon in the United States.

$4.85

Average gasoline tax per gallon in Britain.

Top 10 States in Wind Power Generation Capacity (megawatts)

Texas	10,648
Iowa	4,419
California	4,287
Illinois	2,852
Oregon	2,820
Minnesota	2,718
Washington	2,699
Oklahoma	2,039
Colorado	1,805
New York	1,418

Broker/Dreamstime.com

the production methods companies use. Each of these decisions affects not only the individual or company, but others who share the environment that is being affected.

On a brighter note, economic growth has led to increasing efficiencies in resource use. The growing popularity of hybrid and plug-in electric cars has improved fuel efficiency. Even new technologies in cow feed (such as the infusion of garlic) have reduced the level of harmful methane gases emitted by cows. Yet, clearly we still have many environmental problems that must be addressed, including global climate change, species extinction, overharvesting of fisheries, and overcrowding of highways and parks.

Still, global climate change seems to be an almost intractable problem. Beyond the obvious scientific issues of how to reduce our environmental footprints stands market failure, a concept introduced in Chapter 4. As we saw there, market failure describes how markets fail in specific ways to provide the socially optimal amount of goods and services. In the particular case of global climate change, what makes it so hard to deal with is that several specific market failures come together to make a solution tough to reach.

This chapter starts by examining market failures caused when actions taken by consumers or producers have effects on third parties (externalities), when certain types of goods called public goods provide poor incentives to market participants, and when specific resources are shared. After analyzing these market failures, the chapter then looks at the ways policy tries to solve them in the context of environmental issues. Finally, after you get your hands around market failures and various policies to resolve them, the chapter takes what you have learned and applies it to global climate change, which combines aspects of many market failures.

Externalities

Actions by individuals and firms affect not only those involved, but also can create side effects for others in ways that can be either beneficial or costly. For example, suppose you share an apartment with a neat and organized person. Because your roommate always keeps the apartment clean and uncluttered, you reap the benefits of not having dishes piling up in the sink or potato chip crumbs all over the sofa. Clearly, you benefit from this situation. On the other hand, suppose the occupants of the apartment next door are members of an aspiring heavy metal band. They blast loud music all day, and occasionally have a jam session—and you're forced to hear everything they play. Unless you enjoy that music yourself, your neighbors' actions become a cost for you.

externalities The impact on third parties of some transaction between others in which the third parties are not involved. An external cost (or negative externality) harms the third parties, whereas external benefits (positive externalities) result in gains to them.

Externalities, often called *spillovers,* arise when actions or market transactions by an individual or a firm cause some other party not involved in the activity or transaction to benefit or be harmed. If the activity imposes costs on others, it is called a *negative externality* or an *external cost.* If the activity creates benefits to others, this is a *positive externality* or an *external benefit.* Negative externalities include air and water pollution, littering, and chemical runoff that affect fish stocks. Examples of activities that generate positive externalities include getting a flu shot, acquiring more education, landscaping, and maintaining beehives next to apple orchards.

Both producers and consumers can create externalities and can feel the effects of them. The matrix in Table 1 identifies the origin and impact of some common external effects.

Negative Externalities

When a market transaction harms people not involved in the transaction, negative externalities exist. Pollution of all sorts is the classic example. Firms and consumers rarely consider the impact their production or consumption will have on others. For simplicity, we focus on the pollution caused by production. Figure 1 shows a typical market.

Supply curve S_P represents the manufacturer's marginal private cost (MPC) of production. This supply curve ignores the external costs imposed on others from the pollution generated during production. These external costs might include toxic wastes dumped into lakes or streams, smokestack soot, or the clear-cutting associated with timber harvests. Ignoring these costs, market equilibrium is at point *e,* at which the product is priced at \$6 and 30 units are sold.

Externalities by Origin and Impact

TABLE 1

	Impact: Victims and Beneficiaries of Externality			
	Consumers		**Producers**	
Origin of Externality	**Positive**	**Negative**	**Positive**	**Negative**
Consumers	• Private schools • Immunizations • Landscaping	• Auto pollution • Littering • Smoking	• Flu shot reducing sick days	• Private auto use that adds to road congestion slowing down commercial traffic
	Positive	**Negative**	**Positive**	**Negative**
Producers	• New factory leading to new shops and restaurants in town	• Factory air pollution on wilderness hikers • Pesticide runoff affecting trout fishing	• Honey bees improving apple orchards	• Pollution that harms commercial fishing

Recall from Chapter 4 that one way to measure the well-being of consumers and producers in a market is to measure the consumer surplus and producer surplus. Consumer surplus is the difference between what consumers are willing to pay for a good (shown by the demand curve) and the market price (equal to \$6 in Figure 1). Therefore, consumer surplus is equal to \$45 [((\$9 – \$6) × 30) / 2]. Producer surplus is the difference between the market price and the minimum amount at which sellers are willing to sell a product (shown by the supply curve), and is equal to \$45 as well [((\$6 – \$3) × 30) / 2]. Summing up consumer surplus and producer surplus equals \$90, which is shown as area *ace* in the figure.

Now let's assume that for every unit of the product produced, pollution costs (or effluent) equal to \$2 is generated. Thus, at an output level of 30 units (point *e*), \$60 in pollution

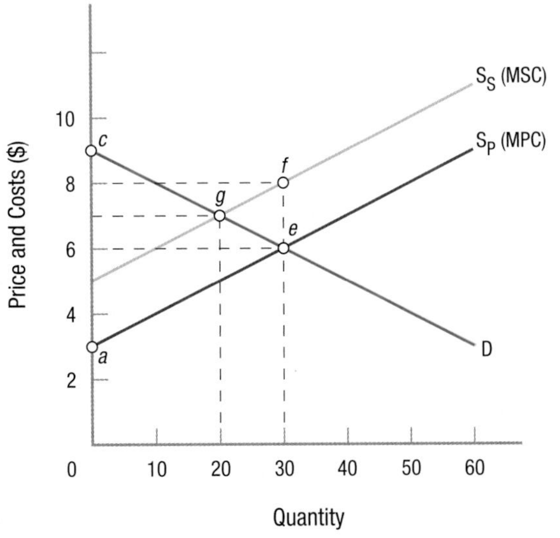

FIGURE 1

The Negative Externality Case

Supply curve S_P represents the manufacturer's supply when only its private costs are considered, ignoring the external costs imposed on others through pollution. Market equilibrium is 30 units sold at \$6 each (point *e*). If each unit of production results in \$2 in pollution costs, then supply curve S_S represents the marginal social costs (MSC) to manufacture the product. Socially optimal output is 20 units sold at \$7 each (point *g*).

costs (or negative externalities) are generated. Subtracting this $60 in pollution from total consumer and producer surplus results in $30 of real social benefit from this output.

This means that the true marginal cost of producing the product, including pollution costs, is equal to supply curve S_S, representing the marginal social cost (MSC) of production. This new supply curve incorporates both the private and social costs of production, thus shifting supply upward by an amount equal to *ef*, or $2. Equilibrium moves to point *g*, at which 20 units of the product are sold at $7. This is the socially optimal production for this product given the pollution it creates.

So why is it better for society than when 30 units were produced? First, notice that when output is 20, the cost of the last unit produced—including the cost of pollution—is $7 (point *g*). This is just equal to the value society attributes to the product. Hence, consumers get just what they want when all costs are considered. Second, notice that consumer and producer surplus at an output of 20 units is $40 [(($9 – $5) × 20) / 2]. More important, it is now higher than the $30 of consumer and producer surplus minus the pollution costs when output was 30 units (point *e*).

Each unit of output produced beyond 20 costs more—taking both private and social costs into account—than its value to consumers.

Imagine a situation in which external costs exceed the consumer and producer surplus from consuming the good. Such a situation might arise when an extremely toxic substance is a by-product of production. Society is better off not permitting production of this good.

What has this analysis shown? First, when negative externalities are present, an unregulated market will produce too much of a good at too low a price. Second, optimal pollution levels are not zero, except in the case just mentioned of extremely toxic agents. In Figure 1, the socially optimal production is 20 units with total pollution costs of $40. Pollution reduction as a good has no price. Even so, we can infer a price, known as a shadow price, equal to the marginal damages—$2 per unit in this case. As we will see later, prices for the "right to pollute" will provide us with better approximations of the costs of pollution.

The Coase Theorem

Ronald Coase was awarded the Nobel Prize in Economics for his seminal paper, "The Problem of Social Cost." Coase has written few articles—less than a dozen—but, as economist Robert Cooter noted, although "most economists maximize the amount they write, Coase maximized the amount others wrote about his work."[1] Indeed, Coase's paper on social cost is one of the most cited works in economics.

Reducing output to the optimal level results in gains to "victims" because pollution is reduced. The reduction in output, however, causes losses to producers. The presence of losses and gains to two distinct parties, Coase argued, introduces the possibility of bargaining, provided that the parties are awarded the property rights necessary for negotiation.

Coase theorem If transaction costs are minimal (near zero), a bargain struck between beneficiaries and victims of externalities will be efficient from a resource allocation perspective. As a result, the socially optimal level of production will be reached.

The **Coase theorem** states that if transaction costs are minimal (near zero), the resulting bargain or allocation of resources will be efficient—output will decline to the optimal level—regardless of the initial allocation of property rights. The socially optimal level of production will be reached, that is, no matter whether polluters are given the right to pollute or victims are given the right to be free of pollution.

Even so, the distribution of benefits or income will be different in these two cases. If victims, for example, are assigned the property rights, their income will grow, but if polluters are assigned these rights, the income of victims will decline.

As Coase noted, for these efficient results to be achieved, transaction costs must approach zero. This means it must be possible for polluters and victims to determine their collective interests accurately, then negotiate and enforce an agreement. In many situations, however, this is simply not feasible. In cases involving air pollution, for instance,

[1] Peter Passell, "Economics Nobel to a Basic Thinker," *New York Times*, October 16, 1991, p. D6.

polluters and victims are so widely dispersed that negotiating is impracticable. In other cases, individuals may be both victims and polluters, making it difficult for an agreement to be reached and enforced.

Another problem associated with assigning rights to one party or another might be called *environmental mugging.* Polluters might at first threaten to pollute more than they anticipate, for instance, to increase their bargaining leverage and, ultimately, their income. Victims, in like manner, might assert exaggerated environmental concerns, again to bid up their compensation. Alternatively, if negotiations should prove to be unfruitful, polluters might start lobbying for legal relief, thus devoting their money to rent-seeking behaviors rather than buying pollution-abatement equipment.

Although the private negotiations Coase proposed have their limitations, his insights proved to be a turning point in environmental policy. Coase challenged the prevailing practice of assuming that victims had a right to be pollution-free. His analysis stressed that it does not matter who the rights are assigned to (the polluter or the pollution-victim, for example). No matter how property rights were assigned, if information was good and transaction costs were low, efficiency would result. Given the costs of pollution, affected parties have an incentive to work out efficient agreements.

This idea was so radical when Coase published "The Problem of Social Cost" in 1960 that another Nobel Prize winner, George Stigler, wondered "how so fine an economist could make such an obvious mistake." Coase was later invited to the University of Chicago to discuss his ideas; Stigler described what transpired[2]:

> *We strongly objected to this heresy. Milton Friedman did most of the talking, as usual. He also did much of the thinking, as usual. In the course of two hours of argument the vote went from twenty against and one for Coase to twenty-one for Coase. What an exhilarating event! I lamented afterward that we had not had the clairvoyance to tape it.*

The Coase theorem has changed the way economists look at many issues, not just environmental problems. In cases in which the costs of negotiation are negligible and the number of parties involved is small, economists and jurists have begun to look more closely at legal rules assigning liability.

NOBEL PRIZE RONALD COASE (1910–2013)

University of Chicago professor Ronald Coase won the Nobel Prize in Economic Sciences in 1991 for "his discovery and clarification of the significance of transaction costs and property rights" in the institutional structure and functioning of the economy. According to his analysis, traditional microeconomic theory was incomplete because it neglected the costs of executing contracts and managing firms. To Coase, these "transaction costs" were the principal reason that firms existed. Economic actors found it cost efficient to create a more complex organization to minimize transaction costs.

Coase also analyzed the economy in terms of the *rights* to use goods and factors (inputs) of production rather than the actual goods and factors themselves. These "property rights" could be defined in different ways according to contracts and rules within organizations. Coase introduced the concept of property rights as an important element of economic analysis.

Born in 1910 in Willesden, a suburb of London, Coase attended the London School of Economics (LSE), where he earned a Bachelor of Commerce degree in 1932, and returned 15 years later and earned a Doctor of Science degree in economics in 1951. Becoming disillusioned with the future of British socialism and taking "a liking for life in America," he migrated to the United States in 1951 and taught at the University of Buffalo. Coase's 1960 article, "The Problem of Social Cost," questioned whether governments could efficiently allocate resources for social purposes through taxes and subsidies. He argued that arbitrarily assigning property rights and using markets to reach a solution was usually better than costly government regulation. This was instantly controversial and led to a lengthy exchange of papers in economics journals. In 1964, Coase joined the faculty at the University of Chicago and became editor of the *Journal of Law and Economics.* The journal was an important catalyst in developing the economic interpretation of legal issues.

Positive Externalities

When private market transactions generate benefits for others, a situation opposite to that just described results. Figure 2 on the next page illustrates a positive externality. Market supply curve S and private demand curve D_P (equal to the marginal private benefit, MPB,

[2] George Stigler, *Memoirs of an Unregulated Economist* (New York: Basic Books, 1988), p. 76.

FIGURE 2

The Positive Externality Case

Market supply curve S and private demand curve D_P represent the market for college education. Equilibrium is at point *e*, and the number of students enrolled is Q_e. Society would benefit, however, if more people would go to college. Demand curve D_S represents the marginal social benefit (MSB), which includes the private demand for college education plus the external benefits that flow from it. Socially optimal enrollment would be Q_1 (point *f*).

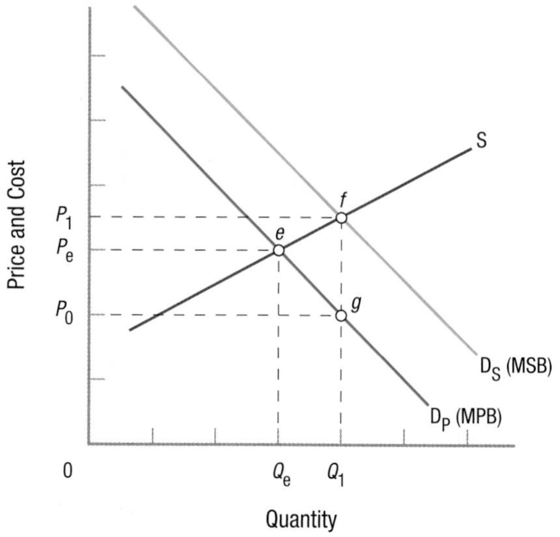

of consumption) represent the market for college education. Equilibrium is at point *e*, with Q_e students enrolling. Society would clearly benefit, however, if more people received a college education: Tax revenues would rise, crime rates would fall, and a better-informed electorate might produce a better-operating democracy.

Taking these considerations into account, social demand curve D_S is the private demand for college education plus the external benefits that flow from it. Socially optimal enrollment would be Q_1 (point *f*). How can society tweak the market so that more students will attend college? Students will demand Q_1 levels of enrollment only if its price is P_0 (point *g*). The public must therefore subsidize college education by *fg* to draw its price down to P_0.

The U.S. government recognizes that college education benefits society at large when it provides low-interest student loans, grants, and scholarships to students attending colleges and universities.

Limitations

Some caveats about our analysis of externalities need to be noted. First, producer and consumer surpluses are good measures of society's welfare if all incomes are weighted equally or the distribution of income is optimal. When income is unequally distributed, gross unfairness created throughout society swamps any improvements from efficiency. Thus, measures of efficiency such as consumer and producer surplus can become unconvincing for public policy. Because no one can agree on the correct distribution of income, economists generally ignore this question and focus on efficiency.

Second, the discussion has focused on the pollution that arises from production, not consumption. The results applied to congestion and littering, however, would be substantially the same.

Third, the examples presented here have assumed, moreover, that pollution has no cumulative effects. And, indeed, smaller amounts of pollution effluence may just flow into the ocean, for instance, with no lasting effects. But the same will not hold true for sustained higher pollution levels.

Fourth, for convenience, we have assumed that we can assign specific amounts to the damages resulting from pollution. In practice, this is not always easy to do.

Fifth, we have assumed that pollution can be reduced only by reducing output, but in real markets, there are other ways to reduce pollution.

Despite these limitations, the analysis presented here helps us focus our attention on ways of reducing the harm done to society by negative externalities.

In summary, the presence of externalities leads to overuse of resources and environmental degradation, causing a **market failure** to occur, when markets fail to provide the socially optimal level of goods and services. Another type of market failure occurs when resources are not privately owned, which we discuss in the next section.

market failure When markets fail to provide the socially optimal level of output, and will provide output at too high or low a price.

CHECKPOINT

EXTERNALITIES

- Externalities arise when the production of one good generates benefits (positive externalities) or costs (negative externalities) for others not involved in the transaction.
- When negative externalities exist, overproduction is the result. When positive externalities are generated, underproduction of the good is the norm.
- The Coase theorem states that if transaction costs are minimal (near zero), no matter which party is provided the property rights to pollution (polluter or victim), the resulting bargain will result in the socially optimal level of pollution.

QUESTION: Compact fluorescent light (CFL) bulbs have grown in popularity as their quality improves and prices fall. But not all consumers are convinced of the benefits of CFL bulbs. Proponents point to the tremendous energy savings, because CFL bulbs require only about 20% of the energy used by incandescent light bulbs, and they last much longer as well. Critics point to the potential dangers of mercury contained in CFL bulbs, along with a less desirable light color emitted by CFL bulbs. In addition to these private benefits and costs, what are some external benefits and external costs that are created by the use of CFL bulbs?

Answers to the Checkpoint question can be found at the end of this chapter.

Public Goods

We saw in the previous section that externalities can lead to markets not providing the socially efficient amount of a good at the optimal price. Either too much or too little of the good is produced, or it is offered at too high or too low a price, leading to a market failure. The presence of externalities is one cause of market failure. This section looks at two other causes of market failure that arise when no individual or firm is able to claim ownership of a product. These goods and services are called *public goods* and *common property resources.*

What Are Public Goods?

Pure **public goods** are nonrival in consumption, and exhibit nonexcludability. **Nonrivalry** means that the consumption of a good or service by one person does not reduce the utility of that good or service to others. **Nonexcludability** means that it is not possible to exclude some consumers from using the good or service once it has been provided.

public goods Goods in which one person's consumption does not diminish the benefit to others from consuming the good (i.e., nonrivalry), and once provided, no one person can be excluded from consuming (i.e., nonexclusion).

nonrivalry The consumption of a good or service by one person does not reduce the utility of that good or service to others.

nonexcludability Once a good or service is provided, it is not possible to exclude others from enjoying that good or service.

By way of contrast, a can of Coke is a rival product. When you drink a can of Coke, no one else can drink that same can. Airline flights exhibit excludability—one must either buy a ticket or obtain an award ticket to board the plane, even if empty seats are available. But consider a lighthouse. Once it is built and in operation, all ships can see the lighthouse and use the light to avoid obstacles. One captain's use of the lighthouse does not prevent another from using it, nor can a ship realistically be excluded from using the lighthouse's services. Hence, the lighthouse is a public good. Other examples of public goods include national defense, accumulated knowledge, standards such as a national currency, protection of property rights, vaccinations, mosquito spraying, and clean air. Table 2 on the next page provides a taxonomy of private and public goods.

Consumers cannot be excluded from a public good once it is provided, therefore they have little incentive to pay for the good in question. Instead, most will essentially be **free riders.** Think of the lighthouse again. If you have a ship and cannot be excluded from the benefits the lighthouse provides, why should you contribute anything to the lighthouse's

free rider The ability of an individual to avoid paying for a public good because he or she cannot be excluded from enjoying the good once provided.

TABLE 2 Taxonomy of Private and Public Goods

	Property Rights	
Characteristics of Goods	**Exclusive**	**Nonexclusive**
Rival	Pure private good • Airline seat • Ice cream bar	Common property resource • Ocean fishery • Highways
Nonrival	Public good with exclusion • Cable TV • Satellite radio	Pure public good • National defense • Public broadcasting

upkeep? But if everyone took this position, there would be no support for the lighthouse, and it would go into decline. With free riders, private producers cannot hope to sell many units of a good, and thus they have no incentive to produce it. Private markets will therefore fail to provide public goods, even if the goods are things everyone would like to see produced. This is why the government or special interest groups must get involved in the provision of products and services that have significant public good characteristics.

The Demand for Public Goods

Assessing the public's demand for public goods is clearly different from that of private goods where we found market demand by horizontally summing private demands. But the fact that once a public good is supplied, no one can be excluded from consuming it, and one person's consumption does not affect another's, plays a crucial role. Figure 3 provides a solution to finding the demand for public goods.

Figure 3 shows demand for a public good by two different consumers. Individual A wants none when the price is $40 and is willing and able to buy 40 units when the price approaches zero. Individual B wants none when the price is $60 and only is willing to buy 30 units when the price nears zero. Because each consumer can consume any given

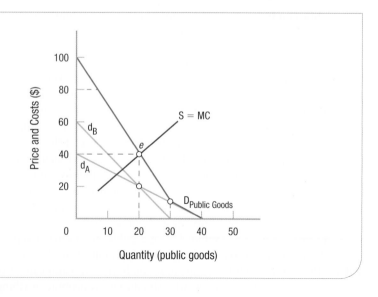

FIGURE 3

Demand for Public Goods: Vertical Summation of Individual Demand Curves

For public goods, exclusion is not possible, individuals can consume the good simultaneously, and market demand is found by summing vertically. Market demand for public goods is really a willingness-to-pay curve because the government will have to provide the good and levy taxes to pay the cost. The total demand for the public good is shown by the heavy line labeled $D_{Public\ Goods}$ and is the vertical summation of individual demands.

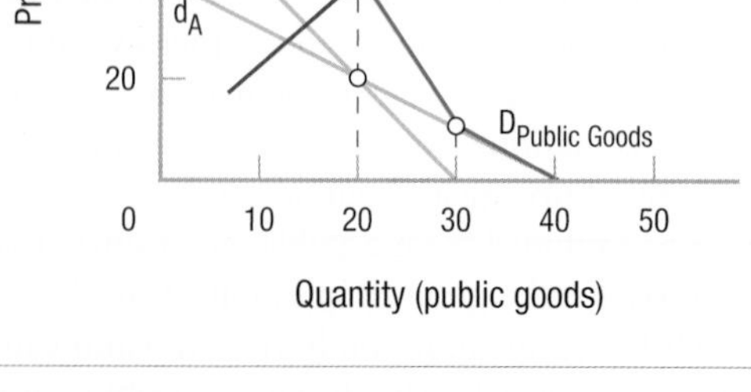

amount of a public good at the same time, the total demand for a public good is found by summing the individual demands *vertically*. To see why, consider when both individuals demand 20 units. This is the point at which the two demand curves cross, and both are willing to pay $20 for 20 units. Thus, total demand for 20 units is $40. The total demand for the public good in Figure 3 is shown by the heavy line labeled $D_{\text{Public Goods}}$ and is the vertical summation of individual demands.

Notice how this differs from our discussion of market demand curves for private goods. For private goods, others could be excluded from consuming any good we bought, therefore demands were horizontally summed. In contrast, with public goods, exclusion is not possible, therefore both individuals can consume the good simultaneously, and market demand is found by summing vertically. Market demand for public goods is really a *willingness-to-pay curve,* because the government will have to provide the good and levy taxes to pay the cost.

Optimal Provision of Public Goods

Providing the optimal amount of public goods is easy in theory and is illustrated in Figure 3. The supply of public goods is equal to the marginal cost curve (S = MC) shown in the figure. Just like the competitive market equilibrium we covered earlier, optimal allocation is where MC = P, and in this instance, it is 20 units of the good at a total price of $40 (point *e*). In this example, the taxes are split equally between individuals A and B. Determining how much tax each person should (or would be willing to) pay is hampered by the fact that once the public good is provided, no one can be excluded, therefore individuals will be unwilling to reveal their true preferences for the good because it might mean that they would have to pay a higher tax.

In reality, providing public goods such as national defense involves the political process. This means that politicians, bureaucrats, special interest groups, and many others generate the decisions on how much of any particular public good to provide. Since the demand for a public good represents the benefits to society and the supply curve represents society's costs, equating marginal benefits and marginal costs yields the optimal amount. But estimating the demand (benefits) from public goods and their costs can be a complex process. Most people desire the benefits of a strong military, but few enjoy paying the taxes required to pay for the cost. Because people cannot be excluded from the good, once provided, they have little incentive to reveal their true preferences, making this type of market failure difficult to overcome.

Common Property Resources

Commonly held resources are subject to nonexclusion but are rival in consumption. The market failure associated with such resources is often referred to as "the **tragedy of the commons.**"[3] The tragedy here is the tendency for commonly held resources to be overused and overexploited. Because the resource is held in common, individuals race to "get theirs" before others can grab it all.

tragedy of the commons
Resources that are owned by the community at large (e.g., parks, ocean fish, and the atmosphere) and therefore tend to be overexploited because individuals have little incentive to use them in a sustainable fashion.

One example of commonly held resources giving rise to problems involves oil fields. Oil reservoirs often span the surface property of many landowners. Because oil reservoirs are regarded as common property, each surface owner has an incentive to drill as many wells as possible and to pump out oil as rapidly as possible. Having too many wells pumping too quickly, however, reduces the oil field's water and gas pressure, thus reducing the total recoverable oil from the reservoir. Each owner's decision to drill a well therefore imposes an external cost on the other owners of land over the reservoir. At one point, this problem grew so severe that it resulted in passage of the 1935 Connally "Hot Oil" Act. This act restricted drilling, regulated the number and location of oil wells, and capped pumping rates.[4]

---

[3] Garrett Hardin, "The Tragedy of the Commons," *Science* 162, 1968, pp. 1243–1248.

[4] Daniel Yergin, *The Prize* (New York: Simon & Schuster), 1991.

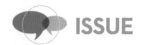

ISSUE

Tragedy of the Commons: The Perfect Fish

Ocean fisheries are a good example of the problem of common property resources. Fish in the ocean were once in excess supply; there was no need to restrict the use of this resource. As global demand for fish rose, improved fishing technologies allowed fishing boats to increase their hauls. Because many of the world's fisheries are still unregulated, one species after another has been fished out in a clearly unsustainable situation.

The Patagonian toothfish, as it is known, lives up to 50 years and can weigh over 200 pounds. This big, ugly, gray-black fish lives in the cold deep waters of the Southern Ocean near Antarctica, and in the 1990s, it became the signature dish of top restaurants in the United States, Japan, and Europe. It became so popular that during the mid-1990s, the annual catch was estimated at 100,000 metric tons.

How did such an ugly fish with such an unappetizing name become so popular? In the late 1970s, Lee Lantz, a Los Angeles fish merchant, visited the docks in Valparaiso, Chile, and spotted a toothfish. He bought a sample and cooked it, but the oily flesh had little taste. Most fish have bladders that they inflate to adjust their buoyancy, reducing the energy it takes to move up and down in the water. Toothfish do not have bladders, but use oil (lighter than water) secreted to create buoyancy. Also, Patagonian toothfish are predators, waiting in ambush for prey. Thus, they do not need a lot of blood rushing through their system. As a result, toothfish meat is oily and white like cod. It is this oiliness—along with the fact that it absorbed any spice—that made the toothfish (now known as Chilean sea bass) a hit with restaurants.

As the reputation of the toothfish spread, so did the take in the ocean. Because this fish is found in the Southern Ocean where it is cold and where few venture, it was highly susceptible to poaching. A full hold of toothfish could fetch $1 million wholesale!

Soon it became clear to many that the species was being seriously overharvested, and chefs began to notice that the filets were getting smaller. The tragedy of the commons was playing out again. Soon chefs from the best restaurants organized a boycott campaign called "Take a Pass on Chilean Sea Bass."

WILDLIFE GmbH/Alamy

Today, limits are set on the catch, and Chilean sea bass is coming back from the brink of extinction. But as G. Bruce Knecht reported in his book *Hooked,* keeping pirates from poaching the toothfish is a dangerous job for the Australian Customs patrols. The toothfish's problem is that it is the perfect fish.

Source: G. Bruce Knecht, *Hooked: Pirates, Poaching, and the Perfect Fish* (Emmaus, PA: Rodale), 2006.

Road congestion is another illustration of the tragedy of the commons. Figure 4 shows a market for usage of a road that is fully used and is right at the tipping point before becoming congested. In Figure 4, demand for driving on this road is D_0, and

FIGURE 4

Road Congestion

Assume that this road is fully used and is right at the tipping point before becoming congested. Demand for driving on this road is D_0, and the marginal cost of using the road—gas, time, and auto expenses—is MC_0. Equilibrium is at point *e*, with Q_0 miles a day being driven. Consumer surplus is area P_0ae for the typical driver. When a new driver begins using the road, this increases the marginal cost of driving to MC_1 for everyone, because the tipping point has been passed, and the road is now congested. Consumer surplus shrinks because of overuse of this common good.

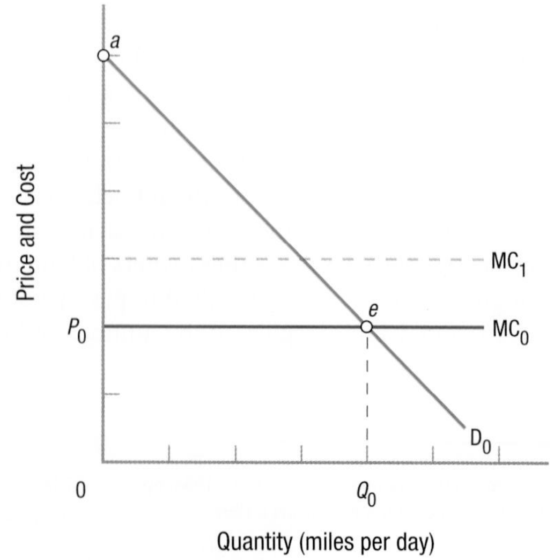

the marginal cost to use the road—gas, time, and auto expenses—is initially MC_0. Equilibrium is at point *e*, with Q_0 miles per day driven. Consumer surplus is area P_0ae for the typical driver.

Now assume that a new driver begins using the road. This increases the marginal costs of driving to MC_1 for everyone, because the tipping point has been passed, and the road is now congested. Consumer surplus shrinks because of overuse of the commons. Note that the new driver did not take these external costs into consideration; the driver assumed that the marginal cost would be equal to MC_0, not MC_1.

Possible solutions to common property resource problems can involve establishing private property rights, using government policy to restrict access to the resource, or informal organizations that restrict each user's benefits from the resource. Reduced congestion, for example, could be achieved by raising the tax on gasoline, subsidizing bus or rapid transit travel, or privatizing roads and allowing the owners to charge tolls.

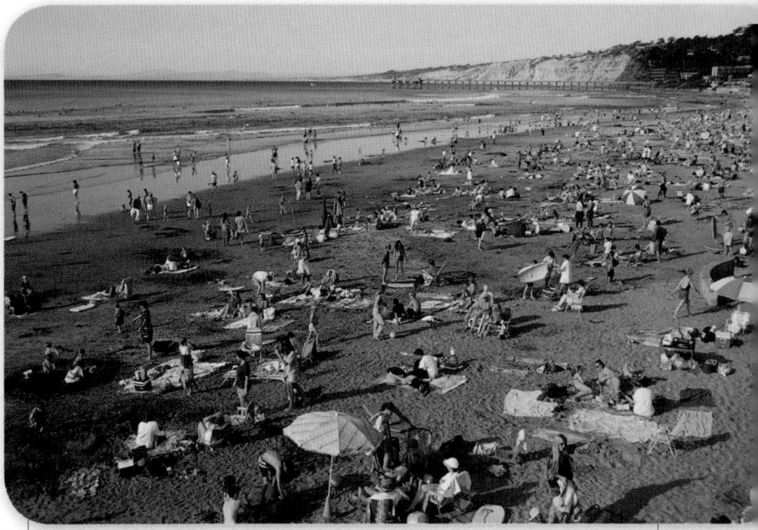
Charles Smith/Corbis

A crowded public beach makes the experience less enjoyable.

The optimal provision of public goods, whether pure public goods or common property resources with significant public goods characteristics, is a significant challenge faced by society. Individuals tend to act in their self-interest when using public goods without contributing to their provision (free-riding) or overusing a resource without considering the impact of such use on others. An example of a public good that has risen to the forefront of policy debate is the environment, which we all share. We turn to environmental policy next.

CHECKPOINT

PUBLIC GOODS

- Pure public goods are nonrival in consumption, and once the good is provided, no one can be excluded from using it.
- The demand for public goods is found by vertically summing individual demand curves.
- Optimal provision of public goods is found where the marginal benefit of public goods (demand) is equal to the marginal cost of provision.
- Determining the optimal provision of public goods is easy in theory, but difficult in practice.
- Common property resources have the characteristics of nonexcludability but are rival. This typically leads to overuse and overexploitation.

QUESTIONS: On most college campuses, the use of the recreation center is open to all registered students without an additional fee. The cost of running the recreation center typically is paid for by an activity fee paid by all students, regardless of whether they use the facilities or not. In what ways does your campus recreation center resemble a public good? In what ways does it not?

Answers to the Checkpoint questions can be found at the end of this chapter.

Environmental Policy

We have seen that market failure can lead to excessive amounts of products that pollute or generate other negative externalities, or to overuse of commonly owned resources that result in environmental degradation. This section puts these market failures together by looking at environmental policy. First, we look at how government policies can fail to improve such situations if the incentives of politicians and policymakers are not aligned with the public interest. Then, we look at the actual policies used by government regulators to reduce pollution, ranging from direct intervention and control to the use of various market instruments. Policymakers also occasionally use publicity and moral suasion to encourage polluters to reduce emissions voluntarily.

Government Failure

Market failure is one reason why unregulated markets may produce inequitable or inefficient results. Government policies, however, do not always make things better. The terrible environmental record the Eastern Bloc countries accumulated during the Soviet era illustrates that, in environmental policy as elsewhere, governments—like markets—can fail.

government failure The result when the incentives of politicians and government bureaucrats do not align with the public interest.

Government failure occurs when (1) public policies do not bring about an optimal allocation of resources, and/or (2) the incentives of politicians and government bureaucrats are not in line with the public interest. As Nobel Prize–winner George Stigler has argued, economic regulation often benefits the group being regulated at the expense of the larger public. Government failures are often more acute in nondemocratic societies. Yet, even in the United States, public policy formation involves a struggle among interest groups, lobbyists, politicians, large corporate interests, and the public at large. The sausage calling itself "public policy" that results from this tug-of-war is often not pretty.

Government failure may result from the practical inability of policymakers to gather enough information to set good policies. Water pollution, for instance, is well understood, resulting in fairly obvious regulatory policies, but the same is not true for issues such as global climate change. Even if we all agree that the Earth is getting warmer and humans are partly to blame, controversy remains about the adequacy of public policy to address this problem. Although calls for government action—"there ought to be a law"—are often justified, we would do well to maintain a healthy skepticism about the ability of the public sector to solve our problems.

Intergenerational Questions

Should politicians consider the interests of voters whose great-grandparents have not yet been born? Environmental issues raise complex questions involving how resources are to be allocated across generations. Some resources, such as sunlight, are continual and renewable. Others, such as forests, fisheries, and the soil are renewable but exhaustible if overexploited. And some resources are nonrenewable, such as oil and coal. These resources are finite and cannot be renewed, but their available stock can be expanded through exploration or the use of new technologies that allow greater extraction or more efficient use.

When we develop environmental policies, we need to consider and evaluate different possible futures. Figure 5 is a reminder of the effects that discount rates have on the present

FIGURE 5

Present Value of \$1,000 to Be Paid in 30 Years Discounted at 1%, 5%, and 10%

This figure is a reminder of the effects discount rates have on the present value of a fixed payment that will come due at a future date. A higher discount rate means that the value today of a future payment will be lower. The higher the discount rate we choose, the lower the value we place on the environmental damage to be suffered by future generations. The lower our discount rate, the more we are willing to protect the health of the future environment.

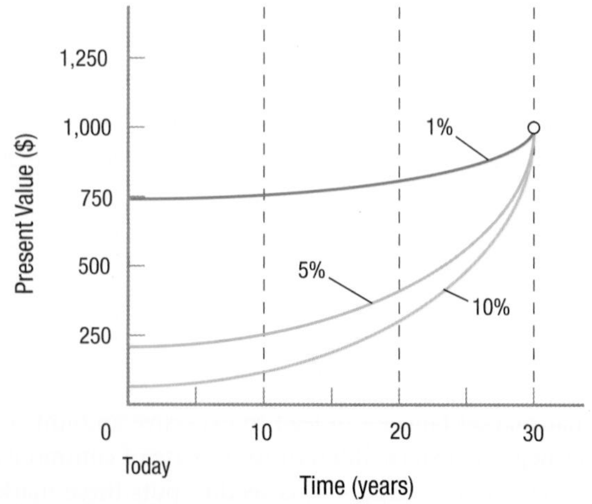

value of a fixed payment that will come due at some date in the future. For environmental policies, the discount rate we choose is crucially important.

A higher discount rate means that the value today of a future payment will be less. At a 10% discount, a payment of $1,000 in 30 years is worth only $42 today, whereas discounting the same $1,000 at 1% yields a present value of $748. The higher the discount rate we choose, the lower the value we place on the environmental damage to be suffered by future generations. The lower our discount rate, conversely, the more we are willing to protect the health of the future environment. As always, crafting good public policies requires striking a balance between the two.

Socially Efficient Levels of Pollution

We have already seen that some pollution is acceptable to society. To require that no one pollute, period, would bring most economic activity as we know it to a halt. Yet, pollution damages our environment. The harmful effects of pollution range from direct threats to our health coming from air and water pollution to reductions in species from deforestation.

The damages that come from pollution are a cost we incur for living: To be alive is to generate some pollution. Our focus is on marginal damage, which resembles the marginal cost curves we have studied earlier. The marginal damage (MD) curve in Figure 6 shows the change in damages that comes from a given change in emission levels. Notice that as emissions levels rise, the added damages rise.

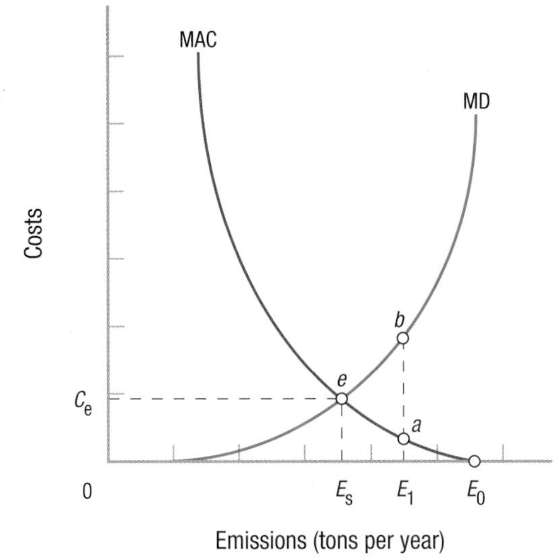

FIGURE 6

Marginal Damages and Marginal Abatement Costs

The marginal damage curve (MD) shows the *change* in damages that come from a given *change* in emission levels. The horizontal axis measures pollution. Note that E_0 is the maximum pollution that can occur without environmental cleanup. The vertical axis measures the environmental costs of this pollution. Marginal abatement costs curve (MAC) begins at zero at E_0, then rises as emission levels are reduced (moving leftward from E_0). Socially optimal pollution is E_S, at a cost to society of C_e (point *e*).

The horizontal axis of Figure 6 measures the tons of pollution emitted into the environment (tons per year). Note that E_0 represents the maximum pollution (no environmental cleanup at all). The vertical axis measures the environmental costs in dollars. These costs represent a dollar value for various environmental losses, including the physical costs of pollution (asthma attacks and other lung diseases), the aesthetic losses (visual impact of clear-cutting), and the losses associated with species reduction.

Abatement costs are the costs associated with reducing emissions. A utility plant dumping effluent into a river can treat the effluent before discharge, but this costs money. In Figure 6, marginal abatement costs (MAC) begin at zero at E_0, then rise as emission levels are reduced (moving leftward from E_0). The MAC curve in Figure 6 is a generalized abatement cost function, but in practice, the costs vary for different sources of pollution and the technologies available for reducing them. Chemical plants face different problems than utilities that release hot water into rivers. Cooling the water before release clearly requires a different technology—and is much easier—than eliminating toxic chemicals from effluent flow.

The socially optimal level of pollution in Figure 6 is E_S, at a cost to society of C_e (point *e*). To see why this is so, assume that we are at pollution level E_1. The cost to reduce another unit of emissions is equal to point *a* (measuring on the vertical axis), while the damage that would result from this pollution is shown at point *b*. Since $b > a$, society is better off if emissions are reduced. Once we begin reducing emissions below E_S, however, abatement costs overtake marginal damages, or the costs of cleanup begin to outweigh the benefits.

The total damage from pollution in Figure 6 is represented by the area beneath the marginal damages curve and to the left of E_S. Total abatement costs, meanwhile, are equal to the area beneath the marginal abatement costs curve and to the right of E_S. Combined, these two costs represent the total social costs from emissions. We turn now to consider how environmental policy can ensure that emissions approach this optimal level.

Overview of Environmental Policies

Over the years, many types of environmental policies have been developed in response to different problems, covering the spectrum from centralized control to decentralized economic incentives. To be effective, all environmental policies must be efficient, fair, and enforceable, and they must provide incentives for improvement in the environment.

command and control policies Environmental policies that set standards and issue regulations, which are then enforced by the legal and regulatory system.

market-based policies Environmental policies that use charges, taxes, subsidies, deposit-refund systems, or tradable emission permits to achieve environmental goals.

As a general rule, the more centralized an environmental policy, the more likely it represents a **command and control** philosophy. This means that a centralized agency sets the rules for emissions, including levels of effluents allowed, usable technologies, and enforcement procedures. Command and control policies usually set standards of conduct that are enforced by the legal and regulatory system. Abatement costs at this point become compliance costs of meeting the standards. Standards are popular because they are simple, they treat all firms in an industry the same way, and they prevent competing firms from polluting.

At the other end of the spectrum are **market-based policies,** which use charges, taxes, subsidies, deposit-refund systems, or tradable emission permits to achieve the same ends. Examples of this approach include water effluent charges, user charges for water and wastewater management, glass and plastic bottle refund systems, and tradable permits for ozone reduction. We begin with a brief look at command and control policies, contrasting them with abatement taxes, then look at the case for tradable emission permits.

Command and Control Policies

Policymakers determine the pollution control or abatement that is best, then introduce the most efficient policies to achieve those ends. Figure 7 shows the supply and demand for pollution abatement. Demand curve $D_A = MB_A$ represents society's demand for abatement;

FIGURE 7

Marginal Cost of Abatement and Abatement Demand

Demand curve D_A represents society's demand for abatement. The marginal benefit from abatement (MB_A) declines as the environment becomes cleaner, because the gains from an ever cleaner environment become smaller and smaller (diminishing returns). The marginal costs of abatement are the costs of reducing pollution. These costs rise with abatement efforts and become high as zero pollution A_0 is approached (again, because of the law of diminishing returns, or increasing costs). Optimal abatement is A_e, costing c_e. This means optimal pollution, $A_0 - A_e$, is greater than zero.

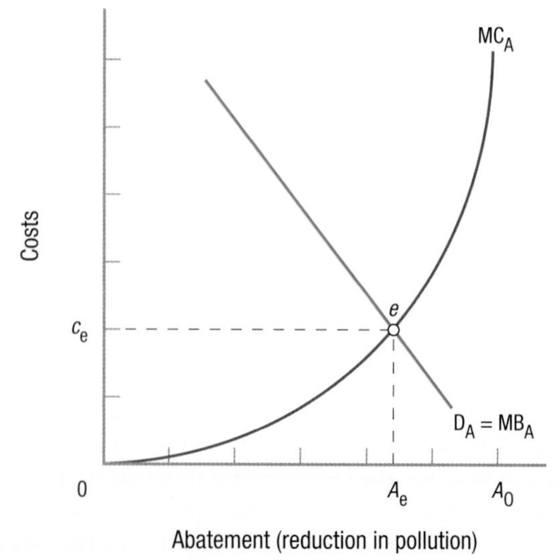

it is a reflection of the marginal damage curve we looked at earlier. Note that the demand curve for abatement is negatively sloped because the *marginal benefit* from abatement declines as the environment becomes cleaner. The gains from an ever cleaner environment eventually become smaller and smaller because of the law of diminishing returns.

The marginal costs of abatement are the costs of cleaning up pollution. These costs rise with abatement efforts and become high as zero pollution, A_0, is approached. Optimal abatement comes at A_e, costing c_e. This means that optimal pollution, $A_0 - A_e$, is greater than zero. Command and control policies could set A_e as the abatement requirement and then set the right standards to meet this requirement. Aiming for abatement higher than A_e would be inefficient, because marginal costs would exceed marginal benefits.

Setting abatement requirements (or standards) equal to A_e in Figure 7 is a classic example of command and control policies. Again, command and control policies that set rigid standards for polluters have long been a favorite of policymakers. Yet, this approach can lead to inefficiencies, because different industries may emit the same (or equivalently dangerous) substances but face different technical problems and costs in reducing their pollution. To minimize the cost of reducing pollution, each source of pollution needs to be reduced to the point at which the marginal cost of abatement is equal for all sources. This can be achieved through market-based policies.

Market-Based Policies

Economists argue that market-oriented, or indirect, approaches to environmental policy are more efficient than command and control policies. Two of the most popular and effective of these indirect approaches are the use of emissions taxes and marketable or tradable permits.

Emissions Taxes An alternative to command and control policies is to enact an emissions tax on every unit of pollution produced to achieve the socially efficient outcome. Taxes of this sort are known as **Pigouvian taxes** (named after Arthur Pigou who developed the idea in 1920). Unlike command and control policies, polluting firms are not limited to a fixed amount of pollution. Instead, by forcing firms to pay for every unit of pollution created, firms would invest in pollution reduction measures up to the point at which the cost of abatement measures is no longer less than the tax. Such policies take into account the fact that some firms are able to reduce pollution at less cost than others. Therefore, it creates efficiencies by allowing firms with higher costs of pollution abatement to pollute more by paying more taxes, while encouraging firms with lower costs of pollution abatement to utilize such measures to reduce their tax burden.

Pigouvian tax A tax that is placed on an activity generating negative externalities in order to achieve a socially efficient outcome.

Returning to Figure 7, achieving the optimal level of pollution abatement, A_e, could be achieved by charging a tax equal to c_e per unit of pollution. Firms would adopt pollution controls up to A_e, because the costs to reduce pollution to this point are less than the tax. Firms would emit only $A_0 - A_e$ pollution. As a result, the same level of abatement is achieved using taxes as with using command and control policies; however, allowing the market to achieve this outcome through taxes allows for a more efficient outcome for the firms involved.

Marketable or Tradable Permits Another way that markets are used to limit pollution is through the use of marketable or tradable permits. Economists first proposed marketable or tradable permits when environmental laws were first being debated and enacted in the 1960s and 1970s. Environmental regulators essentially ignored this suggestion until the 1990s.

Today, tradable permits are used to reduce water effluents in the Fox River in Wisconsin, Tar-Pamlico River in North Carolina, and Dillon Reservoir in Colorado. One of the most successful uses of marketable permits for air pollution, described in the Issue in this section, has reduced the sulfur dioxide (SO_2) emissions in the Midwest that create acid rain in the East. Originally, the cost of this cleanup was expected to be significant, but technical advances steadily reduced abatement costs, causing the price of the permits to decline sharply.

Marketable permits require that a regulatory body set a maximum allowable quantity of effluents allowed, typically called the "cap," and issue permits granting the "right" to pollute a certain amount. These permits can be bought and sold, thus creating the property rights that permit transactions of the sort Coase advocated. Sales are normally between two polluters, with one polluter buying a permit from a more efficient operator. Polluters do not have to be the only purchasers: Victims or environmental groups could conceivably purchase pollution rights and hold them off the market, thereby reducing pollution below the established cap.

Figure 8 illustrates how such a market works. We assume that there are two firms in the market, each producing 10 tons of pollution, and that the government wishes to limit pollution to a total of 10 tons. Without restrictions, firms do zero abatement and total pollution is 20 tons. Setting a goal of 10 tons amounts to cutting pollution in half.

FIGURE 8

Tradable Permits

This figure illustrates how a market for tradable pollution permits works. Assume there are only two firms (X and Y) in the market and the government wishes to limit total pollution to 10 tons. Without restrictions, both firms do zero abatement and pollution is 20 tons. Setting a goal of 10 tons therefore amounts to cutting pollution in half. Assume that the government gives the permits to firm X. Demand curve D_Y represents firm Y's demand for these permits. Given a competitive market for permits, equilibrium will be at point *e* with a permit price equal to $300. Firm Y buys 7 permits and pollutes that amount, and firm X emits 3 tons of pollution.

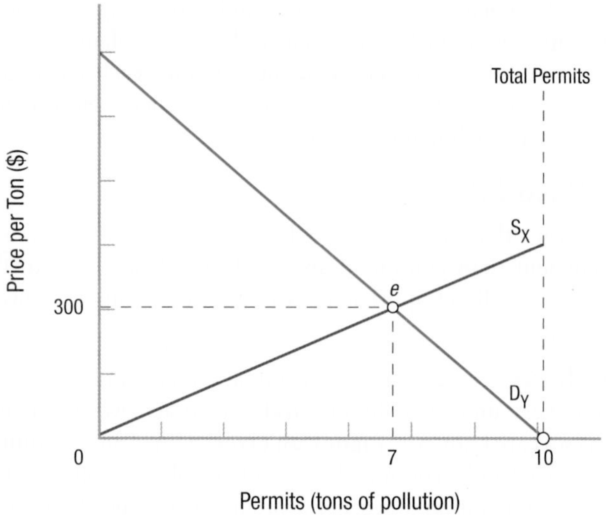

Assume, for simplicity, that the government at first gives the permits to firm X. (Remember that the Coase theorem suggests efficiency is not affected by who owns the rights to pollute.) Demand curve D_Y represents firm Y's demand for these permits. Assume that the market for permits is competitive, thus equilibrium will be at point *e* with a permit price equal to $300. Firm Y buys 7 permits and pollutes that amount, and firm X pollutes 3 tons.

Firm X pollutes less and sells 7 permits to firm Y because it can reduce more of its pollution before its marginal abatement costs reach $300. In this case, firm Y faces high clean-up costs that reach $300 a ton at 3 tons. Thus, it buys 7 tons of pollution rights from firm X. Firm X in this example ends up with the revenue from permit sales, while firm Y's income declines by the same amount ($2,100). Auctioning off the permits produces the same result, but the government receives the revenue.

Keep in mind that regulators could have set a $300 per ton tax on effluents and achieved the same result. One advantage of permits over taxes is that no knowledge of marginal abatement costs is needed to ensure that the tax rate is optimal. The market price of permits will adjust to variances in abatement costs. All the regulator must determine is how much to reduce pollution levels. If reducing pollution by a certain amount, regardless of the cost, is the goal, permits will achieve this goal.

Other Market-Based Policies We have looked at two of the most frequently used market-based policies, taxes and marketable permits. Emission taxes and charges have been used for water effluents, waste management, pesticide packaging, batteries, tires, and other products and processes. User charges are the most common way to finance wastewater treatment facilities.

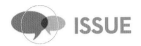

ISSUE

Cap-and-Trade: The Day Liberal Environmentalists and Free-Market Conservatives Agreed

Westend61/SuperStock

Environmental policies in recent decades have epitomized the battle between liberal environmentalists and free-market conservatives, with the former arguing for more limits on pollution while the latter want more market freedom. How then, could the two sides come to an agreement that would satisfy both of their primary objectives?

In the late 1980s, the problem of acid rain reached a boiling point, with heavy pollution from sulfur dioxide emissions causing health issues, polluted lakes and rivers, and reduced visibility. Further, it heightened tensions with Canada, which suffered negative externalities from the pollution from American power plants. With the environmental damage reaching front page news and a fierce political battle on how to fix it, it looked like a lost cause.

Then came a very unlikely alliance between Dan Dukek of the Environmental Defense Fund and Boyden Gray, a multimillionaire conservative who was appointed President Bush's White House counsel in 1988. Gray, a strong proponent of free-market principles, had long supported a method of allowing individuals and firms to buy and sell permits to pollute. The acid rain crisis allowed Dudek and Gray to propose an emissions permit trading program that placed significant caps on sulfur dioxide (placating environmentalists) while eliminating regulations and allowing the marketplace to determine permit prices (placating free-market proponents).

The program became law with the *Clean Air Act of 1990*. When the law, which became known as "cap-and-trade," took effect in 1995, emissions fell and led to significant external cost savings in what has been considered a resounding success in solving a major environmental program using a market-based approach as opposed to a command-and-control approach.

Today, much discussion centers on the proposed use of cap-and-trade to reduce carbon dioxide emissions. Such programs are law in the European Union and elsewhere, but proposals to pass cap-and-trade legislation in the United States since 2008 have been held up, ironically by the same market-based proponents who created the strategy that worked in the past. Opponents of cap-and-trade today argue that cap-and-trade still imposes harsh limits on the broader market, which they support. Yet, without cap-and-trade, resolutions to reduce global warming become less likely. It may take another unlikely alliance before the problem of global warming is solved.

Source: Richard Conniff, "The Political History of Cap and Trade," *Smithsonian*, August 2009.

Federal subsidies, the flip side of taxes or charges, are used when local communities do not have the resources for pollution control. Marketable permits have been most successful in programs to reduce air pollution, as well as those targeting acid rain and ozone reduction. Deposit-refund systems have been used mainly for recyclable products such as cans, bottles, tires, and batteries.

Over the years, most environmental policies have been of the command and control variety. The 1970 Clean Air Act focused on specific forms of air pollution—particulates, carbon monoxide, and so forth—and established air quality standards. Today, economic or market-based approaches to environmental policy are considered more efficient than command and control policies. Most environmental agencies, however, in this country and abroad, have not used these tools until recently.

One reason for this is probably that many people in the regulatory and environmental communities resist viewing environmental resources as commodities to be subjected to market forces of supply and demand. It is market failures, after all, that led to environmental decay in the first place. Why would we want to put the environment on the market? Many pollutants, moreover, are frequently mixed together and their individual impacts are difficult to determine. Consequently, setting the right tax rate or issuing the right number of allowable permits is difficult. Finally, some policymakers balk at giving corporations the right to pollute, even a limited amount.

CHECKPOINT

ENVIRONMENTAL POLICY

- Government failure can occur when politicians and government do not have the right incentives to bring about an optimal allocation of resources.
- The discount rate chosen for environmental policies determines the intergenerational impact of policy.
- The socially optimal level of pollution occurs where the marginal damage is equal to the marginal abatement costs.
- Policymakers determine the optimal pollution levels and then often use command and control policies to set the most efficient regulations or levels of abatement.
- Tradable permits use market forces to bring pollution within limits set by regulators.

QUESTIONS: If a "cap-and-trade" program for carbon dioxide emissions is implemented in the United States, with the overall limit slowly reduced each year, what would happen to the price of permits if all production activity stays the same and the cost of pollution abatement remains unchanged? What would need to happen in order for the price of permits to fall over time?

Answers to the Checkpoint questions can be found at the end of this chapter.

Putting It All Together: An Analysis of Climate Change

Throughout this chapter, we saw how the market failures of externalities, public goods, and common property resources create markets that make it difficult to achieve a socially efficient outcome without some sort of intervention. As a result, governments often are tasked with establishing policies that attempt to incentivize individuals and firms to take actions that lead to a more efficient outcome. But how are such policies established? And how are the effects measured?

Many questions arise that require adequate measurement of how individuals value various objectives. For example, how do we account for the value of biodiversity? How much would we pay to keep certain species from going extinct? Or how much benefit must we obtain to endure living in a polluted city? The answers to these and other questions require the use of a consistent technique to ensure policies are well established to promote social efficiency.

cost-benefit analysis A methodology for decision making that looks at the discounted value of the costs and benefits of a given project.

A common approach taken to develop and debate policies is to use some form of **cost-benefit analysis.** Cost-benefit analysis provides a rational model for policy decisions, forces a focus on alternatives (opportunity costs), draws conclusions about the optimal *scale* of projects, makes the intergenerational aspects explicit through discounting, and takes into account the explicit preferences of individuals. In short, it takes all of the future benefits and costs of a proposed policy and discounts them to the present to determine whether it is worth implementing.

One of the major difficulties with cost-benefit analysis for big public projects and environmental programs is measuring nonmarket or intangible aspects of projects. To resolve these issues, economists use various methods to approximate the values of intangible items, such as how much people pay to avert harm, or even direct surveys among a small but representative portion of the population to determine how individuals value certain aspects of the environment.

Cost-benefit analysis, then, is a rational approach to valuing some things that are hard to put a price on. The issue of climate change is one topic that involves many such variables. Let's analyze in greater detail the issue of global warming, which often is characterized as the mother of all market failures.

Understanding Climate Change

There is growing scientific consensus that without a significant reduction in emissions, global warming from the buildup of greenhouse gases is likely to lead to irreversible damage to the climate, ecosystems, and coastlines.

A sense of urgency surrounds climate change because the state of climate science has advanced to the point where scientists can now put probability estimates on certain impacts of warming, some of which are catastrophic. Current levels of greenhouse gases are roughly 403 parts per million (ppm).[5] This compares to 280 ppm before the Industrial Revolution. Scientists predict that if greenhouse gases exceed 450 ppm, average global temperatures will have risen 2 degrees Celsius since the Industrial Revolution, a change that would lead to dramatic consequences. If the current trend continues, the 450 ppm threshold will be exceeded in less than 25 years.

What will happen as greenhouse gases increase and lead to global warming? Table 3 estimates these effects. The top part of the table shows a range of greenhouse gases from

Greenhouse Gases, Likely Temperature Changes, and Estimated Impacts **TABLE 3**

	Greenhouse Gases (ppm)				
	400	450	550	700	800
	Eventual Temperature Change (relative to preindustrial)				
	1°C	2°C	3°C	4°C	5°C
Food	Rising crop yields in high-latitude developed countries	Rising number of people at risk from hunger	Falling crop yields in developing regions	Major decline in crop yields in all regions	?
Water	Small mountain glaciers disappear	Over a 30% drop in runoff in South Africa and the Mediterranean	Large numbers of people suffer water shortages	Billions of people affected by water shortages	Sea level rise threatens major cities, including New York, Hong Kong, and London
Ecosystems	Ocean coral reef systems damaged	Many ecosystems unable to maintain their current form	Part of Amazon rain forest begins to collapse	20% to 50% species extinction possible	?
Extreme Weather Events	Rising levels of storms, fires, droughts, floods, and heat waves →				
		Rising hurricane intensity →			
Major Irreversible Impacts	Risk of weakening the natural carbon absorption system →				
		Rising risk of large-scale shifts in climate system →			

Source: Nicholas Stern, *The Economics of Climate Change* (Cambridge: Cambridge University Press), 2007.

[5] European Environmental Agency, Atmospheric Greenhouse Gas Concentrations (CSI 013), January 8, 2013.

400 ppm to 800 ppm, with predicted effects on temperature below it. The bottom part estimates the impacts likely to arise with each increase in temperature. The estimated effects of a difference of just 1 or 2 degrees raise serious concerns.

Unique Timing Aspects

The global environment is essentially a common resource with many public goods aspects, and climate change is a huge global negative externality. But what makes analysis and decision making so difficult is the long time horizon that must be considered. Most cost-benefit studies do not look out 50 to 100 years and beyond. This extended time horizon adds a host of difficulties and uncertainties.

Air or water pollution is something that we can see on the horizon, can be measured, is typically localized, and can be altered in a short period of time by some of the approaches discussed earlier. Global warming, in contrast, is not something we can generally see; it is cumulative (this year's CO_2 adds to that from the past to raise concentrations in the future); and once it reaches a certain level, it may lead to extreme consequences that cannot be reversed.

Cleaning up pollution problems typically involves finding that level of abatement at which the marginal costs of abatement equal the marginal benefits from abatement and either taxing, assigning (or auctioning) marketable permits, or using command and control policies to require the optimal level of abatement. However, reducing global warming gases is not a short-term objective, but a cumulative process across many years. Yet, our short-run decisions will have immense impacts in the long run. Small changes in emissions today may have little effect on the current generation, but will have sizable effects many decades out. This aspect of the problem seriously complicates any policymaking and economic analysis.

Public Good Aspects

To compound the problem further, global climate change is a public good. Greenhouse gas emissions "are the purest example of a negative public good; nobody can have less of them because someone else has more; and nobody can be excluded from their malign consequences or the efforts of others to ameliorate them."[6]

One of the solutions is technical innovation that reduces our output of CO_2. But knowledge and technology have large public good aspects, therefore private firms will find it difficult to collect the full returns on their innovation investments that reduce greenhouse gases. Other firms and countries will to some extent be free riders on private innovation, thus society (and the world) may get less than the socially optimal level of innovation. This will mean that a substantial amount of climate change research and development will have to be financed by governments.

Equity Aspects

Why should I do anything for posterity? What has posterity ever done for me?

Groucho Marx

Much of what we do today to reduce global warming will have little immediate impact on our lives. The impacts will show up in the latter half of the century. Any action taken today principally benefits our great-grandchildren. Groucho Marx's joke not withstanding, this fact makes it more difficult to get a political consensus to act.

Also, rich countries will have to make the biggest sacrifices, yet they will not get the biggest benefits from efforts to reduce the impacts of global warming. Suppose that the United States reduces its dependence on carbon. What about China and India? They may decide that growth is worth more than a cleaner environment. At that point, the United States would have to be willing to pay China and India large sums to get them

[6] Martin Wolf, "Curbs on Emissions Will Take a Change of Political Climate," *Financial Times*, November 8, 2006, p. 15.

to decarbonize their economies. How well will that sell to American voters? Probably not well, but it may be what is ultimately necessary.

People in countries both rich and poor living along bodies of water will face floods if current climate forecasts come to pass. However, developing countries which are home to some of the world's poorest people will face the greatest challenge adapting to flooding given their severely limited resources. In addition, developing nations rely heavily on agriculture, one industry that will be hardest hit by the warming of the Earth.

Finding a Solution

Climate change is global, therefore it will take concerted international effort and cooperation to create price signals and markets for carbon, and to develop and promote new technologies, especially in developing countries.

Many economists argue that using fewer fossil fuels today will result in lower spending on environmental protection in the future, like a form of insurance to reduce future harm on the environment. This will require a transition to a low-carbon economy that will require actions such as establishing a worldwide price for carbon that includes its external costs. This can be done using carbon taxes or tradable permits. Initiatives such as the European Union Emissions Trade System (EU ETS), launched in 2005, have taken first steps toward capping emissions levels using tradable permits.

Robert Socolow of Princeton University has suggested that much of the technology needed to reduce our carbon footprint is available today.[7] He and several colleagues suggest that carbon emissions can remain constant over the next 50 years if the following techniques are implemented:

- Use more efficient vehicles and reduce vehicle use in general.
- Build more efficient buildings.
- Capture CO_2 at power plants.
- Use nuclear power.
- Exchange biomass fuels for fossil fuels.
- Use wind and solar power.
- Reduce deforestation.

NOBEL PRIZE
ELINOR OSTROM (1933–2012)

When economists talk about common property resources, they typically discuss the tragedy of the commons and suggest a solution that involves privatization or central government takeover and management of the resource. Elinor Ostrom was awarded the 2009 Nobel Prize in Economic Sciences for challenging this conventional wisdom by showing how *user-managed* resources, where people cooperate to solve a resource issue, can be effective.

Born in 1933 during the depths of the Great Depression and completing her doctorate in political science in 1965, her dissertation looked at a case in which saltwater was seeping into western Los Angeles's water basin. A group of individuals formed a water association to solve the problem by creating rules and injected water along the coast. Their efforts saved the basin. This experience led her to look at other common resource problems from a new perspective.

She used field studies and thousands of case studies by other social scientists along with game theory to determine how these informal organizations evolved and what conditions make them successful.

Her work has determined the requirements for sustainable user-managed common resource property, including (a) rules must clearly define entitlement to the resource, (b) adequate conflict resolution measures must exist, (c) an individual's duty to maintain the resource must be in proportion to his or her benefits, (d) monitoring and sanctioning must be by users or accountable to users, (e) sanctions should be graduated—mild for a first violation and stricter as violations are repeated, (f) governance and decision processes must be democratic, and (g) self-organization is recognized by outside authorities. When these institutional conditions are met, user management of common pool resources typically is successful.

Professor Ostrom's insights and research have opened up an alternative to prevent the tragedy of the commons. Her work will be particularly important as nations begin working together to reduce the potential harm from global climate change, maybe our biggest common resource problem to date.

[7] Robert Socolow et al., "Solving the Climate Problem: Technologies Available to Curb CO_2 Emissions," *Environment*, December 2004, pp. 8–19.

Clearly, undertaking some policies to reduce our carbon footprint as a nation represents an insurance policy on the future. As new climate change information becomes available, policies can be adjusted to reduce the potential costs in the future.

To that end, carbon dioxide emissions are frequently placed on political agendas. However, a slow economic recovery makes it harder to focus people's attention on this issue. Furthermore, questions arise about the initial grant of permits in any cap-and-trade program. Do large established companies with huge capital resources get permits? What about smaller, possibly more innovative alternative energy companies? Do permits get auctioned off, and does this then favor the richer, more established companies? Political issues combine with economic issues to make this a thorny problem for the future.

As with climate change, each of the examples described in this chapter dealt with market failure in which externalities, public goods, or shared resources lead the market away from the socially desirable output. Resolving a market failure generally requires some policy tool, such as the assignment of property rights, regulation, or the creation of market incentives to achieve the ideal outcome. However, determining which policy tool to use often leads to intense debate, making issues of market failure a challenge that societies and their policymakers will continue to face.

CHECKPOINT

PUTTING IT ALL TOGETHER: AN ANALYSIS OF CLIMATE CHANGE

- Global climate change is a huge negative externality with an extremely long time horizon.
- The public goods aspects of climate change make it a truly global problem.
- Balancing the current generation's costs and benefits against the potential harm to future generations raises difficult economic issues.
- Actions taken today to reduce a potential future calamity are a form of insurance.

QUESTION: One of the most difficult aspects of climate change policy is determining how much individuals are willing to sacrifice today for a better environment in the future. What are some factors that may influence whether a person holds a high or low discount rate on the future with regard to environmental policy?

Answers to the Checkpoint question can be found at the end of this chapter.

chapter summary

Section 1: Externalities

Externalities, or spillovers, arise when a transaction benefits or harms parties not involved in the transaction.

Externalities lead to **market failure** when external benefits or external costs push markets away from the socially optimal output.

Jose Luis Pelaez Inc/Getty Images

Taking care of the front lawn creates an external benefit to the neighbors.

Factories spewing dirty smoke create an external cost to the area residents.

Oote Boe 3/Alamy

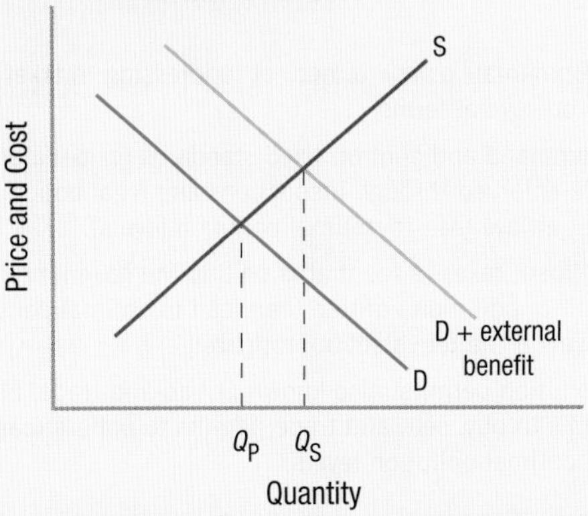

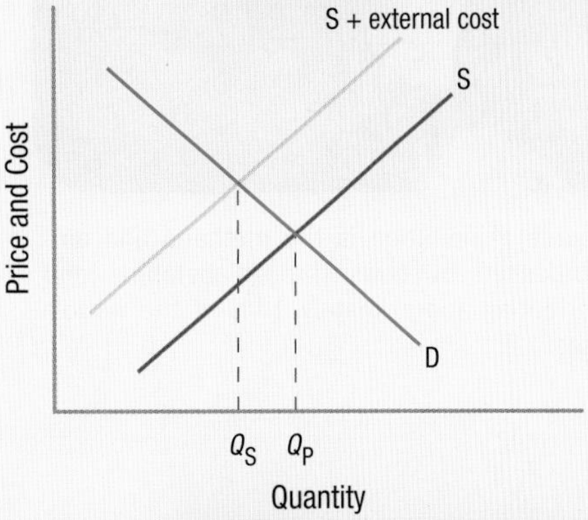

The **Coase theorem** suggests that when transactions costs are near zero, bargaining between parties will lead to an efficient allocation of resources no matter how property rights are allocated.

Example: If students have the right to party, the neighbors can pay the students to stay quiet. If neighbors have the right to a quiet environment, students can pay the neighbors for the right to party. Either way, those with the property rights can exercise their rights or accept payment to forgo the rights.

Bob Krist/Corbis

Section 2: Public Goods

Public goods exhibit two characteristics:

Nonrivalry: One person's consumption of a good does not reduce the availability of that good to others.

Nonexcludability: Once a good has been provided, no consumers can be excluded from consuming the product.

Public goods lead to market failure when individuals lack the incentive to pay for them, leading to such goods being underprovided.

Accent Alaska.com/Alamy

Common property resources are owned by the community, and therefore individuals tend to overuse and overexploit them.

Section 3: **Environmental Policy**

Environmental policies depend on the discount rate chosen for how society values events in the future. A high discount rate places a significant burden on future generations, while a low discount rate places a greater burden on the current generation.

The optimal pollution level in a society is rarely zero. Instead, some pollution is acceptable if the cost of abatement exceeds its benefit. Therefore, optimal pollution levels are found where marginal abatement costs (MAC) equal the marginal damage caused by pollution. As long as the cleanup costs exceed damage, it would be optimal to allow pollution until MAC equals MD at E_S.

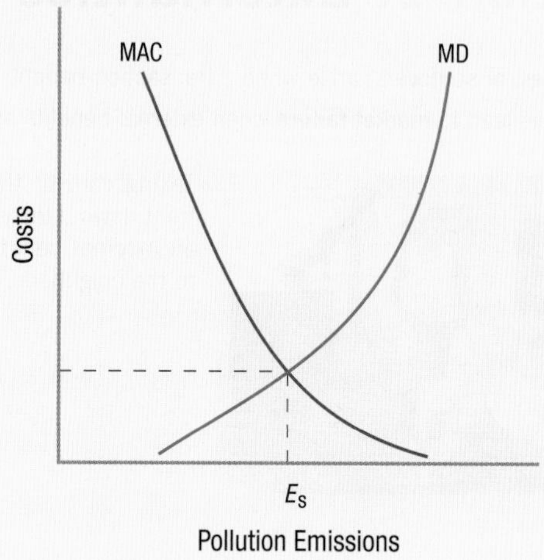

Kevin Britland/Alamy

A surprising source of pollution is the methane and ammonia gases produced by cows through belching and flatulence, contributing approximately 14% of the world's greenhouse gases.

Environmental policy aimed at addressing market failure takes on several forms:

- Command and control: fixed standards for polluters that are enforced through inspections and legal action (does not always lead to optimal pollution levels).
- Effluent taxes: a fee that is paid to the government per unit of pollution emitted (can lead to optimal pollution levels if the fee is set appropriately).
- Pollution permits: also known as cap-and-trade, allows firms to buy, sell, and trade permits to pollute (can lead to optimal pollution levels).

Section 4: **Putting It All Together: An Analysis of Climate Change**

Global climate change is a huge global negative externality accompanied by public goods aspects and extremely long time horizons, making the inherent market failure difficult to address.

Equity issues arise when some countries (often developed) pay significantly more to reduce global climate change than developing countries.

Solutions to global pollution require cooperation between nations and global carbon pricing that is credible and covers the full costs of carbon-based products.

Randy Olson/National Geographic Society/Corbis

Crowded streets filled with polluting vehicles are a common scene in India, contributing to global pollution as the nation develops.

KEY CONCEPTS

externalities, p. 338
Coase theorem, p. 340
market failure, p. 343
public goods, p. 343
nonrivalry, p. 343
nonexcludability, p. 343
free rider, p. 343
tragedy of the commons, p. 345
government failure, p. 348
command and control policies, p. 350
market-based policies, p. 350
Pigouvian tax, p. 351
cost-benefit analysis, p. 354

QUESTIONS AND PROBLEMS

Check Your Understanding

1. When trying to estimate the external benefits of a college education, what kinds of specific benefits would you include?
2. How might the government use market forces to encourage recycling?
3. What makes public goods so different from private goods?
4. Why wouldn't a rural highway in Montana, Freeway 405 in Los Angeles, and the New Jersey Turnpike (toll) all be classified as public goods? Which would be most like a public good and which would be least?
5. Assume that you are convinced that if something isn't done now, global warming is going to create extensive problems and damage at the end of this century. If you were preparing a cost-benefit analysis of the impacts and had a 100-year horizon for your projections, would you use a 3% or an 8% discount rate?
6. What is the tragedy of the commons? How can it be solved?

Applying the Concepts

7. "Internalizing" the cost of negative externalities means that we try to set policies that require each product to include the full costs of its negative spillovers in its price. How do such policies affect product price and industry output and employment? Are these kinds of policies easy to implement in practice? How has globalization of production affected our ability to control pollution?
8. As a way to increase the funds for wildlife conservation, why don't we just auction off (say, on eBay) the right to name a new species when it is discovered? Why not do the same for existing species?
9. We can estimate the emissions caused in one year from automobile use. What can you do to offset these emissions? Buy a *green tag*. These voluntary purchases are akin to carbon offsets traded in Europe. For a small fee, individuals can purchase carbon offsets for their cars or SUVs, or companies can use them as a way to purchase wind power for their stores. Organizations selling the green tag (both for-profit and not-for-profit) provide a decal; most of the fee collected is provided to alternative energy producers as a subsidy, which then can lower their prices to the market to encourage use. Is this a public good being sold privately? Why would individuals or businesses buy a tag when they can free-ride?
10. Garbage dumps are a particular source of a potent global-warming gas, the methane that bubbles up as the garbage decomposes. Does it make sense for companies in the European Union to help Brazilian garbage dumps reduce their releases of methane as a way of meeting their Kyoto obligations?
11. The Presidio, previously a military base in San Francisco, is now a national park. It sits in the middle of San Francisco on some of the most valuable real estate in the United States. Congress, when it created the park, required that it rehabilitate the aging buildings and be self-sufficient within a decade or so, or the land would be sold off

to developers. The park appears to be well on its way to self-sufficiency by leasing the land to private firms—Lucas Films has built a large digital animation studio, and other firms have undertaken similar projects. These projects all must maintain the general character of the park and generate rent that will cover the park's expenses in the future. Would this privatization approach work with most of America's other national parks? Why or why not?

12. Nobel Prize–winner Simon Kuznets once suggested that poor nations tend to pollute more as they grow—until they reach a certain level of income per capita—after which they pollute less. Does this observation by Kuznets seem reasonable? Why or why not?

In the News

13. In 2009, the Cash for Clunkers program was initiated to encourage consumers to trade in their old inefficient cars for a credit to buy new fuel-efficient cars. What are some of the external benefits from such a policy?

14. One's home (whether a house or an apartment) is typically thought of as one's castle. But not so in the condominiums with homeowners associations (HOAs) in Jefferson County, Colorado. In an older four-unit condo, the HOA voted 3–1 to adopt a no-smoking rule (inside the individual condos) after smokers bought one of the units and smoke permeated the walls of the structure. In 2006, a district judge ruled that the HOA's adoption of no-smoking rules was a reasonable restriction on ownership rights, stating that the rules were designed to prevent the odor of cigarettes from penetrating the walls of neighboring condos.

    Considering that there are a small number of people involved (three nonsmoking units, one smoking), you would think that transaction costs would be minimal. Why do you think the homeowners could not work out an agreement (à la Coase) and ended up in court? According to the Coase theorem, would it have made any difference if the judge had ruled against the HOA?

Solving Problems

15. Suppose the market demand and supply for flu shots is shown in the figure below. Not taking into account the external benefits from flu shots, what is the equilibrium price and quantity of flu shots? Now suppose that every flu shot generates $10 in external benefits (from others being less likely to get sick). Show how this positive externality affects the graph (draw in a new curve). Taking into account external benefits, what would be the new equilibrium price and quantity of flu shots?

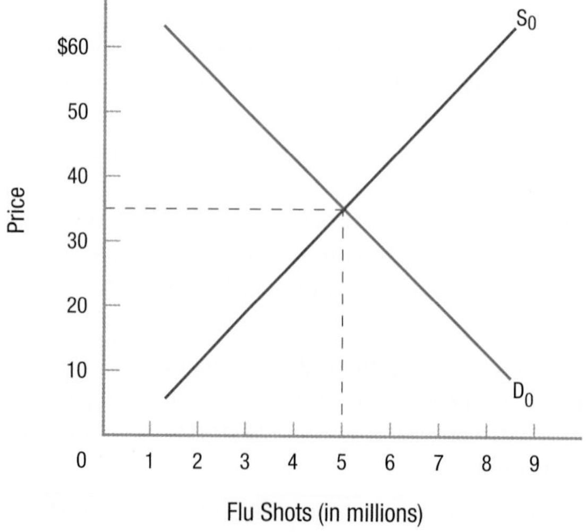

16. Suppose that the individual demand schedules for Al and Jane, the only two residents on a quiet city street, are shown in the table for speed bumps aimed at slowing cars passing through. In a single diagram, plot Al and Jane's individual demand curve, and then plot the total demand curve for each unit of the public good.

Al		Jane	
Quantity	**Marginal benefit**	**Quantity**	**Marginal benefit**
1	$50	1	$100
2	$25	2	$50
3	$10	3	$25
4	$5	4	$10

USING THE NUMBERS

17. According to By the Numbers, between which two years did total sales of hybrid cars increase the most? What factors might have led to this rise in hybrid sales?
18. According to By the Numbers, which two waste products are most recovered (recycled) by percentage, and which two waste products are least recovered?

ANSWERS TO QUESTIONS IN CHECKPOINTS

Checkpoint: Externalities

CFL bulbs create external benefits by reducing the overall use of energy, thus keeping energy prices lower for all consumers. The longer life of CFL bulbs also reduces waste and pollution. CFL bulbs can also create external costs. For example, careless disposal of CFL bulbs may allow mercury, a harmful toxin, to leak into landfills and into the environment, potentially harming all persons.

Checkpoint: Public Goods

If the recreation center on campus allows all students to use it without an additional fee, it resembles some of the characteristics of a public good. Although it can exclude nonstudents from the facility, it is open to all students. Therefore, it is partially nonexcludable. However, if too many students use it, it can become crowded, resembling more of a common property resource.

Checkpoint: Environmental Policy

If the "cap" on total carbon dioxide emissions is reduced each year while economic activity stays the same, permit prices would rise to encourage firms to produce less to meet the cap. In order for permit prices to fall, the costs of pollution abatement must fall due to technological advances, or new production methods (using clean energy) must be introduced to emit lesser carbon dioxide to begin with.

Checkpoint: Putting It All Together: An Analysis of Climate Change

Many answers are valid. But any factor that causes one to place greater emphasis on the future would result in a lower discount rate. Such factors might include having children or grandchildren, a greater desire to preserve Earth's natural beauty, having higher income or a business that relies on the availability of natural resources, or having empathy for future residents. Factors that might result in a high discount rate may include poverty, where emphasis is on improving one's current economic well-being in the future, or other difficult situations (wars and civil strife) that focus more attention on the present than on the future.

14 Network Goods

After studying this chapter you should be able to:

- Describe the similarities and differences among the three main types of networks.
- Explain what a network good is and how consuming a network good generates an external benefit.
- Describe the steps in deriving a demand curve for a network good.
- Describe how networks can rapidly expand or decline due to network effects.
- Describe the strategies firms use to compete in the market for network goods.
- Discuss the role of regulation in promoting network efficiency and competition.
- Explain how compatibility of industry standards can promote competition.
- Explain how interconnection promotes competition in industries with essential facilities.

Tetra Images/Corbis

Mom is calling. Is it this phone I pick up, or this one, or that one?

When you use your AT&T cell phone to call your mother on her Verizon cell phone, do you ever consider what would happen if Verizon refused to connect your call from the AT&T network? Of course not—this just does not happen in the United States. But this is not always the case in other parts of the world. In Nigeria, for example, it is common for cell phone providers to ignore calls placed by callers using competing networks. The result? If you want to call your mom using a different network than hers, it might not work. In countries where customers using different networks are unable to place calls to one another reliably, people often carry multiple phones to make sure they can connect with their families and friends.

As this example illustrates, networks are an important part of our daily lives. In the United States, we often take networks for granted, failing to appreciate that without the efficient functioning of networks, we would be forced to endure a great deal of inconvenience and frustration. Where would you be without the word processing software you use to work collaboratively with others on group projects, or without the social networking site you use to stay in touch with friends?

This chapter studies the role of networks and network goods. Companies that provide network goods engage in competitive strategies to maintain the strength of their networks. Network industries tend to be volatile, and a market leader can quickly evaporate in this type of industry. Do you remember Friendster, AltaVista, Netscape, WordPerfect, and Sega Genesis? Each of these networks was once the market leader in its respective industry, but quickly lost its dominance when an opposing network became stronger.

Network goods are unique in economic analysis. Network goods have a different type of demand curve than we have previously seen, which makes them interesting to economists. More important, because of the nature of network industries, firms that provide network goods often become monopolies in their industries and devise strategies to maintain their monopoly status. However, these seemingly unbeatable monopolies are often short-lived, as was the case with the social networking company Myspace, which had gone from the world's most popular social network to one that is now struggling to reinvent itself as a niche social network. The fleeting nature of some network monopolies raises the question of where network goods fall in the market structure analysis we introduced in Chapters 8 to 10. Are they monopolies, oligopolies, fierce competitors, or somehow a

BY THE NUMBERS

How We Are Connected Today

The importance of networks in the global economy has led to dramatic growth in network goods over the past decade, especially those that use the Internet. As network capabilities continue to expand, industries and markets will transform and people everywhere will adjust to the new way of life.

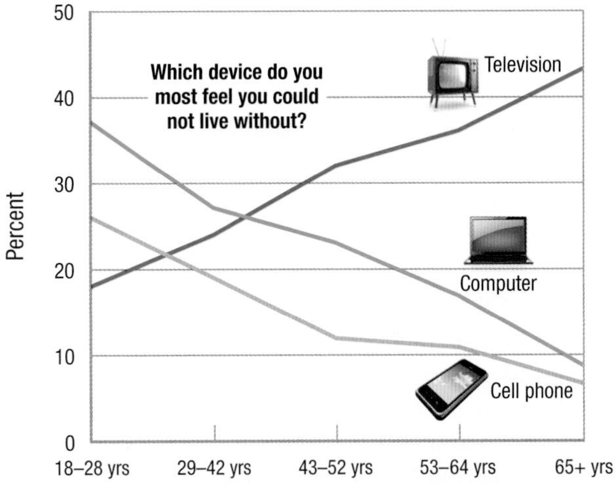

Which device can you not live without? The *New York Times* reported a study by Forrester Research that shows the device (television, computer, cell phone) people of different ages feel they are least able to live without. Older individuals still value the television the most, and younger individuals value computers and cell phones more.

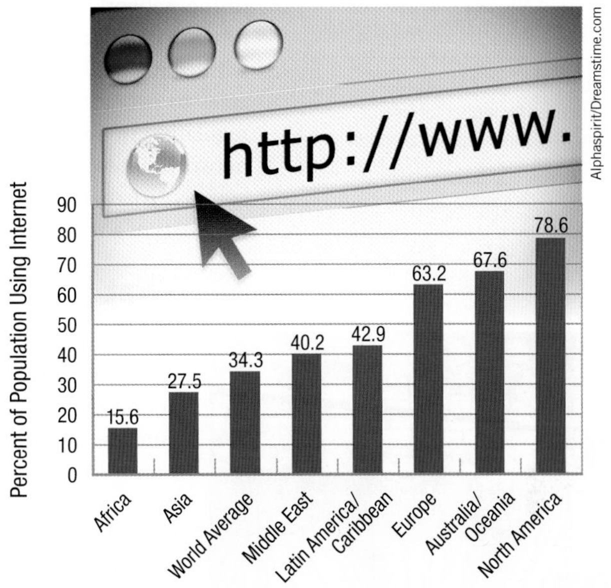

The percentage of people using the Internet as of 2012 varied significantly around the world. However, developing regions are rapidly catching up. Over the past 10 years, while the number of Internet users has doubled in the developed world, it has increased 25-fold in Africa.

500 million
Number of Google Plus users worldwide in 2013.

1.15 billion
Number of Facebook users worldwide in 2013.

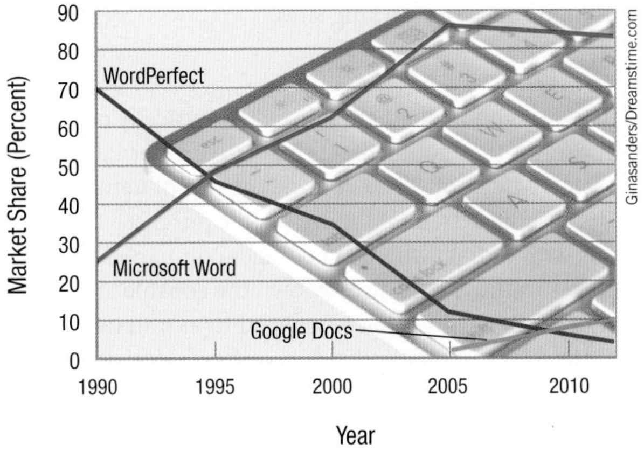

The powerful role of network effects can be seen in the rise and fall of market share for word processing software over the past two decades. In 1990, WordPerfect was the market leader, but saw its market share steadily decline as Microsoft Word became the dominant software provider. However, the recent introduction of Google Docs has begun to take some market share from Microsoft. Will we see another change in market leader in the next decade?

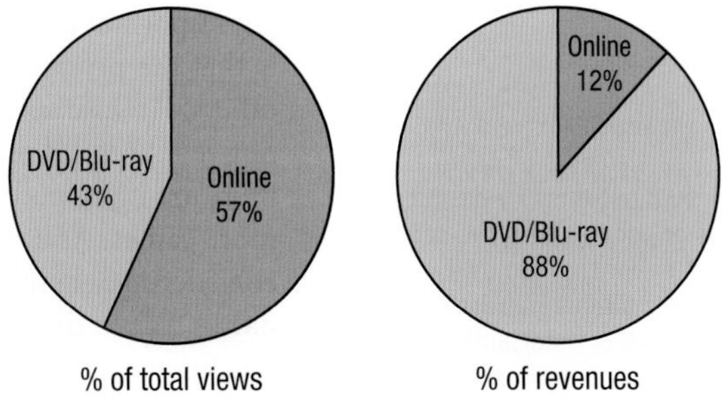

The number of online movie downloads and streaming views surpassed total DVD and Blu-ray movie unit sales for the first time in 2012. However, DVD and Blu-ray sales still generated 88% of revenues in the home-viewing movie market.

network A structure that connects various entities with one another. A network can be physical, virtual, or social.

physical network A network connected by a physical structure such as fiber optics, transportation routes, or satellites.

virtual network A network connected by groups of people using the same type or brand of good.

mixture of these market structures? Also, the market for network goods exhibits externalities, a concept studied in the previous chapter, which influence how firms allocate their resources to maximize profits.

This chapter begins by defining three types of networks and discussing the importance of network effects, a concept related to externalities. We then describe how a network demand curve is derived based on network capacity. We go on to analyze equilibrium in the network industry, and explain how networks can expand or decline quickly due to network effects, which can lead to a successful or failed network. Because of the speed with which networks can expand or decline, firms engage in a variety of competitive strategies to promote and sustain their network. Finally, we look at the role of government regulation in network industries. One example of such regulation is the requirement that networks interconnect, which allows multiple networks, no matter the size, to coexist in a competitive market. But regulation also creates costs, and the tradeoff between the benefits and costs of a regulatory policy helps to determine whether such regulations are necessary.

What Is a Network Good?

Popular Science via Getty Images

Physical networks include telecommunications cables laid across the ocean floor that connect the world. Physical networks are more expensive and less fluid than virtual or social networks.

A **network** is a type of structure that connects various entities with one another. There are three kinds of networks. First, there are **physical networks,** which are connected by fiber optics (such as a telephone network), transportation routes (such as an airline), satellites (such as a GPS network), or other physical connections. Second, there are **virtual networks,** which describe a network connected by groups of people using the same type or brand of good (such as mobile phone service, video game console, search engine, or software). Third, there are **social networks,** which combine elements of physical and virtual networks and describe groups of people using the same product or service who also are connected more directly (for business or entertainment purposes) within the network, such as through the use of "friends" on social networking sites and face-to-face networking in traditional business clubs, country clubs, or health clubs.

Types of Network Goods

A **network good** describes a type of good or service that depends on the existence of a physical network, virtual network, or social network to exist. Although network goods have existed for centuries, the Internet created an immense rise in their importance, given the increased interaction between people and the information they share with one another. Today, network goods are ubiquitous and include but are not limited to smartphones, the Internet, satellite radio, software, digital music, MP3 players, 3D televisions, and social networking sites.

Network Effects

social network A network that combines elements of physical and virtual networks by describing groups of people using the same product or service who also are connected more directly (for business or entertainment purposes) within the network.

network good A good or service that requires the existence of a physical, virtual, or social network to exist.

network externality An external benefit generated from the consumption of a network good.

An important characteristic of a network good, whether connected physically or virtually, is that the production or consumption of that good creates a positive external benefit to others. For example, owning the newest Microsoft Xbox console capable of network play is not very useful if no one else owns the same system. As more people purchase the system, there are more people to play games with online, which encourages companies to develop more games. As a result, the value rises to those who already own the console and to those considering whether to purchase one. This rise in value is referred to as a **network externality.** When this benefit is taken into account in an individual or firm's decision making, it is known as a **network effect.**

Suppose you start a new social networking site for economics majors around the country to interact with one another. Initially, the value of such a network is limited to you and a few classmates who sign up. However, with each additional user, the potential benefit expands and generates spillovers to all users. Similarly, by subscribing to Facebook, you gain access to more than a billion potential "friends" (a clear benefit to you), while you provide an external benefit (albeit quite small unless you're famous) to all 1 billion existing users.

These examples highlight an important difference between a network externality and a positive externality as described in Chapter 13. As we saw in that chapter, a person generating

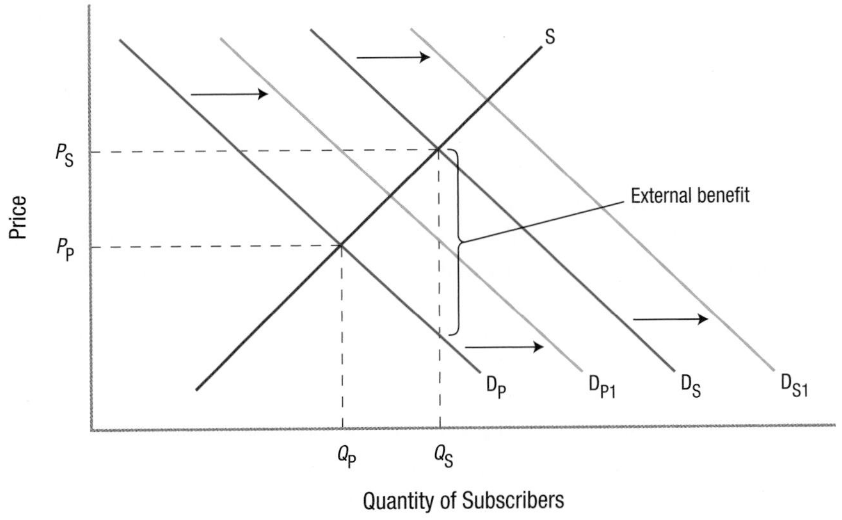

FIGURE 1

External Benefit of Consumption Pulls Private Demand Farther to the Right

Each consumer who joins a network generates an external benefit (the vertical distance between the private demand curve, D_P, and the social demand curve, D_S) enjoyed by all other people within the network. This in turn generates even more demand, shifting D_P and D_S farther to the right, to D_{P1} and D_{S1}, respectively. This effect on demand becomes smaller as more people join the network; a smaller effect is due to diminishing returns to the network externality. The same dynamic effect can work in reverse if a consumer chooses to leave the network.

a positive external benefit does not directly benefit from the externality he or she is creating. However, a network externality benefits all users, including the initial user and even potential users, because the external benefit increases the value of the overall network. This in turn generates even more demand for the network good.

network effect An external benefit generated from the consumption of a network good that is taken into account by individuals and firms in their decision making. It increases the value of a good as more people use or subscribe to a good.

Figure 1 illustrates the network effect described above. The consumer generates an external benefit equal to the vertical distance between the private demand curve, D_P, and the social demand curve, D_S. This external benefit increases the value of the overall network to its existing and potential users. The rise in the value of the network generates even more demand, as shown by the rightward shift of D_P and D_S to D_{P1} and D_{S1}, respectively. Although marginal benefit is not shown, it is important to note that external benefits are subject to diminishing returns. As a network becomes larger, an increase in demand generates fewer additional benefits to others. The benefit added by the 100th user in a new network is greater than the benefit added by the 100-millionth user.

Network effects also can work in reverse. When a consumer leaves a network, the value of the network is reduced to all remaining users, which may lead to a larger leftward shift in demand than is warranted by the loss of only one user. Note that this is not the same as a negative externality, which *imposes a cost* on others and causes the supply curve to shift to the left. In the present case, leaving a network *removes the external benefit* that had been provided to others. The dynamic nature of how network effects influence the demand for network goods affects how a network demand curve is derived.

CHECKPOINT

WHAT IS A NETWORK GOOD?

- Networks can be categorized into physical networks, virtual networks, and social networks.
- A network good is a good whose demand depends on the existence of a physical, virtual, or social network.
- Network externalities are generated when the consumption and/or production of a good leads to additional benefits to all existing users of a good. Taking away these externalities leads to diminished benefits but does not add a cost.
- When network externalities are taken into account in an individual or firm's decision making, they are referred to as network effects. Network effects can lead to a larger rise or a larger decline in demand than would occur in a nonnetwork industry.

QUESTION: Suppose your best friend purchases a new high-tech laptop that allows users to work simultaneously on the same software file. How might your friend's purchase lead to a network effect that generates additional demand?

Answers to the Checkpoint question can be found at the end of this chapter.

Demand Curve for a Network Good

network demand curve A demand curve for a good or service that experiences a network effect, causing it to slope upward at lower quantities before sloping downward once the market matures.

Because the value of network goods is influenced by external benefits, a demand curve for a network good does not look like a typical downward-sloping demand curve. A **network demand curve** reflects the fact that the value of the good initially rises as more people purchase or subscribe to the good, which means that the demand curve has an upward-sloping portion at lower quantities. A general model of demand for network goods is described next.[1]

Demand for a Fixed Capacity Network Good

The model for a network demand curve makes two important assumptions. First, the model assumes that the short-run supply curve is limited to the capacity of the firm's fixed investment, and therefore is vertical. For example, a new entrant in the airline industry starts off with just a few planes, and therefore the number of customers it can serve is fixed until it expands by purchasing more planes. Further, an airline must expand in large increments (that is, it must buy a new airplane that can serve hundreds of passengers a day), rather than by small increments, such as when a baker decides whether to make one more cake. Second, the model assumes that there is a short-run demand curve corresponding to each vertical supply curve that reflects the higher value of a larger network due to network externalities. These assumptions make the analysis easier but do not change the conclusions.

Figure 2 shows how a network market demand curve is developed. We start with a small network with a capacity of Q_0, where demand is small and price (P_0) is determined by the intersection of a vertical supply curve S_0 at Q_0 and demand D_0 for that capacity. As the network expands (supply shifts to the right by an increment to S_1), demand increases because the value to existing and new users increases. This is shown by the

FIGURE 2

A Small Network with Fixed Capacity

A small network has a fixed capacity of Q_0, resulting in a vertical supply curve, S_0. The intersection of S_0 and D_0 results in an equilibrium price of P_0. As the network expands to S_1, the value to existing and new users increases due to network effects causing the demand curve to pivot to D_1. The intersection of S_1 and D_1 leads to a higher equilibrium price of P_1. This differs from a market for a nonnetwork good, in which an increase in supply leads to a lower price.

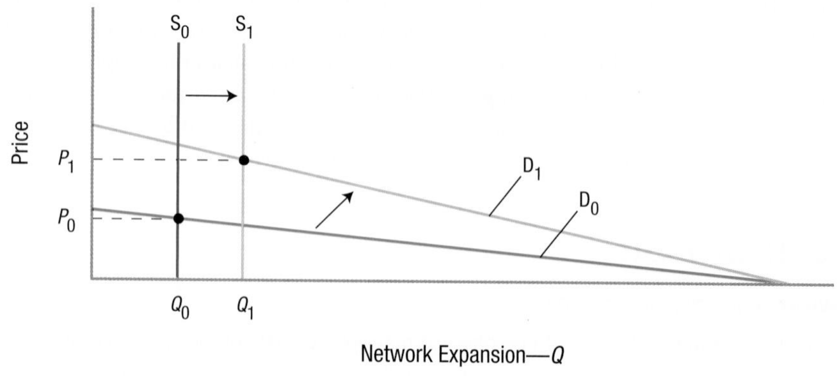

[1] This model is discussed in greater detail in Nicholas Economides, "The Economics of Networks," *International Journal of Industrial Organization,* 1996.

demand curve pivoting higher to D_1 (while intersecting the horizontal axis at the same point as D_0 to indicate a maximum demand for the network good) and reflecting a higher value to initial users and a higher market price at P_1. This differs from a market for a nonnetwork good, in which an increase in supply would not result in an increase in demand. For a nonnetwork good, the increase in supply would lead to a lower price on the demand curve.

Deriving the Full Network Demand Curve

Network effects are strongest in the early stages of a network good's development, as each additional consumer increases the marginal benefit to all consumers of the good. However, this network effect is always opposed by the law of demand we learned in Chapter 3: As price rises, quantity demanded falls. Which effect predominates?

When the quantity of a good provided on the market increases (without any change in demand), the price must fall in order for the market to clear. But the existence of network externalities causes demand to increase when a network expands, allowing prices to rise. Because the price effect and the network effect work in opposition to one another, the market price for a network good depends on which effect is stronger. For most network goods, the network effect dominates the price effect for small quantities, resulting in an upward-sloping portion of the network demand curve, as shown in Figure 3.

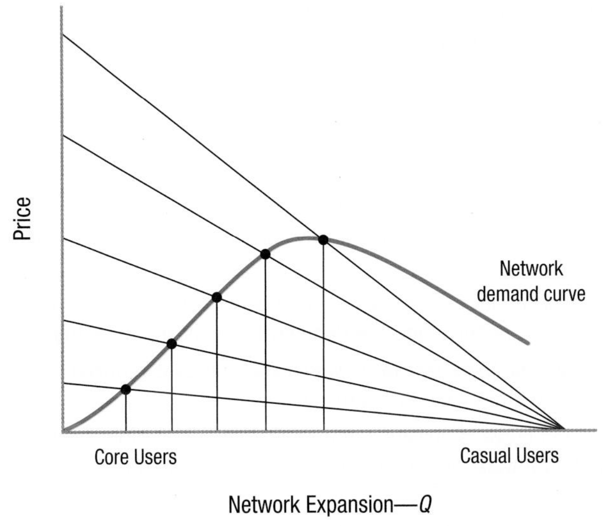

FIGURE 3

A Network Market Demand Curve

Network goods initially have an upward-sloping demand curve as core users build the network by attracting others to buy the good. Once the market matures, a network demand curve becomes downward-sloping as casual users buy the good when the price drops.

As the network expands along the upward-sloping portion of the network demand curve, the price increases as more **core users**—those who benefit most from consuming the good—purchase the good. The demand curve slopes upward as the network effect (which shifts demand to the right as quantity increases, increasing the price) dominates the price effect of an increase in quantity (which reduces the price).

core user A consumer who has a very high willingness to pay for a new product or service and is among the first to purchase it.

As the market for a network good grows and reaches a critical number of consumers to support the network, additional consumers add fewer external benefits due to diminishing returns. These consumers who purchase the network good after it matures are called **casual users** (think of your grandmother buying an iPad only after everyone else in the family has one). Once a network good reaches this stage, the network demand curve slopes downward as the price effect (from the increase in supply due to lower production costs) dominates the network effect.

casual user A consumer who purchases a good only after the good has matured in the market and is more sensitive to price.

By connecting all of the intersections of demand and supply, a network demand curve is generated, which slopes upward from the origin as core users increase the value of the good and then slopes downward once the product matures and casual users buy the good.

Examples of Network Demand Curve Pricing in Our Daily Lives

Jason Kempin/Getty Images

Justin Timberlake allowed his album, *The 20/20 Experience,* to stream online on numerous Web sites, including Spotify and Rdio, at no charge. The album generated a tremendous network effect that helped it sell nearly 1 million *paid* album downloads in its first week of official release in 2013.

What does the presence of a network demand curve mean for prices? It suggests that as a new network good is introduced, the price is kept low to attract new users. As the number of users increases, prices rise because people are willing to pay more for a network good used by more people. Prices continue to rise until the good matures, at which point prices must fall in order to sell a greater quantity.

Consider the following example: When Google launched in 1998, the search engine results displayed were quite bare—no ads, no preferred listings; the cost to use Google was essentially zero. However, as the number of users increased, Google began "charging" people to use the service by placing ads and suggested links alongside the search results. Although not a monetary cost, users pay an opportunity cost when viewing ads.

Another example of network demand curve pricing is a new rock band attempting to gain recognition by initially playing for nothing at local clubs, and/or offering their music free online. Once the band becomes better known, it begins charging for shows and for music downloads. Eventually, a downward-sloping demand curve will return, in which case lower prices are needed to increase quantity demanded. A similar effect can occur when an established musical artist prepares to release a new album. These examples demonstrate the upward- and downward-sloping nature of network demand curves.

CHECKPOINT

DEMAND CURVE FOR A NETWORK GOOD

- The production of network goods is typically carried out in large increments due to high fixed capital costs.
- The short-run equilibrium for a network good occurs at the intersection of a fixed capacity vertical supply curve and the demand curve for that quantity.
- As a network expands, the effect of network externalities is reduced due to diminishing returns as the price effect becomes stronger.
- A network demand curve is upward sloping for smaller quantities (when network effects are strong) and downward sloping for larger quantities (when the network good matures and network effects weaken).
- A network demand curve reflects the role that core users (represented on the upward-sloping portion of the curve) have in building the value of the network.

QUESTION: Why does a network demand curve slope upward for small quantities of a good, then slope downward for higher quantities?

Answers to the Checkpoint question can be found at the end of this chapter.

Market Equilibrium for a Network Good

Now that we have learned how a network demand curve is developed, we can study how market equilibrium is reached in this type of industry. The market equilibrium for a network good occurs once most network effects are realized. Therefore, equilibrium generally is found on the downward-sloping portion of the network demand curve. However, not all network goods reach market equilibrium. As we will soon see, network goods can thrive or fail over a short period of time, making market equilibrium difficult both to achieve and to sustain.

tipping point (or **critical mass**) The quantity from which network effects are strong enough to support the network.

Economies of Scale and Marginal Cost

An important characteristic of network goods is that they generally require a very large fixed cost to produce. Fixed costs can include the cost of writing and producing a new hit song, or the huge cost of building cell phone towers across the country. In Chapters 9 and 10, we saw how monopolies and oligopolies can form when industries exhibit high fixed costs and low marginal costs. Network goods are an excellent example of goods produced in such industries, for once a song is produced or a cell phone tower is built, the cost to serve customers (a firm's marginal cost) is minimal. An outcome from this type of industry is large economies of scale.

Finding an Equilibrium in the Market for Network Goods

Let's assume that the marginal cost of a network good is fixed at P_1, as shown in Figure 4. The equilibrium is point *d*, the intersection of the downward-sloping portion of the network demand curve and the marginal cost curve. To achieve equilibrium, the network for that good must expand from the origin to point *b*, which is called the **tipping point** (or **critical mass**), the quantity from which network effects are strong enough to continue building the network.

virtuous cycle The point at which a network good reaches its tipping point, when network effects cause demand for the good to increase on its own. As more people buy or subscribe to a good or service, it generates even more external benefits and more demand.

vicious cycle When a network good does not reach its tipping point, and therefore does not increase in value enough to retain its customers, customers leave the network, thereby further diminishing the value of the good until all customers leave the network.

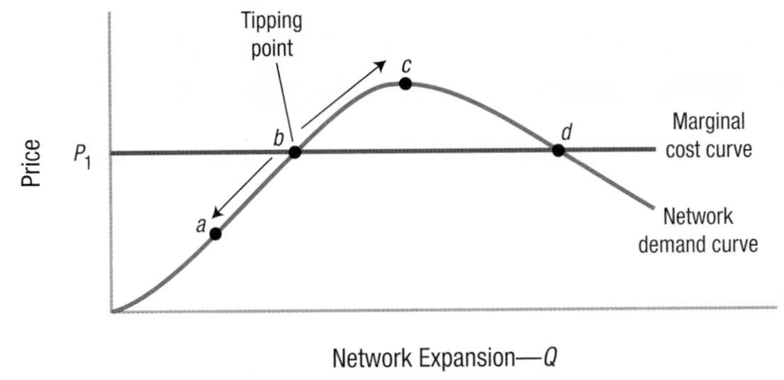

FIGURE 4

Equilibrium in a Market for Network Goods

Point *b* represents the tipping point—the point at which the network has achieved enough momentum to continue expanding until it reaches point *d* (an equilibrium created by a virtuous cycle). However, if a market fails to reach point *b*, a vicious cycle may result, leading to a collapse in market share.

Once a network reaches point *b*, the existence of network effects will continue to generate more demand, allowing the network to expand on its own until it reaches equilibrium at point *d*. This is referred to as a **virtuous cycle,** in which network effects push demand farther to the right, creating even more value for the network.

However, if a network good fails to reach point *b*, or if a new competing network good causes demand to move to a point left of point *b*, a **vicious cycle** can result. In a vicious cycle, people stop consuming a product or service, thereby reducing the value of the product to others, which causes even more people to avoid consuming the good. The result is typically a failed product, shown as a good at point *a* in Figure 4.

An example of a product entering a vicious cycle was the HD DVD format introduced by Toshiba in 2006. Toshiba competed vigorously for market share against Sony's Blu-ray format, but because Toshiba did not reach a critical mass, studios stopped offering their movies in HD DVD format, leading to a vicious cycle and the discontinuation of the format in 2008. Interestingly, several years later Blu-ray entered its own vicious cycle as online streaming of movies made physical media less relevant, leading to fewer movie offerings in Blu-ray format and a steep drop in sales.

Jkirsh/Dreamstime.com

A long line of core users waiting to buy a new product can propel a network good into a virtuous cycle.

Note how the network demand curve slopes upward to point *c*, then downward. What explains this change in slope? Point *c* represents the point of product maturity, when the network effect no longer dominates the price effect. Remember that a demand curve slopes downward due to a price effect—it requires a lower price for people to consume more. However, network effects counter the price effect by raising the value of the good as consumers buy more. At point *c*, the network effect and price effect are equal in magnitude. Thus, the upward-sloping segment represents core users who are less price sensitive, and the downward-sloping segment represents casual users who are more price sensitive.

Networks Goods Can Face a Virtuous Cycle or a Vicious Cycle Very Quickly

The speed at which network effects can influence the success or failure of a product or service can be remarkably fast. As shown in Figure 4, once a firm enters a vicious cycle by moving down the network demand curve to the left of point *b*, it is often difficult to stop the cycle. Meanwhile, firms entering virtuous cycles enjoy what seems to be limitless growth over a very short period.

Table 1 provides examples of network goods that experienced a change in market leader at some point over the last two decades. In some cases the change was gradual (such as the transition from film to digital, because ardent film photographers took many years to make the switch to digital), whereas in other cases the change was almost instantaneous (such as that from the HP Mini to the Apple iPad).

TABLE 1 Examples of Network Goods Facing Virtuous and Vicious Cycles

Industry	Previous Market Leaders	Current Market Leader
Social networking	Friendster (2002–2004) Myspace (2005–2008)	Facebook (2009–)
Internet search engines	AltaVista (1997–2002)	Google (2003–)
Word processing software	WordPerfect (1980–1996)	Microsoft Word (1997–)
Video game consoles	Sega Genesis (1990–1994) PlayStation 1 and 2 (1995–2007) Nintendo Wii (2008–2011)	Microsoft Xbox 360 (2012–)
Internet browsers	Netscape (1995–1998)	Internet Explorer (1999–)
Internet service providers	Prodigy (1991–1994) America Online (1995–2003)	AT&T DSL (2004–)
Photography	Kodak (film) (1936–2004)	Canon (digital) (2005–)
Smartphones	Blackberry (2003–2010)	Apple iPhone (2011–)
Home printers	Epson (dot matrix) (1979–1995)	HP (inkjet/laser) (1996–)
Tablets/netbooks	HP Mini (2008–2009)	Apple iPad (2010–)

Interestingly, the quality of a network good is not always the most important factor in determining the market leader in a network industry. Because network effects are so powerful, consumers sometimes choose an inferior product that many people use over a superior product that fewer people use. For example, some video game enthusiasts claim that Sony's PlayStation 3 is superior in graphics and capabilities to Nintendo's Wii. Yet, the Wii system held its position as market leader for four years, partly due to its lower price but also due to a virtuous cycle it had enjoyed until Microsoft's Xbox 360 took over as the new market leader.

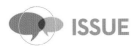

ISSUE

The Broadband Effect: Virtuous and Vicious Cycles in Network Goods

Most Americans rely on broadband Internet connections for work, school, or entertainment. Over 66% of U.S. households in 2012 had a broadband connection, up from just 11% in 2002. Part of this dramatic rise in broadband connectivity has been the result of government efforts to promote broadband usage in all areas of the country, especially in rural areas where it is costly to establish broadband connections.

In 2010, the U.S. Federal Communications Commission (FCC) established the Connect America Fund to promote the goal of ensuring that every household has access to broadband capability. This fund consists of fees collected from all broadband users nationwide and is used to subsidize service in high cost areas such as rural and mountainous communities. The FCC lists the social benefits of such an effort as including improved education, health care, public safety, and civic engagement in rural areas. These ultimately benefit the entire nation.

No doubt, the near universal use of broadband has resulted in significant changes to network industries. For example, network services such as movie and live television streaming, online conferencing, worldwide telecommunications via Skype and other online providers, and instant music and software downloads were all either previously unavailable or excruciatingly time-consuming to use prior to broadband. These services experienced a virtuous cycle as more and more consumers gain access to faster Internet connections, leading to a validation of Metcalfe's Law, which states that the value of a telecommunications network increases exponentially with the number of users.

But not all industries fared well with the rise in broadband usage. Some markets faced a vicious cycle as consumers moved away from certain network goods. These include traditional international

Danieloizo/Dreamstime.com

calling, calling cards, and prepaid phones. Beyond telecommunications, broadband also contributed to the demise of most physical DVD and game rental stores, CD music stores, and software stores, as all of these services can now be obtained online.

Like all industries, goods come and go, and network goods are no different. What is remarkable is how quickly this transformation took place over the last decade. How today's network goods fare in the future will be an interesting question to examine as technological improvements continue to change the way we live.

Because of the speed at which market demand for network goods can occur, no firm is ever "safe" with its market share. Aware of this, businesses often engage in various competitive strategies to increase or secure their market shares. The next section describes some of these strategies.

CHECKPOINT

MARKET EQUILIBRIUM FOR A NETWORK GOOD

- Network goods generally exhibit large economies of scale due to their high fixed costs and low marginal costs of production.
- A network good must reach its tipping point (or critical mass) to enter a virtuous cycle in which network effects generate additional demand until equilibrium is reached.
- Network goods that do not reach their tipping point enter into a vicious cycle, leading to a sharp decline in market share and likely failure of the good.
- Network goods can enter virtuous or vicious cycles in a very short period, such that no good is ever safe from rapid decline.

QUESTION: In 2003, Myspace entered the market and quickly became the world's most popular social networking site. In 2006, with more than 100 million subscribers, Myspace appeared destined to be a successful company over the long run. Enter Facebook, which had been introduced two years earlier as a niche social networking site for college students. Facebook quickly expanded beyond college students to target all consumer markets, and by 2009 Facebook surpassed Myspace, which has since seen a steady decline in subscribers. How does the network demand curve explain the speed at which Myspace rose to prominence and then fell to relative obscurity?

Answers to the Checkpoint question can be found at the end of this chapter.

Competition and Market Structure for Network Goods

The network goods industry provides opportunities for firms to gain substantial market power. Such opportunities often lead to intense competition. A recent example of competition in network goods was the market for high-speed home Internet service between DSL providers (such as AT&T) and cable Internet providers (such as Comcast). With a majority of U.S. households having switched from dial-up Internet services to high-speed providers in the past decade, the race to become the dominant provider was critical to AT&T and Comcast.

AT&T focused on bundling strategies with their U-verse program that incorporates home phone, digital television, and high-speed Internet for one price. Comcast, in addition to their Xfinity program that bundles television, home phone, and Internet, invested heavily in television advertising featuring the Slowskys, a turtle couple that had an aversion to anything fast and was used as a metaphor for DSL-service speed.

This section describes some of the common strategies used to protect network goods from entering a vicious cycle or to increase the likelihood of entering a virtuous cycle. Undoubtedly, as a consumer, you encounter many of these marketing strategies when making decisions about which network goods to purchase. The goal of firms using these strategies is to attract you to their product and to keep you as a customer for a long time.

teaser strategies Attractive up-front deals used as an incentive to entice new customers into a network.

switching cost A cost imposed on consumers when they change products or subscribe to a new network.

Competition and Pricing Strategies

Network goods are characterized as having high fixed costs with low marginal costs. Further, network effects can cause some firms to flourish while causing others to fail, even when little or no quality differences exist between the firms' products. The determinant of market success is not always dependent on the quality of the good, but rather on competitive strategies to capture market share. Low marginal costs means it does not cost much to serve customers once they are committed to a product. Therefore, firms spend significant sums of money to gain new customers and use various strategies to keep existing customers. These strategies include teaser strategies, lock-in strategies, and market segmentation (such as product differentiation and price discrimination).

Wd2007/Dreamstime.com

Zero percent interest lending rate deals abound to attract new customers, but beware, they do not last for long!

Capturing New Customers Using Teaser Strategies **Teaser strategies** are used by firms to gain new customers by offering various sign-up incentives and/or low prices for a short introductory period. Examples of teaser deals include wireless companies offering a free or highly discounted phone when purchasing a two-year wireless plan, cable companies offering six months of free cable or Internet service, banks offering 0% finance charges for a limited time when opening a new credit card account, online music companies offering new customers fifty free music downloads, and software companies allowing new users to sample their products with a 30-day free trial.

Why do companies offer such great deals to new customers? Unlike decisions for non-network goods, such as which brand of cereal to buy—a decision that is relatively easy to switch back and forth—purchasing a network good typically requires a long-term commitment. This can be due to a legal commitment, such as a one- or two-year contract, or it can be due to nonmonetary costs of switching from one product to another.

Have you ever had to switch from a software program that you have used for many years? Once you learn how to use a particular software program or once you are accustomed to a certain email program, it can be a hassle to switch to another. These **switching costs,** which include monetary and nonmonetary costs of switching from one good to another, often are substantial for network goods. Therefore, to provide incentives for consumers to incur these costs to switch, firms must offer attractive up-front deals.

Retaining Existing Customers Using Lock-In Strategies In addition to offering teaser deals to entice new customers, firms also employ strategies to keep existing customers from leaving. **Lock-in strategies** occur after a customer adopts a product, and typically involve the firm engaging in strategies that raise the switching costs of consumers, thereby increasing the likelihood of retaining the customer.

Switching costs include the hassle of learning a new format and its features, dealing with the loss of other features one has become accustomed to, and so forth. In some cases, switching costs may be minimal or offset by benefits; for example, the excitement of purchasing the latest smartphone or computer may outweigh the switching costs of learning how to use it. But consumers generally do not like changing network goods once they are accustomed to one brand.

Common examples of lock-in strategies include the offering of loyalty programs, which reward consumers the more they use or the longer they stay with a company's products. Lock-in strategies also include preventing certain features from being transferred to another product, such as a phone's contact list or saved text messages.

lock-in strategies Techniques used by firms to raise the switching costs for its customers, making it less attractive to leave the network.

market segmentation A strategy of making a single good in different versions to target different consumer markets with varying prices.

versioning A pricing strategy that involves differentiating a good by way of packaging into multiple products for people with different demands.

Using Market Segmentation to Maximize Profits In Chapters 9 and 10, we saw how market power can reduce the elasticity of demand for a firm's product and increase potential profits of monopolies and monopolistically competitive firms. We draw from those analyses by studying how **market segmentation** strategies can be used to increase market share and profits in the market for network goods. Market segmentation is achieved when firms can differentiate their products in a way that allows similar goods to be priced differently to different groups of consumers. In other words, it allows firms to price discriminate, which increases producer surplus (as discussed in Chapter 9).

Because network goods generally have a low marginal cost of production, firms have greater flexibility in segmenting their products to allow for a greater range of prices, each targeting a different subset of the market. Market segmentation strategies in network goods include versioning, intertemporal pricing, peak-load pricing, and bundling strategies.

Versioning refers to pricing strategies that involve differentiating a good by way of packaging it into multiple products for people with different needs. A common

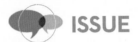

ISSUE

Do Exclusive Marketing Deals Lock In Customers?

Competition among telecommunication providers has flourished since 1984, when the U.S. government forced AT&T, which at the time was the monopoly provider of about 80% of all telephone services, to break apart into seven regional companies and a long-distance company, and to allow competition in long-distance service. Almost immediately, long-distance companies MCI and Sprint began offering long-distance services equal to AT&T's services, and competing vigorously against AT&T for customers. In the 1990s, competition among these three carriers involved advertising in the form of nearly endless sales calls to people's homes, often during dinnertime, which eventually led to the creation of "Do Not Call" registries.

Stewart Cohen/Pam Ostrow/Blend Images/Corbis

Seemingly nonstop telemarketing calls, many from telephone service providers, led to the creation of "Do Not Call" registries and forced firms to find new sales strategies.

Today, competition among wireless carriers is as intense as competition among long-distance carriers was in the 1990s. But with limitations on advertising via sales calls, companies such as Verizon, AT&T, Sprint, and T-Mobile have turned to attractive teaser deals and exclusive phone arrangements with phone makers to offer the newest models of phones only with one wireless provider.

The use of teaser and lock-in strategies (such as preventing a person from keeping his or her phone when transferring wireless service to another provider) represents a new form of competition among network goods providers.

Is this competitive approach better than advertising? On the one hand, consumers today are not bombarded with telephone sales calls as they were in the 1990s, but on the other hand, the ability to switch from one provider to another has taken on additional switching costs.

example is the choice of a wireless plan. Do you choose an unlimited monthly plan, a fixed-minute monthly plan, or a prepaid plan? A single firm can offer each of these plans and price each plan to attract the appropriate subset of customers.

intertemporal pricing A type of versioning in which goods are differentiated by the level of patience of consumers. Less patient consumers pay a higher price than more patient consumers.

A similar but slightly different strategy is **intertemporal pricing.** Like versioning, a firm uses intertemporal pricing strategies to target different groups of consumers by differentiating their product, but in this case, by time. Specifically, they use the fact that some consumers are more impatient than others to buy a product. For example, new books often first appear in bookstores as expensive hardcover editions, then as less expensive paperbacks several months later, followed by the availability of the book for loan from public libraries at no cost for the most patient consumers.

Another example of intertemporal pricing shown in Table 2 is the release of a new movie. A new movie first appears in theaters, followed by on-demand or pay-per-view, then via paid online streaming or DVD rental, then on premium movie channels, and lastly on network TV. With each step, the price to view the movie generally decreases.

TABLE 2 Intertemporal Pricing of a New Movie

Movie Format	Average Wait Time from Movie Release	Approximate Cost to View
Movie theater	Immediate	$10 per person
On-demand/pay-per-view	2 to 3 months	$10 per group of viewers
Paid streaming/DVD rental	6 to 9 months	$5 per group of viewers
Premium channels	6 months to 1 year	Cost of channel subscription
Network TV/Free streaming	1 year or longer	Free (basic TV or Internet access)

Firms that successfully use versioning and intertemporal pricing can price discriminate among consumers by charging less patient consumers, who have lower elasticities of demand, higher prices than those consumers with more patience and higher elasticities of demand. Once consumers with less elastic demand are served, the price is dropped to serve those with more elastic demand. The firm earns more profit by versioning products using time as the differentiating factor.

peak-load pricing A versioning strategy of pricing a product higher during periods of higher demand, and lower during periods of lower demand.

Peak-load pricing focuses less on differentiating a product than it does on charging higher prices when there is greater demand for the product. For example, ticket prices for evening movies and Broadway shows typically are higher than prices for matinees. Most wireless plans come with free or highly discounted evening and weekend usage. And airlines typically charge less for tickets on the nonpeak travel days of Tuesday, Wednesday, and Saturday. Similar to versioning and intertemporal pricing, the use of peak-load pricing attempts to segment the market into consumers with less flexible demand and those with more flexible demand.

Figure 5 illustrates a market with peak-load pricing, where P_P represents the higher prices charged during peak times when demand D_P is greater, whereas P_O is the lower price charged during off-peak times when demand D_O is lower.

bundling A strategy of packaging several products into a single product with a single price. Bundling allows firms to capture customers of related products by making it more attractive to use the same firm's products.

Finally, network industries engage in **bundling** strategies to increase demand for related products. Because network goods generally have low marginal costs to produce, it does not cost the firm much to package several products together. Customers who purchase one product are then more likely to use other products from the same company, thus supporting the firm's network and the value of all its goods. One example is Apple's strategy of bundling many types of software into its Mac operating system. Bundled programs such as Safari, iMovie, iPhoto, iTunes,

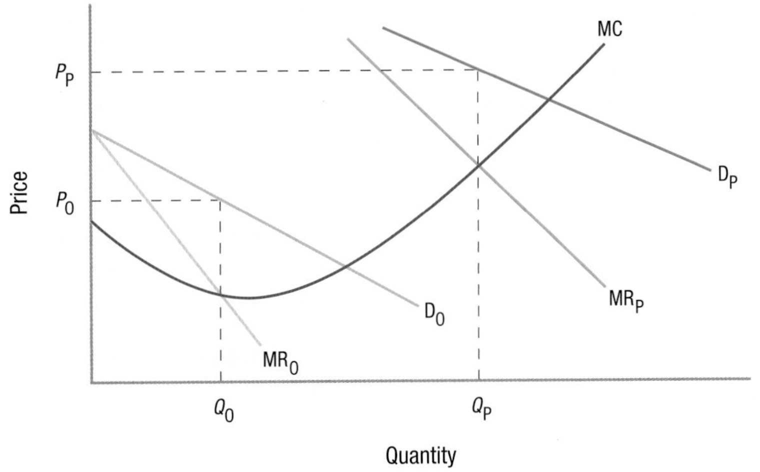

FIGURE 5

Peak-Load Pricing

Demand curve D_P represents a greater demand during peak periods, leading to an optimal price of P_P. During off-peak times, demand D_0 is much lower, leading to a lower price of P_0. Peak-load pricing can occur by time of day (telephone calls, live shows, movies), by day of the week (airline tickets), or by season (ski lift tickets).

and Garage Band provide users with convenient "free" options, thereby reducing the need to use other network providers (such as Adobe and Real), which sell competing media products.

CHECKPOINT

COMPETITION AND MARKET STRUCTURE FOR NETWORK GOODS

- Competition for market share in network goods is often intense as firms attempt to avoid the vicious cycle of a failed network good.
- Teaser strategies include attractive up-front savings to customers willing to switch to another network good provider, while lock-in strategies are used to make it more costly to leave a network good provider.
- Market segmentation involves separating consumers based on their elasticity of demand, with less patient consumers (those with inelastic demands) paying more than patient consumers with elastic demands.
- Versioning is the practice of differentiating a good into multiple products from which consumers can choose. Versioning also can be done by time (intertemporal pricing) or by peak usage (peak-load pricing).
- Firms bundle their goods because the marginal cost of adding additional products is minimal and the benefit from network effects is high if consumers use the included products instead of purchasing them separately from competing firms.

QUESTIONS: Why would a firm selling a network good choose to segment its customers by charging different prices? Wouldn't it make more money by just charging everyone a high price?

Answers to the Checkpoint questions can be found at the end of this chapter.

Should Network Goods Be Regulated?

In a market where firms compete to become the dominant provider, whether as a monopolist or an oligopolist, firms use strategies to strengthen and maintain their market power. In such a market, government must assess the effects of these strategies on consumers. Unlike other firms with market power, those producing network goods face the continuing threat that a new network good might lead them into a vicious cycle. Therefore, competition can exist even when a network good is dominated by a single firm. This brings about the important question of whether or not government should regulate these firms.

Microsoft's market dominance with their Windows operating system, office-suite products (Office), and email and Internet programs (Outlook and Explorer), led the U.S. Department of

Justice, along with governments in the European Union, to investigate whether this dominance was achieved fairly. Specifically, some question Microsoft's bundling tactics, which make it convenient (perhaps too convenient) to adopt its related products once one product is purchased.

The government generally aims to ensure that competition for network goods leads to low prices for consumers, ample choices, and improvements in quality. However, government also must ensure that regulations do not impede productivity or create burdensome costs to firms. Just because a firm is a monopoly does not mean it doesn't face the threat of competition, which can keep firms from exploiting their market power.

One way to promote a competitive environment for network goods is not to break up monopolies, but rather to ensure that firms are prevented from securing exclusive access to a set of consumers. One such regulatory policy is to require interconnection.

Promoting Network Competition with Interconnection

industry standard A common format that is used, for example, in televisions, in digital recorders, or in software programs.

essential facility An input that is needed to produce a product or to allow a person to consume a product.

interconnection The physical linking of a network to another network's essential facilities. Interconnection promotes competition by ensuring that no firm has exclusive access to a set of customers.

Many types of network goods include industry standards or essential facilities. An **industry standard** is a common format that is used, for example, in televisions, in digital recorders, and in software programs. **Essential facilities** are inputs that are needed to produce a product or to allow a person to consume a product. **Interconnection,** the physical linking of a network to another network's essential facilities, helps to promote competition in situations in which firms are able to use their market power to block competitors from entering the industry. When interconnection is required, firms must allow competing providers access to their networks. As discussed in the chapter opener, a Verizon customer, for example, must be able to make a call to an AT&T customer in order for multiple networks to operate efficiently in the same market. For such calls to be possible, they must travel across networks owned by different firms.

Consider the incredible arrangement of networks required to make a telephone call to a friend in another country. To complete this call, parties must work together, starting with a wireless provider or local telephone provider (called a local exchange carrier), connecting to the distance call provider, then the network provider interconnecting to the foreign network operator, and finally connecting to the friend's local exchange carrier. Even more amazing is how the cost of this service has fallen dramatically over the years. How is this possible? We looked at the role of network effects, network competition, and interconnection to explain how competing networks are able to provide efficient and seamless service that in the past could only be possible via large natural monopolies. What is more important is the degree to which global markets are dependent on network technologies that did not exist 15 years ago—technologies that we often take for granted today.

An important role of regulation in network goods is to ensure that providers of essential facilities allow access to competing firms. The most common example of an essential facility is the phone line in your house. Prior to 1984, AT&T owned about 80% of all of these phone lines, and could effectively prevent any competitor from offering phone service because rival firms would not be able to complete a call without access to your (i.e., AT&T's) phone line. In 1984, the U.S. government forced AT&T to break up into smaller firms, and eventually forced these firms to open their networks to competition, paving the way for both land-based and wireless providers to enter the market. The effect on prices was substantial. If you watch an old TV show from the 1970s or early 1980s, you may catch some interesting scenes in which characters make a big deal about calling long distance. Today we don't think twice about calling long distance, or even making international calls. In fact, long-distance calling has lost its identity as a market, leading to the demise of many long-distance companies.

Industry Standards and Network Compatibility

A common issue with network goods is that firms tend to compete vigorously (leading to standards wars) to become the industry standard, thereby "owning" the network. A consequence of this competition is that firms spend large sums of money on marketing strategies to dominate the market (to become a monopoly) rather than to achieve productivity gains and cost reductions typical of more competitive markets. Network compatibility allows competing standards to coexist in a market by ensuring that media can be used on competing formats. For example, a spreadsheet can be shared by a person using a Windows computer and someone using a Mac computer. And the spreadsheet itself can be edited using either Microsoft Excel or Google Docs.

Does Interconnection Improve Efficiency in Network Industries?

A common theme throughout the market structure discussions in Chapters 8 through 10 is that competitive markets generate more consumer surplus than monopoly markets. Further, firms with market power generate deadweight loss. In network industries where monopolies can be created if network effects are strong, interconnection can bring about gains to society by facilitating competition and reducing deadweight loss.

In the long run, interconnection creates a more competitive environment that forces firms to be more efficient, leading to reduced costs. Yet, a more competitive market might limit the network effects and economies of scale that exist with fewer firms. Therefore, implementing regulation to promote competition involves a tradeoff between benefits and costs. In fact, the potential costs of regulation can even exceed the benefits.

Can Poor Regulation Be Worse Than No Regulation?

Throughout this section, it was argued that regulation can promote competition by preventing firms from exploiting their access to essential facilities. However, the benefits of network effects most likely contributed to a firm's dominance in the market. For example, although we enjoy having our choice of wireless carriers, which is a benefit from regulation, such choices do not come without cost.

As discussed in the Issue in the previous section, competition for exclusive contracts with phone makers has made it difficult to use certain providers with certain phones. A similar situation arises in sports broadcasting, in which television networks sign contracts with sports organizations to be the sole broadcaster of games to viewers (such as ESPN's exclusive right to broadcast *Monday Night Football*). Although these cases create minor burdens, other forms of regulation intended to protect consumers have led to major disasters.

The California electricity crisis of 2000–2001 is one such example of poor regulation of a network good. Although the initial objective of placing a price cap (a price ceiling) on electricity prices was to keep prices from rising too rapidly for consumers, it quickly led to strategic responses by producers. Because producers could not raise prices in California to compensate for rising input prices, many firms instead chose to reduce the quantity of electricity provided, creating a huge shortage of electricity. Ultimately, the price ceiling led to massive blackouts and much inconvenience to individuals and businesses for several months.

When determining whether network goods should be regulated or not, the benefits and costs of each policy must be evaluated to determine whether it would be best to implement the policy or to just leave the market alone. In many situations, such as with the California electricity price cap, life might have been brighter (pun intended) without regulation.

CHECKPOINT

SHOULD NETWORK GOODS BE REGULATED?

- The purpose of regulatory policy is to promote a competitive market that will lead to more consumer choices and lower prices.
- One common form of regulation is requiring network providers to allow interconnection with their competitors—that is, allowing access to each other's network and essential facilities.
- Industry standards can lead to intense competition when competing firms attempt to become the dominant standard; however, network compatibility allows competing industry standards to coexist in a market.
- Interconnection facilitates competition and generally improves efficiency by forcing firms to be more productive and cost-effective.
- The costs of regulation, especially poor regulation, can be substantial and can exceed its potential benefits. Any regulatory policy should be evaluated based on the tradeoff between its benefits and costs.

QUESTIONS: The Apple iPod, iPhone, and iPad all serve as MP3 devices that allow individuals to play music that can be downloaded using Apple's iTunes music store and many other music providers. Why is an MP3 player considered an essential facility for playing music? Would regulatory policy ever be needed to prevent Apple from exploiting its essential facility?

Answers to the Checkpoint questions can be found at the end of this chapter.

chapter summary

Section 1: What Is a Network Good?

Networks can consist of physical, virtual, or social networks.

Network goods are either produced within a network or depend on a network for their existence.

Ajv123ajv/Dreamstime.com

Every new user of a social media app increases the value of the network to every existing user and potential user, generating a **network externality.** When these external benefits are taken into account in the decision making by individuals and firms, they are referred to as **network effects.**

Section 2: Demand Curve for a Network Good

Networks typically involve high fixed costs and therefore are produced in large increments, such as adding a new wireless tower that can serve many customers. This leads to a **network demand curve.**

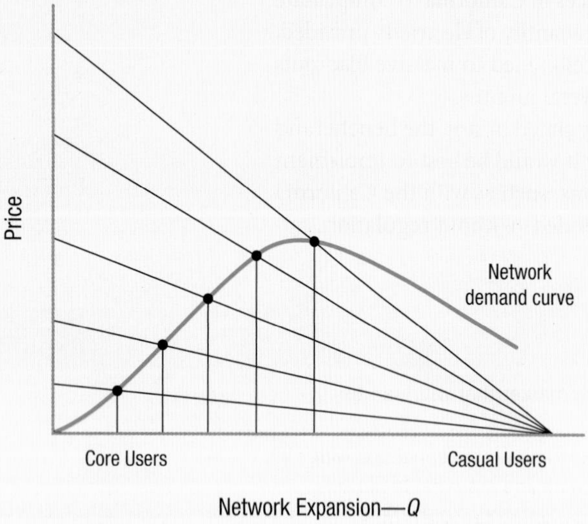

Deriving a Network Demand Curve

A network begins with a vertical short-run supply curve that represents a fixed capacity (a maximum number of customers it can serve), and a corresponding demand curve. As the network expands, the vertical supply curve shifts to the right, and the corresponding demand curve increases due to a network effect.

Two Opposing Effects on Prices in a Network

- **Network effect:** puts upward pressure on prices as output increases
- **Price effect:** puts downward pressure on prices as output increases

A network demand curve has upward-sloping and downward-sloping segments:

- Upward-sloping segment: Shown where the network effect exceeds the price effect, and typically occurs when a network is relatively new. **Core users** of network goods are the target in this part of the network demand curve.
- Downward-sloping segment: Shown where the price effect exceeds the network effect, and typically occurs once a network matures. In this part of the network demand curve, **casual users** join the network.

Lisafx/Dreamstime.com

Even grandma and grandpa eventually fall in love with the newest technology gadget. However, older consumers are more likely to be casual users who buy network goods, such as tablet computers, after the goods have become common in society.

Section 3: Market Equilibrium for a Network Good

A network demand curve contains a **tipping point** (or **critical mass**), defined as the level of output that allows a network to expand further without significant effort by producers. When a tipping point is reached, the power of network effects propels the demand for a network good to a higher equilibrium point. This is referred to as a **virtuous cycle.** If a network good fails to reach its tipping point or falls below its tipping point, a vicious cycle can result as customers leave the network, further decreasing the value of the network to other users.

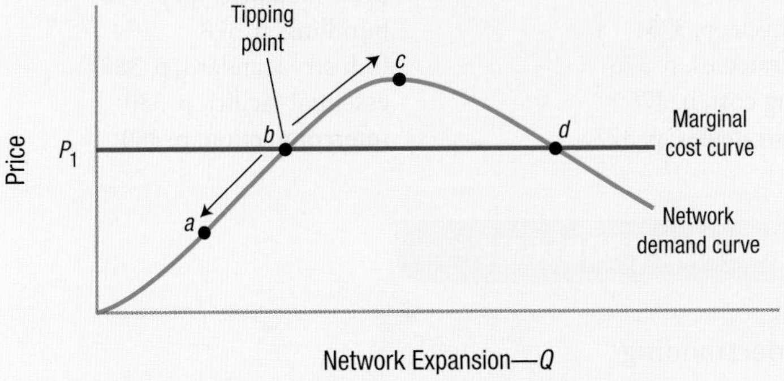

Goods can enter a virtuous cycle or a vicious cycle very quickly, especially if there is a competing network in the market.

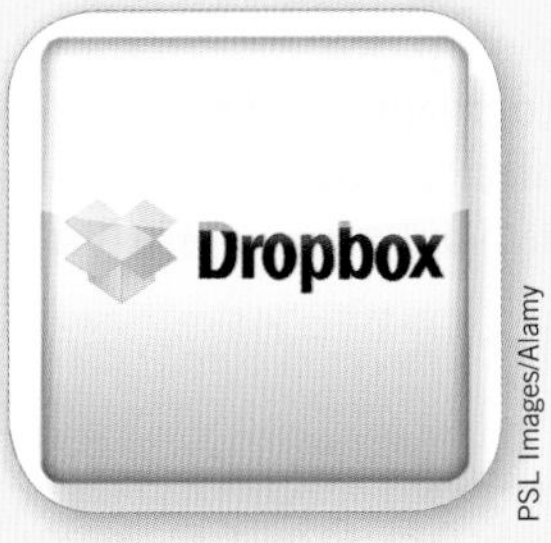

PSL Images/Alamy

Dropbox enjoyed a virtuous cycle in 2012 when over 50 million people signed up for this service that allows users to access and share files on any computer or mobile device.

Section 4: Competition and Market Structure for Network Goods

Firms engage in a variety of marketing strategies to increase the likelihood of entering a virtuous cycle or to avoid entering a vicious cycle. The pressure to gain and retain customers is enhanced by the low marginal cost of production, which makes customers more valuable the longer they use a firm's product.

Cammeraydave/Dreamstime.com

Common strategies used by firms include:

- Teaser strategies
- Lock-in strategies
- Market segmentation by versioning (intertemporal pricing, peak-load pricing, and bundling)

Section 5: Should Network Goods Be Regulated?

Network effects allow successful firms to achieve significant market power, sometimes even a monopoly. To prevent firms from exploiting their market power, governments turn to regulation as a way to limit the abuse of market power.

Poor regulation can sometimes be worse than no regulation. Regulation is not always necessary when the costs of regulation exceed its benefits. The potential of competition itself can prevent monopolies from exploiting their market power.

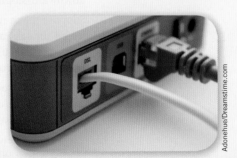

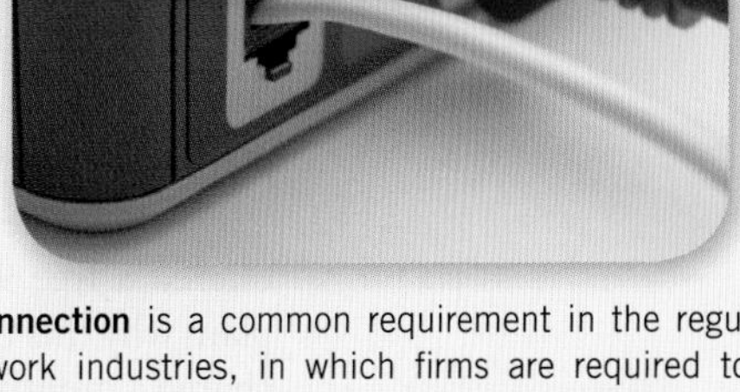

Adonehue/Dreamstime.com

Interconnection is a common requirement in the regulation of network industries, in which firms are required to give competitors access to each other's **essential facilities** such as telephone wires that allow for DSL broadband service.

KEY CONCEPTS

network, p. 368
physical network, p. 368
virtual network, p. 368
social network, p. 368
network good, p. 368
network externality, p. 368
network effect, p. 368
network demand curve, p. 370
core user, p. 371
casual user, p. 371
tipping point (critical mass), p. 373
virtuous cycle, p. 373
vicious cycle, p. 373
teaser strategies, p. 376
switching cost, p. 376
lock-in strategies, p. 377
market segmentation, p. 377
versioning, p. 377
intertemporal pricing, p. 378
peak-load pricing, p. 378
bundling, p. 378
industry standard, p. 380
essential facility, p. 380
interconnection, p. 380

QUESTIONS AND PROBLEMS

Check Your Understanding

1. What is a network externality and how does it differ from a typical externality?
2. Explain why a network demand curve slopes upward for small quantities.
3. List three strategies a firm can use to segment its market for a network good.
4. True or False: Once a firm's network good becomes the market leader, it is extremely unlikely for the firm to lose that position within a five-year period. Explain.
5. Why does the 3DTV industry exhibit large economies of scale? Would there also be network externalities in the consumption of 3DTVs? Explain.
6. If Matt wants to use his AT&T iPhone to call his girlfriend Sue, who uses a MyTouch from T-Mobile, why is interconnection necessary for the call to be completed?

Apply the Concepts

7. Suppose that two community organizations each plan their own public beach volleyball tournament on the same day at the same beach. Each organization wishes to have as many participants as possible. Further, a larger tournament is more fun for the participants. Suppose that a team consists of four players and at least four teams are required to hold a tournament. Explain what the tipping point would be and why a vicious cycle can develop if that number fails to be achieved.
8. If a person decides to unsubscribe from a popular social network, it decreases the value of the network to everyone else. Why wouldn't this action be considered a negative externality?
9. Suppose that expansion of the productive capacity of a firm producing a network good reduces the average cost due to economies of scale, but generates a very large increase in demand due to the network effect. Is this good likely to be on the upward-sloping or downward-sloping portion of the network demand curve? Explain.
10. Suppose that a new Harry Potter book called *The Untold Stories of Harry Potter* is released for sale, and fans line up for days to be the first to buy it. Are these fans core users or casual users in their demand for the new book? How could the book publisher maximize its profit using intertemporal pricing?
11. Suppose that your bank opens up a dozen more automatic teller machines (ATMs) throughout the city, making it much easier to find one. What happens to the demand and supply curves for this network as it expands?
12. Whenever a new car with satellite radio capability is purchased, the buyer is typically offered a free 90-day subscription to a satellite radio service such as SiriusXM. Explain why this offer would be considered a teaser strategy. Why wouldn't SiriusXM just charge a monthly subscription fee from the start?

In the News

13. The 2006 introduction of Google Docs, an online alternative but compatible software to Microsoft Office, forced Microsoft to develop new ideas to maintain its dominant market share. BBC News (May 12, 2010) reported that "Microsoft Takes Aim at Google Docs" by introducing a new online component with its Office 2010 product that offers the same features as Google Docs but with the familiarity of the Office software format. Why would the ability of Google Docs to read and edit a file created using Microsoft Office potentially cause the price of Microsoft Office software to fall?
14. Internet interconnection has become an important issue as countries improve their network infrastructure. According to the International Charging Arrangements for Internet Services (ICAIS) agreement, countries wishing to access U.S. Web sites or use U.S. backbones (Internet networks) must pay the full cost of interconnection (as opposed to, say, telephone interconnection, where each side shares the cost). Why would a country agree to this type of arrangement in the first place (in the 1990s), and what developments have taken place since then that would cause them to now oppose this arrangement?

Solving Problems

15. Suppose Ben values video game X at $100 and video game Y at $20, whereas Paul values video game X at $30 and video game Y at $80. The marginal cost to produce each game is $0. If a firm that produces both games decides to bundle X and Y, what price should it charge, and why is this bundling strategy more profitable than selling each game separately at a single price (assuming price discrimination is not possible)?
16. The accompanying figure shows two demand curves for ski lift tickets, one representing demand during February (peak season) and the other for April (low season). If the ski resort wishes to maximize its profit using peak-load pricing, what price should the ski resort set for lift tickets in February and what price should it set in April?

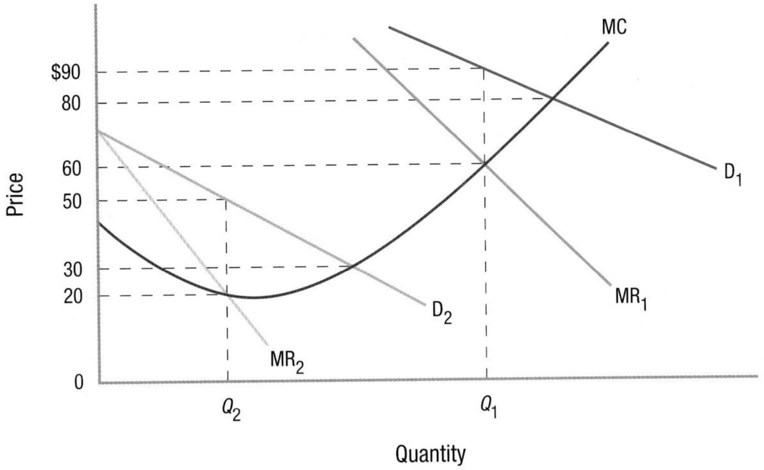

USING THE NUMBERS

17. According to By the Numbers, by what age category does the typical individual perceive television to be harder to live without than a mobile phone? By what age category does television become harder to live without than a computer?
18. According to By the Numbers, in what year did Microsoft Word surpass WordPerfect in terms of market share? In what year did Google Docs surpass WordPerfect? What are the current trends (up or down) for each software program in the last year reported?

ANSWERS TO QUESTIONS IN CHECKPOINTS

Checkpoint: What Is a Network Good?

When your friend purchases a laptop capable of using newer, more elaborate software, it generates a benefit to anyone else (especially you) who would find it useful to collaborate on projects. As a result, your friend's laptop purchase increases the value of the laptop to you (a network effect), increasing the likelihood that you will purchase a similar laptop. And once you purchase the laptop, this will generate additional benefits to your other friends, potentially generating even more demand.

Checkpoint: Demand Curve for a Network Good

A network demand curve gains value based on the number of people who use it. For example, a network good with one consumer is virtually worthless. As more consumers buy the network good, its value rises and the network good becomes attractive to even more consumers. Once a good matures, the network effect weakens and additional consumers will buy the good only after the price drops. Hence, the demand curve slopes downward for higher quantities of the good.

Checkpoint: Market Equilibrium for a Network Good

The network demand curve shows how a good enters a virtuous cycle (where an increase in demand generates network externalities that lead to additional demand) and how it enters a vicious cycle (where a decline in demand reduces the value of the network that leads to further declines in demand). When Myspace was introduced in 2003, it provided new features that its competition (primarily Friendster) didn't offer, and quickly led to a virtuous cycle in which the growth in subscribers increased exponentially over several years. When Facebook entered the market and captured the attention of social networking users, it quickly entered a virtuous cycle as well. Once users began choosing Facebook over Myspace, the drop in Myspace subscriptions quickly led to a vicious cycle and a significant drop in market share.

Checkpoint: Competition and Market Structure for Network Goods

A network good generally has a low marginal cost of production; therefore, any revenue a firm collects, even at low prices, typically increases its profit. By segmenting the market, the firm is separating customers based on their elasticity of demand. Customers with lower elasticities of demand are willing to pay a higher price than customers with higher elasticities of demand. Firms can segment the market by versioning their products. Products can be differentiated by time, peak usage, or bundling to create different versions of the same good at different prices.

Checkpoint: Should Network Goods Be Regulated?

An MP3 player is needed to play digital music, and therefore is considered an essential facility. Because Apple produces its own MP3 player, it could potentially restrict its products to play only music downloaded from its iTunes music store. Doing so would prevent its customers from playing music downloaded from other music providers, restricting competition in the digital music market. If that were the case, then regulatory policy could be implemented to prevent producers of MP3 players from restricting sources from which music can be downloaded. But Apple is unlikely to make this restriction, because it benefits from the ability of people to play music downloaded from iTunes on non-Apple devices.

15 Poverty and Income Distribution

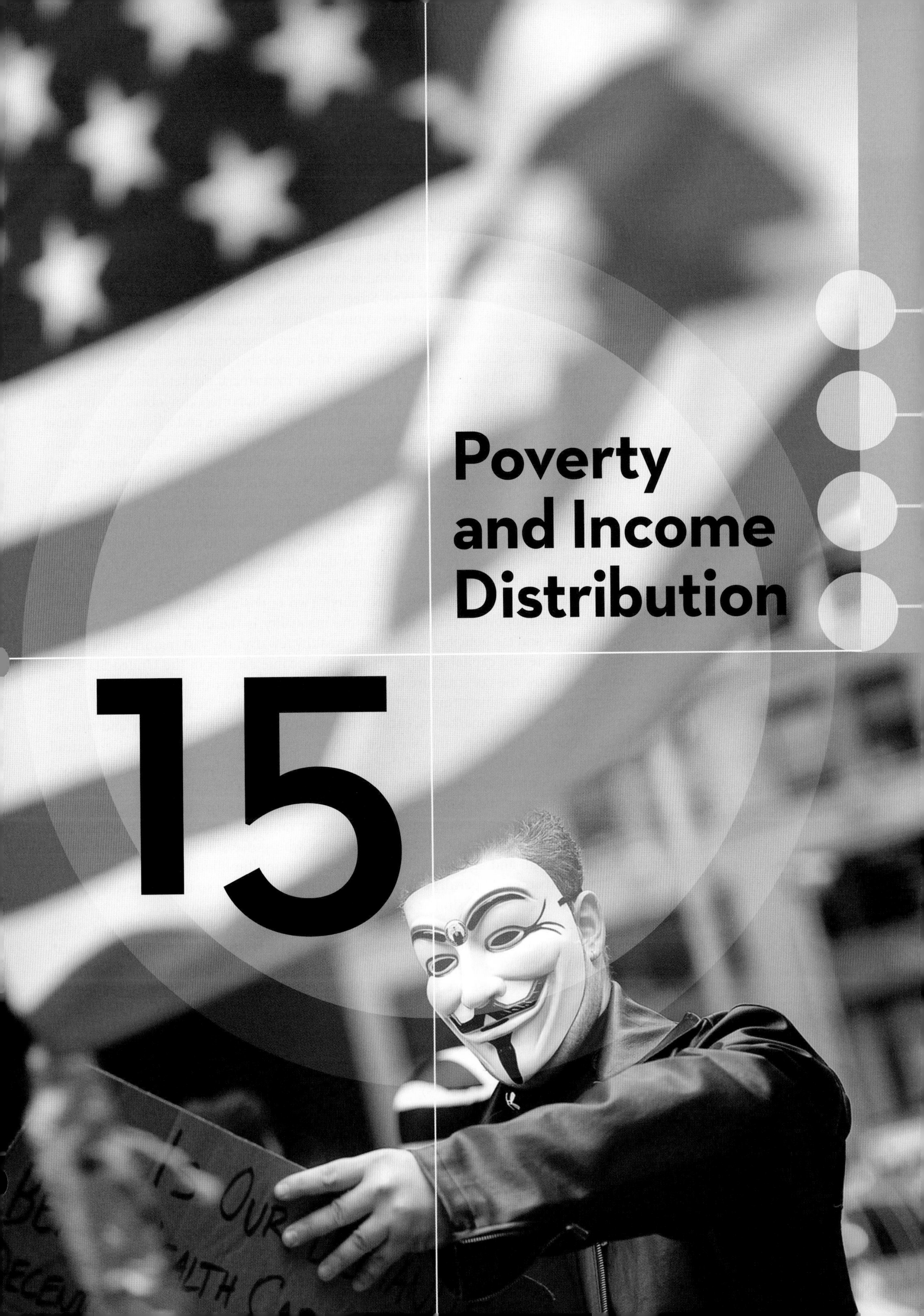

Craig Ruttle/Alamy

After studying this chapter you should be able to:

- Describe the difference between wealth and income.
- Describe the effects of life cycles on income.
- Analyze functional, personal, and family income distributions.
- Use a Lorenz curve and Gini coefficient to measure and describe the distribution of wealth and income.
- Describe the impact of income redistribution efforts.
- Describe the causes of income inequality.
- Describe the means for determining poverty thresholds.
- Describe the two measures for determining depth of poverty for families.
- Describe the prevailing theories on how to deal with poverty and income inequality.

On September 17, 2011, about 1000 protesters gathered in a small park near Wall Street in New York City to voice their concerns about social and economic inequality. What started as a local protest spurred by a social media campaign turned into a global movement known as Occupy.

The concerns raised by the Wall Street protesters and subsequently echoed by protesters in similar rallies in eighty-two countries on six continents dealt with a variety of issues relating to economic hardships that had been exacerbated during the recession of 2007–2009. Specifically, the Occupy movement claimed that the excessive influence of corporations on politics and the concentration of power by financial markets limited the opportunities of the majority of citizens in a democratic society. Supporters also lobbied for the right of citizens to have adequate access to health care, higher education, and a living wage. Above all, they are concerned about rising income inequality, which led to the coining of the slogan, "We are the 99%!" The slogan refers to the belief that economic prosperity has been unfairly concentrated among the richest 1% of the population, leaving the remaining 99% behind.

The issue of income inequality rose to the forefront in the United States as data showed that the richest 1% of the population earned nearly 20% of total income in 2012 and controlled over 40% of all wealth. This is a trend that is not slowing; inequality in the United States and around the world has expanded over the last three decades. Even during the last recession, when incomes of most Americans fell, the incomes of the richest Americans continued to rise.

What are the causes of income inequality? Two opposing theories exist. On the one hand, Occupy supporters claim that income inequality is the direct result of economic opportunities and tax policies that favor the wealthy few over the vast majority. The reductions in income and capital gains taxes on high-income earners in the United States are examples of how the tax structure became less progressive over time. On the other hand, others—including some prominent economists—believe that income inequality is the direct result of robust market incentives that reward entrepreneurial ability and success. These people do not believe income inequality is a result of some social injustice. Instead, they feel that wealth is the reward that comes from the opportunity for anyone to work hard, become successful, and be paid what they are worth to the economy.

Earlier, we saw that when input and product markets are competitive, wages are determined by worker productivity and the market value of output workers produce. This explains why some professional baseball players, who possess a unique ability to throw a 95-mph fastball and attract millions of fans, secure multimillion dollar contracts while teachers, who arguably perform a more valuable service but do so in a profession shared by millions of others with similar skills, earn salaries closer to the average.

Still, many people have trouble accepting that baseball pitchers earn millions, while teachers earn only thousands, and many others eke out subsistence wages. Income inequality is among the most contentious issues facing economists and other social scientists today.

Questions of fairness are normative. They can only be answered through individual value judgments. Economics has no right or wrong answers to offer in this area, but economists frequently contribute to these discussions.

Economic analysis gives us some insight into why income inequality exists. We have already seen how market power, unions, and discrimination can potentially skew income distribution. Even when public policy focuses on reducing these market imperfections, inequalities persist. Regardless of the causes of income inequality, addressing its effects requires special attention to those at the bottom of the income distribution: those who live in poverty.

This chapter looks at income inequality, its trends, its causes, and how it is measured. We then turn our attention to poverty, focusing on how poverty is traditionally measured, and the U.S. Census Bureau's new approach to measuring poverty. Finally, we look at current poverty trends and the causes of poverty. Throughout this chapter, we use economic analysis to provide a framework for analyzing income distribution, poverty, and the public policies used to combat poverty.

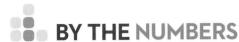

BY THE NUMBERS

Poverty and the Economy

Poverty is a problem facing people in virtually all countries, both rich and poor. Each country uses different methods to address poverty, including assistance for food, housing, health care, and education.

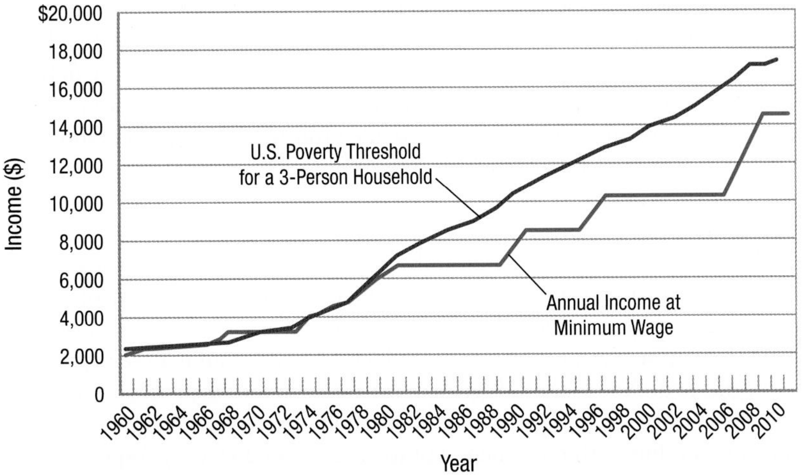

Jeff Greenberg/Alamy

A single-parent working full time at the minimum wage is unable to keep a family out of poverty.

The U.S. federal minimum wage is an example of government policy aimed at curbing poverty. In the 1960s and 1970s, one person working a full-time job at minimum wage was roughly able to keep a family of three out of poverty. Since the 1980s, the minimum wage has not kept up.

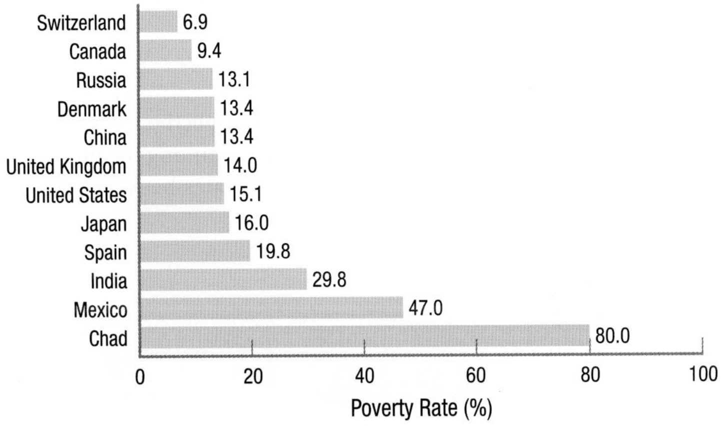

Every country has its own measure of poverty, making a comparison of countries and their *official poverty rate* misleading. For example, Denmark and China both have an official poverty rate of 13.4%. In China, this means a family of four living on less than $1,400 a year; in Denmark, it means living on less than $45,000 a year plus having free health care, education, and retirement benefits.

56,000,000

Number of Medicaid (health care for low-income persons) recipients in 2012

$468

Average monthly U.S. government housing subsidy for a qualified household in 2012

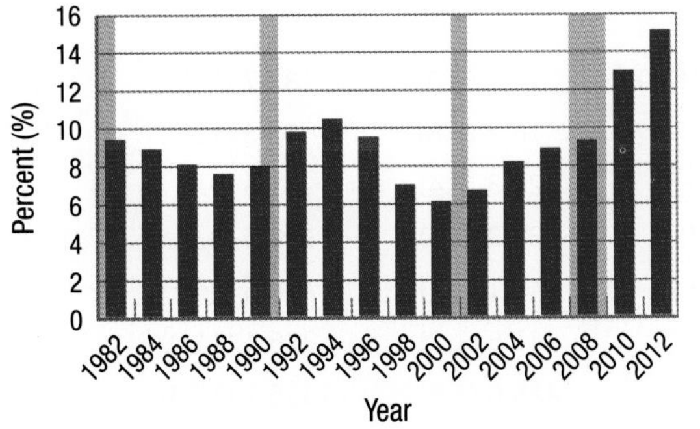

The percentage of Americans receiving food stamps fluctuates with the economy. The last recession and slow recovery caused food stamp usage to rise.

Bob Daemmrich/The Image Works

Unlike food stamps of the past, food stamps today work like a debit card.

The Distribution of Income and Wealth

income A flow measure reflecting the funds received by individuals or households over a period of time, usually a week, month, or year.

wealth A stock measure of an individual's or family's assets, net of liabilities, at a given point in time.

Income is a *flow*, **wealth** is a *stock*. Income measures the receipt of funds by individuals or households over time, usually a week, month, or year. Income is a *flow of funds* measure. Wealth, in contrast, measures a family's assets and net liabilities at a given point in time. You may earn a certain income in 2014, but your net wealth is measured on a specific day, say, December 31, 2014. Many people were wealthy on January 1, 2007, but after suffering the ravages of a falling housing and stock market, they were considerably less wealthy on July 1, 2009.

You can be wealthy with low income if you do not work and your assets are in homes, stocks, and bonds that earn little to no interest or dividends. Alternatively, you can have little wealth, yet a high income, if you are like a rookie professional ballplayer who earns a seven-figure salary but has not yet accumulated assets.

Life Cycle Effects

Family and individual incomes vary significantly over the course of people's lives. Young people just starting their careers and their families often earn only modest incomes. Over their working careers, they become more experienced and their salaries increase, with income peaking roughly between the ages of 45 and 55. At some point between ages 45 and 60, family size begins to decline as the kids grow up and leave home. As people are approaching 60, income also begins declining, although household saving rises as they prepare for retirement. Incomes decline with retirement, but then again, so do family responsibilities.

One result of this economic life cycle is that a society that is growing older can expect to see changes in income distribution as greater numbers of households fall into lower income brackets. The life cycle also has implications for the economic effects of immigration. Newcomers to the United States often possess limited skills, therefore when the country admits more immigrants, it can expect more low-income households. The children of immigrants, however, move up the income distribution ladder.

The Distribution of Income

functional distribution of income The distribution of income for resources or factors of production (land, labor, capital, and entrepreneurial ability).

Income distribution can be considered from several different perspectives. First, we can look at the **functional distribution of income,** which splits income among the inputs (factors) of production. The functional distribution for the United States between 1929 and 2012 is shown in Table 1.

TABLE 1 Functional Distribution of Income (absolute dollars in billions, numbers in parentheses are percentages)

Year	Wages	Proprietor's Income	Rent	Corporate Profits	Net Interest
1929	51.1 (60.3)	14.9 (17.6)	4.9 (5.8)	9.2 (10.8)	4.7 (5.5)
1940	52.1 (65.4)	12.9 (16.2)	2.7 (3.4)	8.7 (10.9)	3.3 (4.1)
1950	154.8 (65.5)	38.4 (16.3)	7.1 (3.0)	33.7 (14.3)	2.3 (1.0)
1960	296.4 (69.4)	51.9 (12.1)	16.2 (3.8)	52.3 (12.2)	10.7 (2.5)
1970	617.2 (73.7)	79.8 (9.5)	20.3 (2.4)	81.6 (9.7)	38.4 (4.6)
1980	1651.7 (73.6)	177.6 (7.9)	31.3 (1.4)	198.5 (8.8)	183.9 (8.2)
1990	3351.7 (72.2)	381.0 (8.2)	49.1 (1.1)	408.6 (8.8)	452.4 (9.7)
2000	5715.2 (71.6)	715.0 (9.0)	141.6 (1.8)	876.4 (11.0)	532.7 (6.7)
2010	8093.9 (69.3)	1059.3 (9.1)	425.0 (3.6)	1435.1 (12.3)	661.9 (5.7)
2012	8795.5 (68.7)	1247.5 (9.7)	555.4 (4.3)	1629.1 (12.7)	583.3 (4.6)

Source: Bureau of Economic Analysis.

Labor's share of national income rose from 1929 to become relatively stable from the 1970s onward, but fell each decade after. The share of income going to small businesses, called "proprietor's income," has declined over this period but has stabilized at slightly under 10%. Rental income's share fell from 1960 to 1990, but has since grown back to over 4%. The share accruing to corporate profits has increased in recent years to over 12%.

As Table 1 illustrates, the biggest fluctuations in income share have been associated with income from interest earned by individuals and firms, and is caused largely by changes in interest rates. It declined into the 1960s, then rose in the 1980s and 1990s, before falling again in the last decade.

Personal or Family Distribution of Income

When most people use the term "the distribution of income," they typically mean **personal or family distribution of income.** This distributional measure is concerned with how much income, in percentage terms, goes to specific segments of the population.

personal or family distribution of income The distribution of income to individuals or family groups (typically quintiles, or fifths, of the population).

To analyze personal and family income distribution, the Census Bureau essentially arrays households from the lowest incomes to the highest. It then splits these households into quintiles, or fifths, from the lowest 20% of households to the highest 20%. After totaling and averaging household incomes for each quintile, the Census Bureau computes the percentage of income flowing to each quintile.

Today, the United States contains approximately 120 million households. Therefore the 24 million households with the lowest incomes compose the bottom quintile, and the 24 million households with the highest incomes compose the upper quintile. Because much of the country's income is concentrated at the top, the Census Bureau breaks down the highest quintile further, showing the percentage of income flowing to the richest 10%, 5%, and 1% of the population.

Table 2 shows the official income distribution estimates for the United States since 1970. These estimates are based "solely on *money income before taxes* and do not include the value of noncash benefits, such as food stamps, Medicaid, public housing, or employer-provided fringe benefits."[1]

Share of Aggregate Income Received by Each Household Quintile: 1970–2011 and the Gini Coefficient — **TABLE 2**

Year	Lowest	Second	Third	Fourth	Highest	Top 10%	Top 5%	Top 1%	Gini Coefficient
1970	4.1	10.8	17.4	24.5	43.3	32.5	19.9	8.5	0.394
1975	4.4	10.5	17.1	24.8	43.2	32.1	20.1	8.2	0.397
1980	4.3	10.3	16.9	24.9	43.7	30.0	20.2	8.8	0.403
1985	4.0	9.7	16.3	24.6	45.3	32.9	23.0	11.2	0.419
1990	3.9	9.6	15.9	24.0	46.6	33.8	23.9	11.9	0.428
1995	3.7	9.1	15.2	23.3	48.7	35.5	25.5	12.2	0.450
2000	3.6	8.9	14.9	23.0	49.6	39.8	30.0	17.3	0.462
2005	3.4	8.6	14.6	23.0	50.4	39.7	30.1	17.4	0.469
2011	3.2	8.4	14.3	23.0	51.1	40.2	31.4	18.7	0.477

Source: U.S. Census Bureau, Current Population Reports, P60-243, *Income, Poverty, and Health Insurance in the United States: 2011* (Washington, DC: U.S. Government Printing Office), 2012.

[1] U.S. Census Bureau, Current Population Reports, P60-243, *Income, Poverty, and Health Insurance in the United States: 2011* (Washington, DC: U.S. Government Printing Office), 2012, p. 3.

Note that if the income distribution were perfectly equal, all quintiles would receive 20% of aggregate income. A quick look at these income distributions over the past four decades suggests that our distribution of income has been growing more unequal. Specifically, the share of income received by the highest quintile has steadily risen since 1970, while the share of income received by each of the four other quintiles has steadily fallen since 1970. Even more notable is how the income flowing to the top 1% has increased the most, with the share of income more than doubling since 1970. Keep in mind that these numbers ignore taxes and transfers (direct payment to households such as welfare and food stamps) that temper income inequality somewhat.

Still, incomes of the richest Americans have fared best over the last generation, and one piece of evidence has been the meteoric rise in CEO salaries. Controlling for inflation, the average salary of a CEO increased eight-fold since 1978, while real wages for workers have barely changed. Such stark differences in worker compensation contributed to the growth of the Occupy movement in recent years and its claims against the power held by the richest 1%.

Compressing distribution data into quintiles allows us to see how distribution has evolved. Economists have developed two primary measures that allow comparisons to be drawn with ease across time and between countries. These measures are Lorenz curves and the Gini coefficient.

Lorenz Curves

Lorenz curves A graphical method of showing the income distribution by cumulating families of various income levels on the horizontal axis and relating this to their cumulative share of total income on the vertical axis.

Lorenz curves cumulate households of various income levels on the horizontal axis, relating this to their cumulated share of total income on the vertical axis. Figure 1, for simplicity, shows a two-person economy. Assume that both people earn 50% of the total income, or that income is divided evenly. Point *a* in Figure 1 marks out this point, resulting in equal distribution curve 0*ac*.

The second curve in Figure 1 shows a two-person economy where the low-income person earns 25% of the total income and the upper income person receives 75% (point *b*). This graph is skewed to the right (curve 0*bc*), indicating an unequal distribution. If this two-person income distribution were as unequal as possible (0% and 100%), the Lorenz curve would be equal to curve 0*dc*.

Figure 2 and its accompanying table offer more realistic Lorenz curves for income and wealth data for the United States in the year 2011. The quintile income distribution in the

FIGURE 1

Lorenz Curves (Two-Person Economy)

If both people in this two-person economy earn 50% of the total income, income will be distributed perfectly equally, shown by the equal distribution curve 0*ac*. Curve 0*bc* represents the same economy in which the low-income person earns 25% of the total income and the upper income person earns 75%. This curve is skewed to the right, indicating an unequal distribution. The most extreme distribution between these two individuals (0% and 100%) is represented by the Lorenz curve 0*dc*.

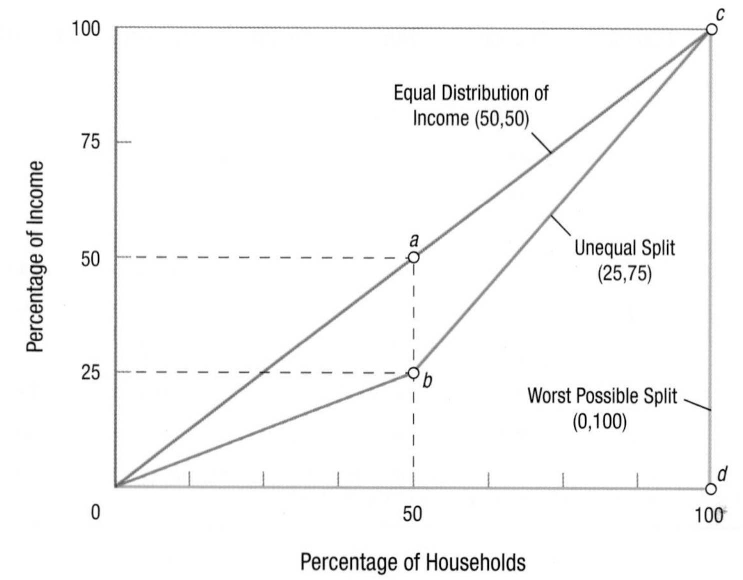

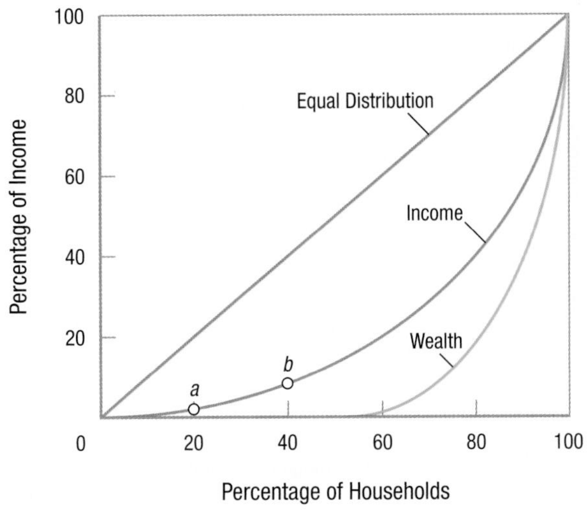

	Income		Wealth	
Quintile	**Income**	**Cum.**	**Wealth**	**Cum.**
Lowest	3.2	3.2	0.1	0.1
Second	8.4	11.6	0.2	0.3
Third	14.3	25.9	3.2	3.5
Fourth	23.0	48.9	7.6	11.1
Highest	51.1	100.0	88.9	100.0

FIGURE 2

Lorenz Curves

The graph shows the most recent Lorenz curves for income and wealth in the United States. The quintile distribution of income, found in the second column of the accompanying table, is cumulated in the third column and then plotted as a Lorenz curve. Notice how wealth is much more unequally distributed than income.

second column of the table is cumulated in the third column and plotted in Figure 2. (To *cumulate* a quintile means to add its percentage of income to the percentages earned by all lower quintiles.)

In Figure 2, for instance, the share of income received by the lowest fifth is 3.2%; it is plotted as point *a*. Next, the lowest two quintiles are summed (3.2 + 8.4 = 11.6) and plotted as point *b*. The process continues until all quintiles have been plotted to create the Lorenz curve.

Figure 2 also plots the Lorenz curve for wealth; it shows how wealth is much more unequally distributed than income. The wealthiest 20% of Americans control nearly 90% of wealth, even though they earn only half of all income.

Gini Coefficient

Lorenz curves give us a good graphical summation of income distributions, but they can be inconvenient to use when comparing distributions between different countries or across time. Economists would like one number that represents an economy's income inequality. The **Gini coefficient** provides such a number.

Gini coefficient A precise method of measuring the position of the Lorenz curve, defined as the area between the Lorenz curve and the equal distribution line divided by the total area below the equal distribution line.

The Gini coefficient provides a precise method of measuring the position of the Lorenz curve. It is defined as the ratio of the area between the Lorenz curve and the equal distribution line, in the numerator, and the total area below the equal distribution line, in the denominator. In Figure 3 on the next page, the Gini coefficient is the ratio of area A to area $(A + B)$.

If the distribution were equal, area A would disappear (equal zero), thus the Gini coefficient would be zero. If the distribution were as unequal as possible, with one individual or household earning all national income, area B would disappear, thus the Gini coefficient would be 1.

As a rule, the lower the coefficient, the more equal the distribution; the higher the coefficient, the more unequal. Looking back at the last column in Table 2, the Gini coefficient confirms that the basic income distribution has become more unequal since 1970. The Gini coefficient has risen from 0.394 in 1970 to 0.477 in 2011.

FIGURE 3

The Gini Coefficient

The Gini coefficient is a precise method of measuring the position of the Lorenz curve. It is defined as the ratio of the area between the Lorenz curve and the equal distribution line, and the total area below the equal distribution line. Thus, the Gini coefficient is equal to the ratio between area *A* and area (*A* + *B*). If distribution were equal, area *A* would be zero, and the Gini coefficient would equal zero. If distribution were as unequal as possible, area *B* would disappear, thus the Gini coefficient would be 1.

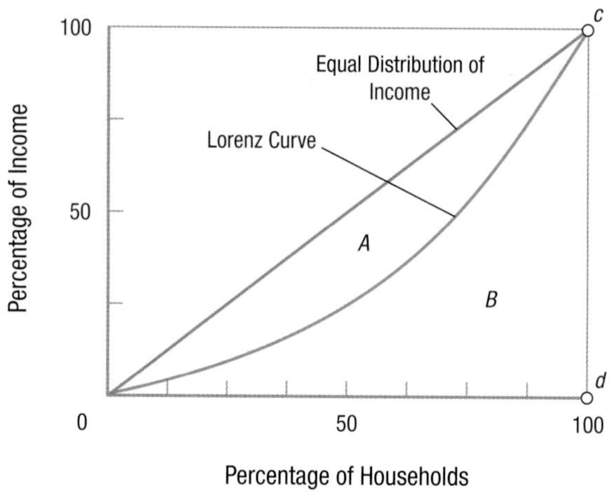

The Impact of Redistribution

In the United States, there is a vast array of income redistribution policies, including the progressive income tax (a tax that taxes higher incomes at a higher rate than lower incomes), housing subsidies, and other transfer payments such as Medicaid and Medicare, Social Security, and traditional welfare programs. Remember that the income distribution data in Table 2 *excluded* such government-provided cash and noncash benefits, and the effects of taxation.

Figure 4 provides an estimate of the impact progressive taxes and transfer payments (cash and in-kind) had on the income distribution in the United States. As we would expect, distribution became more equal: The Gini coefficient declined from 0.477 according to the official measure using gross income to 0.381 after adjusting for taxes and transfer payments.

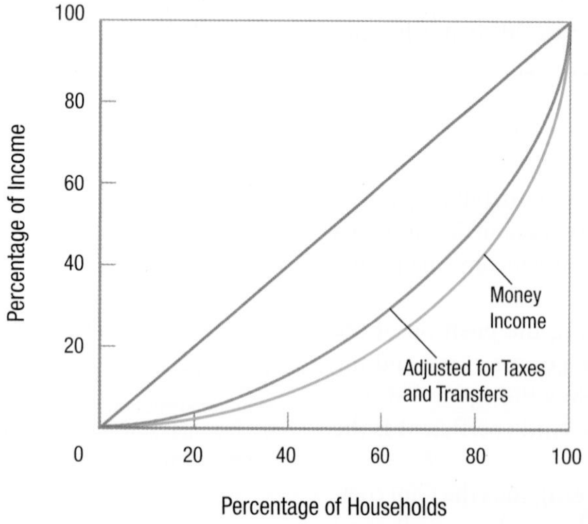

	Money Income		Adjusted Income		Taxes	
Quintile	**Percent**	**Cum.**	**Percent**	**Cum.**	**Percent**	**Cum.**
Lowest	3.2	3.2	6.2	6.2	0.4	0.4
Second	8.4	11.6	11.1	17.3	3.8	4.2
Third	14.3	25.9	15.8	33.1	9.5	13.7
Fourth	23.0	48.9	21.6	54.7	18.4	32.1
Highest	51.1	100.0	45.3	100.0	67.9	100.0

FIGURE 4

Lorenz Curves for the United States: Money Income and Income Adjusted for Taxes and Transfer Payments

These Lorenz curves provide an estimate of the impact progressive taxes and transfer payments (cash and in-kind) had on income distribution in the United States. As one would expect, distribution becomes more equal once taxes and transfer payments are taken into account. In this case, the Gini coefficient declined from 0.477 to 0.381.

Gini Coefficients for Various Countries, 2011 — **TABLE 3**

Country	Gini Coefficient	Country	Gini Coefficient
Australia	0.352	Italy	0.360
Bolivia	0.563	Japan	0.249
Brazil	0.547	Mexico	0.483
Canada	0.326	New Zealand	0.362
Chile	0.521	South Africa	0.631
China	0.425	Spain	0.347
Denmark	0.247	Sweden	0.250
France	0.327	United Kingdom	0.360
Israel	0.392	United States	0.477

Source: World Bank, *World Development Indicators* (Washington, DC: World Bank), 2012.

Table 3 provides some examples of how income distribution varies around the world. Income in European countries is generally more equally distributed than in the United States, while many South American countries have more unequal distributions.

Morten Elm/Dreamstime.com

David Davis/Dreamstime.com

Rio de Janeiro, Brazil, is one of the most beautiful cities in the world, but it also has some of the largest slums in the world.

Redistribution policies are the subject of intense debates. Those on the political right argue that differences in income are the natural result of a market system in which different individuals possess different personal endowments, schooling, and ambition. They believe, moreover, that the incentives of the marketplace are needed to encourage people to work and produce. The opportunities that markets provide mean that some people will be winners and others will lose. These analysts are unconcerned about the distribution of income unless it becomes so unequal that it discourages incentives and reduces efficiency.

Those on the political left argue that public policy should ultimately be guided by human needs. They see personal wealth as being the product of community effort as much as individual effort, and therefore they favor greater government taxation of income and wealth. By and large, European nations have found this argument more compelling than has the United States. This is reflected in the breadth of European social welfare policies. Because there is no correct answer (except possibly keeping distribution away from the extremes), this debate continues.

Causes of Income Inequality

Many factors contribute to income inequality in our society. First, as just mentioned, people are born into different circumstances with differing natural abilities. Families take varying interest in the well-being of their children, with some kids receiving immense inputs of family time and capital, while others receive little. These family choices largely fall outside the realm of public policy.

Human Capital The guarantee of a free public education through high school and huge subsidies to public colleges and universities for all Americans are designed to even out some of the economic differences among families. Still, public education does not eliminate the disparities. Some parents plan their children's education long before they are born, while other parents ignore education altogether.

Table 4 provides evidence of the impact investments in education have on earnings. Those without high school diplomas earned the least, roughly a third less than high school graduates. A college degree resulted in mean earnings nearly 3 times higher than what individuals without high school diplomas earned.

The U.S. economy has become more technologically complex. Manufacturing jobs have dwindled, reducing the demand for these workers, reducing their real wages. Several decades ago, people with low education levels could find highly productive work in manufacturing, with good wages and benefits. Globalization and increased capital mobility, however, have caused many of these jobs to migrate to lower wage countries. The result: Real wages have declined for Americans in many manufacturing occupations.

TABLE 4 Mean Earnings by Highest Degree Earned, 2009

	Mean Earnings by Highest Degree			
	No High School Diploma	High School Graduate	College Graduate	Professional
All Persons	$20,241	$30,627	$56,665	$127,803
Male	23,036	35,468	69,479	150,310
Female	15,514	24,304	43,589	89,897
White	20,457	31,429	57,762	127,942
Black	18,936	26,970	47,799	102,328
Hispanic	19,916	25,998	49,017	79,228

Source: U.S. Census Bureau, Current Population Survey, *2012 Statistical Abstract of the United States,* Table 232.

Our economy is increasingly oriented toward service industries, making investments in human capital more important than ever. The service industry spans more than just burger flipping, maid service, and landscaping. The United States is still the world leader in the design and development of new products, basic scientific research and development, and other professional services. All these industries and occupations have one thing in common: the need for highly skilled and highly educated employees.

Other Factors In an earlier chapter, we saw that economic discrimination leads to an income distribution skewed against those subject to discrimination. Reduced wages then reduce an individual's incentive to invest in human capital because the returns are lower, perpetuating a vicious cycle.

Table 5 outlines some characteristics of households occupying two different income quintiles. By comparing the lowest quintile with the highest, we can see some of the reasons

Distribution of Households by Selected Characteristics within Income Quintiles, 2011 — **TABLE 5**

Characteristic	Lowest Quintile	Highest Quintile
Type of Residence		
Inside metropolitan area	80.4%	90.5%
Inside central city	40.6	29.6
Outside central city	39.8	60.9
Outside metropolitan area	19.6	9.5
Type of Household		
Family households	40.1	86.8
Married-couple families	16.7	78.2
Nonfamily households	59.8	13.2
Householder living alone	56.0	6.6
Age of Householder		
15 to 34 years	23.7	14.6
35 to 54 years	26.9	51.0
55 to 64 years	17.4	22.7
65 years or older	31.9	11.6
Number of Earners		
No earners	61.7	2.9
One earner	33.8	22.2
Two or more earners	4.5	74.9
Work Experience of Householder		
Worked	32.3	87.1
Worked full-time, year-round	18.5	78.2
Worked part-time or part year	13.8	8.9
Did not work	67.7	12.9

Source: U.S. Census Bureau, Current Population Survey, Annual Social and Economic Supplement (Washington, DC: U.S. Government Printing Office), 2012.

for income inequality. As the Census Bureau summarizes these differences, "High-income households tended to be family households that included two or more earners, lived in the suburbs of a large city, and had a working householder between 35 and 54 years old. In contrast, low-income households tended to be in a city with an elderly householder who lived alone and did not work."

The rise in two-earner households over the last two decades accounts for a large part of the growing inequality in income. Note in Table 5 that only 4.5% of the lowest quintile households had two earners, while 74.9% of the highest quintile did. Also, only 2.9% of top quintile householders did not work, but 61.7% of those in the bottom quintile were not working.

It is hardly surprising that households with two people working should tend to have higher incomes than households with only one person or none working. In most households, whether one or two people work represents a choice. Today, clearly more couples are opting for two incomes. This is significant, given that rising income inequality is often cited as evidence that the United States needs to change its public policies to reduce inequalities. Yet, if the rise in inequality is due largely to changes in household attitudes toward work and income, with more couples choosing dual-career households, changes in public policy may not be needed. Rising inequality may simply be a reflection of the changing personal choices of many households.

This overview of income distribution and inequality provides a broad foundation for the remainder of the chapter, which focuses on poverty, its causes, and possible cures.

CHECKPOINT

THE DISTRIBUTION OF INCOME AND WEALTH

- The functional distribution of income splits income among factors of production.
- The family or personal distribution of income typically splits income into quintiles.
- Lorenz curves cumulate households of various income levels on the horizontal axis and their cumulative share of income on the vertical axis.
- The Gini coefficient is the ratio of the area between the Lorenz curve and the equal distribution line to the total area below the equal distribution line. It is used to compare income distribution across time and between countries.
- Income redistribution activities such as progressive taxes, Medicare, Medicaid, and other transfer and welfare programs reduce the Gini coefficient and reduce the inequality in the distribution of income.
- Income inequality is caused by a number of factors, including individual investment in human capital, natural abilities, and discrimination.

QUESTIONS: Economist Charles Murray suggested doing away with all social insurance, including Social Security, Medicare, Medicaid, and other welfare programs, and instead simply giving $10,000 a year to every citizen of the United States over 21 years of age. His purpose was to reduce bureaucracy and the government's role in the decision making of families. Expand his idea slightly by eliminating the age restriction. Would this improve the income distribution in America? Why or why not?

Answers to the Checkpoint questions can be found at the end of this chapter.

Poverty

Thus far, we have examined income distribution in general terms, looking at the spectrum from the top to the bottom. This section focuses on the bottom of the income spectrum—those who live in poverty. First, we look at poverty thresholds and how they are defined. Then we turn to the incidence of poverty and its trends. We then take a brief look at some experimental measures of poverty, considering their impact on measured rates of poverty. Lastly, we discuss the causes of poverty and how poverty can be reduced.

How difficult is life in poverty? A household of four in the United States that lived on less than $23,021 in the year 2011 was considered in poverty. That is equivalent to one wage earner working full-time as a maintenance worker at an apartment complex earning

$11.50 per hour, or about $1,900 per month before taxes. And this is a household living right at the poverty line; many households earn even less. Can a family get by on such meager income? In the United States, about 15% of all households do.

About one in six persons in the United States lives in poverty. For a family of four, this means living on less than $23,000 a year.

A household of four living on $1,900 per month can expect to have $1,675 after payroll and other taxes are deducted. Subtracting the rent on a modest subsidized apartment or a public housing apartment of $600 per month, $250 per month in utilities (electricity, gas, water, trash pickup, telephone, and basic Internet and cable), $250 per month toward a car payment, and $175 per month for fuel and auto insurance, this household has $400 left, or about $100 per week for everything else: food, clothing, school expenses, health care insurance, child care, and entertainment. Not to mention the occasional car repair, doctor and dentist co-payment, or parking ticket. And it certainly does not leave much to buy a $5 cup of coffee.

Living in poverty means that tough choices must be made to make ends meet. Some choose to give up their car and instead rely on public transportation. Others give up cable or the landline telephone. In more severe cases, some households are forced to cut back on food or health care. These choices are faced by one out of six persons in the United States. Why does the world's richest nation have so many poor citizens? Let's start to answer this by looking at how poverty is measured.

Measuring Poverty

poverty thresholds Income levels for various household sizes, below which people are considered to be living in poverty.

Poverty thresholds were developed by Mollie Orshansky in the 1960s. They were based on the Department of Agriculture's Economy Food Plan, the least expensive plan by which a family could feed itself. The Department of Agriculture first surveyed the food-buying patterns of low-income households, using these data to determine the cost of a nutritionally balanced food plan on a low-income budget. Orshansky then extrapolated these costs to determine the cost of maintaining such a food plan for households of various compositions. Finally, to determine the official poverty threshold, Orshansky multiplied the cost of the food plan, adjusted for family size, by three. This multiplier was based on an earlier household survey that had shown the average family of three or more spends roughly a third of its income on food.[2]

Since the 1960s, the poverty thresholds have been updated every year for changes in inflation using the consumer price index (CPI). Table 6 shows the poverty

U.S. Poverty Thresholds, 2011 — **TABLE 6**

One person	$11,484
Two people	14,657
Three people	17,916
Four people	23,021
Five people	27,251
Six people	30,847
Seven people	35,085
Eight people	39,064
Nine people	46,572

Source: U.S. Census Bureau, Current Population Reports, P60-243, *Income, Poverty, and Health Insurance in the United States: 2011* (Washington, DC: U.S. Government Printing Office), 2012.

[2] See Constance F. Citro and Robert T. Michael, *Measuring Poverty: A New Approach* (Washington DC: National Academy Press), 1995, p. 13 and Chapter 2 for more detail on how thresholds are measured.

thresholds for 2011. If a family's income is less than the threshold, every person in the household is considered poor. Official thresholds do not vary geographically. "Income" includes all money income before taxes, including cash benefits, but not capital gains or noncash benefits such as public housing, food stamps, and Medicaid. Later, we will briefly look at some new alternative measures that do adjust for these factors.

The Incidence of Poverty

Poverty rates for the United States since 1960 are shown in Figure 5. Poverty fell rapidly between 1960 and 1975 but has remained roughly stable ever since, fluctuating with the business cycle: rising around recessions (the shaded vertical bars) and falling when times are good.

Poverty rates vary considerably along racial and ethnic lines. Figure 6 charts the poverty rate since 1970. Over most of this time, the poverty rate for blacks and Hispanics was roughly twice the rate for whites. Both of these minority groups benefited, however, from the strong economic growth of the 1990s, their poverty rates dropping from around 30% at the beginning of the decade to around 25% today. White poverty remained fairly steady over the 1990s, fluctuating between 10% and 11%. However, the recession in 2007–2009 and the slow economic recovery pushed the poverty rate for whites above 12%.

These data suggest that robust economic growth is a major force for reducing poverty. The expression "a rising tide floats all boats" would appear to have something to it.

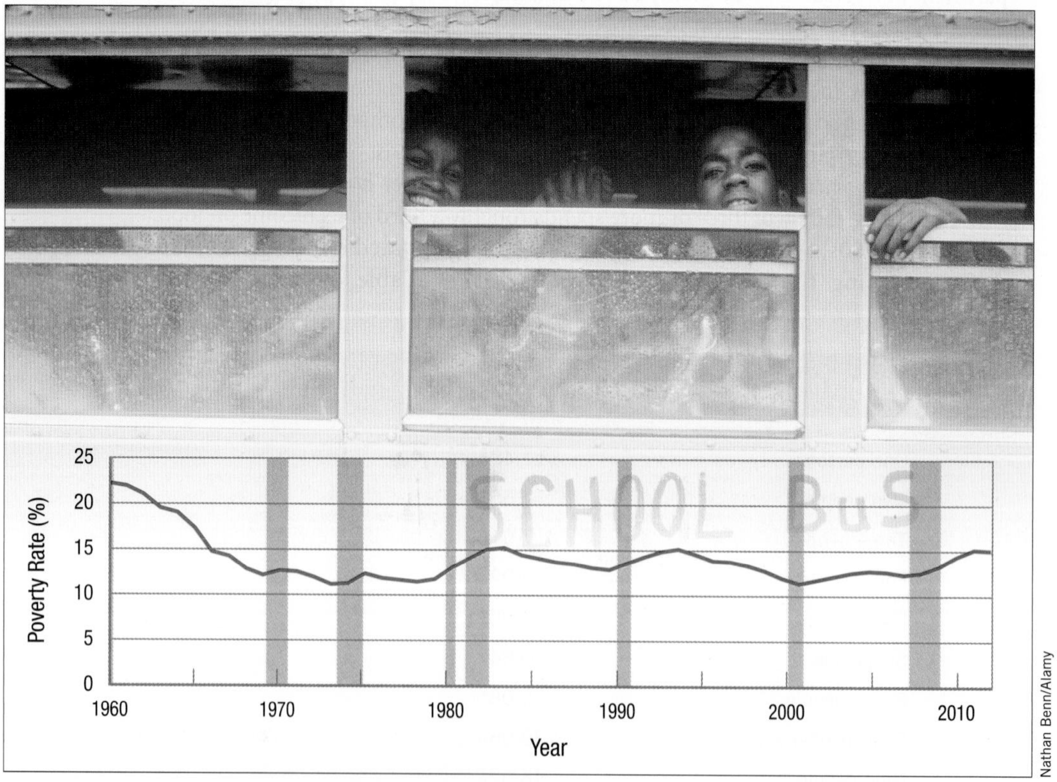

FIGURE 5

Poverty Rates in the United States, 1960–2011

Poverty fell rapidly between 1960 and 1975 but has remained roughly stable ever since.

Source: U.S. Census Bureau, Current Population Reports, P60-243, *Income, Poverty, and Health Insurance in the United States: 2011* (Washington, DC: U.S. Government Printing Office), 2012.

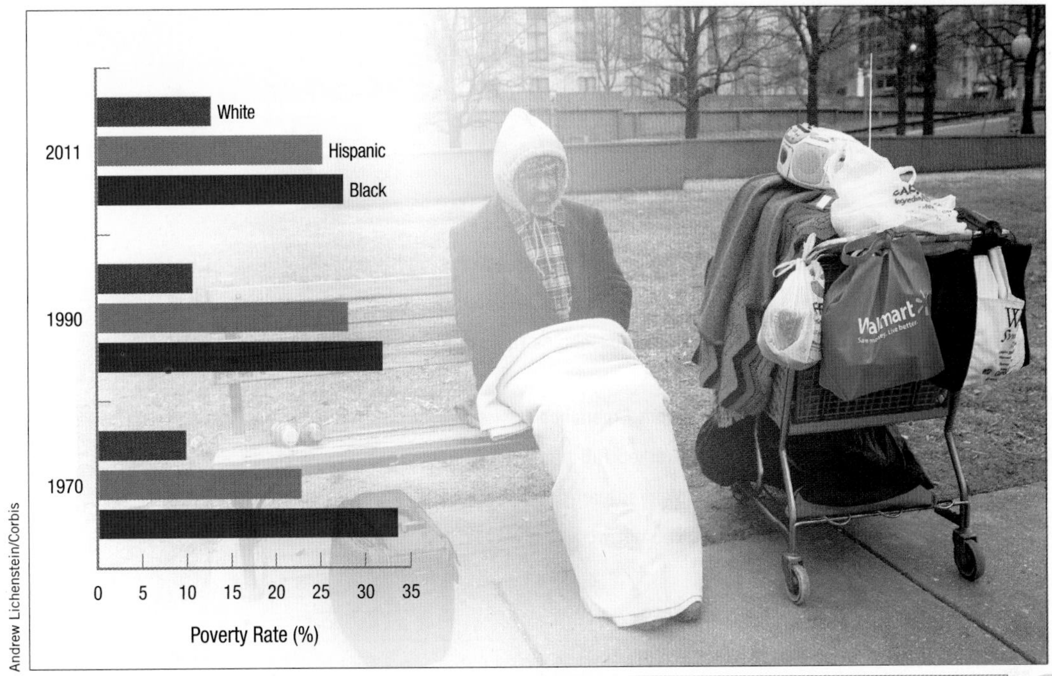

FIGURE 6

Poverty Rates by Race and Ethnic Origin, 1970–2011

Poverty rates vary considerably along racial and ethnic lines. Over most of this period, the poverty rate for blacks and Hispanics was roughly twice the rate for whites. Both of these minority groups benefited, however, from the strong economic growth of the 1990s, their poverty rates dropping from around 30% at the beginning of the decade to around 25% today. White poverty remained fairly steady over the 1990s, fluctuating between 10% and 11%, but rose above 12% after the 2007–2009 recession.

Source: U.S. Census Bureau, Current Population Reports, P60-243, *Income, Poverty, and Health Insurance in the United States: 2011* (Washington, DC: U.S. Government Printing Office), 2012.

Table 7 on the next page shows other characteristics that contribute to poverty. Single parent households have 2 to 5 times the poverty rate of married couples. Not surprisingly, working part-time or not working at all leads to higher poverty rates. And, as we saw in Figure 6, black and Hispanic poverty rates are roughly twice that of whites.

Depth of Poverty

It is one thing to say that a certain percentage of the population is poor. It is another to determine just how poor they are. The poverty threshold for a family of four today is over $23,000. If most poor families have incomes approaching this threshold, we could be confident that poverty was just a transitory stage—one phase of the life cycle—and that many people who are poor today would have higher incomes tomorrow.

But if, conversely, many poor families have incomes below $10,000, our view of poverty would be different, and our public policies aimed at reducing poverty would need to be considerably more robust.

income deficit The difference between the poverty threshold and a family's income.

ratio of income to poverty The ratio of family income to the poverty threshold. Families with ratios below 0.5 are considered severely poor, families with ratios between 0.5 and 1.0 are considered poor, and those families with ratios between 1.0 and 1.25 are considered near poor.

To gain a view of the broad spectrum of poverty, economists have developed two *depth of poverty* measures that describe the economic well-being of lower income families. One measure, the **income deficit,** tells us how far below the poverty threshold a family's income lies. In 2011, the income deficit for families living in poverty averaged $9,576. Using the poverty threshold for a family of four, the average income for a family living in poverty was $13,445.

The second measure of poverty, the one we will focus on, is the **ratio of income to poverty.** It compares family income to the poverty threshold and expresses this comparison as a ratio. Thus, the ratio for families with incomes equal to the poverty threshold equals 1.0;

TABLE 7 People and Families in Poverty by Selected Characteristics, 2011

Characteristic	Poverty Rate
Type of Household	
Married-couple households	6.2%
Female households (no husband)	31.2
Male households (no wife)	16.1
Work Experience	
Worked full time, year round	2.8
Worked part-time, year round	16.3
Did not work	32.9
Race	
White	12.8
Black	27.6
Asian	12.3
Hispanic	25.3

Source: U.S. Census Bureau, Current Population Reports, P60-243, *Income, Poverty, and Health Insurance in the United States: 2011* (Washington, DC: U.S. Government Printing Office), 2012.

the ratio for those living at half the threshold income is 0.5. The Census Bureau considers people who live in families with ratios below 0.5 to be "severely or desperately poor." Those with ratios between 0.5 and 1.0 are "poor," and people with ratios above 1.0 but less than 1.25 (less than 25% above the poverty threshold) are considered to be "near poor."

Of the 46 million poor people in 2011, over 20 million of them were desperately poor, and an additional 15 million were categorized as near poor. These measures (income deficit and the ratio of income to poverty) provide us with a more nuanced picture of poverty.

Alternative Measures of Poverty Many researchers have questioned the relevance of the current method for determining poverty thresholds. The National Academy of Sciences studied the official approach to poverty thresholds and concluded that the measure is flawed because "[it]counts taxes as income, [and] is flawed in the adjustments to the households for different family circumstances."[3]

The study further concluded that the current poverty measure does not distinguish well among working parents, workers generally, nonworkers, or people with higher versus lower health care needs and costs. Finally, noting that the current threshold is just the threshold from "1963 updated for price changes," the panel questioned the value of such a simplistic approach, given how much the U.S. standard of living has changed.

Given the Academy's findings, the Census Bureau developed some new ways of measuring poverty. These alternative measures of poverty differ from the old in basing their estimates on after-tax income plus capital gains and counting as income such noncash benefits as food stamps and housing subsidies plus imputed return on home equity (that

[3] Citro and Michael, *Measuring Poverty,* pp. 97–98.

is, the savings from owning a home versus paying rent each month).

The Census Bureau derived its new estimates of income thresholds from a survey of expenditures on food, clothing, housing, utilities, and other necessities for the typical family of four (two adults and two kids). These figures were then adjusted to reflect differences in family composition and size, given that children consume less than adults, some household economies are associated with larger families, and the first child in a one-adult family costs more to support than the first child in a two-adult family. Under these measures, poverty rates fell by roughly a quarter.

Causes of Poverty

The reasons why poverty persists are wide-ranging. Traditional causes of poverty include a lack of human capital, mental or physical disabilities, and drug addictions that inhibit persons from achieving gainful employment. Reasons also include an unwillingness to work or an apathy toward work that leads to frequent terminations. Another reason for poverty is that some people refuse to relocate for work, despite having the skills and work ethic to escape poverty. This last reason explains why many communities in rural Appalachian states continue to experience high poverty rates: As industries moved out and jobs disappeared, residents chose to remain, seeking jobs that pay meager wages.

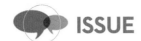

ISSUE

Why Do We Use an Outdated Measure of Poverty?

Aurora Photos/Alamy

Why does the United States still define poverty as 3 times the cost of a *1963* low-income food budget adjusted for inflation? You might think that government policymakers could design a measure that reflects a family's well-being by looking at more than just money income based on some old formula a half-century old.

Based on this measure, poverty rates have fluctuated between 10% and 15% over the last four decades. But in that time, antipoverty programs were generously increased to include reduced tax burdens on the poor, as well as the expansion of food stamp and housing programs, the earned income tax credit, and Medicare, Medicaid, and other programs that have undoubtedly helped the poor. But the measure doesn't reflect this success and as a result provides little guidance to solving poverty. As Professor Rebecca Blank at the University of Michigan observes, "In a very fundamental way, our poverty statistics failed us and made it easy to claim that public spending on the poor had little effect."

Why has the Census Bureau failed to update our poverty measure in the same way that employment, unemployment, consumer prices, national income accounts, and many other economic statistics have been improved? The answer is straightforward and surprising. Through a historical accident, the Executive Office of the President is in charge of the measure. The decision rests with the Office of Management and Budget (OMB), and the president must ultimately approve any change. To date, no White House has been willing to approve any change. If a change in measurement results in falling poverty rates, some will claim manipulation. If a change results in higher poverty rates, the administration risks being seen as a failure on this front. Ultimately, we will probably not see improvement until Congress gives the Census Bureau responsibility for the statistic.

Source: Rebecca Blank, "Presidential Address: How to Improve Poverty Measurement in the United States," *Journal of Policy Analysis and Management,* 2008, pp. 233–254.

As economic and social change took place in recent decades, new factors have contributed to the rise in poverty. First, wages generally have not kept up with rising costs; specifically, a single parent working at the minimum wage cannot escape poverty today, when 40 years ago it was possible. Second, technological changes and globalization have changed employment opportunities and led to unemployment in certain industries that forced people into poverty. Third, rising health costs have led some to give up work to care for an ill family member, forgoing earnings. And finally, changes in family structure, particularly an increase in single parenthood, have made it more difficult to avoid a life of poverty. These reasons and others have encouraged policymakers to rethink approaches to eliminating poverty.

Eliminating Poverty

Poverty can be a relative or an absolute measure. As we saw earlier, the official measure of poverty in the United States is based on an absolute number, the poverty threshold. Some researchers, however, think a relative measure would be more useful, such as labeling the bottom 20% of American households as "poor."

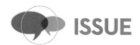

ISSUE

What Is Considered "Poor" Around the World?

Every country uses its own definition of what constitutes being poor. In the United States, the official poverty threshold is calculated as an absolute measure. This means a family of four making $23,000 or less in the year 2011 was considered poor. However, a family of four making $23,000 a year in China or India would be considered quite wealthy in their countries. Compared to many developing countries, being poor in America still allows for a relatively comfortable life.

What is considered poor in America, such as living in a small old house in a rural community, might be considered rich elsewhere, such as in undeveloped areas of Africa where residents do not have access to running water and electricity.

Many countries in the European Union, however, use a relative measure of poverty. In Denmark, a family is considered poor if it earns less than 60% of the median income. With the median household income being over $75,000 a year, this means a family earning less than $45,000 a year is considered poor. In addition, Denmark offers full health care coverage to every citizen and free college tuition. Certainly an American family earning $45,000 a year and receiving free health care and college educations for its children would not be considered poor.

The main culprits for the difficulty in defining and comparing poverty rates between countries involve differences in the cost of living, the role of government, and overall economic development. In rich countries, the cost of living is higher, governments often provide more services, and citizens have a higher expectation of what is considered necessary for survival. In poor countries, the cost of living is low, governments often cannot provide much assistance, and citizens are merely surviving.

To provide a better comparison of poverty across the world, various organizations have devised methods to compare living standards and poverty rates across countries. The United Nations publishes the *Human Development Index* each year, which provides an overall picture of a country's living standard based on factors such as access to education, running water and sanitation, health care, and communications. However, it does not provide a percentage of the country being poor. The World Bank uses an absolute measure with thresholds ranging from $1.25 a day (extreme poverty) to $2 a day, adjusted to the cost of living, to estimate the number of poor in mostly developing countries. Finally, the Organisation for Economic Cooperation and Development (OECD) publishes comparisons of poverty rates among mostly developed countries based on a fixed percentage of median incomes.

The availability of these statistics allows us to compare poverty rates around the world better. Still, difficulties remain when cultural differences influence what is considered vital for survival in each country.

If we decide to use such a measure, poverty will never be eliminated, no matter how wealthy our country might become. A relative measure obscures the fact that poverty in the United States means something different than it does in the developing world. In the United States, being poor might mean scraping by paycheck to paycheck and having to give up such things as cable television or eating out. In some developing countries, being poor might mean literally starving.

The official U.S. poverty threshold for an individual is an income of roughly $30 a day. In the developing world, by contrast, the World Bank and other agencies define poverty as incomes of less than $2 a day. By World Bank standards, poverty has already been eradicated in the United States.

Reducing Income Inequality Regardless of how poverty is defined, the question of how to reduce it is controversial. The political left views income and wealth redistribution as the chief means of reducing poverty. Social justice, they argue, requires that the government provide an extensive safety net for the poor. In their view, services that the government already provides, including public education, housing subsidies, Medicaid, and unemployment compensation, should be greatly expanded.

They say these policies should be supplemented, moreover, by increasing the progressivity of the tax system. This would reduce the inequalities in wealth and income. By increasing the tax burden on the well-to-do, people of modest incomes could lead more meaningful and just lives. It may also reduce acts of desperation, such as shoplifting and home burglaries, representing an external benefit from reducing poverty.

Increasing Economic Growth The opposite side of the political spectrum argues that such programs, when allowed to become too expansive, can be disastrous. Welfare significantly reduces the incentive to work and produce, thereby reducing the economy's output. A vibrant market economy accommodates the wishes of those who want full-time, upwardly mobile careers as well as those who only want just enough work to pursue other goals.

Because wages provide nearly 70% of all income, those on the political right note that there inevitably will be some inequality in a market system. Some people, after all, make bad choices and fail to invest enough in their education or job skills. Yet, the possibility of failure itself provides an incentive to work hard and invest, and the political right sees this sort of efficiency in the economy as being more important than equity or fairness. The best way to cure poverty, they argue, is by implementing policies that increase the economic pie shared by all, not just by splitting up the pie more evenly.

This political dispute has fueled a controversy in economics. One group of economists argues that economic growth raises low incomes at a rate similar to that of average incomes, such that the poor benefit from growth just as much as anyone else. Other economists reply that the shift toward freer markets around the world, combined with the resulting economic growth, has widened inequalities, causing the poor to fall further behind.

Who is right? Jagdish Bhagwati, a well-known development economist, argued that economic growth creates gainful employment, lifting people out of poverty. Further, economic growth increases government revenue, allowing for greater spending on health and education for the poor. He argues that

> *in economic terms, growth [is] an instrument, not a target—the means by which the true targets, like poverty reduction and the social advancement of the masses, would be achieved.*

He adds a caveat, however, that

> *the political sustainability of the growth-first model requires both symbolic and material efforts. While growth does benefit the poor, the rich often benefit disproportionately. So to keep the poor committed to the system as their economic aspirations are aroused, the wealthy would be well advised to indulge less in conspicuous consumption.*[4]

In sum, Bhagwati states that economic growth raises all incomes in absolute terms, including the poor, which reduces poverty. However, relative incomes may continue to suffer, as income inequality can widen with economic growth.

Rawls and Nozick Unfortunately, there is no unified theory of income distribution that takes the various issues we have discussed into account. Earlier chapters suggested that income depends on productivity—in competitive markets, each input (factor) is paid the value of its marginal product.

Human capital analysis adds that as people invest in themselves, their productivity and income rise. Analysis of imperfect input markets, however, shows that income distribution advantages accrue more to those with market power.

Our analysis of economic discrimination suggested several more reasons why incomes may be skewed in favor of some groups rather than others. The bargaining strength of labor unions is yet another factor that can skew income distribution, in this case in favor of union members.

---

[4] Jagdish Bhagwati, "Does Redistributing Income Reduce Poverty?" Project Syndicate, October 27, 2011.

These analyses have focused, in one way or another, on whether certain patterns of income distribution are economically efficient. Yet, how do we know whether various income distributions are equitable or fair? Is there anywhere to turn for theoretical help in addressing this question? The answer is a qualified "yes." Two philosophers, John Rawls and Robert Nozick, published competing views on this subject in the early 1970s.[5]

John Rawls proposed the "maximin principle," in which he argued that society should maximize the welfare of the least well-off individual. He asks us to conduct a thought experiment: Assume that you must decide on the income distribution for your society, without knowing where in the distribution you will end up. Because chance could lead to you being the least well-off individual in the society, Rawls suggests people would favor significant income redistribution under these circumstances.

Robert Nozick argued that it is "illegitimate to use the coercive power of the state to make some better off at the expense of others." To Nozick, justice requires protecting property rights "legitimately acquired or legitimately transferred."[6] Using Nozick's argument, a small group of friends in Finland who developed a game called *Angry Birds* that became a worldwide addiction, and subsequently became wealthy because millions willingly bought premium game subscriptions, cannot be considered unjust. Instead, Nozick would argue it would be unjust if the creators were not rewarded for their innovation that has provided countless hours of fun for so many people.

This debate highlights the perennial tradeoff in economic policy between equity and efficiency, a tradeoff that serves as a bone of contention in nearly every discussion of economic and public policy. Although microeconomics is sometimes beset by controversy, at its best it provides us with a dispassionate framework for analyzing and discussing many issues.

Mobility: Are Poor Families Poor Forever? The poverty rates and income distribution data provide a snapshot in time. How about over time? What is the human side to this? Do people start in poverty or fall into poverty and then stay there, or is there movement out of poverty?

A study by the U.S. Census Bureau tracking over 43,000 American households from 2004 to 2006 provides an answer. The study found that of the households that were living in poverty at the start of 2004, 42% were no longer living in poverty by the end of 2006.[7] Of these households, about half were living just above the poverty line, while the other half did much better and were earning incomes well above the poverty line. The results indicate that mobility between income groups is possible, and that not all who are in poverty stay there forever.

However, additional data from the Census Bureau tells the other side of the story. Although millions of households pull themselves out of poverty each year, millions more find themselves falling into poverty. During the last economic recession and the slow economic recovery that followed, millions of households fell into poverty for the first time, causing the poverty rate to rise above 15% in 2010. The fortunate news is that many of these households will remain in poverty only temporarily as new jobs are created with continued economic growth.

The movements of households in and out of poverty mirror the findings of the University of Michigan's Panel Study of Income Dynamics, which has followed 18,000 individuals since 1968. It shows how fluid the income distribution really is. Data from this

---

[5] John Rawls, *A Theory of Justice* (Oxford: Clarendon), 1972; Robert Nozick, *Anarchy, State and Utopia* (Oxford: Blackwell), 1974.

[6] John Kay, *The Truth about Markets: Their Genius, Their Limits, Their Follies* (London: Penguin Books), 2003, p. 187.

[7] U.S. Census Bureau, Current Population Reports, P70-123, *Dynamics of Economic Well-Being: Poverty, 2004–2006* (Washington, DC: U.S. Government Printing Office), 2011.

study show that within a 10-year period, over half of individuals in the poorest income quintile moved up the income distribution ladder. Surprisingly, the same pattern of mobility appears in the richest quintile: Roughly half were replaced by households from other quintiles. Overall, only one-third to one-half of all households remained in the original quintile after a decade.

Chris Tilly, director of UCLA's Institute for Research on Labor and Employment, states that "poverty is dynamic; not everybody stays in poverty long term. We've always known that people move in and out of poverty, [but] there are people who tend to get stuck."[8] Households that remain in poverty over time, although a relatively small percentage of the population, are the most worrisome. Research by Richard B. Freeman of Harvard tells us that there is a core of poor people who stay poor. This core has physical disabilities, suffers from substance abuse, or is unable to work for a host of other reasons.

These findings suggest that poverty will never be totally eradicated. They also suggest that policies to deal with core poverty should be different from policies that deal with people who start or who have fallen into poverty but are highly likely to escape.

CHECKPOINT

POVERTY

- Poverty thresholds were developed in the 1960s based on a food budget, adjusted for family size, then multiplied by 3.
- Economic growth has been a major force in reducing poverty in the United States.
- The income deficit measures how far below the poverty threshold a family's income lies.
- The other depth of poverty measure is the ratio of income to poverty. If the ratio is below 0.5, the family is considered "severely or desperately poor." A ratio greater than 1.0 but less than 1.25 indicates the family is "near poor."
- The Census Bureau has introduced new measures of poverty that consider health care costs, transportation needs, and child care costs.
- The controversy surrounding reducing poverty centers on whether reducing income inequality or increasing economic growth is the best approach.
- Philosopher John Rawls proposed a "maximin principle" that suggests society should maximize the welfare of the least well-off individual.
- Robert Nozick argued that the state should not use its coercive power to make some people better off at the expense of others.
- Income mobility is quite robust in the United States, with more than half of all families moving up and down the income distribution ladder in any decade.

QUESTIONS: Return to the suggestion by economist Charles Murray that the United States should eliminate all social insurance, including Social Security, Medicare, Medicaid, and other welfare programs, and instead give $10,000 each year to each citizen over 21 years of age. Again, expand his idea by eliminating the age restriction. Would this eliminate poverty in America? Would this satisfy those on the left who wish to reduce inequality in income distribution? What do you think would be the response to such an idea by those on the political right?

Answers to the Checkpoint questions can be found at the end of this chapter.

[8] Ari Bloomekatz, "Poverty Often a Temporary State, U.S. Census Study Finds," *The Los Angeles Times*, March 28, 2011.

chapter summary

Section 1: The Distribution of Income and Wealth

Income: A flow of funds by individuals or households over time.

Wealth: A stock of assets less liabilities at a given point in time.

Spotmatik/Dreamstime.com

A household can have considerable wealth without much income, such as this retired couple who saved over their working careers.

Types of Income Distribution

Functional distribution of income: the distribution of inputs (factors) of production. Wages constitute nearly 70% of income using this approach.

Personal or family distribution of income: the percentage of income flowing to specific segments of the population. Quintiles (20% of the population) are used by the U.S. Census Bureau to measure income distribution.

Income inequality is measured either by constructing a Lorenz curve or by calculating a Gini coefficient for a specific population.

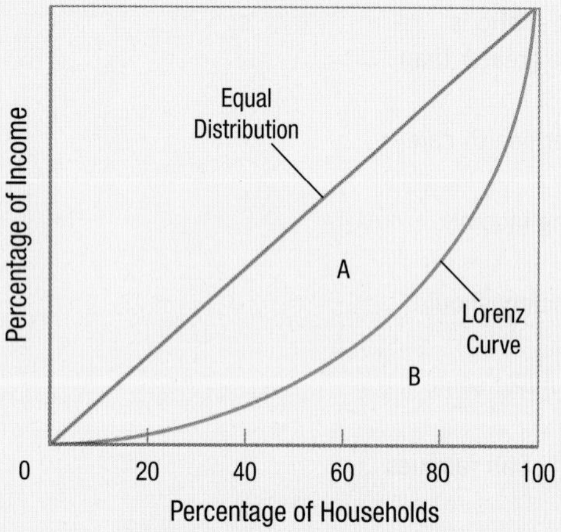

Lorenz curve: shows the cumulative income earned by each segment of the population. The farther the curve is from the 45 degree line, the more unequal the distribution of income.

Gini coefficient: is measured as the ratio between A (area of income inequity) and $A + B$ (total area below equal distribution line). The larger the Gini coefficient, the more unequal the distribution of income.

Since the 1970s, income distribution in the United States has become more unequal. Causes include:

- Differing educational levels
- Economic discrimination
- Market power
- Increase in the number of two-earner households

Stephen Finn/Alamy

Redistribution policies are designed to reduce income inequality. Three common policies are:

1. Progressive taxation: higher tax rates as income increases
2. In-kind transfers: unemployment benefits, welfare, Pell Grants (for college)
3. Noncash benefits: Subsidized or public housing, Medicaid, food stamps

Section 2: Poverty

Poverty is defined differently by each country and by organizations such as the World Bank.

The poverty rate according to the U.S. Census Bureau is the percentage of persons with income below the poverty rate threshold. This includes all money income (before taxes are deducted) and cash benefits and excludes capital gains and noncash benefits.

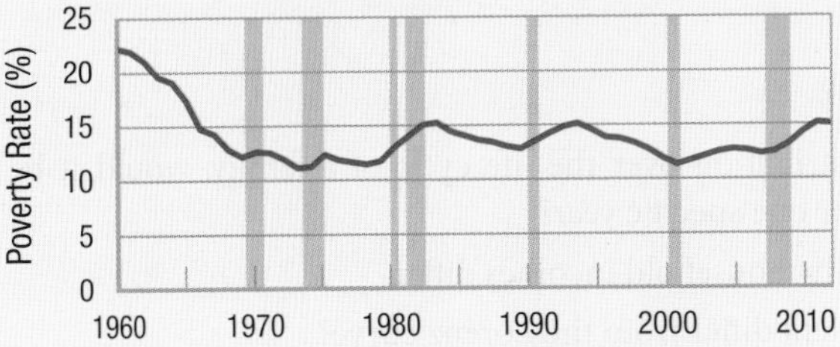

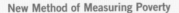

The poverty rate in the United States dropped in the 1960s and 1970s, and has stabilized since, with minor drops during economic expansion and minor rises during recessions.

Hongqi Zhang (aka Michael Zhang)/Dreamstime.com

The depth (or severity) of poverty can be measured using one of two approaches:

Income deficit: How far (in dollars) below the poverty threshold.

Ratio of income to poverty: Measured as the ratio of income compared to the poverty threshold.

0.00–0.50: severely poor (about 6% of Americans)

0.51–1.00: poor

1.01–1.25: near poor

New Method of Measuring Poverty

- includes after-tax money income
- includes noncash benefits (such as food stamps and housing subsidies)
- deducts work-related expenditures (such as transportation and child care) and out-of-pocket medical expenditures

Two Solutions to Reduce Poverty

1. Expand welfare and redistribution programs, and make taxes more progressive.
2. Increase incentives to promote economic growth, which benefits all people, including the poor.

Stuart Key/Dreamstime.com

Rawls: Rawlsian theory states that a society's well-being is only as good as its least fortunate citizen. Therefore, to reduce poverty it advocates for the least amount of income inequality.

Nozick: This theory is based on the argument that property rights (including income) must be protected to provide incentives for growth, which will reduce poverty.

Joel Stettenheim/CORBIS

Considerable movement occurs between income groups (quintiles). About half of all households in a quintile move to a different quintile each decade.

KEY CONCEPTS

income, p. 390
wealth, p. 390
functional distribution of income, p. 390
personal or family distribution of income, p. 391
Lorenz curves, p. 392
Gini coefficient, p. 393
poverty thresholds, p. 399
income deficit, p. 401
ratio of income to poverty, p. 401

QUESTIONS AND PROBLEMS

Check Your Understanding

1. If you look at income distribution over the life cycle of a family, would it be more equally distributed than for one specific year?
2. List some of the reasons why household incomes differ.
3. How does the Gini coefficient differ from the Lorenz curve?
4. Currently the poverty threshold for a family of four is just over $23,000 a year. What does this amount take into account and not take into account?
5. Are the poor in year 2014 just as poor as the poor in 1954? What has changed in 60 years to make poverty different today?
6. What are the primary factors that lead to poverty?

Apply the Concepts

7. Is there an efficiency-equity tradeoff when income is redistributed from the rich to the poor? Explain.
8. What do you think has been the impact on the distribution of income in the United States from the combined impact of the large number of unskilled illegal immigrants and the growing number of dual-earner households?
9. It is probably fair to say that when we classify people as rich or poor at any given moment in time, we are simply describing similar people at different stages in life. Does this life cycle of income and wealth make the income distribution concerns a little less relevant? Why or why not?
10. What would be the change in the distribution of income (Gini coefficient) if the United States decided to permit 10 million new immigrants into the United States who were highly skilled doctors, engineers, executives of large foreign firms, and wealthy foreigners who just want to migrate to the United States? How would the Gini coefficient change if, instead, the United States decided to permit 10 million unskilled foreign workers to enter?
11. Roughly half of all marriages in the United States end in divorce. What is the impact of this divorce rate on the distribution of income and poverty?
12. Poverty rates have declined for blacks and have been relatively stable for everyone else over the last 40 years. But the poverty rate still hovers around 15%. What makes it so difficult to reduce poverty below 10% to 15% of the population?

In the News

13. In 2006, the Nobel Peace Prize went to economist Muhammad Yunus and the Grameen Bank "for their efforts to create economic and social development from below." Yunus led the development of micro loans to poor people without financial security: loans of under $200 to people so poor they could not provide collateral, to use for purchasing basic tools or other basic implements of work. This helped to pull millions of people out of poverty. Discuss how economic prosperity and security for everyone can result in a more peaceful planet.

14. According to the U.S. Department of the Treasury, people in the top income quintile (20%) pay roughly 70% of all federal income taxes, with the remaining 80% paying less than 30%. Further, the bottom half of the population pays less than 10% of all taxes. Many politicians often assert that they want to bring tax relief (presumably with the idea of redistributing income) to "middle- and lower-income" families. Given this distribution of income tax payments, what would middle- and lower-income tax relief look like?

Solving Problems

15. Use the two different distributions of income in the table below to answer the questions that follow.

Quintile	*A*	*B*
Poorest	11.2	10.5
Second	12.0	11.6
Middle	21.2	20.3
Fourth	26.0	25.7
Richest	29.6	31.9

a. Use the grid below and graph the two Lorenz curves.
b. Which curve has a more equal distribution?
c. Are these distributions more or less equal than that for the United States today?

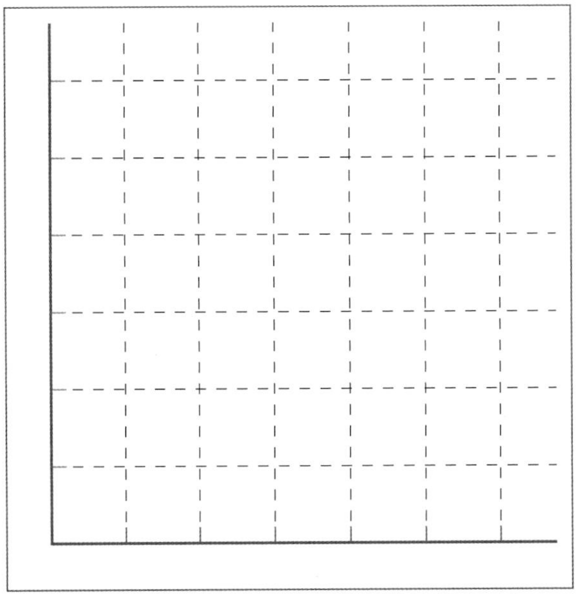

16. The following households each have four persons. Their annual incomes are as follows:

The Aikens:	$25,600
The Browns:	$21,800
The Carlyles:	$18,500
The Donaldsons:	$11,300

Assume that the poverty threshold for a household of four is $23,000. Calculate the income deficit and the income-to-poverty ratio for each family. Classify each family as either not poor, near poor, poor, or severely poor.

USING THE NUMBERS

17. According to By the Numbers, over what period of time did the gap between the full-time minimum wage earnings and the poverty threshold expand the most?
18. According to By the Numbers, about how many Americans used food stamps (now known as SNAP benefits) in the year 2000? How about in the year 2012? (Hint: Use the approximate U.S. population of 300 million to calculate the answers for both years.)

ANSWERS TO QUESTIONS IN CHECKPOINTS

Checkpoint: The Distribution of Income and Wealth

It would clearly improve (make more equal) the before-tax and benefits distribution of income. The impact on the distribution of income after adjusting for current benefits of such a policy would depend on the explicit value of current benefits. Murray suggested that his proposal would cost more for a decade and then begin saving money.

Checkpoint: Poverty

Based on the poverty thresholds, poverty would almost be eliminated by this proposal. In general, the political left would welcome this redistribution except for the elimination of the social safety net. Some people would make bad decisions and not save for retirement or purchase health care coverage, and the political left would still want these services to exist, defeating the idea of the proposal. The political right would worry that once the redistribution scheme is introduced, enough people would reduce their working hours to harm economic growth. Further, the political right would worry that after the redistribution, the safety net would creep back into existence, eroding the benefits of the original idea.

16 International Trade

After studying this chapter you should be able to:

- Describe the benefits of free trade.
- Distinguish between absolute and comparative advantage.
- Describe the economic impacts of trade.
- Describe the terms of trade.
- List the ways in which trade is restricted.
- Discuss the various arguments against free trade.
- Describe the issues surrounding increasing global economic integration.

Every day at the Port of Los Angeles, up to ten mega container ships arrive, each containing 10,000 to 16,000 TEU (*20-foot equivalent units,* or 20 feet × 8 feet × 8.5 feet standard containers) of goods from around the world. A standard tractor trailer can transport two TEUs, which means that up to 80,000 tractor trailers full of goods are brought into the United States each day, *at just one port.*

These cargo ships and trucks transport the goods we enjoy every day that are made in China, France, Brazil, Kenya, Australia, and the 180 other countries with which the United States has trading relations.

Take a quick look in your closet, and count how many countries contributed to your wardrobe—shirts tailored in Hong Kong, shoes made in Italy, sweaters made in Norway, jackets made in China, and the list goes on. On occasion, you might come across something made in the United States, although it is a rarity in the apparel industry. Most Americans wear foreign-made clothing, over half of us drive foreign cars, and even American cars contain many foreign components. Australian wines, Swiss watches, Chilean sea bass, and Brazilian coffee have become common in the United States. We also buy services from other countries, for example, when we travel to Europe and stay in hotels and use its high-speed trains. The opportunity to buy goods and services from other countries gives consumers more variety to choose from, and also provides an opportunity to buy products at lower prices.

Although the United States buys many goods from other countries, it also sells many goods to other countries—just not clothing. The "Made in USA" label is highly respected throughout the world, and the United States sells commercial airplanes, cars and trucks, tractors, high-tech machinery, and pharmaceuticals to individual consumers and businesses in other countries. It also sells agricultural goods and raw materials, such as soybeans, copper, and wood pulp. And it sells services too, such as medical care, tourist services when foreigners visit the United States, higher education (foreign students studying at American colleges), and entertainment, including movies, software, and music.

Trade is now part of the global landscape. Worldwide foreign trade has quadrupled over the past 25 years. In the United States today, the combined value of exports and imports approaches $5 trillion a year. Twenty-five years ago, trade represented under 20% of gross domestic product (GDP); today it accounts for over 30% of GDP. Nearly a tenth of American workers owe their jobs to foreign consumers. Figure 1 shows the current composition of U.S. exports and imports. Note that the United States imports and exports a lot of capital goods—that is, the equipment and machinery used to produce other goods. Also, we export about 50% more services than we import, services such as education and health care. Third, petroleum products represent approximately 13% of imports, totaling $350 billion a year.

FIGURE 1

U.S. Trade by Sector (2012)

This figure shows trade by sector. The United States imports and exports large amounts of capital goods, the equipment and machinery used to produce other goods. Also, nearly one-third of United States exports are services such as education and health care.

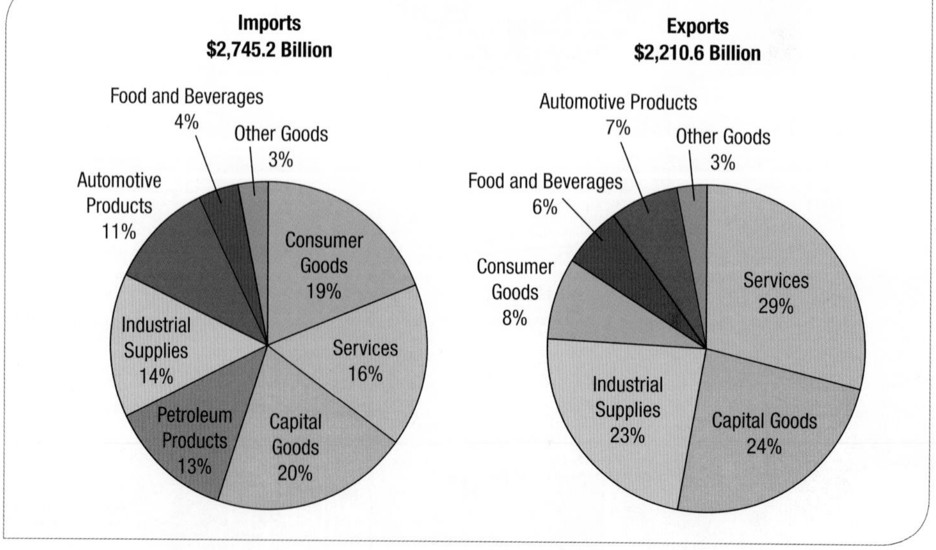

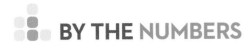

BY THE NUMBERS

International Trade

Most economists would agree that trade has been a net benefit to the world. The 1947 General Agreement on Tariffs and Trade (GATT) lowered tariffs and led to expanded trade and higher standards of living around the world.

Trade deficits (negative trade balances) were not a problem until the mid-1970s, when the United States began importing more than it exported. The recent recession resulted in exports rising while imports fell.

AP Photo/Ben Margot

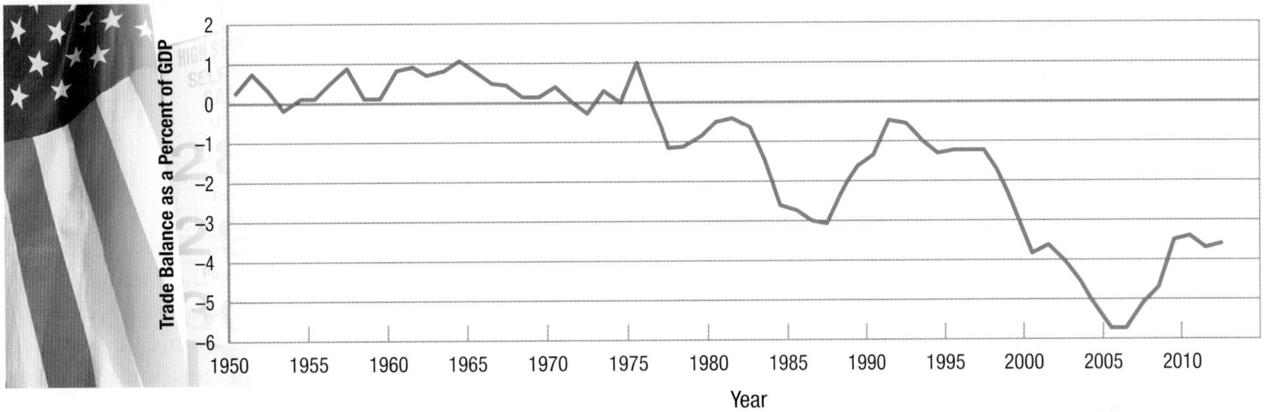

Tariff barriers (a tax on imports) are relatively low in most countries.

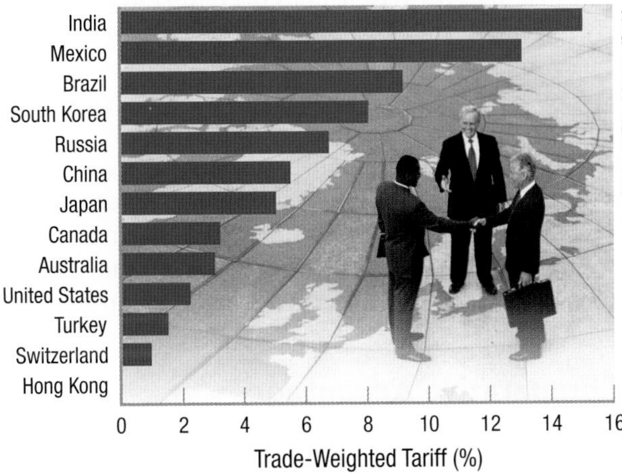

Jon Feingersh/Blend Images/Corbis

Medical tourism is growing because health costs are lower overseas, even including the costs of travel.

Cost of Various Medical Procedures

Procedure	United States	Thailand	Costa Rica
Heart Bypass	$144,317	$22,500	$35,000
Heart Valve	177,665	18,500	31,000
Hip Replacement	100,047	12,000	14,500
Knee Replacement	65,918	10,500	11,700
Hysterectomy	31,474	4,500	7,000
Spinal Fusion	103,761	9,700	22,000

3,150,000

Number of American cars sold in China in 2012.

U.S. public sentiment about lowering trade barriers is mixed, and some even oppose helping displaced workers.

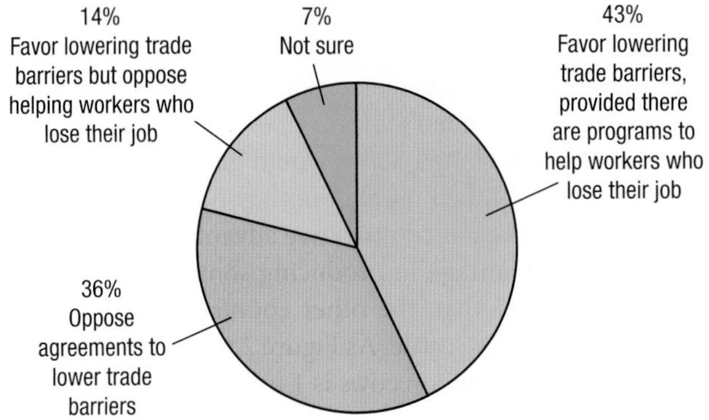

China, once a world powerhouse, slipped in the 20th century but is coming back.

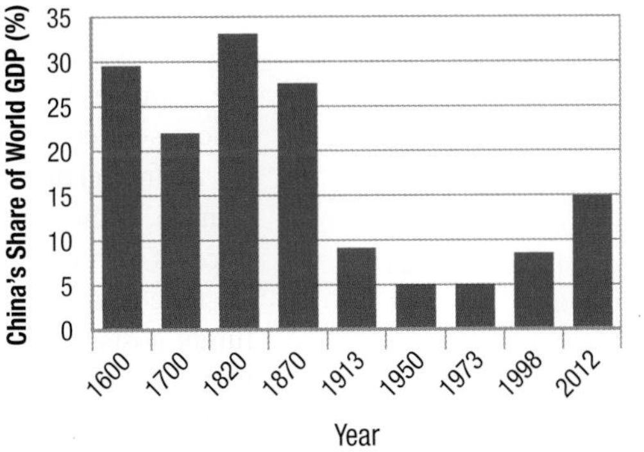

Does all of this world trade make consumers and producers better off? This chapter examines the effects of trade on both the importing (buying) and exporting (selling) countries, and how trade affects the prices and availability of goods and services in each country.

Improved communication and transportation technologies have worked together to promote global economic integration. In addition, most governments around the world have reduced their trade barriers in recent years.

Trade must yield significant benefits or it would not exist. After all, there are no laws requiring countries to trade, just agreements permitting trade and reducing impediments to it. This chapter begins with a discussion of why trade is beneficial. We look at the terms of trade between countries. We then look at the tariffs and quotas sometimes used to restrict trade, calculating their costs. Finally, we will consider some arguments critics have advanced against increased trade and globalization.

The Gains from Trade

autarky A country that does not engage in international trade, also known as a closed economy.

imports Goods and services that are purchased from abroad.

exports Goods and services that are sold abroad.

Economics studies voluntary exchange. People and nations do business with one another because they expect to gain through these transactions. Foreign trade is nearly as old as civilization. Centuries ago, European merchants were already sailing to the Far East to ply the spice trade. Today, people in the United States buy cars from South Korea and electronics from China, along with millions of other products from countries around the world.

Virtually all countries today engage in some form of international trade. Those that trade the least are considered *closed economies*. A country that does not trade at all is called an **autarky.** Most countries, however, are *open economies* that willingly and actively engage in trade with other countries. Trade consists of **imports,** goods and services purchased from other countries, and **exports,** goods and services sold abroad.

Yuri Arcurs/age fotostock

International trade allows consumers to buy goods (such as televisions) produced in many countries. Competition from trade allows for greater variety and lower prices.

Many people assume that trade between nations is a zero-sum game: a game in which, for one party to gain, the other party must lose. Poker games fit this description; one person's winnings must come from another player's losses. This is not true of voluntary trade. Voluntary exchange and trade is a positive-sum game, meaning that both parties to a transaction can gain.

To understand how this works, and thus why nations trade, we need to consider the concepts of absolute and comparative advantage. Note that nations per se do not trade; individuals in specific countries do. We will refer to trade between nations but recognize that individuals, not nations, actually engage in trade. We covered this earlier, in Chapter 2, but it is worthwhile to go through it again.

Absolute and Comparative Advantage

absolute advantage One country can produce more of a good than another country.

comparative advantage One country has a lower opportunity cost of producing a good than another country.

Figure 2 shows hypothetical production possibilities frontiers for the United States and Canada. For simplicity, both countries are assumed to produce only beef and guitars. Given the production possibility frontiers (PPFs) in Figure 2, the United States has an absolute advantage over Canada in the production of both products. An **absolute advantage** exists when one country can produce more of a good than another country. In this case, the United States can produce twice as much beef and 5 times as many guitars as Canada. This is not to say that Canadians are inefficient in producing these goods, but rather that Canada does not have the resources to produce as many goods as the United States does (for one thing, its population is barely a tenth the size of that of the United States).

At first glance, we may wonder why the United States would be willing to trade with Canada. If the United States can produce so much more of both goods, why not just produce its own cattle and guitars? The reason lies in comparative advantage.

One country enjoys a **comparative advantage** in producing some good if its opportunity costs to produce that good are lower than the other country's. In this example, Canada's comparative advantage is in producing cattle. As Figure 2 shows, the opportunity cost for the United States to produce another million cows is 1 million guitars; each added cow essentially costs 1 guitar.

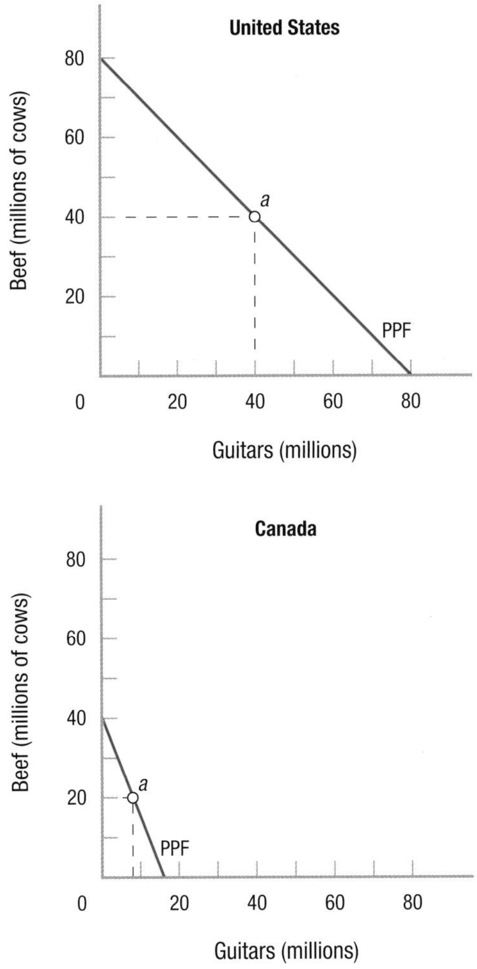

FIGURE 2

Production Possibilities for the United States and Canada

The production possibilities frontiers (PPF) shown here assume that the United States and Canada produce only beef and guitars. In this example, the United States has an absolute advantage over Canada in producing both products; the United States can produce twice as many cattle and 5 times as many guitars as Canada. Canada nonetheless has a comparative advantage over the United States in producing beef.

Contrast this with the situation in Canada. For every guitar Canadian manufacturers forgo making, they can produce 2.5 more cows. This means cows cost only 0.4 guitar in Canada (1/2.5 = 0.4). Canada's comparative advantage is in producing cattle, because a cow costs 0.4 guitar in Canada, while the same cow costs an entire guitar in the United States. By the same token, the United States has a comparative advantage in producing guitars: 1 guitar in the United States costs 1 cow, but the same guitar in Canada costs 2.5 cows.

Table 1 summarizes the opportunity costs of each good in each country and shows which country has the comparative advantage for each good. These relative costs suggest that the United States should focus its resources on guitar production and that Canada should specialize in beef.

TABLE 1 Comparing Opportunity Costs for Beef and Guitar Production

	U.S. Opportunity Cost	Canada Opportunity Cost	Comparative Advantage
Beef production	1 guitar	0.4 guitar	Canada
Guitar production	1 cow	2.5 cows	United States

Gains from Trade

To see how specialization and trade can benefit both countries even when one has an advantage in producing more of both goods, assume that the United States and Canada at first operate at point *a* in Figure 2, producing and consuming their own beef and guitars. As we can see, the United States produces and consumes 40 million cattle and 40 million guitars. Canada produces and consumes 20 million cattle and 8 million guitars. This initial position is similarly shown as points *a* in Figure 3.

FIGURE 3

The Gains from Specialization and Trade to the United States and Canada

Assume Canada specializes in cattle. If the two countries want to continue consuming 60 million cows between them, the United States needs to produce only 20 million. This frees up resources for the United States to begin producing more guitars. Because each cow in the United States costs 1 guitar to produce, reducing beef output by 20 million cattle means that 20 million more guitars can be produced. When the two countries trade their surplus products, both are better off than before.

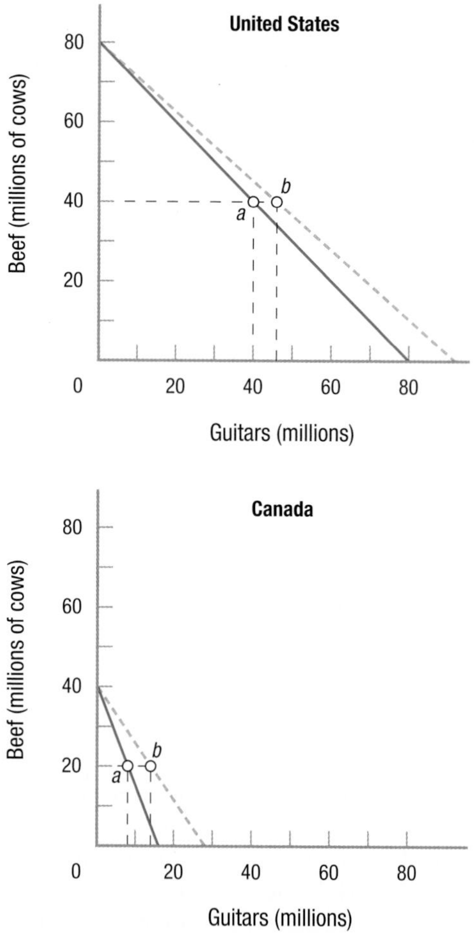

Assume now that Canada specializes in producing cattle, producing all that it can—40 million cows. We will assume that the two countries want to continue consuming 60 million cows between them. This means that the United States needs to produce only 20 million cattle, because Canada is now producing 40 million. This frees up some American resources to produce guitars. Because each cow in the United States costs a guitar, reducing beef output by 20 million cattle means that 20 million more guitars can now be produced.

Thus, the United States is producing 20 million cattle and 60 million guitars. Canada is producing 40 million cattle and no guitars. The combined production of cattle remains the same, 60 million, but guitar production has increased by 12 million (from 48 to 60 million).

The two countries can trade their surplus products and will be better off. This is shown in Table 2. Assuming that they agree to share the added 12 million guitars between them equally, Canada will trade 20 million cattle in exchange for 14 million guitars. Points *b* in Figure 3 show the resulting consumption patterns for each country. Each consumes the same quantity of beef as before trading, but each country now has 6 million more guitars: 46 million for the United States and 14 million for Canada. This is shown in the last column of the table.

The Gains from Trade — TABLE 2

Country and Product	Before Specialization	After Specialization	After Trade
United States			
Cows	40 million	20 million	40 million
Guitars	40 million	60 million	46 million
Canada			
Cows	20 million	40 million	20 million
Guitars	8 million	0	14 million

One important point to remember is that even when one country has an absolute advantage over another, countries still benefit from trade. The gains are small in our example, but they will grow as the two countries approach one another in size and their comparative advantages become more pronounced.

Practical Constraints on Trade At this point, we should take a moment to note some practical constraints on trade. First, every transaction involves costs. These include transportation, communications, and the general costs of doing business. Over the last several

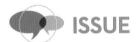

ISSUE

The Challenge of Measuring Imports and Exports in a Global Economy

Before the growth of globalization of manufacturing, the brand names of products would indicate their origin. For example, Sony televisions were made in Japan, Nokia telephones were made in Finland, and a Ford car would be made in the United States using American steel, engines, cloth, and, of course, American labor.

Today, a product's brand name does not tell the entire story. Production has become very complex, with parts sourced from around the world. With such complexities in trade, how then are imports and exports measured?

Do sales of Levi's jeans count as American exports? Although Levi's are an American brand that has for much of its history been produced in the United States, today nearly all Levi's jeans are made in Asia. Therefore, the American-brand jeans we buy count as an *import*. On the other hand, we also consume many products that may seem foreign, but are made in America. The majority of Toyota and Honda cars, for example, are assembled in American factories using American steel, glass, and other materials. The same is true to a lesser extent for luxury brands such as BMW, which produces many compact cars in South Carolina. For all but a few parts (such as the engine and transmission) that are made in Japan or Germany, these cars are as American as apple pie, and are not counted as imports.

In order to measure imports and exports accurately, the United States Bureau of Economic Analysis tabulates data from documents collected by U.S. Customs and Border Protection, which details the appraised value (price paid) for all shipments of goods into and out of the ports of entry (whether by land, air, or sea). The value of imported and exported services is more difficult to measure, and is based on a survey of monthly government and industry reports to determine the value of all services bought from and sold to foreigners.

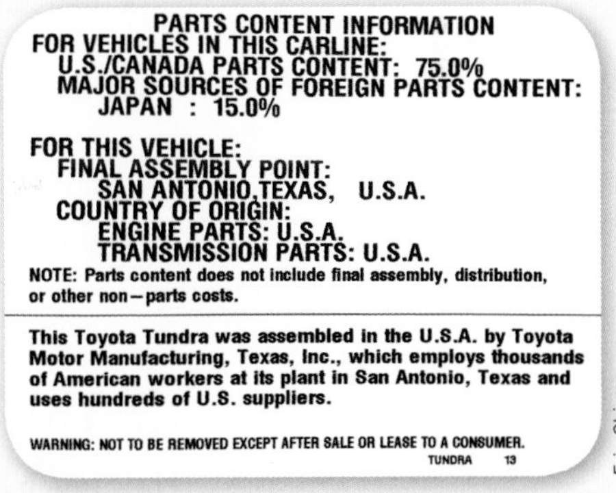
PARTS CONTENT INFORMATION
FOR VEHICLES IN THIS CARLINE:
U.S./CANADA PARTS CONTENT: 75.0%
MAJOR SOURCES OF FOREIGN PARTS CONTENT:
JAPAN : 15.0%
FOR THIS VEHICLE:
FINAL ASSEMBLY POINT:
SAN ANTONIO,TEXAS, U.S.A.
COUNTRY OF ORIGIN:
ENGINE PARTS: U.S.A.
TRANSMISSION PARTS: U.S.A.
NOTE: Parts content does not include final assembly, distribution, or other non–parts costs.
This Toyota Tundra was assembled in the U.S.A. by Toyota Motor Manufacturing, Texas, Inc., which employs thousands of American workers at its plant in San Antonio, Texas and uses hundreds of U.S. suppliers.
WARNING: NOT TO BE REMOVED EXCEPT AFTER SALE OR LEASE TO A CONSUMER.
TUNDRA 13

Eric Chiang

A domestic content label of an "imported" Toyota truck.

The globalized economy has been spurred in large part due to falling transportation and communication costs in the past few decades. Companies face ever greater competition, applying more pressure to reduce production costs. The expansion of the production process to a worldwide factory is just one way our economy has changed, and this trend is likely to continue into the future.

decades, however, transportation and communication costs have declined all over the world, resulting in growing world trade.

Second, the production possibilities frontiers for nations are not linear; rather, they are governed by increasing costs and diminishing returns. Countries find it difficult to specialize only in one product. Indeed, specializing in one product is risky because the market for the product can always decline, new technology might replace it, or its production can be disrupted by changing weather patterns. This is a perennial problem for developing countries that often build their exports and trade around one agricultural commodity.

Although it is true that trading partners benefit from trade, some individuals and groups within each country may lose. Individual workers in those industries at a comparative disadvantage are likely to lose their jobs, and thus may require retraining, relocation, or other help if they are to move smoothly into new occupations.

When the United States signed the North American Free Trade Agreement (NAFTA) with Canada and Mexico, many U.S. workers experienced this sort of dislocation. Some U.S. jobs went south to Mexico because of lower wages. States such as Texas and Arizona experienced greater levels of job dislocation due to their proximity to Mexico. Still, by opening up more markets for U.S. products, NAFTA has stimulated the U.S. economy. The goal is that displaced workers, newly retrained, will end up with new and better jobs, although there is no guarantee this will happen.

CHECKPOINT

THE GAINS FROM TRADE

- An absolute advantage exists when one country can produce more of a good than another country.
- A comparative advantage exists when one country can produce a good at a lower opportunity cost than another country.
- Both countries gain from trade when each specializes in producing goods in which they have a comparative advantage.
- Transaction costs, diminishing returns, and the risk associated with specialization all place some practical constraints on trade.

QUESTIONS: When two individuals voluntarily engage in trade, they both benefit or the trade wouldn't occur—one party wouldn't choose to be worse off after the trade. Is the same true for nations? Is everyone in both nations better off?

Answers to the Checkpoint questions can be found at the end of this chapter.

The Terms of Trade

How much can a country charge when it sells its goods to another country? How much must it pay for imported goods? The terms of trade determine the prices of imports and exports.

To keep things simple, assume that each country has only one export and one import, priced at P_x and P_m. The ratio of the price of the exported goods to the price of the imported goods, P_x/P_m, is the terms of trade. Thus, if a country exports computers and imports coffee, with two computers trading for one ton of coffee, the price of a computer must be one-half the price of a ton of coffee.

terms of trade The ratio of the price of exported goods to the price of imported goods (P_x/P_m).

When countries trade many commodities, the **terms of trade** are defined as the average price of exports divided by the average price of imports. This can get a bit complicated, given that the price of each import and export is quoted in its own national currency, while the exchange rate between the two currencies may be constantly changing. We will ignore these complications by translating currencies into dollars, focusing our attention on how the terms of trade are determined and the impact of trade.

Determining the Terms of Trade

To get a feel for how the terms of trade are determined, let us consider the trade in golf clubs between the United States and South Korea. We will assume the United States has a comparative advantage in producing golf clubs; all prices are given in dollars.

Panel A of Figure 4 shows the demand and supply of sets of golf clubs in the United States. The upward sloping supply curve reflects increasing opportunity costs in golf club production. As the United States continues to specialize in golf club production, resources less suited to this purpose must be employed, resulting in rising costs for golf club production. Because of this rise in costs as ever more resources are shifted to golf clubs, the United States will eventually lose its comparative advantage in golf club production. This represents one limit on specialization and trade.

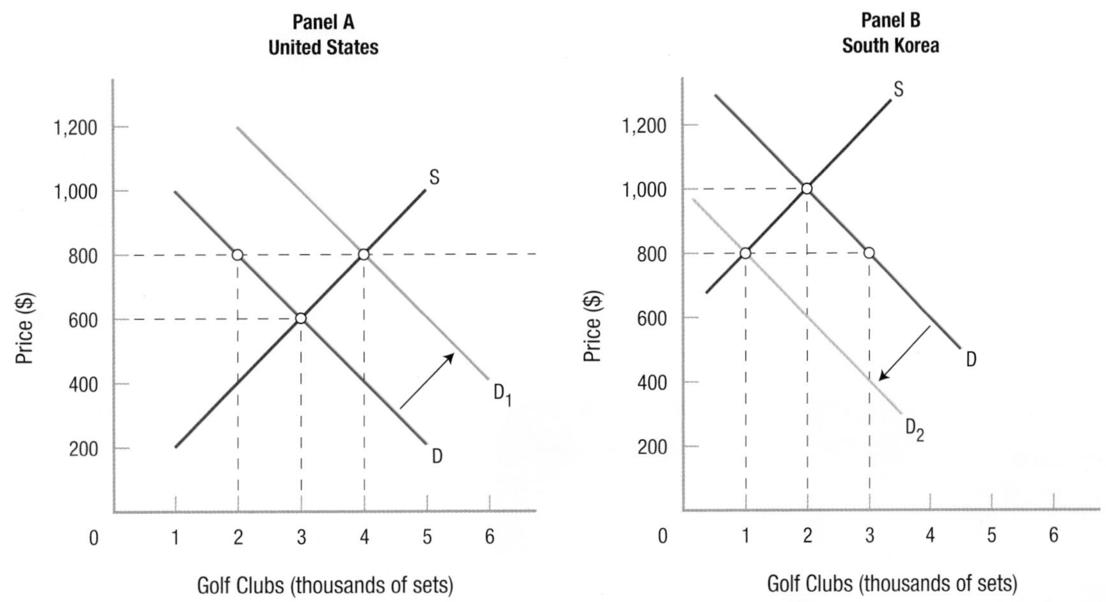

FIGURE 4

Determining the Terms of Trade

Panel A shows the demand and supply of golf clubs in the United States; the upward slope of the supply curve reflects increasing opportunity costs to produce more golf clubs. The United States begins in pretrade equilibrium at $600 and South Korea's initial equilibrium is at $1,000. With trade, Korean consumers will begin buying American golf clubs because of their lower price. American golf club makers will increase production to meet this new demand. Korean golf club firms will see sales of their golf clubs decline as prices begin to fall. Ignoring transport costs, trade will continue until prices reach $800. At this point, American exports (2,000) are just equal to Korean imports (2,000).

Let us assume that the United States begins in pretrade equilibrium, with the price of sets of golf clubs at $600 each. Panel B shows South Korea initially in equilibrium with a higher price of $1,000. Because prices for golf clubs from the United States are lower, when trade begins, Korean consumers will begin buying U.S. golf clubs.

American golf club makers will increase production to meet this new demand. Korean golf club firms, conversely, will see the sales of their golf clubs decline. For now, let us ignore transport costs, such that trade continues until prices reach $800. At this point, U.S. exports (2,000 sets of golf clubs) are just equal to Korean imports. Both countries are now in equilibrium, with the price of golf clubs somewhere between the two pretrade equilibrium prices ($800 in this case).

Imagine this same process simultaneously working itself out with many other goods, including some at which the Koreans have a comparative advantage, such as interactive televisions. As each product settles into an equilibrium price, the terms of trade between these two countries is determined.

The Impact of Trade

Our examination of absolute and comparative advantage has thus far highlighted the benefits of trade. A closer look at Figure 4, however, shows that trade produces winners and losers.

Picking up on the previous example, golf club producers in the United States are happy, having watched their sales rise from 3,000 to 4,000 units. Predictably, management and workers in this industry will favor even more trade with South Korea and the rest of the world. Yet, domestic consumers of golf clubs are worse off, because after trade they purchase only 2,000 sets at the higher equilibrium price of $800.

Contrast this situation in the net exporting country, the United States, with that of the net importer, South Korea. Korean golf club producers are worse off than before because the price of golf clubs fell from $1,000 to $800, and their output was reduced to 1,000 units. Consequently, they must cut jobs, leaving workers and managers in the Korean golf club industry unhappy with its country's trade policies. Korean consumers, however, are beneficiaries of this expanded trade, because they can purchase 3,000 sets of golf clubs at a lower price of $800 each.

These results are not merely hypothetical. This is the story of free trade, which has been played out time and time again: Some sectors of the economy win, and some lose. American consumers have been happy to purchase Korean televisions such as Samsung and LG, given their high quality and low prices. American television producers (such as RCA and Zenith) have not been so pleased, nor have their employees, having watched television factories close and workers displaced as competition from abroad forced these companies out of business.

Mike Flippo/Shutterstock

Wong Maye-E/AP Images

Trade allows American golf club producers to expand sales globally, while Korean golfers benefit from their availability.

Similarly, the ranks of American textile workers have been decimated over the past three decades as domestic clothing producers have increasingly become nothing but designers and marketers of clothes, shifting their production overseas to countries in which wages are lower. American-made clothing is now essentially a thing of the past.

To be sure, American consumers have enjoyed a substantial drop in the price of clothing, because labor forms a significant part of the cost of clothing production. Still, being able to purchase inexpensive T-shirts made in China is small consolation for the unemployed textile worker in North Carolina.

The undoubted pain suffered by the losers from trade often is translated into pressure put on politicians to restrict trade in one way or another. The pain is often felt more strongly than the "happiness" felt by those who benefit from trade.

How Trade Is Restricted

Trade restrictions can range from subsidies provided to domestic firms to protect them against lower priced imports to embargoes by which the government bans any trade with a country. Between these two extremes are more intermediate policies, such as exchange controls that limit the amount of foreign currency available to importers or citizens who travel abroad. Regulation, licensing, and government purchasing policies are all frequently used to promote or ensure the purchase of domestic products. The main reason for these trade restrictions is simple: The industry and its employees actually feel the pain and lobby extensively for protection, while the huge benefits of lower prices are diffused among millions of consumers whose benefits are each so small that fighting against a trade barrier isn't worth their time.

The most common forms of trade restrictions are tariffs and quotas. Panel A of Figure 5 shows the average U.S. tariff rates since 1900. Some economists have suggested that the

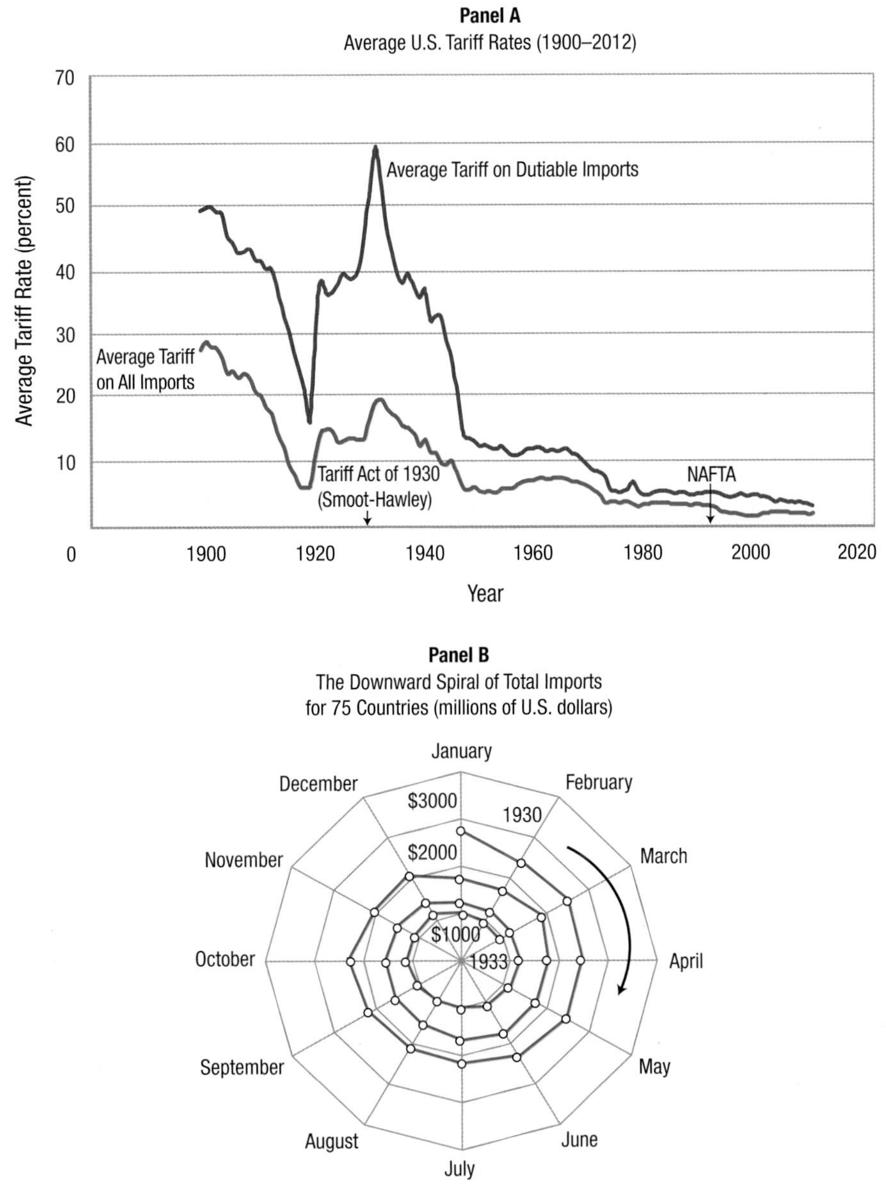

FIGURE 5

Average U.S. Tariff Rates, 1900–2012, and the Downward Spiral of World Imports, 1930–1933

Tariffs and quotas are the most common forms of trade restrictions. Panel A shows that tariff rates in the United States peaked during the Great Depression. Over the last several decades, tariffs have steadily declined to an average of about 2% today. When tariffs jumped with the passage of the Smoot-Hawley Act in 1930, world imports spiraled downward as shown in panel B. As trade between nations declined, incomes, output, and employment also fell worldwide. In panel B, total monthly imports in millions of U.S. dollars for 75 countries is shown spiraling downward from $2,738 million in January 1930 to $1,057 million in March 1933.

Source: Charles Kindleberger, *The World Depression 1929–1939* (Berkeley: University of California Press), 1986, p. 170.

tariff wars that erupted in the 1920s and culminated in the passage of the Smoot-Hawley Act in 1930 were an important factor underlying the severity of the Great Depression. Panel B shows the impact of higher tariffs on worldwide imports from 1930 to 1933. The higher tariffs reduced trade, leading to a reduction in income, output, and employment, and added fuel to the worldwide depression. Since the 1930s, the United States has played a leading role in trade liberalization, with average tariff rates declining to a current rate of roughly 2%.

Effects of Tariffs and Quotas

tariff A tax on imported products. When a country taxes imported products, it drives a wedge between the product's domestic price and its price on the world market.

What exactly are the effects of tariffs and quotas? **Tariffs** are often *ad valorem* taxes. This means that the product is taxed by a certain percentage of its price as it crosses the border. Other tariffs are unit taxes (also known as *specific tariffs*): A fixed tax per unit of the product is assessed at the border. Tariffs are designed to generate revenues and to drive a wedge between the domestic price of a product and its price on the world market. The effects of a tariff are shown in Figure 6.

FIGURE 6

Effects of a Tariff

What are the effects of a typical tariff? Supply and demand curves S and D represent domestic supply and demand. Assume the product's world price of $400 is lower than its domestic price. Imports will therefore be 2,000 units. If the country imposes a tariff of $100 on this product, the domestic price rises to $500, and imports fall to 1,000 units. Domestic consumers now buy less of the product at higher prices. However, the domestic industry is happy because its prices and output have risen. Also, the government collects revenues equal to the shaded area.

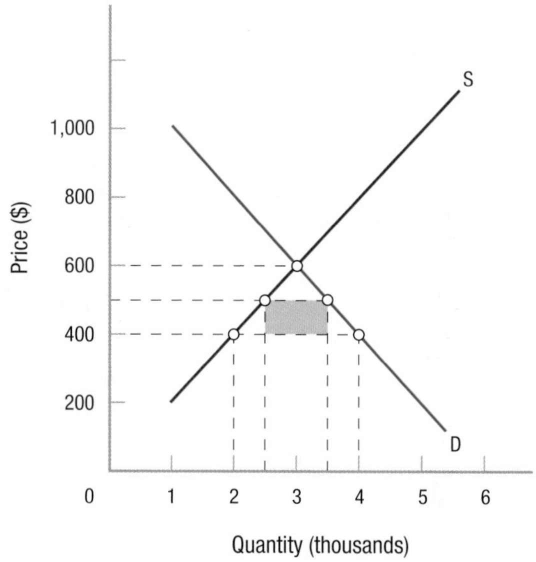

Domestic supply and demand for the product are shown in Figure 6 as S and D. Assume that the product's world price of $400 is lower than its domestic price of $600. Domestic quantity demanded (4,000 units) will consequently exceed domestic quantity supplied (2,000 units) at the world price of $400. Imports to this country will therefore be 2,000 units.

Now assume that the firms and workers in the industry hurt by the lower world price lobby for a tariff and are successful. The country imposes a tariff of $100 per unit on this product. The results are clear. The product's price in this country rises to $500 and imports fall to 1,000 units (3,500 – 2,500). Domestic consumers buy less of the product at higher prices. Even so, the domestic industry is happy, because its prices and output have risen. The government, meanwhile, collects revenues equal to $100,000 ($100 × 1,000), the shaded area in Figure 6. These revenues can be significant: In the 1800s, tariffs were the federal government's dominant form of revenue. It is only in the last century that the federal government has come to rely more on other sources of revenue, including taxes on income, sales, and property.

Figure 7 shows the effects of a **quota.** They are similar to what we saw in Figure 6, except that the government restricts the quantity of imports into the country to 1,000 units. Imports fall to the quota level, and consumers again lose, because they must pay higher prices for less output. Producers and their employees gain as prices and employment in the domestic industry rise. For a quota, however, the government does not collect revenue. Then who gets this revenue? The foreign exporting company gets it in the form of higher prices for its products. This explains why governments prefer tariffs over quotas.

quota A government set limit on the quantity of imports into a country.

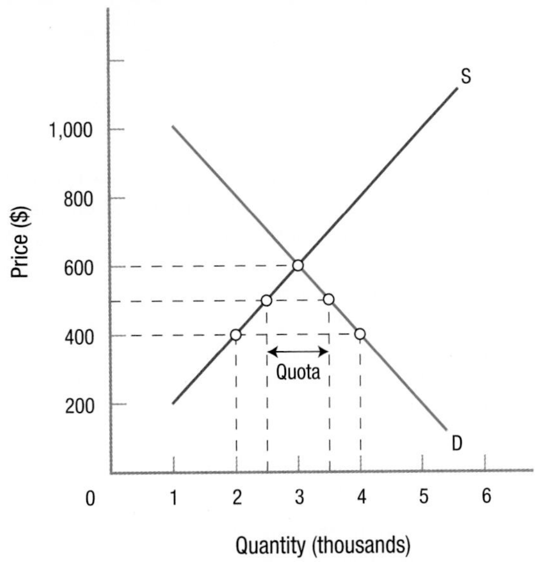

FIGURE 7

Effects of a Quota

What are the effects of a quota? They are similar to the effects of a tariff, except that the government restricts the quantity of imports into the country to 1,000 units. Imports fall to the quota level, and again consumers lose as they must pay higher prices for less output. Producers and their employees gain as prices and employment in the domestic industry rise. With a quota, however, the government does not collect revenues.

The United States imposed quotas on Japanese automobiles in the 1980s. The primary effect of these quotas was initially to raise the minimum standard equipment and price dramatically for some Japanese cars and ultimately to increase the number of Japanese cars made in American factories. If a firm is limited in the number of vehicles it can sell, why not sell higher priced ones where the profit margins are higher? The Toyota Land Cruiser, for instance, was originally a bare-bones SUV selling for under $15,000. With quotas, this vehicle was transformed into a luxury behemoth with all the bells and whistles standard. Although quotas on Japanese automobiles have long expired, Japanese automakers continue to produce a wide array of luxury automobiles today.

One problem with tariffs and quotas is that when they are imposed, large numbers of consumers pay just a small amount more for the targeted products. Few consumers are willing to spend time and effort lobbying Congress to end or forestall these trade barriers from being introduced. Producers, however, are often few in number, and they stand to gain tremendously from such trade barriers. It is no wonder that such firms have large lobbying budgets and provide campaign contributions to political candidates.

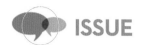

ISSUE

Do Foreign Trade Zones Help or Hurt American Consumers and Workers?

Driving through the gates of the Cartago *Zona Franca* in Costa Rica, one encounters a remarkable sight in a historic Central American town: large factories adorned with the names of large American companies in industries including pharmaceuticals, semiconductors, medical supplies, and household products. What are these companies doing in Costa Rica, and why did they choose to locate within this small gated compound?

In Cartago, as well as in other cities throughout the world, clusters of multinational companies engage in manufacturing activities. These companies are taking advantage of the benefits offered by foreign trade zones, also commonly known as free trade zones or export processing zones.

A foreign trade zone is a designated area in a country where foreign companies can import inputs, without tariffs, to be used for product assembly by local workers who are often paid a fraction of what equivalent workers would be paid in the company's home country. By operating in a foreign trade zone, all inputs coming into a country are exempted from tariffs as long as the finished products (with some exceptions) are then exported from the country. Further, companies are often exempted from other taxes levied by the government.

Countries such as China, the Philippines, and Costa Rica establish foreign trade zones to attract foreign investment, which creates well-paying jobs relative to wages paid by domestic companies. Countries with high literacy rates, like Costa Rica, are especially attractive because their workers can perform semiskilled tasks such as assembling electronic and computer products or handling customer service calls. Foreign trade zones also are prevalent along border towns, such as those in Mexico, where easy transportation to and from the United States allows inputs and products to flow rapidly.

Library of Congress, Prints and Photographs Division, WPA Poster Collection, cph.3g04244

Foreign trade zones have long been a part of the U.S. economy. Today, foreign trade zones exist throughout the country.

Although companies operating in foreign trade zones benefit from lower production costs and the host country benefits from jobs created, not everyone is in favor of foreign trade zones. Various unions in the United States view foreign trade zones as facilitating the offshoring of American jobs. Offshoring (also commonly referred to as outsourcing) occurs when part of the production process (typically the labor-intensive portions) is sent to countries with lower input costs.

What may be surprising, however, is that foreign trade zones and offshoring are not one-way streets. Foreign trade zones are not limited to developing countries with low labor costs. The United States has many foreign trade zones established for the same purpose: to attract foreign companies to invest in manufacturing plants. Although American labor costs are high, they often are lower than wages in European countries or in Japan. By moving production to the United States, European and Japanese companies produce goods such as cars while enjoying the same tax benefits described earlier by American companies operating abroad.

Most of the arguments against offshoring are based on anecdotal evidence—a plant closing here, a closing there, and so on. But in the mid-2000s, the Bureau of Labor Statistics developed a survey to quantify the levels of both offshoring and inshoring (the flow of jobs to the United States by firms from other countries). In the year 2012, statistics showed that the *net* effect was roughly equal, that almost as many jobs were created by foreign companies in the United States as jobs lost from American companies moving production facilities overseas.

As we have seen, there are both winners and losers in trade. But in general, economists found that there is a net increase in income to U.S. residents from offshoring. When all impacts are considered, including savings to consumers from lower product costs, imports of U.S. goods by foreigners, profits to U.S. affiliates, and the value of labor reemployed, the benefits tend to outweigh the costs. Clearly, those who lose their jobs suffer. But with a policy to provide training to displaced workers, the savings from offshoring can lead to greater investment and growth in the long run.

CHECKPOINT

THE TERMS OF TRADE

- The terms of trade are determined by the ratio of the price of exported goods to the price of imported goods.
- The terms of trade are set by the markets in each country and by exports and imports that eventually equalize the prices.

- Trade leads to winners and losers in each country and in each market.
- Trade restrictions vary from subsidies to domestic firms to government bans on the import of foreign products.
- Tariffs are taxes on imports that protect domestic producers and generate revenue for the government.
- Quotas represent restrictions on the volume of particular imports that can come into a country. Quotas do not generate revenue for governments and are infrequently used.

QUESTION: When the government imposes a quota on foreign trucks, who benefits and who loses?

Answers to the Checkpoint question can be found at the end of this chapter.

Arguments Against Free Trade

We have seen the benefits of trade, and have looked at how trade undoubtedly benefits some and harms others. Those who are harmed by trade often seek to restrict trade, primarily in the form of tariffs and quotas. Because trade leads to some loss, those who are harmed by trade have made arguments against free trade.

The arguments against free trade fall into two camps. Traditional economic arguments include protection for infant industries, protection against dumping, low foreign wages, and support for industries judged vital for national defense. More recent arguments focus on globalization (social and economic) concerns that embody political-economy characteristics. These include domestic employment concerns, environmental concerns, and the impact of globalization on working conditions in developing nations. In what follows, we take a critical look at each of these arguments, showing that most of these arguments do not have a solid empirical basis.

Traditional Economic Arguments

Arguments against trade are not new. Despite the huge gains from trade, distortions (subsidies and trade barriers) continue because changing current policies will hurt those dependent on subsidies and trade restrictions, and these firms and workers will show their displeasure in the voting booth. All of these traditional economic arguments against free trade seem reasonable on their face, but on closer examination, they look less attractive.

Infant Industry Argument An **infant industry,** it is argued, is one that is too underdeveloped to achieve comparative advantage or perhaps even to survive in the global market. Such an industry may be too small or undercapitalized, or its management and workers may be too inexperienced, to compete. Unless the industry's government provides it with some protection through tariffs, quotas, or subsidies, it might not survive in the face of foreign competition.

infant industry An industry so underdeveloped that protection is needed for it to become competitive on the world stage or to ensure its survival.

In theory, once the infant industry has been given this protection, it should be able to grow, acquiring the necessary capital and expertise needed to compete internationally. Germany and the United States used high tariffs to protect their infant manufacturing sectors in the 1800s, and Japan continued to maintain import restrictions up until the 1970s.

Although the infant industry argument sounds reasonable, it has several limitations. First, protecting an industry must be done in a way that makes the industry internationally competitive. Many countries coddle their firms, and these producers never seem to develop into "mature," internationally viable firms. Once protection is provided (typically a protective tariff), it is difficult to remove after an industry has matured. The industry and its workers continue to convince policymakers of the need for continued protection.

Second, infant industry protection often tends to focus on capital manufacturing. Countries with huge labor supplies would do better to develop their labor-intensive industries first, letting more capital-intensive industries develop over time. Every country, after all, should seek to exploit its comparative advantages, but it is difficult to determine which industries have a chance of developing a comparative advantage in the future and should be temporarily protected.

Third, many industries seem to be able to develop without protections, therefore countries may be wasting their resources and reducing their incomes by imposing protection measures.

Clearly, the infant industry argument is not valid for advanced economies such as those of the United States, much of Europe, and Japan. The evidence for developing nations shows some benefits but is mixed for the reasons noted above.

dumping Selling goods abroad at lower prices than in home markets, and often below cost.

Antidumping **Dumping** means that goods are sold at lower prices (often *below cost*) abroad than in their home market. This is typically a result of government subsidies.

In the same way that price discrimination improves profits, firms can price discriminate between their home markets and foreign markets. Let's assume that costs of production are $100 per unit for all firms (domestic and foreign). A state subsidy of $30 a unit, for example, reduces domestic costs to $70 per unit and permits the firm to sell its product in world markets at these lower prices. These state subsidies give these firms a cost advantage in foreign markets.

Firms can use dumping as a form of predatory pricing, using higher prices in their domestic markets to support unrealistically low prices in foreign markets. The goal of predatory pricing is to drive foreign competitors out of business. When this occurs, the firm doing the dumping then comes back and imposes higher prices. In the long run, these higher prices thereby offset the company's short-term losses.

Dumping violates American trade laws. If the federal government determines that a foreign firm is dumping products onto the American market, it can impose antidumping tariffs on the offending products. The government, however, must distinguish among dumping, legitimate price discrimination, and legitimate instances of lower cost production arising from comparative advantage.

Low Foreign Wages Some advocates of trade barriers maintain that domestic firms and their workers need to be protected from displacement by cheap foreign labor. Without this protection, it is argued, foreign manufacturers that pay their workers pennies an hour will flood the market with low-cost products. As we have already seen, this argument has something to it: Workers in advanced economies can be displaced by low-wage foreign workers. This is what has happened in the American textile industry.

Once a handful of American clothing manufacturers began moving their production facilities overseas, thereby undercutting domestic producers, other manufacturers were forced to follow them. American consumers have benefited from lower clothing prices, but many displaced textile workers are still trying to get retrained and adapt to work in other industries. More recently, many manufacturing jobs have drifted overseas, and high-technology firms today are shifting some help desk facilities and computer programming to foreign shores.

On balance, however, the benefits of lower priced goods considerably exceed the costs of lost employment. The federal government has resisted imposing protection measures for the sake of protecting jobs, instead funding programs that help displaced workers transition to new lines of work.

National Defense Argument In times of national crisis or war, the United States must be able to rely on key domestic industries, such as oil, steel, and defense. Some have argued that these industries may require some protection even during peacetime to ensure that they are already well established when a crisis strikes and importing key products may be impossible. Within limits, this argument is sound. Still, the United States has the capacity to produce such a wide variety of products that protections for specific industries would seem to be unjustified and unnecessary.

So what are we to make of these traditional arguments? Although they all seem reasonable, they all have deficiencies. Infant industries may be helped in the short run, but protections are often extended well beyond what is necessary, resulting in inefficient firms that are vulnerable on world markets. Dumping is clearly a potential problem, but distinguishing real cases of dumping and comparative advantage has often proven difficult in practice. Low foreign wages are often the only comparative advantage a developing nation has to offer the world economy, and typically, the benefits to consumers vastly outweigh the loss to a particular industry. Maintaining (protecting) industries for national defense has merit and may be appropriate for some countries, but for a country as huge and diversified as the United States, it is probably unnecessary.

Wangsong/Shutterstock

The steel industry is one of several that are considered key domestic industries vital in times of national crisis. Therefore, industry executives frequently argue for protection against foreign competition.

Recent Globalization Concerns

Expanded trade and globalization have provided the world's producers and consumers with many benefits. Some observers, however, have voiced concerns about globalization and its effects on domestic employment, the global environment, and working conditions in developing nations. Let's look at each one of these globalization concerns.

Trade and Domestic Employment Some critics argue that increased trade and globalization spell job losses for domestic workers. We have seen that this can be true. Some firms, unable to compete with imports, will be forced to lay off workers or even close their doors. Even so, increased trade usually allows firms that are exporters to expand their operations and hire new workers. These will be firms in industries with comparative advantages. For the United States, these industries tend to be those that require a highly skilled workforce, resulting in higher wages for American workers.

Clearly, those industries that are adding workers and those that are losing jobs are different industries. For workers who lose their jobs, switching industries can be difficult and time-consuming, and often it requires new investments in human capital. American trade policy recognizes this problem, and the Trade Adjustment Assistance (TAA) program provides workers with job search assistance, job training, and some relocation allowances. In some industries sensitive to trade liberalization, including textiles and agriculture, trade policies are designed to proceed gradually, thus giving these industries and their workers some extra time to adjust.

Possible employment losses in some noncompetitive industries do not seem to provide enough justification for restricting trade. By imposing trade restrictions such as tariffs or quotas in one industry, employment opportunities in many other industries may be reduced. Open, competitive trade encourages producers to focus their production on those areas in which the country stands at a comparative advantage. Free trade puts competitive pressure on domestic firms, forcing them to be more productive and competitive, boosting the flow of information and technology across borders, and widening the availability of inputs for producers. At the end of the day, consumers benefit from these efficiencies, having more goods to choose from and enjoying a higher standard of living.

Trade and the Environment Concerns about globalization, trade, and the environment usually take one of two forms. Some people are concerned that expanded trade and globalization will lead to increased environmental degradation as companies take advantage of lax environmental laws abroad, particularly in the developing world. Others worry that attempts by the government to strengthen environmental laws will be challenged by trading partners as disguised protectionism.

Domestic environmental regulations usually target a product or process that creates pollution or other environmental problems. One concern in establishing environmental regulations, however, is that they not unfairly discriminate against the products of another country. This is usually not a serious problem. Nearly all trade agreements, including the World Trade Organization Agreements and NAFTA, have provisions permitting countries to enforce measures "necessary to protect human, animal or plant life or health" or to conserve exhaustible natural resources. Nothing in our trade agreements prevents the United States from implementing environmental regulations as long as they do not unreasonably discriminate against our trading partners.

Will free trade come at the expense of the environment? Every action involves a tradeoff. Clearly, there can be cases in which the benefits of trade accruing to large numbers of people result in harm to a more concentrated group. However, trade policies can also be complementary to good environmental policies. For example, increased free trade in agriculture encourages countries with fertile lands to specialize in growing crops while discouraging countries from farming marginal lands that require the use of environmentally damaging pesticides and chemicals.

We have seen that trade raises incomes in developed and developing countries. And environmental protection is an income elastic good: As incomes rise, the demand for environmental protections rises and its environmental protection efforts begin to improve.

In poor, developing nations, environmental protection will not at first be a priority. Critics of globalization are concerned that because environmental and labor standards in many developing nations are well below those of the developed countries, there will be pressure to adopt these lower standards in rich nations due to trade and foreign direct investment. But as Bhagwati and Hudec argue, there has been no systematic "race to the bottom" and many corporations often have the highest environmental and labor standards in the developing world.[1] Also, it is worth noting that over time, as incomes rise, environmental protection takes on added importance even in poorer nations. On balance, trade probably benefits the environment over the longer term, as incomes grow in developing nations and environmental protections take on greater importance.

Trade and Its Effect on Working Conditions in Developing Nations Some antiglobalization activists argue that trade between the United States and developing countries, where wages are low and working conditions are deplorable, exploits workers in these developing countries. Clearly, such trade does hurt American workers in low-wage, low-skilled occupations who cannot compete with the even lower wage workers overseas. But it is not clear that workers in developing countries would be helped if the United States were to cut off its trade with those countries that refuse to improve wages or working conditions.

Restricting trade with countries that do not raise wages to levels we think acceptable or bring working conditions up to our standards would probably do more harm than good. Low wages reflect, among other factors, small investments in human capital, low productivity, and meager living standards characteristic of developing nations. Blocking trade with these nations may deprive them of their key chance to grow and to improve in those areas in which we would like to see change.

Liberalized trade policies, economic freedom, and a legal system that respects property rights and foreign capital investment probably provide the best recipe for

---

[1] Jagdish Bhagwati and Robert Hudec (eds.), *Fair Trade and Harmonization, Vol. 1: Economic Analysis* (Cambridge, MA: MIT Press), 1996.

rapid development, economic growth, environmental protection, and improved wages and working conditions.

In summary, trade does result in job losses in some industries, but the gain for consumers and the competitive pressures that trade puts on domestic companies is beneficial to the economy as a whole. Trade raises incomes in developing nations, resulting in a growing demand for more environmentally friendly production processes. Trade is not the reason for low environmental standards in developing countries; they result from low incomes, low standards of living, and poor governmental policies. Trade brings about higher levels of income and ultimately better working conditions.

CHECKPOINT

ARGUMENTS AGAINST FREE TRADE

- The infant industry argument claims that some industries are so underdeveloped that they need protection to survive in a global competitive environment.
- Dumping involves selling products at different prices in domestic and foreign markets, often with the help of subsidies from the government. This is a form of predatory pricing to gain market share in the foreign market.
- Some suggest that domestic workers need to be protected from the low wages in foreign countries. This puts the smaller aggregate loss to small groups ahead of the greater general gains from trade. Also, for many countries, a low wage is their primary comparative advantage.
- Some argue that select industries need protection to ensure that they will exist for national defense reasons.
- Clearly, globalization has meant that some U.S. workers have lost jobs to foreign competition, and some advocates would restrict trade on these grounds alone. But on net, trade has led to higher overall employment. The U.S. government recognizes these issues and has instituted a Trade Adjustment Assistance (TAA) program to help workers who lose their jobs transition to new employment.
- Concern about the environment is often a factor in trade negotiations. Those concerned about globalization want to ensure that firms do not move production to countries with lax environmental laws, while others are concerned that environmental regulation not be used to justify protectionism. Trade ultimately raises income and environmental awareness in developing nations.
- Some antiglobalization activists consider shifting production to countries with low wages as exploitation and demand that wages be increased in other countries. Globalization has typically resulted in higher wages in developing nations, but not up to the standards of developed nations.

QUESTION: Trade between the United States and China increased significantly over the last two decades. China is now the United States' second largest trading partner after Canada. Expanding trade has led to significant reductions in the price of many goods, including technology goods such as computers and tablets. However, some people have been vocal against policies that promote freer trade with China. What are some reasons why people would be against greater trade with China?

Answers to the Checkpoint question can be found at the end of this chapter.

chapter summary

Section 1: The Gains from Trade

Absolute advantage: occurs when one country can produce more of a good than another country.

Comparative advantage: occurs when a country can produce a good at a lower opportunity cost than another country.

Fotokostic/Shutterstock

Nicholas Haig/Dreamstime.com

The United States has a comparative advantage in both soybean production (due to an abundance of fertile land) and commercial aircraft production (due to an abundance of technology and human capital).

Trade is a **positive-sum game,** which means that both countries in a trading relationship can gain compared to not trading.

Section 2: The Terms of Trade

The **terms of trade** determine the prices of imports and exports. When countries trade many commodities, the terms of trade are defined as the average price of exports divided by the price of imports.

The Effect of Trade on Prices

Before trade, the prices charged for one good may be different in the two countries. The country with the lower price is likely to export the good; greater demand for that country's good pushes prices higher. The country with the higher price is likely to import the good; lesser demand for that country's good pushes prices lower. Market forces therefore push prices toward an equilibrium under free trade.

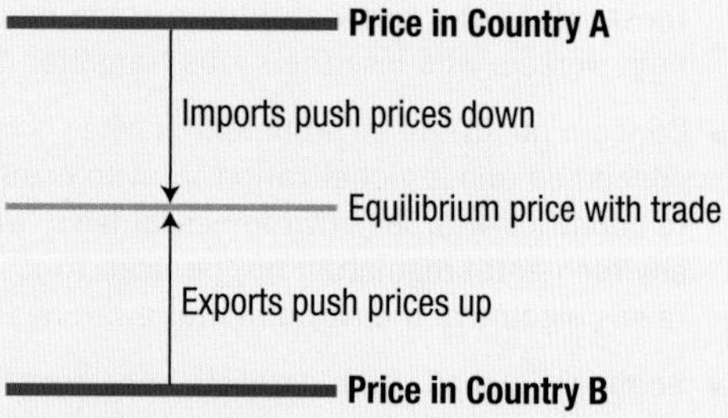

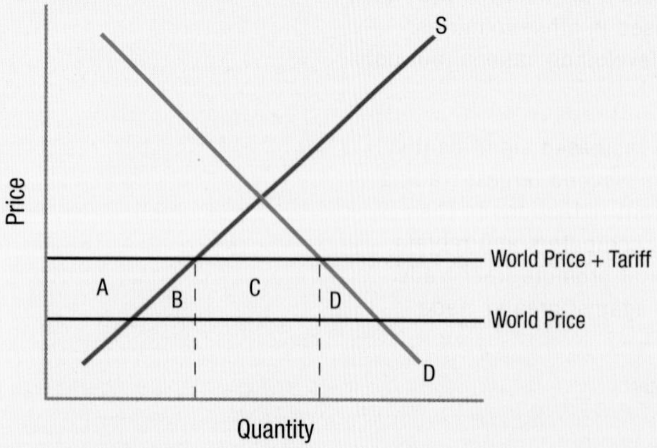

Tariffs are a tax on imports. They raise the domestic price of the good to the *world price + tariff.*

Winners: Domestic producers gain area A. Government gains area C in tariff revenues.

Losers: Domestic consumers lose areas A + B + C + D due to higher prices.

Net Loss: Areas B + D (deadweight loss from the tariff)

Historically, trade barriers have been high. In the 1930s, the Smoot-Hawley Act placed an average tax of 60% on most imported goods, arguably prolonging the Great Depression. Trade barriers have fallen since, and in the past three decades have fallen dramatically to nearly free trade with all countries.

Section 3: Arguments Against Free Trade

Many strong arguments against free trade exist. In each case, trade protection in the form of a tariff or quota is sought to protect the domestic industry.

Infant Industry Argument: States that a new industry requires protection to survive against established foreign competition. The problem is determining when these industries mature.

Antidumping Argument: Occurs when a foreign firm sells its goods below cost or at a price below what it charges in its domestic market.

Key Industries Argument: States that a country must be able to rely on its domestic industries for critical goods such as food, oil, steel, and defense equipment in times of conflict when trade might not be possible.

Environmental Degradation Argument: States that countries producing mass goods allow their environments to deteriorate. However, studies show that as countries develop and incomes grow, demand for environmental protection rises.

Edward Lemery Iii/Dreamstime.com

Topic Photo Agency/Corbis

South Korea sustained environmental degradation during its economic development in the 1980s and 1990s. Today, it invests heavily in environmental protection and sustainable cities like Songdo outside the capital of Seoul.

Michalakis Ppalis/Dreamstime.com

In the early 1980s, Harley-Davidson sought infant industry protection against competition from established lower cost Japanese motorcycles, giving it time to retool its factories to be more competitive.

Protection Against Cheap Labor Argument: Argues that domestic workers need to be protected from cheap foreign labor. Most economists estimate that the benefits from lower priced imports from free trade exceed the costs of lost employment. Further, increased trade generates jobs in export industries.

Exploitation of Foreign Workers Argument: Argues that trading with developing countries where wages are low and working conditions are deplorable exploits workers in these countries. But restricting trade would probably do more harm than good. Trade may be their only chance to grow and improve their standard of living.

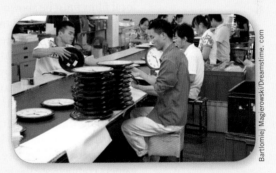

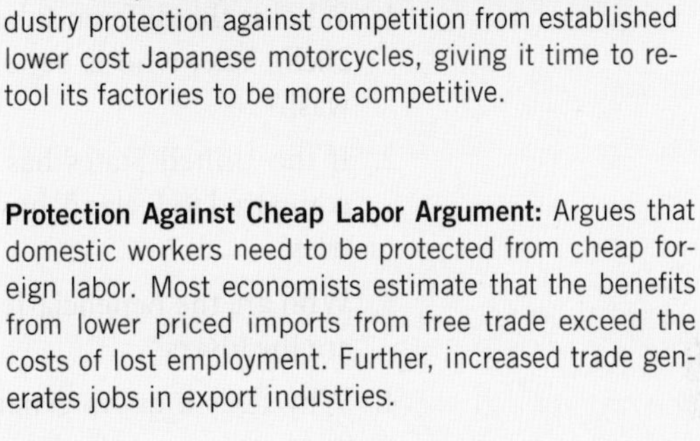

Bartlomiej Magierowski/Dreamstime. com

Although working conditions in factories in developing countries look miserable, they often are better than working conditions before trade. In addition, trade increases demand for workers, which leads to higher wages.

KEY CONCEPTS

autarky, p. 416
imports, p. 416
exports, p. 416
absolute advantage, p. 416
comparative advantage, p. 416
terms of trade, p. 420
tariff, p. 424
quota, p. 425
infant industry, p. 427
dumping, p. 428

QUESTIONS AND PROBLEMS

Check Your Understanding

1. What is the difference between absolute and comparative advantage? Why would Michelle Wie, who is better than you at both golf and laundry, still hire you to do her wash?
2. If the United States has a comparative advantage in the production of strawberries compared to Iceland, how might trade affect the prices of strawberries in the two countries?
3. Who are the beneficiaries from a large U.S. tariff on French and German wines? Who are the losers?
4. Why does a quota generate a larger loss to the importing country than a tariff that restricts imports to the same quantity?
5. What is the difference between an infant industry and a key industry? Why do producers in both industries desire protection against foreign imports?
6. How could free trade between the United States and China potentially lead to *more* jobs in the United States?

Apply the Concepts

7. South Korean film production companies have been protected for half a century by policies enacted to protect an infant industry. But beginning in July 2006, the days that local films *must* be shown by any movie house was reduced to 73 from 146. South Korean film celebrities and the industry fought the changes even though local films commanded half the box office. Why would a country enact special protection for the local film industry? Who would be the major competitor threatening the South Korean film industry? If films made by the local industry must be shown at least 146 days a year, does the local industry have much incentive to develop good films and be competitive with the rest of the world?
8. Expanding trade in general benefits both countries, or they would not willingly engage in trade. But we also know that consumers and society often gain while particular industries or workers lose. Because society and consumers gain, why don't the many gainers compensate the few losers for their loss?
9. Some activist groups are calling for "fair trade laws" by which other countries would be required to meet or approach our environmental standards and provide wage and working conditions approaching those of developed nations in order to be able to trade with us. Is this just another form of rent seeking by industries and unions for protection from overseas competition?
10. Why is there free trade between states in the United States but not necessarily between countries?

11. Remittances from developed countries amount to over $325 billion each year. These funds are sent to their home countries by migrants in developed nations. Is this similar to the gains from trade discussed in this chapter, or are these workers just taking jobs that workers in developed countries would be paid more to do in the absence of the migrants?
12. Suppose Brazil developed a secret process that effectively quadrupled its output of coffee from its coffee plantations. This secret process enabled it to significantly undercut the prices of U.S. domestic producers. Would domestic producers receive a sympathetic ear to calls for protection from Brazil's lower cost coffee? How is this case different from that of protection against cheap foreign labor?

In the News

13. Economist Steven Landsburg (*New York Times,* January 16, 2008, p. A23) made the point that "bullying and protectionism have a lot in common. They both use force (either directly or through the power of the law) to enrich someone else at your involuntary expense. If you're forced to pay $20 an hour to an American for goods you could have bought from a Mexican for $5 an hour, you're being extorted." He also argued, "Surely we have fellow citizens who are hurt by those [trade] agreements, at least in the limited sense that they'd be better off in a world where trade flourishes, except in this one instance. What do we owe those fellow citizens?" The United States has programs to educate and retrain workers displaced by free trade agreements. Do we even owe them that? Why?
14. *The Economist* (November 21, 2009) suggested that in a highly globalized world where production is easily moved to other countries, there is an inherent tension between our desire to reduce carbon emissions to stem global climate change and our commitment to free trade. Do you agree? Why or why not?

Solving Problems

15. The figure below shows the production possibilities frontiers (PPFs) for Italy and India for their domestic production of olives and tea. Without trade, assume that each is consuming olives and tea at point *a*.

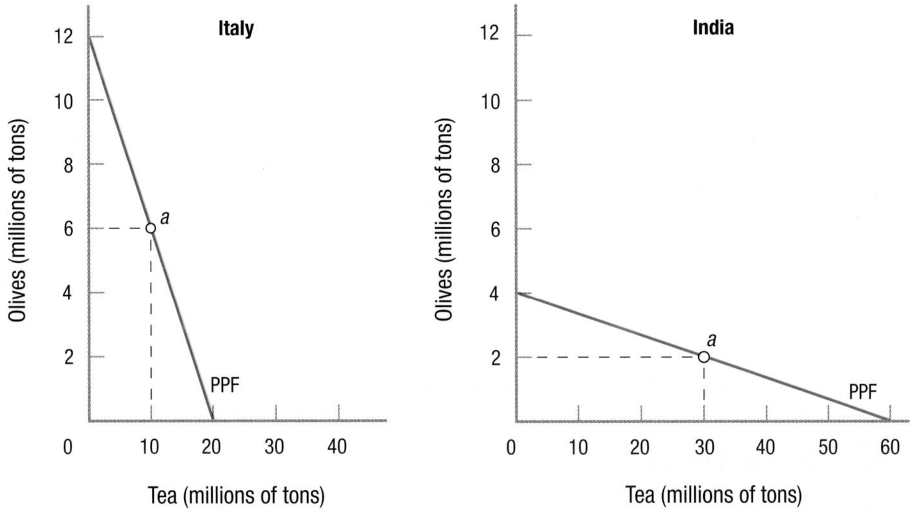

a. If Italy and India were to consider specialization and trade, what commodity would each specialize in? What is India's opportunity cost for tea and olives? What is Italy's opportunity cost for tea and olives?

b. Assume that the two countries agree to specialize entirely in one product (the one for which each country has a comparative advantage), and agree to split the total output between them. Complete the table below. Are both countries better off after trade?

Country and Product	Before Specialization	After Specialization	After Trade
Italy			
Olives	6 million tons	________	________
Tea	10 million tons	________	________
India			
Olives	2 million tons	________	________
Tea	30 million tons	________	________

16. The following figure shows the annual domestic demand and supply for 10 GB compact flash cards for digital cameras.

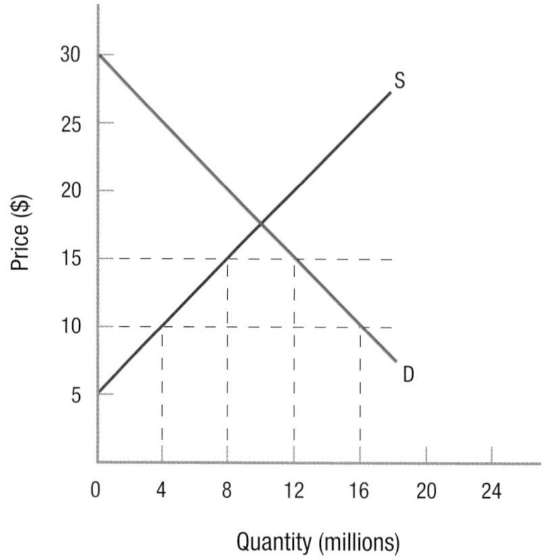

a. Assume that the worldwide price of these 10 GB cards is $10. What percent of United States sales would be imported?

b. Assume the U.S. government puts a $5 tariff per card on imports. How many 10 GB flash cards would be imported into the United States?

c. Given the tariff in question (b), how much revenue would the government collect from this tariff?

d. Given the tariff in question (b), how much more sales revenue would domestic companies enjoy as a result of the tariff?

USING THE NUMBERS

17. According to By the Numbers, approximately when was the last time the United States had a trade surplus? As a percentage of GDP, what was the highest trade surplus the United States has achieved? What was the highest trade deficit the United States has achieved?

18. According to By the Numbers, most of the developed countries (Canada, Australia, the United States, Switzerland, and Hong Kong) have relatively low tariff barriers while much of the developing world still has high tariffs on imports. What reasons might account for why these countries continue to have high tariffs?

ANSWERS TO QUESTIONS IN CHECKPOINTS

Checkpoint: The Gains from Trade

Yes, in general, nations would not trade unless they benefit. However, as we have seen, even though nations as a whole gain, specific groups—industries and their workers who do not have a comparative advantage relative to other countries—lose.

Checkpoint: The Terms of Trade

When a quota is imposed, the first beneficiary is the domestic industry. Competition from foreign competition is limited. If the market is important enough (automobiles), the foreign companies build new plants in the United States and compete as if they are domestic firms. A second beneficiary is foreign competitors, in that they can increase the price or complexity of their products and increase their margins. Losers are consumers and, to some extent, the government, because a tariff could have accomplished the same reduction in imports and the government would have collected some revenue.

Checkpoint: Arguments Against Free Trade

Growth in the volume of trade with China has led to lower prices on many goods Americans enjoy. However, although trade with China has led to significant benefits to Americans, the sentiment is not always positive for a number of reasons. First, many believe that China's low prices (through its low wages as well as government efforts to keep the value of the U.S. dollar strong) forced many American factories to close or move overseas, causing job losses. Second, some believe China holds an unfair advantage due to poor working conditions and low environmental standards. Third, some believe that quality standards for Chinese products are low, leading to safety issues. These and other reasons have created a backlash against efforts to further reduce trade barriers between the two nations. However, these concerns have not diminished the benefits of low prices and the many American jobs generated through increased exports of American-made products to a growing consumer market in China.

Sources for By the Numbers

Chapter 1
Total number of bachelor's degrees granted by major: *Digest of Education Statistics,* National Center for Education Statistics, U.S. Department of Education.

Technology company CEO majors: "Study Finds Most Likely Tech Sector CEO Is Dave the Ivy League Ex-Yahoo Econ Major," *Forbes,* September 28, 2012.

Fortune 100 company CEO majors: "The Education of Fortune 100 CEOs," Curran Career Consulting, January 2011.

Percent of Fortune 500 companies founded by immigrants or their children: "The 'New American' Fortune 500," Partnership For a New American Economy, June 2011.

Average percentage of income spent on various categories: Bureau of Labor Statistics, U.S. Department of Labor.

Median salaries for economics jobs: Payscale.com

Chapter 2
Farm productivity yields: Crop Quick Stats, National Agricultural Statistics Service, U.S. Department of Agriculture.

Cost of firing workers: "You're Fired: What It Costs to Sack a Worker," *The Economist,* September 16, 2008.

U.S. Trade balance: U.S. Department of Commerce.

American attitudes on environment and economic growth: "Who Cares? Don't Count on Public Opinion to Support Mitigation," *The Economist,* December 3, 2009.

Chapter 3
Gaming revenues by state: State of the States: The AGA Survey of Casino Entertainment, American Gaming Association.

Prices of precious metals: cnbc.com

Total value of the worldwide virtual goods market: "Virtual goods revenue to hit $7.3 billion this year," Bloomberg Business Week, November 15, 2010.

Total number of water bottles consumed: Beverage Marketing Corporation, www.beveragemarketing.com

Total sales of bottled water: Beverage Marketing Corporation, www.beveragemarketing.com

College and university enrollment: National Postsecondary Student Aid Study, U.S. Department of Education.

Chapter 4
Rent control price differences: Author estimates using available market data.

Federal telephone support by state: Universal Service Monitoring Report, CC Docket 98-202, Table 1.13, www.FCC.gov

Total U.S. farm support: Farm Subsidy Database, The Environmental Working Group, farm.ewg.org

Minimum wage by state: U.S. Department of Labor.

U.S. farm subsidies: Farm Subsidy Database, The Environmental Working Group, farm.ewg.org

Chapter 5
Elasticity of various goods: Compiled from numerous studies reporting estimates for price elasticity of demand.

Elasticity of food by country: Cross-price elasticities of demand across 114 countries, U.S. Department of Agriculture, March 2010.

Alternative fuels: AutoblogGreen, green.autoblog.com/2010/03/06/u-s-annual-energy-outlook-predicts-alternative-vehicles-wont

Parking alternatives: David A. Hensher and Jenny King (2001), "Parking Demand and Responsiveness to Supply, Price and Location in Sydney Central Business District," *Transportation Research* Part A, Vol. 35, No. 3, March 2001, pp. 177–196.

Average rise in public university tuition: National Center for Education Statistics, U.S. Department of Education.

Average fall in international calling rates: Author calculation using data from the Federal Communications Commission.

Chapter 6
U.S. distribution of household budgets: Bureau of Labor Statistics, U.S. Department of Labor.

Consumer expenditures in various categories: Bureau of Labor Statistics, U.S. Department of Labor.

Total number of passenger cars: U.S. Bureau of Transportation Statistics, U.S. Department of Transportation.

Charitable donations: www.givingUSA.com

Organic foods sales: 2012 Organic Industry Survey, Organic Trade Association.

NBA Jerseys: "Top-Selling NBA Jerseys in the United States and Internationally," *Forbes,* June 21, 2012.

Chapter 7
The cost of industrial robots: Bureau of Labor Statistics, U.S. Department of Labor.

Productivity rates: Bureau of Labor Statistics, U.S. Department of Labor.

Revenue needed to support new semiconductor plant: Author estimate based on various sources.

Time spent on government paperwork: U.S. Government Printing Office, www.gpo.gov

Apple iPad cost breakdown: Digital Manufacturing: How It's Made, www.manufacturingdigital.com/news_archive/tags/apple/apple-ipa

Online flight bookings: U.S. Department of Transportation.

Online flight check-ins: Airline IT Trends Survey, SITA www.sita.aero/surveys-reports/industry-surveys-reports/airline-it-trends-survey-2012

Chapter 8
Farm and farm-related employment by region: U.S. Department of Agriculture, maps.ers.usda.gov/mapimages/ers_reg_color.jpg

Top tea producers: Tip Top Tens, www.tiptoptens.com/2011/05/07/top-10-tea-producing-countries

World tea production: Food and Agricultural Organization of the United Nations.

World coffee production: Food and Agricultural Organization of the United Nations.

Average price of soybeans, wheat, and corn: Economic Research Service, U.S. Department of Agriculture.

Chapter 9
Television viewership by championship: Compiled using various media reports.

Most expensive drugs: www.forbes.com/2010/02/19/expensive-drugs-cost-business-healthcare-rare-diseases.html

Cost of a ride on Virgin Galactic: www.virgingalactic.com

Windows market share: www.netmarketshare.com/operating-system-market-share.aspx?qprid=10&qpcustomd=0

Electricity demand: U.S. Energy Information Administration, U.S. Department of Energy, www.eia.gov/forecasts/aeo/MT_electric.cfm

Chapter 10

Largest fast-food chains: "The Most Popular Fast Food Restaurants in America," Business Insider, July 12, 2012.

Wireless market share: US Wireless Data Market Q1 2011 Update, Chetan Sharma Consulting, www.chetansharma.com

Total number of marathons in the United States: www.MarathonGuide.com

Total number of Nike shoe models produced: www.Solepedia.com

Largest and smallest universities and colleges in the United States: Individual university websites and TopTenz.net

Chapter 11

Pay for undergraduate majors: 2010–11 College Salary Report, Payscale.com

Average salary for women compared to men: "Female Grads Earn $8,000 Less Than Men," CNNMoney, October 23, 2012.

Average cost of benefits as a percent of salary for full-time workers: Bureau of Labor Statistics, U.S. Department of Labor.

Average starting salaries for various professions: NACE 2011 Survey, National Association of Colleges and Employers.

Percent of workers with flexible work hours: Bureau of Labor Statistics, U.S. Department of Labor.

Projected job growth by state: "Which States Are Poised for Job Growth?" *The Wall Street Journal,* October 20, 2011.

Chapter 12

Percentage of high school graduates enrolling in college and percentage of college graduates pursuing postgraduate degrees: *Digest of Education Statistics*, National Center for Education Statistics, U.S. Department of Education.

Total number of patents granted in 1980 and 2012: U.S. Patent Statistics Report, U.S. Patent and Trademark Office.

U.S. venture capital funds by year: Dow Jones Financial Information Services; Thomson Reuters; National Venture Capital Association.

Length of high-speed rail track by country: International Union of Railways.

Chapter 13

Hybrid car sales by year: Alternative Fuels and Advanced Vehicle Data Center; U.S. Department of Energy.

Number of electric bicycles in China: "An Electric Boost for Bicyclists," *The New York Times*, January 31, 2010.

Increase in wind energy generated in the United States: U.S. Energy Information Administration, U.S. Department of Energy.

Annual savings from the use of compact fluorescent bulbs: Energy Star, U.S. Environmental Protection Agency.

Acres of arable land per person in the United States and China: World Development Indicators, The World Bank.

Amount of solid waste by product (recovered and not recovered): Municipal Solid Waste Generation, Recycling, and Disposal in the United States: Facts and Figures for 2011, U.S. Environmental Protection Agency.

Average gasoline tax in the United States: American Petroleum Institute.

Average gasoline tax in Britain: Fuel Duty Rates, HM Revenue & Customs.

European Union Atlantic cod catch by year: European Commission, EU Market Observatory for Fisheries and Aquaculture Products.

Wind generation capacity by state: AWEA 4th Quarter 2012 Public Market Report, American Wind Energy Association.

Chapter 14

Which device can you not live without?: *The New York Times* and Forrester Research.

Internet penetration rates: Internet World Stats, www.internetworldstats.com.

Number of Google Plus users: Google Blog, googleblog.blogspot.com

Number of Facebook users: Facebook, Inc.

Word processing market share: Author estimate based on available market data.

Number of online movie downloads and streaming views: "Internet To Surpass DVD in Movie Consumption, Not Revenue," *The Los Angeles Times*, March 23, 2012.

Chapter 15

U.S. poverty threshold: U.S. Census Bureau, U.S. Department of Commerce.

U.S. minimum wage: Wage and Hour Division, U.S. Department of Labor.

Poverty rates across the world: The World Factbook, Central Intelligence Agency.

Number of Medicaid recipients: Medicaid Spending and Enrollment Detail for CBO's May 2013 Baseline, Congressional Budget Office.

Average monthly U.S. housing subsidy: Author calculation using budget and recipient data from the U.S. Department of Housing and Urban Development.

Percentage of Americans receiving food stamps: Supplemental Nutrition Assistance Program (SNAP) Data System, Economic Research Service, U.S. Department of Agriculture.

Chapter 16

Trade deficit as a percent of GDP: Foreign Trade Division, U.S. Census Bureau, U.S. Department of Commerce.

Trade-weighted tariff barriers: World Development Indicators, The World Bank.

Medical tourism services: Companion Global Healthcare, Inc.

Number of American cars sold in China: Author estimate based on sales reports from Ford, Chrysler, and General Motors.

U.S. public sentiment on lower trade barriers: Constrained Internationalism: Adapting to New Realities: Results of a 2010 National Survey of American Public Opinion, Chicago Council on Global Affairs.

China's share of world GDP: Historical Statistics of the World Economy: 1–2008 AD, Angus Maddison; World Economic Outlook Database, International Monetary Fund.

Glossary

absolute advantage One country can produce more of a good than another country.
accounting profit The difference between total revenue and explicit costs. These are the profits that are taxed by the government.
agency shop Employees are not required to join the union, but must pay dues to compensate the union for its services.
allocative efficiency The mix of goods and services produced is just what the society desires.
altruism Actions undertaken merely out of goodwill or generosity.
antitrust law Laws designed to maintain competition and prevent monopolies from developing.
asymmetric information Occurs when one party to a transaction has significantly better information than another party.
autarky A country that does not engage in international trade, also known as a closed economy.
average cost pricing rule Requires a regulated monopolist to produce and sell output where price equals average total cost. This permits the regulated monopolist to earn a normal return on investment over the long term and therefore remain in business.
average fixed cost Equal to total fixed cost divided by output (FC/*Q*).
average product Output per worker, found by dividing total output by the number of workers employed to produce that output (*Q*/L).
average total cost Equal to total cost divided by output (TC/*Q*). Average total cost is also equal to AFC + AVC.
average variable cost Equal to total variable cost divided by output (VC/*Q*).

barriers to entry Any obstacle that makes it more difficult for a firm to enter an industry, and includes control of a key resource, prohibitive fixed costs, and government protection.
behavioral economics The study of how human psychology enters into economic behavior as a way to explain why individuals sometimes act in predictable ways counter to economic models.
budget line Graphically illustrates the possible combinations of two goods that can be purchased with a given income, given the prices of both goods.
bundling A strategy of packaging several products into a single product with a single price. Bundling allows firms to capture customers of related products by making it more attractive to use the same firm's products.

capital Includes manufactured products such as tractors, welding equipment, and computers that are used to produce other goods and services. The payment to capital is referred to as interest.
cartel An agreement between firms (or countries) in an industry to formally collude on price and output, then agree on the distribution of production.
casual user A consumer who purchases a good only after the good has matured in the market and is more sensitive to price.
ceteris paribus Assumption used in economics (and other disciplines as well), where other relevant factors or variables are held constant.
change in demand Occurs when one or more of the determinants of demand changes, shown as a shift in the entire demand curve.
change in quantity demanded Occurs when the price of the product changes, shown as a movement along an existing demand curve.
change in quantity supplied Occurs when the price of the product changes, shown as a movement along an existing supply curve.
change in supply Occurs when one or more of the determinants of supply change, shown as a shift in the entire supply curve.
closed shop Workers must belong to the union before they can be hired.
Coase theorem If transaction costs are minimal (near zero), a bargain struck between beneficiaries and victims of externalities will be efficient from a resource allocation perspective. As a result, the socially optimal level of production will be reached.
collateral An asset used to secure a loan that can be sold if the borrower fails to repay a loan.
command and control policies Environmental policies that set standards and issue regulations, which are then enforced by the legal and regulatory system.
comparative advantage One country has a lower opportunity cost of producing a good than another country.
complementary goods Goods that are typically consumed together. When the *price* of a complementary good rises, the *demand* for the other good declines, and vice versa. Complements have a negative cross elasticity of demand.
concentration ratio The share of industry shipments or sales accounted for by the top four or eight firms.
constant cost industry An industry that, in the long run, faces roughly the same prices and costs as industry output expands. Some industries can virtually clone their operations in other areas without putting undue pressure on resource prices, resulting in constant operating costs as they expand in the long run.
constant returns to scale A range of output where average total costs are relatively constant. The expansion of fast-food restaurant franchises and movie theaters, which are essentially replications of existing franchises and theaters, reflect this.

consumer surplus The difference between market price and what consumers (as individuals or the market) would be willing to pay. It is equal to the area above market price and below the demand curve.

contestable markets Markets that look monopolistic but where entry costs are so low that the sheer threat of entry keeps prices low.

core user A consumer who has a very high willingness to pay for a new product or service and is among the first to purchase it.

corporation A business structure that has most of the legal rights of individuals, and in addition, can issue stock to raise capital. Stockholders' liability is limited to the value of their stock.

cost-benefit analysis A methodology for decision making that looks at the discounted value of the costs and benefits of a given project.

coupon rate A periodic fixed payment to the bond holder measured as an annual percent of the bond's face value.

cross elasticity of demand Measures how responsive the quantity demanded of one good is to changes in the price of another good. Substitute goods have positive cross elasticities: An increase in the price of one good leads consumers to substitute (buy more of) the other good whose price has not changed. Complementary goods have negative cross elasticities: An increase in the price of a complement leads to a reduction in sales of the other good whose price has not changed.

deadweight loss The reduction in total surplus that results from the inefficiency of a market not in equilibrium.

decreasing cost industry An industry that, in the long run, faces lower prices and costs as industry output expands. Some industries enjoy economies of scale as they expand in the long run, typically the result of technological advances.

demand The maximum amount of a product that buyers are willing and able to purchase over some time period at various prices, holding all other relevant factors constant (the *ceteris paribus* condition).

demand curve A graphical illustration of the law of demand, which shows the relationship between the price of a good and the quantity demanded.

demand for labor Demand for labor is derived from the demand for the firm's product and the productivity of labor.

demand schedule A table that shows the quantity of a good a consumer purchases at each price.

determinants of demand Nonprice factors that affect demand, including tastes and preferences, income, prices of related goods, number of buyers, and expectations.

determinants of supply Nonprice factors that affect supply, including production technology, costs of resources, prices of other commodities, expectations, number of sellers, and taxes and subsidies.

diminishing marginal returns An additional worker adds to total output, but at a diminishing rate.

diseconomies of scale A range of output where average total costs tend to increase. Firms often become so big that management becomes bureaucratic and unable to control its operations efficiently.

dominant strategy Occurs when a player chooses the same strategy regardless of what his or her opponent chooses.

dumping Selling goods abroad at lower prices than in home markets, and often below cost.

economic costs The sum of explicit (out-of-pocket) and implicit (opportunity) costs.

economic discrimination When workers of equal ability are paid different wages or in any other way discriminated against because of race, color, religion, gender, age, national origin, or disability.

economic profit Profit in excess of normal profits. These are profits in excess of both explicit and implicit costs.

economics The study of how individuals, firms, and society make decisions to allocate limited resources to many competing wants.

economies of scale As a firm's output increases, its LRATC tends to decline. This results from specialization of labor and management, and potentially a better use of capital and complementary production techniques.

economies of scope By producing a number of products that are interdependent, firms are able to produce and market these goods at lower costs.

efficiency How well resources are used and allocated. Do people get the goods and services they want at the lowest possible resource cost? This is the chief focus of efficiency.

elastic demand The absolute value of the price elasticity of demand is greater than 1. Elastic demands are very responsive to changes in price. The percentage change in quantity demanded is greater than the percentage change in price.

elastic supply Price elasticity of supply is greater than 1. The percentage change in quantity supplied is greater than the percentage change in price.

elasticity of demand for labor The percentage change in the quantity of labor demanded divided by the percentage change in the wage rate.

entrepreneurs Entrepreneurs combine land, labor, and capital to produce goods and services. They absorb the risk of being in business, including the risk of bankruptcy and other liabilities associated with doing business. Entrepreneurs receive profits for this effort.

equilibrium Market forces are in balance when the quantities demanded by consumers just equal the quantities supplied by producers.

equilibrium price Market equilibrium price is the price that results when quantity demanded is just equal to quantity supplied.

equilibrium quantity Market equilibrium quantity is the output that results when quantity demanded is just equal to quantity supplied.

equity The fairness of various issues and policies.

essential facility An input that is needed to produce a product or to allow a person to consume a product.

explicit costs Those expenses paid directly to another economic entity, including wages, lease payments, taxes, and utilities.

exports Goods and services that are sold abroad.

externalities The impact on third parties of some transaction between others in which the third parties are not involved. An external cost (or negative externality) harms the third parties, whereas external benefits (positive externalities) result in gains to them.

face value The value of a bond that is paid upon maturity. This value is fixed, and therefore not the same as the market value of a bond, which is influenced by changes in interest rates and risk.

financial capital The money required by businesses to purchase inputs for production and to run their operations.

firm An economic institution that transforms resources (factors of production) into outputs.

fixed costs Costs that do not change as a firm's output expands or contracts, often called overhead. These include items such as lease payments, administrative expenses, property taxes, and insurance premiums.

flat tax A tax that is a constant proportion of one's income.

framing bias Describes when individuals are steered into making one decision over another or are convinced they are receiving a higher value for a product than what was paid for it.

free rider The ability of an individual to avoid paying for a public good because he or she cannot be excluded from enjoying the good once provided.

functional distribution of income The distribution of income for resources or factors of production (land, labor, capital, and entrepreneurial ability).

game theory The study of how individuals and firms make strategic decisions to achieve their goals when other parties or factors can influence that outcome.

Gini coefficient A precise method of measuring the position of the Lorenz curve, defined as the area between the Lorenz curve and the equal distribution line divided by the total area below the equal distribution line.

government failure The result when the incentives of politicians and government bureaucrats do not align with the public interest.

Herfindahl-Hirschman index (HHI) A way of measuring industry concentration, equal to the sum of the squares of market shares for all firms in the industry.

horizontal summation Market demand and supply curves are found by adding together how many units of the product will be purchased or supplied at each price.

implicit costs The opportunity costs of using resources that belong to the firm, including depreciation, depletion of business assets, and the opportunity cost of the firm's capital employed in the business.

imports Goods and services that are purchased from abroad.

incentives The factors that motivate individuals and firms to make decisions in their best interest.

incidence of taxation Refers to who bears the economic burden of a tax. The economic entity bearing the burden of a particular tax will depend on the price elasticities of demand and supply.

income A flow measure reflecting the funds received by individuals or households over a period of time, usually a week, month, or year.

income deficit The difference between the poverty threshold and a family's income.

income effect When higher prices essentially reduce consumer income, the quantity demanded for normal goods falls.

income effect (labor) Higher wages mean that you can maintain the same standard of living by working fewer hours. The impact on labor supply is generally negative.

income elasticity of demand Measures how responsive quantity demanded is to changes in consumer income.

increasing cost industry An industry that, in the long run, faces higher prices and costs as industry output expands. Industry expansion puts upward pressure on resources (inputs), causing higher costs in the long run.

increasing marginal returns A new worker hired adds more to total output than the previous worker hired, so that both average and marginal products are rising.

indifference curve Shows all the combinations of two goods where the consumer is indifferent (gets the same level of satisfaction).

indifference map An infinite set of indifference curves in which each curve represents a different level of utility or satisfaction.

industry standard A common format that is used, for example, in televisions, in digital recorders, or in software programs.

inelastic demand The absolute value of the price elasticity of demand is less than 1. Inelastic demands are not very responsive to changes in price. The percentage change in quantity demanded is less than the percentage change in price.

inelastic supply Price elasticity of supply is less than 1. The percentage change in quantity supplied is less than the percentage change in price.

infant industry An industry so underdeveloped that protection is needed for it to become competitive on the world stage or to ensure its survival.

inferior goods Goods that have income elasticities that are negative. When consumer income grows, quantity demanded falls for inferior goods.

intellectual property rights A set of exclusive rights granted to a creator of an invention or creative work, allowing the owner to earn profits over a fixed period of time. The types of protection include patents, copyrights, trademarks, and industrial designs.

interconnection The physical linking of a network to another network's essential facilities. Interconnection promotes competition by ensuring that no firm has exclusive access to a set of customers.

intertemporal pricing A type of versioning in which goods are differentiated by the level of patience of consumers. Less patient consumers pay a higher price than more patient consumers.

investment in human capital Investments such as education and on-the-job training that improve the productivity of labor.

kinked demand curve An oligopoly model that assumes that if a firm raises its price, competitors will not raise theirs; but if the firm lowers its price, all of its competitors will lower their price to match the reduction. This leads to a kink in the demand curve and relatively stable market prices.

labor Includes the mental and physical talents of individuals who produce products and services. The payment to labor is called wages.

laissez-faire A market that is allowed to function without any government intervention.

land Includes natural resources such as mineral deposits, oil, natural gas, water, and land in the usual sense of the word. The payment to land as a resource is called rent.

law of demand Holding all other relevant factors constant, as price increases, quantity demanded falls, and as price decreases, quantity demanded rises.

law of diminishing marginal utility As we consume more of a given product, the added satisfaction we get from consuming an additional unit declines.

law of supply Holding all other relevant factors constant, as price increases, quantity supplied will rise, and as price declines, quantity supplied will fall.

lock-in strategies Techniques used by firms to raise the switching costs for its customers, making it less attractive to leave the network.

long run A period of time sufficient for firms to adjust all factors of production, including plant capacity. Existing firms can expand or build new plants, or firms can enter or exit the industry.

long-run average total cost In the long run, firms can adjust their plant sizes so that LRATC is the lowest unit cost at which any particular output can be produced in the long run.

Lorenz curves A graphical method of showing the income distribution by cumulating families of various income levels on the horizontal axis and relating this to their cumulative share of total income on the vertical axis.

lump-sum tax A fixed amount of tax regardless of income, and is a type of regressive tax.

luxury goods Goods that have income elasticities greater than 1. When consumer income grows, quantity demanded of luxury goods rises more than the rise in income.

macroeconomics The broader issues in the economy such as inflation, unemployment, and national output of goods and services.

marginal cost The change in total costs arising from the production of additional units of output ($\Delta TC/\Delta Q$). Because fixed costs do not change with output, marginal costs are the change in variable costs associated with additional production ($\Delta VC/\Delta Q$).

marginal cost pricing rule Regulators would prefer to have natural monopolists price where P = MC, but this would result in losses (long term) because ATC > MC. Thus, regulators often must use an average cost pricing rule.

marginal factor cost (MFC) The added cost associated with hiring one more unit of labor. For competitive firms, it is equal to the wage; but for monopsonists, it is higher than the new wage (W) because all existing workers must be paid this higher new wage, making MFC > W.

marginal physical product of labor The additional output a firm receives from employing an added unit of labor ($MPP_L = \Delta Q \div \Delta L$).

marginal revenue product The value of another worker to the firm is equal to the marginal physical product of labor (MPP_L) times marginal revenue (MR).

marginal product The change in output that results from a change in labor ($\Delta Q/\Delta L$).

marginal revenue The change in total revenue from selling an additional unit of output. Because competitive firms are price takers, P = MR for competitive firms.

marginal utility The satisfaction received from consuming an additional unit of a given product or service.

marginal utility analysis A theoretical framework underlying consumer decision making. This approach assumes that satisfaction can be measured and that consumers maximize satisfaction when the marginal utilities per dollar are equal for all products and services.

market cap The market value of a firm determined by the current price per share of its stock multiplied by the total number of shares issued.

market failure When markets fail to provide the socially optimal level of output, and will provide output at too high or low a price.

market period Time period so short that the output and the number of firms are fixed. Agricultural products at harvest time face market periods. Products that unexpectedly become instant hits face market periods (there is a lag between when the firm realizes it has a hit on its hands and when inventory can be replaced).

market power A firm's ability to set prices for goods and services in a market.

market segmentation A strategy of making a single good in different versions to target different consumer markets with varying prices.

market structure analysis By observing a few industry characteristics such as number of firms in the industry or the level of barriers to entry, economists can use this information to predict pricing and output behavior of the firm in the industry.

market-based policies Environmental policies that use charges, taxes, subsidies, deposit-refund systems, or tradable emission permits to achieve environmental goals.

markets Institutions that bring buyers and sellers together so they can interact and transact with each other.

maturity The date on which the face value of the bond must be repaid.

microeconomics The decision making by individuals, businesses, industries, and governments.

misallocation of resources Occurs when a good or service is not consumed by the person who values it the most, and typically results when a price ceiling creates an artificial shortage in the market.

monopolistic competition A market structure with a large number of firms producing differentiated products. This differentiation is either real or imagined by consumers and involves innovations, advertising, location, or other ways of making one firm's product different from that of its competitors.

monopolistic exploitation of labor Occurs when workers are paid less than the value of their marginal product because the firm has monopoly power in the product market.

monopoly A one-firm industry with no close product substitutes and with substantial barriers to entry.

monopsonistic exploitation of labor Occurs when workers are paid less than the value of their marginal product because the firm is a monopsonist in the labor market.

monopsony A labor market with one employer.

mutual interdependence When only a few firms constitute an industry, each firm must consider the reactions of its competitors to its decisions.

Nash equilibrium An outcome that occurs when all players choose their optimal strategy in response to all other players' potential moves. At a Nash equilibrium, no player can be better off by unilaterally deviating from the noncooperative outcome.

natural monopoly An industry exhibiting large economies of scale such that the minimum efficient scale of operations is roughly equal to market demand.

network A structure that connects various entities with one another. A network can be physical, virtual, or social.

network demand curve A demand curve for a good or service that experiences a network effect, causing it to slope upward at lower quantities before sloping downward once the market matures.

network effect An external benefit generated from the consumption of a network good that is taken into account by individuals and firms in their decision making. It increases the value of a good as more people use or subscribe to a good.

network externality An external benefit generated from the consumption of a network good.

network good A good or service that requires the existence of a physical, virtual, or social network to exist.

nonexcludability Once a good or service is provided, it is not possible to exclude others from enjoying that good or service.

nonrivalry The consumption of a good or service by one person does not reduce the utility of that good or service to others.

normal goods Goods that have positive income elasticities of less than 1. When consumer income grows, quantity demanded rises for normal goods, but less than the rise in income.

normal profits The return on capital necessary to keep investors satisfied and keep capital in the business over the long run. Equal to zero economic profits; where P = ATC.

normative question A question that is based on societal beliefs on what should or should not take place.

oligopoly A market with just a few firms dominating the industry, where (1) each firm recognizes that it must consider its competitors' reactions when making its own decisions (mutual interdependence), and (2) there are significant barriers to entry into the market.

on-the-job training Training typically done by employers, ranging from suggestions at work to intensive workshops and seminars.

opportunity cost The value of the next best alternative; what you give up to do something or purchase something.

partnership Similar to a sole proprietorship, but involves more than one owner who share the management of the business. Partnerships are also subject to unlimited liability.

peak-load pricing A versioning strategy of pricing a product higher during periods of higher demand, and lower during periods of lower demand.

perfect (first-degree) price discrimination Charging each customer the maximum price each is willing to pay, thereby expropriating all consumer surplus.

perfect competition A market structure with many relatively small buyers and sellers who take the price as given, a standardized product, full information to both buyers and sellers, and no barriers to entry or exit.

personal or family distribution of income The distribution of income to individuals or family groups (typically quintiles, or fifths, of the population).

physical capital All manufactured products that are used to produce goods and services.

physical network A network connected by a physical structure such as fiber optics, transportation routes, or satellites.

Pigouvian tax A tax that is placed on an activity generating negative externalities in order to achieve a socially efficient outcome.

positive question A question that can be answered using available information or facts.

poverty thresholds Income levels for various household sizes, below which people are considered to be living in poverty.

present value The value of an investment (future stream of income) today. The higher the discount rate, the lower the present value today, and vice versa.

price caps Maximum price at which a regulated firm can sell its product. They are often flexible enough to allow for changing cost conditions.

price ceiling A government-set maximum price that can be charged for a product or service. When the price ceiling is set below equilibrium, it leads to shortages.

price discrimination Charging different consumer groups different prices for the same product.

price elasticity of demand A measure of the responsiveness of quantity demanded to a change in price, equal to the percentage change in quantity demanded divided by the percentage change in price.

price elasticity of supply A measure of the responsiveness of quantity supplied to changes in price. An elastic supply curve has elasticity greater than 1, whereas inelastic supplies have elasticities less than 1. Time is the most important determinant of the elasticity of supply.

price floor A government-set minimum price that can be charged for a product or service. When the price floor is set above equilibrium, it leads to surpluses.

price system A name given to the market economy because prices provide considerable information to both buyers and sellers.

price taker Individual firms in perfectly competitive markets get their prices from the market because they are so small they cannot influence market price. For this reason, perfectly competitive firms are price takers and can produce and sell all the output they produce at market-determined prices.

Prisoner's Dilemma A noncooperative game in which players cannot communicate or collaborate in making their decisions, which results in inferior outcomes for both players. Many oligopoly decisions can be framed as a Prisoner's Dilemma.

producer surplus The difference between market price and the price at which firms are willing to supply the product. It is equal to the area below market price and above the supply curve.

product differentiation One firm's product is distinguished from another's through advertising, innovation, location, and so on.

production The process of converting resources (factors of production)-land, labor, capital, and entrepreneurial ability-into goods and services.

production efficiency Goods and services are produced at their lowest resource (opportunity) cost.

production possibilities frontier (PPF) Shows the combinations of two goods that are possible for a society to produce at full employment. Points on or inside the PPF are attainable, and those outside of the frontier are unattainable.

profit Equal to the difference between total revenue and total cost.

profit maximizing rule Firms maximize profit by producing output where MR = MC. No other level of output produces higher profits.

progressive tax A tax that rises in percentage of income as income increases.

public goods Goods in which one person's consumption does not diminish the benefit to others from consuming the good (i.e., nonrivalry), and once provided, no one person can be excluded from consuming (i.e., nonexclusion).

quota A government set limit on the quantity of imports into a country.

rate of return Uses the present value formula, but subtracts costs, then finds the interest rate (discount rate) at which this investment would break even.

rate of return regulation Permits product pricing that allows the firm to earn a normal return on capital invested in the firm.

ratio of income to poverty The ratio of family income to the poverty threshold. Families with ratios below 0.5 are considered severely poor, families with ratios between 0.5 and 1.0 are considered poor, and those families with ratios between 1.0 and 1.25 are considered near poor.

regressive tax A tax that falls in percentage of income as income increases.

rent The return to land as a factor of production. Sometimes called economic rent.

rent seeking Resources expended to protect a monopoly position. These are used for such activities as lobbying, extending patents, and restricting the number of licenses permitted.

resources Productive resources include land (land and natural resources), labor (mental and physical talents of people), capital (manufactured products used to produce other products), and entrepreneurial ability (the combining of the other factors to produce products and assume the risk of the business).

right-to-work laws Laws created by the Taft-Hartley Act that permitted states to outlaw union shops.

scarcity Our unlimited wants clash with limited resources, leading to scarcity. Everyone (rich and poor) faces scarcity because, at a minimum, our time on earth is limited. Economics focuses on the allocation of scarce resources to satisfy unlimited wants.

screening or signaling The use of higher education as a way to let employers know that the prospective employee is intelligent and trainable and potentially has the discipline to be a good employee.

second-degree price discrimination Charging different customers different prices based on the quantities of the product they purchase.

segmented labor markets Labor markets split into separate parts. This leads to different wages paid to different sectors even though both markets are highly competitive.

sequential-move games Games in which players make moves one at a time, allowing players to view the progression of the game and to make decisions based on previous moves.

share of stock A unit of ownership in a business that entitles the shareholder to one vote at shareholder meetings and one share of any dividends paid.

short run A period of time over which at least one factor of production (resource) is fixed, or cannot be changed. Firms can employ more people, have existing employees work overtime, or hire part-time employees to produce more, but this is done in an existing plant.

shortage Occurs when the price is below market equilibrium, and quantity demanded exceeds quantity supplied.

short-run supply curve The marginal cost curve above the minimum point on the average variable cost curve.

shutdown point When price in the short run falls below the minimum point on the AVC curve, the firm will minimize losses by closing its doors and stopping production. Because P < AVC, the firm's variable costs are not covered, therefore by shutting the plant, losses are reduced to fixed costs only.

simultaneous-move games Games in which players' actions occur at the same time, forcing players to make decisions without knowing how the other players will act. These games are analyzed using diagrams called game tables.

social network A network that combines elements of physical and virtual networks by describing groups of people using the same product or service who also are connected more directly (for business or entertainment purposes) within the network.

sole proprietorship A type of business structure composed of a single owner who supervises and manages the business and is subject to unlimited liability.

substitute goods Goods consumers will substitute for one another depending on their relative prices. When the *price* of one good rises and the *demand* for another good increases, they are substitute goods, and vice versa. Substitutes have a positive cross elasticity of demand.

substitution effect When the price of one good rises, consumers will substitute other goods for that good, therefore the quantity demanded for the higher priced good falls.

substitution effect (labor) Higher wages mean that the value of work has increased, and the opportunity costs of leisure are higher, hence work is substituted for leisure.

sunk cost A cost that has been paid and cannot be recovered; therefore, it should not enter into decision making affecting the present or future.

sunk cost fallacy Occurs when people make decisions based on how much was already spent rather than how the decision might affect their current well-being.

supply The maximum amount of a product that sellers are willing and able to provide for sale over some time period at various prices, holding all other relevant factors constant (the *ceteris paribus* condition).

supply curve A graphical illustration of the law of supply, which shows the relationship between the price of a good and the quantity supplied.

supply of labor The amount of time an individual is willing to work at various wage rates.

surplus Occurs when the price is above market equilibrium, and quantity supplied exceeds quantity demanded.

switching cost A cost imposed on consumers when they change products or subscribe to a new network.

tariff A tax on imported products. When a country taxes imported products, it drives a wedge between the product's domestic price and its price on the world market.

teaser strategies Attractive up-front deals used as an incentive to entice new customers into a network.

terms of trade The ratio of the price of exported goods to the price of imported goods (P_x/P_m).

third-degree price discrimination Charging different groups of people different prices based on varying elasticities of demand.

tipping point (or critical mass) The quantity from which network effects are strong enough to support the network.

tit-for-tat strategies A trigger strategy that rewards cooperation and punishes defections. If your opponent lowers its price, you do the same. If your opponent returns to a cooperative strategy, you do the same.

total cost The sum of all costs to run a business. To an economist, this includes out-of-pocket expenses and opportunity costs.

total revenue Price × quantity demanded (sold). If demand is elastic and price rises, quantity demanded falls off significantly and total revenue declines, and vice versa. If demand is inelastic and price rises, quantity demanded does not decline much and total revenue rises, and vice versa.

total surplus The sum of consumer surplus and producer surplus, and a measure of the overall net benefit gained from a market.

total utility The total satisfaction that a person receives from consuming a given amount of goods and services.

tragedy of the commons Resources that are owned by the community at large (e.g., parks, ocean fish, and the atmosphere) and therefore tend to be overexploited because individuals have little incentive to use them in a sustainable fashion.

trigger strategies Action is taken contingent on your opponent's past decisions.

union shop Nonunion hires must join the union within a specified period of time.

unitary elastic supply Price elasticity of supply is equal to 1. The percentage change in quantity supplied is equal to the percentage change in price.

unitary elasticity of demand The absolute value of the price elasticity of demand is equal to 1. The percentage change in quantity demanded is just equal to the percentage change in price.

utility A hypothetical measure of consumer satisfaction.

utility maximizing rule Utility is maximized where the marginal utility per dollar is equal for all products, or $MU_a/P_a = MU_b/P_b = \ldots = MU_n/P_n$.

value of the marginal product The value of the marginal product of labor (VMP_L) is equal to marginal physical product of labor times price, or $MPP_L \times P$.

variable costs Costs that vary with output fluctuations, including expenses such as labor and material costs.

versioning A pricing strategy that involves differentiating a good by way of packaging into multiple products for people with different demands.

vicious cycle When a network good does not reach its tipping point, and therefore does not increase in value enough to retain its customers, customers leave the network, thereby further diminishing the value of the good until all customers leave the network.

virtual network A network connected by groups of people using the same type or brand of good.

virtuous cycle The point at which a network good reaches its tipping point, when network effects cause demand for the good to increase on its own. As more people buy or subscribe to a good or service, it generates even more external benefits and more demand.

wealth A stock measure of an individual's or family's assets, net of liabilities, at a given point in time.

willingness-to-pay An individual's valuation of a good or service, equal to the most an individual is willing and able to pay.

x-inefficiency Protected from competitive pressures, monopolies do not have to act efficiently. Spending on corporate jets, travel, and other perks of business represents x-inefficiency.

yield The annual return to a bond measured as the coupon payment as a percentage of the current price of a bond.

Credits for Chapter Opening Photographs

Chapter 1 John Lund/Matt Holmes/age footstock.

Chapter 2 Sand dunes–Intst/Dreamstime.com; Microchip–Cultura Creative/Alamy

Chapter 3 Piet Mall/Stock4B/Corbis

Chapter 4 Kiyoshi Ota/Reuters/Corbis

Chapter 5 Dedi57/Dreamstime.com

Chapter 6 altrendo images/Getty Images

Chapter 7 Westend61/SuperStock

Chapter 8 Radius Images/Alamy

Chapter 9 Saniphoto/Dreamstime.com

Chapter 10 Craig Van Der Lende/Getty Images

Chapter 11 Photographerlondon/Dreamstime.com

Chapter 12 Richard Kail/Science Source

Chapter 13 WorldFoto/Alamy

Chapter 14 Ajv123ajv/Dreamstime.com

Chapter 15 Timothy A. Clary/AFP/Getty Images

Chapter 16 rodho/Shutterstock

Index

Note: Page numbers followed by f indicate figures; those followed by n indicate notes; those followed by t indicate tables.

Absolute advantage, 41, 416
Accounting profit, 169
Administrative Behavior (Simon), 200
Ad valorem taxes, tariffs as, 424
Advantage
 absolute, 41, 416
 comparative. *See* Comparative advantage
Advertising, product differentiation and, 249–250
AFC. *See* Average fixed cost (AFC)
Affirmative action, 291
Africa, oil production in, 102, 253
AFSCME, 292
AFT, 292
Age Discrimination in Employment Act (1967), 291
Agency shops, 294
Agricultural price supports, 92–93
Airline industry
 as contestable market, 236
 leadership game in, 267
 prices in, 248
Akst, Daniel, 167
Alcoa Aluminum, 218
Allocative efficiency, 6, 32
 in competitive markets, 204–205
AltaVista, 366, 374t
Altruism, 147–148
The Amazing Race, 286
Amazon.com, 54, 223, 297
 eBook market and, 226
American Airlines, 248
American Idol, 286
Americans with Disabilities Act (1990), 291
America Online, 374t
America's Got Talent, 286
Angry Birds, 406
Antidumping, as argument against free trade, 428
Antitrust policy, 233–237
 contestable markets and, 236
 future of, 236–237, 237t
 industry concentration measures and, 234–236
 laws and, 233–234, 234t
 market and market power definition and, 234–236
Apple Computer Inc.
 bundling by, 378–379
 competition by, 180, 256
 eBook market and, 226
 growth of, 167, 180, 317
 profits and, 11
 stock of, 320
 technological change and, 38
 value of brand, 250
Apple iPad, 374, 374t
Apple iPhone, 105, 374t
The Apprentice, 286
Arctic ice caps, 336
Armani, 251
Asymmetric information, market failure and, 87
ATC. *See* Average total cost (ATC)
AT&T, 366, 376
 competition by, 262, 377
 Verizon and, 113, 262, 380
AT&T DSL, 374t
Australia, Gini coefficient for, 395t
Autarky, 416
AVC. *See* Average variable cost (AVC)
Average cost(s), 176, 177f
Average cost pricing rule, 232, 232f
Average fixed cost (AFC), 176, 177f
Average product, 173
Average total cost (ATC), 176, 177f, 178
Average variable cost (AVC), 176, 177, 177f

BackRub, 321
Bank(s), 317–318
Bankruptcy, 327
Bar charts, 20, 20f
Barriers to entry, 218–219
Base method, for calculating percentage changes, 104
Basic economic questions, 28, 30–31
Baumol, William, 39
A Beautiful Mind (Nasar), 257
Bechtolsheim, Andreas von, 321
Becker, Gary, 287–288
Behavioral economics, 144–148
 altruism and, 147–148
 framing bias and, 145–146
 overconfidence and, 146
 overvaluing the present relative to the future and, 146
 sunk cost fallacy and, 145
Belichick, Bill, 257
Benefits. *See also* Cost-benefit analysis
 external, market failure and, 87
 of monopolies, 226
 of union membership, 292
Bentham, Jeremy, 138
Bhagwati, Jagdish, 405, 430
Bias, framing, 145–146
Big Brother, 286
Bing, 216
Blackberry, 374t
"Black Friday," 56
Blank, Rebecca, 403
Blanks, Kyle, 276
Blockbuster Video, 327
Bloomekatz, Ari, 407n
BLS. *See* Bureau of Labor Statistics (BLS)
BMW, 250, 419
Bolivia, Gini coefficient for, 395t
Bonds, 318–319, 319f
Borders, 262, 327
Borrowing, 317–318
Bottled water industry, 52
Brands, 250
Branson, Richard, 310
Brazil
 Gini coefficient for, 395t
 oil production in, 255
Brin, Sergey, 321
Brinksmanship, 267f, 267–268
Broadband connections, 375
Bronco Wine Company, 70
Budget line (budget constraint), 134f, 134–137
 changes to, 135–137
Buffett, Warren, 257
Bundling, 378–379
Bureau of Economic Analysis, 419
Bureau of Labor Statistics (BLS), 287
Burger King, 246
Buyers, number of, demand and, 59

California electricity crisis of 2000–2001, 381
Canada
 Gini coefficient for, 395t
 NAFTA and, 45, 420, 430
 oil production in, 102, 253, 255
Canon, 374t
Canterbery, E. Ray, 68n
Cap-and-trade program, 353
Capital, 31
 debt (bonds), 318–319, 319f
 equity (stocks), 319–320
 financial. *See* Financial capital
 human. *See* Human capital
 marginal efficiency of, 316–317
 physical, 313–315, 314f
 venture, 320–321
Capital accumulation, economic growth and, 36–37, 37f
Capitalist economies, 30
Carnival, 262
Car prices, 136
Cartels, 253–255, 254f
Caryl, Christian, 206n
Casual users, 371
Causation, correlation vs., 26
CBS, 286
CEO salaries, 392
Ceteris paribus assumption, 6
 graphs and, 24
Change in quantity demanded, 60f, 60–61
Change in quantity supplied, 64f, 64–65
Changes in demand, 60f, 60–61
 equilibrium and, 68–71, 69f, 70f, 70t
Changes in supply, 64f, 64–65
 equilibrium and, 68, 69f, 70f, 70–71, 71t
Charles Shaw wines, 70
Charmin, 105
Chevrolet, 113

Chevy Suburban, 102
Chicken games, 267f, 267–268
Chile, Gini coefficient for, 395t
Chilean sea bass, 346
China
climate change and, 356–357
comparative advantage in United States and, 43
economy of, 30
foreign trade zones of, 426
Gini coefficient for, 395t
oil production in, 255
poverty in, 404
China Mobile, 250
Choices, with limited resources, 8
Christie, Chris, 296
Chrome, 216
Circuit City, 262, 327
Citro, Constance F., 399n, 402n
Civil Rights Act (1964), 290, 291
Clayton Act (1914), 234t
Clean Air Act (1970), 353
Clean Air Act (1990), 353
Climate change, 336, 354–358
cost-benefit analysis and, 354
effects of, 355t, 355–356
equity aspects of, 356–357
finding a solution for, 357–358
public good aspects of, 356
timing aspects of, 356
Clinton, Hillary, 257
Closed economies, 416
Closed shops, 294
Coase, Ronald, 340, 341
Coase theorem, 340–341, 352
Coca-Cola Company, 250, 318
Coke recipe and, 219
demand curve of, 105
market value of, 216
product differentiation by, 252
Cochran, Johnnie, 257
Cohn, D'Vera, 280n
Collateral, 318
Collected Works (Samuelson), 87
College education. *See* Education
Comcast, 376
Command and control environmental policy, 340–341, 350f
Common property resources, 345–347, 346f
The Communist Manifesto (Marx and Engels), 306
Comparative advantage, 41–42, 42t
gains from trade and, 416–417, 417f, 417t
in United States and China, 43
Competition
lack of, market failure and, 87
monopolistic. *See* Monopolistic competition
monopolistic competition compared with, 252
monopoly compared with, 224–227
network, promoting with interconnection, 380
network good pricing and, 376–379
perfect. *See* Perfect competition
Complement(s), 113
Complementary goods, 59
Concentration ratios, 235, 235t
Connally "Hot Oil" Act (1935), 345
Connect America Fund, 375
Conniff, Richard, 353n
Constant cost industries, 207, 207f
Constant returns to scale, 180, 180f
Consumer preferences. *See* Preference(s)
Consumer price index (CPI), 399
relative importance of components of, 19, 20f
Consumer surplus
economic efficiency and, 82–84, 83f
gains from trade and, 85f, 85–89, 86f
Contestable markets, 236
Core users, 371
Corporations, 166–167
Correlation, causation vs., 26
Cost(s)
average, 176, 177f
economic, 168
explicit, 168
external, market failure and, 87
implicit, 168
incremental, 174
long-run average total. *See* Long-run average total cost (LRATC)
marginal, 175t, 175–176
of monopolies, 226
opportunity. *See* Opportunity costs
of production. *See* Long-run production costs; Production costs; Short-run production costs
sunk, 145, 168
switching, 376–377
total, 168
of union membership, 292
variable, 174
Costa Rica, foreign trade zones of, 426
Cost-benefit analysis. *See also* Benefits; Cost(s)
of climate change, 354
Costco, 228
Coupon rate, 318
CPI. *See* Consumer price index (CPI)
Craft unions, 292
Critical mass, 372, 373
Crocs, demand for, 58, 59f
Cross elasticity of demand, 112–113
Crovitz, L. Gordon, 204n
Crowding, 347
Crowe, Russell, 257
Cruise ship industry, 167
Curves. *See also* Demand curves; Graphs; Supply curve
shifting, 25f, 25–26

Dairy Queen, 180
Darwin, Charles, 190
Das Kapital (Marx and Engels), 306
Deadweight loss, 86, 224–225, 225f
Debt capital, 318–319, 319f
Decreasing cost industries, 207, 207f
Dell, 180
Delta Airlines, 248
Demand, 55–61
change in quantity demanded and, 60f, 60–61
changes in. *See* Changes in demand
definition of, 56
determinants of, 58–60
elastic, 105, 106f
for fixed capacity network goods, 370f, 370–371
for gasoline, 106
inelastic, 105–106, 106, 106f
for labor. *See* Labor demand
law of, 56–57
for product, labor demand and, 283–284
for public goods, 344f, 344–345
willingness-to-pay and, 55–56, 56f
Demand curves, 57f, 57–58
deriving, 142t, 142–143, 143f
of firm, under monopolistic competition, 248–250, 249f
kinked, 255f, 255–256
linear, elasticity and total revenue along, 111, 112f
network. *See* Network demand curve
perfectly inelastic, 105, 106f
Demand schedule, 57, 57f
Demographic changes, labor market and, 280, 297
Denmark
Gini coefficient for, 395t
poverty in, 404
Depth of poverty, 401–403
Determinants of demand, 58–60
Determinants of supply, 62–64, 65f
Detroit Tigers, 276
Developing nations. *See also specific countries*
working conditions in, international trade and, 430–431
Dillon Reservoir, Colorado, water effluents in, 351
Diminishing marginal returns, 173
Diminishing marginal utility, law of, 139, 140f
Diminishing returns, law of, 173
Diminishing returns effect, 176
Disabilities, legislation protecting people with, 291
Discounting, 315
Discrimination
economic. *See* Economic discrimination
human capital investment and, 325
price. *See* Price discrimination
Diseconomies of scale, 180, 180f
Distribution, 30
Doctorow, Cory, 204
Dominant strategy, 260
"Do Not Call" registries, 377
Dual labor market hypothesis, 287, 288–289, 289f
Duke, Annie, 257
Dukek, Dan, 353
Dumping, 428
Dunkin' Donuts, 164

Earnings. *See also* Income; Income distribution; Poverty; Wage(s)
education and, 19, 20f, 322, 322t

eBay, 82
Economic costs, 168
Economic discrimination, 287–292
Becker's theory of, 287–288
public policy to combat, 290–292
segmented labor markets and, 287, 288–290, 289f
Economic efficiency, consumer and producer surplus and, 82–84, 83f
Economic growth, 35–39
expanding resources and, 36–37
increasing, to reduce poverty, 405
technological change and, 37–38, 38f
Economic loss, 169
Economic profits, 169
monopoly and, 222–223, 223f
in perfect competition, 196, 197f
Economic rent, 312, 312f
Economics
basic questions of, 28, 30–31
definition of, 2
in everyday life, 12
key principles of, 8–13
positive vs. normative questions in, 7
reasons to study, 2, 4
scope of, 2, 4
Economics (Samuelson), 87
The Economics of Discrimination (Becker), 288
Economic systems, 30
Economic theories, 5–6
Economies of scale, 179–180, 180f
market power and, 218–219, 219f
network goods and, 373
Economies of scope, 180–181
Economists, agreement and disagreement among, 13
Economy Food Plan, 399
Edgeworth, Francis Ysidro, 132, 134, 289n
Education. *See also* Human capital
income and, 19, 20f, 322, 322t
international comparison of, 326
as investment, 322–323, 323f
Efficiency, 6
allocative. *See* Allocative efficiency
of capital, marginal, 316–317
economic, consumer and producer surplus and, 82–84, 83f
equity vs., 6–7, 88
of markets, 10–11
production. *See* Production efficiency
Elastic demand, 105, 106f
total revenue and, 110f, 111
Elasticity, 101–125
Elasticity of demand, 104–109
along linear demand curve, 111, 112f
cross, 112–113
income, 112, 113–114
price. *See* Price elasticity of demand
for product, elasticity of demand for labor and, 284
taxes and, 119f, 119–121, 120f
total revenue and, 110–112
Elasticity of demand for labor (E_L), 284–285
Elasticity of supply
price, 115f, 115–118
taxes and, 121f, 121–123, 123t
Elastic supply, 115
Electricity crisis of 2000–2001 (California), 381
Elimination principle, 203
Emissions taxes, 351
Employment. *See also* Labor entries; Wage(s)
discrimination in. *See* Economic discrimination
domestic, international trade and, 429
in United States since 1960, 19, 20f
Employment Non-Discrimination Act (proposed), 291
Energy, renewable, 39
Engels, Friedrich, 306
Entrepreneurs, 31, 166–167
Entrepreneurship, 327–328
Entry, barriers to, 218–219
Envelope curve, 179
Environment. *See also* Climate change; Pollution
international trade and, 429–430
Environmental policy, 347–354
command and control, 340–341, 350f
government failure and, 348
intergenerational questions and, 348f, 348–349
market-based, 350, 351–353
socially efficient levels of pollution and, 349f, 349–350
Epson printers, 374t
Equal Pay Act (1963), 290–291
Equilibrium, 66–71, 67f
changes in supply and demand and, 68–71
deviation from, 85f, 85–87, 86f
investment in human capital and, 324f, 324–325
labor market, competitive, 285f, 285–286
for network goods, 372–376, 373f
Equilibrium price, 66, 67f
for monopoly, 221, 221f
prices below, 86f, 86–87
prices exceeding, 85f, 85–86
Equilibrium quantity, 66, 67f
Equity (fairness), 6
climate change and, 356–357
efficiency vs., 6–7, 88
Equity (financial), private, 320–321
Equity capital, 319–320
ESPN, 381
Essential facilities, 380
European Union Emissions Trade System (EU ETS), 357
Exclusive marketing deals, 377
Executive Office of the President, poverty measures and, 403
Executive Order 10988, 294
Executive Order 11246, 291
Expectations
demand and, 59–60
supply and, 64
Explicit costs, 168
Exports, 416. *See also* International trade
measurement of, 419
External benefits, market failure and, 87
External costs, market failure and, 87
Externalities, 338–343, 339t
Coase theorem and, 340–341
limitations of analysis, 342–343
negative, 338–340
network, 368
positive, 338, 341–342, 342f
Exxon, 106

Facebook, 6, 8, 169
competition by, 226
Greek debt crisis and, 26
growth of, 317
market dominance of, 266
network goods and, 368, 374t
Face value, 318
Factors of production, 31f, 31–32. *See also* Resources
Family distribution of income, 391t, 391–392
Federal Communications Commission (FCC), 375
Federal Trade Commission Act (1914), 234t
Ferguson, Tim, 206n
Financial capital, 317–321
banks and borrowing and, 317–318
bonds and, 318–319, 319f
stocks and, 319–320
venture capital and private equity and, 320–321
Finland, education in, 326
Firms, 164, 166
demand curve of, under monopolistic competition, 248–250, 249f
plant shutdown and, in perfect competition, 198–200, 199f
First-degree price discrimination, 227–228, 228f
Fiscal cliff, 267
Fish markets, 80
Fitch, 318
Five Guys, 246
Fixed costs, 174
average, 176, 177, 177f
in pharmaceutical and software industries, 181
Flat taxes, 118, 118t
Ford, 112, 419
Ford Excursion, 102
Foreign trade zones, 426
Foundations of Economic Analysis (Samuelson), 87
Fox River, Wisconsin, water effluents in, 351
Framing bias, 145–146
France, Gini coefficient for, 395t
Franzia, Fred, 70
Freeman, Richard B., 407
Free riders, 343–344
Free soloing, 2
Free trade, 422, 427–431
recent globalization concerns and, 429–431
traditional arguments against, 427–429
Friedman, Milton, 288
Friendster, 366, 374t
Frontier Airlines, 267
Functional distribution of income, 390t, 390–391
Future, overvaluing the present relative to, 146

Gains from trade, 42–44, 43t, 44t, 416–420
absolute advantage and, 416
comparative advantage and, 416–417, 417f, 417t
consumer and producer surplus and, 85f, 85–89, 86f
Game theory, 256–268
chicken games and, 267f, 267–268
leadership games and, 266–267
Nash equilibrium and, 260–262
Prisoner's Dilemma and, 262–265, 263f
repeated games and, 265–266
sequential-move games and, 258, 266
simultaneous-move games and, 258–260, 259f
Gasoline
demand for, 106
price of, 102. *See also* Oil prices
Gates, Bill, 257
Gender, economic discrimination and, 287
General Motors (GM), 250
Germany
innovation in, 328
tariffs of, 427
GI Bills, 324
Gini coefficient, 393, 394f
Global climate change. *See* Climate change
Global economy. *See also* International trade
innovation and, 328
Global warming, 356. *See also* Climate change
GM. *See* General Motors (GM)
Gmail, 216
Goods
complementary, 59
inferior, 59, 113
luxury (income superior). *See* Luxury goods
network. *See* Network goods
normal, 58, 113
public. *See* Public goods
substitute, 59
Google
growth of, 321
market value of, 216
network goods and, 372, 374t
value of brand, 250
Google+, 216, 226
Google Docs, 216, 380
Gould, Jay, 233
Gould, Stephen Jay, 190n
Government failure, 348
Graphs, 18–21
bar charts, 20, 20f
ceteris paribus assumptions and, 24
information conveyed by, 20–21, 21f
linear relationships and, 22f, 22–23
nonlinear relationships and, 23f, 23–24
pie charts, 19, 20f
reading, 21
scatter plots, 18, 19f
shifting curves and, 25f, 25–26
of simple linear equations, 24–25, 25f
stylized, 21, 22f
time series, 18, 19f
Gratz v. Bollinger, 291
Gray, Boyden, 353
Greek debt crisis, 26
Grim trigger, 265
Grutter v. Bollinger, 291

Half.com, 54
Hardin, Garrett, 345n
Harrah's, 318–319
Hart-Scott-Rodino Act (1976), 236
Herfindahl-Hirschman index (HHI), 235–236
HHI. *See* Herfindahl–Hirschman index (HHI)
Holdouts, 267f, 267–268
Hollister, 252
Home Depot, 258–260, 262
Home prices, 136
Honda, 113, 419
Hooked (Knecht), 346
Horizontal summation, 57f, 58
Housing prices, 136
HP Mini, 374, 374t
HP printers, 374t
Hudec, Robert, 430
Human capital, 322–327
education and earnings and, 322, 322t
education as investment and, 322–323, 323f
equilibrium levels of, 324f, 324–325
implications of human capital theory and, 325
income inequality and, 396t, 396–398
increasing, economic growth and, 36, 37f
on-the-job training and, 325–326
as screening or signaling device, 325
Human Development Index, 404
Hummer H2, 102

IBM (International Business Machines), 318
value of brand, 250
Ice caps, 336
Implicit costs, 168
Imports, 416. *See also* International trade
measurement of, 419
Incentives, 4, 9–10
Incidence of taxation, 119
Income. *See also* Earnings; Income distribution; Income inequality; Poverty; Wage(s)
changes in, budget line and, 135–137, 136f
college education and, 19, 20f
definition of, 390
demand and, 58–59
expectations about, demand and, 59–60
household, sales taxes and, 122
life cycle effects and, 390
nonwage, labor supply and, 281
portion spent, price elasticity of demand and, 107
ratio to poverty, 401–402
Income deficit, 401
Income distribution. *See also* Income inequality; Poverty
functional, 390t, 390–391
Gini coefficient and, 393, 394f
Lorenz curves and, 392f, 392–393, 393f
mobility and, 406–407
personal or family, 391t, 391–392
redistribution policies and, 394f, 394–396, 395t
Income effect
indifference curves and, 159f, 159–160
labor supply and, 279
Income elasticity of demand, 112, 113–114
Income inequality. *See also* Income distribution; Poverty
causes of, 396–398
reducing, 404–405
Income redistribution, 394f, 394–395, 395t
Income superior goods, 113
Increasing cost industries, 205–206, 207f
Increasing marginal returns, 173
Incremental costs, 174
India
climate change and, 356–357
poverty in, 404
Indifference curve(s), 132, 134, 155
income effect and, 159f, 159–160
preferences and, 155f, 155–157
properties of, 156
substitution effect and, 159, 159f, 160
Indifference curve analysis, 132, 134, 148, 155–160
consumer preferences and, 155f, 155–157
optimal consumer choice and, 157, 157f
uses of indifference curves and, 157–160
Indifference maps, 156f, 156–157
Individual labor supply, 278–279, 279f
Industrial agglomeration, 313
Industrial unions, 292
Industries
airline. *See* Airline industry
bottled water, 52
constant cost, 207, 207f
cruise ship, 167
decreasing cost, 207, 207f
increasing cost, 205–206, 207f
infant, as argument against free trade, 427–428
pharmaceutical, fixed costs in, 181
renewable energy, 39
software, fixed costs in, 181
steel, argument for protection from foreign competition, 429
telecommunications, 28
utilities, as natural monopolies, 219
Industry standards, 380
Inelastic demand, 105–106, 106, 106f
total revenue and, 110, 110f
Inelastic supply, 115
Infant industry argument, against free trade, 427–428
Inferior goods, 59, 113
Infomercials, 223
Information, asymmetric, market failure and, 87
Innovation
global economy and, 328
monopoly and, 226
An Inquiry Into the Nature and Causes of the Wealth of Nations (Smith), 12, 190
Insider-outsider theory, 289
Intel Corporation, 38, 179
Intellectual property, antitrust policy and, 236–237
Intellectual property rights, 328
Interconnection

efficiency in network industries and, 381
promoting with network competition, 380
Interest, 31
Internal rate of return, 316–317
International Business Machines. *See* IBM (International Business Machines)
International trade, 413–433, 414f
foreign trade zones and, 426
free trade and. *See* Free trade
gains from trade and. *See* Gains from trade
measurement of, 419
practical constraints on, 419–420
terms of trade and. *See* Terms of trade
of United States, 414, 414f
Internet, market concept and, 54
Internet Explorer, 374t
Intertemporal pricing, 378, 378t
Introduction to the Principles of Morals (Bentham), 138
Investment(s)
in human capital. *See* Human capital
present value approach for comparing, 315–316
rate of return approach for comparing, 316–317
Invisible hand, 11, 12, 80, 85
Iowa Electronic Markets, 88
Israel, Gini coefficient for, 395t
Italy, Gini coefficient for, 395t

Japan
Gini coefficient for, 395t
innovation in, 328
tariffs of, 427
U.S. quota on automobiles imported from, 425
Jiffy Lube, 180
Job(s). *See* Labor *entries*
Job crowding hypothesis, 287, 289
Jobs, Steve, 167, 317
Johnson, Lyndon, 291
JPMorgan Chase, 318

Kay, John, 406n
Kennedy, John F., 87, 294
Keynes, John Maynard, 68n
Kinked demand curve model, 255f, 255–256
Kleenex, 105
Kleiner Perkins Caufield & Byers, 321
Knecht, G. Bruce, 346
Kodak, 374t
Korean Air, 310

Labor, 30
increasing, economic growth and, 36, 37f
marginal physical product of, 282
monopolistic exploitation of, 304
monopsonistic exploitation of, 305
Labor demand, 281–287
elasticity of, 284–285
equilibrium in, 285f, 285–286
factors changing, 283–284
marginal revenue product and, 281–283, 282t
Labor markets, 275–306
demographic changes and, 297
for entertainers, 286
future jobs in U.S. economy and, 297
imperfect, 303–306
jobs of past versus present and, 297
segmented, 287, 288–290, 289f
Labor supply, 278–281
factors changing, 280–281
income effect and, 279
individual, 278–279, 279f
market, 279–280, 280f
substitution effect and, 278–279
Labor unions, 292–296
benefits and costs of membership in, 292
public, future of, 296
types of, 292
in United States, history of, 293f, 293–295, 294f
wage differentials and, 295f, 295–296
Lahart, Justin, 204n
Laissez-faire markets, 89
Laissez-faire economies, 30
Land, 30, 312f, 312–313
Lantz, Lee, 346
Law of demand, 56–57
Law of diminishing marginal utility, 139, 140f
Law of diminishing returns, 173
Law of supply, 62
Lawrence, Andrew, 166n
Leadership games, 266–267
Learning by doing, 181
Legal disputes, Prisoner's Dilemma and, 264
Legislation
anti-discrimination, 290, 291
antitrust, 233–234, 234t
on corporate offshoring, 167
employment, 290–291, 293
environmental, 353
on mergers, 236
protecting common property, 345
trade, 423f, 424
Lehman Brothers, 327
Leisure, 278
Levinson, Mark, 206n
Levi's, 419
LG, 422
Lily Ledbetter Fair Pay Act (2009), 291
Limited liability, 320
Linear equations, simple, graphs of, 24–25, 25f
Linear relationships, graphs of, 22f, 22–23
Linens-N-Things, 262
LinkedIn, 6
Linux, 236
Live Nation, 230
Loanable funds market, 314, 317
Lock-in strategies, 377
Long run, 116, 194
firms and, 169–170
perfect competition in, 200–208
price elasticity of supply and, 116–117, 117f
Long-run average total cost (LRATC), 179
for competitive firm, 205–207, 207f
under monopolistic competition, 252
Long-run production costs, 178–182, 179f
economies and diseconomies of scale and, 179–180, 180f
economies of scope and, 180–181
technology and, 181–182
total, average, 179
Lorenz curves, 392f, 392–393, 393f
Loss(es)
adjusting to, in short run, 202f, 202–203, 203f
deadweight (welfare), 86, 224–225, 225f
economic, 169
minimization of, in perfect competition, 198–200, 199f
Loss leaders, total revenue and, 114
Lotus 123, 236–237
Lowe's, 258–260, 262
LRATC. *See* Long-run average total cost (LRATC)
Lump-sum taxes, 118
Luxury goods, 113
price elasticity of demand and, 107
Lynn, Michael, 147n

Macroeconomics, 5
Major League Baseball, 276
Major League Baseball Players Association, 278
Makers (Doctorow), 204
Marginal analysis, 10
Marginal cost(s), 175t, 175–176, 177f, 178
Marginal cost pricing rule, 232
Marginal efficiency of capital, 316–317
Marginal factor cost (MFC), 304–305
Marginal physical product of labor (MPP_L), 282
Marginal private cost (MPC), 338
Marginal product, 172–173
Marginal returns
diminishing, 173
increasing, 173
Marginal revenue (MR)
for monopolies and competitive firms, 220f, 220–221
in perfect competition, 195
Marginal revenue product (MRP_L), labor demand and, 281–283, 282t
Marginal utility, diminishing, law of, 139, 140f
Marginal utility analysis, 137–144
demand curve derivation and, 142t, 142–143, 143f
limitations of, 143–144
preferences and, 137–142, 138t
Market(s), 52, 54–55
barriers to entry and, 218–219
contestable, 236
definition of, 52
efficiency of, 10–11
fish, 80
Internet and, 54
labor. *See* Labor markets
laissez-faire, 89
loanable funds, 314, 317
price system and, 54
Marketable permits, 351–352, 352f
Market-based environmental policy, 350, 351–353
Market cap, 320
Market-determined price, 221, 221f
Market economies, 30
Market equilibrium. *See* Equilibrium
Market failure, 87–88, 343

Market labor supply curve, 279–280, 280f
Market period, 116
Market power
defining, 234–236
definition of, 218
in product markets, 303f, 303–304
sources of, 218–219
Market segmentation, profit maximization and, 377–379, 378t, 379f
Market structure analysis, 192–195
Market supply curve, 62, 62f
Marshall, Alfred, 68
Marshall, Howard, 12n, 40n
Marx, Groucho, 356
Marx, Karl, 40, 306
Maturity, 318
McCarthy, Mike, 257
McDonald's, 164, 246
market value of, 216
value of brand, 250
MCI, 377
McLean, Malcom, 206
Medicaid, 394, 404
Medicare, 394
Mergers, antitrust laws and, 236
Metcalfe's Law, 375
Mexico
Gini coefficient for, 395t
NAFTA and, 45, 420, 430
oil production in, 102, 255
MFC. *See* Marginal factor cost (MFC)
Michael, Robert T., 399n, 402n
Micklethwait, John, 167n
Microeconomics, 4–5
Microsoft
bundling by, 379–380
competition by, 180, 236
value of brand, 250
Microsoft Excel, 380
Microsoft Word, 374t
Microsoft Xbox, 368, 374, 374t
Midpoints, computing price elasticity of demand using, 108–109
Mill, John Stuart, 40
Millward Brown, 250
Minimum wage, price floors and, 93
Misallocation of resources, 91
Model building, 5–6
Monday Night Football, 381
Monopolistic competition, 248–253, 268t
competition compared with, 252
definition of, 248
price and output under, 250–252, 251f
product differentiation and firm's demand curve and, 248–250, 249f
Monopolistic exploitation of labor, 304
Monopoly, 215–239, 268t
antitrust policy and. *See* Antitrust policy
benefits vs. costs of, 226
competition compared with, 224–227
contestable markets and, 236
definition of, 218
innovation and, 226
marginal revenue for, 220f, 220–221
market power and. *See* Market power
natural, regulation of, 231–233
price discrimination under, 227–231, 228f–230f
pricing and output decisions in, 219–223
rent seeking and, 225–226
Monopoly power. *See* Market power
Monopsonistic exploitation of labor, 305
Monopsony, 303, 304f, 304–306, 305f
Moody's, 318
MPC. *See* Marginal private cost (MPC)
MPP_L. *See* Marginal physical product of labor (MPP_L)
MR. *See* Marginal revenue (MR)
MRP_L. *See* Marginal revenue product (MRP_L)
MTV, 286
Mutual interdependence, 253
Myspace, 236–237, 366, 374t

NAFTA. *See* North American Free Trade Agreement (NAFTA)
Nalebuff, Barry, 261
Nasar, Sylvia, 257
NASDAQ, 320
Nash, John, 257
Nash equilibrium, 257, 260–262
Nation(s). *See also specific countries*
developing, working conditions in, international trade and, 430–431
wealth of, 11–12
National defense argument, against free trade, 428–429
National Football League (NFL), 218
National Hockey League (NHL), chicken game and, 267f, 267–268
National Labor Relations Act (NLRA) (1935), 293
National Labor Relations Board (NLRB), 293
National Venture Capital Association (NVCA), 321
Natural monopolies, 218–219
regulation of, 231–233
Necessities, price elasticity of demand and, 107
Negative externalities, 338–340
Net present value (NPV), of an investment, 315–316
Netscape, 236–237, 366, 374t
Network(s), 368
Network compatibility, 380
Network demand curve, 370–372
derivation of, 371, 371f
examples of pricing, 372
fixed capacity network goods and, 370f, 370–371
Network effects, 368–369, 369f
Network externalities, 368
Network goods, 365–383
competition and pricing strategies for, 376–379
definition of, 368
demand curve for, 370–372
market equilibrium for, 372–376, 373f
network effects and, 368–369, 369f
regulation of, 379–381
types of, 368
New York City
rent controls in, 89
taxis in, 225
New York Stock Exchange, 54, 320
New Zealand, Gini coefficient for, 395t
NFL. *See* National Football League (NFL)
NHL. *See* National Hockey League (NHL)
Nike, 251
Nintendo Wii, 374, 374t
NLRA. *See* National Labor Relations Act (NLRA) (1935)
NLRB. *See* National Labor Relations Board (NLRB)
Nokia, 419
Nonexcludability, 343
Nonlinear relationships, graphs of, 23f, 23–24
Nonmoney perks, labor supply and, 280
Nonrivalry, 343
Normal goods, 58, 113
Normal profits, 169
in perfect competition, 198, 198f
Normative questions, 7
Norris-LaGuardia Act (1932), 293
North American Free Trade Agreement (NAFTA), 45, 420, 430
Northern Europe, oil production in, 102, 253
Nozick, Robert, 406
NPV. *See* Net present value (NPV)
NVCA. *See* National Venture Capital Association (NVCA)

Obama, Barack, 257
Occupational Outlook Handbook, 297
Occupy movement, 388
OECD. *See* Organisation for Economic Cooperation and Development (OECD)
Office Depot, 262
Office of Management and Budget (OMB), poverty measures and, 403
Offshoring, 167, 426
Oil prices
OPEC and, 253, 255
vehicle preferences and, 102
OJT. *See* On-the-job training (OJT)
Oligopoly, 253–256, 268t. *See also* Game theory
cartels and, 253–255, 254f
definition of, 253
kinked demand curve and, 255f, 255–256
OMB. *See* Office of Management and Budget (OMB)
Online betting exchanges, 88
Online technologies, costs and benefits of, 6
On-the-job training (OJT), 325–326
OPEC. *See* Organization of Petroleum Exporting Countries (OPEC)
Open economies, 416
Open-source hardware, 204
Opportunity costs, 8–9
comparative advantage and, 42, 42t, 417, 417f
production possibilities frontier and, 34–35, 35f
Optimal consumer choice, 157
Organisation for Economic Cooperation and Development (OECD),

poverty comparisons and, 404
Organization of Petroleum Exporting Countries (OPEC), 253, 255
Origin of Species (Darwin), 190
Orshansky, Mollie, 399
Ostrom, Elinor, 357
Outback Steakhouse, 180
Output
under monopolistic competition, 250–252, 251f
monopoly pricing and output decisions and, 219–223
under monopoly vs. competition, 224–225, 225f
profit-maximizing. *See* Profit-maximizing output
Outsourcing. *See* Offshoring
Overconfidence, 146
Overfishing, 346
Overhead, 174

Page, Larry, 321
Parker, Trey, 219
Partnerships, 166
Passel, Jeffrey, 280n
Passell, Peter, 288n, 340n
Patagonian toothfish, 346
PATCO, 292
Patrinos, H., 323n
PBS, 88
Peak-load pricing, 378
Ped Egg, 223
Peña, Ramiro, 276
Pep Boys, 318
Percentage(s), measuring elasticity with, 105
Percentage changes, base method for calculating, 104
Perfect competition, 193–210, 268t
definition of, 193–194, 194f
long-run adjustments in, 200–208
marginal revenue for, 220f, 220–221
public interest and, 203–205, 205f
short-run decisions in, 195–201
Perfectly inelastic demand curve, 105, 106f
Perfect price discrimination, 227–228, 228f
Persaud, Raj, 147n
Personal distribution of income, 391t, 391–392
Pet consumerism, 54
Pharmaceutical industry, fixed costs in, 181
Philippines, foreign trade zones of, 426
Physical capital, 313–315, 314f
Physical networks, 368
Pie charts, 19, 20f
Pigou, Arthur, 351
Pigouvian taxes, 351
Planned economies, 30
Plant shutdown, in perfect competition, 198–200, 199f
PlayStation, 374, 374t
Political campaigns, Prisoner's Dilemma and, 264
Pollution
climate change and. *See* Climate change
environmental policy and. *See* Environmental policy
as government failure, 348
as negative externality, 338–341
socially efficient levels of, 349f, 349–350
Positive externalities, 338, 341–342, 342f
Positive questions, 7
Posner, Richard A., 237n
Poverty, 398–407
causes of, 403
depth of, 401–403
eliminating, 403–407
incidence of, 400f, 400–401, 401f, 402t
measurement of, 399t, 399–400, 402–403
ratio of income to, 401–402
Poverty thresholds, 399t, 399–400
international comparison of, 404
PPF. *See* Production possibilities frontier (PPF)
Predictions, by online markets, 88
Preference(s)
demand and, 58, 59f
indifference curves and, 155f, 155–157
utility and, 137–142, 138t
Preference maps, 156f, 156–157
Present, overvaluing relative to the future, 146
Present value, net, of an investment, 315–316
Pressman, Steven, 40n
Price(s). *See also* Pricing
of bottled water, 52
of cars, 136
changes to, budget line and, 135, 135f
elasticity and. *See* Elasticity of demand; Elasticity of supply; Price elasticity of demand
below equilibrium, 86f, 86–87
equilibrium. *See* Equilibrium price
exceeding equilibrium, 85f, 85–86
expectations about, demand and, 59
expectations about, supply and, 64
of gasoline, 102
housing, 136
market-determined, 221, 221f
under monopolistic competition, 250–252, 251f
under monopoly vs. competition, 224–225, 225f
of network goods, competition and, 376–379
of oil. *See* Oil prices
of other inputs, changes in labor demand and, 284
supply and, 63–64
Price caps, 233
Price ceilings, 89–91, 90f
Price discrimination, 221, 227–231
first-degree (perfect), 227–228, 228f
second-degree, 227, 228, 229f
third-degree, 227, 229–231, 230f
Price elasticity of demand, 104–109, 107t
as absolute value, 104–105
computing, 108f, 108–109
determinants of, 107
elastic, 105, 106f
estimates of, 107, 107t
inelastic, 105–106, 106f
measuring with percentages, 105
unitary, 106, 106f
Price elasticity of supply, 115f, 115–118
time and, 116–117
Price floors, 91f, 91–93
Price gouging laws, 92
Price makers, 218. *See also* Monopoly
Price supports, agricultural, 92–93
Price system, 54
Price takers, 193. *See also* Perfect competition
Pricing. *See also* Price(s)
average cost, 232, 232f
intertemporal, 378, 378t
marginal cost, 232
monopoly pricing and output decisions and, 219–223
network demand curve and, 372
peak-load, 378
Principles of Economics (Marshall), 68
Prisoner's Dilemma, 262–265, 263f
classic, 263–264, 264f
examples of outcomes of, 264
resolving, 264–265
Private equity, 320–321
Private Equity Growth Capital Council, 321
"The Problem of Social Cost" (Coase), 341
Procter & Gamble, 181
Prodigy, 374t
Producer surplus
economic efficiency and, 82–84, 83f
gains from trade and, 85f, 85–89, 86f
Product(s). *See also* Goods
average, 173
demand for, labor demand and, 283–284
marginal, 172–173
substitute, 113
total, 171t, 171–172, 172f
Product differentiation, under monopolistic competition, 248–250, 249f
Production
efficiency and, 31f, 31–32
resources and, 30–31
in short run, 171–174
Production costs, 174–182. *See also* Long-run production costs; Short-run production costs
labor's share of, elasticity of demand for labor and, 285
Production efficiency, 6, 31
in competitive markets, 204
Production possibilities frontier (PPF), 32–35, 33f
absolute and comparative advantage and, 40–42, 41f, 42t, 416–417, 417f
economic growth and, 35–39
opportunity cost and, 34–35, 35f
Productivity, changes in, labor demand and, 284
Profit(s), 31, 168
accounting, 169
adjusting to, in short run, 202f, 202–203, 203f
economic. *See* Economic profits
normal. *See* Normal profits
supernormal, 202
Profit maximization
market segmentation and, 377–379, 378t, 379f
in perfect competition, 195–198, 196f, 197f

Profit-maximizing decisions, short-run cost curves for, 177f, 177–178
Profit-maximizing output
for monopoly, 221, 221f
in perfect competition, 195–198, 196f, 197f
Profit-maximizing rule, 196
Progressive taxes, 118, 118t, 122
Psacharopoulos, G., 323n
Public goods, 343–347
climate change and, 356
common property resources as, 345–347, 346f
demand for, 344f, 344–345
description of, 343–344, 344t
market failure and, 88
optimal provision of, 345
Public interest, competition and, 203–205, 205f
Public policy. *See also* Antitrust policy; Legislation
to combat discrimination, 290–292
Public unions, future of, 296

Quantity, equilibrium, 66, 67f
Quantity demanded, change in, 60f, 60–61
Quantity supplied, change in, 64f, 64–65
Quilted Northern, 105
Quotas, import, 423
effects of, 425, 425f

Race
affirmative action and, 291
economic discrimination and, 287
Rate of return, internal, 316–317
Rate of return regulation, 233
Rather, Larry, 206n
Ratio of income to poverty, 401–402
Rawls, John, 406
RCA, 422
Rdio, 372
Reading graphs, 21
Real GDP, annual changes in, 20, 20f
Reality TV, 286
The Real World, 286
Regressive taxes, 118, 118t, 122
Regulation
of natural monopolies, 231–233
of network goods, 379–381
poor, 381
rate of return, 233
Renewable energy industry, 39
Rent, 30, 312, 312f
Rent controls, in New York City, 89
Rent seeking, 225–226
Resources
common property, 345–347, 346f
costs of, supply and, 63
expanding, economic growth and, 36–37
limited, 8
misallocation of, 91
production and, 30–31, 31f, 31–32
user-managed, 357
Returns
diminishing, 173, 176
internal rate of, 316–317
marginal. *See* Marginal returns
to scale, constant, 180, 180f
Revenue. *See* Marginal revenue (MR); Total revenue (TR)
Ricardo, David, 40
Right-to-work laws, 294
Road congestion, 346f, 346–347
Robber barons, 233
Rockefeller, John D., 233
Rodriguez, Alex, 276
Ross, Ian, 12n
Royal Caribbean, 262
Russia
economy of, 30
oil production in, 255

Sales taxes, household income and, 122
Sam's Club, 228
Samsung, 256, 422
Samuel, Graeme, 253
Samuelson, Paul A., 87
San Francisco Giants, 276
Saudi Arabia, education in, 326
Scale, constant returns to, 180, 180f
Scale, diseconomies of, 180, 180f
Scale, economies of. *See* Economies of scale
Scarcity, 4
Scatter plots, 18, 19f
Scope, economies of, 180–181
Scott, 105
Screening device, human capital as, 325
Sea-Land, 206
Second-degree price discrimination, 227, 228, 229f
Sega Genesis, 366, 374t
Segmented labor markets, 287, 288–290, 289f
Sellers, number of, supply and, 64
Sequential-move games, 258, 266
Sequoia Capital, 321
Share of stock, 319
Sharper Image, 262
Shell, 106
Sherman Act (1890), 233, 234t, 236
Shipping containers, 206
Shortages, 67
expectations about, demand and, 59
Short run, 116, 194
adjusting to profits and losses in, 202f, 202–203, 203f
firms and, 169
perfect competition in, 195–201
price elasticity of supply and, 116, 117f
production in, 171–174
Short-run production costs, 174–178
average, 176, 177f
fixed and variable, 174–175
marginal, 175t, 175–176, 177f, 178
for profit-maximizing decisions, 177f, 177–178
total, average, 177f, 178
variable, average, 177, 177f
Short-run supply curve, in perfect competition, 200f, 200–201
Shutdown point, 200
Signaling device, human capital as, 325
Silicon chip manufacture, 28
Simon, Herbert, 200
Simpson, O. J., 257
Simultaneous-move games, 258–260, 259f
Skidelsky, Robert, 68n
Slope
of linear line, 22f, 22–23
of nonlinear curve, 23f, 23–24
Smartphones, 36
costs and benefits of, 6
Smith, Adam, 11, 12, 80, 85, 190
Smoot-Hawley Act (1930), 423f, 424
Socialist countries, 30
Social media. *See also* Facebook; LinkedIn
costs and benefits of, 6
usage across age groups, 20–21, 21f
Social networks, 368
Social Security, 394
Socolow, Robert, 357
Software industry, fixed costs in, 181
Sole proprietorships, 166
Sony, 226, 251, 373, 374, 419
South Africa, Gini coefficient for, 395t
South Korea, education in, 326
South Park, 219
Soviet Union, former, 30
Soy products, comparative advantage in United States and China and, 43
S&P. *See* Standard & Poor's (S&P)
Spain, Gini coefficient for, 395t
Specialization, 9
gains from trade and, 418f, 418–420, 419f
Specific tariffs, 424
Spillovers. *See* Externalities
Sport utility vehicles (SUVs), market for, 102
Spotify, 372
Spreading effect, 176
Sprint, 377
Standard Oil, 233
Standard & Poor's (S&P), 318
Stanford Digital Library Project, 321
Staples, 262
Starbucks, 250
Steel industry, argument for protection from foreign competition, 429
Steenken, Dirk, 206
Stigler, George, 232, 233, 341, 348
Stocks, 319–320
Stone, Matt, 219
Stop Tax Haven Abuse Act (2011), 167
Strathern, Paul, 12n
Strikes, 294, 294f
Stylized graphs, 21, 22f
Subsidies
agricultural, 92–93
number of, supply and, 64
Substitutability
of inputs, elasticity of demand for labor and, 284
price elasticity of demand and, 107
Substitute(s), 113
Substitute goods, 59
Substitution effect
indifference curves and, 159, 159f, 160
labor supply and, 278–279
Sunk cost(s), 145, 168
Sunk cost fallacy, 145

Supernormal profits, 202
Supply, 61–66
change in quantity supplied and, 64f, 64–65
changes in. *See* Changes in supply
definition of, 61
determinants of, 62–64, 65f
elastic, 115
industry, long-run, 205–207, 207f
inelastic, 115
of labor. *See* Labor supply
law of, 62
price elasticity of, 115f, 115–118
unitary elastic, 115
Supply curve, 62
market, 62, 62f
short-run, in perfect competition, 200f, 200–201
Surpluses, 66–67
consumer. *See* Consumer surplus
producer. *See* Producer surplus
total, 85
Survivor, 286
Sushi, 80
SUVs. *See* Sport utility vehicles (SUVs)
Sweden
Gini coefficient for, 395t
innovation in, 328
Switching costs, 376–377

TAA. *See* Trade Adjustment Assistance (TAA) program
Taft-Hartley Act (1947), 294
Target, 262
Tariffs, 423f, 423–424
effects of, 424f, 424–425
to protect infant industries, 427
specific, 424
Tar-Pamlico River, North Carolina, water effluents in, 351
Tastes. *See* Preference(s)
Taxes, 118–123
ad valorem, tariffs as, 424
elasticity of demand and, 119f, 119–121, 120f
elasticity of supply and, 121f, 121–123, 123t
emissions, 351
flat, 118, 118t
incidence of, 119
lump-sum, 118
number of, supply and, 64
profits and, 169
progressive, 118, 118t, 122
regressive, 118, 118t, 122
sales, household income and, 122
unit, tariffs as, 424
Taxis, in New York City, 225
Tax policy, incentives and, 9
Teamsters, 292
Teaser strategies, 376–377
Technology
economic growth and, 37–38, 38f
long-run average total cost and, 181
supply and, 63
Telecommunications industry, 28
Telemarketing, 377
Terms of trade, 420–427
determining, 421f, 421–422
impact of trade and, 422
trade restrictions and, 422–424, 423f
Third-degree price discrimination, 227, 229–231, 230f
Ticketmaster, 230
Tilly, Chris, 407
Timberlake, Justin, 372
Time. *See also* Long run; Short run; *entries beginning with terms* Long-run *and* Short-run
overvaluing the present relative to the future, 146
price elasticity of demand and, 107
price elasticity of supply and, 116–117, 117f
timing and climate change and, 356
Time series graphs, 18, 19f
Tipping, 147
Tipping point, 372, 373
Tit-for-tat strategy, 265–266
T-Mobile, 377
Toshiba, 373
Total cost, 168
average, 176, 177f, 178
Total product, 171t, 171–172, 172f
Total revenue (TR), 168
along linear demand curve, 111, 112f
elasticity of demand and, 110–112
loss leaders and, 114
Total surplus, 85
Total utility, 138
Toyota, 419, 425
Honda and, 113
pricing by, 112
value of brand, 250
Toyota Prius, 105, 164
TR. *See* Total revenue (TR)
Tradable permits, 351–352, 352f
Trade. *See also* International trade
free. *See* Free trade
gains from. *See* Gains from trade
practical constraints on, 45
Trade Adjustment Assistance (TAA) program, 429
Trade agreements, 430
Trade disputes, Prisoner's Dilemma and, 264
Tradeoffs, 8. *See also* Opportunity costs
Trade restrictions, 422–424, 423f
Trader Joe's, 70
Tragedy of the commons, 345–347, 346f
Training, on-the-job, 325–326
Transactions, 54
A Treatise on the Family (Becker), 288
Trembling hand trigger, 265
Trigger strategies, 265
True Religion, 252
Truman, Harry S, 13
The 20/20 Experience (Timberlake), 372
Two-Buck Chuck, 70

UAW, 292
Unions. *See* Labor unions
Union shops, 294
Unitary elasticity of demand, 106, 106f
total revenue and, 111, 111t
Unitary elastic supply, 115
United Airlines, 248, 267
United Kingdom, Gini coefficient for, 395t
United Nations, poverty comparisons and, 404
United States
comparative advantage in China and, 43
education in, 326
foreign trade zones of, 426
Gini coefficient for, 395t
international trade of, 414, 414f
NAFTA and, 45, 420, 430
oil production in, 102, 255
poverty threshold in, 404
quota on Japanese automobiles and, 425
tariffs of, 427
U.S. Customs and Border Protection, 419
U.S. Postal Service, 226
Unit taxes, tariffs as, 424
University of Michigan, 291
User-managed resources, 357
Util(s), 138
Utilities industries, as natural monopolies, 219
Utility, 137–138
marginal. *See* Marginal utility; Marginal utility analysis
maximizing, 140–142, 141t
preferences and, 137–142, 138t
total, 138
Utility maximizing rule, 141
Utility theory, 132

Value of the marginal product (VMP_L), 282
Variable costs, 174
average, 176
Venture capital, 320–321
Verizon, 366
AT&T and, 113, 262, 380
competition by, 262, 377
Versioning, 377–378
Vicious cycle, 373, 374t, 374–375
Virgin Galactic, 310
Virgin Group, 310
Virtual networks, 368
Virtuous cycle, 373, 374t, 374–375
VMP_L. *See* Value of the marginal product (VMP_L)

Wage(s), 30. *See also* Earnings; Income
in alternative jobs, labor supply and, 280–281
foreign, low, as argument against free trade, 428
Wage differentials, 289–290
union vs. nonunion, 295f, 295–296
Wagner Act (1935), 293
Walgreens, 223
Wal-Mart, 11, 82, 262
Walt Disney, 250
Warsh, David, 87n
Water pollution, as government failure, 348
"Waves of innovation," 39
Wealth
definition of, 390
of nations, 11–12
Welfare loss, 86, 224–225, 225f
Wendy's, 246
Wilkinson, Nick, 266n
Willingness-to-pay (WTP)
consumer and producer surplus and, 82–84, 83f
market demand and, 55–56, 56f
market demand for public goods as, 345

Wolf, Martin, 356n
Wooldridge, Adrian, 167n
WordPerfect, 236–237, 366, 374t
Working conditions, in developing nations, international trade and, 430–431
Work stoppages, 294, 294f
World Bank, poverty comparisons and, 404
World Trade Organization Agreements, 430
Wozniak, Steve, 167, 317
Wrangler, 252
WTP. *See* Willingness-to-pay (WTP)
Wu, Lawrence, 105n

X-inefficiency, 226

Yahoo!, 216
Yellow dog contracts, 293
Yergin, Daniel, 345n
Yield, 318
YouTube, 216

Zenith, 422
Zuckerberg, Mark, 8, 169, 317